Medical Termino
Essentials

Nina Thierer, CMA, BS, CPC

Ivy Tech Community College of Indiana
Fort Wayne, Indiana

Lisa Breitbard, LVN, CMA

 **Higher Education**

Boston   Burr Ridge, IL   Dubuque, IA   Madison, WI   New York   San Francisco   St. Louis
Bangkok   Bogotá   Caracas   Kuala Lumpur   Lisbon   London   Madrid   Mexico City
Milan   Montreal   New Delhi   Santiago   Seoul   Singapore   Sydney   Taipei   Toronto

Higher Education

MEDICAL TERMINOLOGY ESSENTIALS

Published by McGraw-Hill, a business unit of The McGraw-Hill Companies, Inc., 1221 Avenue of the Americas, New York, NY 10020. Copyright © 2007 by The McGraw-Hill Companies, Inc. All rights reserved. No part of this publication may be reproduced or distributed in any form or by any means, or stored in a database or retrieval system, without the prior written consent of The McGraw-Hill Companies, Inc., including, but not limited to, in any network or other electronic storage or transmission, or broadcast for distance learning.

Some ancillaries, including electronic and print components, may not be available to customers outside the United States.

This book is printed on acid-free paper.

1 2 3 4 5 6 7 8 9 0 VNH/VNH 0 9 8 7 6

ISBN-13 978–0–07–313403–1

ISBN-10 0–07–313403–1

Publisher, Career Education: *David T. Culverwell*
Publisher, Allied Health: *Michelle Watnick*
Senior Sponsoring Editor: *Roxan Kinsey*
Managing Developmental Editor: *Jonathan Plant*
Senior Marketing Manager: *Nancy Anselment Bradshaw*
Senior Project Manager: *Kay J. Brimeyer*
Senior Production Supervisor: *Sherry L. Kane*
Lead Media Project Manager: *Audrey A. Reiter*
Senior Media Producer: *Renee Russian*
Designer: *Laurie B. Janssen*
Cover Designer: *Ron Bissell, Creative Measures Design, Inc.*
(USE) Cover Image: *©PhotoDisc V72*
Senior Photo Research Coordinator: *Lori Hancock*
Supplement Producer: *Tracy L. Konrardy*
Compositor: *Electronic Publishing Services Inc., NYC*
Typeface: *11/13 Goudy*
Printer: *Von Hoffmann Corporation*

PHOTO CREDITS
Chapter Four:
Figure 4.5: © James Stevenson/Photo Researchers, Inc.; **4.7(left):** © Chassenet/Photo Researchers, Inc.; **4.7(right):** © James Stevenson/Photo Researchers, Inc.
Chapter Five:
Figure 5.11: © CNRI/Science Photo Library/Photo Researchers, Inc.
Chapter Six:
Figure 6.3: © Voisin/Photo Researchers, Inc.; **6.10:** © Blair Steitz/Photo Researchers
Chapter Seven:
Figure 7.2: © Lou Bopp; **7.5:** © Saturn Stills/Photo Researchers, Inc.
Chapter Eight:
Figure 8.5: © The McGraw-Hill Companies, Inc. /Bob Coyle, photographer; **8.8:** © Dr. M.A. Ansary/ Photo Researchers, Inc.
Chapter Thirteen:
Figure 13.4: © Nabisco/Photo Researchers, Inc.
Chapter Fifteen:
Figure 15.2: © SPL/Photo Researchers, Inc.
Chapter Sixteen:
Figure 16.4: © Blair Seitz/Photo Researchers, Inc; **16.7, 16.8, 16.9:** National Eye Institute Bethesda MD.
Chapter Eighteen:
Figure 18.1: © Paul Biddle & Tim Malyon/Photo Researchers, Inc.; **18.2:** © Françoise Saze/Photo Researchers, Inc.

www.mhhe.com

Contents

CHAPTER 4

The Integumentary System   61

CHAPTER 5

The Musculoskeletal System   91

CHAPTER 6

The Cardiovascular System   136

CHAPTER

11

The Male Reproductive System 298

CHAPTER

12

The Blood System 314

CHAPTER

13

The Lymphatic and Immune Systems 341

CHAPTER

17

Terms in Pharmacology   453

Acknowledgments

Reviewers of the Thierer–Breitbard Medical Terminology Series

Dr. Judy Adams
Department of Public and Allied Health
Bowling Green State University
Bowling Green, OH

Barbara G. Brice, Ph.D., RHIA
Associate Professor, Clark Atlanta
University
Atlanta, GA

Mona M. Burke, RHIA
Bowling Green State University—
Firelands College
Huron, OH

Barbara Desch, LVN, AHI
San Joaquin Valley College
Visalia, CA

Jennifer M. Evans
South Seattle Community College
Seattle, WA

Shawnie Haas, RN, CCRN, MBA
Yakima Valley Community College
Yakima, WA

**JoAnne E. Habenicht, MPA, RT
(RTM)**
Manhattan College
Riverdale, NY

Georgia D. Hammill
Vatterott College
Tulsa, OK

Judy Johnson, RN
Nashville State Community College
Nashville, TN

Patricia Kalvelage, MS
Governors State University
University Park, IL

Judith Karls
Madison Area Technical College
Madison, WI

Paula LaGrass, J.D.
Ohio Business College, Sandusky
Campus
Sandusky, OH

Vicki Legg, MS, ATC
Marietta College
Marietta, OH

Anne M. Loochtan
Columbus State Community College
Columbus, OH

Nelly Mangarova
Heald College
Milpitas, CA

Evelyn Kay Mayer
Tri-State Business Institute
Erie, PA

Ann Minks
Medical Terminology & Transcription
Instructor
Lake Washington Technical College
Kirkland, WA

Neil H. Penny, MS, OTR/L
Alvernia College
Reading, PA

Ellen J. Rarick
EduTek College
Stow, OH

**Donna J. Slovensky, PhD, RHIA,
FAHIMA**
University of Alabama at Birmingham
Birmingham, AL

Deborah M. Sulkowski, CMA
Pittsburgh Technical Institute
Oakdale, PA

Marilu Vazquez, M.D., M.S.
University of Texas Health Sciences
Center
San Antonio, TX

Lela Weaver, Health Educator
Northwestern College
Sacramento, CA

Kathryn L. Whitley, MSN, FNP
Associate Professor
Patrick Henry Community College
Martinsville, VA

CD-ROM Reviewers

Shawnie Haas, RN, CCRN, MBA
Yakima Valley Community College
Yakima, WA

Judy Johnson, RN
Nashville State Community College
Nashville, TN

Judith Karls
Madison Area Technical College
Madison, WI

Anne Loochtan
Columbus State Community College
Columbus, OH

Nelly Mangarova
Heald College
Milpitas, CA

Ann Minks
Lake Washington Technical College
Kirkland, WA

David Lee Sessoms, Jr., M.Ed., CMA
Miller-Motte Technical College
Cary, NC

Deborah M. Sulkowski, CMA
Pittsburgh Technical Institute
Oakdale, PA

Sharion Thompson
Sanford Brown Institute
Middleburg Heights, OH

Dyan Whitlow Underhill, MHA, BS
Miller-Motte Technical College
Cary, NC

Lela Weaver, Health Educator
Northwestern College
Sacramento, CA

Spanish Language Audio CD Reviewer

Lilia Torres, CMA
Florida Career College
The Pines Campus, FL
Pembroke Pines, FL

To the Student

Medical Terminology Essentials is designed for you, the students in the allied health curriculum, who need to know the language of health care. Its purpose is to help you succeed in your chosen health care careers by familiarizing you with how medical words are formed and by providing a systematic learning structure.

Before this section takes you through a short, instructive journey on how the book is set up and how it will work best for you, take the time to go through some general tips for success in school.

How Can I Succeed in This Class?

If you're reading this, you're on the right track.

> *"You are the same today that you are going to be five years from now except for two things: the people with whom you associate and the books you read."*

Charles Jones

Right now, you're probably leafing through this book feeling just a little overwhelmed. You're trying to juggle several other classes (which probably are equally daunting), possibly a job, and on top of it all, a life.

This special section—To the Student—has been designed specifically to help you focus. It's here to help you learn how to manage your time and your studies to succeed.

Start Here.

It's true—you are what you put into your studies. You have a lot of time and money invested in your education; you've been planning since high school, working an extra job or through summer vacations to save your money. Don't blow it now by only putting in half of the effort this class requires. Succeeding in this class (and life) requires:

- a commitment—of time and perseverance
- knowing and motivating yourself
- getting organized
- managing your time

This specially designed section will help you learn how to be effective in these areas, as well as offer guidance in:

- getting the most out of your class
- thinking through—and applying—the material
- getting the most out of your textbook
- finding extra help when you need it

A Commitment—of Time and Perseverance

Learning—and mastering—takes time and patience. Nothing worthwhile comes easily. Be committed to your studies and you will reap the benefits in the long run.

Consider this: your education is building the foundation for your future—a future in your chosen profession. Sloppy and hurried work now will only lead to lack of success later. Two or four years of committed education time now is nothing compared to the lifetime that awaits you.

Side note: A good rule of thumb is to allow a minimum of 2 hours of study time each week for every hour you spend in class.

For instance, 3 hours of class deserve 6 hours of weekly study time. If you set aside time each day to study, you will be investing a little time every day, including the weekend. Study time includes completing exercises, reading the text, practicing words, listening to tapes, and reviewing notes.

Insight 1.1 Why Study Medical Terminology?

If you were moving to a foreign country where very few people spoke English, you would make every effort to learn the language of that country. You have chosen a course of study in allied health or health care and you will need to know the language that is used in that discipline. Medical terminology covers the specific words and phrases you will need to learn to function effectively and understand the "language" of health care.

Knowing and Motivating Yourself

What type of learner are you? When are you most productive? Know yourself and your limits and work within them. Know how to motivate yourself to give your all to your studies and achieve your goals. Quite bluntly, you are the one who will benefit most from your success. If you lack self-motivation and drive, you will be the first person to suffer.

Know yourself: There are many types of learners, and no right or wrong way of learning. Which category do you fall into?

Visual Learner—You respond best to "seeing" processes and information. Particularly focus on text illustrations and charts, course handouts. Check to see if there are animations on the course or text Web site to help you. Also, consider drawing diagrams in your notes to illustrate concepts.

Auditory Learner—You work best by listening to—and possibly recording—the class lecture and by talking information through with a study partner. Your study sessions should include a flash card drill with a study partner or family member.

Tactile/Kinesthetic Learner—You learn best by being "hands on." You'll benefit by applying what you've learned during class time. Think of ways to apply your critical thinking skills in a variety of situations. Perhaps a text Web site or interactive CD-ROM will also help you.

Identify your own personal preferences for learning and seek out the resources that will best help you with your studies. Also, learn by recognizing your weaknesses and try to compensate for them while you work to improve them.

Getting Organized

It's simple, yet it's fundamental. It seems the more organized you are, the easier things come. Take the time before your course begins to look around and analyze your life and your study habits. Get organized now and you'll find you have a little more time—and a lot less stress.

- Find a calendar system that works for you. The best kind is one that you can take with you everywhere. To be truly organized, you should integrate all aspects of your life into this one calendar—school, work, leisure.
- By the same token, keep everything for your course or courses in one place—and at your fingertips. A three-ring binder works well because it allows you to add or organize handouts and notes from class in any order you prefer. Incorporating your own custom tabs helps you flip to exactly what you need at a moment's notice.
- Find your space. Find a place that helps you be organized and focused. If it's your desk in your room or elsewhere in your home, keep it clean. Clutter adds confusion and stress and wastes time.

A Helpful Hint—add extra "padding" into your deadlines to yourself. If you have a test on Friday, set a goal for yourself to have most of the studying done by Wednesday. Then, take time on Thursday to look over the work again, with a fresh eye. Review anything you had trouble remembering and be ready for the test on Friday.

Managing Your Time

Managing your time is the single most important thing you can do to help yourself. And, it's probably one of the most difficult tasks to successfully master.

You are taking this course because you want to succeed in life. You are preparing for a career. In school, you are expected to work much harder and to learn much more than you ever have before. To be successful you need to invest in your education with a commitment of time.

How Time Slips Away

People tend to let an enormous amount of time slip away from them, mainly in three ways:

1. **Procrastination,** putting off chores simply because you don't feel in the mood to do them right away
2. **Distraction,** getting sidetracked by the endless variety of other things that seem easier or more fun to do, often not realizing how much time they eat up
3. **Underestimating the value of small bits of time,** thinking it's not worth doing any work because you have something else to do or somewhere else to be in 20 minutes or so.

We all lead busy lives. But we all make choices as to how we spend our time. Choose wisely and make the most of every minute you have by implementing these tips.

- **Know yourself and when you'll be able to study most efficiently.** When are you most productive? Are you a late nighter? Or an early bird? Plan to study when you are most alert and can have some uninterrupted time. This could include a quick 5-minute review before class or a one-hour problem solving study session with a friend.

- **Create a set study time for yourself daily.** Having a set schedule for yourself helps you commit to studying, and helps you plan instead of cram.
- **Organize *all* of your activities in one place.** Find—and use—a planner that is small enough to carry with you everywhere. This can be a $2.50 paper calendar or a more expensive electronic version. They all work on the same premise.
- **Less is more. Schedule study time using shorter, focused blocks with small breaks.** Doing this offers two benefits:
  1. You will be less fatigued and gain more from your effort, and
  2. Studying will seem less overwhelming and you will be less likely to procrastinate.
- **Do plan time for leisure, friends, exercise, and sleep.** Studying should be your main focus, but you need to balance your time—and your life.
- Make sure you log your projects and homework deadlines in your personal calendar.
- "Plot" your assignments on your calendar or task list. If you have a report, for instance, break the assignment down into smaller targets. For example, set a goal for a first draft, second draft, and final copy.
- Try to complete tasks ahead of schedule. This will give you a chance to carefully review your work before you hand it in (instead of at 1 a.m. when you are half awake). You'll feel less stressed in the long run.
- Prioritize! In your calendar or planner, highlight or number key projects; do them first, and then cross them off when you've completed them. Give yourself a pat on the back for getting them done!
- Review your calendar and reprioritize daily.
- Try to resist distractions by setting and sticking to a designated study time (remember your commitment!). Distractions may include friends, surfing the Internet, or even a pet lizard.
- Multitask when possible—you may find a lot of extra time you didn't think you had. Review material in your head while walking to class, doing laundry, or during "mental down time." (Note—mental down time does NOT mean in the middle of lecture.)

Side note: Plan to study and plan for leisure. Being well balanced will help you focus when it is time to study.

Tip: Try combining social time with studying (a study partner) or social time with mealtime or exercise (dine or work out with a friend). Being a good student doesn't mean you have to be a hermit. It does mean you need to know how to smartly budget your time.

Learn to Manage or Avoid Time Wasters

DON'T
- Don't let friends manage your time

Tip: Kindly ask, "Can we talk later?" when you are trying to study; this will keep you in control of your time without alienating your friends.

- Don't get sucked into the Internet

It's easy to lose hours in front of the computer surfing the Web. Set a time limit for you self and stick to it.

DO

- Do use small bits of time to your advantage

Example: Arrive to class five minutes early and review notes. Review your personal calendar for upcoming due dates and events while eating meals or waiting for appointments.

- Do balance your life—sleep, study, and leisure are all important. Keep each in balance.

Getting the Most out of Classes

Believe it or not, instructors want you to succeed. They put a lot of effort into helping you learn and preparing their classes. Attending class is one of the simplest, most valuable things you can do to help yourself. But it doesn't end there; getting the most out of your classes means being organized. Here's how:

Prepare Before You Go to Class

Really! You'll be amazed at how much better you understand the material when you preview the chapter before you go to class. Don't feel overwhelmed by this suggestion. One tip that may help you—plan to arrive at class 5-15 minutes early. Bring your text with you and skim the chapter before class begins. This will at the very least give you an overview of what may be discussed.

Be a Good Listener

Most people think they are good listeners, but few really are. Are you?

Obvious but important points to remember:

- You can't listen if you are talking.
- You aren't listening if you are daydreaming.
- Listening and comprehending are two different things. If you don't understand something your instructor is saying, ask a question or jot a note and visit the instructor after hours. Don't feel dumb or intimidated; you probably aren't the only person who "doesn't get it."

Take Good Notes

- Use a standard size notebook, or better yet, a three-ring binder with loose leaf notepaper. The binder will allow you to organize and integrate your notes and handouts, make use of easy-to-reference tabs, etc.
- Use a standard black or blue ink pen to take your initial notes. You can annotate later using a pencil, which can be erased if need be.
- Start a new page for each class or note-taking session (yes—you can and should also take notes from your textbook).
- Label each page with the date and a heading for each day.
- Focus on main points and try to use an outline format to take notes to capture key ideas and organize sub-points.
- Leave lots of white space in your note-taking. A solid page of notes is difficult to study.
- Review and edit your notes shortly after class—at least within 24 hours—to make sure they make sense and that you've recorded core thoughts. You may also want to compare your notes with a study partner later to make sure neither of you have missed anything.

Get a Study Partner

Having a study partner has many benefits. First, he/she can help you keep your commitment to this class. By having set study dates, you can combine study and social time, and maybe even make it fun! In addition, you now have two sets of eyes and ears and two minds to help digest the information from class and from the text. Talk through concepts, compare notes, and quiz each other.

An obvious note: Don't take advantage of your study partner by skipping class or skipping study dates. You soon won't have a study partner—or a friend!

Helpful hint: Take your text to class, and keep it open to the topics being discussed. You can take brief notes in your textbook margin or reference textbook pages in your notebook to help you study later.

How to Study for an Exam

- Rereading is not studying.
- Be an active learner—
  - Read.
  - Be an active participant in class; ask questions.
  - Finish reading all material—text, notes, handouts—at least three days prior to the exam.
  - Three days prior to the exam, set aside time each day to do self-testing, practice problems, review notes, and use critical thinking skills to understand the material.
  - Analyze your weaknesses, and create an "I don't know this yet" list. Focus on strengthening these areas and narrow your list as you study.
  - Create your own study tools such as flash cards and checklists and practice defining key terms.
- Make up a mock test. If you were the instructor, what questions would you put on the test? You will be surprised at how accurate you will be.

Useful tools to help: the end-of-chapter reviews, questions and practice problems; text Web site; student CD-ROM; and your study partner.

VERY IMPORTANT

Be sure to sleep and eat well before the exam.
If you are determined to fail, just follow these few simple instructions:

1. Skip class, or if you do attend, arrive fashionably late.
2. Don't buy the book, or if you buy it, don't read it.
3. Don't bother studying if you have to be somewhere else in 20 minutes; that's not enough time to get anything done.
4. Big test coming up? Beat the stress by relaxing with friends, going out for a few beers, or hanging out in an Internet chat room. Be sure to complain to your chat room friends about how there's not way you can pass the test tomorrow.
5. Don't ask questions in class; you're probably the only one who doesn't know the answer, and everyone else will think you're stupid.
6. Don't visit the instructor in his or her office; instructors don't want to be bothered.
7. If you miss a class, trust your friends' notes to be complete and accurate.
8. Be sure to pull an all-nighter before the exam; you don't have time to sleep.

9. Don't strain your brain trying to do the chapter review. Look up the answers and fill them in. You can fool your friends into thinking you're really smart (as long as they don't see your test grade).

10. When you study with friends, have a good time—chat about things unrelated to your study topic.

11. The time to begin studying for an exam is the day before the test. Four hours ought to be plenty.

Getting the Most Out of Your Textbook

McGraw-Hill and the authors of this book, Nina Thierer and Lisa Breitbard, have invested their time, research, and talents to help you succeed. The goal is to make learning easier for you.

Here's How:

Throughout the pages of *Medical Terminology Essentials* you'll find an organized learning system. Follow it throughout your course and you will become a proficient "speaker" of the language of health care.

A Journey Through *Medical Terminology Essentials*

Forming Medical Terms

The first three chapters of the book introduce the way that most medical terms are formed. Most medical terms are built from word parts, often derived from Latin and Greek terms. These three chapters introduce many of the major word parts used in the formation of medical terms.

Chapter 1 gives the major combining forms used in medical terminology except for the combining forms that are more specific to each body part. Those combining forms are learned in each chapter that covers a different body system.

Chapter 2 provides the majority of general prefixes and suffixes that are used to form medical terms. Learning these prefixes and suffixes will enable you to break apart built-up terms that you are not familiar with and understand their meanings by knowing the meaning of the parts.

Chapter 3 introduces you to the body systems you will be studying throughout this book. It also covers the most commonly used body system word parts, which are then repeated in the individual body system chapters. This concentrated repetition is designed to reinforce the body system approach to medical word building.

Using the Systematic Learning Approach

Chapters 4 through 16 are the body system chapters. The format of these chapters is designed to acquaint you with an overview of each body system, including coverage of its basic anatomy and physiology. At the same time, each chapter teaches the specific terms and word parts used in the medical terminology. Each body system chapter is presented in the following format:

A. Objectives
B. Structure and Function
C. Combining Forms
D. Diagnostic, Procedural, and Laboratory Terms
E. Pathological Terms
F. Surgical Terms
G. Terminology in Action
H. Using the Internet
I. Chapter Review
J. Answers to Chapter Exercises

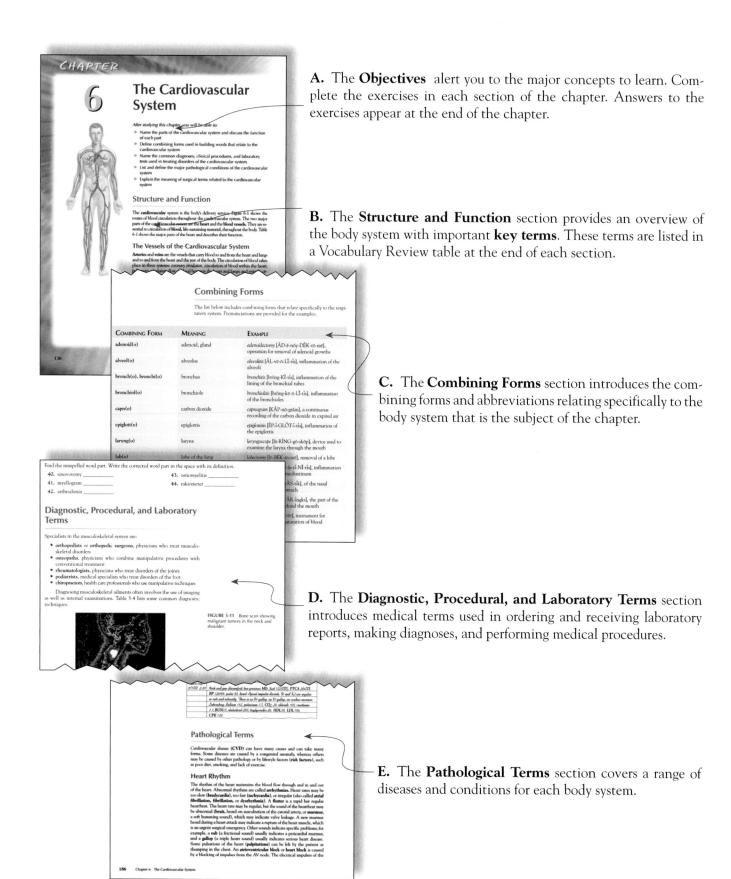

A. The **Objectives** alert you to the major concepts to learn. Complete the exercises in each section of the chapter. Answers to the exercises appear at the end of the chapter.

B. The **Structure and Function** section provides an overview of the body system with important **key terms**. These terms are listed in a Vocabulary Review table at the end of each section.

C. The **Combining Forms** section introduces the combining forms and abbreviations relating specifically to the body system that is the subject of the chapter.

D. The **Diagnostic, Procedural, and Laboratory Terms** section introduces medical terms used in ordering and receiving laboratory reports, making diagnoses, and performing medical procedures.

E. The **Pathological Terms** section covers a range of diseases and conditions for each body system.

F. The **Surgical Terms** section provides an overview of common surgical procedures performed for each body system.

G. The **Terminology in Action** are an additional opportunity for critical thinking.

H. Using the Internet offers you an opportunity to gather information from a medical Web site and familiarize yourself with medical offerings on the Internet.

I. The **Chapter Review** gives a complete listing of key terms and combining forms learned in the chapter.

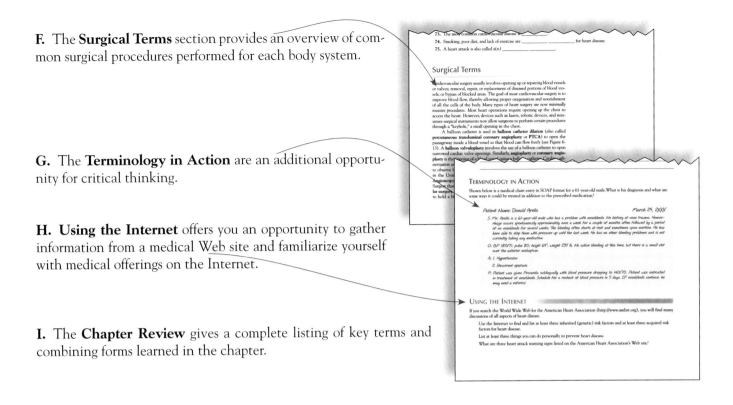

J. Answers to Chapter Exercises allow self-study and instant feedback so you can determine how well you learned the material.

Special Features

Each chapter contains some special features that reinforce learning, provide additional information, or expose you to realistic situations that you may encounter in your chosen allied health profession.

A. Case Studies throughout the text provide you with realistic health care situations. The case studies shows you how terminology and abbreviations are used in a realistic context.

B. Critical Thinking following the case studies and in some other special sections, you are asked critical thinking questions. Critical thinking skills are essential to the development of your decision-making skills as a future allied health care professional.

C. More About boxes throughout the book provide some medical information that would not normally appear within a medical terminology text.

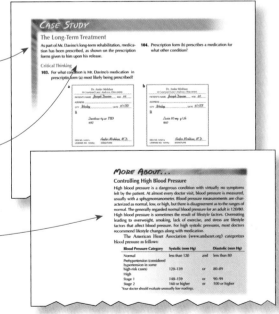

some of the abnormalities that may show up on ECGs. A **Holter monitor** is a portable type of electrocardiograph or instrument that performs an electrocardiogram over a 24-hour period.

Various diagnostic procedures can be performed by producing some type of image. Taking x-rays after a dye has been injected is called **angiocardiography** (x-ray of the heart and its large blood vessels), **angiography** (x-ray of the heart's large blood vessels), **arteriography** (x-ray of a specific artery), **aortography** (x-ray of the aorta), or **venography** or **phlebography** (x-ray of a specific vein). The tests are called an angiocardiogram, angiogram, arteriogram, aortogram, or venogram or phlebogram. A **ventriculogram** is an x-ray showing the ventricles. Ventriculograms measure stroke volume (**SV**), the amount of blood going out of a ventricle in one contraction; cardiac output (**CO**), the amount of blood ejected from a ventricle every minute; and the **ejection fraction**, the percentage of volume of the contents of the left ventricle ejected with each contraction. Another x-ray test, **digital subtraction angiography** (**DSA**), requires two angiograms with different contrast material to compare the results of the two tests in a computer.

Ultrasound tests, or ultrasonography or **sonography**, produce images by measuring the echoes of sound waves against various structures. **Doppler ultrasound** measures blood flow in certain blood vessels. **Echocardiography** records sound waves to show the structure and movement of the heart. The test itself is called an echocardiogram. Figure 6-10 shows an echocardiogram.

Radioactive substances that are injected into the patient can provide information in a **cardiac scan**, a test that measures movement of areas of the heart, or in nuclear medicine imaging. **Positron emission tomography** (**PET**) **scans** are one form of nuclear imaging. A PET scan of the heart reveals images of the heart's blood flow and its cellular metabolism. Another form of

MORE ABOUT...

Electrocardiograms

The electrocardiograph can have twelve leads, which are placed at specific points on the patient's body to monitor electrical activity of the heart. Six of the leads go on the arms and legs and six of the leads go at specific points on the chest. The chest leads are marked with specific codes. For example, V_1 goes in the fourth intercostal space to the right of the sternum. Each lead traces the electrical activity from a different angle.

The Web site www.heartsite.com has a search item called tests. Click on echocardiogram and any other test listed to learn more details about these tests.

D. Internet References appear in many places in the margin of the text. These references direct you to the Internet to learn more about the material being studied and to familiarize yourself with using the Internet to enhance your knowledge—something that will be helpful to you both personally and professionally throughout your life. Although all Web sites have been checked, some Web sites become inactive. In such cases, if the Web site does not work, use a search engine on your computer to find another source. Simply insert a related word and go to some suggested sites to find more information.

Warning: Using the Internet can be helpful but it may also be harmful. Some people are posting false and even damaging or misleading medical information on the Internet. Check the source of the site to make sure it is a trustworthy medical resource. Avoid advertisements, clubs, and articles written by anyone asking for a donation. Use common sense—if it sounds too good to be true, it usually is false. Also, if someone is trying to sell you something, beware of buying medical items on the Internet without sound medical advice. Never substitute the advice of someone you don't know on the Internet for the advice you can get from a medical professional.

Specialized Chapter

Chapter 17 Terms in Pharmacology may be assigned at any time during the course.

Additional Study Resources

In addition to the textbook, McGraw-Hill offers the following study resources to enhance your learning of medical terminology:

- An interactive student CD-ROM. The next section gives instructions for using the CD-ROM.
- A set of English audio CDs. The two English audio CDs (available for purchase) are organized by chapter sections. You can use these to test your ability to spell and pronounce all key terms in the book.
- An Online Learning Center (OLC) Web site. The Web site (www. mhhe.com/medtermessentials) includes an Information Center with general information about the medical terminology program. It includes an instructor's side with resources for classroom testing and management. For you, the student, it includes major checkpoints from the text along with additional learning activities. These additional activities will reinforce what you learned in the text and what you practiced on the student CD-ROM.

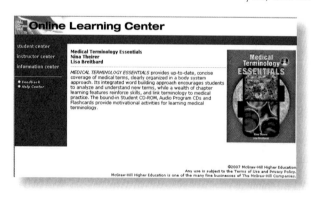

- A Spanish-English audio CD. To use this audio CD effectively, listen to the Spanish words while you look at the selected Spanish terms in the appropriate body system chapter. If you want to read the definition in Spanish, refer to the Spanish glossary on the Web site (www.mhhe.com/medtermessentials).

USING THE CD-ROM

The Medical Terminology Essentials Student CD-ROM is an interactive tutorial designed to complement the student textbook. In it you will find key terms, flashcards, drag and drop word building and labeling exercises, and games (such as Hangman and That's Epidemic) that are designed to challenge you.

System Requirements

To run this product, your computer must meet the following minimum specifications:

- Pentium II or higher processor
- Microsoft Windows 98 Second Edition, Millennium Edition (ME), 2000, or XP (Windows XP recommended)
- 64 MB of RAM or higher (128 required for Windows XP)
- 800x600 or higher desktop display
- 16-bit or higher desktop color (24-bit or 32-bit highly recommended)
- Internet Explorer 5.5 or higher required (6.0 or higher recommended)
- Windows Media Player 7.1 or higher required (9.0 or higher recommended)

Installation

The installation and setup program checks your computer to make sure it meets the minimum specifications to run the Medical Terminology Essentials Student CD-ROM.

To run the installation program:

1. Insert the CD-ROM into your CD-ROM drive.
2. The "AutoRun" program should start automatically, asking you if you would like to install the program.

- If you have already installed the program, AutoRun will ask if you want to run the program instead.
- If AutoRun does not start automatically, you will need to follow these steps:

1. Click the Windows Start menu and go to Run.
2. In the Run: box, type D:\autorun.exe (where D is the letter of your CD-ROM drive).
3. Click OK.
4. To run the program after it is installed, go to the Windows Start menu, point your mouse to Programs (or All Programs), point your mouse to Medical Terminology, and click the icon for Medical Terminology.

The Help Section

Once you have installed the software, you are strongly encouraged to read and review the Help section of this software. The Help section will explain in detail all of the features and activities. It will also discuss frequently asked questions and offer troubleshooting tips. To access Help, click on the Help button found on the top right of your computer screen.

Software Support

If you are experiencing difficulties with this product, please visit the McGraw-Hill Higher Education Support Web site at http://www.mhhe.com/support.

Learning Terminology

After studying this chapter, you will be able to:

▶ Explain how medical terms are developed
▶ Describe the process of pluralizing terms
▶ Describe how to interpret pronunciation marks
▶ Define the four word parts used to build medical terms
▶ Define common medical combining forms
▶ List basic legal and ethical issues for health-related professionals
▶ Describe how medical documentation is compiled
▶ Describe HIPAA in relation to allied health

The Language of Medicine

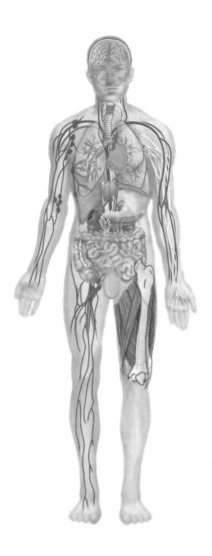

Many everyday terms that we use to describe our health and our medical care go back to the early history of civilization. The language of medicine dates to the time when people had only spoken language, not written. Like all people who followed after them, they gave names to parts of their bodies, to illnesses, and to the cures they used. Some of these names survive in the roots and words still used today in medical terminology. For example, the ancient Greeks thought of the disease we call "cancer" as something eating at a person on the inside, and so named the condition *karkinos*, meaning both crab and cancer. Medical terminology began to become standardized when Hippocrates (460–377 B.C.), a Greek physician, set about to organize an approach to medicine. The Hippocratic oath that is generally attributed to him has been in use for over 2,000 years.

> *I swear by Apollo the physician and Asklepios, and health, and All-Heal, and all the gods and goddesses, that, according to my ability and judgment.*
>
> *I will keep this Oath and this stipulation—to reckon him who taught me this Art equally dear to me as my parents, to share my substance with him, and relieve his necessities if required, to look upon his offspring in the same footing as my own brothers, and to teach them this Art, if they shall wish to learn it, without fee or stipulation; and that by precept, lecture, and every other mode of instruction, I will impart a knowledge of the Art to my own sons, and those of my teachers, and to disciples bound by a stipulation and oath according to the law of medicine, but to none others.*
>
> *I will follow that system of regimen which, according to my ability and judgment, I consider for the benefit of my patients, and abstain from whatever is deleterious and mischievous, I will give no deadly medicine to any one if asked, nor suggest any such counsel; and in like manner I will not give to a woman a pessary to produce abortion. With purity and holiness I will pass my life and practice my Art.*
>
> *I will not cut persons laboring under the stone, but will leave this to be done by men who are practitioners of this work. Into whatever houses I enter, I will go into*

The Hippocratic Oath

Some aspects of the Hippocratic Oath are still debated today. For example, the phrase "I will give no deadly medicine to any one if asked" is a subject of debate now that modern medicine is capable of prolonging a life that is extremely painful and difficult. The question of whether a physician should help to end the life of a suffering patient is an extremely difficult one. Should patients have the right to choose *euthanasia,* that is, to be helped to die? There are many reasonable arguments on both sides of the issue. A pessary, a vaginal suppository used to induce abortion, was forbidden under the Hippocratic oath. Today, abortion is legally available in the United States, but the question of whether it should be legal is debated widely. Other points of the Oath, about not seducing females or males, keeping confidences, and abstaining from the deleterious (doing no harm), form the basic ethical standards of modern medicine.

them for the benefit of the sick, and will abstain from every voluntary act of mischief and corruption; and, further, from the seduction of females or males, of freemen and slaves. Whatever, in connection with my professional practice, or not in connection with it, I see or hear, in the life of men, which ought not to be spoken of abroad, I will not divulge, as reckoning that all such should be kept secret. While I continue to keep this Oath unviolated, may it be granted to me to enjoy life and the practice of the Art, respected by all men, in all times! But should I trespass and violate this Oath, may the reverse be my lot!

Origins of Medical Terminology

Many medical terms originate directly from ancient Greek or Latin terms. Table 1-1 shows a sampling of words taken directly from those languages. Notice how the terms have retained their meaning over the centuries. Other languages form words in the same way. For example, the word nerve is derived from the Latin *nervus.* In Spanish, the word *nervio* is also derived from the same Latin word. (In Appendix D, you will find a Spanish-English glossary of some of the key terms used in this book. In many cases, you will find the words very similar to their English counterparts.)

Later, people of many cultures used these ancient terms in their languages. Even though the appearance of the words changed, the roots from which the words developed remained the original Greek or Latin terms. Over the ensuing centuries, people involved in medicine and the development of treatments tended to look for Greek or Latin words or roots to describe their newest discoveries. Hence, many medical terms used today are based on ancient Greek and Latin. Word building became and remains the primary way to describe new medical discoveries.

The study of the origin of words is called *etymology.* General language terms tend to change dramatically. It takes a talented word detective to find the actual root of a word that has undergone centuries of change. Remember that most languages, up until the last 500 years, were spoken by most of the population, but were available in written form to only a few. Although books

TABLE 1-1 Derivations of Terms

Modern Term	Historical Derivation
artery	Latin *arteria*; Greek *arteria*
cardi(o), the heart	Greek *kardia*
cell	Latin *cella*, chamber
gene	Greek *genos*, birth
hernia	Latin *hernia*, rupture
ligament	Latin *ligamentum*
nerve	Latin *nervus*
sinus	Latin *sinus*, cavity
tendon	Latin *tendo*
vein	Latin *vena*

had been around for many centuries, printed material was not available to the general population until the advent of the printing press in the sixteenth century. Even then, it took some time for large numbers of people to become readers of newspapers, journals, and books. Passing word knowledge on only through spoken communication often results in words being pronounced very differently and, ultimately, changing. An example is the word *heart*. It is derived from Old English *heorte*, which ultimately comes from an early Germanic word, related to Greek *kardia*, meaning heart, and found in words like *cardiac*, *cardiology*, and *cardiogram*.

The change in medical terms has generally been less drastic. Most people who have studied medicine since Greek and Roman times have also studied the Latin and Greek languages as part of learning medical terminology. So, a suffix, *-tomy*, which means "cutting," may be used in modern types of surgery (*phlebotomy*, incision into a vein), but the basic meaning is still the original one, "cutting." Throughout this text, you will learn the parts of words that enable you to understand many medical terms.

HISTORY OF MEDICAL TERMS EXERCISES

Fill in the Blanks

1. If a word is derived from an Old English word, it might also be related to a _____ or _____ word that means the same thing.

2. The first organized approach to medicine was formalized by _____.

3. The Hippocratic Oath forbade both _____ and _____, two issues still debated today.

4. Two languages studied throughout the history of medicine are _____ and _____.

5. When a word is passed through spoken language only, it is more likely to be altered than if it is passed through _____ language.

TABLE 1-2   Formation of Plurals

Singular Words	Pluralizing Rules	Plural Words
joint, face, angioma, cancer, muscle, paraplegic	Add -s to words ending in any vowel or consonant except s, x, z, or y.	joints, faces, angiomas, cancers, muscles, paraplegics
abscess, reflex	Add -es to words ending in s, x, or z.	abscesses, reflexes
vasectomy	Remove the y and add -ies to words ending in -y preceded by a consonant. When an ending -y is preceded by a vowel, the usual plural suffix is -s.	vasectomies
appendix, radix	Remove the x and add -ces to Latin words ending in x.	appendices, radices
fossa	Add -e to Latin terms ending in -a.	fossae
staphylococcus	Remove -us and add -i to Latin words ending in -us	staphylococci
ganglion, datum	Remove -on and add -a to Greek words ending in -on; remove -um from and add -a to Latin words ending in -um.	ganglia, data
neurosis	Change -sis to -ses in Greek words ending in -sis.	neuroses

Creating Plurals

Most English plurals are formed by adding -s or -es to a word. This is also true of many medical terms (cancer, cancers; abscess, abscesses). However, medical terms derived from ancient Greek and Latin often use the regular plural forms from those languages (bursa, bursae; embolus, emboli). Some of these ancient plural forms were eventually replaced by adding -s or -es. As you study the text, you will learn which plurals are commonly used as well as irregular plurals (foot, feet; tooth, teeth). Table 1-2 shows the formation of plurals.

Spelling and Pronunciation of Medical Terms

Misspellings and mispronunciations in a medical setting can result in life-threatening situations. A misspelled or a misunderstood abbreviation for a medicine dosage was responsible for the death of several children in a cancer ward. Several new AIDS medications are close enough in sound to other drugs as to make prescribing, particularly by telephone, difficult. A physician ordered a prescription for an AIDS drug, saquinavir, for an AIDS patient. The pharmacy filled a prescription for a sedative, Sinequan, and the patient became critically ill. Aside from the possibility of written mistakes, people in health care must remain vigilant in checking and rechecking verbal instructions. Misspellings that result in harm to a patient may become legal issues. Patients have the right to expect a certain standard of

For quick checking of terms, you can use www.medical-spell-checker.com, which is not an official Web site but is provided free for Internet users. It is important to note that such sites are supported by advertising, so use them carefully.

Medical Errors

Both government and the health care industry are investigating ways to avoid the increasing number of medical errors (mistakes). Several companies have now devised an electronic method for entering prescriptions (known as CPOE, computerized physician order entry) with only doctors having passwords; the amounts and drug names are double-checked by the program. Some health care services centers now require every direction or order given by phone to be read back at least once for confirmation. Some surgeons insist that a patient actually write "yes" on the correct limb to be operated on before they will proceed.

> For more information on medical errors, go to www.ahrq.gov and search for medical errors.

care. Misunderstandings caused by incorrect or misspelled words may be disastrous in certain circumstances. For example, some hospitals and doctors' offices require that written forms requesting an electrocardiogram include the abbreviation EKG instead of ECG because of the possible confusion of a written "C" with an "E" as in EEG (electroencephalogram).

Learning how to spell and pronounce medical terms is a matter of practice. In this text, spellings and pronunciations are given in both the vocabulary review sections of each chapter and in the end-of-chapter review sections. Familiarizing yourself with correct spellings of terms is a matter of practice and of seeing the terms over and over again. Pronouncing a word out loud each time you see the pronunciation will help familiarize you with the sound of the word. (Note: Not everyone agrees on every pronunciation, and there may be regional variations. If your instructor has a particular preference, follow that preference.) Also, use your own medical dictionary as a reference when you have a question. It is a good idea to know some basic terms in other languages such as Spanish when you work in an area where many people mainly speak that language. Since Spanish is the second most common language spoken in the United States today, the Web site for this textbook has a Spanish-English glossary for your reference.

In this text, there are two ways we help you learn to pronounce words. First, we capitalize one syllable of all words with two or more syllables so you can tell where the heaviest accent falls. For example, the word *femoral* is pronounced FEM-or-al, with the accent on the first syllable. Next, we add marks, called *diacritical marks,* to the vowels to guide you in pronouncing them. Vowels are either long or short, as shown in Table 1-3.

Long and short vowels are just a guide to help you pronounce the words correctly. English dictionaries have much more extensive pronunciation systems, with many degrees of vowel sounds. For the purposes of learning medical terminology, long and short marks provide enough guidance.

Some spelling differences occur in different fields of allied health. For example, medical transcriptionists follow AAMT (The American Association for Medical Transcription) style. In this style, diseases, procedures, and conditions that are named after people are spelled without the possessive form. For example, *Alzheimer's disease* is spelled *Alzheimer disease* and *Fontan's operation* is spelled *Fontan operation.* The AMA (American Medical Association) has also adopted this practice. However, U.S. government Web sites still use the possessive form, as do most organizations (for example, Alzheimer's Foundation of America). Appendix D gives some examples of these style differences.

TABLE 1-3 Pronunciation Guide

Vowel	Long (–) or Short (˘)	Examples of Pronunciation
a	long ā	pace, plate, atrium
e	long ē	feline, easy, beat
i	long ī	dine, line, I, bite
o	long ō	boat, wrote, rose
u	long ū	cute, cube
a	short ă	rap, cat, mar
e	short ĕ	ever, pet
i	short ĭ	pit, kitten
o	short ŏ	pot, hot
u	short ŭ	put, cut

PRONUNCIATION EXERCISES

Saying What You Mean

In the following list of words, the accented syllable is shown in capital letters. The vowels need a long or short mark added. As an exercise in how familiar you already are with medical words, add the diacritical marks to the vowels. Check the answers at the end of the chapter.

6. anemia [a-NE-me-a]
7. angioplasty [AN-je-o-plas-te]
8. bursitis [ber-SI-tis]
9. disease [di-ZEZ]
10. hemoglobin [HE-mo-GLO-bin]
11. lymphoma [lim-FO-ma]
12. neuritis [nu-RI-tis]
13. osteoporosis [OS-te-o-po-RO-sis]
14. paraplegia [par-a-PLE-je-a]
15. pulse [puls]

16. radiation [ra-de-A-shun]
17. reflex [RE-fleks]
18. retina [RET-i-na]
19. rheumatism [RU-ma-tizm]
20. sciatica [si-AT-i-ka]
21. septum [SEP-tum]
22. sinus [SI-nus]
23. therapy [THAR-a-pe]
24. typhoid [TI-foyd]
25. vaccine [VAK-sen]

Forming Medical Terms

Many medical terms are formed from two or more word parts. There are four word parts to learn about in the study of medical terminology.

- A **word root** is the fundamental portion of a word that contains the basic meaning. For example, the word root *cardi-* means "heart."
- **Combining forms** are the word root and a combining vowel that enable two parts to be connected. For example, the word root *cardi-* +

the combining vowel -o- can form words relating to the basic meaning "heart," such as *cardiology*, the practice that studies, diagnoses, and treats disorders of the heart. It is often easier to understand medical terms by looking at the suffix first. Thus, *-logy*, the study of, plus the prefix *cardio-* gives you a quick understanding of the definition.

- **Prefixes** are word parts attached to the beginning of a word or word root that modify the meaning of that word root. For example, the prefix *peri-*, meaning "around, near, surrounding," helps to form the word *pericardium*, meaning "around or surrounding the heart." Common prefixes used in medical terminology are discussed in Chapter 2 as well as in the body systems chapters.
- **Suffixes** are word parts attached to the end of a word or word root that modify the meaning of that word root. For example, the suffix *-oid*, meaning "like or resembling," helps to form the word *fibroid*, meaning "made of fibrous tissue." Common suffixes used in medical terminology are discussed in Chapter 2 as well as in the body systems chapters.

By familiarizing yourself with the word parts in this chapter and in Chapters 2 and 3, you will find the separate chapters about body systems easier to understand. Once you have learned the basic words, combining forms, and word parts in the systems chapters, you will be able to define many of the medical terms you will encounter as a health care professional.

Word Roots and Combining Forms

Most medical word roots come directly from Greek and Latin terms. The history of a word is called its *etymology*. The list that follows includes common medical combining forms with meanings that are not specifically part of a body system or may apply both to general terms and to specific body systems. (Body systems combining forms are discussed in later chapters.) Many of the combining forms in this chapter form medical terms when used with word parts or other terms. In Chapter 2, you will study prefixes and suffixes. Once you master all three basic word parts, along with roots, you will have the basic tools necessary for understanding medical terms.

Combining Form	Meaning	Example
actin(o)	light	*actinotherapy* [ĂK-tĭn-ō-THĀR-ă-pē], ultraviolet light therapy used in dermatology
aer(o)	air; gas	*aerogen* [ĀR-ō-jĕn], gas-producing microorganism
alge, alges(i), algio, algo	pain	*algospasm* [ĂL-gō-spăzm], pain caused by a spasm
andro	masculine	*androblastoma* [ĂN-drō-blăs-TŌ-mă], testicular tumor
ather(o)	plaque; fatty substance	*atheroma* [ăth-ĕr-Ō-mă], swelling on the surface of an artery from a fatty deposit

Combining Form	Meaning	Example
bacteri(o)	bacteria	*bacteriogenic* [băk-TĒR-ē-ō-JĔN-ĭk], caused by bacteria
bar(o)	weight; pressure	*barostat* [BĂR-ō-stăt], pressure-regulating device
bas(o), basi(o)	base	*basophilic* [BĀ-sō-FĬL-ĭk], having an affinity for basic dyes (said of tissue)
bio-	life	*biopsy* [BĪ-ŏp-sē], sampling of tissue from living patients
blasto	immature cells	*glioblastoma* [GLĪ-ō-blăs-TŌ-mă], growth consisting of immature neural cells
calc(o), calci(o)	calcium	*calcipenia* [kăl-sĭ-PĒ-nē-ă], calcium deficiency
carcin(o)	cancer	*carcinogen* [kăr-SĬN-ō-jĕn], cancer-producing substance
chem(o)	chemical	*chemolysis* [kĕm-ŎL-ĭ-sĭs], chemical decomposition
chlor(o)	chlorine, green	*chloruresis* [klō-yū-RĒ-sĭs], excretion of chloride in urine
chondri(o), chondr(o)	cartilage, grainy, gritty	*chondrocyte* [KŎN-drō-sīt], cartilage cell
chrom(o), chromat(o)	color	*chromatogenous* [krō-mă-TŎJ-ĕ-nŭs], producing color
chrono	time	*chronometry* [krō-NŎM-ĕ-trē], measurement of time intervals
cry(o)	cold	*cryocautery* [KRĪ-ō-KĂW-tĕr-ē], destruction of tissue by freezing
crypt(o)	hidden; obscure	*cryptogenic* [krĭp-tō-JĔN-ĭk], of obscure origin
cyan(o)	blue	*cyanopsia* [sī-ă-NŎP-sē-ă], condition following a cataract operation in which all objects appear blue
cycl(o)	circle; cycle; ciliary body	*cyclectomy* [sī-KLĔK-tō-mē], removal of a part of a ciliary body
cyst(o), cysti	bladder, cyst, cystic duct	*cystoid* [SĬS-tŏyd], bladder-shaped
cyt(o)	cell	*cytoarchitecture* [SĪ-tō-ĂR-kĭ-tĕk-chūr], arrangement of cells in tissue
dextr(o)	right, toward the right	*dextrocardia* [DĔKS-trō-KĂR-dē-ă], displacement of the heart to the right
dips(o)	thirst	*dipsomania* [dĭp-sō-MĀ-nē-ă], alcoholism

Combining Form	Meaning	Example
dors(o), dorsi	back	*dorsalgia* [dōr-SĂL-jē-ă], upper back pain
echo	reflected sound	*echocardiogram* [ĕk-ō-KĂR-dē-ō-grăm], ultrasound recording of the heart
electr(o)	electricity; electric	*electrocardiogram* [ē-lĕk-trō-KĂR-dē-ō-grăm], graphic record of heart's electrical currents
eosin(o)	red; rosy	*eosinophilic* [ē-ō-sĭn-ō-FĬL-ĭk], staining readily with certain dyes
erythr(o)	red, redness	*erythroclasis* [ĕr-ĭ-THRŎK-lă-sĭs], fragmentation of red blood cells
esthesio	sensation, perception	*esthesiometry* [ĕs-thē-zē-ŎM-ĕ-trē], measurement of tactile sensibility
etio	cause	*etiopathology* [Ē-tē-ō-pă-THŎL-ō-jē], study of the cause of an abnormality or disease
fibr(o)	fiber	*fibroplastic* [fī-brō-PLĂS-tĭk], producing fibrous tissue
fluor(o)	light; luminous; fluorine	*fluorochrome* [FLŪR-ō-krōm], fluorescent contrast medium
fungi	fungus	*fungicide* [FŬN-jĭ-sīd], substance that destroys fungi
galact(o)	milk	*galactophoritis* [gă-LĂK-tō-fō-RĪ-tĭs], inflammation of the milk ducts
gen(o)	producing; being born	*genoblast* [JĔN-ō-blăst], nucleus of a fertilized ovum
gero, geront(o)	old age	*gerontology* [jār-ŏn-TŎL-ō-jē], study of the problems of aging
gluco	glucose	*glucogenic* [glū-kō-JĔN-ĭk], producing glucose
glyco	sugars	*glycopenia* [glī-kō-PĒ-nē-ă], sugar deficiency
gonio	angle	*goniometer* [gō-nē-ŎM-ĕ-tĕr], instrument for measuring angles
granul(o)	granular	*granuloma* [grăn-yū-LŌ-mă], small, granular lesion
gyn(o), gyne, gyneco	women	*gynopathy* [gī-NŎP-ă-thē], disease peculiar to women
home(o), homo	same; constant	*homeoplasia* [HŌ-mē-ō-PLĀ-zhē-ă], formation of new, similar tissue

COMBINING FORM	MEANING	EXAMPLE
hydr(o)	hydrogen, water	*hydrocephaly* [hī-drō-SĔF-ă-lē], condition characterized by excessive fluid accumulation in the head
hypn(o)	sleep	*hypnogenesis* [hĭp-nō-JĔN-ĕ-sĭs], induction of sleep
iatr(o)	physician; treatment	*iatrogenic* [ī-ăt-rō-JĔN-ĭk], produced or caused by treatment or diagnostic procedure
immun(o)	safe; immune	*immunodeficient* [ĬM-yū-nō-dē-FĬSH-ĕnt], lacking in some essential immune function
kinesi(o), kineso	motion	*kinesiology* [kĭ-nē-sē-ŎL-ō-jē], study of movement
lact(o), lacti	milk	*lactogen* [LĂK-tō-jĕn], agent that stimulates milk production
latero	lateral, to one side	*lateroduction* [LĂT-ĕr-ō-DŬK-shŭn], movement to one side
leuk(o)	white	*leukoblast* [LŪ-kō-blăst], immature white blood cell
lip(o)	fat	*lipoblast* [LĬ-pō-blăst], embryonic fat cell
lith(o)	stone	*lithotomy* [lĭ-THŎT-ō-mē], operation for removal of stones
log(o)	speech, words, thought	*logopathy* [lŏg-ŎP-ă-thē], speech disorder
macr(o)	large; long	*macromelia* [măk-rō-MĒ-lē-ă], abnormally large limb
medi(o)	middle; medial plane	*mediolateral* [MĒ-dē-ō-LĂT-ĕr-ăl], relating to the medial plane and one side of the body
meg(a), megal(o)	large; million	*megaloencephaly* [MĔG-ă-lō-ĕn-SĔF-ă-lē], abnormally large brain
melan(o)	black; dark	*melanoderma* [MĔL-ă-nō-DĔR-mă], abnormal skin darkening
mes(o)	middle; median	*mesocephalic* [MĔZ-ō-sĕ-FĂL-ĭk], having a medium-sized head
micr(o)	small; one-millionth; tiny	*microorganism* [MĪ-krō-ŌR-găn-ĭzm], tiny organism
mio	smaller; less	*miopragia* [mī-ō-PRĀ-jē-ă], lessened functional activity
morph(o)	structure; shape	*morphology* [mōr-FŎL-ō-jē], study of the structure of animals and plants

Combining Form	Meaning	Example
narco	sleep; numbness	*narcolepsy* [NĂR-kō-lĕp-sē], sleep disorder
necr(o)	death; dying	*necrology* [nĕ-KRŎL-ō-jē], study of the cause of death
noct(i)	night	*nocturia* [nŏk-TŪ-rē-ā], urination at night
nucle(o)	nucleus	*nucleotoxin* [NŪ-klē-ō-TŎK-sĭn], poison that acts upon a cell nucleus
nyct(o)	night	*nyctalopia* [nĭk-tă-LŌ-pē-ă], reduced ability to see at night
oncho, onco	tumor	*oncolysis* [ŏng-KŎL-ĭ-sĭs], destruction of a tumor
orth(o)	straight; normal	*orthodontics* [ōr-thō-DŎN-tĭks], dental specialty concerned with correction of tooth placement
oxy	sharp; acute; oxygen	*oxyphonia* [ŏk-sē-FŌN-nē-ă], shrillness of voice
path(o)	disease	*pathogen* [PĂTH-ō-jĕn], disease-causing substance
phago	eating; devouring; swallowing	*phagocyte* [FĂG-ō-sīt], cell that ingests bacteria and other particles
pharmaco	drugs; medicine	*pharmacology* [FĂR-mă-KŎL-ō-jē], the science of drugs, including their sources, uses, and interactions
phon(o)	sound; voice; speech	*phonometer* [fō-NŎM-ĕ-tĕr], instrument for measuring sound
phot(o)	light	*photometer* [fō-TŎM-ĕ-tĕr], instrument for measuring light
physi, physio	physical; natural	*physiotherapy* [FĬZ-ē-ō-THĀR-ă-pē], physical therapy
plasma, plasmo	formative; plasma	*plasmapheresis* [PLĂZ-mă-fĕ-RĒ-sĭs], separation of blood into parts
pseud(o)	false	*pseudodiabetes* [SŪ-dō-dī-ă-BĒ-tēz], false positive test for sugar in the urine
pyo	pus	*pyocyst* [PĪ-ō-sĭst], cyst filled with pus
pyreto	fever	*pyretogenous* [pī-rĕ-TŎJ-ĕ-nŭs], causing fever
pyro	fever; fire; heat	*pyrogenic* [pī-rō-JĔN-ĭk], causing fever
radio	radiation; x-ray; radius	*radiography* [RĀ-dē-ŎG-ră-fē], x-ray examination

Combining Form	Meaning	Example
salping(o)	tube	*salpingectomy* [săl-pĭn-JĔK-tō-mē], removal of the fallopian tube
schiz(o)	split; division	*schizophrenia* [skĭz-ō-FRĔ-nē-ă, skĭts-ō-FRĔ-nē-ă], a group of mental disorders often with a disorder in perception
scler(o)	hardness; hardening	*scleroderma* [sklēr-ō-DĔR-mă], thickening and hardness of the skin
scolio	crooked; bent	*scoliometer* [skō-lē-ŎM-ě-těr], instrument for measuring curves
somat(o)	body	*somatogenic* [SŌ-mă-tō-JĔN-ĭk], originating in the body
somn(o), somni	sleep	*somnambulism* [sŏm-NĂM-byū-lĭzm], sleepwalking
sono	sound	*sonomotor* [sŏn-ō-MŌ-těr], relating to movements caused by sound
spasmo	spasm	*spasmolytic* [SPĂZ-mō-LĬT-ĭk], agent that relieves spasms
spher(o)	round; spherical	*spherocyte* [SFĒR-ō-sīt], spherical red blood cell
spir(o)	breath; breathe	*spiroscope* [SPĪ-rō-skōp], device for measuring lung capacity
staphyl(o)	grapelike clusters	*staphylococcus* [STĂF-ĭ-lō-KŎK-ŭs], a group of bacteria that cause of a variety of infections
steno	narrowness	*stenocephaly* [stĕn-ō-SĔF-ă-lē], narrowness of the head
strepto	twisted chains; streptococci	*streptococcus* [strĕp-tō-KŎK-ŭs], a group of organisms that can cause various infections
styl(o)	peg-shaped	*styloid* [STĪ-lŏyd], peg-shaped; said of a bony growth
syring(o)	tube	*syringitis* [sĭ-rĭn-JĪ-tĭs], inflammation of the eustachian tube
terato	monster (as a malformed fetus)	*teratogen* [TĔR-ă-tō-jĕn], agent that causes a malformed fetus
therm(o)	heat	*thermometer* [thěr-MŎM-ě-těr], an instrument for measuring temperature
tono	tension; pressure	*tonometer* [tō-NŎM-ě-těr], instrument for measuring pressure

Combining Form	Meaning	Example
top(o)	place; topical	*topography* [tō-PŎG-ră-fē], description of a body part in terms of a specific surface area
tox(i), toxico, toxo	poison; toxin	*toxipathy* [tŏk-SĬP-ă-thē], disease due to poisoning
tropho	food; nutrition	*trophocyte* [TRŎF-ō-sīt], cell that provides nutrition
vivi	life	*viviparous* [vī-VĬP-ă-rŭs], giving birth to living young
xeno	stranger	*xenophobia* [zĕn-ō-FŌ-bē-ă], extreme fear of strangers or foreigners
xer(o)	dry	*xeroderm* [ZĔ-rō-dŭrm], dry skin
zo(o)	life	*zooblast* [ZŌ-ō-blăst], animal cell

Legal and Ethical Issues

Health care workers share some special obligations, both legally and ethically. Many legal decisions have upheld the right of patients to privacy in the health care setting. Patients also have the right to sue over maltreatment. Ethical standards require that patients and their families are treated fairly. "Fair" may include giving the best care, keeping clear records, or respecting patients' rights. The American Hospital Association's Patient's Bill of Rights gives twelve guidelines for medical staff, administrative personnel, and patients. Although these are specifically meant for hospitals, most of the following guidelines provide a clear, ethical standard for patients' rights in all health care settings.

- The right to considerate and respectful care.
- The right to relevant, current, and understandable information about their diagnosis, treatment, and prognosis.
- The right to make decisions about the planned care and the right to refuse care.
- The right to have an advance directive (such as a living will) concerning treatment if they become incapacitated.
- The right to privacy in all procedures, examinations, and discussions of treatment.
- The right to confidential handling of all information and records about their care.
- The right to look over and have all records about their care explained.
- The right to suggest changes in the planned care or to transfer to another facility.

- The right to be informed about the business relationships among the hospital and other facilities that are part of the treatment and care.
- The right to decide whether to take part in experimental treatments.
- The right to understand their care options after a hospital stay.
- The right to know about the hospital's policies for settling disputes and to examine and receive an explanation of all charges.

As a worker in health care, you may be a clinical worker who provides direct care, or you may be an administrative worker who usually has access to, or responsibility for, patient records. In either case, the adherence to all legal and ethical standards is a fundamental requirement of your job. Many issues are legislated differently around the country. You must follow the rules of the state and institution for which you work. Never take it upon yourself to make medical decisions for which you have not been trained and are not qualified.

HIPAA and Allied Health Professions

In 1996, Congress passed the Health Insurance Portability and Accountability Act of 1996 (HIPAA). This law protects health insurance coverage for workers and their families when they change or lose their jobs. The act also requires the Department of Health and Human Services to establish national standards for electronic health care transactions and national identifiers for providers, health plans, and employers. It also addresses the security and privacy of health data. The goal of the law is to improve the efficiency and effectiveness of the nation's health care system by encouraging the widespread use of electronic data interchange in health care.

For more information about the Patient's Bill of Rights, go to the American Hospital Association's Web site (www.aha.org).

There are a number of Web sites where you can learn about HIPAA (www.cms.gov; www.hhs.gov). You can also do a search for the keyword HIPAA and you will come up with many more sites.

MORE ABOUT...

HIPAA and Privacy

The following are examples of possible violations of patient privacy under HIPAA regulations and some suggestions about how to avoid them.

- Telephone conversations with (or regarding) patients should not be held within earshot of the reception room or other patients. This is why phone triage is set apart from patient areas.
- A conversation with the patient being escorted down the hall to the exam or treatment room should not include the reason the patient is being seen, how treatment is progressing, or whether they followed the prep instructions for this visit. Limit the conversation until there is a private environment.
- Patient records, documents, telephone messages, lab reports, etc. should be sorted, processed, and/or filed promptly. If there is a need to retain the documents for processing or reference, the documents should be stored in an area apart from patient flow.
- When scheduling a procedure by phone, it should be done away from areas of high traffic, preferably in a private office.

Working in Health Care

The Crestview Walk-In Medical Center is a nonemergency clinic. It employs three doctors, four nurses, three medical assistants, and two receptionists. All twelve employees have access to the many patient records kept in the files and in the computers at Crestview. The small conference room at the back of the facility doubles as a lunchroom. Most of the staff bring their snacks and lunches to work because Crestview is in a suburban neighborhood that does not have many stores or restaurants nearby.

All the employees have one thing in common—the patients. When they gather in the conference room for meetings, the teams discuss how to handle their cases. However, when the room becomes a lunchroom, all patient discussion stops. The facility has a strict policy that allows discussion of cases only in a professional setting. Everyone observes the ethical and legal codes that forbid staff from discussing cases outside the facility and outside the domain of a work situation.

Critical Thinking

26. Why should the facility have a policy about discussing specific cases among the staff? What should it be?
27. Based on what you understand about the roles of the physicians, nurses, medical assistants, and receptionists, who do you think should have access to patient files?

Using Medical Terminology

Many careers depend on a sound knowledge of medical terminology. Written or electronic records are developed and used by many people involved in health care services. Spoken directions are used to communicate orders for health care and administrative procedures in the health care setting. The role of each health care professional usually includes the duties that each person is or is not allowed to do. For example, physicians diagnose, treat, and prescribe medications for the treatment of diseases. Nurses administer medications, track vital signs, and give care, but are not allowed to prescribe medication. Other health care employees (medical assistant, patient care technician) combine administrative and clinical duties in various health care settings. People in health information management perform many of the administrative tasks that allow facilities to get paid or reimbursed in the complicated world of health care. The systems chapters, case studies, and career pages in this text will introduce you to people working in the health care environment.

From the time someone calls or visits a physician's office, that patient's medical record is involved. The medical assistant or receptionist first gathers or updates personal information about the patient, such as name, address, and insurance information, as well as learns the patient's chief complaint, or reason for the visit. The medical documentation continues to grow as the provider (the physician, nurse, nurse-practitioner, and so on) sees the patient, gathers the pertinent medical history and performs a physical examination, reaches a diagnosis, and provides procedures appropriate for the condition or illness. If a patient is hospitalized, or additional laboratory or x-ray services are needed, hospital workers, laboratory technicians, and radiologists may perform procedures, which must be documented. The patient's medical record then provides the basis for payment for these services.

Coders and billing clerks then fill out the paperwork necessary to enable the provider to get paid.

Documentation of health care services must be complete for both ethical and legal reasons. Many health care careers require an understanding of documentation. Documentation in the form of medical records typically uses many terms learned in medical terminology courses. Most health care institutions train employees to become familiar with their own documentation formats. However, each institution may have its own format for records.

Formats for records depend on state law, the institution's responsibilities, the configuration of its computer systems, and its coding and billing practices. One plan of organization is the SOAP approach. SOAP stands for *subjective, objective, assessment,* and *plan.* When first dealing with a patient, the health care practitioner receives the subjective information from the patient (how the patient feels, what the symptoms are). Next, the health care practitioner performs an examination (takes temperature, blood pressure, pulse) and orders tests (blood and urine tests, allergy tests), thereby getting the objective facts needed for a diagnosis. The assessment stage is the examination of all data and the reaching of a conclusion (the diagnosis). Finally, a plan—treatments, medications, tests, and patient education—is determined and put into action for ongoing evaluation. Figure 1-1 is an example of a SOAP medical record. Another method of documentation is chronological, in which patient interactions are listed in chronological order with the earliest date at the top (Figure 1-2). Figure 1-3 shows documentation for a specific procedure—with the procedure, the person performing it, and what took place.

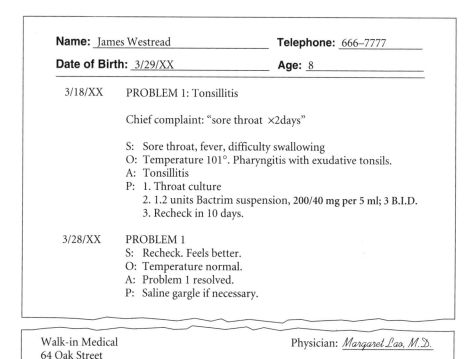

Name: James Westread   **Telephone:** 666–7777

Date of Birth: 3/29/XX   **Age:** 8

3/18/XX   PROBLEM 1: Tonsillitis

Chief complaint: "sore throat ×2days"

S: Sore throat, fever, difficulty swallowing
O: Temperature 101°. Pharyngitis with exudative tonsils.
A: Tonsillitis
P: 1. Throat culture
    2. 1.2 units Bactrim suspension, 200/40 mg per 5 ml; 3 B.I.D.
    3. Recheck in 10 days.

3/28/XX   PROBLEM 1
S: Recheck. Feels better.
O: Temperature normal.
A: Problem 1 resolved.
P: Saline gargle if necessary.

Walk-in Medical
64 Oak Street
Wellington, NY 00001
(444) 555–7777

Physician: *Margaret Lao, M.D.*

Patient No. 89808CQ

FIGURE 1-1 The SOAP method of keeping medical records.

Patient name _Angela O'Toole_	Age _57_	Current Diagnosis _angina_

DATE/TIME	
10/10/XX	Patient presents with increased chest pain, particularly after meals. Sent to lab
	for echocardiogram; BP 143/84. Leonard Glasser, M.D.
10/14/XX	Phone consultation with patient—echocardiogram shows status quo. Suspect
	acid reflux, tell patient to add Tagamet to medications. Leonard Glasser, M.D.
10/21/XX	Patient call—experiencing relief. Continue present medication and Tagamet.
	Leonard Glasser, M.D.

FIGURE 1-2   A chronological medical record.

PROCEDURE: _Gastroscopy_	**PATIENT:** _Holly Berger_
STAFF: _Dr. Walker_	**ID no.:** _888–22–8888_

DATE	
9/28/XX	Instrument—GIF100 video gastroscope
	Premedication: 2% Cetacaine spray locally; Demerol 50 mg; Valium 20 mg IV;
	Atropine 0.4 mg IM.
	History: 51 year-old white female with longstanding Crohn's disease, status post
	resection of the terminal ileum and proximal colon in 1971. The patient has been
	complaining of epigastric and right-sided abdominal pain with occasional
	nausea, vomiting over the last 3 weeks. Upper GI series and small bowel follow
	through showed narrowing of the duodenal bulb and post-bulbar segment and
	then approximately 8 cm. irregular stenotic area in the right side of the abdomen,
	probably at the area of the previous anastomosis and the right proximal
	jejunal stricture.
	Procedure: The patient was brought to the endoscopy suite on a gurney. Her
	oropharynx was sprayed with 2% Cetacaine and then she was placed in the left
	lateral decubitus position.

FIGURE 1-3   A medical record of a gastroscopy, a surgical procedure.

SNOMED

Many health care providers and government agencies are involved in an international attempt to standardize medical terminology for use in electronic medical records. The adoption of SNOMED (Systematized Nomenclature of Medicine) Clinical Terms®, better known as SNOMED CT®, is a major step toward this goal. Eventually, it is expected that all medical coding and electronic transfer of medical data will use SNOMED as the basis for medical terms. SNOMED is gradually being standardized and is being uploaded into a database on the Internet continually. It is available in a number of languages. Currently, it is in use in Britain. It is expected that people who do medical coding will be using it for electronic records in the United States in the near future.

For more information, visit SNOMED's Web site (www.snomed.org).

SNOMED contains many unique terms. It is a system that breaks down terms to capture many more diseases, treatments, therapies, procedures, and outcomes than was ever possible in the past. Since SNOMED is an electronic system, all healthcare providers who use it must be using paperless systems. Since most U.S. hospitals now use paper medical records, the widespread implementation of SNOMED is still in the future.

ICD

The set of diagnosis codes in the coding reference called *The International Classification of Diseases, 9th Revision, Clinical Modification* is the current standard for coding patient records and death certificates. Eventually, it is thought that ICD will be combined with SNOMED once all healthcare records are electronic.

Abbreviations

Throughout this text, you will learn common medical abbreviations which are given following any terms or phrases that have familiar abbreviations. In Chapter 17, you will learn abbreviations used in pharmacology. In addition, Appendix B lists you a variety of common medical abbreviations. In recent years, several organizations have come out with recommendations regarding the use of certain abbreviations that have caused confusion leading to medical errors. Appendix B also lists "forbidden" abbreviations as well as abbreviations that are to be avoided.

Complementary and Alternative Medicine

Most medical practices in the United States are run under *conventional medicine* standards. These are standards taught in medical schools and endorsed by organizations such as the American Medical Association (AMA). Around the world, other cultures have health care traditions that have developed over hundreds or even thousands of years. Some practitioners in the United States have incorporated some of these traditions into or alongside their practice of medicine. Such inclusion is called *complementary medicine*. Other health care providers practice forms of medicine outside the realm of conventional medicine. Such practices fall under the category of *alternative medicine*.

The whole field of complementary and alternative medicine (CAM) has generated a lot of interest in the United States. It is estimated that approximately 40 percent of the U. S. population uses some form of complementary and/or alternative medicine. The National Institutes for Health has set up the National Center for Complementary and Alternative Medicine (NCCAM) to provide information, support research, and set standards (http://nccam.nih.gov).

In the field of health care, many people work in CAM practices. Some examples are chiropractic offices, nutritional practices, and therapeutic massage. Some insurance companies now cover certain CAM therapies. Coding systems for CAM therapies have been developed. One such system can be found at Alternative Link's Web site (www.alternativelink.com). As the use of CAM becomes even more popular, insurance companies will probably pay for more therapies and coding will become standardized.

Using Medical Terminology Exercises

Analyzing the Record

Write S for subjective, O for objective, A for assessment, and P for plan after each of the following phrases.

28. I feel nauseous _____

29. Allergy medicine prescribed _____

30. Has dermatitis (rash) _____

31. My arm aches _____

32. Has hypertension _____

Check Your Knowledge

Circle T for true of F for false.

33. Nurses never add to a patient's record. T F

34. A medical assistant should understand the doctor's notes. T F

35. A patient record is a confidential document. T F

36. Objective information is always given by the patient. T F

37. A plan for treatment must never be changed. T F

38. HIPAA governs the patient's bill of rights. T F

39. SNOMED is used only in the United States. T F

40. Privacy in the medical office is the responsibility of everyone who works there. T F

41. Combining forms are the same as prefixes. T F

42. A word's history is called its etymology. T F

Using the Internet

At the Electronic Privacy Information Center site (http://epic.org/privacy/medical/), you will find discussions of current cases, articles, and advice on safeguarding medical records. Click one of the site's topics. Write a paragraph explaining the issue being discussed.

Answers to Chapter Exercises

1. Greek, Latin
2. Hippocrates
3. euthanasia, abortion
4. Greek, Latin
5. written
6. ă-NĒ-mē-ă
7. ĂN-jē-ō-plăs-tē
8. bĕr-SĪ-tĭs
9. dĭ-ZĒZ
10. hē-mō-GLŌ-bĭn
11. lĭm-FŌ-mă
12. nū-RĪ-tĭs
13. ŎS-tē-ō-pō-RŌ-sĭs
14. păr-ă-PLĒ-jē-ă
15. pŭls
16. rā-dē-Ā-shŭn
17. RĒ-flĕks
18. RĔT-ĭ-nă
19. RŪ-mă-tĭzm

20. sĭ-ĂT-ĭ-kă
21. SĔP-tŭm
22. SĪ-nŭs
23. THĀR-ă-pē
24. TĪ-fŏyd
25. VĂK-sēn
26. There needs to be a policy because unsupervised discussion of cases in an informal setting can lead to breaches of confidentiality. The policy should limit discussion to case review (often supervised) and answering of specific questions.
27. Specific members of the staff need access to patient files. Facility policy should make the rules of access

clear enough that the staff understands the legal and ethical implications of confidentiality.

28. S
29. P
30. O
31. S
32. A
33. F
34. T
35. T
36. F
37. F
38. F
39. F
40. T
41. F
42. T

Prefixes and Suffixes in Medical Terms

2

After studying this chapter, you will be able to:

▶ Define common medical prefixes
▶ Define common medical suffixes
▶ Describe how word parts are put together to form words

Medical Prefixes and Suffixes

In Chapter 1, you learned about the four basic word parts—word roots, combining forms, prefixes, and suffixes, and you learned the important medical roots and combining forms. In this chapter, you learn the important medical prefixes and suffixes and how word parts are put together to form medical terminology.

Prefixes

Prefixes are word parts that modify the meaning of the word or word root. They attach to the beginning of words. Prefixes tend to indicate size, quantity, position, presence of, and location. When trying to understand a word with a prefix, you can take apart the word, find the meaning of each part, and take a guess at the meaning of the original word. For example, terms for paralysis include *paraplegia, hemiplegia,* and *quadriplegia.* By taking apart the three terms, you can deduce the meaning of each of these three medical terms.

> para- = abnormal; involving two parts + -plegia = paralysis
> hemi- = half
> quadri- = four

Sometimes you need to choose the most likely definition, or you need to reason out a meaning that is not quite the prefix plus the root but is a meaning that makes sense. *Paraplegia* is paralysis of the two lower limbs; *hemiplegia* is paralysis of one side; and *quadriplegia* is paralysis of all four limbs. The meaning "limbs" is not contained specifically in the prefix but it is understood from the combination of the numbers in the prefix's meaning and the root meaning paralysis—so "two paralysis" is paralysis of the two lower limbs (since you cannot have paralysis of just the upper limbs).

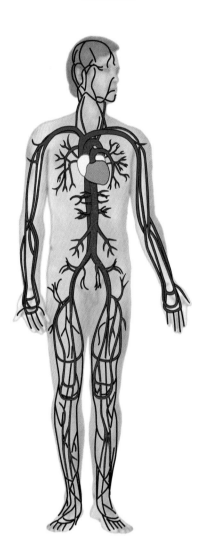

To learn more about paralysis and what is being done to cure it, go to the National Spinal Cord Injury Association's Web site (www.spinalcord.org).

PREFIX	MEANING	EXAMPLE
a-	without	*asepsis* [ā-SĔP-sĭs], without living organisms
ab-, abs-	away from	*abduct* [ăb-DŬKT], to draw away from a position
ad-	toward, to	*adduct* [ă-DŬKT], to draw toward the body, as a limb
ambi-	both, around	*ambidextrous* [ăm-bē-DĔKS-trŭs], having ability on both the right and left sides (said of the hands)
an-	without	*anencephalic* [ăn-ĕn-sĕ-FĂL-ĭk], without a brain
ana-	up, toward	*anaphylactic* [ĂN-ă-fĭ-LĂK-tĭk], exaggerated reaction to an antigen or toxin
ante-	before	*antemortem* [ĂN-tē-mŏr-tĕm], before death
anti-	against	*antibacterial* [ĂN-tē-băk-TĒR-ē-ăl], preventing the growth of bacteria
apo-	derived, separate	*apobiosis* [ăp-ō-bī-Ō-sĭs], death of a part of a living organism
aut(o)-	self	*autoimmune* [ăw-tō-ĭ-MYŪN], against an individual's own tissue
bi-	twice, double	*biparous* [BĬP-ă-rŭs], bearing two young
brachy-	short	*brachyesophagus* [BRĂK-ē-ĕ-sŏf-ă-gŭs], abnormally short esophagus
brady-	slow	*bradycardia* [brăd-ē-KĂR-dē-ă], abnormally slow heartbeat
cata-	down	*cataplexy* [KĂT-ă-plĕk-sē], sudden extreme muscle weakness
circum-	around	*circumoral* [sĕr-kŭm-ŌR-ăl], around the mouth
co-, col-, com-, con-, cor-	together	*codominant* [kō-DŎM-ĭ-nănt], having an equal degree of dominance (said of two genes)
contra-	against	*contraindicated* [kŏn-tră-ĭn-dĭ-KĀ-tĕd], not recommended
de-	away from	*demyelination* [dē-MĪ-ĕ-lĭ-NĀ-shŭn], loss of myelin
di-, dif-, dir-, dis-,	not, separated	*disarticulation* [dĭs-ăr-tĭk-yū-LĀ-shŭn], amputation of a joint
dia-	through	*diaplacental* [dī-ă-plă-SĔN-tăl], passing through the placenta

Prefix	Meaning	Example
dys-	abnormal; difficult	*dysfunctional* [dĭs-FŬNK-shŭn-ăl], functioning abnormally
ect(o)-	outside	*ectopic* [ĕk-TŎP-ĭk], occurring outside the normal place, as a pregnancy occurring outside of the uterus
end(o)-	within	*endoabdominal* [ĔN-dō-ăb-DŎM-ĭ-năl], within the abdomen
epi-	over	*epicondyle* [ĕp-ĭ-KŎN-dīl], projection over or near the condyle
eu-	well, good, normal	*eupepsia* [yū-PĔP-sē-ă], normal digestion
ex-	out of, away from	*exhale* [ĔKS-hāl], breathe out
exo-	external, on the outside	*exogenous* [ĕks-ŎJ-ĕ-nŭs], produced outside of the organism
extra-	without, outside of	*extracorporeal* [ĕks-tră-kōr-PŎ-rē-ăl], outside of the body
hemi-	half	*hemiplegia* [hĕm-ĭ-PLĒ-jē-ă], paralysis on one side of the body
hyper-	above normal; overly	*hyperactive* [hī-pĕr-ĂK-tĭv], abnormally restless and inattentive
hypo-	below normal, beneath	*hypoglycemia* [hī-pō-glī-SĒ-mē-ă], low blood sugar
infra-	positioned beneath	*infrasternal* [ĭn-fră-STĔR-năl], below the sternum
inter-	between	*interdental* [ĭn-tĕr-DĔN-tăl], between the teeth
intra-	within	*intramuscular* [ĬN-tră-MŬS-kyū-lăr], within the substance of the muscles
iso-	equal, same	*isometric* [ī-sō-MĔT-rĭk], of the same dimensions
mal-	bad; inadequate	*malabsorption* [măl-ăb-SŎRP-shŭn], inadequate absorption
meg(a)-, megal(o)-	large	*megacephaly* [mĕg-ă-SĔF-ă-lē], abnormal enlargement of the head
mes(o)-	middle, median	*mesoderm* [MĔZ-ō-dĕrm], the middle layer of skin
meta-	after	*metacarpus* [MĔT-ă-KĂR-pŭs], bones attached to the carpus

Prefix	Meaning	Example
micr(o)-	small, microscopic	*microplasia* [mī-krō-PLĀ-zhē-ă], stunted growth, as in dwarfism
mon(o)-	single	*monomania* [mŏn-ō-MĀ-nē-ă], obsession with a single thought or idea
multi-	many	*multiarticular* [MŬL-tē-ăr-TĬK-yū-lăr], involving many joints
olig(o)-	few; little; scanty	*oligospermia* [ŏl-ĭ-gō-SPĔR-mē-ă], low sperm count
pan-, pant(o)-	all, entire	*panarthritis* [păn-ăr-THRĪ-tĭs], arthritis involving all joints
par(a)-	beside; abnormal; involving two parts	*parakinesia* [păr-ă-kĭ-NĒ-zhē-ă], motor abnormality
per-	through, intensely	*peraxillary* [pĕr-ĂK-sĭ-lār-ē], through the axilla
peri-	around, about, near	*periappendicitis* [PĔR-ē-ă-pĕn-dĭ-SĪ-tĭs], inflammation of the tissue surrounding the appendix
pluri-	several, more	*pluriglandular* [plū-rĭ-GLĂN-dū-lăr], of several glands
poly-	many	*polyarteritis* [pŏl-ē-ăr-tĕr-Ī-tĭs], inflammation of a number of arteries
post-	after, following	*postmortem* [pōst-MŌR-tĕm], after death
pre-	before	*prenatal* [prē-NĀ-tăl], before birth
pro-	before, forward	*prodrome* [PRŌ-drōm], a symptom or group of symptoms that occurs before a disease shows up
quadra-, quadri-	four	*quadriplegia* [kwăh-drĭ-PLĒ-jē-ă], paralysis of all four limbs
re-	again, backward	*reflux* [RĒ-flŭks], backward flow
retro-	behind, backward	*retroversion* [rĕ-trō-VĔR-shŭn], a turning backward, as of the uterus
semi-	half	*semicomatose* [sĕm-ē-KŌ-mă-tōs], drowsy and inactive, but not in a full coma
sub-	less than, under, inferior	*subcutaneous* [sŭb-kyū-TĀ-nē-ŭs], beneath the skin
super-	more than, above, superior	*superacute* [sū-pĕr-ă-KYŪT], more acute
supra-	above, over	*supramaxillary* [sū-pră-MĂK-sĭ-lār-ē], above the maxilla

Prefix	Meaning	Example
syl-, sym-, syn-, sys-	together	*symbiosis* [sĭm-bē-Ō-sĭs], mutual interdependence
tachy-	fast	*tachycardia* [TĂK-i-KAR-de-a], rapid heartbeat
trans-	across, through	*transocular* [trăns-ŎK-yū-lăr], across the eye
ultra-	beyond, excessive	*ultrasonic* [ŭl-tră-SŎN-ĭk], relating to energy waves of higher frequency than sound waves
un-	not	*unconscious* [ŭn-KŎN-shŭs], not conscious
uni-	one	*uniglandular* [yū-nĭ-GLĂN-dū-lăr], involving only one gland

Suffixes

Suffixes can also be combining forms. In the section "Prefixes," the example meaning paralysis, *-plegia*, is both a suffix and a combining form. It both attaches to the end of the word and carries the underlying meaning of the word such as *cardioplegia*, paralysis of the heart.

Many suffixes have several variations that can make the compound word a noun, verb, adjective, or adverb. For example:

an intense fear of closed spaces is *claustrophobia* (noun)

relating to or having such a condition is *claustrophic* (adjective)

Some suffixes form both verbs and nouns so it may be important to look at the sentence in which it appears to determine the exact meaning. For example, *hemorrhage* can mean both "to bleed profusely" (verb) or "profuse bleeding" (noun). In the sentence, "It is possible to hemorrhage profusely from certain injuries," *hemorrhage* is a verb. In the sentence, "The hemorrhage was caused by an injury to his leg," *hemorrhage* is a noun.

Suffix	Meaning	Example
-ad	toward	*cephalad* [SĔF-ă-lăd], toward the head
-algia	pain	*neuralgia* [nū-RĂL-jē-ă], nerve pain
-asthenia	weakness	*neurasthenia* [nūr-ăs-THĒ-nē-ă], condition with vague symptoms, such as weakness
-blast	immature, forming	*astroblast* [ĂS-trō-blăst], immature cell
-cele	hernia	*cystocele* [SĬS-tō-sēl], hernia of the urinary bladder
-cidal	destroying, killing	*suicidal* [sū-ĭ-SĬD-ăl], likely to kill oneself
-cide	destroyer of, killer of	*suicide* [SŪ-ĭ-sĭd], killing of oneself; *bacteriocide* [băk-TĒR-ē-ō-sĭd], agent that destroys bacteria

Suffix	Meaning	Example
-clasis	breaking	*osteoclasis* [ŎS-tē-ŎK-lă-sĭs], intentional breaking of a bone
-clast	breaking instrument	*osteoclast* [ŎS-tē-ō-klăst], instrument used in osteoclasis
-crine	secreting	*endocrine* [ĔN-dō-krĭn], gland that secretes hormones into the bloodstream
-crit	separate	*hematocrit* [HĒ-mă-tō-krĭt, HĔM-ă-tō-krĭt], percentage of volume of a blood sample that is composed of cells
-cyte	cell	*thrombocyte* [THRŎM-bō-sīt], blood platelet
-cytosis	condition of cells	*erythrocytosis* [ĕ-RĬTH-rō-sī-tō-sĭs], condition with an abnormal number of red blood cells in the blood
-derma	skin	*scleroderma* [sklēr-ō-DĔR-mă], hardening of the skin
-desis	binding	*arthrodesis* [ăr-THRŎD-ĕ-sĭs, ăr-thrō-DĒ-sĭs], stiffening of a joint
-dynia	pain	*neurodynia* [nūr-ō-DĬN-ē-ă], nerve pain
-ectasia	expansion; dilation	*neurectasia* [nūr-ĕk-TĀ-zhē-ă], operation with dilation of a nerve
-ectasis	expanding; dilating	*bronchiectasis* [brŏng-kē-ĔK-tă-sĭs], condition with chronic dilation of the bronchi
-ectomy	removal of	*appendectomy* [ăp-ĕn-DĔK-tō-mē], removal of the appendix
-edema	swelling	*lymphedema* [lĭmf-ĕ-DĒ-mă], swelling as a result of obstructed lymph nodes
-ema	condition	*empyema* [ĕm-pī-Ē-mă], pus in a body cavity
-emesis	vomiting	*hematemesis* [hē-mă-TĔM-ĕ-sĭs], vomiting of blood
-emia	blood	*uremia* [yū-RĒ-mē-ă], excess urea in the blood
-emic	relating to blood	*uremic* [yū-RĒ-mĭk], having excess urea in the blood
-esthesia	sensation	*paresthesia* [păr-ĕs-THĒ-zhē-ă], abnormal sensation, such as tingling
-form	in the shape of	*uniform* [YŪ-nĭ-fŏrm], having the same shape throughout
-gen	producing, coming to be	*carcinogen* [kăr-SĬN-ō-jĕn], cancer-causing agent

Suffix	Meaning	Example
-genesis	production of	*pathogenesis* [păth-ō-JĔN-ĕ-sĭs], production of disease
-genic	producing	*iatrogenic* [ī-ăt-rō-JĔN-ĭk], induced by treatment
-globin	protein	*hemoglobin* [hē-mō-GLŌ-bĭn], protein of red blood cells
-globulin	protein	*immunoglobulin* [ĭm-yū-nō-GLŎB-yū-lĭn], one of certain structurally related proteins
-gram	a recording	*encephalogram* [ĕn-SĔF-ă-lō-grăm], brain scan
-graph	recording instrument	*encephalograph* [ĕn-SĔF-ă-lō-grăf], instrument for measuring brain activity
-graphy	process of recording	*echocardiography* [ĔK-ō-kăr-dē-ŎG-ră-fē], use of ultrasound to examine the heart
-iasis	pathological condition or state	*psoriasis* [sō-RĪ-ă-sĭs], chronic skin disease
-ic	pertaining to	*gastric* [GĂS-trĭk], relating to the stomach
-ics	treatment, practice, body of knowledge	*orthopedics* [ōr-thō-PĒ-dĭks], medical practice concerned with treatment of skeletal disorders
-ism	condition, disease, doctrine	*dwarfism* [DWŌRF-ĭzm], condition including abnormally small size
-itis (*pl.*, **-itides**)	inflammation	*nephritis* [nĕ-FRĪ-tĭs], kidney inflammation; *neuritides* [nū-RĬT-ĭ-dēz], inflammations of nerves
-kinesia	movement	*bradykinesia* [brăd-ĭ-kĭn-Ē-zhē-ă], decrease in movement
-kinesis	movement	*hyperkinesis* [hī-pĕr-kĭ-NĒ-sĭs], excessive muscular movement
-lepsy	condition of	*catalepsy* [KĂT-ă-lĕp-sē], condition with having seizures of extreme rigidity
-leptic	having seizures	*cataleptic* [kăt-ă-LĔP-tĭk], person with catalepsy
-logist	one who practices	*dermatologist* [dĕr-mă-TŎL-ō-jĭst], one who practices dermatology
-logy	study, practice	*dermatology* [dĕr-mă-TŎL-ō-jē], study and treatment of skin disorders
-lysis	destruction of	*electrolysis* [ē-lĕk-TRŎL-ĭ-sĭs], permanent removal of unwanted hair
-lytic	destroying	*thrombolytic* [thrŏm-bō-LĬT-ĭk], dissolving a thrombus
-malacia	softening	*osteomalacia* [ŎS-tē-ō-mă-LĀ-shē-ă], gradual softening of bone
-mania	obsession	*monomania* [mŏn-ō-MĀ-nē-ă], obsession with one idea

Suffix	Meaning	Example
-megaly	enlargement	*cephalomegaly* [SĔF-ă-lō-MĔG-ă-lē], abnormal enlargement of the head
-meter	measuring device	*ophthalmometer* [ŏf-thăl-MŎM-ĕ-tĕr], device for measuring cornea curvature
-metry	measurement	*optometry* [ŏp-TŎM-ĕ-trē], specialty concerned with measurement of eye function
-oid	like, resembling	*cardioid* [KĂR-dē-ŏyd], resembling a heart
-oma (pl., -omata)	tumor, neoplasm	*myoma* (*pl.*, *myomata*) [mī-Ō-mă (mī-ō-MĂ-tă)], neoplasm of muscle tissue
-opia	vision	*diplopia* [dĭ-PLŌ-pē-ă], double vision
-opsia	vision	*chloropsia* [klō-RŎP-sē-ă], condition of seeing objects as green
-opsy	view of	*biopsy* [BĪ-ŏp-sē], removal of living tissue for analysis
-osis (pl., -oses)	condition, state, process	*halitosis* [hăl-ĭ-TŌ-sĭs], chronic bad breath
-ostomy	opening	*colostomy* [kō-LŎS-tō-mē], surgical opening in the colon
-oxia	oxygen	*anoxia* [ăn-ŎK-sē-ă], lack of oxygen
-para	bearing	*primipara* [prī-MĬP-ăr-ă], woman who has given birth once
-paresis	slight paralysis	*monoparesis* [mŏn-ō-pă-RĒ-sĭs], paralysis of only one extremity
-parous	producing; bearing	*viviparous* [vī-VĬP-ă-rŭs], bearing living young
-pathy	disease	*osteopathy* [ŏs-tē-ŎP-ă-thē], bone disease
-penia	deficiency	*leukopenia* [lū-kō-PĒ-nē-ă], condition with fewer than normal white blood cells
-pepsia	digestion	*dyspepsia* [dĭs-PĔP-sē-ă], impaired digestion
-pexy	fixation, usually done surgically	*nephropexy* [NĔF-rō-pĕk-sē], surgical fixation of a floating kidney
-phage, -phagia, -phagy	eating, devouring	*polyphagia* [pŏl-ē-FĀ-jē-ă], excessive eating
-phasia	speaking	*aphasia* [ă-FĀ-zhē-ă], loss of or reduction in speaking ability
-pheresis	removal	*leukapheresis* [lū-kă-fĕ-RĒ-sĭs], removal of leukocytes from drawn blood
-phil	attraction; affinity for	*cyanophil* [SĪ-ăn-nō-fĭl], element that turns blue after staining
-philia	attraction; affinity for	*hemophilia* [hē-mō-FĬL-ē-ă], blood disorder with tendency to hemorrhage
-phobia	fear	*acrophobia* [ăk-rō-FŌ-bē-ă], fear of heights
-phonia	sound	*neuraphonia* [nūr-ă-FŌ-nē-ă], loss of sounds
-phoresis	carrying	*electrophoresis* [ē-lĕk-trō-FŌR-ē-sĭs], movement of particles in an electric field

SUFFIX	MEANING	EXAMPLE
-phoria	feeling; carrying	*euphoria* [yū-FŌR-ē-ă], feeling of well-being
-phrenia	of the mind	*schizophrenia* [skĭz-ō-FRĔ-nē-ă, skĭt-sō-FRĔ-nē-ă], term for a common psychosis
-phthisis	wasting away	*hemophthisis* [hē-MŎF-thĭ-sĭs], anemia
-phylaxis	protection	*prophylaxis* [prō-fĭ-LĂK-sĭs], prevention of disease
-physis	growing	*epiphysis* [ĕ-PĬF-ĭ-sĭs], part of a long bone distinct from and growing out of the shaft
-plakia	plaque	*leukoplakia* [lū-kō-PLĀ-kē-ă], white patch on the mucous membrane
-plasia	formation	*dysplasia* [dĭs-PLĀ-zhē-ă], abnormal tissue formation
-plasm	formation	*protoplasm* [PRŌ-tō-plăzm], living matter
-plastic	forming	*hemoplastic* [hē-mō-PLĂS-tĭk], forming new blood cells
-plasty	surgical repair	*rhinoplasty* [RĪ-nō-plăs-tē], plastic surgery of the nose
-plegia	paralysis	*quadriplegia* [KWĂH-drĭ-PLĒ-jē-ă], paralysis of all four limbs
-plegic	one who is paralyzed	*quadriplegic* [kwăh-drĭ-PLĒ-jĭk], person who has quadriplegia
-pnea	breath	*eupnea* [yūp-NĒ-ă], easy, normal respiration
-poiesis	formation	*erythropoiesis* [ĕ-RĬTH-rō-pŏy-Ē-sĭs], formation of red blood cells
-poietic	forming	*erythropoietic* [ĕ-RĬTH-rō-pŏy-ĕt-ĭk], forming new red blood cells
-poietin	one that forms	*erythropoietin* [ĕ-RĬTH-rō-pŏy-ĕ-tĭn], an acid that aids in the formation of red blood cells
-porosis	lessening in density	*osteoporosis* [ŎS-tē-ō-pō-RŌ-sĭs], lessening of bone density
-ptosis	falling down; drooping	*blepharoptosis* [blĕf-ă-RŎP-tō-sĭs], drooping eyelid
-rrhage	discharge heavily	*hemorrhage* [HĔM-ō-răj], to bleed profusely
-rrhagia	heavy discharge	*tracheorrhagia* [trā-kē-ō-RĀ-jē-ă], hemorrhage from the trachea
-rrhaphy	surgical suturing	*herniorrhaphy* [HĔR-nē-ŌR-ă-fē], surgical suturing of a hernia
-rrhea	a flowing, a flux	*dysmenorrhea* [dĭs-mĕn-ŌR-ē-ă], difficult menstrual flow
-rrhexis	rupture	*cardiorrhexis* [kăr-dē-ō-RĔK-sĭs], rupture of the heart wall
-schisis	splitting	*spondyloschisis* [spŏn-dĭ-LŎS-kĭ-sĭs], failure of fusion of the vertebral arch in an embryo

SUFFIX	MEANING	EXAMPLE
-scope	instrument (especially one used for observing or measuring)	*microscope* [MĪ-krō-skōp], instrument for viewing small objects
-scopy	use of an instrument for observing	*microscopy* [mī-KRŎS-kō-pē], use of microscopes
-somnia	sleep	*insomnia* [ĭn-SŎM-nē-ă], inability to sleep
-spasm	contraction	*esophagospasm* [ĕ-SŎF-ă-gō-spăzm], spasm of the walls of the esophagus
-stalsis	contraction	*peristalsis* [pĕr-ĭ-STĂL-sĭs], movement of the intestines by contraction and relaxation of its tube
-stasis	stopping; constant	*homeostasis* [HŌ-mē-ō-STĀ-sĭs], state of equilibrium in the body
-stat	agent to maintain a state	*bacteriostat* [băk-TĒR-ē-ō-stăt], agent that inhibits bacterial growth
-static	maintaining a state	*hemostatic* [hē-mō-STĂT-ĭk], stopping blood flow within a vessel
-stenosis	narrowing	*stenostenosis* [STĔN-ō-stĕ-NŌ-sĭs], narrowing of the parotid duct
-stomy	opening	*colostomy* [kō-LŎS-tō-mē], surgical opening in the colon
-tome	cutting instrument, segment	*osteotome* [ŎS-tē-ō-tōm], instrument for cutting bone
-tomy	cutting operation	*laparotomy* [LĂP-ă-RŎT-ō-mē], incision in the abdomen
-trophic	nutritional	*atrophic* [ā-TRŌF-ĭk], of a wasting state, often due to malnutrition
-trophy	nutrition	*dystrophy* [DĬS-trō-fē], changes that result from inadequate nutrition
-tropia	turning	*esotropia* [ĕs-ō-TRŌ-pē-ă], crossed eyes
-tropic	turning toward	*neurotropic* [nūr-ō-TRŎP-ĭk], localizing in nerve tissue
-tropy	condition of turning toward	*neurotropy* [nū-RŎT-rō-pē], affinity of certain contrast mediums for nervous tissue
-uria	urine	*pyuria* [pī-YŪ-rē-ă], pus in the urine
-version	turning	*retroversion* [rĕ-trō-VĔR-zhŭn], a turning backward (said of the uterus)

Putting It All Together

All medical terms have a word root, which is the element that gives the essential meaning to the word. For example, *card-* is a word root meaning heart. In the word *pericarditis*, the prefix *peri-* and the suffix *-itis* are

MORE ABOUT...

Detecting Compound Words

An easy way to define compound words is to start at the end of the word, look at the suffix to determine its meaning, and then look at the word root. The word root will contain a combining vowel if the suffix begins with a consonant. If not, the combining vowel (usually "o") will be removed. An example is *neuritis.* The suffix *-itis* means "inflammation of." The word root *neur-,* nerve, does not need a combining vowel because *-itis* begins with a vowel. Therefore, *neuritis* is inflammation of a nerve. To repeat the basic rules: If a suffix begins with a vowel, do NOT use the "o." If the suffix begins with a consonant, retain the "o." Then figure out the meaning of any prefixes.

added to the word root to form the whole word meaning an inflammation (*-itis*) of the area surrounding (*peri-*) the heart (*card-*). The word root can also appear in a combining form, which is the root plus a combining vowel or vowels. For example, *cardiology* is formed from *cardio-* (the word root *card-* plus the combining vowels *-i-* and *-o-*) plus the suffix *-logy* meaning the study of the heart.

WORD PARTS EXERCISES

Build Your Medical Vocabulary

Using the lists in this chapter and in Chapter 1, write the appropriate prefix, suffix, or combining form in the blank for each word part. The definition of each word part needed is given immediately under the blank. Item 1 is completed as an example.

1. ____osteo____myel____itis____
    (bone)   (inflammation)

2. _____ cardio _____
    (within)   (recording)

3. _____ dactyly
    (together)

4. _____ violet
    (beyond)

5. _____ sensitive
    (overly)

6. entero _____ _____
            (disease)   (causing)

7. _____ dermic
    (beneath)

8. _____ therapy
    (sleep)

9. _____ ost _____
    (bladder)   (inflammation)

10. _____ tonsillar
    (above)

11. _____ cranio _____
    (half)   (cutting)

12. _____ _____
    (old people)   (fear)

13. _____ glandular
    (within)

14. _____ blast
    (white)

15. _____ _____
    (structure)   (study of)

16. arterio _____
            (suture)

17. dermato _____
           (hemorrhage)

18. _____ flexion
           (half)

19. _____ algesia
           (heat)

20. fibr _____
           (resembling)

21. _____ organsim
           (tiny)

22. onco _____
           (study of)

23. subcost _____
                (pain)

24. blepharo _____
                (paralysis)

25. _____ myx _____
           (fiber)   (tumor)

Find a Match

Each of the words in the left-hand column contains a word part that matches one of the definitions in the right-hand column. Write the letter of the answer that best fits into the left-hand column. Exercise 26 is completed as an example.

26. __o__ antipsychotic   a. in the shape of

27. ____ polycystic   b. without

28. ____ acephaly   c. enlargement

29. ____ tenosynovitis   d. abnormally low

30. ____ myotrophy   e. nutrition

31. ____ laryngoscope   f. self

32. ____ dysgnosia   g. outside of

33. ____ decontamination   h. inflammation

34. ____ chyliform   i. instrument for viewing

35. ____ autoinfection   j. abnormal

36. ____ cardiomegaly   k. between

37. ____ extrasensory   l. away from

38. ____ intercerebral   m. condition

39. ____ osteoporosis   n. many

40. ____ hyposthenia   o. against

Find the Word Part

Complete the word for which the definition is given. Add a word part(s) learned in this chapter.

41. Any disease of the hair: tricho _____

42. Repair of a nose defect: rhino _____

43. Removal of the appendix: append _____

44. Having a jaw that protrudes abnormally forward: _____ gnathic

45. Disease of the heart: cardio _____

46. Inflammation of the bronchi: bronch _____

47. Outer layer of a cell: _____ blast

48. Rib-shaped: costi _____

49. Bone-forming cell: osteo _____

50. Above the nose: _____ nasal

51. Study of the skin: dermato _____

52. Loss of the voice: _____ phonia

53. Study of tissue: hist _____

54. Inflammation of the ovary: ovar _____

55. Inflammation of the ear: ot _____

56. Specialist in the treatment of disorders of the nervous system: neuro _____

57. Incision into a vein: phlebo _____

58. Study of the mind: psycho _____

59. Enlargement of the spleen: spleno _____

60. Removal of the kidney: nephr _____

Separate the Word Parts

Break apart the following words and define each part in the space allowed. You will want to study the list in Chapter 1 before you do this exercise.

61. exocrine _____

62. endocranium _____

63. antidepressant _____

64. somatotropic _____

65. pseudesthesia _____

66. dextrotropic _____

67. algesic _____

68. dyspepsia _____

69. litholysis _____

70. cryolysis _____

Add the suffix

Complete each of the following terms by adding the appropriate suffix at the end of the word.

71. blood vessel disease: angio _____

72. nearsighted vision: my _____

73. poor breathing: dys _____

74. bone density deficiency: osteo _____

75. lymph tumor: lymph _____

76. paralysis of one side: hemi _____

continued

77. practitioner who treats the elderly: geronto _____

78. softening of cartilage: chondro _____

79. instrument for blood pressure measurement: sphygmano _____

80. breast reconstruction: mammo _____

Using the Internet

Go to the Centers for Disease Control's site (www.cdc.gov). Click on several of the topics on the site and find at least ten combining forms, suffixes, and prefixes that you learned about in this chapter and in Chapter 1.

Answers to Chapter Exercises

1. osteomyelitis
2. endocardiography
3. syndactyly
4. ultraviolet
5. hypersensitive
6. enteropathogenic
7. hypodermic
8. hypnotherapy
9. cystitis
10. supratonsillar
11. hemicraniotomy
12. gerontophobia
13. intraglandular
14. leukoblast
15. morphology
16. arteriorrhaphy
17. dermatorrhagia
18. semiflexion
19. thermalgesia
20. fibroid
21. microorganism
22. oncology
23. subcostalgia
24. blepharoplegia
25. fibromyxoma
26. o
27. n
28. b

29. h
30. e
31. i
32. j
33. l
34. a
35. f
36. c
37. g
38. k
39. m
40. d
41. trichopathy
42. rhinoplasty
43. appendectomy
44. prognathic
45. cardiopathy
46. bronchitis
47. ectoblast
48. costiform
49. osteoblast
50. supranasal
51. dermatology
52. aphonia
53. histology
54. ovaritis
55. otitis
56. neurologist

57. phlebotomy
58. psychology
59. splenomegaly
60. nephrectomy
61. exo-, outside of; crine-, secreting
62. endo-, within; cranium
63. anti-, against; depressant
64. somato-, body; -tropic, turning toward
65. pseud-, false; -esthesia, sensation
66. dextro-, right; -tropic, turning toward
67. alges-, pain; -ic, pertaining to
68. dys-, abnormal; -pepsia, digestion
69. litho, stone; -lysis, destruction of
70. cryo-, cold; -lysis, destruction of
71. angiopathy
72. myopia
73. dyspnea
74. osteopenia
75. lympnoma
76. hemiplegia
77. gerontologist
78. chondromalacia
79. sphygmanometer
80. mammoplasty

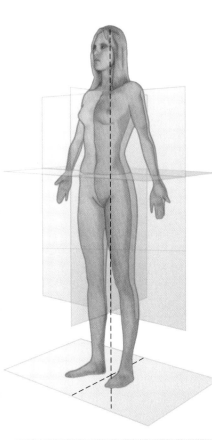

CHAPTER

3

Body Structure

After studying this chapter, you will be able to:

▶ Define the elements of human body structure
▶ Describe the planes of the body
▶ Locate the body cavities and list organs that are contained within each cavity
▶ Recognize combining forms that relate to elements and systems of the body

Body Structure and Organization

The body is organized from its smallest element, the **cell,** to the collection of systems, with all its interrelated parts. The entire body is made of cells that vary in size, shape, and function, but all cells have one thing in common: they need food, water, and oxygen to live and function.

Cells

The basic structure of a cell (Figure 3-1) includes three parts:

1. The *cell membrane* is the outer covering of the cell.
2. The *nucleus* is the central portion of each cell. It directs the cell's activities and contains the *chromosomes*. The chromosomes are the bearers of *genes*—those elements that control inherited traits such as eye color, height, inherited diseases, gender, and so on.
3. Surrounding the nucleus is the *cytoplasm*, a substance that contains the material to instruct cells to perform different essential tasks, such as reproduction and movement.

To see some videos about living cells, go to www.cellsalive.com and click on animal cells.

Tissues

Groups of cells that work together to perform the same task are called **tissue.** The body has four types of tissue:

- **Connective tissue** holds and connects body parts together. Examples are bones, ligaments, and tendons.
- **Epithelial tissue** covers the internal and external body surfaces. Skin and linings of internal organs (such as the intestines) are epithelial tissue.
- **Muscle tissue** expands and contracts, allowing the body to move.
- **Nervous tissue** carries messages to and from the brain and spinal cord to and from all parts of the body.

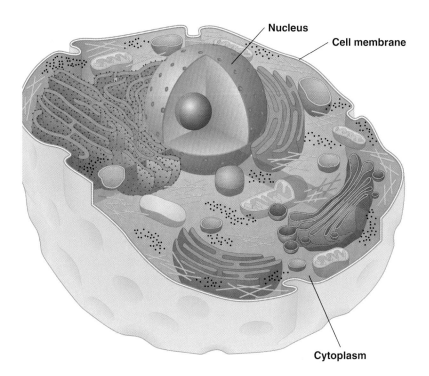

FIGURE 3-1 The human body is made up of cells. Cells have three basic parts—a cell membrane, a nucleus, and cytoplasm.

Labels in figure: Nucleus, Cell membrane, Cytoplasm

Organs

Groups of tissue that work together to perform a specific function are called **organs.** Examples are the *kidneys*, which maintain water and salt balance in the blood, and the *stomach*, which breaks down food into substances that the circulatory system can transport throughout the body as nourishment for its cells.

Systems

Groups of organs that work together to perform one of the body's major functions form a **system.** The terminology for each body system is provided in a separate chapter.

- The **integumentary system** consists of the skin and the accessory structures derived from it—hair, nails, sweat glands, and oil glands. (See Chapter 4.)
- The **musculoskeletal system** supports the body, protects organs, and provides body movement. It includes muscles, bones, and cartilage. (See Chapter 5.)
- The **cardiovascular system** includes the heart and blood vessels, which pump and transport blood throughout the body. Blood carries nutrients to and removes waste from the tissues. (See Chapter 6.)
- The **respiratory system** includes the lungs and the airways. This system performs respiration. (See Chapter 7.)
- The **nervous system** consists of the brain, spinal cord, and peripheral nerves. The nervous system regulates most body activities and sends and receives messages from the sensory organs. (See Chapter 8.) The two major sensory organs are covered in the sensory system. (See Chapter 16.)
- The **urinary system** includes the kidneys, ureters, bladder, and urethra. It eliminates metabolic waste, helps to maintain acid-base and water-salt balances, and helps regulate blood pressure. (See Chapter 9.)

To play a game online that sees if you know where the organs are in the human body, go to www.scugog-net.com/room108/money/organ600.htm and try your luck.

- The **reproductive system** controls reproduction and heredity. The female reproductive system includes the ovaries, vagina, uterine (fallopian) tubes, uterus, and mammary glands. (See Chapter 10.) The male reproductive system includes the testes, penis, prostate gland, vas deferens, and the seminal vesicles. (See Chapter 11.)
- The **blood system** includes the blood and all its components. (See Chapter 12.)
- The **lymphatic and immune systems** includes the lymph, the glands of the lymphatic system, lymphatic vessels, and the nonspecific and specific defenses of the immune system. (See Chapter 13.)
- The **digestive system** includes all the organs of digestion and excretion of waste. (See Chapter 14.)
- The **endocrine system** includes the glands that secrete hormones for regulation of many of the body's activities. (See Chapter 15.)
- The **sensory system** covers the eyes and ears and those parts of other systems that are involved in the reactions of the five senses. (See Chapter 16.)

Cavities

The body has two main cavities (spaces)—the dorsal and the ventral. The **dorsal cavity,** on the back side of the body, is divided into the **cranial cavity,** which holds the brain, and the **spinal cavity,** which holds the spinal cord. The **ventral cavity,** on the front side of the body, is divided (and separated by a muscle called the **diaphragm**) into the **thoracic cavity,** which holds the heart, lungs, and major blood vessels, and the **abdominal cavity,** which holds the organs of the digestive and urinary systems. The bottom portion of the abdominal cavity is called the **pelvic cavity.** It contains the reproductive system. Figure 3-2 shows the body cavities.

FIGURE 3-2 The body has two main cavities—the dorsal and the ventral cavities. Each of these is further divided into smaller cavities as shown here.

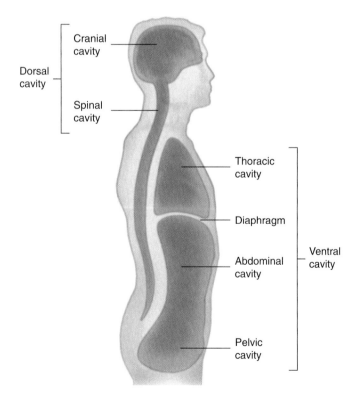

Vocabulary Review

In the previous section, you learned terms relating to body structure and organization. Before going on to the exercises, review the terms below and refer to the previous section if you have any questions. Pronunciations are provided for certain terms. Sometimes information about where the word came from is included after the term. These etymologies (word histories) are for your information only. You do not need to memorize them.

Term	Definition
abdominal [ăb-DŎM-ĭ-năl] **cavity**	Body space between the abdominal walls, above the pelvis, and below the diaphragm.
blood [blŭd] **system** Old English *blud*.	Body system that includes blood and all its component parts.
cardiovascular [KĂR-dē-ō-VĂS-kyū-lăr] **system**	Body system that includes the heart and blood vessels; circulatory system.
cell [sĕl] Latin *cella*, storeroom	Smallest unit of a living structure.
connective [kŏn-NĔK-tĭv] **tissue**	Fibrous substance that forms the body's supportive framework.
cranial [KRĀ-nē-ăl] **cavity**	Space in the head that contains the brain.
diaphragm [DĪ-ă-frăm]	Muscle that divides the abdominal and thoracic cavities.
digestive [dī-JĔS-tĭv] **system**	Body system that includes all organs of digestion and waste excretion, from the mouth to the anus.
dorsal [DŌR-săl] **cavity**	Main cavity on the back side of the body containing the cranial and spinal cavities.
endocrine [ĔN-dō-krĭn] **system**	Body system that includes glands which secrete hormones to regulate certain body functions.
epithelial [ĕp-ĭ-THĒ-lē-ăl] **tissue**	Tissue that covers or lines the body or its parts.
integumentary [ĭn-tĕg-yū-MĔN-tă-rē] **system**	Body system that includes skin, hair, and nails.
lymphatic [lĭm-FĂT-ĭk] **and immune** [ĭ-MYŪN] **systems**	Body system that includes lymph, the glands of the lymphatic system, lymphatic vessels, and the specific and nonspecific defenses of the immune system.
muscle [MŬS-ĕl] **tissue** Latin *musculus*, muscle, mouse	Tissue that is able to contract and relax.
musculoskeletal [MŬS-kyū-lō-SKĔL-ĕ-tăl] **system**	Body system that includes muscles, bones, and cartilage.
nervous [NĔR-vŭs] **system**	Body system that includes the brain, spinal cord, and nerves and controls most body functions by sending and receiving messages.
nervous tissue	Specialized tissue that forms nerve cells and is capable of transmitting messages.

Term	Definition
organ [ŌR-găn]	Group of specialized tissue that performs a specific function.
pelvic [PĔL-vĭk] **cavity**	Body space below the abdominal cavity that includes the reproductive organs.
reproductive [RĒ-prō-DŬK-tĭv] **system**	Either the male or female body system that controls reproduction.
respiratory [RĔS-pĭ-ră-tōr-ē, rĕ-SPĪR-ă-tōr-ē] **system**	Body system that includes the lungs and airways and performs breathing.
sensory [SĔN-sŏ-rē] **system**	Body system that includes the eyes and ears and those parts of other systems involved in the reactions of the five senses.
spinal [SPĪ-năl] **cavity**	Body space that contains the spinal cord.
system [SĬS-tĕm]	Any group of organs and ancillary parts that work together to perform a major body function.
thoracic [thō-RĂS-ĭk] **cavity**	Body space above the abdominal cavity that contains the heart, lungs, and major blood vessels.
tissue [TĬSH-ū]	Any group of cells that work together to perform a single function.
urinary [YŪR-ĭ-nār-ē] **system**	Body system that includes the kidneys, ureters, bladder, and urethra and helps maintain homeostasis by removing fluid and dissolved waste.
ventral [VĔN-trăl] **cavity**	Major cavity in the front of the body containing the thoracic, abdominal, and pelvic cavities.

BODY STRUCTURE AND ORGANIZATION EXERCISES

Find the Match

Match the system to its function.

1. _____ cardiovascular system
2. _____ digestive system
3. _____ endocrine system
4. _____ blood system
5. _____ integumentary system
6. _____ lymphatic and immune system
7. _____ musculoskeletal system
8. _____ nervous system
9. _____ reproductive system
10. _____ respiratory system
11. _____ urinary system

a. performs breathing
b. removes fluid and dissolved waste
c. sends and receives messages
d. pumps and circulates blood to tissues
e. consists of blood and its elements
f. covers the body and its internal structures
g. provides defenses for the body
h. breaks down food
i. regulates through production of hormones
j. controls reproduction
k. supports organs and provides movement

Complete the Sentence

12. The basic element of the human body is a(n) _____.

13. Groups of these basic elements form _____ .

14. Tissue that covers the body or its parts is called _____ tissue.

15. The brain is contained within the _____ cavity.

16. The muscle separating the two main parts of the ventral cavity is called the _____.

17. The spinal and cranial cavities make up the _____ cavity.

18. The space below the abdominal cavity is called the _____ cavity.

19. The system that helps eliminate fluids is the _____ system.

20. The system that breaks down food is called the _____ system.

Directional Terms, Planes, and Regions

In making diagnoses or prescribing treatments, health care providers use standard terms to refer to different areas of the body. These terms describe each anatomical position as a point of reference. The anatomical position always means the body is standing erect, facing forward, with upper limbs at the sides and with the palms facing forward. For example, if a pain is described as in the *right lower quadrant* (RLQ), medical personnel immediately understand that to mean the lower right portion of the patient's body. Certain terms refer to a direction going to or from the body or in which the body is placed. Others divide the body into imaginary planes as a way of mapping the body when the person is in the anatomical position. Still others refer to specific regions of the body.

Directional Terms

Directional terms locate a portion of the body or describe a position of the body. The front side (**anterior** or **ventral**) and the back side (**posterior** or **dorsal**) are the largest divisions of the body. Figure 3-3 shows the body regions of the anterior and posterior sections. Each of these regions contain many parts of the body that will be discussed as part of the body systems of which they are a part.

Some terms indicate a position relative to something else. **Inferior** means below another structure; for example, the vagina is inferior to (or below) the uterus. **Superior** means above another structure; for example, the stomach is superior to the large intestine. **Lateral** means to the side; for example, the eyes are lateral to the nose. **Medial** means middle or near the medial plane of the body; for example, the nose is medial to the eyes. **Deep** means through the surface (as in a deep cut), while **superficial** means on or near the surface (as a scratch on the skin). **Proximal** means near the point of attachment to the trunk; for example, the proximal end of the thighbone joins the hip bone. **Distal** means away from the point of attachment to the trunk; for example, the distal end of the thighbone forms the knee. Figure 3-4 shows the directional terms.

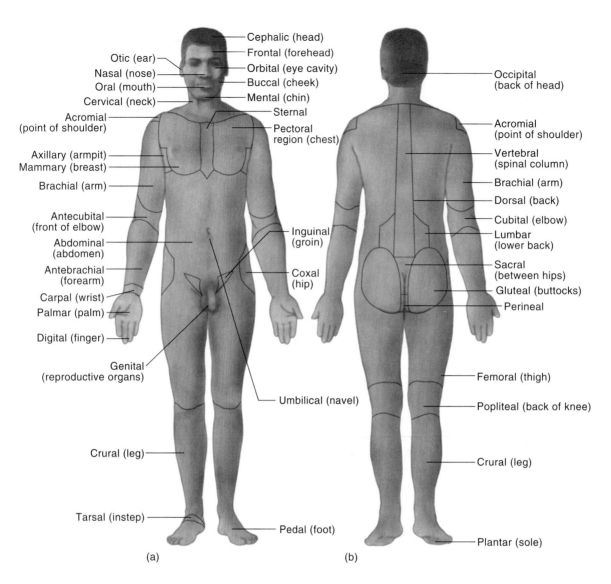

FIGURE 3-3 Anterior (a) and posterior (b) regions. The parts shown in each of the regions are discussed in the body systems chapters throughout the book.

For examination purposes, patients are either **supine** (lying on their spine face upward) or **prone** (lying on the abdomen with their face down). Figure 3-5 shows a patient lying in supine position and Figure 3-6 shows one in prone position.

Planes of the Body

For anatomical and diagnostic discussions, some standard terms are used for the planes and positions of the body. The imaginary planes of the body when it is vertical and facing front are: **frontal (coronal) plane,** which divides the body into anterior and posterior positions; **sagittal (lateral) plane,** which is the plane parallel to the medial and divides the body into left and right sections; **medial** or **midsagittal plane,** which divides the body into equal left and right halves; and **transverse (cross-sectional) plane,** which intersects the body horizontally and divides the body into upper and lower sections. Figure 3-7 shows the planes of the body.

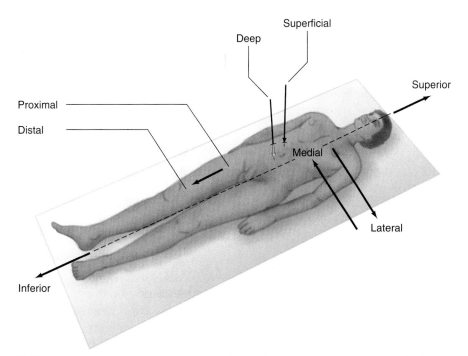

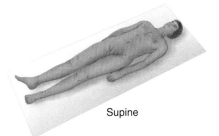

FIGURE 3-5 A patient lying in a supine position with the spinal cord facing down.

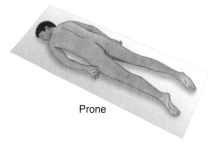

FIGURE 3-6 A patient lying in a prone position with the spinal cord facing up.

FIGURE 3-4 Directional terms used when referring to locations on the body.

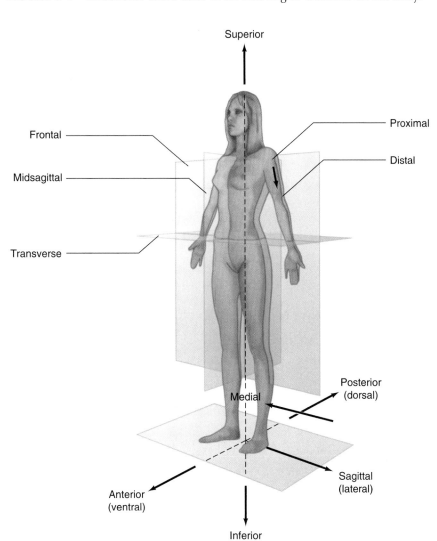

FIGURE 3-7 The planes of and directions from the body.

Areas of the Body

Pain is sometimes felt in only one region of the body (as a muscle pull in the RUQ or right upper quadrant). Other times, internal pain is felt in an area that is not the actual source of the pain. This is known as "referred pain" or synalgia. Such pain usually emanates from nerves or other deep structures within the body.

Regions of the Body

Health care practitioners usually refer to a specific organ, area, or bone when speaking of the upper body. In the back, the spinal column is divided into specific regions (cervical, thoracic, lumbar, sacral, and coccygeal). Chapter 5 describes the spinal column in detail. The middle portion of the body (abdominal and pelvic cavities) is often the site of pain. Doctors use two standard sections to describe this area of the body. The larger section is divided into four quarters with the navel being the center point (Figure 3-8).

- **Right upper quadrant** (RUQ): On the right anterior side; contains part of the liver, the gallbladder, and parts of the pancreas and intestinal tract.
- **Right lower quadrant** (RLQ): On the right anterior side; contains the appendix, parts of the intestines, and parts of the reproductive organs in the female.
- **Left upper quadrant** (LUQ): On the left anterior side; contains the stomach, spleen, and parts of the liver, pancreas, and intestines.
- **Left lower quadrant** (LLQ): On the left anterior side; contains parts of the intestines and parts of reproductive organs in the female.

The smaller divisions of the abdominal and pelvic areas are the nine regions, each of which correspond to a region near a specific point in the body (Figure 3-9).

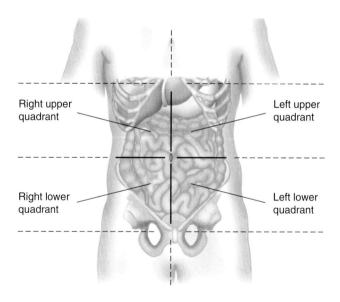

FIGURE 3-8 The four quadrants of the abdominopelvic area.

- **Epigastric region:** the area above the stomach.
- **Hypochondriac regions** (left and right): the two regions just below the cartilage of the ribs, immediately over the abdomen.
- **Umbilical region:** the region surrounding the umbilicus (navel).
- **Lumbar regions** (left and right): the two regions near the waist.
- **Hypogastric region:** the area just below the umbilical region.
- **Iliac (inguinal) regions** (left and right): the two regions near the upper portion of the hip bone.

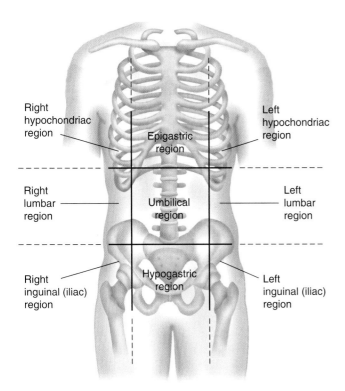

FIGURE 3-9 The regions of the abdominopelvic area.

VOCABULARY REVIEW

In the previous section, you learned terms relating to directional terms, planes, and regions of the body. Before going on to the exercises, review the terms below and refer to the previous section if you have any questions. Pronunciations are provided for certain terms. Sometimes information about where the word came from is included after the term. The etymologies (word histories) are for your information only. You do not need to memorize them.

Term	Definition
anterior [ăn-TĒR-ē-ŏr]	At or toward the front (of the body).
coronal [KŌR-ŏ-năl] **plane**	Imaginary line that divides the body into anterior and posterior positions.

Term	Definition
cross-sectional plane	Imaginary line that intersects the body horizontally.
deep	Away from the surface (of the body).
distal [DĬS-tăl]	Away from the point of attachment to the trunk.
dorsal [DŌR-săl]	At or toward the back of the body.
epigastric [ĕp-ĭ-GĂS-trĭk] **region**	Area of the body immediately above the stomach.
frontal [FRŬN-tăl] **plane**	Imaginary line that divides the body into anterior and posterior positions.
hypochondriac [hī-pō-KŎN-drē-ăk] **regions**	Left and right regions of the body just below the cartilage of the ribs and immediately above the abdomen.
hypogastric [hī-pō-GĂS-trĭk] **region**	Area of the body just below the umbilical region.
iliac [ĬL-ē-ăk] **regions**	Left and right regions of the body near the upper portion of the hip bone.
inferior [ĭn-FĒR-ē-ōr]	Below another body structure.
inguinal [ĬN-gwĭ-năl] **regions**	Left and right regions of the body near the upper portion of the hip bone.
lateral [LĂT-ĕr-ăl]	To the side.
lateral plane	Imaginary line that divides the body perpendicularly to the medial plane.
left lower quadrant (LLQ)	Quadrant on the lower left anterior side of the patient's body.
left upper quadrant (LUQ)	Quadrant on the upper left anterior side of the patient's body.
lumbar [LŬM-băr] **regions**	Left and right regions of the body near the abdomen.
medial [MĒ-dē-ăl]	At or near the middle (of the body).
medial plane	Imaginary line that divides the body into equal left and right halves.
midsagittal [mĭd-SĂJ-ĭ-tăl] **plane**	*See* medial plane.
posterior	At or toward the back side (of the body).
prone	Lying on the stomach with the face down.
proximal [PRŎK-sĭ-măl]	At or near the point of attachment to the trunk.
right lower quadrant (RLQ)	Quadrant on the lower right anterior side of the patient's body.

Term	Definition
right upper quadrant (RUQ)	Quadrant on the upper right anterior side of the patient's body.
sagittal [SĂJ-ĭ-tăl] plane	Imaginary line that divides the body into right and left portions.
superficial [sū-pĕr-FĬSH-ăl]	At or near the surface (of the body).
superior [sū-PĒR-ē-ōr]	Above another body structure.
supine [sū-PĪN]	Lying on the spine facing upward.
transverse plane	Imaginary line that intersects the body horizontally.
umbilical [ŭm-BĬL-ĭ-kăl] region	Area of the body surrounding the umbilicus.
ventral [VĔN-trăl]	At or toward the front (of the body).

CASE STUDY

Locating a Problem

Dr. Lena Woodrow checked the chart of the next patient, Darlene Gordon. Darlene had called yesterday with a vague pain in her LUQ. She also experienced some nausea and general discomfort. Dr. Woodrow had suggested she make a morning appointment.

Critical Thinking

21. What organs might be causing pain in the LUQ?
22. Is it possible for the source of the pain to be located elsewhere in the body?

DIRECTIONAL TERMS, PLANES, AND REGIONS EXERCISES

Check Your Knowledge

Circle T for true or F for false.

23. The epigastric region is below the hypogastric region. T F
24. The heart is deeper than the ribs. T F
25. The leg is inferior to the foot. T F
26. The nose is superior to the eyes. T F
27. The right lower quadrant contains the appendix. T F
28. The coronal plane divides the body horizontally. T F
29. The lateral plane is another name for the sagittal plane. T F
30. The wrist is proximal to the shoulder. T F
31. The spleen is in the left upper quadrant. T F

Complete the Diagram

32. Using any of the terms below, fill in the blanks on the following diagram.

Distal

Supine

Inferior

Deep

Superficial

Anterior

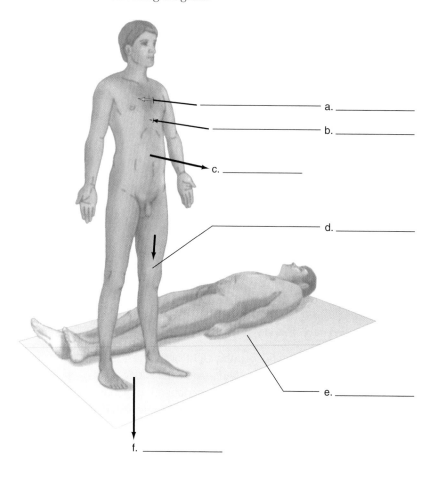

a. _____

b. _____

c. _____

d. _____

e. _____

f. _____

Combining Forms

Chapters 1 and 2 introduced many word roots, combining forms, prefixes, and suffixes used in medical terminology. The combining forms in this chapter relate to elements and systems of the body described here. Once you familiarize yourself with the word parts in Chapters 1, 2, and 3, you will understand many medical terms.

COMBINING FORM	MEANING	EXAMPLE
abdomin(o)	abdomen	*abdominoplasty* [ăb-DŎM-ĭ-nō-plăs-tĕ], surgical repair of the abdomen
aden(o)	gland	*adenitis* [ăd-ĕ-NĪ-tĭs], inflammation of a gland
adip(o)	fat	*adiposis* [ĂD-ĭ-pōs], condition of excessive accumulation of fat

Combining Form	Meaning	Example
adren(o)	adrenal glands	*adrenotoxin* [ă-drē-nō-TŎK-sĭn], a substance toxic to the adrenal glands
angi(o)	vessel	*angiomegaly* [ĂN-jē-ō-MĔG-ă-lē], enlargement of blood vessels
aort(o)	aorta	*aortitis* [ā-ōr-TĪ-tĭs], inflammation of the aorta
appendic(o)	appendix	*appendicitis* [ă-pĕn-dĭ-SĪ-tĭs], inflammation of the appendix
arteri(o)	artery	*arteriosclerosis* [ăr-TĔR-ē-ō-sklĕr-Ō-sĭs], hardening of the arteries
arteriol(o)	arteriole	*arteriolosclerosis* [ăr-tĕr-ē-Ō-lō-sklĕr-Ō-sĭs], hardening of the arterioles, often seen in conjunction with chronic high blood pressure
arthr(o)	joint; articulation	*arthralgia* [ăr-THRĂL-jē-ă], severe joint pain
cardi(o)	heart; esophageal opening of the stomach	*cardiomegaly* [kăr-dē-ō-MĔG-ă-lē], enlargement of the heart; *cardiectomy* [kăr-dē-ĔK-tō-mē], excision of the cardiac portion of the stomach
cephal(o)	head	*cephalomegaly* [SĔF-ă-lō-MĔG-ă-lē], enlargement of the head
cerebell(o)	cerebellum	*cerebellitis* [sĕr-ĕ-bĕl-Ī-tĭs], inflammation of the cerebellum
cerebr(o)	cerebrum	*cerebrotomy* [sĕr-ĕ-BRŎT-ō-mē], incision into the brain
cervic(o)	neck; cervix	*cervicodynia* [SĔR-vĭ-kō-DĬN-ē-ă], neck pain
chir(o)	hand	*chiropractic* [kī-rō-PRĂK-tĭk], theory that uses manipulation of the spine to restore and maintain health
chol(e), cholo	bile	*cholelith* [KŌ-lē-lĭth], gallstone
col(o), colon(o)	colon	*colonoscopy* [kō-lŏn-ŎS-kō-pē], visual examination of the colon
crani(o)	cranium	*craniotomy* [krā-nē-ŎT-ō-mē], opening into the skull
cyst(i), cysto	bladder; cyst	*cystoscopy* [sĭs-TŎS-kō-pē], examination of the interior of the bladder
cyt(o)	cell	*cytology* [sī-TŎL-ō-jē], study of cells
dent(i), dento	tooth	*dentiform* [DĔN-tĭ-fŏrm], tooth-shaped
derm(o), derma, dermat(o)	skin	*dermatitis* [dĕr-mă-TĪ-tĭs], inflammation of the skin

Combining Form	Meaning	Example
duoden(o)	duodenum	*duodenoscopy* [dū-ō-dĕ-NŎS-kō-pē], examination of the interior of the duodenum
encephal(o)	brain	*encephalomyeloneuropathy* [ĕn-SĔF-ă-lō-MĪ-ĕ-lō-nū-RŎP-ă-thē], disease involving the brain, spinal cord, and nerves
gastr(o)	stomach	*gastritis* [găs-TRĪ-tĭs], inflammation of the stomach
gingiv(o)	gum	*gingivitis* [jĭn-jĭ-VĪ-tĭs], inflammation of the gums
gloss(o)	tongue	*glossodynia* [GLŎS-ō-DĬN-ē-ă], pain in the tongue
hem(a), hemat(o), hemo	blood	*hematoma* [hē-mă-TŌ-mă], mass of clotted blood
hidr(o)	sweat	*hidropoeisis* [HĪ-drō-pŏy-Ē-sĭs], production of sweat
histi(o), histo	tissue	*histolysis* [hĭs-TŎL-ĭ-sĭs], breakdown of tissue
ischi(o)	ischium	*ischialgia* [ĭs-kē-ĂL-jē-ă], hip pain
kerat(o)	cornea	*keratitis* [kĕr-ă-TĪ-tĭs], inflammation of the cornea
labi(o)	lip	*labioplasty* [LĀ-bē-ō-plăs-tē], plastic surgery of a lip
lapar(o)	abdominal wall	*laparomyositis* [LĂP-ă-rō-mī-ō-SĪ-tĭs], inflammation of the abdominal muscles
laryng(o)	larynx	*laryngitis* [lăr-ĭn-JĪ-tĭs], inflammation of the larynx
linguo	tongue	*linguocclusion* [lĭng-gwō-KLŪ-zhŭn], displacement of a tooth toward the tongue
lymph(o)	lymph	*lymphuria* [lĭm-FŪ-rē-ă], discharge of lymph into the urine
my(o)	muscle	*myocarditis* [MĪ-ō-kăr-DĪ-tĭs], inflammation of the muscle tissue of the heart
myel(o)	spinal cord; bone marrow	*myelopathy* [mī-ĕ-LŎP-ă-thē], disease of the spinal cord
nephr(o)	kidney	*nephritis* [nĕ-FRĪ-tĭs], inflammation of the kidneys
neur(o)	nerve	*neuritis* [nū-RĪ-tĭs], inflammation of a nerve
odont(o)	tooth	*odontalgia* [ō-dŏn-TĂL-jē-ă], toothache

Combining Form	Meaning	Example
ophthalm(o)	eye	*ophthalmoscope* [ŏf-THĂL-mō-skōp], device for examining interior of the eyeball
opto, optico	eye; sight	*optometer* [ŏp-TŎM-ĕ-tĕr], instrument for measuring eye refraction
or(o)	mouth	*orofacial* [ōr-ō-FĀ-shăl], relating to the mouth and face
orchi(o), orchid(o)	testis	*orchialgia* [ōr-kē-ĂL-jē-ă], pain in the testis
ost(e), osteo	bone	*osteochondritis* [ŎS-tē-ō-kŏn-DRĪ-tĭs], inflammation of a bone and its cartilage
ot(o)	ear	*otitis* [ō-TĪ-tĭs], inflammation of the ear
ped(o), pedi	foot; child	*pedicure* [PĔD-ĭ-kyūr], treatment of the feet; *pedophilia* [pĕ-dō-FĬL-ē-ă], abnormal sexual attraction to children
pharyng(o)	pharynx	*pharyngitis* [făr-ĭn-JĪ-tĭs], inflammation of the pharynx
phleb(o)	vein	*phlebitis* [flĕ-BĪ-tĭs], inflammation of a vein
plasma, plasmo, plasmat(o)	plasma	*plasmacyte* [PLĂZ-mă-sīt], plasma cell
pleur(o), pleura	rib; side; pleura	*pleurography* [plūr-ŎG-ră-fē], imaging of the pleural cavity
pneum(a), pneumat(o), pneum(o), pneumon(o)	lungs; air; breathing	*pneumonitis* [nū-mō-NĪ-tĭs], inflammation of the lungs
pod(o)	foot	*podiatrist* [pō-DĪ-ă-trĭst], specialist in diseases of the foot
psych(o), psyche	mind	*psychomotor* [sī-kō-MŌ-tĕr], relating to psychological influence on body movement
pulmon(o)	lung	*pulmonitis* [pūl-mō-NĪ-tĭs], inflammation of the lungs
reni, reno	kidney	*reniform* [RĔN-ĭ-fŏrm], kidney-shaped
rhin(o)	nose	*rhinitis* [rī-NĪ-tĭs], inflammation of the nasal membranes
splen(o)	spleen	*splenectomy* [splē-NĔK-tō-mē], removal of the spleen
spondyl(o)	vertebra	*spondylitis* [spŏn-dĭ-LĪ-tĭs], inflammation of a vertebra
stern(o)	sternum	*sternalgia* [stĕr-NĂL-jē-ă], sternum pain

COMBINING FORM	MEANING	EXAMPLE
steth(o)	chest	*stethoscope* [STĔTH-ō-skōp], device for listening to chest sounds
stom(a), stomat(o)	mouth	*stomatopathy* [stō-mă-TŎP-ă-thē], disease of the mouth
ten(o), tendin(o), tendo, tenon(o)	tendon	*tenectomy* [tĕ-NĔK-tō-mē], *tenonectomy* [tĕn-ō-NĔK-tō-mē], removal of part of a tendon
thorac(o), thoracico	thorax, chest	*thoracalgia* [thōr-ă-KĂL-jē-ă], chest pain
vas(o)	blood vessel, duct	*vasoconstrictor* [VĀ-sō-kŏn-STRĬK-tŏr], agent that narrows blood vessels
vasculo	blood vessel	*vasculopathy* [văs-kyū-LŎP-ă-thē], disease of the blood vessels
veni, veno	vein	*venipuncture* [VĔN-ĭ-pŭngk-shūr, VĒ-nĭ-pŭnkg-shūr], puncture of a vein, as with a needle
ventricul(o)	ventricle	*ventriculitis* [vĕn-trĭk-yū-LĪ-tĭs], inflammation of the ventricles in the brain
vertebro	vertebra	*vertebrosacral* [vĕr-tĕ-brō-SĀ-krăl], relating to the vertebra and the sacrum

COMBINING FORMS AND ABBREVIATIONS EXERCISES

Build Your Medical Vocabulary

Match each compound term with its meaning.

33. _____ adrenomegaly

34. _____ gingivoplasty

35. _____ angiography

36. _____ osteosclerosis

37. _____ arteriospasm

38. _____ cephalalgia

39. _____ rhinedema

40. _____ laryngectomy

41. _____ abdominothoracic

42. _____ hemostat

a. agent that stops the flow of blood

b. spasm of an artery

c. headache

d. surgical repair of the gums

e. removal of the larynx

f. relating to the abdomen and thorax

g. abnormal hardening of bone

h. radiography of blood vessels

i. enlargement of the adrenal glands

j. swelling in the nose

Add a Suffix

Add the suffix needed to complete the statement.

43. An inflammation of an artery is called arter _____.

44. Suturing of a tendon is called teno _____.

45. Death of muscle is called myo _____.

46. A name for any disorder of the spinal cord is myelo _____.

47. Cervic_____ means neck pain.

48. Angio_____ means repair of a blood vessel.

49. Softening of the walls of the heart is called cardio _____.

50. Incision into the chest is called a thoraco _____.

51. Enlargement of the kidney is called nephro _____.

52. Any disease of the mouth is called stomato_____

USING THE INTERNET

Go to the National Institutes of Health's Web site (http://www.health.nih.gov/) and click on one of the body systems you have learned about in this chapter. Find the name of at least two diseases of that body system.

CHAPTER REVIEW

The material that follows is to help you review all the material in this chapter as well as to challenge you to think critically about the material you have studied. In addition, this would be a good time to review the chapter on the student CD-ROM and to examine any further related material on the book's Web site (www.mhhe.com/medterm2e).

DEFINITIONS

Define the following terms and combining forms. Review the chapter before starting. Make sure you know how to pronounce each term as you define it. Check your answers in this chapter or in the glossary/index at the end of the book.

TERM	DEFINITION
abdominal [ăb-DŎM-ĭ-năl] cavity	_____
abdomin(o)	_____
aden(o)	_____
adip(o)	_____
adren(o)	_____
angi(o)	_____
anterior [ăn-TĒR-ē-ŏr]	_____
aort(o)	_____
appendic(o)	_____
arteri(o)	_____
arteriol(o)	_____
arthr(o)	_____
blood [blŭd] system	_____
cardi(o)	_____
cardiovascular [KĂR-dē-ō-VĂS-kyū-lăr] system	_____
cell [sĕl]	_____
cephal(o)	_____
cerebell(o)	_____
cerebr(o)	_____
cervic(o)	_____
chir(o)	_____
chol(e), cholo	_____
col(o), colon(o)	_____
connective [kŏn-NĚK-tĭv] tissue	_____
coronal [KŌR-ō-năl] plane	_____
cranial [KRĀ-nē-ăl] cavity	_____

TERM	DEFINITION
crani(o)	_____
cross-sectional plane	_____
cyst(i), cysto	_____
cyt(o)	_____
deep	_____
dent(i), dento	_____
derm(o), derma, dermat(o)	_____
diaphragm [DĪ-ă-frăm]	_____
digestive [dī-JĔS-tĭv] system	_____
distal [DĬS-tăl]	_____
dorsal [DŌR-săl]	_____
dorsal cavity	_____
duoden(o)	_____
encephal(o)	_____
endocrine [ĔN-dō-krĭn] system	_____
epigastric [ĕp-ĭ-GĂS-trĭk] region	_____
epithelial [ĕp-ĭ-THĒ-lē-ăl] tissue	_____
frontal plane	_____
gastr(o)	_____
gingiv(o)	_____
gloss(o)	_____
hem(a), hemat(o), hemo	_____
hidr(o)	_____
histi(o), histo	_____
hypochondriac [hī-pō-KŎN-drē-ăk] regions	_____
hypogastric [hī-pō-GĂS-trĭk] region	_____
iliac [ĬL-ē-ăk] regions	_____
inferior [ĭn-FĒR-ē-ōr]	_____
inguinal [ĬN-gwĭ-năl] regions	_____
integumentary [ĭn-tĕg-yū-MĔN-tă-rē] system	_____
ischi(o)	_____
kerat(o)	_____
labi(o)	_____
lapar(o)	_____
laryng(o)	_____

TERM	DEFINITION
lateral [LĂT-ĕr-ăl]	
lateral plane	
left lower quadrant (LLQ)	
left upper quadrant (LUQ)	
linguo	
lumbar [LŬM-băr] regions	
lymph(o)	
lymphatic [lĭm-FĂT-ĭk] and immune [ĭ-MYŪN] systems	
medial [MĒ-dē-ăl]	
medial plane	
midsagittal [mĭd-SĂJ-ĭ-tăl] plane	
muscle [MŬS-ĕl] tissue	
musculoskeletal [mŭs-kyū-lō-SKĔL-ĕ-tăl] system	
my(o)	
myel(o)	
nephr(o)	
nervous [NĔR-vŭs] system	
nervous tissue	
neur(o)	
odont(o)	
ophthalm(o)	
opto, optico	
or(o)	
orchi(o), orchid(o)	
organ [ŌR-găn]	
ost(e), osteo	
ot(o)	
ped(o), pedi	
pelvic [PĔL-vĭk] cavity	
pharyng(o)	
phleb(o)	
plasma, plasmo, plasmat(o)	
pleur(o), pleura	
pneum(a), pneumat(o), pneum(o), pneumon(o)	
pod(o)	
posterior	

Term	Definition
prone	
proximal [PRŎK-sĭ-măl]	
psych(o), psyche	
pulmon(o)	
reni, reno	
reproductive [rē-prō-DŬK-tĭv] system	
respiratory [RĔS-pĭ-ră-tōr-ē, rĕ-SPĪR-ă-tōr-ē] system	
rhin(o)	
right lower quadrant (RLQ)	
right upper quadrant (RUQ)	
sagittal [SĂJ-ĭ-tăl] plane	
sensory [SĔN-sō-rē] system	
spinal [SPĪ-năl] cavity	
splen(o)	
spondyl(o)	
stern(o)	
steth(o)	
stom(a), stomat(o)	
superficial	
superior	
supine [sū-PĪN]	
system [SĬS-tĕm]	
ten(o), tendin(o), tendo, tenon(o)	
thorac(o), thoracico	
thoracic [thō-RĂS-ĭk] cavity	
tissue [TĬSH-ū]	
transverse plane	
umbilical [ŭm-BĬL-ĭ-kăl] region	
urinary [YŪR-ĭ-nār-ē] system	
vas(o)	
vasculo	
veni, veno	
ventral [VĔN-trăl]	
ventral cavity	
ventricul(o)	
vertebro	

Word Building

Build the Right Term

Using the word lists and vocabulary reviews in Chapters 1, 2, and 3, construct a medical term that fits each of the following definitions. The number following each definition tells you the number of word parts—combining forms, suffixes, or prefixes—you will need to use.

53. Disease of the heart muscle (3)

54. Reconstruction of an artery wall (2)

55. Incision into the stomach (2)

56. muscle pain (2)

57. Study of poisons (2)

58. Condition with extreme sweating (3)

59. Inflammation of the tissue surrounding a blood vessel (3)

60. Producing sugar (2)

61. Morbid fear of blood (2)

62. Paralysis of the heart (2)

63. Plastic surgery of the skin (2)

64. narcolepsy (2)

Define the Terms

Using the information you have learned in Chapters 1, 2, and 3, and without consulting a dictionary, give the closest definition you can for each of the following terms.

65. otorhinolaryngology

66. rhinomegaly

67. cystitis

68. oncology

69. fibroma

70. renirrhagia

71. antiparasitic

72. neuropathy

73. retropharynx

74. lipocardiac

Find a Match

Match the combining form with its definition.

75. adip(o)		a.	kidney
76. cervic(o)		b.	mouth
77. cephal(o)		c.	neck
78. gastr(o)		d.	fat
79. dent(i)		e.	bone

80. ren(i)

81. pod(o)

82. or(o)

83. oste(o)

f. head

g. stomach

h. foot

i. tooth

Find What's Wrong

In each of the following terms, one or more word parts are misspelled.
Replace the misspelled word part(s) and write the correct term in the space provided.

84. meningiitus

85. polmonary

86. abdomenal

87. cardiomagaley

88. ensephaloscope

89. mielopathy

90. larynjectomy

91. hipnosis

92. optimetrist

93. hemoglobine

94. athrodesis

95. yatrogenic

96. carcinsoma

97. paraplejic

98. mezomorph

99. simbiosis

100. schizofrenia

Find the Specialty

For each of the following diagnoses, name the appropriate specialist who would generally treat the condition. If you do not know the meaning of any of these conditions, look them up in the glossary/index at the back of the book.

101. myocarditis

102. dermatitis

103. bronchitis

104. ovarian cysts

105. prostatitis

106. cancer

107. glaucoma

108. colitis

109. neuritis

110. allergy to bee sting

Answers to Chapter Exercises

1. d
2. h
3. i
4. e
5. f
6. g
7. k
8. c
9. j
10. a
11. b
12. cell
13. tissue
14. epithelial
15. cranial
16. diaphragm
17. dorsal
18. pelvic
19. urinary
20. digestive
21. stomach, spleen, intestines, liver, pancreas
22. Yes, pain may be "referred," felt in one part of the body but actually coming from another part.
23. F
24. T
25. F
26. F
27. T
28. F
29. T
30. F
31. T
32.

a. Deep
b. Superficial
c. Anterior
d. Distal
e. Supine
f. Inferior

33. i
34. d
35. h
36. g
37. b
38. c
39. j
40. e
41. f
42. a
43. itis
44. rrhaphy
45. necrosis
46. pathy
47. algia
48. plasty
49. malacia
50. tomy
51. megaly
52. pathy
53. cardiomyopathy
54. arterioplasty
55. gastrotomy
56. myalgia or myodynia
57. toxicology
58. hyperhidrosis
59. periangitis
60. glucogenic
61. hemophobia
62. cardioplegia
63. dermatoplasty or dermoplasty
64. sleep condition
65. study of the ear, nose, and throat
66. abnormally enlarged nose
67. inflammation of the bladder
68. study of cancer
69. tumor in fibrous tissues
70. kidney hemorrhage
71. destructive to parasites
72. any nerve disorder
73. back part of the pharynx
74. relating to a fatty heart
75. d
76. c
77. f
78. g
79. i
80. a

81. h
82. b
83. e
84. meningitis
85. pulmonary
86. abdominal
87. cardiomegaly
88. encephaloscope
89. myelopathy
90. laryngectomy
91. hypnosis
92. optometrist
93. hemoglobin
94. arthrodesis
95. iatrogenic
96. carcinoma
97. paraplegic
98. mesomorph
99. symbiosis
100. schizophrenia
101. cardiologist
102. dermatologist
103. pulmonologist
104. gynecologist
105. urologist
106. oncologist
107. ophthalmologist
108. gastroenterologist
109. neurologist
110. allergist

The Integumentary System

4

After studying this chapter, you will be able to:

► Name the parts of the integumentary system and discuss the function of each part

► Define the combining forms used in building words that relate to the integumentary system

► Name the common diagnoses, laboratory tests, and clinical procedures used in testing and treating disorders of the integumentary system

► List and define the major pathological conditions of the integumentary system

► Define surgical terms related to the integumentary system

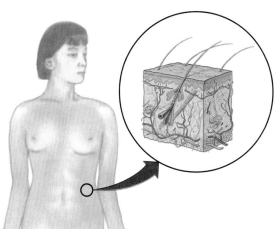

Structure and Function

The integumentary system includes the skin or **integument,** the *hair*, the **nails,** the **sweat glands** (also called the *sudoriferous glands*), and the oil-producing glands (also called the **sebaceous glands**). This system covers and protects the body, helps regulate the body's temperature, excretes some of the body's waste materials, and includes the body's sensors for pain and sensation. Figure 4-1a shows a cross-section of skin with the parts of the integumentary system labeled. Figure 4-1b is a diagram showing the three layers of skin and what they contain.

Skin

The skin is the largest body organ. The average adult has about 21.5 square feet of skin. The four major functions of the skin are:

1. It protects the body from fluid loss and injury and from the intrusion of harmful microorganisms and ultraviolet (UV) rays of the sun.
2. It helps to maintain the proper internal temperature of the body.
3. It serves as a site for excretion of waste materials through perspiration.
4. It is an important sensory organ.

The skin has three main layers, each with sublayers:

1. The **epidermis**, the outer layer, is made up of cells called **squamous epithelium.** The epidermis has several **strata**, or sublayers.
   a. The top sublayer is the **stratum corneum.** the cells in this sublayer fill with a barrier called **keratin.**

FIGURE 4-1a The integumentary system consists of the skin with all its layers, hair, nails, and glands.

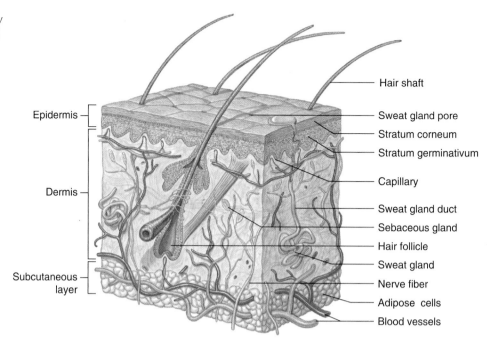

- Hair shaft
- Sweat gland pore
- Stratum corneum
- Stratum germinativum
- Capillary
- Sweat gland duct
- Sebaceous gland
- Hair follicle
- Sweat gland
- Nerve fiber
- Adipose cells
- Blood vessels

Epidermis

Dermis

Subcutaneous layer

FIGURE 4-1b A diagram showing the three layers of skin and what they contain.

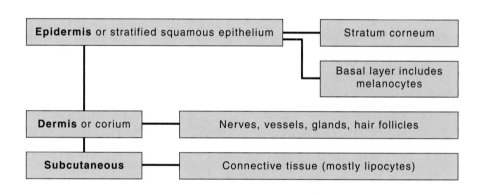

Epidermis or stratified squamous epithelium	Stratum corneum
	Basal layer includes melanocytes
Dermis or corium	Nerves, vessels, glands, hair follicles
Subcutaneous	Connective tissue (mostly lipocytes)

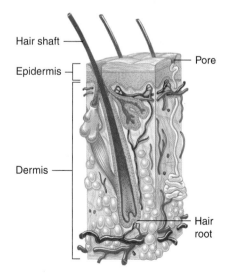

- Hair shaft
- Epidermis
- Pore
- Dermis
- Hair root

FIGURE 4-2 Detail of hair growing out of the epidermis.

b. The bottom sublayer is the **stratum germinativum.** It contains cells called **melanocytes,** which produce the pigment **melanin.**

2. The **dermis** or **corium** is the middle layer. It contains **collagen.** It has two sublayers.
   a. The top one is the **papillary layer.**
   b. The bottom one is the **reticular layer.**
3. The bottom layer of the skin is the **subcutaneous layer** or **hypodermis.** It contains **adipose** or fatty tissue.

Hair

Hair grows out of the epidermis to cover various parts of the body. Hair serves to cushion and protect the areas it covers. Figure 4-2 shows a detail of hair growing out of the epidermis. Hair has two parts.

1. The **hair shaft** protrudes above the skin.
2. The **hair root** is beneath the skin's surface. It contains the **hair follicles.**

Nails

Nails are made of hard keratin and cover parts of fingers and toes. The base of most nails has a **lunula**, a whitish half-moon, and nails are surrounded by a **cuticle.**

Glands

There are five major types of glands in the integumentary system:

1. The **sweat glands** or *sudoriferous glands* secrete outward and are, therefore, a type of **exocrine gland.** The excretion of sweat is called **diaphoresis.** Sweat is secreted through the **pores** of the skin.
2. The small sweat glands or **eccrine glands** excrete a colorless liquid.
3. The **apocrine glands** secrete sweat from the armpits.
4. **Ceruminous glands** secrete wax in the ears.
5. **Sebaceous glands** secrete an oily substance called **sebum.**

VOCABULARY REVIEW

In the previous section, you learned terms relating to the integumentary system. Before going on to the exercise section, read the definitions below. Pronunciations are provided for certain terms.

Term	Definition
adipose [ĂD-ĭ-pōs]	Fatty; relating to fat.
apocrine [ĂP-ō-krĭn] **glands**	Glands that secrete sweat, as from the armpits.
ceruminous [sĕ-RŪ-mĭn-ŭs] **glands**	Glands that secrete a waxy substance on the surface of the ear.
collagen [KŎL-lă-jĕn]	Substance that forms connective tissue in the body.
corium [KŌ-rē-ŭm]	*See* dermis.
cuticle [KYŪ-tĭ-kl]	Thin band of epidermis that surrounds the edge of nails, except at the top.
dermis [DĔR-mĭs]	Layer of skin beneath the epidermis.
diaphoresis [DĪ-ă-fō-RĒ-sĭs]	Excretion of fluid by the sweat glands; sweating.
eccrine [ĔK-rĭn] **glands**	Sweat glands that occur all over the body, except where the apocrine glands occur.
epidermis [ĕp-ĭ-DĔR-mĭs, epi- + dermis]	Outer portion of the skin containing several strata.
exocrine [ĔK-sō-krĭn, exo- + crine] **glands**	Glands that secrete toward the outside of the body.
hair follicle [FŎL-ĭ-kl]	Tubelike sac out of which the hair shaft develops.
hair root	Portion of the hair beneath the skin surface.
hair shaft	Portion of the hair visible above the skin surface.

Term	Definition
hypodermis [hī-pō-DĔR-mĭs, hypo- + dermis]	Subcutaneous skin layer; layer below the dermis.
integument [ĭn-TĔG-yū-mĕnt]	Skin and all the elements that are contained within and arise from it.
keratin [KĔR-ă-tĭn]	Hard, horny protein that forms nails and hair.
lunula (*pl.*, **lunulae**) [LŪ-nū-lă (LŪ-nū-lē)]	Half-moon shaped area at the base of the nail plate.
melanin [MĔL-ă-nĭn]	Pigment produced by melanocytes that determines skin, hair, and eye color.
melanocyte [MĔL-ă-nō-sīt, melano- + -cyte]	Cell in the epidermis that produces melanin.
nail	Thin layer of keratin that covers the distal portion of fingers and toes.
papillary [PĂP-ĭ-lār-ē] **layer**	Top sublayer of the dermis.
pore	Opening or hole, particularly in the skin.
reticular [rĕ-TĬK-yū-lăr] **layer**	Bottom sublayer of the dermis.
sebaceous [sĕ-BĀ-shŭs] **glands**	Glands in the dermis that open to hair follicles and secrete sebum.
sebum [SĒ-bŭm]	Oily substance, usually secreted into the hair follicle.
squamous epithelium [SKWĂ-mŭs ĕp-ĭ-THĒ-lē- ŭm]	Flat, scaly layer of cells that makes up the epidermis.
stratum (*pl.*, **strata**) [STRĂT-ŭm (STRĂ-tă)]	Layer of tissue, especially a layer of the skin.
stratum corneum [KŌR-nē-ŭm]	Top sublayer of the epidermis.
stratum germinativum [jĕr-mĭ-NĀT-ĭ-vŭm]	Bottom sublayer of the epidermis.
subcutaneous [sŭb-kyū-TĀ-nē-ŭs] **layer**	Bottom layer of the skin containing fatty tissue.
sweat glands	Coiled glands of the skin that secrete perspiration to regulate body temperature and excrete waste products.

STRUCTURE AND FUNCTION EXERCISES

Build Your Medical Vocabulary

1. The dermis is a layer of skin. Using your knowledge of prefixes learned in Chapter 2, put the following words in order according to how close they are to the outside of the body.

    a. hypodermis _____

    b. epidermis _____

    c. dermis _____

2. Another name for skin is the _____.

Complete the Diagram

3. Fill in the missing labels on the figure shown here.

   a. _____

   b. _____

   c. _____

   d. _____

   e. _____

   a. _____

   b. _____

   c. _____

   d. _____

   e. _____

Fill in the Blanks

Complete the sentences below by filling in the blank(s).

4. The thin layer of skin around the edge of a nail is called a(n) _____.

5. Hair follicles are found in the _____ (layer of the skin).

6. The outer layer of skin is the _____.

7. The top sublayer of the dermis is called the _____ _____.

8. Small sweat glands found all over the body are called _____ glands.

9. The subcutaneous layer consists of _____ tissue.

10. Sebaceous glands secrete _____.

CASE STUDY

The Dermatologist's Office

Madeline Charles arrived at the office a few minutes early. She knew that Dr. Lin had a busy morning scheduled, and she wanted to set up before the doctor arrived. As secretary to Dr. Lin, Madeline handles incoming calls, scheduling, billing, new patient information forms, and insurance matters. She reports to James Carlson, the CMA and office manager for this small office. James assists the doctor with patients, oversees the work Madeline does, and helps when Madeline's load is too great. This morning, the first three patients are scheduled at 8:30, 9:00, and 9:30. Madeline looks at the schedule, realizes that one of the patients is new, and gets the folders for the other two. She sets up the clipboard with the forms the new patient will have to complete and attaches the privacy practices statement of the office (a requirement of the HIPAA laws). She had previously asked the new patient to arrive 15 minutes early in order to have time to fill out the necessary forms.

Bob Luis, the first patient, is 48 years old and has a long history of diabetes (a disease of the endocrine system discussed in Chapter 15). He sees Dr. Lin several times a year for treatment of skin irritations that do not seem to heal. Yesterday, Mr. Luis called with a specific problem. He has an extensive rash on his left ankle. It sounded serious enough to warrant an appointment for the next morning. When Mr. Luis arrives, James escorts him to an examination room and helps him prepare for his visit.

Critical Thinking

11. What do we know about Mr. Luis's condition that would warrant an immediate appointment with Dr. Lin?

12. Does a dermatologist treat a disease such as diabetes, or only symptoms related to the integumentary system?

Combining Forms

The list below includes combining forms related to the integumentary system. Pronunciations are included for the examples.

COMBINING FORM	MEANING	EXAMPLE
adip(o)	fatty	*adiposis* [ăd-ĭ-PŌ-sĭs], excessive accumulation of body fat
dermat(o)	skin	*dermatitis* [dĕr-mă-TĪ-tĭs], inflammation of the skin
derm(o)	skin	*dermabrasion* [dĕr-mă-BRĀ-zhŭn], surgical procedure to remove acne scars and marks, using an abrasive product to remove part of the skin
hidr(o)	sweat, sweat glands	*hidrosis* [hī-DRŌ-sĭs], production and excretion of sweat
ichthy(o)	fish, scaly	*ichthyosis* [ĭk-thē-Ō-sĭs], congenital skin disorder characterized by dryness and peeling
kerat(o)	horny tissue	*keratosis* [kĕr-ă-TŌ-sĭs], skin lesion covered by a horny layer of tissue
lip(o)	fatty	*liposuction* [lĭp-ō-SŬK-shŭn], removal of unwanted fat by suctioning through tubes placed under the skin
melan(o)	black, very dark	*melanoma* [mĕl-ă-NŌ-mă], malignancy arising from cells that form melanin
myc(o)	fungus	*mycosis* [mī-KŌ-sĭs], any condition caused by fungus
onych(o)	nail	*onychotomy* [ŏn-ĭ-KŎT-ō-mē] incision into a nail
pil(o)	hair	*pilocystic* [pī-lō-SĬS-tĭk], relating to a skin cyst with hair
seb(o)	sebum, sebaceous glands	*seborrhea* [sĕb-ō-RĒ-ă], excessive sebum caused by overactivity of the sebaceous glands
steat(o)	fat	*steatitis* [stē-ă-TĪ-tĭs], inflammation of fatty tissue
trich(o)	hair	*trichopathy* [trī-KŎP-ă-thē], disease of the hair
xanth(o)	yellow	*xanthoma* [zăn-THŌ-mă], yellow growth on or discoloration of the skin
xer(o)	dry	*xeroderma* [zēr-ō-DĔR-mă], excessive dryness of the skin

CASE STUDY

Understanding Information

While Dr. Lin is examining Bob Luis, his first patient, the new patient arrives for her 9:00 appointment. Madeline explains which parts of the forms have to be filled out, asks for the patient's insurance card so she can copy it, and completes the file for Dr. Lin before 9:00. Meanwhile, Dr. Lin hands Madeline his notes with a diagnosis for Bob Luis, including a new prescription for treatment of xeroderma. In addition, Dr. Lin gives Mr. Luis samples of a cream to relieve itching.

Critical Thinking

13. Why does the new patient have to fill out forms with questions about family history?
14. Mr. Luis is to be given samples of a prescription cream to try. Can the medical assistant decide which samples to give him?

COMBINING FORMS AND ABBREVIATIONS EXERCISES

Build Your Medical Vocabulary

Build a word for each of the following definitions. Use the combining forms in this chapter and the ones you have learned earlier.

15. Plastic surgery of the skin: _____
16. Inflammation of the skin and veins: _____
17. Horny growth on the epidermis: _____
18. Fungal eruption on the skin: _____
19. Excess pigment in the skin: _____
20. Fungal infection of the nail: _____
21. Surgical repair of the nail: _____
22. Of the hair follicles and sebaceous glands: _____
23. Pigment-producing cell: _____
24. Examination of the hair: _____
25. Removal of fat by cutting: _____
26. Relating to both fatty and cellular tissue: _____
27. Study of hair: _____
28. Disease of the nail: _____
29. Poison produced by certain fungi: _____
30. Virus that infects fungi: _____
31. Yellow coloration of the skin: _____
32. Condition of extreme dryness: _____
33. Removal or shedding of the horny layer of the epidermis: _____
34. Abnormally darkened skin: _____
35. Lessening of the rate of sweating: _____

Root Out the Meaning

Separate the following terms into word parts; define each word part.

36. trichoma _____
37. xerosis _____
38. mycocide _____
39. onychoid _____

Diagnostic, Procedural, and Laboratory Terms

The field of **dermatology** studies, diagnoses, and treats ailments of the skin. The first diagnostic test is usually visual observation of the surface of the skin.

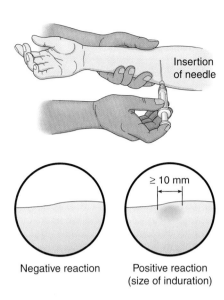

Negative reaction

≥ 10 mm

Positive reaction
(size of induration)

FIGURE 4-3 A Mantoux test is performed by injecting a small dose of tuberculin intradermally. A positive result is a small raised bump on the skin. No reaction indicates that tuberculosis is not present.

The American Lung Association (www.lungusa.org) has extensive information about tuberculosis.

Clinical procedures and laboratory tests can result in diagnosis and treatment of specific skin conditions.

Diagnostic Procedures and Tests

Once a visual assessment has been made, the dermatologist determines which procedures and tests will help find the underlying cause of a skin problem. Samples of **exudate** (material that passes out of tissues) or pus may be sent to a laboratory for examination.

Skin is a reliable place to test for various diseases and allergies. A suspected *allergen*, something that provokes an allergic reaction, is mixed with a substance that can be used in tests. That substance containing the allergen is called an *antigen*. Skin tests are typically performed in one of three ways:

1. The **patch test** calls for placing a suspected antigen on a piece of gauze and applying it to the skin. If a reaction results, the test is considered positive.
2. The **scratch test** (in which a suspected antigen is scratched onto the skin, and redness or swelling within ten minutes indicates a positive reaction).
3. The **intradermal test** (in which a suspected antigen is injected between layers of skin). Infectious diseases may also be detected by an intradermal test. Some common intradermal tests are:
   a. The **Mantoux test** for diagnosing tuberculosis. In the Mantoux test, **PPD** (a purified protein derivative of tuberculin) is injected intradermally. Figure 4-3 shows a Mantoux test.
   b. The **tine test** (also called **TB tine**), a screening test for tuberculosis, injects the tuberculin using a tine (an instrument with a number of pointed ends).
   c. The **Schick test** is a test for diphtheria, in which a small amount of toxin is injected into the skin of one arm and a small amount of deactivated toxin is injected into the skin of the other arm for comparison.

VOCABULARY REVIEW

In the previous section, you learned terms relating to diagnosis, clinical procedures, and laboratory tests. Before going on to the exercise section, read the definitions below. Pronunciations are provided for certain terms.

Term	Definition
dermatology [dĕr-mă-TŎL-ō-jē]	Medical specialty that deals with diseases of the skin.
exudate [ĔKS-yū-dāt]	Any fluid excreted out of tissue, especially fluid excreted out of an injury to the skin.
intradermal [ĬN-tră-DĔR-măl] **test**	Test that injects antigen or protein between layers of skin.
Mantoux [măn-TŪ] **test**	Test for tuberculosis in which a small dose of tuberculin is injected intradermally with a syringe.
patch test	Test for allergic sensitivity in which a small dose of antigen is applied to the skin on a small piece of gauze.

Term	Definition
PPD	Purified protein derivative of tuberculin.
Schick [shǐk] test	Test for diphtheria.
scratch test	Test for allergic sensitivity in which a small amount of antigen is scratched onto the surface of the skin.
tine [tīn] test, TB tine	Screening test for tuberculosis in which a small dose of tuberculin is injected into a series of sites within a small space with a tine (instrument that punctures the surface of the skin).

Case Study

Testing for Allergic Reactions

Several days ago, Dr. Lin had given a series of scratch tests to a teenager who had allergic skin rashes. The doctor had noted all the places where redness or swelling appeared within ten minutes.

He had also noted the negative reactions, where no changes appeared within thirty minutes. There were also some mild, inconclusive reactions. Dr. Lin reviewed the results of the tests. He asked Madeline to send a report to the patient and to set up a phone appointment to discuss the results. Madeline thought the results looked interesting. She didn't know that people could be allergic to so many things at once. However, Madeline knows she cannot discuss this patient's case with anyone not allowed to see that specific medical record. So, while it may be something interesting to talk to some of her friends about, she will not say anything.

Critical Thinking

40. What does a negative reaction to a scratch test indicate?
41. If the patient avoids the allergens that gave the most positive reactions, what is likely to happen to the rashes?

DIAGNOSTIC, PROCEDURAL, AND LABORATORY TERMS EXERCISES

Check Your Knowledge

Circle T for true and F for false.

42. The Mantoux test detects allergies. T F
43. An intradermal test may detect an infectious disease. T F
44. PPD is used in the Mantoux test. T F
45. An intradermal injection usually reaches into the hypodermis. T F

Fill in the Blanks

Complete the sentences below by filling in the blanks.

46. Samples of _____ may be sent to a laboratory for examination.
47. Scratch tests are often used to detect _____.
48. Suspected antigens are injected between layers of skin in a(n) _____ test.

Pathological Terms

The skin is a place where abnormalities, such as **cysts,** occur and some internal diseases show dermatological symptoms. **Lesions** are areas of tissues that are altered because of a pathological condition. Figure 4-4 shows various types of skin lesions. Table 4-1 is a list of many types of lesions. They are characterized as *primary,* appearing on previously normal skin; *secondary,* abnormalities resulting from changing primary lesions; or *vascular,* blood vessel lesions showing through the skin.

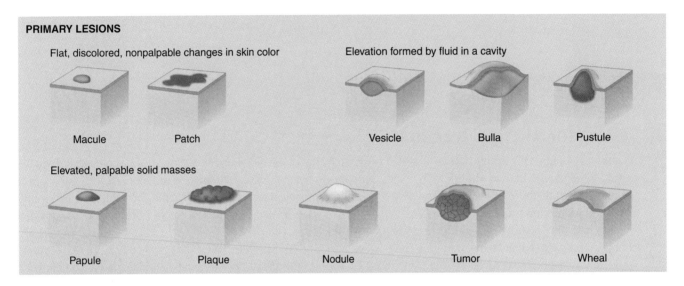

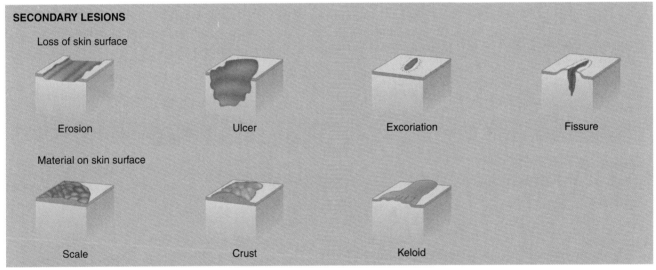

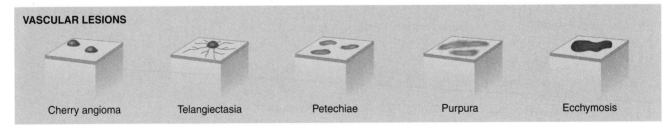

FIGURE 4-4   Various types of skin lesions.

TABLE 4-1 Skin lesions.

Lesion	Type	Major Characteristic
macule or **patch**	primary	area of discoloration
papule or *pimple*	primary	elevated solid mass
plaque	primary	small patch on skin
nodule	primary	large pimple or small node
polyp	primary	mass that projects upward
tumor	primary	abnormal tissue growth
wheal	primary	slightly elevated area of skin
bulla	primary	large blister
pustule	primary	small mass containing pus
vesicle	primary	small mass containing liquid
pilonidal cyst	primary	elevated mass containing hair
sebaceous cyst	primary	elevated mass containing sebum
excoriation	secondary	shallow area of skin that is worn away
fissure	secondary	deep crack in the skin's surface
ulcer	secondary	wound with loss of tissue
decubitus ulcer or **pressure sore**	secondary	chronic skin ulcer
erosion	secondary	wearing away of skin
scale	secondary	thin plates formed on the skin's surface
crust	secondary	dried blood or pus
keloid	secondary	scar tissue
cicatrix	secondary	internal scarring
cherry angioma	vascular	dome-shaped lesion
telegiectasia	vascular	dilation of small blood vessels showing through the skin

Symptoms, Abnormalities, and Conditions

Symptoms of disease can appear on the skin. Skin conditions or rashes can develop from viruses, infections, allergies, injuries, or irritations. Figure 4-5 shows one skin condition. Table 4-2 lists some common skin conditions, their causes, and characteristics. Exposure of the skin to heat, chemicals, electricity, radiation, or other irritants may cause a **burn.** Burns are classified by the amount or level of skin involvement.

> The National Skin Centre in Singapore (www.nsc.gov.sg) provides a guide to many skin diseases.

1. **First-degree burns** are superficial burns of the epidermis without blistering, but with redness and swelling. Sunburn is an example of a first-degree burn.

FIGURE 4-5 Vitiligo is a loss of pigment in certain areas of the skin.

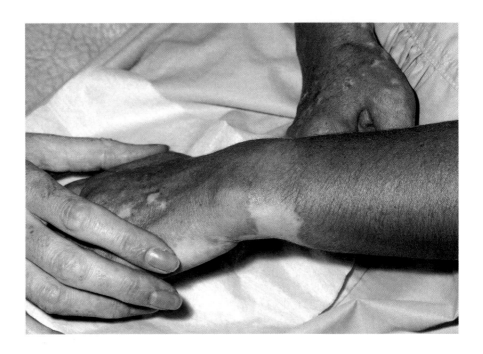

TABLE 4-2 Skin conditions or rashes.

Condition or Rash	Cause	Characteristics
rubeola	measles virus	rash
rubella	German measles	rash
roseola	virus	small, rosy patches on the skin
varicella or *chicken pox*	varicella virus	small pustules
impetigo or **pyoderma**	infection	pus-containing skin rash
tinea or **ringworm**	fungal infection	**pruritus** or intense itching
candidiasis	yeast fungus	fungal rash
dermatitis	irritation or allergy	general term for skin irritation
urticaria or **hives**	usually allergy	red blotches on skin
eczema	usually allergy	acute skin irritation
ecchymosis	injury	bluish-purple skin mark
petechiae	injury	tiny, pinpoint ecchymoses
purpura	various causes	extensive hemorrhages into the skin
rosacea	vascular disorder	red blotches, particularly on the face
furuncle	infection	pustule in a hair follicle
carbuncle	infection	pus-producing inflammation underneath the skin
abscess	infection	pus and inflammation

TABLE 4-2 Skin conditions or rashes (*cont.*).

Condition or Rash	Cause	Characteristics
gangrene	infection-loss of blood supply	death of tissue
depigmentation	often caused by disease	loss of pigmentation
vitiligo	usually disease	large areas of lack of pigmentation
leukoderma	usually disease	white patches
albinism	congenital condition	lack of pigmentation
nevus or birthmark	congenital condition	pigmented skin lesion
chloasma	associated with pregnancy	large, pigmented facial patches
herpes simplex virus Type 1, cold sore, or fever blister	virus	sore around the mouth
herpes simplex virus Type 2 or genital herpes	sexually transmitted disease	genital sores
herpes zoster or shingles	inflammation of nerves	skin blisters
verruca or wart	virus	small, raised area on the skin
acne or acne vulgaris	overproduction of sebum	pimples on the face and upper back
comedones or blackheads	present in acne	pimples with a dark center
whiteheads	present in acne	pimples with a white center
scleroderma	chronic disease	skin thickening
psoriasis	often caused by stress	skin inflammation
seborrhea or *dandruff*	excessive production of sebum	scaly scalp eruption

2. **Second-degree burns** involve the epidermis and dermis and involve blistering. The wound is sensitive to touch and very painful.
3. **Third-degree burns** involve complete destruction of the skin, sometimes reaching into the muscle and bone and causing extensive scarring.

Figure 4-6 shows the "rule of 9s," which is used to determine the extent of burning.

Some skin conditions are caused by insects. **Pediculosis** is an inflammation with lice, often on the head (*pediculosis capitis*) or the genital area (*pediculosis pubis*). **Scabies,** a contagious skin eruption, is caused by mites.

Inflammations of the nail can be caused by infection, irritation, or fungi. **Onychia** or **onychitis** is a nail inflammation. **Paronychia** is an inflammation in the nail fold. A general term for disease of the nails is **onychopathy.**

Some abnormal growths or **neoplasms** are benign. The most common benign neoplasms are a **callus,** a hard, thickened area of skin; a **corn,** hardening or thickening of skin on a toe; **keratosis,** overgrowth of horny tissue on skin, such as overgrowth due to excessive sun exposure (especially **actinic keratosis**); and **leukoplakia,** thickened white patches of epithelium.

The National Psoriasis Foundation (www.psoriasis.org) provides information about new treatments for psoriasis on their Web site.

FIGURE 4-6 Burns are categorized by the extent and depth of burning.

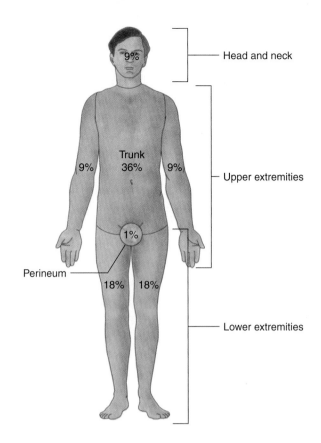

Some neoplasms are malignant. **Basal cell carcinoma** is cancer of the basal layer of the epidermis; **squamous cell carcinoma** affects the squamous epithelium. **Kaposi's sarcoma** is often associated with AIDS. The incidence of **malignant melanoma** is rapidly increasing. Figure 4-7 shows a benign mole and a malignant melanoma.

In most instances, hair loss is hereditary or due to a side effect of medication. However, **alopecia,** or hair loss, can be a pathological condition, as in **alopecia areata,** a condition in which hair falls out in patche, is caused by mites.

MORE ABOUT...

Burns

When burning occurs, the faster treatment starts, the better the outcome. Here are some tips for the following types of burns:

- **Heat burns.** It is important to smother any flames immediately. So if your clothing is on fire, stop, drop, and roll to smother the flames.
- **Liquid scald burns.** Run cool water over the burn for 10 to 20 minutes. Do not use ice.
- **Chemical burns.** Immediately call the Poison Control Center or 911 to find out how to treat burns from a chemical.
- **Electrical burns.** Make sure the person is removed from the electrical source of the burn. If the person is not breathing, call 911 and begin CPR (discussed in Chapter 7).

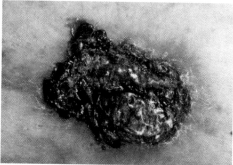

FIGURE 4-7 A benign mole and a malignant melanoma. Notice the darkness and the irregular borders of the malignancy.

VOCABULARY REVIEW

In the previous section, you learned terms relating to pathology. Before going on to the exercises, read the definitions below. Pronunciations are provided for certain terms.

Term	Definition
abscess [ĂB-sĕs] Latin *abscessus*, a going away	Localized collection of pus and other exudate, usually accompanied by swelling and redness.
acne [ĂK-nē]	Inflammatory eruption of the skin.
acne vulgaris [vŭl-GĀR-ĭs]	*See* acne.
actinic keratosis [ăk-TĬN-ĭk KĔR-ă-tō-sĭs]	Overgrowth of horny skin that forms from over-exposure to sunlight.
albinism [ĂL-bĭ-nĭzm] albin(o) + -ism, state	Rare, congenital condition causing either partial or total lack of pigmentation.
alopecia [ăl-ō-PĒ-shē-ă]	Hair loss.
alopecia areata [ă-rē-Ā-tă]	Loss of hair in patches.
basal cell carcinoma [BĀ-săl sĕl kăr-sĭn-Ō-mă]	Slow-growing cancer of the basal cells of the epidermis, usually a result of sun damage.
birthmark	Lesion (especially a hemangioma) visible at or soon after birth; nevus.
blackhead	*See* comedo.
bulla (*pl.*, **bullae**) [BŬL-ă (BŬL-ī)]	Bubble-like blister on the surface of the skin.
burn	Damage to the skin caused by exposure to heat, chemicals, electricity, radiation, or other skin irritants.
callus [KĂL-ŭs] Latin	Mass of hard skin that forms as a cover over broken skin on certain areas of the body, especially the feet and hands.

Term	Definition
candidiasis [kăn-dĭ-DĪ-ă-sĭs]	Yeastlike fungus on the skin.
carbuncle [KĂR-bŭng-kl]	Infected area of the skin producing pus and usually accompanied by fever.
cherry angioma [ăn-jē-Ō-mă]	A dome-shaped vascular angioma lesion that usually occurs in the elderly.
chloasma [klō-ĂZ-mă] Greek *chloazo*, to become green	Group of fairly large, pigmented facial patches, often associated with pregnancy.
cicatrix [SĬK-ă-trĭks] Latin	Growth of fibrous tissue inside a wound that forms a scar; also, general term for scar.
cold sore	Eruption around the mouth or lips; herpes simplex virus Type 1.
comedo (*pl.*, **comedos, comedones**) [KŌM-ē-dō, kō-MĒ-dō (KŌM-ē-dōz, kō-mē-DŌ-nĕz)]	Open hair follicle filled with bacteria and sebum; common in acne; blackhead.
corn	Growth of hard skin, usually on the toes.
crust	Hard layer, especially one formed by dried pus, as in a scab.
cyst [sĭst]	Abnormal sac containing fluid.
decubitus (*pl.*, **decubiti**) [dě-KYŪ-bǐ-tŭs (dě-KYŪ-bǐ-tī)], **decubitus ulcer**	Chronic ulcer on skin over bony parts that are under constant pressure; pressure sore.
depigmentation [dē-pǐg-měn-TĀ-shŭn]	Loss of color of the skin.
dermatitis [děr-mă-TĪ-tǐs] dermat-, skin + -itis	Inflammation of the skin.
ecchymosis (*pl.*, **ecchymoses**) [ěk-ǐ-MŌ-sǐs (ěk-ǐ-MŌ-sēz)] Greek	Purplish skin patch (bruise) caused by broken blood vessels beneath the surface.
eczema [ĔK-sē-mă, ĔG-zē-mă]	Severe inflammatory condition of the skin, usually of unknown cause.
erosion	Wearing away of the surface of the skin, especially when caused by friction.
excoriation [ěks-KŌ-rē-Ā-shŭn]	Injury to the surface of the skin caused by a scratch, abrasion, or burn, usually accompanied by some oozing.
fever blister	Eruption around the mouth or lips; herpes simplex virus Type 1.
first-degree burn	Least severe burn, causes injury to the surface of the skin without blistering.
fissure [FĬSH-ŭr] Latin	Deep slit in the skin.

Term	Definition
furuncle [FYŪ-rŭng-kl]	Localized skin infection, usually in a hair follicle and containing pus; boil.
gangrene [GĂNG-grēn]	Death of an area of skin, usually caused by loss of blood supply to the area.
genital herpes	*See* herpes simplex virus Type 2.
herpes [HĚR-pēz]	An inflammatory skin disease caused by viruses of the family Herpesviridae.
herpes simplex virus Type 1	Herpes that recurs on the lips and around the area of the mouth, usually during viral illnesses or states of stress.
herpes simplex virus Type 2	Herpes that recurs on the genitalia; can be easily transmitted from one person to another through sexual contact.
herpes zoster [ZŎS-tĕr]	Painful herpes that affects nerve roots; shingles.
hives	*See* urticaria.
impetigo [ĭm-pĕ-TĪ-gō]	A type of pyoderma.
Kaposi's sarcoma [KĂ-pō-sēz săr-KŌ-mă]	Skin cancer associated with AIDS.
keloid [KĒ-lŏyd]	Thick scarring of the skin that forms after an injury or surgery.
keratosis [kĕr-ă-TŌ-sĭs] kerat(o)- + -osis	Lesion on the epidermis containing keratin.
lesion [LĒ-zhŭn]	Wound, damage, or injury to the skin.
leukoderma [lū-kō-DĔR-mă] leuko- + -derma	Absence of pigment in the skin or in an area of the skin.
leukoplakia [lū-kō-PLĀ-kē-ă] leuko- + -plakia, plaque	White patch of mucous membrane on the tongue or cheek.
macule [MĂK-yūl]	Small, flat, noticeably colored spot on the skin.
malignant melanoma [mĕl-ă-NŌ-mă]	Virulent skin cancer originating in the melanocytes, usually caused by overexposure to the sun.
neoplasm [NĒ-ō-plăzm]	Abnormal tissue growth.
nevus (*pl.*, **nevi**) [NĒ-vŭs (NĒ-vī)]	Birthmark.
nodule [NŎD-yūl]	Small knob of tissue.
onychia, onychitis [ō-NĬK-ē-ă, ŏn-ĭ-KĪ-tĭs] onycho-, nail + -ia, condition; onych(o)- + -itis	Inflammation of the nail.

Term	Definition
onychopathy [ōn-ĭ-KŎP-ă-thē] onycho- + -pathy, disease	Disease of the nail.
papule [PĂP-yūl]	Small, solid elevation on the skin.
paronychia [păr-ŏ-NĬK-ē-ă]	Inflammation, with pus, of the fold surrounding the nail plate.
patch	Small area of skin differing in color from the surrounding area; plaque.
pediculosis [pĕ-DĬK-yū-LŌ-sĭs]	Lice infestation.
petechia (*pl.*, **petechiae**) [pē-TĒ-kē-ă, pē-TĔK-ē-ă (pē-TĒ-kē-ē)]	A tiny hemorrhage beneath the surface of the skin.
pilonidal [pī-lō-NĪ-dă] **cyst**	Cyst containing hair, usually found at the lower end of the spinal column.
plaque [plăk]	*See* patch.
polyp [PŎL-ĭp]	Bulging mass of tissue that projects outward from the skin surface.
pressure sore	*See* decubitus ulcer.
pruritus [prū-RĪ-tŭs]	Itching.
psoriasis [sō-RĪ-ă-sĭs]	Chronic skin condition accompanied by scaly lesions with extreme pruritus.
purpura [PŬR-pū-ră]	Skin condition with extensive hemorrhages underneath the skin covering a wide area.
pustule [PŬS-tūl]	Small elevation on the skin containing pus.
pyoderma [pī-ō-DĔR-mă] pyo-, pus + -derma	Any inflammation of the skin that produces pus.
ringworm	Fungal infection; tinea.
rosacea [rō-ZĀ-shē-ă]	Vascular disease that causes blotchy, red patches on the skin, particularly on the nose and cheeks.
roseola [rō-ZĒ-ō-lă]	Skin eruption of small, rosy patches, usually caused by a virus.
rubella [rū-BĚL-ă]	Disease that causes a viral skin rash; German measles.
rubeola [rū-BĒ-ō-lă]	Disease that causes a viral skin rash; measles.
scabies [SKĀ-bēz]	Skin eruption caused by a mite burrowing into the skin.

Term	Definition
scale	Small plate of hard skin that falls off.
scleroderma [sklēr-ō-DĔR-mă] sclero-, hardness + -derma	Thickening of the skin caused by an increase in collagen formation.
sebaceous [sĕ-BĀ-shŭs] **cyst**	Cyst containing yellow sebum.
seborrhea [sĕb-ō-RĒ-ă] sebo-, sebum + -rrhea	Overproduction of sebum by the sebaceous glands.
second-degree burn	Moderately severe burn that affects the epidermis and dermis; usually involves blistering.
shingles [SHĬN-glz]	Viral disease affecting peripheral nerves and caused by herpes zoster.
squamous cell carcinoma [SKWĂ-mŭs sĕl kăr-sĭn-NŌ-mă]	Cancer of the squamous epithelium.
telangiectasia [tĕl-ĂN-jē-ĕk-TĀ-zhē-ă]	A permanent dilation of the small blood vessels.
third-degree burn	Most severe type of burn; involves complete destruction of an area of skin.
tinea [TĬN-ē-ă]	Fungal infection; ringworm.
tumor [TŪ-mŏr]	Any mass of tissue; swelling.
ulcer [ŬL-sĕr]	Open lesion, usually with superficial loss of tissue.
urticaria [ŬR-tĭ-KĀR-ē-ă]	Group of reddish wheals, usually accompanied by pruritus and often caused by an allergy.
varicella [vār-ĭ-SĔL-ă]	Contagious skin disease, usually occurring during childhood, and often accompanied by the formation of pustules; chicken pox.
verruca (*pl.*, **verrucae**) [vĕ-RŪ-kă (vĕ-RŪ-kē)]	Flesh-colored growth, sometimes caused by a virus; wart.
vesicle [VĔS-ĭ-kl]	Small, raised sac on the skin containing fluid.
vitiligo [vĭt-ĭ-LĪ-gō]	Condition in which white patches appear on otherwise normally pigmented skin.
wart [wōrt]	*See* verruca.
wheal [hwēl]	Itchy patch of raised skin.
whitehead [WHĪT-hĕd]	Closed comedo that does not contain the dark bacteria present in blackheads.

Treating Adolescent Acne

Dr. Lin's new patient, Maria Cardoza, is 17 years old and has a persistent case of acne. She had been treating it with soap and Oxy-10 with limited success in the past couple of years, but recently her condition has worsened and her pediatrician recommended that she see Dr. Lin. After careful examination and removal of some comedones, Dr. Lin prescribed a course of antibiotics and asked Maria to return in three weeks. Dr. Lin put the following notes on Maria's record:

"Mild-to-moderate acne on the face, neck, and upper back. Lesions consist of macules, papules, mild oily comedones, and an occasional nodule, but no cysts or boils. Erythromycin, 400 mg., t.i.d. for 3 months. Recheck in 3 months."

Critical Thinking

49. Dr. Lin recommended that Maria wash her face with soap three times a day. Acne occurs in the sebaceous glands. How will frequent washing help?
50. As Maria gets older, why might her acne improve even without treatment?

PATHOLOGICAL TERMS EXERCISES

Build Your Medical Vocabulary

Put C for correct in the blank next to each word that is spelled correctly. Put the correct spelling next to words that are spelled incorrectly.

51. varicella _____
52. purpora _____

53. urticaria _____
54. rosola _____

Add the missing suffix to the following terms.

55. Nail inflammation: onych _____
56. Skin condition: dermat _____
57. Black tumor: melan _____

58. Hair disease: tricho _____
59. White skin: leuko _____

Check Your Knowledge

Circle T for true or F for false.

60. Basal cell carcinoma is characterized by blackened areas on the skin. T F
61. All neoplasms are malignant. T F
62. A nevus is a third-degree burn. T F
63. Pruritus can be present in many skin conditions. T F
64. Rubella causes a viral skin rash. T F
65. Warts may be caused by a virus. T F
66. Seborrhea is abnormal pigmentation. T F
67. The herpes virus is not curable and recurs at various times. T F
68. Food allergies can cause skin eruptions. T F

Fill in the blanks.

69. Herpes simplex virus Type 1 usually occurs around the area of the _____.

70. Herpes simplex virus Type 2 usually occurs on the _____.

Surgical Terms

Skin surgery includes the repair of various conditions. Sutures, stitches, or staples hold skin together while healing takes place. Various types of **plastic surgery** may involve reconstructing areas of the skin, as after severe burns or radiation. Some such surgeries use **skin grafts.** Other types of skin surgery result in the removal of a part of a growth to test for the presence of cancer. Growths are also removed to keep a cancer from spreading. Table 4-3 shows various kinds of surgeries related to the integumentary system.

TABLE 4-3 Skin surgeries.

Type of Surgery	Characteristics
autograft	skin graft using one's own skin
allograft or homograft	skin graft using skin from another person
heterograft or xenograft	skin graft using donor skin from an animal
cryosurgery	removal of tissue using liquid nitrogen
dermabrasion	removal of the top layers of skin with brushes or emery papers
debridement or curettage	removal of dead skin by scraping
cauterization	burning of an area to stop bleeding
electrodesiccation	drying of an area with electrical current
fulguration	destruction of tissue with electric sparks
biopsy (bx)	cutting of tissue for microscopic examination

VOCABULARY REVIEW

In the previous section, you learned terms relating to surgery. Before going on to the exercises, read the definitions below. Pronunciations are provided for certain terms.

Term	Definition
allograft [ĂL-ō-grăft] allo-, other + graft	*See* homograft.
autograft [ĂW-tō-grăft] auto-, self + graft	Skin graft using skin from one's own body.
biopsy [BĪ-ŏp-sē] bi(o)-, life + -opsy, view of	Excision of tissue for microscopic examination.
cauterization [KĂW-tĕr-ĭ-ZĀ-shŭn]	The application of heat to an area to cause coagulation and stop bleeding.
cryosurgery [KRĪ-ō-SĔR-jĕr-ē] cryo-, cold + surgery	Surgery that removes tissue by freezing it with liquid nitrogen.

Term	Definition
curettage [kyū-rĕ-TĂZH]	Removal of tissue from an area, such as a wound, by scraping.
debridement [dā-brēd-MŎN]	Removal of dead tissue from a wound.
dermabrasion [dĕr-mă-BRĀ-zhŭn] derm- + abrasion	Removal of wrinkles, scars, tattoos, and other marks by scraping with brushes or emery papers.
electrodesiccation [ē-LĔK-trō-dĕ-sĭ-KĀ-shŭn]	Drying with electrical current.
fulguration [fŭl-gŭ-RĀ-shŭn]	Destruction of tissue using electric sparks.
heterograft [HĔT-ĕr-ō-grăft] hetero-, other + graft	Skin graft using donor skin from one species to another; xenograft.
homograft [HŌ-mō-grăft] homo-, alike + graft	Skin graft using donor skin from one person to another; allograft.
plastic surgery	Repair or reconstruction (as of the skin) by means of surgery.
skin graft	Placement of fresh skin over a damaged area.
xenograft [ZĔN-ō-grăft] xeno-, foreign + graft	*See* heterograft.

CASE STUDY

Skin Biopsy

Dr. Lin has hospital hours scheduled for tomorrow morning. He will see two patients in the one-day surgery unit for minor operations. The first patient is to have cryosurgery for removal of several moles. Later, Dr. Lin will take a biopsy from a suspicious-looking skin patch of a patient who was treated earlier for a basal cell carcinoma. The pathology report follows:

The specimen consists of two ellipses of skin, each stated to be from the left upper arm. The larger measures 1.7 × 0.7 cm and has a slightly raised and roughened outer surface. Sections of skin exhibit a dermal nodular lesion consisting of interlacing bundles of elongated cells surrounded by fibrous stroma.

Critical Thinking

71. If the patch turns out to be a malignant melanoma, will that be more serious than the patient's earlier diagnosis?
72. What steps can you take to avoid permanent skin damage?

SURGICAL TERMS EXERCISES

Build Your Medical Vocabulary

Fill in the blanks in the statements that follow.

73. The repair of various conditions or the changing of one's appearance surgically is called _____ surgery.
74. Cauterizing a wound helps to stop _____.
75. The use of one's own skin to cover a wound is called a/an _____.
76. The use of someone else's skin to cover a wound is called a/an _____ or _____.

TERMINOLOGY IN ACTION

The letter shown below is a referral from a general practitioner to a dermatologist's office. As a learning exercise, define from memory the terms from the integumentary system that you find in the letter.

Dr. Alicia Williams

45 Essex Street

Anywhere, TX 99999

Dear Dr. Williams:

In the near future, you will be seeing a patient of mine, Lee Hong. He has been seen by me several times for treatment of verruca on his hands. They have been resistant to liquid nitrogen treatment.

On examination of his hands, there is an approximate 3-mm growth over the dorsum of the index finger and a small lesion on the thumb of his right hand. In addition, I noticed a change in a mole on his left thigh. Please check this mole.

Thank you for assisting in the care of this patient.

Sincerely,

Alicia Williams

Alicia Williams, MD

USING THE INTERNET

Go to the National Cancer Institute's Web site for skin cancer (http://www.nci.nih.gov/cancerinfo/types/skin). Find two treatments for skin cancer that are presently being used. Discuss one research article on skin cancer presented at the site.

CHAPTER REVIEW

DEFINITIONS

Define the following terms and combining forms. Review the chapter before starting, and check your answers by looking in the vocabulary reviews in this chapter. Make sure you know how to pronounce each term. The blue words in curly brackets are references to the Spanish glossary on the Web site.

TERM	DEFINITION
abscess [ĂB-sĕs] {absceso}	
acne [ĂK-nē] {acné}	
acne vulgaris [vŭl-GĀR-ĭs] {acné vulgar}	
actinic keratosis [ăk-TĬN-ĭk kĕr-ă-TŌ-sĭs]	
adip(o)	
adipose [ĂD-ĭ-pōs] {adiposo}	
allograft [ĂL-ō-grăft] {aloinjerto}	
albinism [ĂL-bĭ-nĭzm] {albinismo}	
alopecia [ăl-ō-PĒ-shē-ă] {alopecia}	
alopecia areata [ă-rē-Ā-tă]	
apocrine [ĂP-ō-krĭn] glands	
autograft [ĂW-tō-grăft] {autoinjerto}	
basal cell carcinoma [BĀ-săl sĕl kăr-sĭn-Ō-mă]	
biopsy [BĪ-ŏp-sē] (bx) {biopsia}	
birthmark	
blackhead {punto Negro}	
bulla (pl., bullae) [BŬL-ă (BŬL-ī)] {bulla}	
burn {quemadura}	
callus [KĂL-ŭs] {callo}	
candidiasis [kăn-dĭ-DĪ-ă-sĭs] {candidiasis}	
carbuncle [KĂR-bŭng-kl] {carbunco}	
cauterize [KĂW-tĕr-īz] {cauterizar}	

TERM	DEFINITION
ceruminous [sĕ-RŪ-mĭn-ŭs] glands	
cherry angioma [ăn-jē-Ō-mă]	
chloasma [klō-ĂZ-mă] {cloasma}	
cicatrix [SĬK-ă-trĭks] {cicatriz}	
cold sore	
collagen [KŎL-lă-jĕn] {colágeno}	
comedo (pl., comedos, comedones) [KŌM-ē-dō, kō-MĒ-dō (KŌM-ē-dōz, kō-mē-DŌ-nĕz)]	
corium [KŌ-rē-ŭm] {corium}	
corn {callo}	
crust {costra}	
cryosurgery [KRĪ-ō-SĔR-jĕr-ē] {criocirugía}	
curettage [kyū-rĕ-TĂZH]	
cuticle [KYŪ-tĭ-kl] {cutícula}	
cyst [sĭst] {quiste}	
debridement [dā-brēd-MŎN]	
decubitus (pl., decubiti) [dĕ-KYŪ-bĭ-tŭs (dĕ-KYŪ-bĭ-tī)], decubitus ulcer	
depigmentation [dē-pĭg-mĕn-TĀ-shŭn]	
dermabrasion [dĕr-mă-BRĀ-zhŭn] {dermabrasión}	
dermatitis [dĕr-mă-TĪ-tĭs] {dermatitis}	
dermat(o)	
dermatology [dĕr-mă-TŎL-ō-jē] {dermatologia}	
dermis [DĔR-mĭs] {dermis}	
derm(o)	
diaphoresis [DĪ-ă-fō-RĒ-sĭs] {diaforesis}	
ecchymosis (pl., ecchymoses) [ĕk-ĭ-MŌ-sĭs (ĕk-ĭ-MŌ-sēz)] {equimosis}	
eccrine [ĔK-rĭn] glands {glándulas ecrinas}	
eczema [ĔK-sē-mă, ĔG-zē-mă] {eccema}	
electrodesiccation [ē-LĔK-trō-dĕ-sĭ-KĀ-shŭn]	

Term	Definition
epidermis [ĕp-ĭ-DĚR-mĭs] {epidermis}	
erosion {erosion}	
excoriation [ĕks-KŌ-rē-Ā-shŭn] {excoriación}	
exocrine [ĚK-sō-krĭn] glands	
exudate [ĚKS-yū-dāt] {exudado}	
fever blister	
first-degree burn	
fissure [FĬSH-ŭr] {fisura}	
fulguration [fŭl-gū-RĀ-shŭn] {fulguración}	
furuncle [FYŪ-rŭng-kl] {furúnculo}	
gangrene [GĂNG-grēn] {gangrena}	
genital herpes	
hair follicle [FŎL-ĭ-kl]	
hair root {raiz del pelo}	
hair shaft	
herpes [HĚR-pēz] {herpes}	
herpes simplex virus Type 1	
herpes simplex virus Type 2	
herpes zoster [ZŎS-tĕr]	
heterograft [HĚT-ĕr-ō-grăft] {heteroinjerto}	
hidr(o)	
hives {urticaria}	
homograft [HŌ-mō-grăft] {homoinjerto}	
hypodermis [hĭ-pō-DĚR-mĭs] {hipodermis}	
ichthy(o)	
impetigo [ĭm-pĕ-TĪ-gō] {impétigo}	
integument [ĭn-TĚG-yū-mĕnt] {integumento}	
intradermal [ĭn-tră-DĚR-măl] test {intradérmico}	
Kaposi's sarcoma [KĂ-pō-sēz săr-KŌ-mă]	
keloid [KĒ-lŏyd] {queloide}	

keratin [KĔR-ă-tĭn] {queratina} _____

kerat(o) _____

keratosis [kĕr-ă-TŌ-sĭs] {queratosis} _____

lesion [LĒ-zhŭn] {lesión} _____

leukoderma [lū-kō-DĔR-mă] {leucodermia} _____

leukoplakia [lū-kō-PLĀ-kē-ă] {leucoplaquia} _____

lip(o) _____

lunula (pl., lunulae) [LŪ-nū-lă (LŪ-nū-lē)] {lúnula} _____

macule [MĂK-yūl] {macula} _____

malignant melanoma [mĕl-ă-NŌ-mă] _____

Mantoux [măn-TŪ] test _____

melan(o) _____

melanin [MĔL-ă-nĭn] {melanina} _____

melanocyte [MĔL-ă-nō-sīt] {melanocito} _____

myc(o) _____

nail {uña} _____

neoplasm [NĒ-ō-plăzm] {neoplasma} _____

nevus (pl., nevi) [NĒ-vŭs (NĒ-vī)] {nevo} _____

nodule [NŎD-yūl] {nódulo} _____

onych(o) _____

onychia, onychitis [ō-NĬK-ē-ă, ŏn-ĭ-KĪ-tĭs] {oniquia} _____

onychopathy [ŏn-ĭ-KŎP-ă-thē] {onicopatia} _____

papillary [PĂP-ĭ-lār-ē] layer _____

papule [PĂP-yūl] {pápula} _____

paronychia [păr-ŏ-NĬK-ē-ă] {paroniquia} _____

patch {placa} _____

patch test _____

pediculosis [pĕ-DĬK-yū-LŌ-sĭs] {pediculosis} _____

TERM	DEFINITION
petechia (*pl.*, petechiae) [pē-TĒ-kē-ă, (pē-TĒ-kē-ē)] {petequia}	
pil(o)	
pilonidal [pī-lō-NĪ-dăl] cyst	
plaque [plăk] {placa}	
plastic surgery	
polyp [PŎL-ĭp] {pólipo}	
pore {poro}	
PPD	
pressure sore	
pruritus [prū-RĪ-tŭs] {prurita}	
psoriasis [sō-RĪ-ă-sĭs] {psoriasis}	
purpura [PŬR-pū-ră] {púrpura}	
pustule [PŬS-tūl] {pústula}	
pyoderma [pī-ō-DĔR-mă] {pioderma}	
reticular [rĕ-TĬK-yū-lăr] layer	
ringworm {tiña}	
rosacea [rō-ZĀ-shē-ă] {rosácea}	
roseola [rō-ZĒ-ō-lă]	
rubella [rū-BĔL-ă] {rubéola}	
rubeola [rū-BĒ-ō-lă] {rubéola}	
scabies [SKĀ-bēz] {sarna}	
scale {costra}	
Schick [shĭk] test	
scleroderma [sklēr-ō-DĔR-mă] {esclerodermia}	
scratch test	
sebaceous [sĕ-BĀ-shŭs] cyst	
sebaceous glands	
seb(o)	
seborrhea [sĕb-ō-RĒ-ă] {seborrea}	
sebum [SĒ-bŭm] {sebo}	
second-degree burn	
shingles [SHĬN-glz] {culebrilla}	
skin graft {injerto de la piel}	
squamous cell carcinoma [SKWĂ-mŭs sĕl kăr-sĭn-NŌ-mă]	

TERM	DEFINITION
squamous epithelium [ĕp-ĭ-THĒ-lē-ŭm]	_____
steat(o)	_____
stratum (*pl.*, strata) [STRĂT-ŭm (STRĂ-tă)] {estrato}	_____
stratum corneum [KŌR-nē-ŭm]	_____
stratum germinativum [jĕr-mĭ-NĀT-ĭ-vŭm]	_____
subcutaneous [sŭb-kyū-TĀ-nē-ŭs] layer	_____
sweat glands	_____
telangiectasia [tĕl-ĂN-jē-ĕk-TĀ-zhē-ă]	_____
third-degree burn	_____
tine [tīn] test, TB tine	_____
tinea [TĬN-ē-ă] {tiña}	_____
trich(o)	_____
tumor [TŪ-mŏr] {tumor}	_____
ulcer [ŬL-sĕr] {úlcera}	_____
urticaria [ŬR-tĭ-KĀR-ē-ă] {urticaria}	_____
varicella [vār-ĭ-SĔL-ă] {varicela}	_____
verruca (*pl.*, verrucae) [vĕ-RŪ-kă (vĕ-RŪ-kē)] {verruga}	_____
vesicle [VĔS-ĭ-kl] {vesícula}	_____
vitiligo [vĭt-ĭ-LĪ-gō] {vitiligo}	_____
wart [wōrt] {verruga}	_____
wheal [hwēl] {roncha}	_____
whitehead [WHĪT-hĕd] {punto blanco}	_____
xanth(o)	_____
xenograft [ZĔN-ō-grăft] {xenoinjerto}	_____
xer(o)	_____

Answers to Chapter Exercises

1. a. 3; b. 1; c. 2
2. integument
3.
   a. epidermis
   b. stratum corneum
   c. sebaceous gland
   d. hair follicle
   e. subcutaneous layer (hypodermis)
4. cuticle
5. dermis
6. epidermis
7. papillary layer
8. eccrine
9. adipose
10. sebum
11. He is a diabetic and has a stubborn skin rash, which may become infected.
12. symptoms
13. Family history can give clues to hereditary disorders.
14. No, only a medical doctor may prescribe prescription medication, whether in sample form or not.
15. dermatoplasty or dermoplasty
16. dermophlebitis
17. keratoderma
18. mycodermatitis
19. melanoderma
20. onychomycosis
21. onychoplasty
22. pilosebaceous
23. melanocyte
24. trichoscopy
25. lipotomy
26. adipocellular
27. trichology
28. onychopathy
29. mycotoxin
30. mycovirus
31. xanthoderma
32. xerosis
33. keratolysis
34. melanoderma
35. hidromeiosis
36. tricho-, hair + -oma, tumor
37. xer(o)-, dry + -osis, condition
38. myco-, fungus + -cide, killing
39. onych(o)-, nail + -oid, resembling
40. Patient does not have allergies to the allergens being tested.
41. The rashes would subside or even disappear.
42. F
43. T
44. T
45. F
46. exudate or pus
47. allergies
48. intradermal
49. Washing helps to remove excess sebum from the skin.
50. Hormonal changes that occur as one ages affect the occurrence of acne.
51. C
52. purpura
53. C
54. roseola
55. -itis
56. -osis
57. -oma
58. -pathy
59. -derma
60. F
61. F
62. F
63. T
64. T
65. T
66. F
67. T
68. T
69. mouth
70. genitalia
71. yes
72. Avoid baking in the sun; use protectant lotions; wear a hat outside.
73. plastic
74. bleeding
75. autograft
76. allograft, homograft

The Musculoskeletal System

5

After studying this chapter, you will be able to:

▶ Name the parts of the musculoskeletal system and discuss the function of each part

▶ Define combining forms used in building words that relate to the musculoskeletal system

▶ Name the common diagnoses, laboratory tests, and clinical procedures used in treating disorders of the musculoskeletal system

▶ List and define the major pathological conditions of the musculoskeletal system

▶ Define surgical terms related to the musculoskeletal system

Structure and Function

The **musculoskeletal system** forms the framework that holds the body together, enables it to move, and protects and supports all the internal organs. This system includes **bones, joints,** and **muscles.** Figure 5-1 shows the musculoskeletal system.

Bones

Bones are made of **osseous tissue.** The cells of bone called **osteocytes.** The hardening process and development of the osteocytes is called **ossification.** This process is largely dependent on *calcium, phosphorus,* and *vitamin D.* During fetal development, bones are softer and flexible and are composed of **cartilage** until the hardening process begins.

    Bone-forming cells are called **osteoblasts.** As bone tissue develops, some of it dies and is reabsorbed by **osteoclasts** (also called **bone phagocytes**).

    There are many types of bones. The **long bones** form the arms and legs. They consist of a **diaphysis** or shaft. At each end of the shaft, an *epiphysis,* or shaped area, is where bones connect to other bones via ligaments and muscles. The space between the diaphysis and each epiphysis, called the **metaphysis,** develops as one grows. In that space, an **epiphyseal plate** of cartilage is covered by **articular cartilage** that provides protection.

    The outer portion of long bones is **compact bone** which surrounds **cancellous bone** (also called **spongy bone**). This covers the **medullary cavity,** which has a lining called the **endosteum.** The outside of the bone is covered by the **periosteum.** Figure 5-2 shows the parts of a long bone.

    Table 5-1 shows the five most common categories of bones.

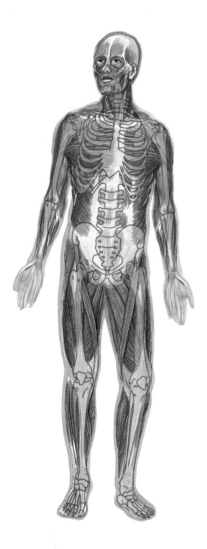

Calcium is important for the formation of bones. It is recommended that you pay attention to your daily calcium intake throughout your life, since lack of calcium is a factor in certain diseases, such as osteoporosis. To find out about the recommended levels, go to the National Osteoporosis Foundation's Web site (www.nof.org) and click on prevention.

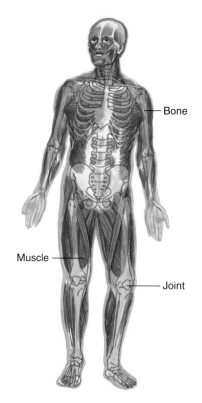

FIGURE 5-1 Muscles and bones hold the body together, enable it to move, and protect and support the internal organs.

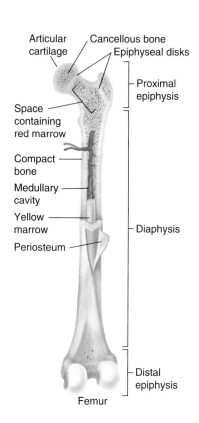

FIGURE 5-2 Parts of a long bone. The legs and arms are made up of long bones.

TABLE 5-1 Five common categories of bone

Type of Bone	Where Found	Characteristics
long bones	extremities of the body—legs and arms	outer portion is compact bone and ends connect to other bones
short bones	small bones of the wrists, ankles, and toes	outer portion is compact bone; inner portion is cancellous bone
flat bones	cover organs or provide surface for muscles—shoulders, pelvis, and skull	large, somewhat flat surfaces
irregular bones	ears, vertebrae, face	specialized bones with irregular shapes
sesamoid bones	hands, feet, knees	formed in tendons near joints

The **skeleton** of the body is made up of bones and joints. A mature adult has 206 bones that work together with joints and muscles to move the various parts of the body.

Commonly, bones have various extensions and depressions that serve as sites for attaching muscles and tendons. The seven different kinds of bone extensions are:

1. The **bone head,** the end of a bone, often rounded, that attaches to other bones or connective material and is covered with cartilage.

2. The **crest,** a bony ridge.
3. The **process,** any bony projection to which muscles and tendons attach.
4. The **tubercle,** a slight elevation on a bone's surface where muscles or ligaments are attached.
5. The **trochanter,** a bony extension near the upper end of the femur where muscle is attached.
6. A **tuberosity,** a large elevation on the surface of a bone for the attachments of muscles or tendons.
7. A **condyle,** a rounded surface protrusion at the end of a bone.

Figure 5-3 shows some of the extensions on a long bone.

Depressions in bone also allow bones to attach to each other. In addition, they are the passageways for blood vessels and nerves throughout the body. The most common types of depressions in bone are:

1. A **fossa,** a shallow pit in bone
2. A **foramen,** an opening through bone for blood vessels and nerves.
3. A **fissure,** a deep cleft in bone
4. A **sulcus,** a groove or furrow on the surface of a bone
5. A **sinus,** a hollow space or cavity in a bone.

Figure 5-4 shows the types of bone depressions.

Marrow is soft connective tissue and serves important functions in the production of blood cells.

Bones of the Head

Cranial bones form the *skull* or *cranium*. These bones join at points called **sutures.** The bones of the head include cavities, depressions, and extensions with specific purposes. Figure 5-5 shows the sinus cavities. Table 5-2 lists the major structures of the head.

Spinal Column

The **spinal column** (also called the **vertebral column**) consists of five sets of **vertebrae.** Each vertebra is a bone segment with a thick, **cartilaginous disk** (also called **intervertebral disk** or **disk,** also *disc*) that separates the vertebrae. In the

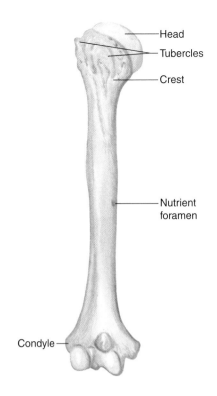

FIGURE 5-3 Bone extensions on a long bone.

Bone marrow can be transplanted from one person to another to help in curing certain diseases. To find out more about bone marrow donation, go to the Bone Marrow Foundation's Web site (www.bonemarrow.org).

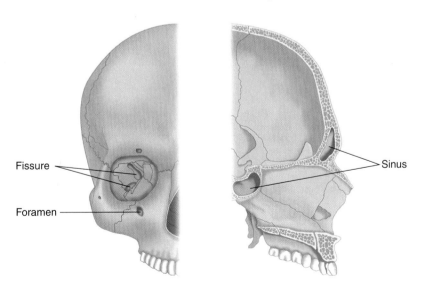

FIGURE 5-4 Several types of bone depressions.

FIGURE 5-5 The bones of the sinus cavities.

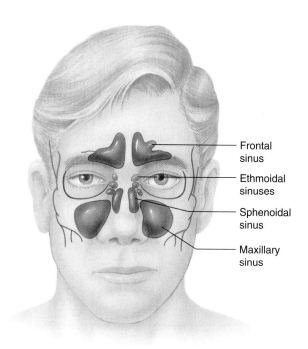

- Frontal sinus
- Ethmoidal sinuses
- Sphenoidal sinus
- Maxillary sinus

TABLE 5-2 Major structures of the head.

Bone or Other Structure	Location or Purpose	Characteristics
fontanelle	skull of a newborn	soft spot that closes eventually
frontal bone	forehead and roof of eye socket	
ethmoid bone	nasal cavity and eye orbits	
parietal bone	top and upper sides of the skull	
temporal bone	lower part of skull and lower sides	includes openings for ears
temporomandibular joint (TMJ)	connects temporal bone to **mandible** (lower jawbone)	
mastoid process	bone behind the ear	round extension
styloid process	protusion from the temporal bone	peg-shaped protrusion
occipital bone	back of skull	has opening called the **foramen magnum** through which spinal cord passes
sphenoid bone	base of the skull	holds the frontal, occipital, and ethmoid bones together
sella turcica	depression in the sphenoid bone	holds the pituitary gland
frontal sinuses	cavities above the eyes	
sphenoid sinuses	cavities above and behind the nose	
ethmoid sinuses	a group of small sinuses at the side of the **nasal cavity**	
maxillary sinuses	cavities on either side of the nasal cavity	

TABLE 5-2 Major structures of the head (*cont.*).

Bone or Other Structure	Location or Purpose	Characteristics
nasal bones	form the nose bridge	
lacrimal bones	hold the lacrimal gland and the canals for the tear ducts	
mandibular bone or mandible	lower jawbone; holds the sockets for the lower teeth	
maxillary bone	upper jawbone; holds sockets for the upper teeth	
vomer	nasal septum	
zygomatic bones	cheek bones	
palatine bones	form the nasal cavity and the hard palate	

middle of the disk is a fibrous mass called the **nucleus pulposus.** The disks cushion the vertebrae and help in movement and flexibility of the spinal column. The space between the **vertebral body** and the back of the vertebra is called the **neural canal.** This is the space through which the spinal cord passes. At the back of the vertebra, the **spinous process, transverse process,** and **lamina** form the posterior side of the spinal column.

The five divisions of vertebrae are:

1. The **cervical vertebrae,** the seven vertebrae of the neck bone, which include the first vertebra (T1, first thoracic vertebra), called the **atlas,** and the second vertebra (T2, second thoracic vertebra), called the **axis.**
2. The **thoracic vertebrae** (also called the **dorsal vertebrae**), the twelve vertebrae that connect to the ribs.
3. The **lumbar vertebrae,** the five bones of the middle back.
4. The **sacrum,** the curved bone of the lower back.
5. The **coccyx,** the tailbone.

Figure 5-6 shows the divisions of the spinal column.

Bones of the Chest

The bones of the chest or **thorax** include weight-transferring sections of bones. The upper group is formed by the **clavicle** (anterior collar bone) and the **scapula** (posterior shoulder bone). The point at which they join is the

MORE ABOUT...

The Atlas and the Axis

The ancient Greeks thought that the god Atlas supported the heavens on his shoulders. When the first vertebra was named, it too was called atlas because it supports the head. The axis is so-called because it forms the pivot point on which the atlas can rotate (as when one shakes the head "no").

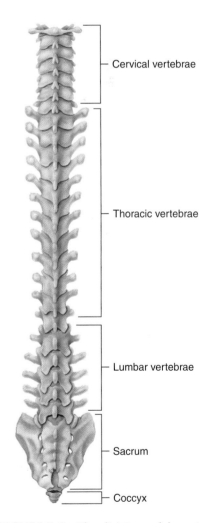

FIGURE 5-6 The divisions of the spinal column.

acromion. Below that is the **sternum** or **breastbone,** out from which extends the twelve pairs of **ribs.** The first seven pairs of ribs are called **true ribs.** Below that is a weight-transferring section called the *pelvic girdle.*

Bones of the Pelvis

Below the thoracic cavity is the pelvis, a ring of bone and ligament. The **pelvic girdle** is a large bone that forms the hips and supports the trunk of the body. It is composed of three fused bones, including the **ilium, ischium,** and **pubes** (the anteroinferior portion of the hip bone). It is also the point of attachment for the legs.

Inside the pelvic girdle is the **pelvic cavity.** In the pelvic cavity are located the female reproductive organs, the sigmoid colon, the bladder, and the rectum. The area where the two pubic bones join is called the **pubic symphysis.**

Bones of the Extremities

The arms and legs fit into the bones of the trunk of the body at one end and end in the fingers and toes at the other. Figures 5-7 and 5-8 show the bones of the extremities. Table 5-3 lists the bones of the extremities.

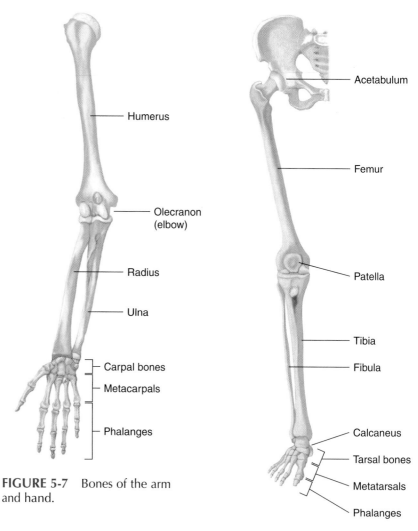

FIGURE 5-7 Bones of the arm and hand.

FIGURE 5-8 Bones of the leg and foot.

TABLE 5-3 Bones of the extremities.

Bone, Depression, or Protrusion	Where Located
humerus	attaches to the scapula and clavicle
ulna	larger of the two lower arm bones
olecranon or **elbow**	bony protrusion on the ulna
radius	smaller bone between the elbow and wrist
carpus or *wrist*	attached to the radius and palm
metacarpals	five palm bones that radiate to fingers
phalanges (*sing.*, **phalanx**)	finger or toe bones
acetabulum	depression in hip bone into which thigh fits
femur	thigh bone
tibia or **shin**	one of the two bones of the lower leg
fibula	one of the two bones of the lower leg
patella	kneecap
malleolus (*pl.*, **malleoli**)	bony protrusion at the bottom of each lower leg bone
tarsal bones	help form the **ankle, tarsus** or instep, and **calcaneus** or heel
metatarsals	bones that connect the tarsal bones to the phalanges or toe bones

Joints

Joints are also called **articulations,** points where bones connect. **Diarthroses** are joints that move freely, such as the knee joint. **Amphiarthroses** are cartilaginous joints that move slightly, such as the joints between vertebrae. **Synarthroses** do not move; examples are the fibrous joints between the skull bones. **Symphyses** are cartilaginous joints that unite two bones firmly; an example is the pubic symphysis.

Bones are connected to other bones with **ligaments,** bands of fibrous tissue. **Tendons** are bands of fibrous tissue that connect muscles to bone. **Synovial joints** are covered with a **synovial membrane,** which secretes **synovial fluid,** a joint lubricant. Some spaces between tendons and joints have a **bursa,** a sac lined with a synovial membrane. Figure 5-9 shows the three types of joints and the parts of a joint.

Muscles

Muscles contract and extend to provide body movement. The **voluntary (striated) muscles,** such as those in the arms and legs, can be contracted at

Body Movement

Bones, joints, and muscles allow parts of the body to move in certain directions. To determine if movement can be done correctly, medical practitioners in a variety of fields look at the range of motion of the parts of the body. Also, testing for range of motion of the body involves placement in certain positions.

- *Flexion*—the bending of a limb.
- *Extension*—the straightening of a limb.
- *Rotation*—the circular movement of a part, such as the neck.
- *Abduction*—movement away from the body.
- *Adduction*—movement toward the body
- *Supination*—a turning up, as of the hand.
- *Pronation*—a turning down, as of the hand.
- *Dorsiflexion*—a bending up, as of the ankle.
- *Plantar flexion*—a bending down, as of the ankle.

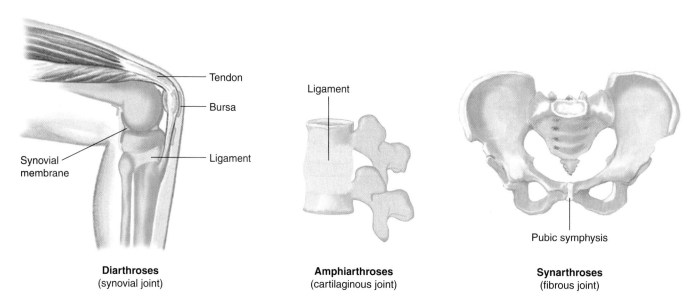

Diarthroses
(synovial joint)

Amphiarthroses
(cartilaginous joint)

Synarthroses
(fibrous joint)

FIGURE 5-9   Types of and parts of a joint.

will. The **involuntary (smooth** or **visceral) muscles** control movement that is not regulated by will, such as respiration, urination, and digestion. **Cardiac muscle,** which controls the contractions of the heart, is the only involuntary muscle that is also striated.

Most muscles are covered by **fascia,** a band of connective tissue. Muscles attach to a stationary bone at a point called the **origin.** They attach to a movable bone at a point called the **insertion.** Figure 5-10 shows the various types of muscle.

MORE ABOUT...

Muscles

Normal muscles contract and extend during routine movement and exercise. In unusual circumstances, muscles can *atrophy* (waste away). This can happen from a number of diseases that affect muscles and movement or from lack of use, as in a sedentary lifestyle. People who are paralyzed and find it difficult to get help moving muscles generally have areas where muscle atrophies. On the other hand, overuse of muscles can cause *hyperplasia,* an abnormal increase in muscle cells.

Building muscle by exercising is generally a healthy thing to do. However, some athletes take dangerous shortcuts to building muscle. They take *anabolic steroids* or supplements containing products similar to anabolic steroids that build muscle quickly. Unfortunately, these products can have devastating health and emotional consequences, sometimes even fatal ones. Also, athletes who take these illegal substances often have an unfair advantage in competition over those who don't. These substances are outlawed in most competitive sports.

For more information about steroid abuse, go to the National Institute on Drug Abuse's Web site on steroid abuse (www.steroidabuse.org).

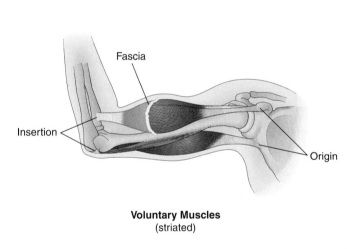

Voluntary Muscles
(striated)

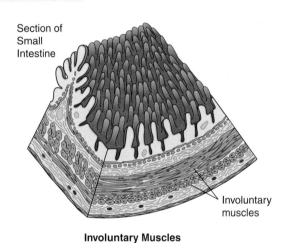

Involuntary Muscles
(smooth or visceral)

FIGURE 5-10 Types and parts of muscle.

VOCABULARY REVIEW

In the previous section, you learned terms relating to the musculoskeletal system. Before going on to the exercises, read the definitions below. Pronunciations are provided for certain terms.

Term	Definition
acetabulum [ăs-ĕ-TĂB-yū-lŭm]	Cup-shaped depression in the hip bone into which the top of the femur fits.

Term	Definition
acromion [ă-KRŌ-mē-oñ]	Part of the scapula that connects to the clavicle.
amphiarthrosis (*pl.*, **amphiarthoses**) [ĂM-fĭ-ăr-THRŌ-sĭs (ĂM-fĭ-ăr-THRŌ-sĕs)]	Cartilaginous joint having some movement at the union of two bones.
ankle [ĂNG-kl]	Hinged area between the lower leg bones and the bones of the foot.
articular [ăr-TĬK-yū-lăr] **cartilage**	Cartilage at a joint.
articulation [ăr-tĭk-yū-LĀ-shŭn]	Point at which two bones join together to allow movement.
atlas [ĂT-lăs]	First cervical vertebra.
axis [ĂK-sĭs]	Second cervical vertebra.
bone	Hard connective tissue that forms the skeleton of the body.
bone head	Upper, rounded end of a bone.
bone phagocyte [FĂG-ō-sīt]	Bone cell that ingests dead bone and bone debris.
bursa (*pl.*, **bursae**) [BŬR-să(BŬR-sē)]	Sac lined with a synovial membrane that fills the spaces between tendons and joints.
calcaneus [kăl-KĀ-nē-ŭs]	Heel bone.
cancellous [KĂN-sĕ-lŭs] **bone**	Spongy bone with a latticelike structure.
cardiac [KĂR-dē-ăk] **muscle**	Striated involuntary muscle of the heart.
carpus [KĂR-pŭs]	Wrist.
cartilage [KĂR-tĭ-lăj]	Flexible connective tissue found in joints, fetal skeleton, and the lining of various parts of the body.
cartilaginous [kăr-tĭ-LĂJ-ĭ-nŭs] **disk**	Thick, circular mass of cartilage between the vertebrae of the spinal column.
cervical [SĔR-vĭ-kl] **vertebrae**	Seven vertebrae of the spinal column located in the neck.
clavicle [KLĂV-ĭ-kl]	Curved bone of the shoulder that joins to the scapula; collar bone.
coccyx [KŎK-sĭks]	Small bone consisting of four fused vertebrae at the end of the spinal column; tailbone.
compact bone	Hard bone with a tightly woven structure.
condyle [KŎN-dīl]	Rounded surface at the end of a bone.
crest	Bony ridge.
diaphysis [dī-ĂF-ĭ-sĭs]	Long middle section of a long bone; shaft.

Term	Definition
diarthroses (*sing.*, **diarthrosis**) [dī-ăr-THRŌ-sēz (dī-ăr-THRŌ-sĭs]	Freely movable joints.
disk [dĭsk]	*See* cartilaginous disk.
dorsal vertebrae	*See* thoracic vertebrae.
elbow [ĔL-bō]	Joint between the upper arm and the forearm.
endosteum [ĕn-DŎS-tē-ŭm]	Lining of the medullary cavity.
epiphyseal [ĕp-ĭ-FĬZ-ē-ăl] **plate**	Cartilaginous tissue that is replaced during growth years, but eventually calcifies and disappears when growth stops.
ethmoid [ĔTH-mŏyd] **bone**	Irregular bone of the face attached to the sphenoid bone.
ethmoid sinuses	Sinuses on both sides of the nasal cavities between each eye and the sphenoid sinus.
fascia (*pl.*, **fasciae**) [FĂSH-ē-ă (FĂSH-ē-ē)]	Sheet of fibrous tissue that encloses muscles.
femur [FĒ-mūr]	Long bone of the thigh.
fibula [FĬB-yū-lă]	Smaller long bone of the lower leg.
fissure [FĬSH-ŭr]	Deep furrow or slit.
flat bones	Thin, flattened bones that cover certain areas, as of the skull.
fontanelle [FŎN-tă-nĕl]	Soft, membranous section on top of an infant's skull.
foramen [fō-RĀ-mĕn]	Opening or perforation through a bone.
fossa (*pl.*, **fossae**) [FŎS-ă (FŎS-ē)]	Depression, as in a bone.
frontal [FRŬN-tăl] **bone**	Large bone of the skull that forms the top of the head and forehead.
frontal sinuses	Sinuses above the eyes.
humerus [HYŪ-mĕr-ŭs]	Long bone of the arm connecting to the scapula on top and the radius and ulna at the bottom.
ilium [ĬL-ē-ŭm]	Wide portion of the hip bone.
insertion	Point at which a muscle attaches to a movable bone.
intervertebral [ĭn-tĕr-VĔR-tĕ-brăl] **disk**	*See* cartilaginous disk.
involuntary muscle	Muscle not movable at will.
irregular bones	Any of a group of bones with a special shape to fit into certain areas of the skeleton, such as the skull.
ischium [ĬS-kē-ŭm]	One of three fused bones that form the pelvic girdle.

Term	Definition
joint [jŏynt]	Place of joining between two or more bones.
lacrimal [LĂK-rĭ-măl] **bone**	Thin, flat bone of the face.
lamina (*pl.*, **laminae**) [LĂM-ĭ-nă (LĂM-ĭ-nē)]	Thin, flat part of either side of the arch of a vertebra.
ligament [LĬG-ă-mĕnt]	Sheet of fibrous tissue connecting and supporting bones; attaches bone to bone.
long bone	Any bone of the extremities with a shaft.
lumbar [LŬM-băr] **vertebrae**	Five vertebrae of the lower back.
malleolus (*pl.*, **malleoli**) [mă-LĒ-ō-lŭs (mă-LĒ-ō-lī)]	Rounded protrusion of the tibia or fibula on either side of the ankle.
mandible [MĂN-dĭ-bl]	U-shaped bone of the lower jaw.
mandibular [măn-DĬB-yū-lăr] **bone**	*See* mandible.
marrow [MĂR-ō]	Connective tissue filling the medullary cavity, often rich in nutrients.
mastoid [MĂS-tŏyd] **process**	Protrusion of the temporal bone that sits behind the ear.
maxillary [MĂK-sĭ-lār-ē] **bone**	Bone of the upper jaw.
maxillary sinus	Sinus on either side of the nasal cavity below the eyes.
medullary [MĚD-ū-lār-ē] **cavity**	Soft center cavity in bone that often holds marrow.
metacarpal [MĚT-ă-KĂR-păl]	One of five bones of the hand between the wrist and the fingers.
metaphysis [mĕ-TĂF-ĭ-sĭs]	Section of a long bone between the epiphysis and diaphysis.
metatarsal [MĚT-ă-TĂR-săl] **bones**	Bones of the foot between the instep (arch) and the toes.
muscle [MŬS-ĕl]	Contractile tissue that plays a major role in body movement.
musculoskeletal [MŬS-kyū-lō-SKĚL-ĕ-tăl] **system**	System of the body including the muscles and skeleton.
nasal bones	Bones that form the bridge of the nose.
neural [NŪR-ăl] **canal**	Space through which the spinal cord passes.
nucleus pulposus [NŪ-klē-ŭs pŭl-PŌ-sŭs]	Fibrous mass in the center portion of the intervertebral disk.
occipital [ŏk-SĬP-ĭ-tăl] **bone**	Bone that forms the lower back portion of the skull.

Term	Definition
olecranon [ō-LĔK-ră-nŏn]	Curved end of the ulna to which tendons of the arm muscles attach; bony prominence of the elbow.
origin	Point at which muscles attach to stationary bone.
osseous [ŎS-ē-ŭs] **tissue**	Connective tissue into which calcium salts are deposited.
ossification [ŎS-ĭ-fĭ-KĀ-shŭn]	Hardening into bone.
osteoblast [ŎS-tē-ō-blăst]	Cell that forms bone.
osteoclast [ŎS-tē-ō-klăst]	Large cell that reabsorbs and removes osseous tissue.
osteocyte [ŎS-tē-ō-sīt]	Bone cell.
palatine [PĂL-ă-tīn] **bone**	Bone that helps form the hard palate and nasal cavity; located behind the maxillary bones.
parietal [pă-RĪ-ĕ-tăl] **bone**	Flat, curved bone on either side of the upper part of the skull.
patella [pă-TĔL-ă]	Large, sesamoid bone that forms the kneecap.
pelvic [PĔL-vĭk] **cavity**	Cup-shaped cavity formed by the large bones of the pelvic girdle; contains female reproductive organs, sigmoid colon, bladder, and rectum.
pelvic girdle	Hip bones.
pelvis [PĔL-vĭs]	Cup-shaped ring of bone and ligaments at the base of the trunk.
periosteum [pĕr-ē-ŎS-tē-ŭm]	Fibrous membrane covering the surface of bone.
phalanges (*sing.*, **phalanx**) [fă-LĂN-jēz (FĂ-lăngks)]	Long bones of the fingers and toes.
process [PRŌ-sĕs, PRŎS-ĕs]	Bony outgrowth or projection.
pubes [PYŪ-bĭs]	Anteroinferior portion of the hip bone.
pubic symphysis [PYŪ-bĭk SĬM-fă-sĭs]	Joint between the two public bones.
radius [RĀ-dē-ŭs]	Shorter bone of the forearm.
rib	One of twenty-four bones that form the chest wall.
sacrum [SĀ-krŭm]	Next-to-last spinal vertebra made up of five fused bones; vertebra that forms part of the pelvis.
scapula [SKĂP-yū-lă]	Large flat bone that forms the shoulder blade.
sella turcica [SĔL-ă TŬR-sĭ-kă]	Bony depression in the sphenoid bone where the pituitary gland is located.

Term	Definition
sesamoid [SĔS-ă-mŏyd] **bone**	Bone formed in a tendon over a joint.
shin [shĭn]	Anterior ridge of the tibia.
short bones	Square-shaped bones with approximately equal dimensions on all sides.
sinus [SĪ-nŭs]	Hollow cavity, especially either of two cavities on the sides of the nose.
skeleton [SKĔL-ĕ-tŏn]	Bony framework of the body.
smooth muscle	Fibrous muscle of internal organs that acts involuntarily.
sphenoid [SFĒ-nŏyd] **bone**	Bone that forms the base of the skull.
sphenoid sinus	Sinus above and behind the nose.
spinal column	Column of vertebrae at the posterior of the body, from the neck to the coccyx.
spinous [SPĪ-nŭs] **process**	Protrusion from the center of the vertebral arch.
spongy bone	Bone with an open latticework filled with connective tissue or marrow.
sternum [STĔR-nŭm]	Long, flat bone that forms the midline of the anterior of the thorax.
striated [strī-ĀT-ĕd] **muscle**	Muscle with a ribbed appearance that is controlled at will.
styloid [STĪ-lŏyd] **process**	Peg-shaped protrusion from a bone.
sulcus (*pl.,* **sulci**) [SŬL-kŭs (SŬL-sī)]	Groove or furrow in the surface of bone.
suture [SŪ-chūr]	Joining of two bone parts with a fibrous membrane.
symphysis [SĬM-fĭ-sĭs]	Type of cartilaginous joint uniting two bones.
synarthrosis [SĬN-ăr-THRŌ-sĭs]	Fibrous joint with no movement.
synovial [sĭ-NŌ-vē-ăl] **fluid**	Fluid that serves to lubricate joints.
synovial joint	A joint that moves.
synovial membrane	Connective tissue lining the cavity of joints and producing the synovial fluid.
tarsus, tarsal [TĂR-sŭs, TĂR-săl] **bones**	Seven bones of the instep (arch of the foot).
temporal [TĔM-pō-răl] **bone**	Large bone forming the base and sides of the skull.
temporomandibular [TĔM-pō-rō-măn-DĬB-yū-lăr] **joint (TMJ)**	Joint of the lower jaw between the temporal bone and the mandible.

Term	Definition
tendon [TĔN-dŏn]	Fibrous band that connects muscle to bone or other structures.
thoracic [thō-RĂS-ĭk] **vertebrae**	Twelve vertebrae of the chest area.
thorax [THŌ-răks]	Part of the trunk between the neck and the abdomen; chest.
tibia [TĬB-ē-ă]	Larger of the two lower leg bones.
transverse process	Protrusion on either side of the vertebral arch.
trochanter [trō-KĂN-tĕr]	Bony protrusion at the upper end of the femur.
true ribs	Seven upper ribs on each side of the chest that attach to the sternum.
tubercle [TŪ-bĕr-kl]	Slight bony elevation to which a ligament or muscle may be attached.
tuberosity [TŪ-bĕr-ŎS-ĭ-tē]	Large elevation in the surface of a bone.
ulna [ŬL-nă]	Larger bone of the forearm.
vertebra (*pl.*, **vertebrae**) [VĔR-tĕ-bră (VĔR-tĕ-brē)]	One of the bony segments of the spinal column.
vertebral body	Main portion of the vertebra, separate from the arches of the vertebra.
vertebral column	Spinal column.
visceral [VĬS-ĕr-ăl] **muscle**	Smooth muscle.
voluntary muscle	Striated muscle.
vomer [VŌ-mĕr]	Flat bone forming the nasal septum.
zygomatic [ZĪ-gō-MĂT-ĭk] **bone**	Bone that forms the cheek.

CASE STUDY

Seeing a Specialist

Mary Edgarton was referred to Dr. Alana Wolf, a rheumatologist, by her internist. Mary's five-month bout of joint pain, swelling, and stiffness had not shown improvement. Dr. Wolf gave her a full musculoskeletal examination to check for swelling, abnormalities, and her ability to move her joints. Even though Mary remains a fairly active person, her movement in certain joints is now limited. She shows a moderate loss of grip strength.

In checking earlier for a number of systemic diseases, Mary's internist felt that Mary's problems were the result of some disease of her musculoskeletal system. Many of the laboratory tests that were forwarded to Dr. Wolf showed normal levels.

Critical Thinking

1. What lubricates the joints, allowing movement?
2. Exercise is usually recommended to alleviate musculoskeletal problems. Is it possible to exercise both involuntary and voluntary muscles?

Check Your Knowledge

Fill in the blanks.

3. The large bones of the extremities are _____ bones.

4. The outer portion of a long bone is _____ _____.

5. Soft connective tissue with high nutrient content in the center of some bones is called _____ .

6. An infant's skull generally has soft spots known as _____ .

7. Disks in the spinal column have a soft, fibrous mass in the middle called the _____ _____ .

8. The scapula and the clavicle join at a point called the _____ .

9. Ribs that attach to the sternum are called _____ _____ .

10. Another name for kneecap is _____ .

11. The largest tarsal is called the _____ or heel.

12. The only muscle that is both striated and involuntary is the _____ muscle.

Circle T for true or F for false.

13. Compact bone is another name for cancellous bone. T F

14. Tendons are parts of bones. T F

15. The mandible is the upper jawbone. T F

16. The twelve vertebrae that connect to the ribs are the dorsal vertebrae. T F

17. Joints are lubricated with synovial fluid. T F

Combining Forms

The list below includes combining forms that relate specifically to the musculoskeletal system. Pronunciations are provided for the examples.

COMBINING FORM	MEANING	EXAMPLE
acetabul(o)	acetabulum	*acetabulectomy* [ĂS-ĕ-tăb-yū-LĔK-tō-mē], excision of the acetabulum
acromi(o)	end point of the scapula	*acromioscapular* [ă-KRŌ-mē-ō-SKĂP-yū-lăr], relating to the acromion and the body of the scapula
ankyl(o)	bent, crooked	*ankylosis* [ĂNG-kĭ-LŌ-sĭs], fixation of a joint in a bent position, usually resulting from a disease
arthr(o)	joint	*arthrogram* [ĂR-thrō-grăm], x-ray of a joint
brachi(o)	arm	*brachiocephalic* [BRĀ-kē-ō-sĕ-FĂL-ĭk], relating to both the arm and head

COMBINING FORM	MEANING	EXAMPLE
burs(o)	bursa	*bursitis* [bŭr-SĪ-tĭs], inflammation of a bursa
calcane(o)	heel	*calcaneodynia* [kăl-KĀ-nē-ō-DĬN-ē-ă], heel pain
calci(o)	calcium	*calciokinesis* [KĂL-sē-ō-kĭ-NĒ-sĭs], mobilization of stored calcium in the body
carp(o)	wrist	*carpopedal* [KĂR-pō-PĔD-ăl], relating to the wrist and foot
cephal(o)	head	*cephalomegaly* [SĔF-ă-lō-MĔG-ă-lē], abnormally large head
cervic(o)	neck	*cervicodynia* [SĔR-vĭ-kō-DĬN-ē-ă], neck pain
chondr(o)	cartilage	*chondroplasty* [KŎN-drō-plăs-tē], surgical repair of cartilage
condyl(o)	knob, knuckle	*condylectomy* [kŏn-dĭ-LĔK-tō-mē], excision of a condyle
cost(o)	rib	*costiform* [KŎS-tĭ-fŏrm], rib-shaped
crani(o)	skull	*craniotomy* [krā-nē-ŎT-ō-mē], incision into the skull
dactyl(o)	fingers, toes	*dactylitis* [dăk-tĭ-LĪ-tĭs], inflammation of the finger(s) or toe(s)
fasci(o)	fascia	*fasciotomy* [făsh-ē-ŎT-ō-mē], incision through a fascia
femor(o)	femur, thigh	*femorocele* [FĔM-ō-rō-sēl], hernia near the top of the thigh
fibr(o)	fiber	*fibroma* [fĭ-BRŌ-mă], benign tumor in fibrous tissue
humer(o)	humerus	*humeroscapular* [HYŪ-mĕr-ō-SKĂP-yū-lăr], relating to both the humerus and the scapula
ili(o)	ilium	*iliofemoral* [ĬL-ē-ō-FĔM-ō-răl], relating to the ilium and the femur
ischi(o)	ischium	*ischiodynia* [ĬS-kē-ō-DĬN-ē-ă], pain in the ischium
kyph(o)	hump; bent	*kyphoscoliosis* [KĪ-fō-skō-lē-Ō-sĭs], kyphosis and scoliosis combined
lamin(o)	lamina	*laminectomy* [LĂM-ĭ-NĔK-tō-mē], removal of part of one or more of the thick cartilaginous disks between the vertebrae
leiomy(o)	smooth muscle	*leiomyosarcoma* [LĪ-ō-MĪ-ō-săr-KŌ-mă], malignant tumor of smooth muscle

COMBINING FORM	MEANING	EXAMPLE
lumb(o)	lumbar	*lumboabdominal* [LŬM-bō-ăb-DŎM-ĭ-năl], relating to the lumbar and abdominal regions
maxill(o)	upper jaw	*maxillofacial* [măk-SĬL-ō-FĀ-shăl], pertaining to the jaws and face
metacarp(o)	metacarpal	*metacarpectomy* [MĚT-ă-kăr-PĔK-tō-mē], excision of a metacarpal
my(o)	muscle	*myocardium* [mī-ō-KĂR-dē-ŭm], cardiac muscle in the middle layer of the heart
myel(o)	spinal cord; bone marrow	*myelocyst* [MĪ-ĕ-lō-sĭst], cyst that develops in bone marrow
oste(o)	bone	*osteoarthritis* [ŎS-tē-ō-ăr-THRĪ-tĭs], arthritis characterized by erosion of cartilage and bone and joint pain
patell(o)	knee	*patellectomy* [PĂT-ĕ-LĔK-tō-mē], excision of the patella
ped(i), ped(o)	foot	*pedometer* [pĕ-DŎM-ĕ-tĕr], instrument for measuring walking distance
pelv(i)	pelvis	*pelviscope* [PĔL-vĭ-skōp], instrument for viewing the pelvic cavity
phalang(o)	finger or toe bone	*phalangectomy* [făl-ăn-JĔK-tō-mē], removal of a finger or toe
pod(o)	foot	*podalgia* [pō-DĂL-jē-ă], foot pain
pub(o)	pubis	*puborectal* [PYŪ-bō-RĔK-tăl], relating to the pubis and the rectum
rachi(o)	spine	*rachiometer* [rā-kē-ŎM-ĕ-tĕr], instrument for measuring spine curvature
radi(o)	forearm bone	*radiomuscular* [RĀ-dē-ō-MŬS-kyū-lăr], relating to the radius and nearby muscles
rhabd(o)	rod-shaped	*rhabdosphincter* [RĂB-dō-SFĬNGK-tĕr], striated muscular sphincter
rhabdomy(o)	striated muscle	*rhabdomyolysis* [RĂB-dō-mī-ŎL-ĭ-sĭs], acute disease that includes destruction of skeletal muscle
scapul(o)	scapula	*scapulodynia* [SKĂP-yū-lō-DĬN-ē-ă], scapula pain
scoli(o)	curved	*scoliokyphosis* [SKŌ-lē-ō-kī-FŌ-sĭs], lateral and posterior curvature of the spine

COMBINING FORM	MEANING	EXAMPLE
spondyl(o)	vertebra	*spondylitis* [spŏn-dĭ-LĪ-tĭs], inflammation of a vertebra
stern(o)	sternum	*sternodynia* [stĕr-nō-DĬN-ē-ă], sternum pain
synov(o)	synovial membrane	*synovitis* [sĭn-ō-VĪ-tĭs], inflammation of a synovial joint
tars(o)	tarsus	*tarsomegaly* [tăr-sō-MĔG-ă-lē], congenital abnormality with overgrowth of a tarsal bone
ten(o), tend(o), tendin(o)	tendon	*tenodynia* [tĕn-ō-DĬN-ē-ă], tendon pain; *tendoplasty* [TĔN-dō-plăs-tē], surgical repair of a tendon; *tendinitis* [tĕn-dĭ-NĪ-tĭs], tendon inflammation
thorac(o)	thorax	*thoracoabdominal* [THŌR-ă-kō-ăb-DŎM-ĭ-năl], relating to the thorax and the abdomen
tibi(o)	tibia	*tibiotarsal* [tĭb-ē-ō-TĂR-săl], relating to the tarsal and tibia bones
uln(o)	ulna	*ulnocarpal* [ŬL-nō-KĂR-păl], relating to the ulna and the wrist
vertebr(o)	vertebra	*vertebroarterial* [VĔR-tĕ-brō-ăr-TĒR-ē-ăl], relating to a vertebral artery or to a vertebra and an artery

Combining Forms Exercises

Build Your Medical Vocabulary

Complete the words using combining forms listed in this chapter.

18. Joint pain: _____ dynia

19. Plastic surgery of the skull: _____ plasty

20. Of the upper jaw and its teeth: _____ dental

21. Relating to the large area of the hip bone and the tibia: _____ tibial

22. Operation on the instep of the foot: _____ tomy

23. Relating to the head and chest: cephalo _____

24. Production of fibrous tissue: _____ plasia

25. Inflammation of the foot: _____ itis

26. Incision into the spine: _____ centesis

27. Incision through the sternum: _____ tomy

CASE STUDY

Checking Medication

Dr. Wolf's next patient, Laura Spinoza, is in for a follow-up visit for fibromyalgia, a disease that causes chronic muscle pain. In addition, Laura has tested positive for CTS (carpal tunnel syndrome). The patient suffers from depression, for which she is currently being treated. Laura has had earlier reactions to some of the medications meant to relieve the symptoms of fibromyalgia. She is receiving new prescriptions for the fibromyalgia as well as directions for an exercise program. Dr. Wolf sent a follow-up letter to Laura's primary care physician after her visit.

Critical Thinking

28. Dr. Wolf gets referrals from general practitioners and internists. As a specialist in rheumatology, most of her cases involve diseases of the musculoskeletal system. Refer to the letter from Dr. Wolf and use the combining forms list to provide definitions of two diseases given as examples.

29. Laura has a physical condition in addition to fibromyalgia. What is it?

Alana Wolf, M.D.
285 Riverview Road
Belle Harbor, MI 09999

March 12, 20XX

Dr. Robert Johnson
16 Tyler Court
Newtown, MI 09990

Dear Dr. Johnson

I saw Laura Spinoza on March the 7th for evaluation of her fibromyalgia. I reviewed her history with her and discussed her treatment for depression. The history suggests that there has not been any new development of an inflammatory rheumatic disease process within the last two years. She does have right thumb-carpal pain, which represents some osteoarthritis. Headaches are frequent but she is receiving no specific therapy. Her sleep pattern remains disturbed at times.

Her height was 62 inches, her weight was 170 lbs, while her BP was 162/100 in the right arm in the reclining position. Pelvic and rectal examinations were not done. The abdominal examination revealed some mild tenderness in the right lower quadrant without other abnormalities. The musculoskeletal examination revealed rotation and flexion to the left with no other cervical abnormalities. The remainder of the musculoskeletal examination revealed hypermobility in the elbow and knees and slight bony osteoarthritic enlargement of the thumb-carpal joint. Slight deformity was noted in the right knee with mild patellar-femoral crepitus. Severe bilateral pas planus was present, with the right foot more involved than the left, and ankle vagus deformity with mild bony osteoarthritic enlargement of both 1st MTP joints.

Hope these thoughts are helpful. I want to thank you for the consultation. If I can be of future service with her or other rheumatic-problem patients, please do not hesitate to contact me.

Alana Wolf, MD

Alana Wolf, M.D.

Find the Word Parts

Give the term that fits the definition given below. Each term must contain at least one of the combining forms given in the previous section. You may refer to the Appendix of combining forms at the back of the book.

30. Joint pain _____ .

31. Removal of a bursa _____ .

32. Inflammation of cartilage _____ .

33. Removal of a vertebra _____ .

34. Bone-forming cell _____ .

35. Abnormal bone hardening _____ .

36. Plastic surgery on the neck _____ .

37. Inflammation of the spinal cord _____ .

38. Foot spasm _____ .

39. Of the ulna and the carpus _____ .

Find the misspelled word part. Write the corrected word part in the space with its definition.

40. sinovotomy _____

41. myellogram _____

42. arthrodunia _____

43. ostiomyelitis _____

44. rakiometer _____

Diagnostic, Procedural, and Laboratory Terms

Specialists in the musculoskeletal system are:

- **orthopedists** or **orthopedic surgeons**, physicians who treat musculoskeletal disorders
- **osteopaths**, physicians who combine manipulative procedures with conventional treatment
- **rheumatologists,** physicians who treat disorders of the joints
- **podiatrists**, medical specialists who treat disorders of the foot
- **chiropractors**, health care professionals who use manipulative techniques

Diagnosing musculoskeletal ailments often involves the use of imaging as well as internal examinations. Table 5-4 lists some common diagnostic techniques.

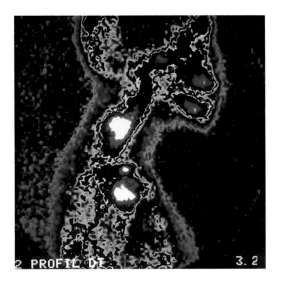

FIGURE 5-11 Bone scan showing malignant tumors in the neck and shoulder.

TABLE 5-4 Musculoskeletal diagnostic techniques.

Dignostic Terms	Description
arthrography	examination of joints
arthroscopy	internal examination of joints
diskography	radiographic examination of disks
myelography	radiographic examination of the spinal cord
electromyogram	imaging of muscle activity
magnetic resonance imaging (MRI)	graphic imaging—used in musculoskeletal examinations as well as other body systems
bone scan (see Figure 5-11)	computerized scan to detect bone tumors
Tinel's sign	a sensation felt when tapping an injured nerve
rheumatoid factor test	laboratory test for rheumatoid arthritis
serum creatine phosphokinase	laboratory test for skeletal injury
serum calcium and serum phosphorus	found in tests for substances in bone
uric acid test	laboratory test for gout
goniometer (see Figure 5-12)	device to measure joint motion
densitometer	imaging device for testing bone density

FIGURE 5-12 A goniometer is used to measure the range of motion of a joint.

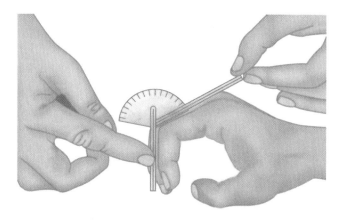

VOCABULARY REVIEW

In the previous section, you learned terms relating to diagnosis, clinical procedures, and laboratory tests. Before going on to the exercises, read the definitions below. Pronunciations are provided for certain terms.

Term	Definition
arthrography [ăr-THRŎG-ră-fē] arthro-, joint + -graphy, process of recording	Radiography of a joint.

Term	Definition
arthroscopy [ăr-THRŎS-kō-pē] arthro- + -scopy	Examination with an instrument that explores the interior of a joint.
bone scan	Radiographic or nuclear medicine image of a bone.
chiropractor [kī-rō-PRĂK-tōr]	Health care professional who works to align the spinal column so as to treat certain ailments.
densitometer [dĕn-sĭ-TŎM-ĕ-tĕr]	Device that measures bone density using light and x-rays.
diskography [dĭs-KŎG-ră-fē]	Radiographic image of an intervertebral disk by injection of a contrast medium into the center of the disk.
electromyogram [ē-lĕk-trō-MĪ-ō-grăm] electro- + myo- + -gram	A graphic image of muscular action using electrical currents.
goniometer [gō-nē-ŎM-ĕ-tĕr]	Instrument that measures angles or range of motion in a joint.
myelography [MĪ-ĕ-LŎG-ră-fĕ] myelo- + -graphy	Radiographic imaging of the spinal cord.
orthopedist [ōr-thō-PĒ-dĭst], **orthopedic** [ōr-thō-PĒD-ĭk] **surgeon**	Physician who examines, diagnoses, and treats disorders of the musculoskeletal system.
osteopath [ŎS-tē-ō-păth] osteo- + -path(y)	Physician who combines manipulative treatment with conventional therapeutic measures.
podiatrist [pō-DĪ-ă-trĭst]	Medical specialist who examines, diagnoses, and treats disorders of the foot.
rheumatoid factor test	Test used to detect rheumatoid arthritis.
rheumatologist [rū-mă-TŎL-ō-jĭst]	Physician who examines, diagnoses, and treats disorders of the joints and musculoskeletal system.
serum calcium [SĒR-ŭm KĂL-sĭ-ŭm]	Test for calcium in the blood.
serum creatine phosphokinase [KRĒ-ă-tēn fŏs-fō-KĪ-nās]	Enzyme active in muscle contraction; usually phosphokinase is elevated after a myocardial infarction and in the presence of other degenerative muscle diseases.
serum phosphorus [FŎS-fōr-ŭs]	Test for phosphorus in the blood.
Tinel's [tĭ-NĔLZ] **sign**	"Pins and needles" sensation felt when an injured nerve site is tapped.
uric [YŪR-ĭk] **acid test**	Test for acid content in urine; elevated levels may indicate gout.

CASE STUDY

Preventing Disease

Louella Jones (age 48) visited her gynecologist, Dr. Phillips, for her annual examination. During the past year, Louella had stopped menstruating. She had some symptoms of menopause, but they did not bother her tremendously. Louella is tall and very thin. Dr. Phillips sent her for a bone density test. The densitometer measured the density of Louella's bones and found that there was a slight increase in her bones' porosity from three years ago. Dr. Phillips suggested hormone replacement therapy and a program of weight-bearing exercises. However, Louella wanted more information about the treatment's potential impact on her body before beginning therapy.

Critical Thinking

45. Why are bone density measurements important in the diagnosis?

46. Louella wanted more information before taking medication and starting an exercise program. What kind of information might she be given?

DIAGNOSTIC, PROCEDURAL, AND LABORATORY TERMS EXERCISES

Test Your Knowledge

Answer the following questions.

47. Tests for calcium and phosphorus are given to determine blood levels of these minerals. What significance do these minerals have for the musculoskeletal system? _____

_____

_____

_____

48. Is it likely that a chiropractor would order a uric acid test? Why or why not?_____

_____

_____

49. Would a bone scan be likely to show bone cancer? _____

50. How is an osteopath like a chiropractor? _____

_____

51. What might a goniometer show about a muscle's action? _____

_____

Pathological Terms

Musculoskeletal disorders arise from congenital conditions, injury, degenerative disease, or other systemic disorders. A common injury, a **fracture,** is a break or crack in bones. There are many different types of fractures:

- A **closed fracture** is a break with no open wound.
- An **open (compound) fracture** is a break with an open wound.
- A **simple (hairline** or **closed) fracture** does not move any part of the bone out of place.

- A **complex fracture** is a separation of part of the bone and usually requires surgery for repair.
- A **greenstick fracture** is an incomplete break of a soft (usually, a child's) bone.
- An **incomplete fracture** is a break that does not go entirely through any type of bone.
- A **comminuted fracture** is a break in which the bone is fragmented or shattered.
- A **Colles' fracture** is a break of the distal part of the radius.
- A **complicated fracture** involves extensive soft tissue injury.
- An **impacted fracture** occurs when a fragment from one part of a fracture is driven into the tissue of another part.
- A **pathological fracture** occurs at the site of bone already damaged by disease.
- A **compression fracture** is a break in one or more vertebrae caused by a compressing or squeezing of the space between the vertebrae.

Figure 5-13 shows various types of fractures.

The National Library of Medicine has an online encyclopedia where you can learn more about almost any medical subject. Go to their Medline encyclopedia (www.nlm.nih.gov/medlineplus) and search for fractures to learn more about types and treatments for fractures.

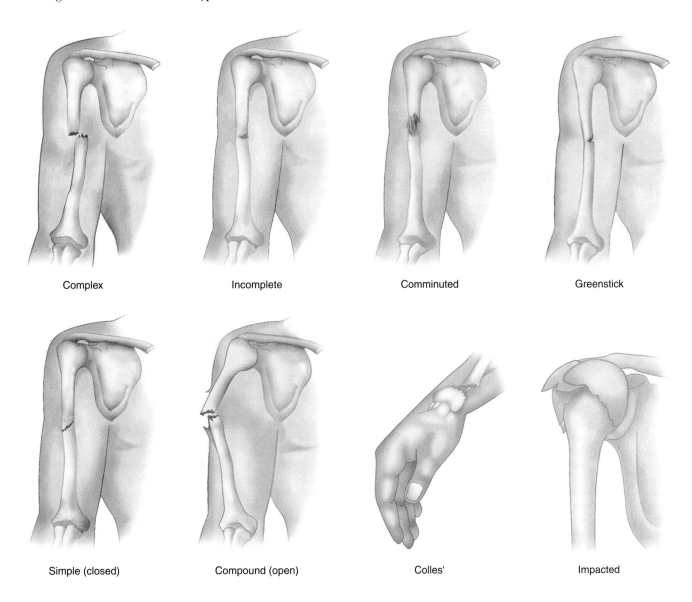

Complex   Incomplete   Comminuted   Greenstick

Simple (closed)   Compound (open)   Colles'   Impacted

FIGURE 5-13   Some different types of fractures.

Musculoskeletal disorders may come from the musculoskeletal system itself or may result from disorders of other body systems. Some conditions such as a **spastic** muscle may occur. Some can be treated by **physical therapy.** Table 5-5 lists various musculoskeletal disorders.

TABLE 5-5 Musculoskeletal disorders.

Condition, Disease, or Disorder	Where Located or Source	Characteristics or Causes
spina bifida	birth defect in the spine	developmental and physical disabilities
rickets	leg deformities	vitamin D deficiency
calcar or **spur**	bony projection	abnormal growth out of bone
sprain	ligament	injury
strain	muscle	overuse or improper use
carpal tunnel syndrome (CTS)	hand	repetitive motion injury
tendonitis, tendonitis	tendon	inflammation
dislocation	point where bones meet	injury or sudden, strenuous movement
subluxation	point where bones meet	partial dislocation
osteoporosis	bones	loss of bone density
herniated disk	vertebrae	injury or disease, may lead to **sciatica**, lower back pain
contracture	muscles	disease or injury to muscle fibers
ostealgia or **osteodynia**	bones	pain
myalgia or **myodynia**	muscles	pain
arthralgia	joints	pain
ankylosis	joints	stiffness
spasm	muscles	disease
hypertrophy	muscle	abnormal increased size
hypotonia	muscle	abnormally reduced muscle tension
dystonia	muscle	abnormally increased muscle tension
rigor or **rigidity**	muscle	abnormal stiffness, usually from a disease
atrophy	muscle	shrinking from disease
muscular dystrophy	muscle	degenerative disease
myositis	muscle	inflammation
bursitis	bursa	inflammation
bunion	bursa of the big toe	inflammation

TABLE 5-5 Musculoskeletal disorders *(cont.).*

Condition, Disease, or Disorder	Where Located or Source	Characteristics or Causes
epiphysitis	epiphysis	inflammation
arthritis	joint	inflammation
rheumatoid arthritis	connective tissue	systemic autoimmune disease
osteoarthritis or degenerative arthritis	joint cartilage	degenerative disease
gout or gouty arthritis	joint pain	disease
podagra	big toe	painful disease
osteomyelitis	bone	infection
chondromalacia	cartilage	softening as from a herniated disk
spinal curvature, kyphosis, lordosis, scoliosis	abnormal posture conditions	pain; may be a result of poor nutrition, disease, or poor posture
phantom pain or phantom limb	at any paralyzed or amputated site	pain felt in missing or paralyzed limbs
myoma, myeloma, leiomyoma, leiomyosarcoma, rhabdomyoma, rhabdomyosarcoma	muscles	tumors
osteoma, osteosarcoma	bones	tumors

MORE ABOUT...

Fractures

Some types of fractures are possible indicators of child abuse. This is particularly true of *spiral fractures,* fractures caused by twisting an extremity until the bone breaks. This type of fracture is usually investigated as to its cause in a child. Also, if a child's x-rays show a number of old fractures, child abuse may be suspected. Unfortunately, there are some diseases that cause continual bone fracturing and, as a result, some people have been falsely accused of child abuse in such cases.

Go to the Arthritis Foundation's Web site (www.arthritis.org) to learn about arthritis research.

Carpal tunnel syndrome usually requires some rest period. For people who work on computers this may be difficult. There are alternative devices, such as the hands-free mouse (it uses head motion) available at www.ctsplace.com.

MORE ABOUT...

Cartilage

The replacement of damaged or lost cartilage is now possible. The procedure is to remove some of a patient's cartilage through a small incision, grow more cartilage in the laboratory using the patient's own cells, and inject them back into the small incision.

MORE ABOUT...

What Fractures Can Tell Us

Fractures can be caused by many types of injuries or diseases. Osteoporosis in older people may result in hip fractures which, in many cases, are thought to precede the actual fall. A twisting fracture may result from a twisting injury in a sports game. A comminuted fracture may result from the impact of a car crash. The type of fracture often gives clues as to how the initial injury occurred.

VOCABULARY REVIEW

In the previous section, you learned terms relating to pathology. Before going on to the exercises, read the definitions below. Pronunciations are provided for certain terms.

Term	Definition
ankylosis [ĂNG-kĭ-LŌ-sĭs]	Stiffening of a joint, especially as a result of disease.
arthralgia [ăr-THĂL-jē-ă]	Severe joint pain.
arthritis [ăr-THRĪ-tĭs]	Any of various conditions involving joint inflammation.
atrophy [ĂT-rō-fē]	Wasting away of tissue, organs, and cells, usually as a result of disease or loss of blood supply.
bunion [BŬN-yŭn]	An inflamed bursa at the foot joint, between the big toe and the first metatarsal bone.
bursitis [bŭr-SĪ-tĭs]	Inflammation of a bursa.
calcar [KĂL-kăr]	Spur.
carpal [KĂR-păl] tunnel syndrome (CTS)	Pain and paresthesia in the hand due to repetitive motion injury of the median nerve.
chondromalacia [KŎN-drō-mă-LĀ-shē-ă]	Softening of cartilage.
closed fracture	Fracture with no open skin wound.
Colles' [kōlz] fracture	Fracture of the lower end of the radius.
comminuted [KŎM-ĭ-nū-tĕd] fracture	Fracture with shattered bones.
complex fracture	Fracture with part of the bone displaced.
complicated fracture	Fracture involving extensive soft tissue injury.
compound fracture	Fracture with an open skin wound; open fracture.
compression fracture	Fracture of one or more vertebrae caused by compressing of the space between the vertebrae.
contracture [kŏn-TRĂK-chūr]	Extreme resistance to the stretching of a muscle.
degenerative arthritis	Arthritis with erosion of the cartilage.
dislocation	Movement of a joint out of its normal position as a result of an injury or sudden, strenuous movement.
dystonia [dĭs-TŌ-nē-ă]	Abnormal tone in tissues.
epiphysitis [ĕ-pĭf-ĭ-SĪ-tĭs]	Inflammation of the epiphysis.
fracture [FRĂK-chŭr]	A break, especially in a bone.
gouty arthritis, gout [GŎWT-ē, gŏwt]	Inflammation of the joints; usually caused by uric acid crystals.
greenstick fracture	Fracture with twisting or bending of the bone but no breaking; usually occurs in children.

Term	Definition
hairline fracture	Fracture with no bone separation or fragmentation.
herniated [HĔR-nē-ā-tĕd] disk	Protrusion of an intervertebral disk into the neural canal.
hypertrophy [hī-PĔR-trō-fē]	Abnormal increase as in muscle size.
hypotonia [HĪ-pō-TŌ-nē-ă]	Abnormally reduced muscle tension.
impacted fracture	Fracture in which a fragment from one part of the fracture is driven into the tissue of another part.
incomplete fracture	Fracture that does not go entirely through a bone.
kyphosis [kī-FŌ-sĭs]	Abnormal posterior spine curvature.
leiomyoma [LĪ-ō-mī-Ō-mă]	Benign tumor of smooth muscle.
leiomyosarcoma [LĪ-ō-MĪ-ō-săr-KŌ-mă]	Malignant tumor of smooth muscle.
lordosis [lōr-DŌ-sĭs]	Abnormal anterior spine curvature resulting in a sway back.
muscular dystrophy [MŬS-kyū-lăr DĬS-trō-fē]	Progressive degenerative disorder affecting the musculoskeletal system and, later, other organs.
myalgia [mī-ĂL-jē-ă]	Muscle pain.
myeloma [mī-ĕ-LŌ-mă]	Bone marrow tumor.
myodynia [MĪ-ō-DĬN-ē-ă]	Muscle pain.
myoma [mī-Ō-mă]	Benign muscle tumor.
myositis [mī-ō-SĪ-tĭs]	Inflammation of a muscle.
open fracture	Fracture with an open skin wound; compound fracture.
ostealgia [ŏs-tē-ĂL-jē-ă]	Bone pain.
osteoarthritis [ŎS-tē-ō-ăr-THRĪ-tĭs]	Arthritis with loss of cartilage.
osteodynia [ŏs-tē-ō-DĬN-ē-ă]	Bone pain.
osteoma [ŏs-tē-Ō-mă]	Benign bone tumor, usually on the skull or mandible.
osteomyelitis [ŎS-tē-ō-mī-ĕ-LĪ-tĭs]	Inflammation of the bone marrow and surrounding bone.
osteoporosis [ŎS-tē-ō-pō-RŌ-sĭs]	Degenerative thinning of bone.
osteosarcoma [ŎS-tē-ō-săr-KŌ-mă]	Malignant tumor of bone.
pathological fracture	Fracture occurring at the site of already damaged bone.
phantom limb; phantom pain	Pain felt in a paralyzed or amputated limb.
physical therapy	Movement therapy to restore use of damaged areas of the body.

Term	Definition
podagra [pō-DĂG-ră]	Pain in the big toe, often associated with gout.
rhabdomyoma [RĂB-dō-mĭ-Ō-mă]	Benign tumor in striated muscle.
rhabdomyosarcoma [RĂB-dō-mĭ-ō-săr-KŌ-mă]	Malignant tumor in striated muscle.
rheumatoid [RŪ-mă-tŏyd] **arthritis**	Autoimmune disorder affecting connective tissue.
rickets [RĬK-ĕts]	Disease of the skeletal system, usually caused by vitamin D deficiency.
rigidity	Stiffness.
rigor [RĬG-ōr]	Stiffening.
sciatica [sī-ĂT-ĭ-kă]	Pain in the lower back, usually radiating down the leg, from a herniated disk or other injury or condition.
scoliosis [skō-lē-Ō-sĭs]	Abnormal lateral curvature of the spinal column.
simple fracture	Fracture with no open skin wound.
spasm [spăzm]	Sudden, involuntary muscle contraction.
spastic [SPĂS-tĭk]	Tending to have spasms.
spina bifida [SPĪ-nă BĬF-ĭ-dă]	Congenital defect with deformity of the spinal column.
spinal curvature	Abnormal curvature of the spine.
sprain [sprān]	Injury to a ligament.
spur [spŭr]	Bony projection growing out of a bone; calcar.
strain [strān]	Injury to a muscle as a result of improper use or overuse.
subluxation [sŭb-lŭk-SĀ-shŭn]	Partial dislocation, as between joint surfaces.
tendinitis, tendonitis [tĕn-dĭn-ĪT-ĭs]	Inflammation of a tendon.

CASE STUDY

Making a Referral

Dr. Millet, a chiropractor, sees many patients for back pain. His treatments consist primarily of spinal manipulation, heat, and nutritional and exercise counseling. He currently sees a group of patients, mainly middle-aged men, who complain of sciatica. He has been able to relieve the pain for about 50 percent of them. The others seem to have more persistent pain. Dr. Millet is not allowed to prescribe medications because he is not a licensed medical doctor. He refers some of his patients to Dr. Wolf, a specialist, who believes that Dr. Millet provides a valuable service.

Critical Thinking

52. Chiropractic is one way for some people to manage pain. Why might spinal manipulation help?
53. If spinal manipulation does not work, why should the patient see a medical specialist?

PATHOLOGICAL TERMS EXERCISES

Build Your Medical Vocabulary

Match the word roots on the left with the proper definition on the right.

54. ____ myo-   **a.** bone
55. ____ myelo-   **b.** hand
56. ____ rhabdo-   **c.** rod-shaped
57. ____ osteo-   **d.** joint
58. ____ arthro-   **e.** bone marrow
59. ____ chiro-   **f.** muscle

Know the Word Parts

Match the following terms with the letter that gives the best definition.

60. ____ myeloma   **a.** malignant tumor of smooth muscle
61. ____ myoma   **b.** benign tumor in striated muscle
62. ____ leiomyoma   **c.** benign tumor of smooth muscle
63. ____ leiomyosarcoma   **d.** benign muscle tumor
64. ____ rhabdomyoma   **e.** malignant bone tumor
65. ____ rhabdomyosarcoma **f.** bone marrow tumor
66. ____ osteoma   **g.** malignant tumor in striated muscle
67. ____ osteosarcoma   **h.** benign tumor, usually on the skull or mandible

Check Your Knowledge

Complete the sentences below by filling in the blanks.

68. A patient with painful joints and bulges around the knuckles probably has _____.

69. Fractures that are most likely to occur in young children are called _____ fractures.

70. Osteoporosis is usually a disease found in _____ women.

71. Playing tennis too vigorously may cause _____ of the elbow.

72. Repetitive motion may cause _____ _____ _____.

73. A muscle tumor is a(n) _____.

74. A slipped disk is called _____.

75. A compound fracture is a break accompanied by a(n) _____ wound.

76. Arthritis is a general term for a number of _____ diseases.

77. Paralysis may be caused by an injury to the _____.

Surgical Terms

Orthopedic surgery may involve repair, grafting, replacement, excision, or reconstruction of parts of the musculoskeletal system. Surgeons also make incisions to take biopsies. Almost any major part of the musculoskeletal system can now be surgically replaced. **Amputation,** removal of a limb, may be necessary. **Prosthetic devices** now routinely replace knees and hips. **Bone grafting** can repair a defect. An **orthosis** or **orthotic** may be used to provide support.

Fractures are treated by **casting, splinting,** surgical manipulation, or placement in **traction. Reduction** is the return of a part to its normal position.

Osteoplasty is repair of a bone. **Osteoclasis** is the breaking of bone for the purpose of repairing it. **Osteotomy** is an incision into a bone. **Tenotomy** is the cutting into a tendon to repair a muscle. **Myoplasty** is muscle repair. **Arthroplasty** is joint repair. **Arthrocentesis** is a puncture into a joint. A **synovectomy** is the removal of part or all of the synovial membrane of a joint. **Arthrodesis** and **spondylosyndesis** are two types of fusion. A **bursectomy** is the removal of a bursa. A **bunionectomy** is the removal of a bunion.

> Historically, before the advent of antibiotics, limb amputations were often necessary due to infections or wounds that would have no way to heal. Now, amputations are much rarer. New techniques of bone repair and infection control make it more likely that they can be avoided.

VOCABULARY REVIEW

In the previous section, you learned terms relating to surgery. Before going on to the exercises, read the definitions below. Pronunciations are provided for certain terms.

Term	Definition
amputation [ĂM-pyū-TĀ-shŭn]	Cutting off of a limb or part of a limb.
arthrocentesis [ĂR-thrō-sĕn-TĒ-sĭs]	Removal of fluid from a joint with use of a puncture needle.
arthrodesis [ăr-thrō-DĒ-sĭs]	Surgical fusion of a joint to stiffen it.
arthroplasty [ĂR-thrō-plăs-tē]	Surgical replacement or repair of a joint.
bone grafting	Transplantation of bone from one site to another.
bunionectomy [bŭn-yŭn-ĔK-tō-mē]	Removal of a bunion.
bursectomy [bŭr-SĔK-tō-mē]	Removal of a bursa.
casting	Forming of a cast in a mold; placing of fiberglass or plaster over a body part to prevent its movement.
myoplasty [MĪ-ō-plăs-tē]	Surgical repair of muscle tissue.
orthosis, orthotic [ōr-THŌ-sĭs, ōr-THŎT-ĭk]	External appliance used to immobilize or assist the movement of the spine or limbs.
osteoclasis [ŎS-tē-ŎK-lā-sĭs]	Breaking of a bone in order to repair or reposition it.
osteoplasty [ŎS-tē-ō-plăs-tē] osteo- + -plasty	Surgical replacement or repair of bone.
osteotomy [ŏs-tē-ŎT-ō-mē] osteo- + -tomy	Cutting of bone.

Term	Definition
prosthetic [prŏs-THĔT-ĭk] **device**	Artificial device used as a substitute for a missing or diseased body part.
reduction	Return of a part to its normal position.
splinting	Applying a splint to immobilize a body part.
spondylosyndesis [SPŎN-dĭ-lō-sĭn-DĒ-sĭs]	Fusion of two or more spinal vertebrae.
synovectomy [sĭn-ō-VĔK-tō-mē] synovi(o)- + -ectomy	Removal of part or all of a joint's synovial membrane.
tenotomy [tĕ-NŎT-ō-mē] teno- + -tomy	Surgical cutting of a tendon.
traction [TRĂK-shŭn]	Dragging or pulling or straightening of something, as a limb, by attachment of elastic or other devices.

CASE STUDY

Musculoskeletal Injury

John Positano, a track star at a large university, suffered a knee injury during a meet. The team physician prescribed rest and medication first, to be followed by a gradual program of physical therapy. John missed about six weeks of meets and seemed fine until the end of the season, when a particularly strenuous run in which he twisted his knee left him writhing in pain. It was the same knee on which fluid had accumulated during the previous week. X-rays showed no fractures. Later, after examination by a specialist, arthroscopic surgery was recommended. John had to go through another rehabilitative program (rest, medication, and physical therapy) after the surgery.

Critical Thinking

78. A program of physical therapy was prescribed for John. Which one of his tests was most important in determining whether or not he could exercise?
79. Is physical therapy always appropriate for a musculoskeletal injury?

SURGICAL TERMS EXERCISES

Build Your Medical Vocabulary

Form two surgical words for each of the following word roots by adding suffixes learned in Chapter 2.

80. osteo- _____

81. arthro- _____

82. myo- _____

Find a Match

Match the terms in the second column to the terms in the first.

83. _____ amputation
84. _____ prosthesis
85. _____ orthosis, orthotic
86. _____ traction
87. _____ casting
88. _____ splinting
89. _____ myoplasty
90. _____ osteoplasty
91. _____ osteotomy
92. _____ arthroplasty

a. replacement device
b. molding
c. muscle repair
d. bone cutting
e. limb removal
f. bone repair
g. external supporting or immobilizing device
h. wrapping to immobilize
i. pulling to straighten
j. joint repair

TERMINOLOGY IN ACTION

After an x-ray given in the emergency room, Ellen was told that she would need to be seen by the orthopedist on call. The notes in her chart are as follows:

X-RAY: X-ray of the right wrist reveals distal radial fracture with about 20 degrees dorsal angulation and displaced about 30% from normal position. There is no ulnar fracture. Right knee x-ray shows a fracture of the patella with no displacement of the fragments.

From the notes, describe what she has fractured and what you think the treatment will be.

USING THE INTERNET

Osteoporosis can be a serious affliction of late adulthood. Visit the National Osteoporosis Foundation's Web site (http://www.nof.org). From what you read at the site, what can you do to prevent osteoporosis as you age?

CHAPTER REVIEW

The material that follows is to help you review all the material in this chapter.

DEFINITIONS

Define the following terms and combining forms. Review the chapter before starting. Make sure you know how to pronounce each term as you define it. The blue words in curly brackets are references to the Spanish glossary on the Web site.

WORD	DEFINITION
acetabul(o)	
acetabulum [ăs-ĕ-TĂB-yū-lŭm] {acetábulo}	
acromi(o)	
acromion [ă-KRŌ-mē-ōn] {acromion}	
amphiarthrosis [ĂM-fī-ăr-THRŌ-sĭs] {anfiartrosis}	
amputation [ĂM-pyū-TĀ-shŭn] {amputación}	
ankle [ĂNG-kl] {tobillo}	
ankyl(o)	
ankylosis [ĂNG-kĭ-LŌ-sĭs] {anquilosis}	
arthr(o)	
arthralgia [ăr-THRĂL-jē-ă] {artralgia}	
arthritis [ăr-THRĬ-tĭs] {artritis}	
arthrocentesis [ĂR-thrō-sĕn-TĒ-sĭs] {artrocentesis}	
arthrodesis [ăr-thrō-DĒ-sĭs]	
arthrography [ăr-THRŎG-ră-fē]	
arthroplasty [ĂR-thrō-plăs-tē]	
arthroscopy [ăr-THRŌS-kŏ-pē]	
articular [ăr-TĬK-yū-lăr] cartilage	
articulation [ăr-tĭk-yū-LĀ-shŭn] {articulación}	
atlas [ĂT-lăs] {atlas}	
atrophy [ĂT-rō-fē] {atrofia}	
axis [ĂK-sĭs] {axis}	
bone {hueso}	

WORD	DEFINITION
bone grafting	
bone head	
bone phagocyte [FĂG-ō-sīt]	
bone scan	
brachi(o)	
bunion [BŬN-yŭn] {bunio}	
bunionectomy [bŭn-yŭn-ĔK-tō-mē] {bunionectomía}	
burs(o)	
bursa (pl., bursae) [BŬR-să (BŬR-sē)] {bursa}	
bursectomy [bŭr-SĔK-tō-mē] {bursectomía}	
bursitis [bŭr-SĪ-tĭs] {bursitis}	
calcane(o)	
calcaneus [kăl-KĀ-nē-ŭs] {calcáneo}	
calcar [KĂL-kăr] {calcar}	
calci(o)	
cancellous [KĂN-sĕ-lŭs] {canceloso} bone	
cardiac [KĂR-dē-ăk] muscle	
carp(o)	
carpal [KĂR-păl] tunnel syndrome (CTS)	
carpus [KĂR-pŭs], carpal bone	
cartilage [KĂR-tĭ-lăj] {cartílago}	
cartilaginous [kăr-tĭ-LĂJ-ĭ-nŭs] disk	
casting {colado}	
cephal(o)	
cervic(o)	
cervical [SĔR-vĭ-kăl] vertebrae	
chiropractor [kī-rō-PRĂK-tĕr] {quiropráctico}	
chondr(o)	
chondromalacia [KŎN-drō-mă-LĀ-shē-ă] {condromalacia}	
clavicle [KLĂV-ĭ-kl] {clavicula}	
closed fracture	

WORD	DEFINITION
coccyx [KŎK-sĭks] {cóccix}	
Colles' [kōlz] fracture	
comminuted [KŎM-ĭ-nū-těd] fracture	
compact bone	
complex fracture	
complicated fracture	
compound fracture	
compression fracture	
condyl(o)	
condyle [KŎN-dīl]	
contracture [kŏn-TRĂK-chŭr]	
corticosteroid	
cost(o)	
crani(o)	
crest {cresta}	
dactyl(o)	
degenerative arthritis	
densitometer [děn-sĭ-TŎM-ě-těr]	
diaphysis [dī-ĂF-ĭ-sĭs] {diáfisis}	
diarthroses [dī-ăr-THRŌ-sēz]	
disk [dĭsk] {disco}	
diskography [dĭs-KŎG-ră-fē] {discografía}	
dislocation {dislocación}	
dorsal vertebrae	
dystonia [dĭs-TŌ-nē-ă] {distonia}	
elbow [ĔL-bō] {codo}	
electromyogram [ē-lěk-trō-MĪ-ō-grăm] {electromiógrafo}	
endosteum [ěn-DŎS-tē-ŭm] {endostio}	
epiphyseal [ěp-ĭ-FĬZ-ē-ăl] plate	
epiphysitis [ě-pĭf-ĭ-SĪ-tĭs] {epifisitis}	
ethmoid [ĔTH-mŏyd] bone	
ethmoid sinuses	
fasci(o)	

WORD	DEFINITION
fascia (*pl.*, fasciae [FĂSH-ē-ă (FĂSH-ē-ē)] {fascia}	_____
femor(o)	_____
femur [FĒ-mūr] {fémur}	_____
fibr(o)	_____
fibula [FĬB-yū-lă] {peroné}	_____
fissure [FĬSH-ŭr] {fisura}	_____
flat bones	_____
fontanelle [FŎN-tă-něl] {fontanela}	_____
foramen [fō-RĀ-měn] {agujero}	_____
fossa (*pl.*, fossae) [FŎS-ă (FŎS-ē)] {fosa}	_____
fracture [FRĂK-chŭr] {fractura}	_____
frontal [FRŬN-tăl] bone	_____
frontal sinuses	_____
goniometer [gō-nē-ŎM-ě-těr] {goniómetro}	_____
gouty arthritis, gout [GŎWT-ē, gŏwt]	_____
greenstick fracture	_____
hairline fracture	_____
herniated [HĔR-nē-ā-těd] disk	_____
humer(o)	_____
humerus [HYŪ-měr-ŭs] {húmero}	_____
hypertrophy [hī-PĔR-trō-fē]	_____
hypotonia [HĪ-pō-TŌ-nē-ă]	_____
ili(o)	_____
ilium [ĬL-ē-ŭm] {ilium}	_____
impacted fracture	_____
incomplete fracture	_____
insertion {inserción}	_____
intervertebral [ĭn-těr-VĔR-tě-brăl] disk	_____
involuntary muscle	_____
irregular bones	_____
ischi(o)	_____
ischium [ĬS-kē-ŭm] {isquión}	_____

WORD	DEFINITION
joint [jŏynt] {empalme}	
kyph(o)	
kyphosis [kī-FŌ-sĭs] {cifosis}	
lacrimal [LĂK-rĭ-măl] bone	
lamin(o)	
lamina (pl., laminae) [LĂM-ĭ-nă (LĂM-ĭ-nē)] {lamina}	
leiomy(o)	
leiomyoma [LĪ-ō-mī-Ō-mă]	
leiomyosarcoma [LĪ-ō-MĪ-ō-săr-KŌmă]	
ligament [LĬG-ă-mĕnt] {ligamento}	
long bone	
lordosis [lōr-DŌ-sĭs] {lordosis}	
lumb(o)	
lumbar [LŬM-băr] vertebrae	
malleolus (pl., malleoli) [mă-LĒ-ō-lŭs (mă-LĒ-ō-lī)]	
mandible [MĂN-dĭ-bl] {mandíbula}	
mandibular [măn-DĬB-yū-lăr] bone	
marrow [MĂR-ō] {médula}	
mastoid [MĂS-tŏyd] process	
maxill(o)	
maxillary [MĂK-sĭ-lār-ē] bone	
maxillary sinus	
medullary [MĔD-ū-lār-ē] cavity	
metacarp(o)	
metacarpal [MĔT-ă-KĂR-păl] {metacarpiano}	
metaphysis [mĕ-TĂF-ĭ-sĭs] {metáfisis}	
metatarsal [MĔT-ă-tăr-săl] bones	
muscle [MŬS-ĕl] {músculo}	
muscular dystrophy [MŬS-kyū-lăr DĬS-trō-fē] {distrofia muscular}	
musculoskeletal [MŬS-kyū-lō-SKĔL-ĕ-tăl] {musculoesquelético} system	
my(o)	

Word	Definition
myalgia [mī-ĂL-jē-ă] {mialgia}	
myel(o)	
myelography [MĪ-ĕ-LŎG-ră-fē] {mielografia}	
myeloma [mī-ĕ-LŌ-mă] {mieloma}	
myodynia [MĪ-ō-DĬN-ē-ă] {miodinia}	
myoma [mī-Ō-mă] {mioma}	
myoplasty [MĪ-ō-plăs-tē]	
myositis [mī-ō-SĪ-tĭs] {miositis}	
nasal bones	
neural [NŪR-ăl] canal	
nucleus pulposus [NŪ-klē-ŭs pŭl-PŌ-sŭs]	
occipital [ŏk-SĬP-ĭ-tăl] bone	
olecranon [ō-LĔK-ră-nŏn] {olecranon}	
open fracture	
origin {origen}	
orthopedist [ōr-thō-PĒ-dĭst], orthopedic [ōr-thō-PĒ-dĭk] {ortopedista} surgeon	
orthosis [ōr-THŌ-sĭs], orthotic [ōr-THŎT-ĭk] {ortosis, ortótica}	
osseus [ŎS-ē-ŭs] tissue	
ossification [ŎS-ĭ-fĭ-KĀ-shŭn] {ossificación}	
oste(o)	
ostealgia [ŏs-tĕ-ĂL-jē-ă] {ostealgia}	
osteoarthritis [ŎS-tē-ō-ăr-THRĪ-tĭs] {osteoartritis}	
osteoblast [ŎS-tē-ō-blăst] {osteoblasto}	
osteoclasis [ŎS-tē-ŎK-lā-sĭs] {osteoclasia}	
osteoclast [ŎS-tē-ō-klăst] {osteoclasto}	
osteocyte [ŎS-tē-ō-sīt] {osteocito}	
osteodynia [ŏs-tē-ō-DĬN-ē-ă] {osteodinia}	
osteoma [ŏs-tē-Ō-mă] {osteoma}	

WORD	DEFINITION

osteomyelitis [ŎS-tē-ō-mī-ĕ-LĪ-tĭs]
{osteomielitis}

osteopath [ŎS-tē-ō-păth] {osteópata}

osteoplasty [ŎS-tē-ō-plăs-tē]
{osteoplastia}

osteoporosis [ŎS-tē-ō-pō-RŌ-sĭs]
{osteoporosis}

osteosarcoma [ŎS-tē-ō-săr-KŌ-mă]
{osteosarcoma}

osteotomy [ŏs-tē-ŎT-ō-mē] {osteotomía}

palatine [PĂL-ă-tīn] bone

parietal [pă-RĪ-ĕ-tăl] bone

patell(o)

patella [pă-TĔL-ă] {rótula}

pathological fracture

ped(i), ped(o)

pelv(i)

pelvic [PĔL-vĭk] cavity

pelvic girdle

pelvis [PĔL-vĭs] {pelvis}

periosteum [pĕr-ē-ŎS-tē-ŭm] {periostio}

phalang(o)

phalanges (sing., phalanx) [fă-LĂN-jēz
(FĂ-lăngks)] {falangeo}

phantom limb; phantom pain

physical therapy

pod(o)

podagra [pō-DĂG-ră] {podagra}

podiatrist [pō-DĪ-ă-trĭst] {podiatra}

process [PRŌS-sĕs, PRŎS-ĕs]

prosthetic [prŏs-THĔT-ĭk] device

pub(o)

pubes [PYŪ-bĭs] {pubis}

pubic symphysis [PYŪ-bĭk SĬM-fĭ-sĭs]

rachi(o)

radi(o)

radius [RĀ-dē-ŭs] {radio}

WORD	DEFINITION

reduction {reducción} _____

rhabd(o) _____

rhabdomy(o) _____

rhabdomyoma [RĂB-dō-mī-Ō-mă]
  {rabdomioma} _____

rhabdomyosarcoma [RĂB-dō-mī-ō-
  săr-KŌ-mă] {rabdomiosarcoma} _____

rheumatoid arthritis _____

rheumatoid factor test _____

rheumatologist [rū-mă-TŎL-ō-jĭst]
  {reumatólogo} _____

rib {costilla} _____

rickets [RĬK-ĕts] {raquitismo} _____

rigidity {rigidez} _____

rigor [RĬG-ōr] {rigor} _____

sacrum [SĀ-krŭm] {sacro} _____

scapul(o) _____

scapula [SKĂP-yū-lă] {escápula} _____

sciatica [sī-ĂT-ĭ-kă] {ciática} _____

scoli(o) _____

scoliosis [skō-lē-Ō-sĭs] {escolisis} _____

sella turcica [SĔL-ă-TŬR-sĭ-kă]
  {silla turcica} _____

serum calcium _____

serum creatine phosphokinase [SĒR-ŭm
  KRĒ-ă-tēn fŏs-fō-KĪ-nās] _____

serum phosphorus _____

sesamoid [SĔS-ă-mŏyd] bone _____

shin [shĭn] {espinilla} _____

short bones _____

simple fracture _____

sinus [SĪ-nŭs] {seno} _____

skeleton [SKĔL-ĕ-tŏn] {esqueleto} _____

smooth muscle _____

spasm [spăzm] {espasmo} _____

spastic [SPĂS-tĭk] {espástico} _____

sphenoid [SFĒ-nŏyd] bone _____

WORD	DEFINITION
sphenoid sinus	
spina bifida [SPĪ-nă BĬF-ĭ-dă] {espina bífido}	
spinal column	
spinal curvature	
spinous [SPĪ-nŭs] process	
splinting {ferulización}	
spondyl(o)	
spondylosyndesis [SPŎN-dĭl-lō-sĭn-DĒ-sĭs]	
spongy bone	
sprain [sprān]	
spur [spŭr]	
stern(o)	
sternum [STĔR-nŭm] {esternón}	
strain [strān] {distender}	
striated [strī-ĀT-ĕd] muscle	
styloid [STĪ-lŏyd] process	
subluxation [sŭb-lŭk-SĀ-shŭn] {subluxación}	
sulcus (pl., sulci) [SŬL-kŭs, [SŬL-sī] {surco}	
suture [SŪ-chūr] {sutura}	
symphysis [SĬM-fĭ-sĭs] {sinfisis}	
synarthrosis [SĬN-ăr-THRŌ-sĭs] {sinartrosis}	
synov(o)	
synovectomy [sĭn-ō-VĔK-tō-mē] {sinovectomi}	
synovial [sĭ-NŌ-vē-ăl] fluid	
synovial joint	
synovial membrane	
tars(o)	
tarsus, tarsal [TĂR-sŭs, TĂR-săl] bones	
temporal [TĔM-pō-RĂL] bone	
temporomandibular [TĔM-pō-rō-măn-DĬB-yū-lăr] joint	

WORD	DEFINITION
ten(o), tend(o), tendin(o)	_____
tendinitis, tendonitis {tendonitis}	_____
tendon [TĔN-dŏn] {tendon}	_____
tenotomy [tĕ-NŎT-ō-mē] {tenotomía}	_____
thorac(o)	_____
thoracic [thō-RĂS-ĭk] vertebrae	_____
thorax [THŌ-răks] {tórax}	_____
tibi(o)	_____
tibia [TĬB-ē-ă] {tibia}	_____
Tinel's [tĭ-NĔLZ] sign	_____
traction [TRĂK-shŭn] {tracción}	_____
transverse process	_____
trochanter [trō-KĂN-tĕr] {trocánter}	_____
true ribs	_____
tubercle [TŪ-bĕr-kl] {tubérculo}	_____
tuberosity [TŪ-bĕr-ŏs-ĭ-tē] {tuberosidad}	_____
uln(o)	_____
ulna [ŬL-nă] {ulna}	_____
uric [YŪR-ĭk] acid test	_____
vertebr(o)	_____
vertebra (_pl._, vertebrae) [VĔR-tĕ-bră (VĔR-tĕ-brē)] {vertebra}	_____
vertebral [vĕr-TĔ-brăl, VĔR-tĕ-brăl] body	_____
vertebral column	_____
visceral [VĬS-ĕr-ăl] muscle	_____
voluntary muscle	_____
vomer [VŌ-mĕr] {vómer}	_____
zygomatic [ZĪ-gō-MĂT-ĭk] bone	_____

Answers to Chapter Exercises

1. Synovial fluid lubricates joints.
2. Yes, exercise can increase breathing and heart rate which can exercise certain involuntary muscles. Voluntary muscles may be exercised at will.
3. long
4. compact bone
5. marrow
6. fontanelles
7. nucleus pulposus
8. acromion
9. true ribs
10. patella
11. calcaneus
12. cardiac
13. F
14. F
15. F
16. T
17. T
18. arthro
19. cranio
20. maxillo
21. ilio
22. tarso
23. thoracic
24. fibro
25. pod
26. rachio
27. sterno
28. fibromyalgia, pain in the fibrous tissue of muscles; osteoarthritis, arthritis of the bone
29. carpel tunnel syndrome
30. arthralgia, arthrodynia
31. bursectomy
32. chondritis
33. spondylectomy or vertebrectory
34. osteoblast
35. osteosclerosis

36. cervicoplasty
37. myelitis
38. podospasm
39. ulnocarpal
40. synovo-, synovial fluid; synovial membrane
41. myelo-, spinal cord; bone marrow
42. -dynia, pain
43. osteo-, bone
44. rachio-, spine
45. Porous bone can result in breakage.
46. alternative treatment plans, side effects, potential benefits, potential risks, and the negative effect of not taking the medicine
47. These elements are crucial to bone formation.
48. No. Chiropractors are concerned with spinal manipulation.
49. Yes, the picture of the bone should show abnormalities.
50. Both believe in spinal manipulation.
51. A goniometer can measure range of motion of a joint.
52. It may help ease pain by loosening and realigning.
53. Because the pain may be due to a condition other than back misalignment.
54. f.
55. e.
56. c.
57. a.
58. d.
59. b.
60. f

61. d
62. c
63. a
64. b
65. g
66. h
67. e
68. arthritis
69. greenstick
70. older
71. tendinitis (tendonitis)
72. carpal tunnel syndrome
73. myoma
74. spondylolisthesis
75. open
76. joint
77. spinal cord
78. The x-rays showed no fractures; therefore, no area needed to be held in place for a long period of time to allow the bone to heal.
79. No, not if there are certain kinds of fractures that must heal before movement is attempted.

Answers to 80–83 may vary. Sample answers are shown below.

80. osteotomy, osteoplasty, osteoclasis
81. arthroplasty, arthrotomy
82. myotomy, myoplasty
83. e
84. a
85. g
86. i
87. b
88. h
89. c
90. f
91. d
92. j

6 The Cardiovascular System

After studying this chapter, you will be able to:

▶ Name the parts of the cardiovascular system and discuss the function of each part

▶ Define combining forms used in building words that relate to the cardiovascular system

▶ Name the common diagnoses, clinical procedures, and laboratory tests used in treating disorders of the cardiovascular system

▶ List and define the major pathological conditions of the cardiovascular system

▶ Explain the meaning of surgical terms related to the cardiovascular system

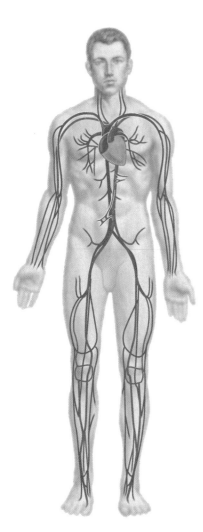

Structure and Function

The **cardiovascular** system is the body's delivery service. Figure 6-1 shows the routes of blood circulation throughout the cardiovascular system. The two major parts of the cardiovascular system are the **heart** and the **blood vessels.** They are essential to circulation of **blood,** life-sustaining material, throughout the body. Table 6-1 shows the major parts of the heart and describes their function.

The Vessels of the Cardiovascular System

Arteries and **veins** are the vessels that carry blood to and from the heart and lungs and to and from the heart and the rest of the body. The circulation of blood takes place in three systems: *coronary circulation*, circulation of blood within the heart; *pulmonary circulation*, flow of blood between the heart and lungs; and *systemic circulation*, flow of blood between the heart and the cells of the body.

Coronary Circulation

The **coronary arteries,** which branch off the **aorta** (the body's largest artery and the artery through which blood exits the heart), supply blood to the heart muscle. The amount of blood pumped to the heart through the coronary arteries is about 100 gallons per day. Figure 6-2 diagrams coronary circulation.

Pulmonary Circulation

The **pulmonary arteries** carry blood that is low in oxygen (*deoxygenated blood*) from the right **ventricle** of the heart to the lungs to get oxygen. Blood that is rich in oxygen (*oxygenated blood*) flows from the lungs to the left **atrium** of the heart through the **pulmonary veins.**

TABLE 6-1 Major parts of the heart.

Part of the Heart	Where Located	Function
pericardium	sac surrounding the heart, part of the heart wall	protection
epicardium	outermost layer of heart tissue	holds in *pericardial fluid*
myocardium	second layer of the heart wall	muscular tissue
endocardium	inner layer of the heart wall	holds the chambers and valves of the heart
right atrium	upper part of the right chamber of the heart	
right ventricle	lower part of the right chamber of the heart	
left atrium	upper part of the left chamber of the heart	
left ventricle	lower part of the left chamber of the heart	
septum	partition between the two chambers of the heart	
valves	within and at the edge of the heart	control the blood flow within and to and from the heart
arteries	vessels that carry blood away from the heart	transport oxygenated blood
veins	vessels that carry blood toward the heart	transport deoxygenated blood except in pulmonary circulation (see Figure 6-2)
endothelium	lining of arteries	secrete substances into the blood
lumen	space within arteries through which blood flows	
atrioventricular valves	two valves between the atria and ventricles	control blood flow through the heart
tricuspid valve	atrioventricular valve on the right side of the heart	
bicuspid or mitral valve	atrioventricular valve on the left side of the heart	
seminlunar valves	at the edge of the heart	prevent backflow of blood into the heart
pulmonary valve	one of the two semilunar valves	
aortic valve	one of the two semilunar valves	

Systemic Circulation

The heart pumps blood through the arteries to the cells of the body. The blood moves in a surge caused by the muscular contraction of the heart. This surge is called the **pulse.**

Specialized arteries carry the oxygen-rich blood to different areas of the body.

The Web site www.heartinfo.org has heart animations that illustrate different parts of the heart and how they are affected by disease and surgery.

- The **carotid artery** supplies the head and neck.
- The **femoral artery** supplies the thigh.
- The **popliteal artery** supplies the back of the knee.

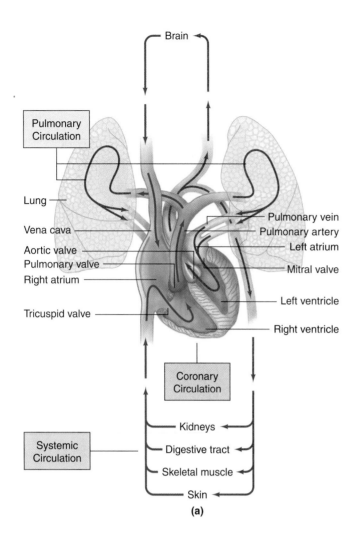

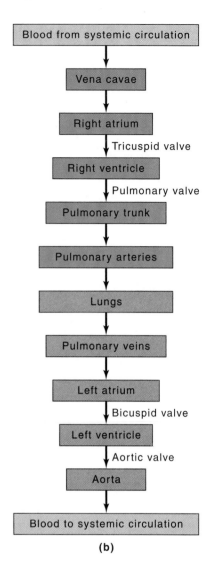

FIGURE 6-1 The heart pumps blood throughout the cardiovascular system via the blood vessels, arteries, and veins.

- The **arterioles** are smaller vessels that branch off the arteries.
- The **capillaries** are supplied by the arterioles and, in turn, send waste products, such as **carbon dioxide (CO_2),** from the cells.

The veins take the deoxygenated blood back to the heart. Important veins are:

- The **venules** are smaller branches of veins leading from the capillaries to the veins.
- The **saphenous veins** transport deoxygenated blood from the legs.
- The **superior vena cava** collects blood from the upper part of the body.
- The **inferior vena cava** collects blood from the lower part of the body.

Blood pressure **Blood pressure** measures the force of the blood surging against the walls of the arteries. Each heartbeat consists of two parts. The first is the contraction, called **systole,** and the second is the relaxation, the **diastole.**

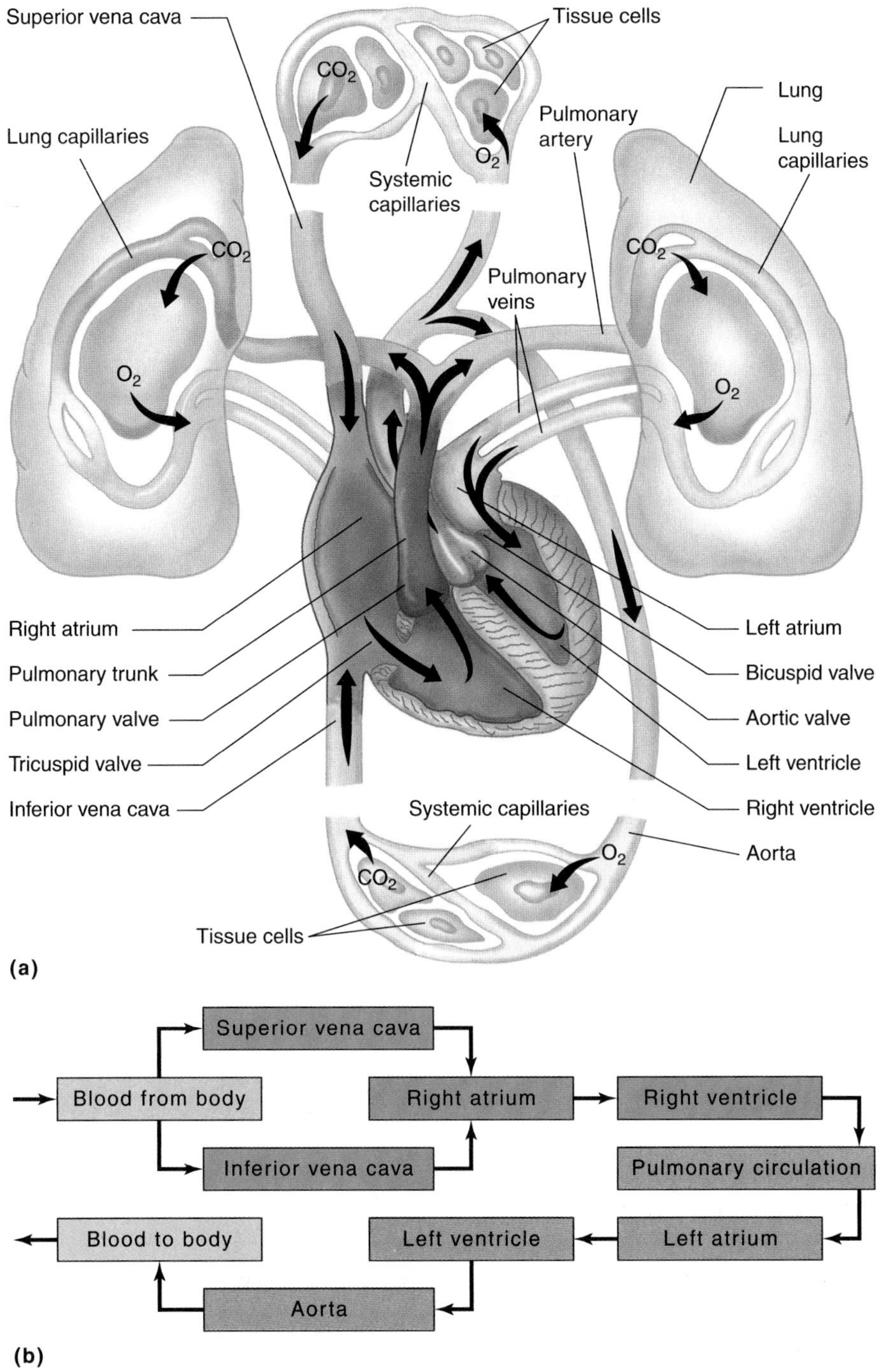

FIGURE 6-2 Coronary circulation is the circulation of blood within the heart (a). The flowchart (b) gives an overview of this type of circulation.

(a)

(b)

Conduction System   The **conduction system** controls the electrical impulses that cause the heart to contract. The region of the conduction system is called the **sinoatrial (SA) node** and is known as the heart's **pacemaker**. The contractions take place in the myocardium, which cycles through **polarization** (resting state) to **depolarization** (contracting state) to **repolarization** (recharging from contracting to resting) in the heartbeat. The electrical current from the SA node passes to a portion of the interatrial septum called the **atrioventricular (AV) node,** which sends the charge to a group of specialized muscle fibers called the **atrioventricular bundle,** also called the **bundle of His.**

Heart rate can vary depending on a person's health, physical activity, or emotions at any one time. The repeated beating of the heart takes place

The National Heart, Lung, and Blood Institute's Web site (www.nhlbi.nih.gov) can be searched for good information about blood pressure.

MORE ABOUT...

Controlling High Blood Pressure

High blood pressure is a dangerous condition with virtually no symptoms felt by the patient. At almost every doctor visit, blood pressure is measured, usually with a sphygmomanometer. Blood pressure measurements are characterized as normal, low, or high, but there is disagreement as to the ranges of normal. The generally regarded normal blood pressure for an adult is 120/80. High blood pressure is sometimes the result of lifestyle factors. Overeating leading to overweight, smoking, lack of exercise, and stress are lifestyle factors that affect blood pressure. For high systolic pressures, most doctors recommend lifestyle changes along with medication.

The American Heart Association (www.amheart.org) categorizes blood pressure as follows:

Blood Pressure Category	Systolic (mm Hg)		Diastolic (mm Hg)
Normal	less than 120	and	less than 80
Prehypertension (considered hypertension in some high-risk cases)	120–139	or	80–89
High			
Stage 1	140–159	or	90–99
Stage 2	160 or higher	or	100 or higher

*Your doctor should evaluate unusually low readings.

in the **cardiac cycle,** during which the heart contracts and relaxes as it circulates blood. Normal heart rhythm is called **sinus rhythm.**

Fetal Circulation

The circulatory system of the fetus bypasses pulmonary circulation, because fetal lungs do not function until after birth. Three structures are important to fetal circulation.

1. The **ductus venosus** is the connection from the umbilical vein to the fetus's inferior vena cava.
2. Deoxygenated blood flows from the fetal heart through the **ductus arteriosus**.
3. The septum between the atria of the fetal heart has a small opening called the **foramen ovale,** which allows blood to flow from the right atrium into the left atrium. After birth, this opening closes.

VOCABULARY REVIEW

In the previous section, you learned terms relating to the cardiovascular system. Before going on to the exercises, read the definitions below. Pronunciations are provided for certain terms.

Term	Definition
aorta [ā-OR-tă]	Largest artery of the body; artery through which blood exits the heart.

Term	Definition
aortic [ā-ŌR-tĭk] **valve**	Valve between the aorta and the left ventricle.
arteriole [ăr-TĒ-rē-ōl]	A tiny artery connecting to a capillary.
artery [ĂR-tĕr-ē]	A thick-walled blood vessel that, in systemic circulation, carries oxygenated blood away from the heart.
atrioventricular [Ā-trē-ō-vĕn-TRĬK-yū-lăr] **bundle**	Bundle of fibers in the interventricular septum that transfers charges in the heart's conduction system; also called bundle of His.
atrioventricular (AV) node	Specialized part of the interatrial septum that sends a charge to the bundle of His.
atrioventricular valve	One of two valves that control blood flow between the atria and ventricles.
atrium (*pl.*, **atria**) [Ā-trē-ŭm (Ā-trē-ă)]	Either of the two upper chambers of the heart.
bicuspid [bī-KŬS-pĭd] **valve**	Atrioventricular valve on the left side of the heart.
blood [blŭd]	Essential fluid made up of plasma and other elements that circulates throughout the body; delivers nutrients to and removes waste from the body's cells.
blood pressure	Measure of the force of blood surging against the walls of the arteries.
blood vessel	Any of the tubular passageways in the cardiovascular system through which blood travels.
bundle of His [hĭz, hĭs]	*See* atrioventricular bundle.
capillary [KĂP-ĭ-lār-ē]	A tiny blood vessel that forms the exchange point between the arterial and venous vessels.
carbon dioxide (CO$_2$)	Waste material transported in the venous blood.
cardiac cycle	Repeated contraction and relaxation of the heart as it circulates blood within itself and pumps it out to the rest of the body or the lungs.
cardiovascular [KĂR-dē-ō-VĂS-kyū-lĕr]	Relating to or affecting the heart and blood vessels.
carotid [kă-RŎT-ĭd] **artery**	Artery that transports oxygenated blood to the head and neck.
conduction system	Part of the heart containing specialized tissue that sends charges through heart fibers, causing the heart to contract and relax at regular intervals.
coronary [KŌR-ō-nār-ē] **artery**	Blood vessel that supplies oxygen-rich blood to the heart.
depolarization [dē-pō-lă-rĭ-ZĀ-shŭn]	Contracting state of the myocardial tissue in the heart's conduction system.
diastole [dī-ĂS-tō-lē]	Relaxation phase of a heartbeat.

Term	Definition
ductus arteriosus [DŬK-tŭs ăr-tēr-ē-Ō-sŭs]	Structure in the fetal circulatory system through which blood flows to bypass the fetus's nonfunctioning lungs.
ductus venosus [vĕn-Ō-sŭs]	Structure in the fetal circulatory system through which blood flows to bypass the fetal liver.
endocardium [ĕn-dō-KĂR-dē-ŭm]	Membranous lining of the chambers and valves of the heart; the innermost layer of heart tissue.
endothelium [ĕn-dō-THĒ-lē-ŭm]	Lining of the arteries that secretes substances into the blood.
epicardium [ĕp-ĭ-KĂR-dē-ŭm]	Outermost layer of heart tissue.
femoral [FĔM-ŏ-răl, FĒ-mŏ-răl] **artery**	An artery that supplies blood to the thigh.
foramen ovale [fō-RĀ-mĕn ō-VĂ-lē]	Opening in the septum of the fetal heart that closes at birth.
heart [hărt]	Muscular organ that receives blood from the veins and sends it into the arteries.
inferior vena cava [VĒ-nă KĂ-vă, KĀ-vă]	Large vein that draws blood from the lower part of the body to the right atrium.
left atrium	Upper left heart chamber.
left ventricle	Lower left heart chamber.
lumen [LŪ-mĕn]	Channel inside an artery through which blood flows.
mitral [MĪ-trăl] **valve**	*See* bicuspid valve.
myocardium [mī-ō-KĂR-dē-ŭm]	Muscular layer of heart tissue between the epicardium and the endocardium.
pacemaker	Term for the sinoatrial (SA) node; also, an artificial device that regulates heart rhythm.
pericardium [pĕr-ĭ-KĂR-dē-ŭm]	Protective covering of the heart.
polarization [pō-lăr-ĭ-ZĀ-shŭn]	Resting state of the myocardial tissue in the conduction system of the heart.
popliteal [pŏp-LĬT-ē-ăl] **artery**	An artery that supplies blood to the cells of the area behind the knee.
pulmonary [PŬL-mō-năr-ē] **artery**	One of two arteries that carry blood that is low in oxygen from the heart to the lungs.
pulmonary valve	Valve that controls the blood flow between the right ventricle and the pulmonary arteries.
pulmonary vein	One of four veins that bring oxygenated blood from the lungs to the left atrium.
pulse [pŭls]	Rhythmic expansion and contraction of a blood vessel, usually an artery.

Term	Definition
repolarization [rē-pō-lăr-ĭ-ZĀ-shŭn]	Recharging state; transition from contraction to resting that occurs in the conduction system of the heart.
right atrium	Upper right chamber of the heart.
right ventricle	Lower right chamber of the heart.
saphenous [să-FĒ-nŭs] **vein**	Any of a group of veins that transport deoxygenated blood from the legs.
semilunar [sĕm-ē-LŪ-năr] **valve**	One of the two valves that prevent the backflow of blood flowing out of the heart into the aorta and the pulmonary artery.
septum (*pl.*, **septa**) [SĔP-tŭm (SĔP-tă)]	Partition between the left and right chambers of the heart.
sinoatrial [sĭ-nō-Ā-trē-ăl] **(SA) node**	Region of the right atrium containing specialized tissue that sends electrical impulses to the heart muscle, causing it to contract.
sinus rhythm	Normal heart rhythm.
superior vena cava	Large vein that transports blood collected from the upper part of the body to the heart.
systole [SĬS-tō-lē]	Contraction phase of the heartbeat.
tricuspid [trī-KŬS-pĭd] **valve**	Atrioventricular valve on the right side of the heart.
valve [vălv]	Any of various structures that slow or prevent fluid from flowing backward or forward.
vein [vān]	Any of various blood vessels carrying deoxygenated blood toward the heart, except the pulmonary vein.
ventricle [VĚN-trĭ-kl]	Either of the two lower chambers of the heart.
venule [VĚN-yūl, VĒ-nūl]	A tiny vein connecting to a capillary.

CASE STUDY

A Cardiovascular Emergency

On a hot summer afternoon, Joseph Davino entered the emergency room at Stone General Hospital with severe shortness of breath (SOB). Dr. Mary Woodard was the cardiologist on call that day. She immediately started examining Mr. Davino and made a preliminary diagnosis based upon the physical assessment and the patient's history. She learned that Mr. Davino is 44 years old, is a smoker, is overweight, and has a sedentary lifestyle.

Mr. Davino's past medical history shows that he has a high cholesterol level, has a history of angina, and takes medication to control high blood pressure. The physical exam shows normal temperature and a blood pressure of 190/100. Dr. Woodard orders an ECG and cardiac enzymes.

Critical Thinking

1. Shortness of breath may indicate cardiovascular disease. What lifestyle factors put Mr. Davino at risk?
2. Was Mr. Davino's blood pressure normal?

Spell It Correctly

For each of the following words, write C if the spelling is correct. If it is not, write the correct spelling.

3. atriaventricular _____

4. capillairy _____

5. ductus arteriosus _____

6. Purkine fibers _____

7. myocardium _____

8. arteryole _____

9. bundle of His _____

10. popliteal _____

11. sistole _____

Test Your Knowledge

Complete the sentences below by filling in the blanks.

12. A vessel that carries oxygenated blood is a(n) _____.

13. Deoxygenated blood flows through the _____.

14. The innermost layer of heart tissue is called the _____.

15. The two atrioventricular valves control the flow of blood between the _____ and the _____.

16. Carbon dioxide is carried back to the heart via the _____.

17. Three lifestyle factors that may result in high blood pressure are _____, _____, and _____.

18. The fetal circulatory system does not include _____ circulation.

19. The lining of the arteries that secretes substances into the blood is called the _____.

20. Pulmonary circulation is the flow of blood between the _____ and _____.

21. The head and neck receive oxygen-rich blood via the _____ _____.

22. Fill in the missing part in the following sequence: pulmonary arteries $\rightarrow$ _____ $\rightarrow$ pulmonary veins.

Combining Forms

The list below includes combining forms that relate specifically to the cardiovascular system. Pronunciations are provided for the examples.

COMBINING FORM	MEANING	EXAMPLE
angi(o)	blood vessel	*angiogram* [ĂN-jē-ō-grăm], image of a blood vessel
aort(o)	aorta	*aortitis* [ā-ōr-TĪ-tĭs], inflammation of the aorta
arteri(o), arter(o)	artery	*arteriosclerosis* [ăr-TĒR-ē-ō-sklĕr-Ō-sĭs], hardening of the arteries

COMBINING FORM	MEANING	EXAMPLE
ather(o)	fatty matter	*atherosclerosis* [ĂTH-ĕr-ō-sklĕr-Ō-sĭs], hardening of the arteries with irregular plaque deposits
atri(o)	atrium	*atrioventricular* [Ā-trē-ō-vĕn-TRĬK-yū-lăr], relating to the atria and ventricles of the heart
cardi(o)	heart	*cardiomyopathy* [KĂR-dē-ō-mī-ŎP-ă-thē], disease of the heart muscle
hemangi(o)	blood vessel	*hemangioma* [hĕ-MĂN-jē-ō-mă], abnormal mass of blood vessels
pericardi(o)	pericardium	*pericarditis* [PĔR-ĭ-kăr-DĪ-tĭs], inflammation of the pericardium
phleb(o)	vein	*phlebitis* [flĕ-BĪ-tĭs], inflammation of a vein
sphygm(o)	pulse	*sphygmomanometer* [SFĬG-mō-mă-NŎM-ĕ-tĕr], instrument for measuring blood pressure
thromb(o)	blood clot	*thrombocytosis* [THRŎM-bō-sī-TŌ-sĭs], abnormal increase in blood platelets in the blood
vas(o)	blood vessel	*vasodepressor* [VĀ-sō-dē-PRĔS-ŏr], agent that lowers blood pressure by relaxing blood vessels
ven(o)	vein	*venography* [vē-NŎG-ră-fē], radiographic imaging of a vein

COMBINING FORMS EXERCISES

Build Your Medical Vocabulary

Build a word for each of the following definitions. Use the combining forms in this chapter as well as those in Chapters 1, 2, and 3.

23. Disease of the heart muscle _____

24. Inflammation of the membrane surrounding the heart _____

25. X-ray of a vein _____

26. Inflammation of a vein _____

27. Operation for reconstruction of an artery _____

28. A disease involving both blood vessels and nerves _____

29. Tending to act on the blood vessels _____

30. Of cardiac origin _____

31. Enlargement of the heart _____

32. Inflammation of the artery with a thrombus _____

CASE STUDY

Reading the Record

The nurse on duty the night of Mr. Davino's admittance observed that his blood pressure dropped gradually from 190/100 to 160/90. The nurse, Joan Aquino, marked each change of blood pressure on his record. In addition to blood pressure, she also took Mr. Davino's temperature and pulse every two hours. All his measurements seemed to show improvement, except that Mr. Davino was running a slight fever. However, Joan did not like Mr. Davino's appearance. His skin had a gray pallor and he seemed very disoriented. Dr. Mirkhan, the cardiologist on call that night, spoke with Nurse Aquino and looked over the results of the tests ordered earlier. The doctor also made the notes shown on the record.

Critical Thinking

33. Nurse Aquino made very specific comments to Dr. Mirkhan about her observations of Mr. Davino's appearance. What are the two items that Nurse Aquino noticed?
34. Referring to Mr. Davino's chart below, figure out how long Mr. Davino's temperature remained slightly elevated.

MEDICAL RECORD	PROGRESS NOTES
DATE 8/15/XX	3:30 pm Chest clear to auscultation bilaterally with mild crackles; Heart rate and rhythm regular; no audible murmur; no rubs; ECG, blood gases, and SED rate were ordered. Recommended transfer to CCU.—A. Mirkhan, M.D.
8/15/XX	4 pm BP 190/100; temp 100.4°; no urine in catheter bag.—J. Aquino, R.N.
8/15/XX	5 pm BP 182/95; temp 100.5°; still no urine in catheter bag; if no urine by 8 pm, notify Dr. Mirkhan.—J. Aquino, R.N.
8/15/XX	6 pm BP 176/97; temp 100.6°; catheter bag empty.—J. Aquino, R.N.
8/15/XX	7 pm Catheter bag empty.—J. Aquino, R.N.
8/15/XX	8 pm BP 168/94; temp 100.7°; catheter bag empty; paged Dr. Mirkhan.—J. Aquino, R.N.
8/15/XX	9 pm BP 162/96; temp 100.8°; start IV; ECG; blood gases.—A. Mirkhan, M.D.
8/15/XX	10 pm Catheter bag contains 50 ml of urine; patient resting comfortably.—J. Aquino, R.N.
8/15/XX	11 pm Catheter bag contains about 200 ml of urine; patient still sleeping.—J. Aquino, R.N.
8/15/XX	12 pm Woke patient; BP 160/90; temp 100.2°; 300 ml of urine.—J. Aquino, R.N.

PATIENT'S IDENTIFICATION *(For typed or written entries give: Name—last, first, middle; grade; rank; hospital or medical facility)* REGISTER NO. WARD NO. 4B

Use the following combining forms and the suffixes and prefixes you learned in Chapters 1, 2, and 3 to fill in the missing word parts: atrio-, arterio-, phlebo-, thrombo-, veno-

35. _____ itis, inflammation of a vein
36. _____ ectomy, surgical removal of a thrombus
37. _____ plasty, vein repair
38. _____ megaly, enlargement of the atrium
39. _____ graph, radiograph of veins

Give the term that fits each definition. Each term must contain at least one of the combining forms shown in the previous section. You may also refer to Chapters 1, 2, and 3.

40. Enlargement of the heart _____

41. Relating to the heart and lungs _____

42. Establishing an opening into the pericardium _____

43. Inflammation of the endocardium _____

44. Repair of a vein _____

45. Paralysis of a blood vessel _____

46. Suturing of a blood vessel _____

Check Your Knowledge

Complete the sentences below by filling in the blanks.

47. An inflammation of a vein is _____.

48. Atherosclerosis is hardening of the _____.

49. A venogram is an x-ray of a(n) _____.

50. Removal of an artery is a(n) _____.

51. A cardiologist treats _____ disease.

Diagnostic, Procedural, and Laboratory Terms

Doctors who specialize in the diagnosis and treatment of cardiovascular disease (*cardiology*) are called *cardiologists*. The cardiologist often starts an examination with **auscultation** (listening to sounds within the body through a stethoscope). Some abnormal sounds a physician may hear are a *murmur*, a *bruit*, or a *gallop*. Each sound is a clue to the patient's condition. A **sphygmomanometer** is then usually used to measure blood pressure.

Diagnosis of the cardiovascular system is done either by procedures and diagnostic tests or by laboratory examination of certain factors in the blood. Table 6-2 lists some procedures and tests of the cardiovascular system. Figure 6-3 shows an ECG. Figures 6-4 and 6-5 show normal and abnormal result.

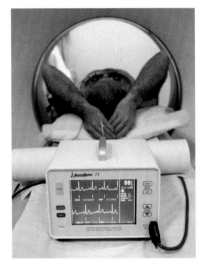

FIGURE 6-3 An ECG produces a picture of the heartbeat in the form of a graph. Six leads are used in most ECGs. Some ECGs are performed using more leads, such as twelve, to map electrical changes in other areas of the heart.

TABLE 6-2 Cardiovascular tests.

Procedure or Test	Description	Purpose
stress test or *exercise tolerance test (ETT)*	measurements taken while patient exercises on a treadmill	to diagnose coronary artery disease or assess heart attack risk
electrocardiography (ECG, EKG) or *electrocardiogram*	mapping of electrical changes in the heart on a machine called an electrocardiograph	to check for heart abnormalities
Holter monitor	portable electrocardiograph machine	monitors heart activity over a 24-hour period
angiocardiography	x-ray of the heart and large blood vessels	
angiography	x-ray of the large blood vessels	

TABLE 6-2 Cardiovascular tests (*cont.*).

Procedure or Test	Description	Purpose
aortography	x-ray of the aorta	
arteriography	x-ray of a specific artery	
venography or phlebography	x-ray of a specific vein	
ventriculogram	x-ray of the ventricles	measures the *cardiac output* (CO) and **ejection fraction**, both of which indicate the functioning of the ventricles
digital subtraction angiography (DSA)	two angiograms	compares the results of two tests
sonography	images by sound waves	
Doppler ultrasound	imaging test using ultrasound	to measure blood flow
echocardiography	records sound waves	shows heart structure and movement
cardiac scan	imaging test using nuclear medicine	shows movement in areas of the heart
positron emission tomography (PET)	nuclear imaging	shows blood flow in the heart
multiple-gated acquisition (MUGA) angiography	non-invasive nuclear imaging	assess cardiac muscle function
cardiac MRI (magnetic resonance imaging)	detailed image of the heart and large blood vessels	
cardiac catheterization	insertion of a catheter through an artery or vein into the heart	to get blood samples and take measurements

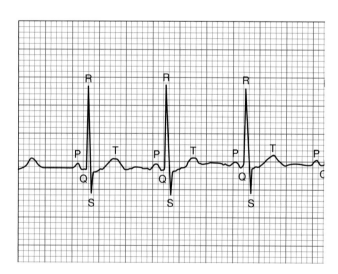

FIGURE 6-4 A normal ECG. The waves of electrical changes in the heart are mapped as P, QRS, and T waves. The P wave is electrical change occurring in the atria, the QRS wave represents change in the ventricles, and the T wave represents relaxation of the ventricles.

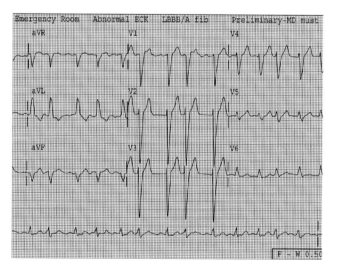

FIGURE 6-5 An abnormal ECG taken in the emergency room. Note the irregularities compared to Figure 6-4. These irregularities show atrial fibrillation and a blockage. In atrial fibrillation, the heart's rhythm is irregular, with as many as 350 beats per minute. It results from the atria discharging blood simultaneously. If not treated with medication, it can result in heart failure. Heart blockage represents a delay in the heart's conduction system.

```
                Laboratory Report
                 Emhar Diagnostics
                Three Riverview Drive
                  Wesley, OH 66666
                   (800) 999–0000

PATIENT NAME   Mary Helfer
PATIENT ID    777-888-6666
DATE RECEIVED  06/14/XXXX
DATE REPORTED  06/15/XXXX
```

	RESULTS		
TEST	OUT OF RANGE	WITHIN RANGE	REFERENCE RANGE/UNITS
HDL	36 mg/dL		>40 mg/dL
LDL	192 mg/dL		<130mg/dL
Triglycerides	204 mg/dL		40–199 mg/dL
Cholesterol	208 mg/dL		120–199mg/dL

FIGURE 6-6 This lipid profile reveals the need to cut cholesterol in the patient's diet.

MORE ABOUT...

Electrocardiograms

The electrocardiograph can have twelve leads, which are placed at specific points on the patient's body to monitor electrical activity of the heart. Six of the leads go on the arms and legs and six of the leads go at specific points on the chest. The chest leads are marked with specific codes. For example, V_1 goes in the fourth intercostal space to the right of the sternum. Each lead traces the electrical activity from a different angle.

Laboratory Tests

Laboratory tests are crucial for determining what may be happening to a patient or for evaluating risk factors for heart disease. Drug therapy, clinical procedures, and lifestyle changes may all be recommended largely on the basis of laboratory test results.

The flow of blood in the arteries is affected by the amount of **cholesterol** and **triglycerides** (fatty substances or *lipids*) contained in the blood. *Low-density lipoproteins (LDL)* and *very low-density lipoproteins (VLDL)* cause cholesterol to form blockages in the arteries. *High-density lipoproteins (HDL)* actually remove lipids from the arteries. A **lipid profile** (a series of laboratory tests performed on a blood sample) gives the lipid, triglyceride, glucose, and other values that help in evaluating a patient's risk factors. Figure 6-6 is an example of a patient's lipid profile.

Another important laboratory test of blood is the **cardiac enzyme test** or **study** (also called a **serum enzyme test**), which measures the levels of enzymes released into the blood. The three enzymes that help evaluate the condition of the patient are *GOT* (*glutamic oxaloacetic transaminase*), *CPK* (*creatine phosphokinase*), and *LDH* (*lactate dehydrogenase*).

The Web site www.heartsite.com has a search item called tests. Click on echocardiogram and any other test listed to learn more details about these tests.

MORE ABOUT...

Cholesterol

Cholesterol is just one of the risk factors for heart disease but it is one that can be changed by lifestyle and/or medication. That is why many researchers focus on cholesterol levels and ratios. It is generally thought that low LDL levels and high HDL levels are healthier. However, some studies suggest that even HDL levels can get too high.

To learn more about cardiac enzyme tests, visit the information site of the BBC (www.bbc.co.uk/health/talking/tests/blood_cardiac_enzymes.shtml).

VOCABULARY REVIEW

In the previous section, you learned terms relating to diagnosis, clinical procedures, and laboratory tests. Before going on to the exercises, read the definitions below. Pronunciations are provided for certain terms.

Term	Definition
angiocardiography [ăn-jē-ō-kăr-dē-ŎG-ră-fē]	Viewing of the heart and its major blood vessels by x-ray after injection of a contrast medium.
angiography [ăn-jē-ŎG-ră-fē] angio- + -graphy	Viewing of the heart's major blood vessels by x-ray after injection of a contrast medium.
aortography [ā-ōr-TŎG-ră-fē] aorto- + -graphy	Viewing of the aorta by x-ray after injection of a contrast medium.
arteriography [ăr-tēr-ē-ŎG-ră-fē] arterio- + -graphy	Viewing of a specific artery by x-ray after injection of a contrast medium.
auscultation [ăws-kŭl-TĀ-shŭn]	Process of listening to body sounds via a stethoscope.
cardiac catheterization [kăth-ĕ-tĕr-ĭ-ZĀ-shŭn]	Process of passing a thin catheter through an artery or vein to the heart to take blood samples, inject a contrast medium, or measure various pressures.
cardiac enzyme tests/studies	Blood tests for determining levels of enzymes during a myocardial infarction; serum enzyme tests.
cardiac MRI (Magnetic Resonance Imaging)	Viewing of the heart by magnetic resonance imaging.
cardiac scan	Process of viewing the heart muscle at work by scanning the heart of a patient into whom a radioactive substance has been injected.
cholesterol [kō-LĔS-tĕr-ōl]	Fatty substance present in animal fats; cholesterol circulates in the bloodstream, sometimes causing arterial plaque to form.
digital subtraction angiography	Use of two angiograms done with different dyes to provide a comparison between the results.
Doppler [DŎP-lĕr] **ultrasound**	Ultrasound test of blood flow in certain blood vessels.
echocardiography [ĕk-ō-kăr-dē-ŎG-ră-fē] echo- + cardio- + -graphy	Use of sound waves to produce images showing the structure and motion of the heart.
ejection fraction	Percentage of the volume of the contents of the left ventricle ejected with each contraction.
electrocardiography [ē-lĕk-trō-kăr-dē-ŎG-ră-fē] electro- + cardio- + -graphy	Use of the electrocardiograph in diagnosis.
Holter [HŌL-tĕr] **monitor**	Portable device that provides a 24-hour electrocardiogram.
lipid profile [LĬP-ĭd] Greek *lipos*, fat	Laboratory test that provides the levels of lipids, triglycerides, and other substances in the blood.

Term	Definition
multiple-gated acquisition (MUGA) angiography	Radioactive scan showing heart function.
phlebography [flĕ-BŎG-ră-fē] phlebo-, vein + -graphy	Viewing of a vein by x-ray after injection of a contrast medium.
positron emission tomography [tō-MŎG-ră-fē] **(PET) scan**	Type of nuclear image that measures movement of areas of the heart.
serum enzyme tests	Laboratory tests performed to detect enzymes present during or after a myocardial infarction.
sonography [sō-NŎG-ră-fē]	Production of images based on the echoes of sound waves against structures.
sphygmomanometer [SFĬG-mō-mă-NŎM-ĕ-tĕr]	Device for measuring blood pressure.
stress test	Test that measures heart rate and functions while the patient is exercising on a treadmill.
triglyceride [trī-GLĬS-ĕr-īd]	Fatty substance; lipid.
venography [vē-NŎG-ră-fē] veno-, vein + -graphy	Viewing of a vein by x-ray after injection of a contrast medium.
ventriculogram [vĕn-TRĬK-yū-lō-grăm] ventricle + -gram, a recording	X-ray of a ventricle taken after injection of a contrast medium.

CASE STUDY

Diagnosing the Problem

Dr. Woodard, the admitting physician, had made notations on the patient's chart. The doctor on call that night was Dr. Mirkhan, a cardiologist. He agreed with Nurse Aquino that the patient's pallor and disorientation warranted further tests. First, Dr. Mirkhan reviewed the ECG that Dr. Woodard had ordered. Then, he ordered some more laboratory tests to help in his diagnosis of Mr. Davino's current condition. He made the additions to Mr. Davino's record.

Critical Thinking

52. From the notations added to the chart, is his cholesterol still high?
53. Which of his laboratory tests shows an abnormal level that can often be corrected by dietary changes?

MEDICAL RECORD	PROGRESS NOTES
DATE 8/15/XX	3:30 pm Have reviewed nursing notes. Chest clear to auscultation bilaterally with mild crackles; Heart rate and rhythm regular; no audible murmur; no rubs; ECG, blood gases, and SED rate were ordered. Recommend transfer to CCU.—A. Mirkhan, M.D.
8/15/XX	9 pm BP 162/96; temp 100.8°; start IV; ECG, blood gases.—A. Mirkhan, M.D.
8/16/XX	2 am ECG—sinus rhythm with Q waves in 2AVF; mild ST elevation in V2 and V3; cholesterol 296; SED rate 15 mm/1 hr.—A. Mirkhan, M.D.

Apply What You Learn

Dr. Mirkhan also works in private practice. Patients' notes from his practice that follow give you an idea of the types of clinical problems he treats.

54. What is Marvin's diagnosis? _____

55. List five laboratory tests Dr. Mirkhan reviewed on 9/7/xx.

_____

_____

_____

_____

_____

Patient name *Angela O'Toole*	Age *57*	Current Diagnosis *angina*

DATE/TIME	
9/7/XX 9:30	*Exercise thallium test with no post-exercise changes; continue current medication.*

Patient name *Marvin Hochstadter*	Age *64*	Current Diagnosis *arteriosclerosis*

DATE/TIME	
9/7/XX 10:15	*Two-year post angioplasty; SOB; cardiac pain; schedule cardiac catheterization.*

Patient name *Lou Lawisky*	Age *49*	Current Diagnosis *unstable angina*

DATE/TIME	
9/7/XX 1:20	*Negative stress cardiolite scan to 12 MET; peak heart rate of 153/min with no ischemia or infarction; epigastric burning, no angina; recommend Tagamet to control reflux.*

Patient name *Marlena Castelli*	Age *68*	Current Diagnosis *R/O MI*

DATE/TIME	
9/7/XX 2:30	*Neck and jaw discomfort; two previous MIs (last 1/23/XX); PTCA 2/6/XX; BP 126/84, pulse 88, heart: Apical impulse discrete. S1 and S2 are regular in rate and intensity. There is an S4 gallop, no S3 gallop, no cardiac murmur. Laboratory: Sodium 142, potassium 3.7, CO_2 29, chloride 103, creatinine 1.1, BUN 13, cholesterol 293, triglycerides 28; HDL 35; LDL 156; CPK 133.*

Pathological Terms

Cardiovascular disease (CVD) can have many causes and can take many forms. Some diseases are caused by a congenital anomaly, whereas others may be caused by other pathology or by lifestyle factors **(risk factors),** such as poor diet, smoking, and lack of exercise.

Heart Rhythm

The rhythm of the heart maintains the blood flow through and in and out of the heart. Table 6-3 lists disorders associated with the heart's rhythm.

TABLE 6-3 Rhythm disorders.

Disorder	Description	Cause
arrhythmia	abnormal rhythm	
bradycardia	abnormally slow heart rate	
tachycardia	abnormally fast heart rate	
atrial fibrillation, dysrhythmia, or fibrillation	irregular heart rhythm	
flutter	rapid but regular heartbeat	
murmur	humming sound which may indicate valve leakage	
bruit	abnormal sound heard on auscultation	
rub	frictional sound	pericardial murmur
gallop	triple heart sound	serious heart disease
palpitations	thumping in the chest	
atrioventricular block or heart block	blocking of impulses from the AV node	
premature atrial contractions (PACs) or premature ventricular contractions (PVCs)	irregularities in the heart's contractions	

Blood Pressure

Abnormalities in blood pressure (**hypertensive heart disease**) can damage the heart as well as other body systems. If the blood pressure is too high (**hypertension** or **high blood pressure**) or too low (**hypotension** or **low blood pressure**), the blood vessels do not have the proper pressure of blood flowing through them. **Essential hypertension** is high blood pressure that is *idiopathic* or without any known cause. **Secondary hypertension** has a known cause, such as a high-salt diet, renal disease, adrenal gland disease, and so on.

Diseases of the Blood Vessels

Blood vessels can become diseased, as when **plaque,** buildup of fatty material, is deposited on the wall of an artery. Table 6-4 lists diseases of the blood vessels. Figure 6-7 shows a thrombus and an embolus.

Coronary Artery Disease

Coronary artery disease (CAD) refers to any condition that reduces the nourishment the heart receives from the blood flowing through the arteries of the heart. Such diseases include **aortic stenosis** or narrowing of the aorta. **Coarctation of the aorta** is also an abnormal narrowing of the aorta. **Stenosis** is any narrowing of a blood vessel. **Pulmonary artery stenosis** slows the flow of

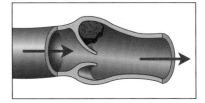
A thrombus.

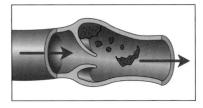
An embolus.

FIGURE 6-7 A thrombus is a stationary blood clot, while an embolus is a traveling mass of material that blocks a blood vessel.

TABLE 6-4 Diseases of blood vessels.

Disease or Condition	Description
atheroma	plaque on an artery wall
atherosclerosis	hardening of the arteries
embolus	mass in the bloodstream that causes a blockage
thrombus	stationary blood clot
thrombophlebitis	inflammation of a vein with a thrombus
thrombosis	presence of a thrombus in a blood vessel
deep vein thrombosis	thrombus in a deep vein
thrombotic occlusion	closing of a vessel by a thrombus
constriction	narrowing of a vessel
aneurysm	weakness in an artery wall that balloons and can burst
arteriosclerosis	hardening and loss of elasticity of the arteries
claudication	limping
intermittent claudication	irregular attacks of claudication
peripheral vascular disease	disease of the vessels of the lower extremities
infarction	sudden loss of blood supply to a vessel
necrosis or infarct	area of dead tissue caused by an infarction
perfusion deficit	lack of blood flow through a vessel
ischemia	area of blood insufficiency
cyanosis	bluish skin color due to deficiency in blood oxygenation
Raynaud's phenomenon	spasm in finger arteries
varicose veins	twisted or enlarged veins
hemorrhoids	varicose veins in the anus
phlebitis	inflammation of a vein
arteritis	inflammation of an artery
petechiae	minute hemorrhages in skin blood vessels

blood to the lungs. **Angina** or **angina pectoris** (sometimes referred to as cardiac pain) can result from lack of oxygen to the heart muscle.

General Heart and Lung Diseases

When the heart suffers an attack that causes insufficient blood flow to the heart or ischemia, one is said to have a *coronary* or *heart attack*. These are informal terms for a **myocardial infarction (MI)**. **Cardiac arrest** or **asystole** is a sudden stopping of the heart. Such an attack can be fatal. Attacks may be caused by an **occlusion,** a closing of a blood vessel.

More About...

Familiar Terms for Heart Disease

Cardiovascular disease is a common ailment of middle and old age. Many familiar terms are used by lay people to describe common cardiovascular diseases and procedures. A myocardial infarction may be called a *coronary* or a *heart attack*. Arteriosclerosis is often referred to as *hardening of the arteries*. Congestive heart failure may be called *heart failure*. *Vein stripping* is a common term for removal of veins for transplanting elsewhere or for treating varicosities.

> Select coronary artery disease on the Texas Heart Institute's Web site (www.tmc.edu/thi/index.html) to read more about the risks of CAD.

Some diseases of the heart are specific inflammations, such as **endocarditis, myocarditis, pericarditis,** or **bacterial endocarditis.** Other conditions of the heart have to do with fluid accumulation. **Congestive heart failure** occurs when the heart is unable to pump the necessary amount of blood. **Pulmonary edema** or accumulation of fluid in the lungs can result from this failure. Fluid accumulation in the pericardial sac causes compression of the heart called **cardiac tamponade.**

An **intracardiac tumor** is a tumor in a heart chamber. **Cardiomyopathy** is disease of the heart muscle.

Valve Conditions

The heart valves control the flow of blood into, through, and out of the heart. **Aortic regurgitation** or **reflux** is a backward flow of blood through the aortic valve. An abnormal narrowing of the opening of the mitral valve (**mitral stenosis**) affects the opening and closing of the valve. **Mitral insufficiency** or **reflux** is a backward flow of blood through the mitral valve. Similarly, **mitral valve prolapse** is a backward flow of blood, but it is due to the abnormal protrusion of one or both of the mitral cusps into the left atrium. **Tricuspid stenosis** is an abnormal narrowing of the opening of the tricuspid valve.

Sometimes, infections or inflammation may cause valve damage. **Valvulitis** is the general term for a heart valve inflammation. **Rheumatic heart disease** is damage to the heart, usually to the valves, caused by an untreated streptococcal infection. Some infections can cause a clot (**vegetation**) on a heart valve or opening.

Congenital Heart Conditions

Congenital heart disease results from a condition present at birth. Some common conditions are **patent ductus arteriosus,** a disease in which a small duct remains open at birth; **septal defect,** an abnormal opening in the septum between the atria or ventricles; and **tetrology of Fallot,** a combination of four heart abnormalities.

Vocabulary Review

In the previous section, you learned terms relating to pathology. Before going on to the exercises, read the definitions below. Pronunciations are provided for certain terms.

Term	Definition
aneurysm [ĂN-yū-rĭzm]	Ballooning of the artery wall caused by weakness in the wall.

Term	Definition
angina [ĂN-jĭ-nă, ăn-JĪ-nă]	Angina pectoris.
angina pectoris [PĔK-tōr-ĭs, pĕk-TOR-ĭs]	Chest pain, usually caused by a lowered oxygen or blood supply to the heart.
aortic regurgitation [rē-GŬR-jĭ-TĀ-shŭn] or **reflux** [RĒ-flŭks]	Backward flow or leakage of blood through a faulty aortic valve.
aortic stenosis [stĕ-NŌ-sĭs]	Narrowing of the aorta.
arrhythmia [ā-RĬTH-mē-ă] a- + rhythm	Irregularity in the rhythm of the heartbeat.
arteriosclerosis [ăr-TĒR-ē-ō-sklĕr-Ō-sĭs] arterio- + sclerosis	Hardening of the arteries.
arteritis [ăr-tĕr-Ī-tĭs] arter- + -itis	Inflammation of an artery or arteries.
asystole [ā-SĬS-tō-lē]	Cardiac arrest.
atheroma [ăth-ĕr-Ō-mă]	A fatty deposit (plaque) in the wall of an artery.
atherosclerosis [ĂTH-ĕr-ō-sklĕr-ō-sĭs] athero- + sclerosis	Hardening of the arteries caused by the buildup of atheromas.
atrial fibrillation [fĭ-brĭ-LĀ-shŭn]	An irregular, usually rapid, heartbeat caused by overstimulation of the AV node.
atrioventricular block atrio- + ventricle	Heart block; partial or complete blockage of the electrical impulses from the atrioventricular node to the ventricles.
bacterial endocarditis	Bacterial inflammation of the inner lining of the heart.
bradycardia [brād-ē-KĂR-dē-ă]	Heart rate of fewer than 60 beats per minute.
bruit [brū-Ē]	Sound or murmur, especially an abnormal heart sound heard on auscultation, especially of the carotid artery.
cardiac arrest	Sudden stopping of the heart; also called asystole.
cardiac tamponade [tăm-pō-NĀD]	Compression of the heart caused by fluid accumulation in the pericardial sac.
cardiomyopathy [KĂR-dē-ō-mĭ-ŎP-ă-thē] cardio- + myo- + -pathy	Disease of the heart muscle.
claudication [klăw-dĭ-KĀ-shŭn]	Limping caused by inadequate blood supply during activity; usually subsides during rest.
coarctation [kō-ărk-TĀ-shŭn] **of the aorta**	Abnormal narrowing of the aorta.
congenital [kŏn-JĔN-Ĭ-tăl] **heart disease**	Heart disease (usually a type of malformation) that exists at birth.
congestive [kŏn-JĔS-tĭv] **heart failure**	Inability of the heart to pump enough blood out during the cardiac cycle; collection of fluid in the lungs results.

Term	Definition
constriction [kŏn-STRĬK-shŭn]	Compression or narrowing caused by contraction, as of a vessel.
coronary artery disease (CAD)	Condition that reduces the flow of blood and nutrients through the arteries of the heart.
cyanosis [sī-ă-NŌ-sĭs]	Bluish or purplish coloration, as of the skin, caused by inadequate oxygenation of the blood.
deep vein thrombosis [thrŏm-BŌ-sĭs]	Formation of a thrombus (clot) in a deep vein, such as a femoral vein.
dysrhythmia [dĭs-RĬTH-mē-ă] dys- + rhythm	Abnormal heart rhythm.
embolus [ĔM-bō-lŭs]	Mass of foreign material blocking a vessel.
endocarditis [ĔN-dō-kăr-DĪ-tĭs] endo-, within + card-, heart + -itis, inflammation	Inflammation of the endocardium, especially an inflammation caused by a bacterial (for example, staphylococci) or fungal agent.
essential hypertension	High blood pressure without any known cause.
fibrillation [fĭ-brĭ-LĀ-shŭn]	Random, chaotic, irregular heart rhythm.
flutter	Regular but very rapid heartbeat.
gallop	Triple sound of a heartbeat, usually indicative of serious heart disease.
heart block	*See* atrioventricular block.
hemorrhoids [HĔM-ō-rŏydz]	Varicose condition of veins in the anal region.
high blood pressure	*See* hypertension.
hypertension [HĪ-pĕr-TĔN-shŭn] hyper- + tension	Chronic condition with blood pressure greater than 140/90.
hypertensive heart disease	Heart disease caused, or worsened, by high blood pressure.
hypotension [HĪ-pō-TĔN-shŭn] hypo- + tension	Chronic condition with blood pressure below normal.
infarct [ĬN-fărkt]	Area of necrosis caused by a sudden drop in the supply of arterial or venous blood.
infarction [ĭn-FĂRK-shŭn]	Sudden drop in the supply of arterial or venous blood, often due to an embolus or thrombus.
intermittent claudication	Attacks of limping, particularly in the legs, due to ischemia of the muscles.
intracardiac [ĭn-tră-KĂR-dē-ăk] **tumor** intra- + cardiac	A tumor within one of the heart chambers.

Term	Definition
ischemia [ĭs-KĒ-mē-ă]	Localized blood insufficiency caused by an obstruction.
low blood pressure	*See* hypotension.
mitral [MĪ-trăl] insufficiency or reflux	Backward flow of blood due to a damaged mitral valve.
mitral stenosis	Abnormal narrowing at the opening of the mitral valve.
mitral valve prolapse	Backward flow of blood into the left atrium due to protrusion of one or both mitral cusps into the left atrium during contractions.
murmur	Soft heart humming sound heard between normal beats.
myocardial infarction (MI) myocardi(um) + -al	Sudden drop in the supply of blood to an area of the heart muscle, usually due to a blockage in a coronary artery.
myocarditis [MĪ-ō-kăr-DĪ-tĭs] myocard(ium) + -itis	Inflammation of the myocardium.
necrosis [nĕ-KRŌ-sĭs]	Death of tissue or an organ or part due to irreversible damage; usually a result of oxygen deprivation.
occlusion [ŏ-KLŪ-zhŭn]	The closing of a blood vessel.
palpitations [păl-pĭ-TĀ-shŭnz]	Uncomfortable pulsations of the heart felt as a thumping in the chest.
patent ductus arteriosus [PĂ-tĕnt DŬK-tŭs ăr-tēr-ē-Ō-sĭs]	A condition at birth in which the ductus arteriosus, a small duct between the aorta and the pulmonary artery, remains abnormally open.
perfusion deficit	Lack of flow through a blood vessel, usually caused by an occlusion.
pericarditis [PĔR-ĭ-kăr-DĪ-tĭs] pericard(ium) + -itis	Inflammation of the pericardium.
peripheral vascular disease	Vascular disease in the lower extremities, usually due to blockages in the arteries of the groin or legs.
petechiae (*sing.*, petechia) [pĕ-TĒ-kē-ē, pĕ-TĔK-ē-ē, (pĕ-TĒ-kē-ă, pĕ-TĔK-ē-ă)]	Minute hemorrhages in the skin.
phlebitis [flĕ-BĪ-tĭs] phleb-, vein + -itis	Inflammation of a vein.
plaque [plăk]	Buildup of solid material, such as a fatty deposit, on the lining of an artery.
premature atrial contractions (PACs)	Atrial contractions that occur before the normal impulse; can be the cause of palpitations.

Term	Definition
premature ventricular contractions (PVCs)	Ventricular contractions that occur before the normal impulse; can be the cause of palpitations.
pulmonary artery stenosis	Narrowing of the pulmonary artery, preventing the lungs from receiving enough blood from the heart to oxygenate.
pulmonary edema	Abnormal accumulation of fluid in the lungs.
Raynaud's phenomenon [rā-NŌZ]	Spasm in the arteries of the fingers causing numbness or pain.
rheumatic heart disease	Heart valve and/or muscle damage caused by an untreated streptococcal infection.
risk factor	Any of various factors considered to increase the probability that a disease will occur; for example, high blood pressure and smoking are considered risk factors for heart disease.
rub	Frictional sound heard between heartbeats, usually indicating a pericardial murmur.
secondary hypertension	Hypertension having a known cause, such as kidney disease.
septal defect	Congenital abnormality consisting of an opening in the septum between the atria or ventricles.
stenosis [stĕ-NŌ-sĭs]	Narrowing, particularly of blood vessels or of the cardiac valves.
tachycardia [TĂK-ĭ-KĂR-dē-ă]	Heart rate greater than 100 beats per minute.
tetralogy of Fallot [fă-LŌ]	Set of four congenital heart abnormalities appearing together that cause deoxygenated blood to enter the systemic circulation: ventricular septal defect, pulmonary stenosis, incorrect position of the aorta, and right ventricular hypertrophy.
thrombophlebitis [THRŎM-bō-flĕ-BĪ-tĭs] thrombo- + phleb- + -itis	Inflammation of a vein with a thrombus.
thrombosis [thrŏm-BŌ-sĭs]	Presence of a thrombus in a blood vessel.
thrombotic [thrŏm-BŎT-ĭk] occlusion	Narrowing caused by a thrombus.
thrombus [THRŎM-bŭs]	Stationary blood clot in the cardiovascular system, usually formed from matter found in the blood.
tricuspid stenosis	Abnormal narrowing of the opening of the tricuspid valve.
valvulitis [văl-vyū-LĪ-tĭs]	Inflammation of a heart valve.

Term	Definition
varicose [VĂR-ĭ-kōs] **vein**	Dilated, enlarged, or twisted vein, usually on the leg.
vegetation [vĕj-ĕ-TĀ-shŭn]	Clot on a heart valve or opening, usually caused by infection.

CASE STUDY

Applying Medical Technology to Reimbursement

Mr. Davino had a follow-up visit in Dr. Mirkhan's office. The doctor's billing clerk received the records and notes for Mr. Davino. Mr. Davino's insurance company will pay the claim once the doctor's office submits it for payment. A section of the claim is shown below

Critical Thinking

56. On the claim, what is the procedure code for the service provided to Mr. Davino?

57. On the claim, what is the code for Mr. Davino's diagnosis?

24. A DATE(S) OF SERVICE						B Place of Service	C Type of Service	D PROCEDURES, SERVICES, OR SUPPLIES (Explain Unusual Circumstances) CPT/HCPCS MODIFIER	E DIAGNOSIS CODE	F $ CHARGES	G DAYS OR UNITS	H EPSDT Family Plan	I EMG	J COB	K RESERVED FOR LOCAL USE
From MM	DD	YY	To MM	DD	YY										
08	15	XXXX						82803	414.0	74 00	1				

25. FEDERAL TAX I.D. NUMBER	SSN EIN	26. PATIENT'S ACCOUNT NO.	27. ACCEPT ASSIGNMENT? (For govt. claims, see back)	28. TOTAL CHARGE	29. AMOUNT PAID	30. BALANCE DUE
12-34-56789	[X] [ ]	000-77-9999	[X] YES [ ] NO	$ 74 00	$	$ 74 00

31. SIGNATURE OF PHYSICIAN OR SUPPLIER INCLUDING DEGREES OR CREDENTIALS (I certify that the statements on the reverse apply to this bill and are made a part thereof.) SIGNED *Andar Mirkhan, M.D.* DATE 08/22/XXXX	32. NAME AND ADDRESS OF FACILITY WHERE SERVICES WERE RENDERED (if other than home or office) *Glenview Clinic 14 Woodrow Blvd. Andover, OH 66666*	33. PHYSICIAN'S OR SUPPLIER'S NAME, ADDRESS, ZIP CODE & TELEPHONE NO. *Andar Mirkhan, M.D. 16 Courtyard Lane Andover, Ohio 66666* PIN# *B4OS987* GRP# *3218B*

(APPROVED BY AMA COUNCIL ON MEDICAL SERVICE 8/88)   **PLEASE PRINT OR TYPE**   FORM HCFA-1500 (12-90) FORM OWCP-1500   FORM RRB-1500

PATHOLOGICAL TERMS EXERCISES

Make an Educated Guess

For each of the following four situations, insert the likely age of the patient from the following age ranges. Use each range only once.

A. 0–2   C. 40–55

B. 11–18   D. 67–90

58. A patient going into surgery for a septal defect _____

59. Arteriosclerosis with pulmonary edema _____

60. Cardiac arrest of an athlete during a stressful game _____

61. Hypertension due to stress _____

Check Your Knowledge

Complete the sentences below by filling in the blanks.

62. Heart rhythms may be dangerously fast (called _____) or dangerously slow (called _____).

63. Atrial fibrillation is another name for _____ or _____, irregular rhythm.

64. An embolus travels in the blood while a(n) _____ is stationary.

65. An abnormal sound heard on auscultation is called a(n) _____.

66. An abnormal heartbeat with a soft humming sound is called a(n) _____.

67. The most common cardiovascular disease is _____.

68. Smoking, poor diet, and lack of exercise are _____ _____ for heart disease.

69. A heart attack is also called a(n) _____ _____.

Surgical Terms

Cardiovascular surgery usually involves opening up or repairing blood vessels or valves; removal, repair, or replacement of diseased portions of blood vessels; or bypass of blocked areas. Table 6-5 describes terms related to cardiovascular surgery. Figures 6-8 and 6-9 show devices sometimes used in cardiovascular surgery. Figure 6-10 shows a phlebotomist.

TABLE 6-5 Terms in cardiovascular surgery.

Surgical Term	Description	Purpose
balloon catheter dilation, percutaneous transluminal coronary angioplasty (PTCA), angioplasty, or coronary angioplasty	insertion of a balloon catheter inside a blood vessel	to allow the free flow of blood
balloon valvuloplasty	insertion of a balloon catheter in a narrowed valve opening	to widen a narrow valve opening
angioscopy	insertion of a fiberoptic catheter into a blood vessel	to view the interior of a blood vessel
endovascular surgery	use of *cardiac catheterization*, threading of a catheter through an artery or vein	may be used to insert a **stent, drug-eluting stent,** or an **intravascular stent** to hold the passageway open

TABLE 6-5 Terms in cardiovascular surgery (*cont.*).

Surgical Term	Description	Purpose
bypass, coronary bypass	creation of a detour around a blockage	to allow blood to flow freely
coronary artery bypass graft (CABG)	attaching of a vessel or **graft** in a bypass operation	
cardiopulmonary bypass	use of a heart-lung bypass machine during an operation	
heart transplant	replacement of a diseased heart	
valve replacement	replacement of a heart valve	
thrombectomy	removal of a thrombus	
embolectomy	removal of an embolus	
atherectomy	removal of an atheroma	
arteriotomy	removal of an artery	
hemorrhoidectomy	removal of hemorrhoids	
endartectomy	removal of diseased artery lining	
valvotomy	incision into a valve to remove a clot	
valvuloplasty	repair of a valve	
venipucture or **phlebotomy**	small puncture of a vein to remove blood	
anastomosis	connecting of blood vessels or implanting of devices, such as *pacemakers*	

Narrowed artery with balloon catheter positioned.

Inflated balloon presses against arterial wall.

FIGURE 6-8 Balloon catheter dilation.

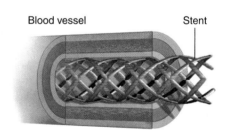

FIGURE 6-9 Drug-eluting stent.

MORE ABOUT...

Surgical Devices

New surgical devices are being developed all the time. The Da Vinci System is a robotic device that uses a tiny camera with multiple lenses inserted into the patient's chest, providing a three-dimensional image of the heart. The surgeon, at a nearby computer workstation, watches through a viewer to see inside the chest as a pair of joysticks control two robotic arms. The arms hold specially designed surgical instruments that mimic the actual movement of the surgeon's hands on the joysticks. This allows for minimal incision into the patient.

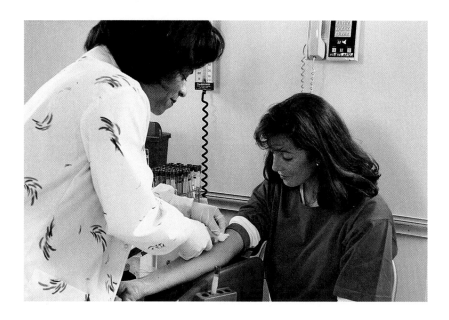

FIGURE 6-10 Phlebotomists must follow standard precautions when drawing blood.

VOCABULARY REVIEW

In the previous section, you learned terms relating to surgery. Before going on to the exercises, read the definitions below. Pronunciations are provided for certain terms.

Term	Definition
anastomosis [ă-năs-tō-MŌ-sĭs]	Surgical connection of two blood vessels to allow blood flow between them.
angioplasty [ĂN-jē-ō-plăs-tē] angio- + -plasty	Opening of a blocked blood vessel, as by balloon dilation.
angioscopy [ăn-jē-ŎS-kō-pē] angio- + -scopy	Viewing of the interior of a blood vessel using a fiberoptic catheter inserted or threaded into the vessel.

Term	Definition
arteriotomy [ăr-tēr-ē-ŎT-ō-mē] arterio- + -tomy	Surgical incision into an artery, especially to remove a clot.
atherectomy [ăth-ĕ-RĔK-tō-mē] ather- + -ectomy	Surgical removal of an atheroma.
balloon catheter dilation	Insertion of a balloon catheter into a blood vessel to open the passage so blood can flow freely.
balloon valvuloplasty [VĂL-vyū-lō-PLĂS-tē]	Procedure that uses a balloon catheter to open narrowed orifices in cardiac valves.
bypass	A structure (usually a vein graft) that creates a new passage for blood to flow from one artery to another artery or part of an artery; used to create a detour around blockages in arteries.
cardiopulmonary [KĂR-dē-ō-PŬL-mŏ-nēr-ē] **bypass**	Procedure used during surgery to divert blood flow to and from the heart through a heart-lung machine and back into circulation.
coronary angioplasty	*See* angioplasty.
coronary bypass surgery	*See* bypass.
drug-eluting stent	Stent that contains medication.
embolectomy [ĕm-bō-LĔK-tō-mē] embol(us) + -ectomy	Surgical removal of an embolus.
endarterectomy [ĕnd-ăr-tēr-ĔK-tō-mē] end-, within + arter-, artery + -ectomy	Surgical removal of the diseased portion of the lining of an artery.
endovascular [ĕn-dō-VĂS-kyū-lăr] **surgery** endo-, within + vascular	Any of various procedures performed during cardiac catheterization, such as angioscopy and atherectomy.
graft	Any tissue or organ implanted to replace or mend damaged areas.
heart transplant	Implantation of the heart of a person who has just died into a person whose diseased heart cannot sustain life.
hemorrhoidectomy [HĔM-ō-rŏy-DĔK-tō-mē] hemorrhoid + -ectomy	Surgical removal of hemorrhoids.
intravascular stent intra- + vascular	Stent placed within a blood vessel to allow blood to flow freely.
percutaneous transluminal [pĕr-kyū-TĀ-nē-ŭs trăns-LŪ-mĭn-ăl] **coronary angioplasty (PTCA)**	*See* balloon catheter dilation.
phlebotomy [flĕ-BŎT-ō-mē] phlebo- + -tomy	Drawing blood from a vein via a small incision.
stent [stĕnt]	Surgically implanted device used to hold something (as a blood vessel) open.

Term	Definition
thrombectomy [thrŏm-BĔK-tō-mē] thromb- + -ectomy	Surgical removal of a thrombus.
valve replacement	Surgical replacement of a coronary valve.
valvotomy [văl-VŎT-ō-mē]	Incision into a cardiac valve to remove an obstruction.
valvuloplasty [VĂL-vyū-lō-PLĂS-tē]	Surgical reconstruction of a cardiac valve.
venipuncture [VĔN-ĭ-pŭnk-chŭr, VĒ-nĭ-PŬNK-chŭr] veni- + puncture	Small puncture into a vein, usually to draw blood or inject a solution.

CASE STUDY

Surgery Helps

Mr. Davino's progress is poor after three days in the hospital. After determining that his heart has extensive blockages, the doctors decide to perform a CABG on him. Mr. Davino has a smooth postoperative recovery. He is told that he must make some lifestyle changes and will have to attend a cardiac rehabilitation center as an outpatient.

Critical Thinking

70. What are some of the lifestyle changes the staff at the cardiac rehabilitation center will probably recommend?

71. Evaluate your own general cardiovascular health based on your lifestyle. What changes should you make to prevent heart disease?

SURGICAL TERMS EXERCISES

Check Your Knowledge

Define the following terms.

72. Anastomosis is _____

73. Valvuloplasty is _____

74. Valvotomy is _____

75. Embolectomy is _____

76. Angioplasty is _____

Spell It Correctly

Check the spelling of the following terms. If the term is spelled correctly, put "C" in the blank. If not, put the correct spelling.

78. thromboctomy _____

79. atherectomy _____

80. arteritomy _____

81. angiascopy _____

82. hemorrhoidectomy _____

83. valvitomy _____

84. veinipuncture _____

85. valvuloplasty _____

86. coronery _____

TERMINOLOGY IN ACTION

Shown below is a medical chart entry in SOAP format for a 61-year-old male. What is his diagnosis and what are some ways it could be treated in addition to the prescribed medication?

Patient Name: Donald Arelio   March 29, 2XXX

S: Mr. Arelio is a 61-year-old male who has a problem with nosebleeds. No history of nose trauma. Hemorrhage occurs spontaneously approximately once a week for a couple of months often followed by a period of no nosebleeds for several weeks. The bleeding often starts at rest and sometimes upon exertion. He has been able to stop them with pressure up until the last week. He has no other bleeding problems and is not currently taking any medication.

O: BP 180/71; pulse 80; height 69"; weight 235 lb. No active bleeding at this time, but there is a small clot over the anterior midseptum.

A: 1. Hypertension

   2. Recurrent epistaxis

P: Patient was given Procardia sublingually with blood pressure dropping to 140/70. Patient was instructed in treatment of nosebleeds. Schedule for a recheck of blood pressure in 5 days. IF nosebleeds continue, he may need a referral.

USING THE INTERNET

If you search the World Wide Web for the American Heart Association (http://www.amhrt.org), you will find many discussions of all aspects of heart disease.

Use the Internet to find and list at least three inherited (genetic) risk factors and at least three acquired risk factors for heart disease.

List at least three things you can do personally to prevent heart disease.

What are three heart attack warning signs listed on the American Heart Association's Web site?

CHAPTER REVIEW

The material that follows is to help you review all the material in this chapter.

DEFINITIONS

Define the following terms and combining forms. Review the chapter before starting. Make sure you know how to pronounce each term as you define it. The blue words in curly brackets are references to the Spanish glossary on the Web site.

TERM	DEFINITION
anastomosis [ă-năs-tō-MŌ-sĭs] {anastomosis}	
aneurysm [ĂN-yū-rĭzm] {aneurisma}	
angina [ĂN-jĭ-nă, ăn-JĪ-nă] {angina}	
angina pectoris [PĔK-tōr-ĭs, pĕk-TŌR-ĭs] {angina de pecho}	
angi(o)	
angiocardiography [ăn-jē-ō-kăr-dē-ŎG-ră-fē]	
angiography [ăn-jē-ŎG-ră-fē]	
angioplasty [ĂN-jē-ō-plăs-tē] {angioplastia}	
angioscopy [ăn-jē-ŎS-kō-pē] {angioscopia}	
aorta [ā-ŌR-tă] {aorta}	
aort(o)	
aortic regurgitation [ā-ŌR-tĭk rē-GŬR-jĭ-TĀ-shŭn] or reflux [RĒ-flŭks]	
aortic stenosis [stĕ-NŌ-sĭs]	
aortic valve	
aortography [ā-ōr-TŎG-ră-fē]	
arrhythmia [ā-RĬTH-mē-ă] {arritmia}	
arteri(o), arter(o)	
arteriography [ăr-tēr-ē-ŎG-ră-fē]	
arteriole [ăr-TĒ-rē-ōl] {arteriola}	
arteriosclerosis [ăr-TĒR-ē-ō-sklĕr-Ō-sĭs] {arteriosclerosis}	

TERM	DEFINITION
arteriotomy [ăr-tēr-ē-ŎT-ō-mē]	
arteritis [ăr-tēr-Ī-tĭs] {arteritis}	
artery [ĂR-tēr-ē] {arteria}	
asystole [ā-SĬS-tō-lē] {asistolia}	
ather(o)	
atherectomy [ăth-ĕ-RĔK-tō-mē]	
atheroma [ăth-ĕr-Ō-mă] {ateroma}	
atherosclerosis [ĂTH-ĕr-ō-sklĕr-ō-sĭs] {arteriosclerosis}	
atri(o)	
atrial fibrillation [Ā-trē-ăl fĭ-brĭ-LĀ-shŭn]	
atrioventricular [Ā-trē-ō-vĕn-TRĬK-yū-lăr] block	
atrioventricular bundle	
atrioventricular node (AV node)	
atrioventricular valve	
atrium (pl., atria) [Ā-trē-ŭm (Ā-trē-ă)] {atrium}	
auscultation [ăws-kŭl-TĀ-shŭn] {auscultación}	
bacterial endocarditis	
balloon catheter dilation	
balloon valvuloplasty [VĂL-vyū-lō-PLĂS-tē]	
bicuspid [bī-KŬS-pĭd] valve	
blood [blŭd] {sangre}	
blood pressure	
blood vessel	
bradycardia [brād-ē-KĂR-dē-ă] {bradicardia}	
bruit [brū-Ē] {ruido}	
bundle of His [hĭz, hĭs]	
bypass	
capillary [KĂP-ĭ-lār-ē] {capilar}	
carbon dioxide (CO_2) {dióxido de carbono}	
cardi(o)	

TERM	DEFINITION
cardiac arrest	
cardiac catheterization [kăth-ĕ-tĕr-ĭ-ZĀ-shŭn]	
cardiac cycle	
cardiac enzyme studies	
cardiac MRI (Magnetic Resource Imaging)	
cardiac scan	
cardiac tamponade [tăm-pō-NĀD]	
cardiomyopathy [KĂR-dē-ō-mī-ŎP-ă-thē] {cardiomiopatía}	
cardiopulmonary [KĂR-dē-ō-PŬL-mŏ-nār-ē] bypass	
cardiovascular [KĂR-dē-ō-VĂS-kyū-lăr]	
carotid [kă-RŎT-ĭd] artery	
cholesterol [kō-LĔS-tĕr-ōl] {colesterol}	
claudication [klăw-dĭ-KĀ-shŭn] {claudicación}	
coarctation [kō-ărk-TĀ-shŭn] of the aorta	
conduction system	
congenital heart disease	
congestive heart failure	
constriction [kŏn-STRĬK-shŭn] {constricción}	
coronary angioplasty	
coronary [KŌR-ō-nār-ē] artery	
coronary artery disease (CAD)	
coronary bypass surgery	
cyanosis [sī-ă-NŌ-sĭs] {cianosis}	
deep vein thrombosis [thrŏm-BŌ-sĭs]	
depolarization [dē-pō-lă-rĭ-ZĀ-shŭn] {despolarización}	
diastole [dī-ĂS-tō-lē] {diástole}	
digital subtraction angiography	
Doppler [DŎP-lĕr] ultrasound	
drug-eluting stent	

TERM	DEFINITION

ductus arteriosus [DŬK-tŭs ăr-tēr-ē-Ō-sŭs] _____

ductus venosus [věn-Ō-sĭs] _____

dysrhythmia [dĭs-RĬTH-mē-ă] {disritmia} _____

echocardiography [ĕk-ō-kăr-dē-ŎG-ră-fē] {ecocardiografía} _____

ejection fraction _____

electrocardiography [ē-lĕk-trō-kăr-dē-ŎG-ră-fē] _____

embolectomy [ĕm-bō-LĔK-tō-mē] _____

embolus [ĔM-bō-lŭs] {émbolo} _____

endarterectomy [ĕnd-ăr-tēr-ĔK-tō-mē] _____

endocarditis [ĔN-dō-kăr-DĪ-tĭs] {endocarditis} _____

endocardium [ĕn-dō-KĂR-dē-ŭm] {endocardio} _____

endothelium [ĕn-dō-THĒ-lē-ŭm] {endotelio} _____

endovascular surgery _____

epicardium [ĕp-ĭ-KĂR-dē-ŭm] {epicardio} _____

essential hypertension _____

femoral [FĔM-ŏ-răl, FĒ-mŏ-răl] artery _____

fibrillation [fĭ-brĭ-LĀ-shŭn] {fibrilación} _____

flutter {aleteo} _____

foramen ovale [fō-RĀ-měn ō-VĂ-lē] _____

gallop {galope} _____

graft _____

heart [hărt] {corazón} _____

heart block _____

heart transplant _____

hemangi(o) _____

hemorrhoidectomy [HĔM-ō-rŏy-DĔK-tō-mē] {hemorroidectomía} _____

hemorrhoids [HĔM-ō-rŏydz] {hemorroides} _____

TERM	DEFINITION
high blood pressure {presión arterial alta}	_____
Holter [HŌL-tĕr] monitor	_____
hypertension [HĪ-pĕr-TĔN-shŭn] {hipertensión}	_____
hypertensive heart disease	_____
hypotension [HĪ-pō-TĔN-shŭn] {hipotensión}	_____
infarct [ĬN-fărkt] {infarto}	_____
infarction [ĭn-FĂRK-shŭn] {infarto}	_____
inferior vena cava [VĒ-nă KĂ-vă, KĀ-vă]	_____
intermittent claudication	_____
intracardiac [ĭn-tră-KĂR-dē-ăk] tumor	_____
intravascular stent	_____
ischemia [ĭs-KĒ-mē-ă] {isquemia}	_____
left atrium	_____
left ventricle	_____
lipid [LĬP-ĭd] profile	_____
low blood pressure {presión arterial baja}	_____
lumen [LŪ-mĕn] {lumen}	_____
mitral [MĪ-trăl] insufficiency or reflux	_____
mitral stenosis	_____
mitral [MĪ-trăl] valve	_____
mitral valve prolapse	_____
multiple-gated acquisition (MUGA) angiography	_____
murmur {soplo}	_____
myocardial infarction (MI)	_____
myocarditis [MĪ-ō-kăr-DĪ-tĭs] {miocarditis}	_____
myocardium [mī-ō-KĂR-dē-ŭm] {miocardio}	_____
necrosis [nĕ-KRŌ-sĭs] {necrosis}	_____
occlusion [ŏ-KLŪ-zhŭn] {oclusión}	_____
pacemaker {marcapaso}	_____

TERM	DEFINITION
palpitations [păl-pĭ-TĀ-shŭnz] {palpitaciones}	
patent ductus arteriosus [PĂ-tĕnt DŬK-tŭs ăr-tēr-ē-Ō-sĭs]	
percutaneous transluminal [pĕr-kyū-TĀ-nē-ŭs trăns-LŪ-mĭn-ăl] coronary angioplasty (PTCA)	
perfusion deficit	
pericardi(o)	
pericarditis [PĔR-ĭ-kăr-DĪ-tĭs] {pericarditis}	
pericardium [pĕr-ĭ-KĂR-dē-ŭm] {pericardio}	
peripheral vascular disease	
petechiae (sing., petechia) [pĕ-TĒ-kē-ē, pĕ-TĔK-ē-ē (pĕ-TĒ-kē-ă, pĕ-TĔK-ē-ă)] {petequia}	
phleb(o)	
phlebitis [flĕ-BĪ-tĭs] {flebitis}	
phlebography [flĕ-BŎG-ră-fē] {flebografía}	
phlebotomy [flĕ-BŎT-ō-mē] {flebotomía}	
plaque [plăk] {placa}	
polarization [pō-lăr-ĭ-ZĀ-shŭn] {polarización}	
popliteal [pŏp-LĬT-ē-ăl] artery	
positron emission tomography [tō-MŎG-ră-fē] (PET) scan	
premature atrial contractions (PACs)	
premature ventricular contractions (PVCs)	
pulmonary [PŬL-mō-nār-ē] artery {arteria pulmonar}	
pulmonary artery stenosis	
pulmonary edema	
pulmonary valve	
pulmonary vein	
pulse [pŭls] {pulso}	

TERM	DEFINITION
Raynaud's [rā-NŌZ] phenomenon	_____
repolarization [rē-pō-lăr-ĭ-ZĀ-shŭn] {repolarización}	_____
rheumatic heart disease	_____
right atrium	_____
right ventricle	_____
risk factor	_____
rub {roce}	_____
saphenous [să-FĒ-nŭs] vein	_____
secondary hypertension	_____
semilunar [sĕm-ē-LŪ-năr] valve	_____
septal defect	_____
septum (pl., septa) [SĔP-tŭm (SĔP-tă)] {tabique}	_____
serum enzyme tests	_____
sinoatrial [sī-nō-Ā-trē-ăl] node (SA node)	_____
sinus rhythm	_____
sonography [sō-NŎG-ră-fē] {sonografía}	_____
sphygm(o)	_____
sphygmomanometer [SFĬG-mō-mă-NŎM-ĕ-tĕr] {esfigmomanómetro}	_____
stenosis [stĕ-NŌ-sĭs] {estenosis}	_____
stent [stĕnt]	_____
stress test	_____
superior vena cava	_____
systole [SĬS-tō-lē] {sístole}	_____
tachycardia [TĂK-ĭ-KĂR-dē-ă] {taquicardia}	_____
tetralogy of Fallot [fă-LŌ]	_____
thromb(o)	_____
thrombectomy [thrŏm-BĔK-tō-mē] {trombectomia}	_____
thrombophlebitis [THRŎM-bō-flĕ-BĪ-tĭs] {tromboflebitis}	_____
thrombosis [thrŏm-BŌ-sĭs] {trombosis}	_____
thrombotic [thrŏm-BŎT-ĭk] occlusion	_____

TERM	DEFINITION
thrombus [THRŎM-bŭs] {trombo}	
tricuspid [trī-KŬS-pĭd] stenosis	
tricuspid valve	
triglyceride [trī-GLĬS-ĕr-īd] {triglicérido}	
valve [vălv] {válvula}	
valve replacement	
valvotomy [văl-VŎT-ō-mē]	
valvulitis [văl-vyū-LĪ-tĭs] {valvulitis}	
valvuloplasty [VĂL-vyū-lō-PLĂS-tē] {valvuloplastia}	
varicose [VĂR-ĭ-kōs] vein	
vas(o)	
vegetation [vĕj-ĕ-TĀ-shŭn] {vegetación}	
vein [vān] {vena}	
ven(o)	
venipuncture [VĚN-ĭ-pŭnk-chŭr, VĒ-nĭ-PŬNK-chŭr] {venipuntura}	
venography [vē-NŎG-ră-fē] {venografía}	
ventricle [VĚN-trĭ-kl] {ventrículo}	
ventriculogram [vĕn-TRĬK-yū-lō-grăm]	
venule [VĚN-yūl, VĒ-nŭl] {vénula}	

Answers to Chapter Exercises

1. overweight, sedentary, smoker
2. no
3. atrioventricular
4. capillary
5. C
6. Purkinje fibers
7. C
8. arteriole
9. C
10. C
11. systole
12. artery
13. veins
14. endocardium
15. atria and ventricles
16. blood
17. poor diet, smoking, and lack of exercise
18. pulmonary
19. endothelium
20. heart and lungs
21. carotid artery
22. lungs
23. cardiomyopathy
24. pericarditis
25. venogram
26. phlebitis
27. arterioplasty
28. vasoneuropathy
29. vasotropic or angiotropic
30. cardiogenic
31. cardiomegaly

32. thromboarteritis
33. Skin color and disorientation
34. 8 hours
35. phlebitis
36. thrombectomy
37. phleboplasty, venoplasty
38. atriomegaly
39. phlebograph, venograph
40. cardiomegaly
41. cardiopulmonary
42. pericardiostomy
43. endocarditis
44. phleboplasty, venoplasty
45. vasoparalysis
46. angiorrhaphy
47. phlebitis
48. arteries
49. vein
50. arteriotomy
51. heart
52. yes
53. cholesterol
54. arteriosclerosis
55. exercise thallium test, sodium, potassium, CO2, chloride, creatinine, BUN, cholesterol, trigliycerides, HDL, LDL, CPK,
56. 82803
57. 414.0
58. A
59. D
60. B

61. C
62. tachycardia, bradycardia
63. arrhythmia, dysrhythmia
64. thrombus
65. bruit
66. murmur
67. hypertension
68. risk factors
69. myocardial infarction
70. dietary changes, quit smoking, exercise program, stress reduction
71. depends on individual, but maintaining a healthy lifestyle will help prevent heart disease
72. surgical connection of two blood vessels
73. repair of a cardiac valve
74. incision into a cardiac valve to remove an obstruction
75. surgical removal of an embolus
76. opening of a blocked blood vessel, as by balloon dilation
77. thrombectomy
78. C
79. arteriotomy
80. angioscopy
81. C
82. valvotomy
83. venipuncture
84. C
85. coronary

7

The Respiratory System

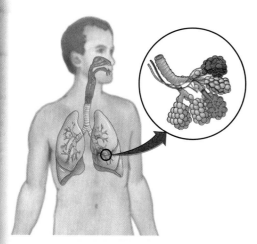

After studying this chapter, you will be able to:

▶ Name the parts of the respiratory system and discuss the function of each part

▶ Define combining forms used in building words that relate to the respiratory system and its parts

▶ Name the common diagnoses, clinical procedures, and laboratory tests used in treating disorders of the respiratory system

▶ List and define the major pathological conditions of the respiratory system

▶ Explain the meaning of surgical terms related to the respiratory system

Structure and Function

The **respiratory system** is the body's breathing, or *respiration*, system. It involves the exchange of oxygen and waste gases between the atmosphere and the body and its cells. **External respiration** is breathing or exchanging air between the body and the outside environment. **Internal respiration** is the bringing of oxygen to the cells and removing carbon dioxide from them.

The respiratory system includes the **respiratory tract** (passageways through which air moves in and out of the lungs), the **lungs**, and the muscles that move air into and out of the lungs (Figures 7-1a and 7-1b).

The Respiratory Tract

The respiratory tract is also known as the *airway*, the route through which air enters the lungs and the route via which air exits the body. **Inspiration** (breathing in or **inhalation**) brings air from the outside environment into the **nose** or mouth. During **exhalation** or **expiration**, air is expelled from the lungs back through the respiratory tract into the environment. Table 7-1 lists the terms related to the respiratory tract.

Once air enters the airway and lungs, the **bronchi** further divide into many smaller branches called **bronchioles**. Inside the lungs, the structures resemble tree branches, with smaller parts branching off. At the end of each bronchiole is a cluster of air sacs. Each air sac is called an **alveolus**

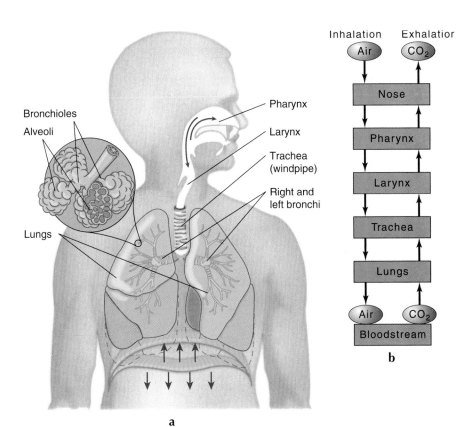

Inhalation · Air
Exhalation · CO₂

Nose → Pharynx → Larynx → Trachea → Lungs

Air · CO₂

Bloodstream

b

a

Bronchioles
Alveoli
Lungs

Pharynx
Larynx
Trachea (windpipe)
Right and left bronchi

FIGURE 7-1 (a) The respiratory system performs the process of inhaling air and exhaling carbon dioxide. (b) The diagram shows the pathways of inhaled air (containing oxygen) and exhaled air (containing carbon dioxide).

The Science Museum of Minnesota (www.smm.org/sound/activity/ssl14.htm) has a simple experiment to show you how vocal cords work as well as a video of vocal cords in action.

TABLE 7-1 Terms of the respiratory tract.

Term	Description	Function
nostrils or **external nares**	external openings at the base of the nose	
nasal septum	strip of cartilage that divides the nose into two halves	
nasal cavity	cavity into which air enters and exits through the nose	
paranasal sinuses	sinuses where outside air is warmed	
cilia	hairs in the nasal cavity	filter out foreign bodies
pharynx (throat)	passageway for both air and food	
nasopharynx	part of the pharynx	contains the **pharyngeal tonsils** or **adenoids**
soft palate	muscular sheet that separate parts of the pharynx	
oropharynx	back part of the mouth	contains the **palatine tonsils**
laryngopharynx or **hypopharynx**	bottom section of the pharynx	divides the respiratory tract into the esophagus (for the passage of food) and the passageway for air
larynx or **voice box**	passageway for air	

TABLE 7-1 Terms of the respiratory tract (*cont.*).

Term	Description	Function
epiglottis	flap of cartilage covering the opening of the larynx (called the **glottis**)	prevents food from going into the larynx
vocal cords (Figure 7-3)	strip of tissue that vibrate	produce sound
thyroid cartilage or **Adam's apple**	cartilaginous structure	supports the larynx
trachea or **windpipe**	passageway for air	
bronchi (*sing.*, **bronchus**)	two tubes that connect the trachea to the lungs and through which air flows	
mediastinum	point of division at which trachea divides into the bronchi	

FIGURE 7-2   The abdominal thrust maneuver is taught in CPR classes.

At the Heimlich Institute's Web site (www.heimlichinstitute.org), you can learn more about saving people and even pets who have something blocking their airway.

MORE ABOUT...

Aspiration

Occasionally, food or saliva can be aspirated by inhaling, laughing, or talking with food, gum, or fluid in the mouth. An unconscious person who is lying on his or her back may aspirate some saliva or possibly blood as in a trauma. The body's automatic response to aspiration is violent coughing or choking in an attempt to expel the material. If total obstruction occurs, then the abdominal thrust maneuver (also known as the Heimlich maneuver and shown in Figure 7-2) must be used.

(plural, **alveoli**). There are about 300 million alveoli in the lungs. The one-celled, thin-walled alveoli are surrounded by capillaries, with which they exchange gases.

The Structure of the Lungs

The lungs (Figure 7-4) take up most of the thoracic cavity (or **thorax**), reaching from the collarbone to the diaphragm. Table 7-2 lists the parts of the lungs.

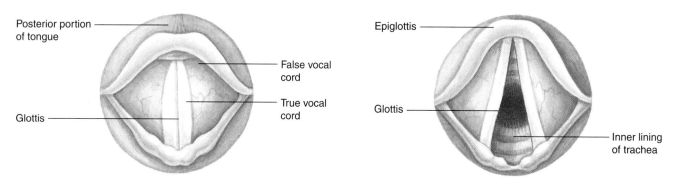

FIGURE 7-3   Vocal cords are the primary instruments of sound. The drawing on the left shows the position of the vocal cords when the voice is high in pitch and the picture on the right illustrates the vocal cords when the voice is low in pitch.

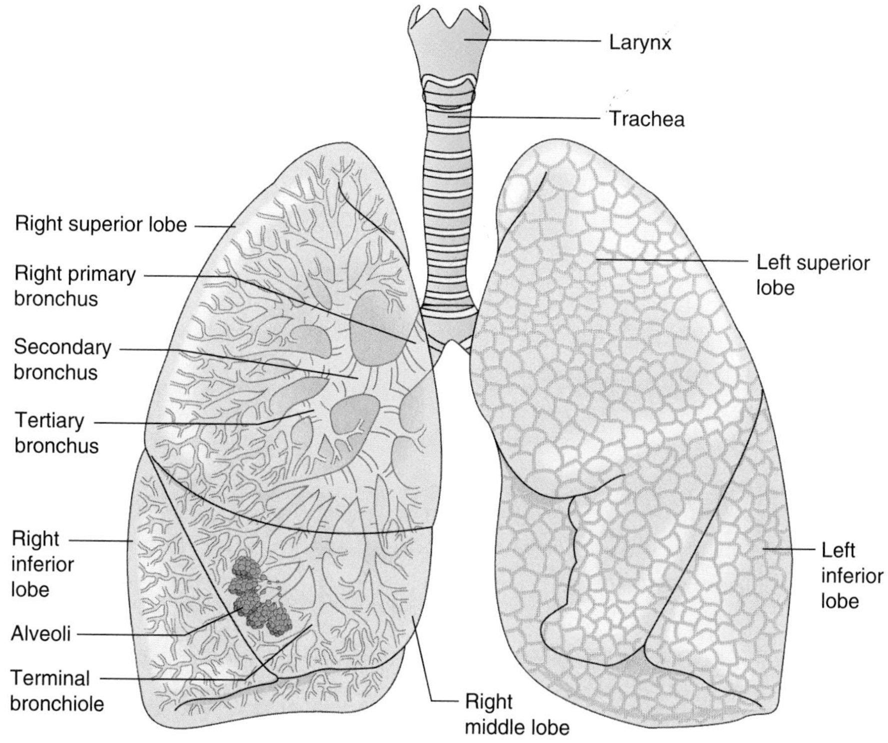

FIGURE 7-4 The alveoli are at the end of the terminal bronchioles inside the lungs. The lungs have three lobes on the right and two on the left.

Labels on figure: Larynx, Trachea, Right superior lobe, Right primary bronchus, Secondary bronchus, Tertiary bronchus, Right inferior lobe, Alveoli, Terminal bronchiole, Right middle lobe, Left superior lobe, Left inferior lobe

TABLE 7-2 Parts of the lungs.

Part	Description	Function
pleura (*pl.*, pleurae)	moist double layer of membrane covering the lungs	protects the lungs
parietal pleura	outer layer of pleura	
visceral pleura	inner layer of pleura	
pleural cavity	space between the parietal pleura and the visceral pleura	filled with fluid that prevents friction
apex	topmost section of lung	
hilum or hilus	middle section of lung	
base	lower section of lung	
superior lobe	one of the three lobes of the right lung and one of the two lobes of the left lung	
middle lobe	one of the three lobes of the right lung	
inferior lobe	one of the three lobes of the right lung and one of the two lobes of the left lung	

Muscles for Breathing

Inhalation and exhalation is accomplished by changing the capacity of the thoracic cavity. The major muscles for changing this capacity are the **diaphragm** and the **intercostal muscles** (the muscles between the ribs).

MORE ABOUT...

Lung Capacity

Normal inspiration brings about 500 milliliters of air into the lungs. Normal expiration expels about the same amount from the lungs. Forced inspiration brings extra air (even up to six times the normal amount) into the lungs. Forced expiration can expel up to three times the normal amount of air from the lungs.

Some quantity of air always remains in the lungs so that newly inhaled air mixes with the remaining air. This helps to maintain the proper concentrations of oxygen and carbon dioxide in the lungs.

VOCABULARY REVIEW

In the previous section, you learned terms relating to the respiratory system. Before going on to the exercises, read the definitions below. Pronunciations are provided for certain terms.

Term	Definition
Adam's apple	Thyroid cartilage, supportive structure of the larynx; larger in males than in females.
adenoids [ĂD-ĕ-nŏydz]	Collection of lymphoid tissue in the nasopharynx; pharyngeal tonsils.
alveolus (*pl.*, alveoli) [ăl-VĒ-ō-lŭs (ăl-VĒ-ō-lī)]	Air sac at the end of each bronchiole.
apex [Ā-pĕks]	Topmost section of the lung.
base [bās]	Bottom section of the lung.
bronchiole [BRŎNG-ē-ōl]	Fine subdivision of the bronchi made of smooth muscle and elastic fibers.
bronchus (*pl.*, bronchi) [BRŎNG-kŭs (BRŎNG-kī)]	One of the two airways from the trachea to the lungs.
cilia [SĬL-ē-ă]	Hairlike extensions of a cell's surface that usually provide some protection by sweeping foreign particles away.
diaphragm [DĪ-ă-frăm]	Membranous muscle between the abdominal and thoracic cavities that contracts and relaxes during the respiratory cycle
epiglottis [ĔP-ĭ-GLŎT-ĭs]	Cartilaginous flap that covers the larynx during swallowing to prevent food from entering the airway.
exhalation [ĕks-hă-LĀ-shŭn]	Breathing out.
expiration [ĕks-pĭ-RĀ-shŭn]	Exhalation.
external nares [NĀR-ēz]	*See* nostrils.
external respiration	Exchange of air between the body and the outside environment.

Term	Definition
glottis [GLŎT-ĭs]	Part of the larynx consisting of the vocal folds of mucous membrane and muscle.
hilum, hilus [HĪ-lŭm, HĪ-lŭs]	Midsection of the lung where the nerves and vessels enter and exit.
hypopharynx [HĪ-pō-FĂR-ĭngks]	Laryngopharynx.
inferior lobe [ĭn-FĒ-rē-ōr lōb]	Bottom lobe of the lung.
inhalation [ĭn-hă-LĀ-shŭn]	Breathing in.
inspiration [ĭn-spĭ-RĀ-shŭn]	Inhalation.
intercostal muscles [ĭn-tĕr-KŎS-tăl MŬS-ĕlz]	Muscles between the ribs.
internal respiration	Exchange of oxygen and carbon dioxide between the cells.
laryngopharynx [lă-RĬNG-gō-făr-ĭngks]	Part of the pharynx below and behind the larynx.
larynx [LĂR-ĭngks]	Organ of voice production in the respiratory tract, between the pharynx and the trachea; voice box.
lung [lŭng]	One of two organs of respiration (left lung and right lung) in the thoracic cavity, where oxygenation of blood takes place.
mediastinum [MĒ-dē-ăs-TĪ-nŭm]	Median portion of the thoracic cavity; septum between two areas of an organ or cavity.
middle lobe	Middle section of the right lung.
nasal cavity [NĀ-zăl KĂV-ĭ-tē]	Opening in the external nose where air enters the body.
nasal septum [SĔP-tŭm]	Cartilaginous division of the external nose.
nasopharynx [NĀ-zō-FĂR-ĭngks]	Portion of the throat above the soft palate.
nose [nōz]	External structure supported by nasal bones and containing nasal cavity.
nostrils [NŎS-trĭlz]	External openings at the base of the nose; also called external nares.
oropharynx [ŌR-ō-FĂR-ĭngks]	Back portion of the mouth, a division of the pharynx.
palatine tonsils [PĂL-ă-tĭn TŎN-sĭlz]	Lymphatic tissue that works as part of the immune system.
paranasal sinuses [păr-ă-NĀ-săl SĪ-nŭs-ĕz]	Area of the nasal cavity where external air is warmed by blood in the mucous membrane lining.
parietal pleura [pă-RĪ-ĕ-tăl PLŪR-ă]	Outer layer of the pleura.
pharyngeal tonsils [fă-RĬN-jē-ăl TŎN-sĭlz]	Adenoids.
pharynx [FĂR-ĭngks]	Passageway at back of mouth for air and food; throat.

Term	Definition
pleura (*pl.*, **pleurae**) [PLŪR-ă (PLŪR-ē)]	Double layer of membrane making up the outside of the lungs.
pleural cavity [PLŪR-ăl KĂV-ĭ-tē]	Space between the two pleura.
respiratory [RĔS-pĭ-ră-tōr-ē, rĕ-SPĪR-ă-tōr-ē] **system**	The body's system for breathing.
respiratory tract	Passageways through which air moves into and out of the lungs.
septum [SĔP-tŭm]	Cartilaginous division, as in the nose.
soft palate [sŏft PĂL-ăt]	Flexible muscular sheet that separates the nasopharynx from the rest of the pharynx.
superior lobe	Topmost lobe of each lung.
thorax [THŌ-răks]	Chest cavity.
throat [thrōt]	*See* pharynx.
thyroid cartilage [THĪ-rŏyd KĂR-tĭ-lĭj]	*See* Adam's apple.
trachea [TRĀ-kē-ă]	Airway from the larynx into the bronchi; windpipe.
visceral pleura [VĬS-ĕr-ăl PLŪR-ă]	Inner layer of the pleura.
vocal cords	Strips of epithelial tissue that vibrate and play a major role in the production of sound.
voice box	*See* larynx.
windpipe	*See* trachea.

CASE STUDY

Breathing Emergencies

The emergency department at Midvale Central Hospital often sees patients who complain of breathing problems. The physicians on duty are trained to listen to sounds with a stethoscope to determine the immediate needs of the patient. Many of the patients at Midvale are elderly. Respiratory problems are the number-one reason for seeking emergency help.

Critical Thinking

1. How might an elderly person's weakened muscles affect respiration?

2. Midvale is a retirement community in the South. About six times a year, the state department of environmental protection issues pollution or smog warnings, with suggestions that children, the elderly, and those with chronic illnesses stay indoors, preferably with air conditioning. Polluted air diminishes what gas necessary for respiration?

STRUCTURE AND FUNCTION EXERCISES

Complete the Picture

3. Label the parts of the respiratory system on the following diagram.

   a. _____

   b. _____

   c. _____

Bronchioles

c. _____

Pharynx

Larynx

a. _____

Right and left bronchi

b. _____

Check Your Knowledge

Complete the sentences below by filling in the blanks.

4. Exchanging air between the body and the outside environment is called _____ _____.

5. Foreign bodies entering the respiratory tract are filtered through _____.

6. The nose is divided into two halves by the _____ _____.

7. Food is prevented from going into the larynx by the _____.

8. A simple technique that has saved many people from death is the _____ _____ _____.

9. At the end of each bronchiole is a small cluster of _____ _____ called _____.

10. The right lung has _____ lobes.

11. The left lung has _____ lobes.

12. The muscle that lowers itself to allow more space when one is breathing in is called the _____.

13. The muscles between the ribs that also aid in breathing are called _____ muscles.

Circle T for true or F for false.

14. The respiratory tract is the major area involved in internal respiration. T F

15. The throat is a passageway for both air and food. T F

16. The pharynx contains the vocal cords. T F

17. Each bronchus enters one lung. T F

18. The pleura are moist layers of membrane surrounding the lungs. T F

19. Humans must have both lungs to live. T F

20. Only the right lung has a middle lobe. T F

21. The hilum is the topmost portion of the lung. T F

22. The larynx is another name for the windpipe. T F

23. The soft palate is at the bottom of the mouth. T F

Spell It Correctly

Write the correct spelling in the blank to the right of any misspelled words. If the word is already correctly spelled, write C.

24. nasopharyngx _____

25. trachae _____

26. resperation _____

27. alveoli _____

28. diagphram _____

29. epiglottus _____

30. pharinx _____

31. mediastinum _____

32. tonsills _____

33. bronchis _____

Combining Forms

The list below includes combining forms that relate specifically to the respiratory system. Pronunciations are provided for the examples.

COMBINING FORM	MEANING	EXAMPLE
adenoid(o)	adenoid, gland	*adenoidectomy* [ĂD-ĕ-nŏy-DĔK-tō-mē], operation for removal of adenoid growths
alveol(o)	alveolus	*alveolitis* [ĂL-vē-ō-ō-LĪ-tĭs], inflammation of the alveoli
bronch(o), bronchi(o)	bronchus	*bronchitis* [brŏng-KĪ-tĭs], inflammation of the lining of the bronchial tubes
bronchiol(o)	bronchiole	*bronchiolitis* [brŏng-kē-ō-ō-LĪ-tĭs], inflammation of the bronchioles
capn(o)	carbon dioxide	*capnogram* [KĂP-nō-grăm], a continuous recording of the carbon dioxide in expired air
epiglott(o)	epiglottis	*epiglottitis* [ĔP-ĭ-GLŎT-ī-tĭs], inflammation of the epiglottis
laryng(o)	larynx	*laryngoscope* [lă-RĬNG-gō-skōp], device used to examine the larynx through the mouth
lob(o)	lobe of the lung	*lobectomy* [lō-BĔK-tō-mē], removal of a lobe
mediastin(o)	mediastinum	*mediastinitis* [MĒ-dē-ăs-tī-NĪ-tĭs], inflammation of the tissue of the mediastinum
nas(o)	nose	*nasogastric* [nā-zō-GĂS-tĭk], of the nasal passages and the stomach
or(o)	mouth	*oropharynx* [ŌR-ō-FĂR-ĭngks], the part of the pharynx that lies behind the mouth
ox(o), oxi-, oxy	oxygen	*oximeter* [ŏk-SĬM-ĕ-tĕr], instrument for measuring oxygen saturation of blood

Combining Form	Meaning	Example
pharyng(o)	pharynx	*pharyngitis* [făr-ĭn-JĪ-tĭs], inflammation in the pharynx
phon(o)	voice, sound	*phonometer* [fō-NŎM-ĕ-tĕr], instrument for measuring sounds
phren(o)	diaphragm	*phrenitis* [frĕn-Ī-tĭs], inflammation in the diaphragm
pleur(o)	pleura	*pleuritis* [plū-RĪ-tĭs], inflammation of the pleura
pneum(o), pneumon(o)	air, lung	*pneumolith* [NŪ-mō-lĭth], calculus in the lungs; *pneumonitis* [nū-mō-NĪ-tĭs], inflammation of the lungs
rhin(o)	nose	*rhinitis* [rī-NĪ-tĭs], inflammation of the nose
spir(o)	breathing	*spirometer* [spī-RŎM-ĕ-tĕr], instrument used to measure respiratory gases
steth(o)	chest	*stethoscope* [STĔTH-ō-skōp], instrument for listening to sounds in the chest
thorac(o)	thorax, chest	*thoracotomy* [thōr-ă-KŎT-ō-mē], incision into the chest wall
tonsill(o)	tonsils	*tonsillectomy* [TŎN-sĭ-LĔK-tō-mē], removal of one entire tonsil or of both tonsils
trache(o)	trachea	*tracheoscopy* [trā-kē-ŎS-kō-pē], inspection of the interior of the trachea

CASE STUDY

Coping with COPD

The emergency room nurse admitted Mr. DiGiorno, a patient from a nursing home. He was having difficulty breathing and complained of chest pains. The nurse checked his record and found that he has been positive for chronic obstructive pulmonary disorder (COPD) for five years. This patient has had four hospital admissions in the last six months. He is overweight, smokes, and is sedentary. He takes medications for his COPD.

Critical Thinking

34. What lifestyle factors might play a role in Mr. DiGiorno's disease?
35. Mr. DiGiorno's chest pains may indicate cardiovascular disease. How might this affect internal respiration?

COMBINING FORMS EXERCISES

Build Your Medical Vocabulary

Complete the words by putting a combining form in the blank.

36. Removal of the adenoids: _____ ectomy.

37. Surgical puncture of the thoracic cavity: _____centesis.

38. Opening into the trachea: _____otomy.

39. Inflammation of the tonsils: _____tis.

40. Inflammation of the pericardium and surrounding mediastinal tissue: _____pericarditis.

41. Suture of the lung: _____rrhaphy.

42. Relating to the nose and mouth: _____nasal.

43. Inflammation of the pharynx: _____itis.

44. Disease of the vocal cords affecting speech: _____pathy.

45. Instrument that measures carbon dioxide in expired air: _____meter.

46. Bronchial inflammation: _____itis.

47. Inflammation of tissue surrounding the bronchi: peri_____itis.

48. Relating to the pericardium and pleural cavity: pericardio_____.

49. Incision into a lobe: _____otomy.

50. Measurement of oxygen in blood: _____metry.

51. Compound of oxygen and a chloride: _____chloride.

52. Swelling in the bronchial area: _____edema.

53. Destruction of an alveolus: _____clasia.

54. Chest pain: _____algia.

55. Incision into the throat: _____tomy.

Match the Root

Match the respiratory combining forms in the list on the right with the definitions in the list on the left.

56. _____ pain arising in air sacs in the lungs   a. broncho

57. _____ instrument to study vocal folds   b. capno

58. _____ record of heart sounds   c. lob

59. _____ nasal obstruction   d. alveol(o)

60. _____ contraction of the bronchus   e. pharyngo

61. _____ abnormally dilated windpipe   f. laryngo

62. _____ repair of the pharynx   g. phono

63. _____ fissure of the chest wall   h. thoraco

64. _____ inflammation of a lobe   i. rhino

65. _____ instrument for graphing carbon dioxide   j. tracheo

Diagnostic, Procedural, and Laboratory Terms

Disorders of the respiratory system can be diagnosed in several ways. First, a physician usually listens to the lungs with a stethoscope, a process called **auscultation.** Next, the respiratory rate is determined by counting the number of respirations per minute. The physician may use **percussion**, tapping over the lung area.

Pulmonary function tests measure the mechanics of breathing. Breathing may be tested by a **peak flow meter** (Figure 7-5). A **spirometer** is a pulmonary function testing machine.

Visual images of the chest and parts of the respiratory system play an important role in diagnosing respiratory ailments. Chest x-rays, MRIs, and lung scans can detect abnormalities, such as masses and restricted blood flow within the lungs. A **bronchography** provides a radiological picture of the trachea and bronchi.

Parts of the respiratory system can also be observed by *endoscopy,* insertion of an **endoscope** (a viewing tube) into a body cavity. A **bronchoscope** is used for *bronchoscopy,* which is performed to examine airways or retrieve specimens, such as fluid retrieved in **bronchial alveolar lavage** or material for biopsy that is retrieved by **bronchial brushing** (a brush inserted through the bronchoscope). In **nasopharyngoscopy,** a flexible endoscope is used to examine nasal passages and the pharynx. **Laryngoscopy** is the procedure for examining the mouth and larynx, and **mediastinoscopy** for examining the mediastinum area and all the organs within it.

FIGURE 7-5   Peak flow meter.

Laboratory Tests

Throat cultures are commonly used to diagnose streptococcal infections. A **sputum sample** or **culture** may be taken and cultured to identify any disease-causing organisms. **Arterial blood gases (ABGs)** measure the levels of pressure of oxygen (O_2) and carbon dioxide (CO_2) in arterial blood. A **sweat test** measures the amount of salt in sweat and is used to confirm cystic fibrosis.

The FDA has a "Bad Bug Book" on one of its Web sites (http://vm.cfsan. fda.gov/~mow/intro.html) where you can learn more about streptococcal infections.

MORE ABOUT...

Streptococcal Infections

Throat cultures are commonly given to children with sore throats. The presence of a streptococcal infection is usually treated with antibiotics because the presence of such an infection can cause health problems (such as heart and kidney damage) if left unchecked.

VOCABULARY REVIEW

In the previous section, you learned terms relating to diagnosis, clinical procedures, and laboratory tests. Before going on to the exercises, read the definitions below. Pronunciations are provided for certain terms.

Term	Definition
arterial [ăr-TĒR-ē-ăl] blood gases (ABGs)	Laboratory test that measures the levels of oxygen and carbon dioxide in arterial blood.
auscultation [ăws-kŭl-TĀ-shŭn]	Listening to internal sounds with a stethoscope.

Term	Definition
bronchial alveolar lavage [BRŎNG-kē-ăl ăl-VĒ-ō-lăr lă-VĂZH]	Retrieval of fluid for examination through a bronchoscope.
bronchial brushing	Retrieval of material for biopsy by insertion of a brush through a bronchoscope.
bronchography [brŏng-KŎG-ră-fē] broncho- + -graphy	Radiological picture of the trachea and bronchi.
bronchoscope [BRŎNG-kō-skōp] broncho- + -scope	Device used to examine airways.
endoscope [ĔN-dō-skōp] endo- + -scope	Tube used to view a body cavity.
laryngoscopy [LĂR-ĭng-GŎS-kō-pē] laryngo- + -scopy	Visual examination of the mouth and larynx using an endoscope.
mediastinoscopy [MĒ-dē-ăs-tĭ-NŎS-kō-pē] mediastino- + -scopy	Visual examination of the mediastinum and all the organs within it using an endoscope.
nasopharyngoscopy [NĀ-zō-fă-rĭng-GŎS-kō-pē] naso- + pharyngo- + -scopy	Examination of the nasal passages and the pharynx using an endoscope.
peak flow meter	Device for measuring breathing capacity.
percussion [pĕr-KŬSH-ŭn]	Tapping on the surface of the body to see if lungs are clear.
pulmonary function tests	Tests that measure the mechanics of breathing.
spirometer [spī-RŎM-ĕ-tĕr] spiro- + -meter	Testing machine that measures the lungs' volume and capacity.
sputum [SPŪ-tŭm] **sample** or **culture**	Culture of material that is expectorated (brought back up as mucus).
sweat test	Test for cystic fibrosis that measures the amount of salt in sweat.
throat culture	Test for streptococcal or other infections in which a swab taken on the surface of the throat is placed in a culture to see if certain bacteria grow.

DIAGNOSTIC, PROCEDURAL, AND LABORATORY TERMS EXERCISES

Check Your Knowledge

Complete the sentences below by filling in the blanks.

66. The mechanics of breathing are measured by _____ _____ tests.

67. A test that can confirm the presence of cystic fibrosis is called a(n) _____ _____.

68. A tube for viewing a body cavity is called a(n) _____.

69. An instrument for viewing a body cavity is a(n) _____.

70. A stethoscope is necessary for _____, listening to the lungs.

71. Streptococcal infections can be detected in a _____ _____.

72. Tapping the skin over the lung area to check whether the lungs are clear is called _____.

73. Asthmatics often use a _____ _____ _____ to check breathing capacity.

74. Disease-causing organisms in sputum can be identified in a(n) _____ _____.

75. A device that measures the lung volume and capacity is called a(n) _____.

Root Out the Meaning

Add the appropriate combining form from the list in this chapter.

76. _____ scopy means viewing of the pharynx.

77. _____ gram means a record of carbon dioxide in expired air.

78. _____ ectomy means removal of the larynx.

79. _____ itis means inflammation of a lobe.

80. _____ plegia means paralysis of the larynx.

CASE STUDY

Laboratory Testing

Mr. DiGiorno was admitted to Midvale Hospital from the emergency room. His radiological/laboratory data read as follows:

A chest x-ray showed a pneumonic infiltrate in the left lower lobe with some parapneumonic effusion. Follow-up chest x-rays showed progression of infiltrate and then slight clearing. Serial ECGs (ECGs given one after another in succession) showed the development of T-wave inversions anterolaterally compatible with ischemia or a pericardial process. The WBC was 10,000; HCT, 37; platelets, 425,000; PT and PTT were normal. Blood gases showed a pH of 7.43, PCO_2 37, PO_2 71. Sputum culture could not be obtained.

Critical Thinking

81. Why do you think blood gas tests were ordered for Mr. DiGiorno?

82. What part of his blood measured 10,000?

Pathological Terms

The respiratory system is the site for many inflammations, disorders, and infections.

Normal breathing (**eupnea**) may become affected by diseases or conditions and change to one of the following breathing difficulties:

- **Bradypnea**, slow breathing
- **Tachypnea**, fast breathing
- **Hypopnea**, shallow breathing
- **Hyperpnea**, abnormally deep breathing
- **Dyspnea**, difficult breathing

MORE ABOUT...

SARS

SARS first appeared in Asia in 2003 and was fairly quickly contained by a worldwide cooperative response. Travel to and from countries where SARS first appeared was either restricted or people were checked before and after travel. In general, people with the disease were quarantined. SARS begins with a high fever (temperature greater than 100.4°F [> 38.0°C]). Other symptoms may include headache and body aches. After 2 to 7 days, SARS patients may develop a dry cough. Most patients develop pneumonia. It is hoped that a vaccine can be developed before the next outbreak.

The American Academy of Allergy, Asthma, and Immunology (www.aaaai. org) has up-to-date information about asthma.

Normal bronchiole

Asthmatic bronchiole, showing constriction

FIGURE 7-6 Asthma causes a narrowing of the bronchi.

- **Apnea,** absence of breathing
- **Orthopnea,** difficulty in breathing, especially while lying down.

Other irregular breathing patterns may indicate various conditions. Table 7-3 give some irregular breathing patterns and what they may indicate.

Upper respiratory infection is a term that covers an infection of some or all of the upper respiratory tract. There are many infections, disorders, and conditions that occur or affect the respiratory tract. Table 7-4 lists some of them.

Chronic obstructive pulmonary disease (COPD) is a term for any disease with chronic obstruction of the bronchial tubes and lungs. Chronic bronchitis and emphysema are two COPD disease processes. In addition to bronchitis, the bronchial tubes can be the site of **asthma** bronchial airway obstruction (Figure 7-6), causing an irritable airway. **Paroxysmal** (sudden spasmodic) movement of the airway can occur in asthma as well as in other respiratory conditions. **Hemoptysis** is a lung or bronchial hemorrhage that results in the spitting of blood. **Cystic fibrosis** is a chronic airway obstruction caused by disease of the exocrine glands.

TABLE 7-3 Irregular breathing patterns.

Breathing Pattern	Characteristics	Indications
Cheynes-Stokes respiration	irregular breathing with periods of apnea	heart failure
crackles or rales	popping sounds	lung collapse and other disorders
wheezes or ronchi	frictional breathing sounds	asthma or emphysema
stridor	high-pitched crowing sound	airway obstruction; infection
dysphonia	hoarseness	laryngitis
singultus	hiccupping	
hyperventilation	excessive breathing in and out	anxiety or overexertion
hypoventilation	abnormally low movement of air in and out	may cause **hypercapnia,** excessive carbon dioxide in the lungs
hypoxemia	deficient oxygen in the blood	
hypoxia	deficient oxygen in tissue	

TABLE 7-4 Infections, disorders, and conditions of the respiratory tract.

Infection, disorder, condition	Description	Characteristics or Cause
croup	acute respiratory syndrome in infants and children	
diphtheria	acute bacterial infection of the throat and upper respiratory tract	
severe acute respiratory distress (SARS)	contagious viral disease	
nosebleed or epistaxis	rupture of blood vessels in the nose causing bleeding	trauma or spontaneous occurrence
rhinorrhea	nasal discharge	infection or inflammation
whooping cough or pertussis	severe bacterial infection of the pharynx, larynx, and trachea	spasmodic coughing with a whooping sound
adenoiditis	inflammation of the adenoids	
bronchitis/chronic bronchitis	inflammation of the bronchi/ chronic inflammation of the bronchi	
laryngitis	inflammation of the larynx	
epiglottitis	inflammation of the epiglottis	infection or trauma
pharyngitis (sore throat)	inflammation of the throat	
pleuritis or pleurisy	inflammation of the pleura	
pneumonitis	inflammation of the lung	
rhinitis	inflammation of the nose	
sinusitis	inflammation of the sinuses	
tonsillitis	inflammation of the tonsils	
tracheitis	inflammation of the trachea	

Carcinomas, frequently caused by smoking, can also be found in the respiratory system. Lung cancer is one of the leading causes of death in the United States.

Lung disorders may occur in the alveoli: for example, **atelectasis**, a collapsed lung or part of a lung; **emphysema**, hyperinflation of the air sacs often caused by smoking; and **pneumonia**, acute infection of the alveoli. Pneumonia is a term for a number of infections. Table 7-5 details several types of pneumonia.

Tuberculosis is a highly infectious disease caused by rod-shaped bacteria **(bacilli)**. A **pulmonary abscess** is a large collection of pus in the lungs, and **pulmonary edema** is a buildup of fluid in the air sacs and bronchioles. Several environmental agents cause **pneumoconiosis**, a lung condition caused by dust in the lungs. **Black lung** or **anthracosis** is caused by coal dust. **Asbestosis** is caused by asbestos particles released during construction. **Silicosis** is caused by the silica dust from grinding rocks or glass.

Learn about the risks of lung cancer by going to the Web site www.lungcancer.org.

The Centers for Diseases Control has a Division of Tuberculosis Elimation that maintains a Web site (www.cdc.gov/nchstp/tb/) with information about control of this disease.

TABLE 7-5 Some types of pneumonia.

Type of Pneumonia	Location	Cause
bacterial pneumonia	lungs	usually streptococcus bacteria
bronchial pneumonia, bronchopneumonia	walls of the smaller bronchial tubes	may be postoperative or from tuberculosis
chronic pneumonia	lungs	any recurrent inflammation or infection
double pneumonia	both lungs at the same time	bacterial infection
pneumoncystis carinii pneumonia	lungs	usually seen in AIDS patients
viral pneumonia	lungs	caused by viral infection

Disorders of the pleura, other than pleuritis, include **pneumothorax**, an accumulation of air or gas in the pleural cavity; **empyema**, pus in the pleural cavity; **hemothorax**, blood in the pleural cavity; **pleural effusion**, an escape of fluid into the pleural cavity; and, rarely, **mesothelioma**, a cancer associated with asbestosis.

The respiratory system may be disturbed by spasms that cause coughing or constriction. When severe, these spasms can be life-threatening. **Bronchospasms** occur in the bronchi (as seen in asthma), and **laryngospasms** occur in the larynx.

VOCABULARY REVIEW

In the previous section, you learned terms relating to pathology. Before going on to the exercises, read the definitions below. Pronunciations are provided for certain terms.

Term	Definition
adenoiditis [ĂD-ĕ-nŏy-DĪ-tĭs	Inflammation of the adenoids.
anthracosis [ăn-thră-KŌ-sĭs]	Lung disease caused by long-term inhalation of coal dust; black lung disease.
apnea [ĂP-nē-ă]	Cessation of breathing.
asbestosis [ăs-bĕs-TŌ-sĭs]	Lung disorder caused by long-term inhalation of asbestos (as in construction work).
asthma [ĂZ-mă]	Chronic condition with obstruction or narrowing of the bronchial airways.
atelectasis [ăt-ĕ-LĔK-tă-sĭs]	Collapse of a lung or part of a lung.

Term	Definition
bacilli (*sing.*, **bacillus**) [bă-SĬL-ī (bă-SĬL-ĭs)]	A type of bacteria that causes tuberulosis.
black lung	*See* anthracosis.
bradypnea [brăd-ĭp-NĒ-ă]	Abnormally slow breathing.
bronchitis [brŏng-KĪ-tĭs]	Inflammation of the bronchi.
bronchospasm [BRŎNG-kō-spăzm]	Sudden contraction in the bronchi that causes coughing.
Cheyne-Stokes respiration [chān stōks rĕs-pĭ-RĀ-shŭn]	Irregular breathing pattern with a period of apnea followed by deep, labored breathing that becomes shallow, then apneic.
chronic bronchitis	Recurring or long-lasting bouts of bronchitis.
chronic obstructive pulmonary disease (COPD)	Disease of the bronchial tubes or lungs with chronic obstruction.
crackles [KRĂK-ls]	Popping sounds heard in lung collapse or other conditions; rales.
croup [krūp]	Acute respiratory syndrome in children or infants accompanied by seal-like coughing.
cystic fibrosis [SĬS-tĭk fī-BRŌ-sĭs]	Disease that causes chronic airway obstruction and also affects the bronchial tubes.
diphtheria [dĭf-THĒR-ē-ă]	Acute infection of the throat and upper respiratory tract caused by bacteria.
dysphonia [dĭs-FŌ-nē-ă]	Hoarseness usually caused by laryngitis.
dyspnea [dĭsp-NĒ-ă, DĬSP-nē-ă]	Difficult breathing.
emphysema [ĕm-fă-SĒ-mă, ĕm-fă-ZĒ-mă]	Chronic condition of hyperinflation of the air sacs; often caused by prolonged smoking.
empyema [ĕm-pī-Ē-mă]	Pus in the pleural cavity.
epiglottitis [ĕp-ĭ-glŏt-Ī-tĭs]	Inflammation of the epiglottis.
epistaxis [ĔP-ĭ-STĂK-sĭs]	Bleeding from the nose, usually caused by trauma or a sudden rupture of the blood vessels of the nose.
eupnea [yūp-NĒ-ă, YŪP-nē-ă]	Normal breathing.
hemoptysis [hē-MŎP-tĭ-sĭs]	Lung or bronchial hemorrhage resulting in the spitting of blood.
hemothorax [hē-mō-THŌR-ăks]	Blood in the pleural cavity.
hypercapnia [hī-pĕr-KĂP-nē-ă]	Excessive buildup of carbon dioxide in lungs, usually associated with hypoventilation.
hyperpnea [hī-pĕrp-NĒ-ă]	Abnormally deep breathing.
hyperventilation [HĪ-pĕr-vĕn-tĭ-LĀ-shŭn]	Abnormally fast breathing in and out, often associated with anxiety.
hypopnea [hī-PŎP-nē-ă]	Shallow breathing.

Term	Definition
hypoventilation [HĪ-pō-věn-ĭ-LĀ-shŭn]	Abnormally low movement of air in and out of the lungs.
hypoxemia [hī-pŏk-SĒ-mē-ă]	Deficient amount of oxygen in the blood.
hypoxia [hī-PŎK-sē-ă]	Deficient amount of oxygen in tissue.
laryngitis [lăr-ĭn-JĪ-tĭs]	Inflammation of the larynx.
laryngospasm [lă-RĬNG-gō-spăsm]	Sudden contraction of the larynx, which may cause coughing and may restrict breathing.
mesothelioma [MĚZ-ō-thē-lē-Ō-mă]	Rare cancer of the lungs associated with asbestosis.
nosebleed	*See* epistaxis.
orthopnea [ōr-thŏp-NĒ-ă, ōr-THŎP-ne-ă]	Difficulty in breathing, especially while lying down.
paroxysmal [păr-ŏk-SĬZ-măl]	Sudden, as a spasm or convulsion.
pertussis [pĕr-TŬS-ĭs]	Severe infection of the pharynx, larynx, and trachea caused by bacteria; whooping cough.
pharyngitis [făr-ĭn-JĪ-tĭs]	Inflammation of the pharynx; sore throat.
pleural effusion [PLŬR-ăl ĕ-FYŪ-zhŭn]	Escape of fluid into the pleural cavity.
pleuritis, pleurisy [plū-RĪ-tĭs, PLŪR-ĭ-sē]	Inflammation of the pleura.
pneumoconiosis [NŪ-mō-kō-nē-Ō-sĭs]	Lung condition caused by inhaling dust.
pneumonia [nū-MŌ-nē-ă]	Acute infection of the alveoli.
pneumonitis [nū-mō-NĪ-tĭs]	Inflammation of the lung.
pneumothorax [nū-mō-THŌR-ăks]	Accumulation of air or gas in the pleural cavity.
pulmonary abscess [PŬL-mō-nār-ē ĂB-sĕs]	Large collection of pus in the lungs.
pulmonary edema [PŬL-mō-nār-ē ĕ-DĒ-mă]	Fluid in the air sacs and bronchioles usually caused by failure of the heart to pump enough blood to and from lungs.
rales [răhlz]	*See* crackles.
rhinitis [rī-NĪ-tĭs]	Nasal inflammation.
rhinorrhea [rīn-nō-RĒ-ă]	Nasal discharge.
rhonchi [RŎNG-kī]	*See* wheezes.
silicosis [sĭl-ĭ-KŌ-sĭs]	Lung condition caused by silica dust from grinding rocks or glass or other materials used in manufacturing.
singultus [sĭng-GŬL-tŭs]	Hiccuping.
sinusitis [sī-nū-SĪ-tĭs]	Inflammation of the sinuses.

Term	Definition
stridor [STRĪ-dōr]	High-pitched crowing sound heard in certain respiratory conditions.
tachypnea [tăk-ĭp-NĒ-ă]	Abnormally fast breathing.
tonsillitis [TŎN-sĭ-LĪ-tĭs]	Inflammation of the tonsils.
tracheitis [trā-kē-Ī-tĭs]	Inflammation of the trachea.
tuberculosis [tū-bĕr-kyū-LŌ-sĭs]	Acute infectious disease caused by bacteria called bacilli.
upper respiratory infection	Infection of all or part of upper portion of respiratory tract.
wheezes [HWĒZ-ĕz]	Whistling sounds heard on inspiration in certain breathing disorders, especially asthma.
whooping cough [HŎOP-ĭng kăwf]	*See* pertussis.

CASE STUDY

X-rays for Pneumonia

Many of the elderly patients admitted to the hospital through the emergency room are suffering from pneumonia. Their chest x-rays will show evidence of the disease. Usually, after a course of antibiotics, the patients are x-rayed again. If the x-rays are not clear a second time, some other underlying problem, such as an abnormal growth or latent disease, may be suspected.

Critical Thinking

83. Why is a bedridden person more susceptible to pneumonia than a patient who is ambulatory?
84. Patients with any kind of respiratory infection often have breathing problems when lying down. Why can lying down cause breathing problems?

PATHOLOGICAL TERMS EXERCISES

Match the Condition

Match the words in the column on the left with the definition in the column on the right.

85. _____ pleurisy, pleuritis

86. _____ epistaxis

87. _____ dysphonia

88. _____ hypoxemia

89. _____ hypercapnia

90. _____ anthracosis

91. _____ pleural effusion

92. _____ pertussis

93. _____ tachypnea

94. _____ apnea

a. whooping cough

b. deficient oxygen in blood

c. black lung

d. pleural inflammation

e. hoarseness

f. inability to breathe

g. nosebleed

h. fast breathing

i. too much carbon dioxide

j. fluid in the pleural cavity

Check Your Knowledge

Circle T for true or F for false.

95. Foreign material comes into the body during internal respiration. T F

96. Dysphonia is associated with laryngitis. T F

97. Diphtheria, pertussis, and tuberculosis are all caused by bacteria. T F

98. A pleural effusion is a type of cancer. T F

99. Respiratory spasms may cause uncontrollable coughing. T F

100. Bronchospasms occur during tonsillitis. T F

101. Tuberculosis cannot be passed from one person to another. T F

102. Atelectasis is another name for a nosebleed. T F

103. Inflammation of the voice box is called laryngitis. T F

104. Hypopnea is abnormally deep breathing. T F

Fill In the Blanks

105. Inflammation of the throat is called _____.

106. Any lung condition caused by dust is called _____.

107. Chronic bronchial airway obstruction is a symptom of _____.

108. The sounds heard in atelectasis are _____ or _____.

109. Many respiratory conditions are caused or made worse by _____,
an addictive habit.

Surgical Terms

When breathing is disrupted or chronic infections of the respiratory tract occur, surgical procedures can provide relief. Ear, nose, and throat (ENT) doctors or **otorhinolaryngologists** specialize in disorders of the upper respiratory tract. Sometimes it is necessary to remove parts of the respiratory system. A **tonsillectomy** is excision of the tonsils (often to stop recurrent tonsillitis). An **adenoidectomy** is removal of the adenoids; a **laryngectomy** removes the larynx (usually to stop cancerous growth); a **pneumonectomy** is the excision of a lung; and a **lobectomy** is the excision of a lobe of a lung (as when cancer is present).

Surgical repair can relieve respiratory problems caused by trauma, abnormalities, growths, or infections. A **bronchoplasty** is the repair of a bronchus; **laryngoplasty** is the repair of the larynx; **rhinoplasty** is the repair of the bones of the nose; **septoplasty** is the repair of the nasal septum; and **tracheoplasty** is the repair of the trachea.

Incisions into parts of the respiratory system are sometimes necessary. **Thoracic surgeons** are the specialists who usually perform such procedures. A **laryngotracheotomy** is an incision of the larynx and trachea; **pneumo-**

bronchotomy is an incision of the lung and bronchus; **septostomy** is the creation of an opening in the nasal septum; **sinusotomy** is an incision of a sinus; **thoracotomy** is an incision into the chest cavity; **thoracostomy** is the establishment of an opening in the chest cavity to drain fluid; and **tracheotomy** is an incision into the trachea, usually to provide an airway (Figure 7-7). Surgical punctures provide a means to aspirate or remove fluid. **Laryngocentesis** is a surgical puncture of the larynx; **pleurocentesis** is a surgical puncture of pleural space; and **thoracocentesis** is a surgical puncture of the chest cavity.

Artificial openings into the respiratory tract may allow for alternative airways as in a **tracheostomy** (artificial tracheal opening) or a **laryngostomy** (artificial laryngeal opening). An **endotracheal intubation** is the insertion of a tube through the nose or mouth, pharynx, and larynx and into the trachea to establish an airway. A **pleuropexy** is performed to attach the pleura in place surgically, usually in case of injury or deterioration.

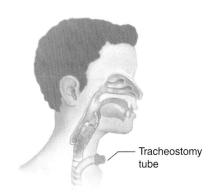

Tracheostomy
tube

FIGURE 7-7 A tracheostomy provides an emergency airway.

VOCABULARY REVIEW

In the previous section, you learned terms relating to surgery. Before going on to the exercises, read the definitions below. Pronunciations are provided for certain terms.

Term	Definition
adenoidectomy [ĂD-ĕ-nŏy-DĔK-tō-mē] adenoid-, adenoids + -ectomy, removal	Removal of the adenoids.
bronchoplasty [BRŎNG-kō-plăs-tē] broncho-, bronchus + -plasty, repair	Surgical repair of a bronchus.
endotracheal intubation [ĔN-dō-TRĀ-kē-ăl ĭn-tū-BĀ-shŭn] **(ET)** endo- within + trache-, trachea + -al, pertaining to	Insertion of a tube through the nose or mouth, pharynx, and larynx and into the trachea to establish an airway.
laryngectomy [LĂR-ĭn-JĔK-tō-mē] laryng-, larynx + -ectomy	Removal of the larynx.
laryngocentesis [lă-RĬNG-gō-sĕn-TĒ-sĭs] laryngo- , larynx + -centesis, puncture	Surgical puncture of the larynx.
laryngoplasty [lă-RĬNG-gō-plăs-tē] laryngo- + -plasty	Repair of the larynx.
laryngostomy [LĂR-ĭng-GŎS-tō-mē] laryngo- + -stomy, mouth	Creation of an artificial opening in the larynx.
laryngotracheotomy [lă-RĬNG-gō-trā-kē-ŎT-ō-mē] laryngo- + tracheo-, trachea + -tomy, cutting	Incision into the larynx and trachea.
lobectomy [lō-BĔK-tō-mē] lob-, lobe + -ectomy	Removal of one of the lobes of a lung.
otorhinolaryngologist [ō-tō-RĪ-nō-lăr-ĭng-GŎL-ō-jĭst] oto-, ear + rhino-, nose + laryngo- + -logist, specialist	Medical doctor who diagnoses and treats disorders of the ear, nose, and throat.

Term	Definition
pleurocentesis [PLŪR-ō-sĕn-TĒ-sĭs] pleuro-, pleura + -centesis	Surgical puncture of pleural space.
pleuropexy [PLŪR-ō-PĔK-sē] pleuro- + -pexy, a fixing	Fixing in place of the pleura surgically, usually in case of injury or deterioration.
pneumobronchotomy [NŪ-mō-brŏng-KŎT-ō-mē] pneumo-, lung + broncho- + -tomy	Incision of the lung and bronchus.
pneumonectomy [NŪ-mō-NĔK-tō-mē] pneumon-, lung + -ectomy	Removal of a lung.
rhinoplasty [RĪ-nō-plăs-tē] rhino-, nose + -plasty	Surgical repair of the bones of the nose.
septoplasty [SĔP-tō-plăs-tē] sept(um) + -plasty	Surgical repair of the nasal septum.
septostomy [sĕp-TŎS-tō-mē] sept(um) + -stomy	Creation of an opening in the nasal septum.
sinusotomy [sīn-ū-SŎT-ō-mē] sinus + -tomy	Incision of a sinus.
thoracic [thō-RĂS-ĭk] **surgeon**	Surgeon who specializes in surgery of the thorax.
thoracocentesis [THŌR-ă-kō-sĕn-TĒ-sĭs] thoraco-, thorax + -centesis	Surgical puncture of the chest cavity.
thoracostomy [thōr-ă-KŎS-tō-mē] thoraco- + -stomy	Establishment of an opening in the chest cavity.
thoracotomy [thōr-ă-KŎT-ō-mē] thraco- + -tomy	Incision into the chest cavity.
tonsillectomy [TŎN-sĭ-LĔK-tō-mē] tonsill-, tonsils + ectomy	Removal of the tonsils.
tracheoplasty [TRĀ-kē-ō-PLĂS-tē] tracheo-, trachea + plasty	Repair of the trachea.
tracheostomy [TRĀ-kē-ŌS-tō-mē] tracheo- + -stomy	Creation of an artificial opening in the trachea.
tracheotomy [trā-kē-ŎT-ō-mē] tracheo- + -tomy	Incision into the trachea.

SURGICAL TERMS EXERCISES

Check Your Knowledge

Match the terms in the left column with the definitions in the right column.

110. _____ rhinoplasty   **a.** artificial laryngeal opening

111. _____ pleuropexy   **b.** removal of a lobe of the lung

112. ____ adenoidectomy
113. ____ tracheostomy
114. ____ tracheotomy
115. ____ laryngectomy
116. ____ lobectomy
117. ____ laryngostomy
118. ____ pleurocentesis
119. ____ septostomy

c. puncture of the pleura
d. creation of an opening in the nasal septum
e. incision into the trachea
f. removal of the adenoids
g. repair of the nose
h. attaching of the pleura
i. removal of the larynx
j. artificial tracheal opening

Fill In the Blanks

120. An incision into the chest cavity is a _____.
121. An airway can be provided by an emergency _____.
122. Cancer of the lung may require a _____ or _____.
123. Surgical attaching of the pleura in place is called _____.
124. The nasal septum is repaired during _____.

CASE STUDY

Asthma Emergencies

Emergency rooms are also visited frequently by people with asthma. A severe asthmatic attack requires medication and close monitoring or it can be fatal. Once the patient is stabilized, various tests may be necessary to determine the pathology in the lungs. June Lytel is a 10-year-old who has asthma. Recently she has had tonsillitis. Four months ago, another case of tonsillitis caused inflammation of her upper respiratory tract. She had two emergency room visits for asthma attacks during the URI. Her physician, an ENT, is also a surgeon.

Critical Thinking

125. Why is it important that her doctor is a surgeon?
126. How might surgery help avoid future URIs?

TERMINOLOGY IN ACTION

Shown below is a referral letter for a 65-year-old patient with severe emphysema. Write a brief description of the disease and discuss the most likely cause of the disease.

Dr. Youssef Muhammed
12 Park Street
Dexter, MI 99999
Dear Dr. Mohammed:

Mr. Alima will be making an appointment to see you in the very near future. He is a 65-year-old male who has had emphysema for many years. Recently it has become quite severe. At this time, he presents with complaints of weakness, even with the most minimal exertion.

(continued)

I have not instituted any change in his therapy as he plans to see you within the week and will follow your recommendations.

I am enclosing my office notes for your review. Please do not hesitate to contact me if you need further information.

Sincerely,

Allison Jankman, MD

Enclosure

USING THE INTERNET

Go to the American Lung Association's Web site (http://www.lungusa.org). Write a short paragraph about research being done on one disease of the respiratory system.

CHAPTER REVIEW

The material that follows is to help you review all the material in this chapter.

DEFINITIONS

Define the following terms and combining forms. Review the chapter before starting. Make sure you know how to pronounce each term as you define it. The blue words in curly brackets are references to the Spanish glossary on the Web site.

WORD	DEFINITION
Adam's apple	
adenoid(o)	
adenoidectomy [ĂD-ĕ-nŏy-DĔK-tō-mē] {adenoidectomía}	
adenoiditis [ĂD-ĕ-nŏy-DĪ-tĭs] {adenoiditis}	
adenoids [ĂD-ĕ-nŏydz] {adenoides}	
alveol(o)	
alveolus (pl., alveoli) [ăl-VĒ-ō-lŭs (ăl-VĒ-ō-lī)] {alvéolo}	
anthracosis [ăn-thră-KŌ-sĭs] {antracosis}	
apex [Ā-pĕks] {apex}	
apnea [ĂP-nē-ă] {apnea}	
arterial blood gases (ABGs)	
asbestosis [ăs-bĕs-TŌ-sĭs] {asbestosis}	
asthma [ĂZ-mă] {asma}	
atelectasis [ăt-ĕ-LĔK-tă-sĭs] {atelectasia}	
auscultation [ăws-kŭl-TĀ-shŭn] {auscultación}	
bacilli (sing., bacillus) [bă-SĬL-Ī (bă-SĬL-ĭs)] {bacilo}	
base [bās] {base}	
black lung	
bradypnea [brăd-ĭp-NĒ-ă] {bradipnea}	
bronch(o), bronchi(o)	
bronchial alveolar lavage [BRŎNG-kē-ăl ăl-VĒ-ō-lăr lă-VĂZH]	

WORD	DEFINITION
bronchial brushing	_____
bronchiol(o)	_____
bronchiole [BRŎNG-kē-ōl] {bronquiolo}	_____
bronchitis [brŏng-KĪ-tĭs] {bronquitis}	_____
bronchography [brŏng-KŎG-ră-fē] {broncografía}	_____
bronchoplasty [BRŎNG-kō-plăs-tē]	_____
bronchoscope [BRŎNG-kō-skōp] {broncoscopio}	_____
bronchospasm [BRŎNG-kō-spăzm] {broncoespasmo}	_____
bronchus (_pl._, bronchi) [BRŎNG-kŭs (BRŎNG-kī)] {bronquio}	_____
capn(o)	_____
Cheyne-Stokes respiration [chān stōks rĕs-pĭ-RĀ-shŭn]	_____
chronic bronchitis	_____
chronic obstructive pulmonary disease (COPD)	_____
cilia [SĬL-ē-ă]	_____
crackles [KRĂK-ls]	_____
croup [krūp] {crup}	_____
cystic fibrosis [SĬS-tĭk fĭ-BRŌ-sĭs]	_____
diaphragm [DĪ-ă-frăm] {diafragma}	_____
diphtheria [dĭf-THĒR-ē-ă] {difteria}	_____
dysphonia [dĭs-FŌ-nē-ă] {dissfonía}	_____
dyspnea [dĭsp-NĒ-ă, DĬSP-nē-ă] {disnea}	_____
emphysema [ĕm-fă-SĒ-mă, ĕm-fă-ZĒ-mă] {enfisema}	_____
empyema [ĕm-pī-Ē-mă] {empiema}	_____
endoscope [ĔN-dō-skōp] {endoscopio}	_____
endotracheal intubation [ĕn-dō-TRĀ-kē-ăl ĭn-tū-BĀ-shŭn] (ET)	_____
epiglott(o)	_____
epiglottis [ĔP-ĭ-GLŎT-ĭs] {epiglotis}	_____
epiglottitis [ĕp-ĭ-glŏt-Ī-tĭs] {epiglotitis}	_____

WORD	DEFINITION

epistaxis [ĔP-ĭ-STĂK-sĭs] _____

eupnea [yūp-NĒ-ă, YŪP-nē-ă]
{eupnea} _____

exhalation [ĕks-hă-LĀ-shŭn]
{exahalación} _____

expiration [ĕks-pĭ-RĀ-shŭn] {espiración} _____

external nares [ĕks-TĔR-năl NĀR-ēz] _____

external respiration _____

glottis [GLŎT-ĭs] {glotis} _____

hemoptysis [hē-MŎP-tĭ-sĭs] _____

hemothorax [hē-mō-THŌR-ăks]
{hemotórax} _____

hilum (also hilus) [HĪ-lŭm (HĪ-lŭs)]
{hilio} _____

hypercapnia [hī-pĕr-KĂP-nē-ă] _____

hyperpnea [hī-pĕrp-NĒ-ă] _____

hyperventilation [HĪ-pĕr-vĕn-tĭ-
LĀ-shŭn] {hiperventilación} _____

hypopharynx [HĪ-pō-FĂR-ĭngks]
{hipofaringe} _____

hypopnea [hī-PŎP-nē-ă] _____

hypoventilation [HĪ-pō-vĕn-tĭ-LĀ-
shŭn] {hipoventilación} _____

hypoxemia [hī-pŏk-SĒ-mē-ă]
{hipoxemia} _____

hypoxia [hī-PŎK-sē-ă] {hypoxia} _____

inferior lobe [ĭn-FĒ-rē-ōr lōb] _____

inhalation [ĭn-hă-LĀ-shŭn]
{inhalación} _____

inspiration [ĭn-spĭ-RĀ-shŭn]
{inspiración} _____

intercostal muscles [ĭn-tĕr-KŎS-
tăl MŬS-ĕlz] _____

internal respiration _____

laryng(o) _____

laryngectomy [LĂR-ĭn-JĔK-tō-mē] _____

laryngitis [lăr-ĭn-JĪ-tĭs] {laryngitis} _____

laryngocentesis [lă-RĬNG-gō-sĕn-TĒ-sĭs] _____

Word	Definition
laryngopharynx [lă-RĬNG-gō-făr-ĭngks]	
laryngoplasty [lă-RĬNG-gō-plăs-tē] {laringoplastia}	
laryngoscopy [LĂR-ĭng-GŎS-kō-pē] {laringoscopia}	
laryngospasm [lă-RĬNG-gō-spăsm]	
laryngostomy [LĂR-ĭng-GŎS-tō-mē] {laringostomía}	
laryngotracheotomy [lă-RĬNG-gō-trā-kē-ŎT-ō-mē]	
larynx [LĂR-ĭngks] {laringe}	
lob(o)	
lobectomy [lō-BĔK-tō-mē] {lobectomía}	
lung [lŭng] {pulmón}	
mediastin(o)	
mediastinoscopy [MĒ-dē-ăs-tĭ-NŎS-kō-pē]	
mediastinum [MĒ-dē-ăs-TĪ-nŭm] {mediastino}	
mesothelioma [MĔZ-ō-thē-lē-Ō-mă] {mesotelioma}	
middle lobe	
nas(o)	
nasal cavity [NĀ-zăl KĂV-ĭ-tē]	
nasal septum [NĀ-zăl SĔP-tŭm]	
nasopharyngoscopy [NĀ-zō-fă-rĭng-GŎS-kō-pē] {nasofaringoscopio}	
nasopharynx [NĀ-zō-FĂR-ĭngks] {nasofaringe}	
nose [nōz] {nariz}	
nosebleed {epistaxis}	
nostrils [NŎS-trĭlz] {naris}	
or(o)	
oropharynx [ŌR-ō-FĂR-ĭngks] {orofaringe}	
orthopnea [ōr-thŏp-NĒ-ă, ōr-THŎP-nē-ă] {ortopnea}	

WORD	DEFINITION
otorhinolaryngologist [ō-tō-RĪ-nō-lăr-ĭng-GŎL-ō-jĭst]	_____
ox(o), oxi, oxy	_____
palatine tonsils [PĂL-ă-tīn TŎN-sĭlz]	_____
paranasal sinuses [păr-ă-NĀ-săl SĪ-nŭs-ĕz]	_____
parietal pleura [pă-RĪ-ĕ-tăl PLŪR-ă]	_____
paroxysmal [păr-ŏk-SĪZ-măl] {paraxístico}	_____
peak flow meter	_____
percussion [pĕr-KŬSH-ŭn] {percusión}	_____
pertussis [pĕr-TŬS-ĭs] {pertussis}	_____
pharyng(o)	_____
pharyngeal tonsils [fă-RĬN-jē-ăl TŎN-sĭlz]	_____
pharyngitis [făr-ĭn-JĪ-tĭs] {faringitis}	_____
pharynx [FĂR-ĭngks] {faringe}	_____
phon(o)	_____
phren(o)	_____
pleur(o)	_____
pleura (_pl._, pleurae) [PLŪR-ă (PLŪR-ē)] {pleura}	_____
pleural cavity [PLŪR-ăl KĂV-ĭ-tē]	_____
pleural effusion [PLŪR-ăl ĕ-FYŪ-zhŭn]	_____
pleuritis, pleurisy [plū-RĪ-tĭs, PLŪR-ĭ-sē] {pleuritis}	_____
pleurocentesis [PLŪR-ō-sĕn-TĒ-sĭs]	_____
pleuropexy [PLŪR-ō-PĔK-sē]	_____
pneum(o), pneumon(o)	_____
pneumobronchotomy [NŪ-mō-brŏng-KŎT-ō-mē]	_____
pneumoconiosis [NŪ-mō-kō-nē-Ō-sĭs] {neumoconiosis}	_____
pneumonectomy [NŪ-mō-NĔK-tō-mē] {neumonectomía}	_____
pneumonia [nū-MŌ-nē-ă] {neumonía}	_____
pneumonitis [nū-mō-NĪ-tĭs] {neumonitis}	_____

WORD	DEFINITION

pneumothorax [nū-mō-THŌR-ăks]
{neumotórax} _____

pulmonary abscess [PŬL-mō-nār-ē
ĂB-sĕs] _____

pulmonary edema [PŬL-mō-nār-ē ĕ-
DĒ-mă] _____

pulmonary function tests _____

rales [răhlz] {rales} _____

respiratory [RĔS-pĭ-ră-tōr-ē, rĕ-SPĪR-
ă-tōr-ē] system _____

respiratory tract _____

rhin(o) _____

rhinitis [rī-NĪ-tĭs] {rinitis} _____

rhinoplasty [RĪ-nō-plăs-tē] {rinoplastia} _____

rhinorrhea [rī-nō-RĒ-ă] {rinorrea} _____

rhonchi [RŎNG-kī] {ronquidos} _____

septoplasty [SĔP-tō-plăs-tē]
{septoplastia} _____

septostomy [sĕp-TŎS-tō-mē]
{septostomía} _____

septum [SĔP-tŭm] {tabique} _____

silicosis [sĭl-ĭ-KŌ-sĭs] _____

singultus [sĭng-GŬL-tŭs] {singulto} _____

sinusitis [sī-nŭ-SĪ-tĭs] {sinusitis} _____

sinusotomy [sīn-ū-SŎT-ō-mē]
{sinosotomía} _____

soft palate [sŏft PĂL-ăt] _____

spir(o) _____

spirometer [sī-RŎM-ĕ-tĕr] {espirómetro} _____

sputum [SPŬ-tūm] sample or culture _____

steth(o) _____

stridor [STRĪ-dōr] {estridor} _____

superior lobe _____

sweat test _____

tachypnea [tăk-ĭp-NĒ-ă] {taquipnea} _____

thorac(o) _____

thoracic [thō-RĂS-ĭk] surgeon _____

thoracocentesis [THŌR-ă-kō-sĕn-TĒ-sĭs] {toracocentesis} _____

thoracostomy [thōr-ă-KŎS-tō-mē] {torascostomía} _____

thoracotomy [thōr-ă-KŎT-ō-mē] {toracotomía} _____

thorax [THŌ-răks] {tórax} _____

throat [thrōt] {garganta} _____

throat culture _____

thyroid cartilage [THĪ-rŏyd KĂR-tĭ-lĭj] _____

tonsill(o) _____

tonsillectomy [TŎN-sĭ-LĔK-tō-mē] {tonsilectomía} _____

tonsillitis [TŎN-sĭ-LĪ-tĭs] {tonsilitis} _____

trache(o) _____

trachea [TRĀ-kē-ă] {tráquea} _____

tracheitis [trā-kē-Ī-tĭs] _____

tracheoplasty [TRĀ-kē-ō-PLĂS-tē] {traqueoplastia} _____

tracheostomy [TRĀ-kē-ŎS-tō-mē] {traquestomía} _____

tracheotomy [trā-kē-ŎT-ō-mē] {traqueotomía} _____

tuberculosis [tū-bĕr-kyū-LŌ-sĭs] {tuberculosis} _____

upper respiratory infection _____

visceral pleura [VĬS-ĕr-ăl PLŪR-ă] _____

vocal cords _____

voice box _____

wheezes [HWĒZ-ĕz] {sibilancias} _____

whooping cough [HŎOP-ĭng kăwf] _____

windpipe _____

Answers to Chapter Exercises

1. Muscles in the diaphragm control the amount of air inhaled and exhaled. Weakened muscles may lead to shallow breathing.
2. oxygen
3. a. Trachea
   b. Lungs
   c. Alveoli
4. external respiration
5. cilia
6. nasal septum
7. epiglottis
8. abdominal thrust maneuver
9. air sacs / alveoli
10. three
11. two
12. diaphragm
13. intercostal
14. F
15. T
16. F
17. T
18. T
19. F
20. T
21. F
22. F
23. F
24. nasopharynx
25. trachea
26. respiration
27. C
28. diaphragm
29. epiglottis
30. pharynx
31. C
32. tonsils
33. bronchus
34. smoking, sedentary, weight, heart disease, age.
35. Internal respiration is the exchange of oxygen and carbon dioxide between the blood and the cells. The heart pumps oxygenated blood throughout the body, and internal respiration requires an efficient cardiovascular system.
36. adenoidectomy
37. thoracocentesis
38. tracheotomy
39. tonsillitis
40. mediastinopericarditis
41. pneumonorrhaphy
42. oronasal
43. pharyngitis
44. phonopathy
45. capnometer
46. bronchitis
47. peribronchitis
48. pericardiopleural
49. lobotomy
50. oximetry
51. oxychloride
52. bronchoedema
53. alveoloclasia
54. thoracalgia
55. pharyngotomy
56. d
57. f
58. g
59. i
60. a
61. j
62. e
63. h
64. c
65. b
66. pulmonary function
67. sweat test
68. endoscope
69. endoscope
70. auscultation
71. throat culture
72. percussion
73. peak flow meter
74. sputum sample or culture
75. spirometer
76. pharyngo
77. capno
78. laryng
79. lob
80. laryngo
81. Mr. DiGiorno has both cardiovascular and respiratory problems. Blood gas tests show how his internal respiration is working.
82. WBC or white blood count
83. The bedridden person's muscles are weaker; breathing is shallower; there is reduced fresh air.
84. Fluids from the infection may still reside in the respiratory system. Lying down causes them to collect rather than to be expelled.
85. d
86. g
87. e
88. b
89. i
90. c
91. j
92. a
93. h
94. f
95. F
96. T
97. T
98. F
99. T
100. F
101. F
102. F
103. T
104. F
105. pharyngitis
106. pneumoconiosis
107. asthma
108. crackles / rales
109. smoking
110. g
111. h

Answers to Chapter Exercises (continued)

112. f
113. j
114. e
115. i
116. b
117. a

118. c
119. d
120. thoracotomy
121. tracheotomy
122. lobectomy or pneumonectomy
123. pleuropexy

124. septoplasty
125. She may need a tonsillectomy.
126. If the tonsils are removed, they cannot spread infection.

The Nervous System

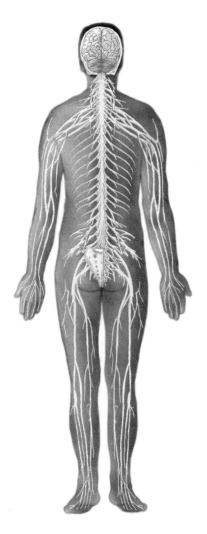

After studying this chapter, you will be able to:

▶ Name the parts of the nervous system and discuss the function of each part

▶ Define the combining forms used in building words that relate to the nervous system

▶ Name the common diagnoses, laboratory tests, and clinical procedures used in testing and treating disorders of the nervous system

▶ List and define the major pathological conditions of the nervous system

▶ Define surgical terms related to the nervous system

Structure and Function

The nervous system directs the function of all the human body systems (Figure 8-1). The nervous system is divided into two subsystems: the central nervous system (CNS) and the peripheral nervous system (PNS).

A **nerve cell** or **neuron** is the basic element of the nervous system. All neurons have three parts:

1. The **cell body,** which has branches or fibers that reach out to send or receive impulses.
2. **Dendrites,** which are thin branching extensions of the cell body. They conduct nerve impulses *toward* the cell body.
3. The **axon,** which conducts nerve impulses *away* from the cell body. It is generally a single branch covered by fatty tissue called the **myelin sheath,** itself covered by the **neurilemma.** At the end of the axon, there are **terminal end fibers.**

Nerve impulses jump from one neuron to the next over a space called a **synapse.** The nerve impulse is stimulated to jump over the synapse by a **neurotransmitter,** any of various substances in the terminal end fibers.

All neurons also have two basic properties—**excitability,** the ability to respond to a **stimulus** (anything that arouses a response), and **conductivity,** the ability to transmit a signal. Neurons are microscopic entities that form bundles called **nerves,** which carry electrical messages to the organs and muscles of the body. The three types of neurons are:

1. **Efferent (motor) neurons,** which convey information to the muscles and glands from the central nervous system

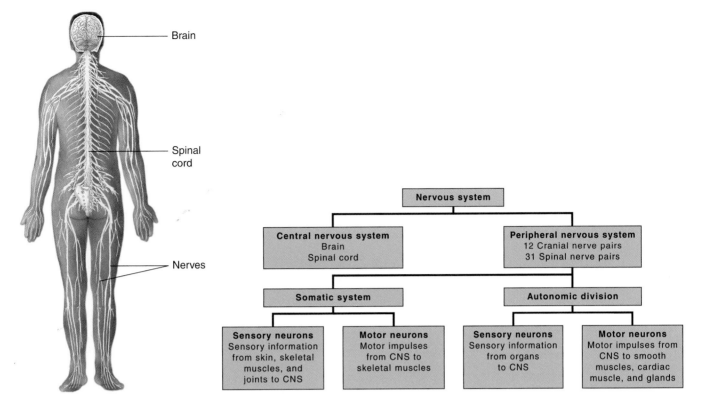

FIGURE 8-1 (a) The nervous system directs the function of all the human body systems. (b) The chart illustrates the functions controlled by the various parts of the nervous system.

2. **Afferent (sensory) neurons,** which carry information from sensory receptors to the central nervous system
3. **Interneurons,** which carry and process sensory information.

Nerve cells send **nerve impulses** to tissue or organs called **receptors.** In addition to nerve cells, other cells in the nervous system support, connect, protect, and remove debris from the system. These cells, **neuroglia** or **neuroglial cells,** do not transmit impulses. Each of the three types of neuroglia serves different purposes.

1. Star-shaped **astroglia** (or **astrocytes**) maintain nutrient and chemical levels in neurons.
2. **Oligodendroglia** produce myelin and help in supporting neurons.
3. **Microglia** are phagocytes—cells that remove debris.

Figure 8-2 shows neuroglia.

Central Nervous System

The **central nervous system (CNS)** consists of the brain and spinal cord.

Brain

The human adult **brain** has four major divisions (Figure 8-3).

1. The **brainstem** is made up of the **midbrain,** the **pons,** and the **medulla oblongata,** all involved with many basic body functions.

FIGURE 8-2 The three types of neuroglia shown here perform different functions in the nervous system.

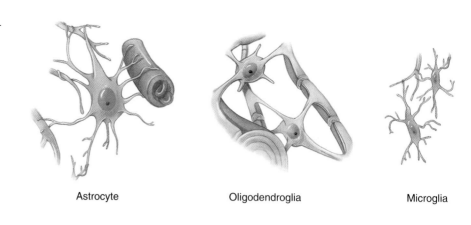

Astrocyte   Oligodendroglia   Microglia

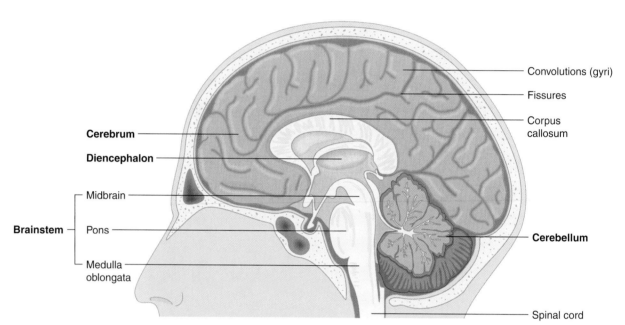

Convolutions (gyri)

Fissures

Corpus callosum

Cerebrum

Diencephalon

Midbrain

Brainstem

Pons

Cerebellum

Medulla oblongata

Spinal cord

FIGURE 8-3 The parts of the brain.

2. The **cerebellum** is the area that coordinates musculoskeletal movement.
3. The **cerebrum** is the largest area of the brain. It contains two hemispheres with an outer portion called the **cerebral cortex.** The cerebral cortex has many **fissures** (also called **sulci**) and **convolutions** (also called **gyri**). Below the cerebral cortex is an area of gray matter called the **basal ganglia.** The left and right hemispheres of the cerebellum are each divided into four parts or lobes:
   a. The **frontal lobe** controls voluntary movements and certain emotions.
   b. The **parietal lobe** controls the senses.
   c. The **temporal lobe** controls memory, equilibrium and some emotions.
   d. The **occipital lobe** controls vision and some expression.
   The two hemispheres are connected by the **corpus callosum.**
4. The **diencephalon** is deep within the brain and contains the **thalamus, hypothalamus, epithalamus,** and the **ventral thalamus.**

   The brain sits inside the **cranium** or skull, a strong bony structure that protects it. The area between the brain and the cranium is filled with **cerebrospinal fluid (CSF),** a watery liquid that is also contained in the **ventricles.**

Spinal Cord

The **spinal cord** extends from the medulla oblongata of the brain to the area around the second lumbar vertebra in the lower back. The spinal cord is contained within the vertebral column. Figure 8-4 illustrates a section of the spinal cord.

Meninges

The **meninges** (*sing.* **meninx**) are three layers of connective tissue membrane that cover the brain and spinal cord. The outer layer, the **dura mater,** is a tough, fibrous membrane that covers the entire length of the spinal cord. The middle layer, the **arachnoid,** is a weblike structure that runs across the space (called the **subdural space**) containing cerebrospinal fluid. The **pia mater,** the innermost layer of meninges, is a thin membrane containing many blood vessels. The space between the pia mater and the bones of the spinal cord is called the **epidural space.**

Severe spinal cord injuries usually result in some type of paralysis. Research is under way to grow replacement cells for injured nerves. It is expected that some types of paralysis will be cured by 2010.

Peripheral Nervous System

The peripheral nervous system includes the 12 pairs of **cranial nerves** that carry impulses to and from the brain and the 31 pairs of **spinal nerves** that carry messages to and from the spinal cord and the torso and extremities of the body. Table 8-1 lists the cranial nerves and their functions.

For an easy way to remember and even test your cranial nerves, go to http://faculty.washington.edu/chudler/cranial.html.

The 31 pairs of spinal nerves are grouped according to the segments of the spinal cord out of which they extend. Table 8-2 lists those groups and the regions served by the nerves of each group. The peripheral nerves are further divided into two subsystems—the somatic and autonomic nervous systems.

Somatic Nervous System

Nerves of the **somatic nervous system** receive and process sensory input from the skin, muscles, tendons, joints, eyes, tongue, nose, and ears. They also excite the voluntary contraction of skeletal muscles.

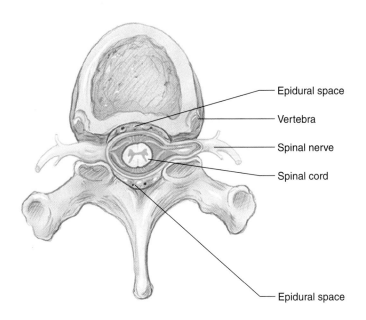

FIGURE 8-4 A section of the spinal column showing a vertebra.

- Epidural space
- Vertebra
- Spinal nerve
- Spinal cord
- Epidural space

TABLE 8-1 The twelve pairs of cranial nerves and their function.

Pair of Cranial Nerves	Primary Type of Nerve	Function
I olfactory	sensory	involved in sense of smell
II optic	sensory	involved in sense of vision
III oculomotor	motor	involved in movement of eyes, controlling both the exterior and interior parts
IV trochlear	motor	involved in muscles that move the eyes
V trigeminal	sensory and motor	involved in eyes, tear glands, scalp, forehead, teeth, gums, lips, and muscles of the mouth
VI abducens	motor	involved with muscle conditioning
VII facial	sensory and motor	involved with taste, facial expressions, tear glands, and salivary glands
VIII vestibulocochlear	sensory	involved in equilibrium and hearing
IX glossopharyngeal	sensory and motor	involved in pharynx, tonsils, tongue, and carotid arteries; stimulates salivary glands
X vagus	sensory and motor	involved in speech, swallowing, heart muscles, smooth muscles, and certain glands
XI accessory (cranial and spinal)	motor	involved in muscles of the soft palate, pharynx, larynx, neck, and back
XII hypoglossal	motor	involved in muscles that move the tongue

TABLE 8-2 Major spinal nerve divisions and their functions.

Region of Spinal Cord	Location	Functions of Nerves
cervical	neck	involved in muscles of the back of the head and neck and in the diaphragm
brachial	lower neck, axilla	involved in the muscles and skin of the neck, shoulder, arm, and hand
lumbar	posterior abdominal wall	involved in abdominal skin and muscles
sacral	posterior pelvic wall	involved in the muscles of the buttocks, thighs, feet, legs, and voluntary sphincters
coccygeal	coccyx and surrounding area	skin in coccyx region

Autonomic Nervous System

Nerves of the **autonomic nervous system** carry impulses from the central nervous system to glands, various smooth (involuntary) muscles, cardiac muscle, and various membranes.

The autonomic nerves are further divided into the **sympathetic nervous system** and the **parasympathetic nervous system**.

VOCABULARY REVIEW

In the previous section, you learned terms relating to the nervous system. Before going on to the exercises, read the definitions below. Pronunciations are provided for certain terms.

Term	Definition
afferent [ĂF-ĕr-ĕnt] **(sensory) neuron**	Neuron that carries information from the sensory receptors to the central nervous system.
arachnoid [ă-RĂK-nŏyd]	Middle layer of meninges.
astrocyte, [ĂS-trō-sīt], **astroglia** [ăs-TRŎG-lē-ă]	A type of neuroglia that maintains nutrient and chemical levels in neurons.
autonomic [ăw-tō-NŎM-ĭk] **nervous system**	Part of the peripheral nervous system that carries impulses from the central nervous system to glands, smooth muscles, cardiac muscle, and various membranes.
axon [ĂK-sōn]	Part of a nerve cell that conducts nerve impulses away from the cell body.
basal ganglia [BĀ-săl GĂNG-glē-ă]	Large masses of gray matter within the cerebrum.
brain [brān]	Body organ responsible for controlling the body's functions and interactions with outside stimuli.
brainstem	One of the four major divisions of the brain; division that controls certain heart, lung, and visual functions.
cell body	Part of a nerve cell that has branches or fibers that reach out to send or receive impulses.
central nervous system (CNS)	The brain and spinal cord.
cerebellum [sĕr-ĕ-BĔL-ūm]	One of the four major divisions of the brain; division that coordinates musculoskeletal movement.
cerebral cortex [SĔR-ē-brăl KŌR-tĕks]	Outer portion of the cerebrum.
cerebrospinal [SĔR-ĕ-brō-spī-năl] **fluid (CSF)**	Watery fluid that flows throughout the brain and around the spinal cord.
cerebrum [SĔR-ĕ-brŭm, sĕ-RĒ-brŭm]	One of the four major divisions of the brain; division involved with emotions, memory, conscious thought, moral behavior, sensory interpretations, and certain bodily movement.
conductivity [kŏn-dŭk-TĬV-ĭ-tē]	Ability to transmit a signal.
convolutions [kŏn-vō-LŪ-shŭnz]	Folds in the cerebral cortex; gyri.
corpus callosum [KŌR-pŭs kă-LŌ-sŭm]	Bridge of nerve fibers that connects the two hemispheres of the cerebrum.
cranial [KRĀ-nē-ăL] **nerves**	Any of 12 pairs of nerves that carry impulses to and from the brain.

Term	Definition
cranium [KRĀ-nē-ŭm]	Bony structure that the brain sits in.
dendrite [DĔN-drīt]	A thin branching extension of a nerve cell that conducts nerve impulses toward the cell body.
diencephalon [dī-ĕn-SĔF-ă-lŏn]	One of the four major structures of the brain; it is the deep portion of the brain and contains the thalamus.
dura mater [DŪ-ră MĀ-tĕr]	Outermost layer of meninges.
efferent [ĔF-ĕr-ĕnt] **(motor) neuron**	Neuron that carries information to the muscles and glands from the central nervous system.
epidural [ĕp-ĭ-DŪ-răl] **space**	Area between the pia mater and the bones of the spinal cord.
epithalamus [ĔP-ĭ-THĂL-ă-mŭs]	One of the parts of the diencephalon; serves as a sensory relay station.
excitability [ĕk-SĪ-tă-BĬL-ĭ-tē]	Ability to respond to stimuli.
fissure [FĬSH-ŭr]	One of many indentations of the cerebrum; sulcus.
frontal lobe	One of the four parts of each hemisphere of the cerebrum.
gyrus (*pl.*, **gyri**) [JĪ-rŭs (JĪ-rī)]	*See* convolution.
hypothalamus [HĪ-pō-THĂL-ă-mŭs]	One of the parts of the diencephalon; serves as a sensory relay station.
interneuron [ĬN-tĕr-NŪ-rŏn]	Neuron that carries and processes sensory information.
medulla oblongata [mĕ-DŪL-ă ŏb-lŏng-GĂ-tă]	Part of the brain stem that regulates heart and lung functions, swallowing, vomiting, coughing, and sneezing.
meninges (*sing.*, **meninx**) [mĕ-NĬN-jēz (MĒ-nĭngks)]	Three layers of membranes that cover and protect the brain and spinal cord.
microglia [mī-KRŎG-lē-ă]	A type of neuroglia that removes debris.
midbrain	Part of the brainstem involved with visual reflexes.
myelin sheath [MĪ-ĕ-lĭn shēth]	Fatty tissue that covers axons.
nerve [nĕrv]	Bundle of neurons that bear electrical messages to the organs and muscles of the body.
nerve cell	Basic cell of the nervous system having three parts: cell body, dendrite, and axon; neuron.
nerve impulse	Released energy that is received or transmitted by tissue or organs and that usually provokes a response.
neurilemma [nūr-ĭ-LĔM-ă]	Membranous covering that protects the myelin sheath.
neuroglia [nū-RŎG-lē-ă], **neuroglial** [nū-RŎG-lē-ăl] **cell**	Cell of the nervous system that does not transmit impulses.

Term	Definition
neuron [NŪR-ŏn]	Basic cell of the nervous system having three parts; nerve cell.
neurotransmitters [NŪR-ō-trăns-MĬT-ĕrz]	Various substances located in tiny sacs at the end of the axon.
occipital lobe [ŏk-SĬP-ĭ-tăl lōb]	One of the four parts of each hemisphere of the cerebrum.
oligodendroglia [ŌL-ĭ-gō-dĕn-DRŎG-lē-ă]	A type of neuroglia that produces myelin and helps to support neurons.
parasympathetic [păr-ă-sĭm-pă-THĔT-ĭk] **nervous system**	Part of the autonomic nervous system that operates when the body is in a normal state.
parietal lobe [pă-RĪ-ĕ-tăl lōb]	One of the four parts of each hemisphere of the cerebrum.
pia mater [PĪ-ă, PĒ-ă MĀ-tĕr, MĂ-tĕr]	Innermost layer of meninges.
pons [pŏnz] Latin, bridge	Part of the brainstem that controls certain respiratory functions.
receptor [rē-SĔP-tĕr]	Tissue or organ that receives nerve impulses.
somatic [sō-MĂT-ĭk] **nervous system**	Part of the peripheral nervous system that receives and processes sensory input from various parts of the body.
spinal cord	Ropelike tissue that sits inside the vertebral column and from which spinal nerves extend.
spinal nerves	Any of 31 pairs of nerves that carry messages to and from the spinal cord and the torso and extremities.
stimulus (*pl.*, **stimuli**) [STĬM-yū-lŭs (STĬM-yū-lī)]	Anything that arouses a response.
subdural [sŭb-DŪR-ăl] **space**	Area between the dura mater and the pia mater across which the arachnoid runs.
sulcus (*pl.*, **sulci**) [SŬL-kŭs (SŬL-sī)]	*See* fissure.
sympathetic [sĭm-pă-THĔT-ĭk] **nervous system**	Part of the autonomic nervous system that operates when the body is under stress.
synapse [SĬN-ăps]	Space over which nerve impulses jump from one neuron to another.
temporal lobe [TĔM-pŏ-răl lōb]	One of the four parts of each hemisphere of the cerebrum.
terminal end fibers	Group of fibers at the end of an axon that passes the impulses leaving the neuron to the next neuron.

Term	Definition
thalamus [THĂL-ă-mŭs]	One of the four parts of the diencephalon; serves as a sensory relay station.
ventral thalamus	One of the four parts of the diencephalon; serves as a sensory relay station.
ventricle [VĔN-trĭ-kl]	Cavity in the brain for cerebrospinal fluid.

CASE STUDY

Neurological Problem

Jose Gutierrez is a patient of Dr. Marla Chin, an internist. He is scheduled for his six-month checkup and medication review. Mr. Gutierrez has a history of heart disease and skin carcinoma. In the past few months he has been having trouble buttoning his shirts and remembering things. He has also developed a limp. Dr. Chin orders some tests.

Critical Thinking

1. Mr. Gutierrez has some new problems. According to his symptoms, what areas of the brain might have been affected by some disorder?

2. Dr. Chin does a thorough checkup and asks both Mr. Gutierrez and his wife many questions about such things as respiratory function, sleep habits, and so on. How will the answers to the questions help Dr. Chin determine the next steps to take?

STRUCTURE AND FUNCTION EXERCISES

Know the Position

3. The brain and spinal cord are protected by three layers of meninges. Name the three layers in order from inside the skull to the brain.

   a. _____

   b. _____

   c. _____

Find a Match

Match the definition in the right-hand column to the word in the left-hand column.

4. ____ neuroglia

5. ____ meninges

6. ____ neuron

7. ____ thalamus

8. ____ excitability

9. ____ ventricle

10. ____ basal ganglia

a. gray matter

b. weblike meningeal layer

c. part of the diencephalon

d. cell that does not transmit impulses

e. fissures

f. area between pia mater and spinal bones

g. responsiveness to stimuli

11. ____ sulci   **h.** protective membranes

12. ____ arachnoid   **i.** cell that transmits impulses

13. ____ epidural space   **j.** cavity for fluid

Complete the Thought

Fill in the blanks.

14. Organs that receive nerve impulses are called _____.

15. Each axon is covered by a _____ _____.

16. Neuron structures that conduct nerve impulses toward the cell body are called _____.

17. Neuron structures that conduct nerve impulses away from the cell body are called _____.

18. The spinal cord connects to the brain at the _____ _____.

19. The part of the brain with two hemispheres is called the _____.

20. The part of the brainstem that controls certain respiratory functions is called the _____.

21. The bony structure protecting the brain is the _____.

22. Ventricles hold _____ _____.

23. The deep portion of the brain is called the _____.

Spell It Correctly

Write the correct spelling in the blank to the right of each word. If the word is already correctly spelled, write C.

24. meninxes _____

25. thalomus _____

26. ganoglia _____

27. gyri _____

28. synapse _____

29. axen _____

30. neurilemma _____

31. convulotions _____

32. neurglia _____

33. cerebrellum _____

Combining Forms

The list below includes combining forms that relate specifically to the nervous system. Pronunciations are provided for the examples.

Combining Form	Meaning	Example
cerebell(o)	cerebellum	*cerebellitis* [sĕr-ĕ-bĕl-Ī-tĭs], inflammation of the cerebellum
cerebr(o), cerebri	cerebrum	*cerebralgia* [sĕr-ĕ-BRĂL-jē-ă], pain in the head
crani(o)	cranium	*craniofacial* [KRĀ-nē-ō-FĀ-shăl], relating to the face and the cranium
encephal(o)	brain	*encephalitis* [ĕn-sĕf-ă-LĪ-tĭs], inflammation of the brain

COMBINING FORM	MEANING	EXAMPLE
gangli(o)	ganglion	*gangliform* [GĂNG-glē-fŏrm], having the shape of a ganglion
gli(o)	neuroglia	*gliomatosis* [glī-ō-mă-TŌ-sĭs], abnormal growth of neuroglia in the brain or spinal cord
mening(o), meningi(o)	meninges	*meningocele* [mĕ-NĬNG-gō-sēl], protrusion of the spinal meninges above the surface of the skin; *meningitis* [mĕn-ĭn-JĪ-tĭs], inflammation of the meninges
myel(o)	bone marrow, spinal cord	*myelomalacia* [MĪ-ĕ-lō-mă-LĀ-shē-ă], softening of the spinal cord
neur(o), neuri	nerve	*neuritis* [nū-RĪ-tĭs], inflammation of a nerve
spin(o)	spine	*spinoneural* [spī-nō-NŪ-răl], relating to the spine and the nerves that extend from it
thalam(o)	thalamus	*thalamotomy* [thăl-ă-MŎT-ō-mē], incision into the thalamus to destroy a portion causing or transmitting sensations of pain
vag(o)	vagus nerve	*vagectomy* [vă-JĔK-tō-mē], surgical removal of a portion of the vagus nerve; *vagotomy* [vă-GŎT-ō-mē], surgical severing of the vagus nerve
ventricul(o)	ventricle	*ventriculitis* [vĕn-trĭk-yū-LĪ-tĭs], inflammation of the ventricles of the brain

CASE STUDY

Referral to a Neurologist

Dr. Chin takes some blood tests and decides to send Mr. Gutierrez to a neurologist, Dr. Martin Stanley, for an evaluation. Dr. Stanley reviews Dr. Chin's notes and finds that Mr. Gutierrez has no history of stroke, but is experiencing numbness in his fingers and has some difficulty walking. Dr. Stanley will test for stroke, but since Mr. Gutierrez has a history of normal blood pressure, he suspects another disorder.

Critical Thinking

34. Why is Mr. Gutierrez referred to a neurologist?
35. Can numbness and limping be caused by a disorder of the cardiovascular system?

COMBINING FORMS EXERCISES

Root Out the Meaning

Find at least two nervous system combining forms in each word. Write the combining forms and their definitions in the space provided.

36. encephalomyelitis:

37. craniomeningocele:

38. glioneuroma:

39. cerebromeningitis:

40. spinoneural:

41. neuroencephalomyelopathy:

Trace the Root

Add the combining form that completes the word.

42. Acting upon the vagus nerve: _____tropic.

43. Tumor consisting of ganglionic neurons: ganglio_____oma.

44. Myxoma containing glial cells: _____myxoma.

45. Relating to nerves and meninges: neuro_____eal.

In each word, find the combining form that relates to the nervous system and give its definition.

46. parencephalia _____

47. angioneurectomy _____

48. cephalomegaly _____

49. myelitis _____

50. meningocyte _____

51. neurocyte _____

52. craniomalacia _____

53. vagotropic _____

54. glioblast _____

55. cerebrosclerosis _____

Diagnostic, Procedural, and Laboratory Terms

Many of the diagnostic tests used to examine the nervous system include electrodiagnostic procedures. An **electroencephalogram (EEG)** is a record of the electrical impulses of the brain (Figure 8-5). **Evoked potentials** are electrical waves observed in an electroencephalogram. Peripheral nervous system diseases can sometimes be detected by shocking the peripheral nerves and timing the conductivity of the shock. This procedure is called **nerve conduction velocity.** Polysomnography (PSG) is a recording of electrical and movement patterns during sleep to diagnose sleep disorders, such as *sleep apnea*, a dangerous breathing disorder.

Various types of imaging are used to visualize the structures of the brain and spinal cord. *Magnetic resonance imaging (MRI)* is the use of magnetic fields and radio waves to visualize structures. *Magnetic resonance angiography (MRA)* is the imaging of blood vessels to detect various abnormalities. **SPECT (single photon emission computed tomography) brain scan** is a procedure that produces brain images using radioactive isotopes. **PET (positron emission tomography)** is a procedure that produces excellent brain images using radioactive isotopes and tomography. **Computerized (axial) tomography (CT or CAT) scans** use tomography to show cross-sectional radiographic images.

X-rays are used to diagnose specific malformations or disorders. A **myelogram** is an x-ray of the spinal cord after a contrast medium is injected. A **cerebral angiogram** is an x-ray of the brain's blood vessels after a contrast medium is injected. An **encephalogram** is a record made by a study of the

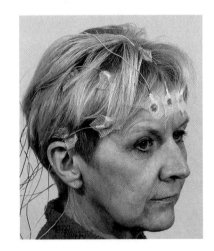

FIGURE 8-5 An electroencephalogram (EEG) records the brain's impulses. The impulses are collected from electrodes placed around the patient's head.

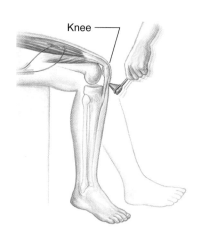

FIGURE 8-6 Tapping just below the knee usually causes a reflex reaction similar to the one shown here.

Knee

brain's ventricles. Sound waves are used to create brain images in a **transcranial sonogram** for diagnosing and managing head and stroke trauma.

Reflexes are involuntary muscular contractions in response to a stimulus. Reflex testing can aid in the diagnosis of certain nervous system disorders. **Babinski's reflex** is a reflex on the plantar surface of the foot. In most physical examinations, the reflex of each knee is tested for responsiveness (Figure 8-6).

Cerebrospinal fluid that has been withdrawn from between two lumbar vertebrae during a **lumbar (spinal) puncture** can be studied for the presence of various substances, which may indicate certain diseases.

VOCABULARY REVIEW

In the previous section, you learned terms relating to diagnosis, clinical procedures, and laboratory tests. Before going on to the exercises, read the definitions below. Pronunciations are provided for certain terms.

Term	Definition
Babinski's [bă-BĬN-skēz] **reflex**	Reflex on the plantar surface of the foot.
cerebral angiogram	X-ray of the brain's blood vessels after a dye is injected.
computerized (axial) tomography [(ĂKS-ē-ăl) tō-MŎG-ră-fē] **(CT or CAT) scan**	Radiographic imaging that produces cross-sectional images.
electroencephalogram [ē-LĔK-trō-ĕn-SĔF-ă-lō-grăm] **(EEG)**	Record of the electrical impulses of the brain.
encephalogram [ĕn-SĔF-ă-lō-grăm]	Record of the radiographic study of the ventricles of the brain.
evoked potentials [ē-VŌKT pō-TĔN-shălz]	Record of the electrical wave patterns observed in an EEG.
lumbar [LŬM-băr] **(spinal) puncture**	Withdrawal of cerebrospinal fluid from between two lumbar vertebrae.
myelogram [MĪ-ĕ-lō-grăm]	X-ray of the spinal cord after a contrast medium has been injected.

Term	Definition
nerve conduction velocity	Timing of the conductivity of an electrical shock administered to peripheral nerves.
PET (positron emission tomography) [(PŎZ-Ĭ-trŏn ē-MĬ-shŭn tō-MŎG-ră-fē)]	Imaging of the brain using radioactive isotopes and tomography.
polysomnography [PŎL-ē-sŏm-NŎG-ră-fē] (PSG)	Recording of electrical and movement patterns during sleep.
reflex [RĒ-flĕks]	Involuntary muscular contraction in response to a stimulus.
SPECT (single photon emission computed tomography) brain scan	Brain image produced by the use of radioactive isotopes.
transcranial sonogram [trănz-KRĀ-nē-ăl SŎN-ō-grăm]	Brain images produced by the use of sound waves.

CASE STUDY

Ordering Treatment

Dr. Stanley orders an electroencephalogram of Mr. Gutierrez's brain. He also orders some additional blood tests. Dr. Stanley performs a number of reflex tests. The abnormalities present confirm Dr. Stanley's initial suspicion of Parkinson's disease. He prescribes several medications and schedules a visit for Mr. Gutierrez in three weeks to discuss his progress. He asks Mr. Gutierrez to keep a daily log of his walking ability, any vision changes, his speech, and tremors for the three weeks until his appointment.

Critical Thinking

56. Why does Dr. Stanley want Mr. Gutierrez to keep a log?
57. What might Mr. Gutierrez's abnormal reflex tests indicate?

DIAGNOSTIC, PROCEDURAL, AND LABORATORY TERMS EXERCISES

Check Your Knowledge

Circle T for true and F for false.

58. SPECT is imaging of the spinal cord. T F
59. Reflexes are voluntary muscular contractions. T F
60. An encephalogram is a record of a study of the ventricles of the brain. T F
61. A lumbar puncture removes blood. T F
62. PET is an extremely accurate imaging system. T F
63. Evoked potentials are electrical waves. T F
64. A myelogram and an angiogram are both taken after injection of a contrast medium. T F
65. PSG is taken during waking hours. T F
66. Encephalography uses sound waves to produce brain images. T F

Pathological Terms

Neurologial disorders can be caused by trauma, congenital abnormalities, infectious disorders, degenerative diseases, or vascular conditions.

Trauma Disorders

A **concussion** is an injury to the brain from an impact with an object. A severe concussion can lead to **coma,** abnormally deep sleep with little or no response to stimuli. Coma can also result from other causes, such as stroke. A more serious trauma than concussion is a **brain contusion,** a bruising of the surface of the brain without penetration into the brain. A *subdural hematoma* (between the dura mater and the arachnoid or at the base of the dura mater) is a tumorlike collection of blood often caused by trauma. Injuries that result in penetration of the brain through the skull are usually extremely serious and often fatal.

Trauma to the brain can occur by breaking down of the blood-brain barrier. Go to http://faculty.washington.edu/chudler/bbb.html for some of the ways this can happen.

Congenital Disorders

Congenital diseases of the brain or spinal cord can be devastating and have an impact on the activities of daily living. **Spina bifida** is a defect in the spinal column sometimes with a **meningocele** (protrusion of the spinal meninges above the surface of the skin) or a **meningomyelocele** (protrusion of the meninges and spinal cord). **Tay-Sachs disease** is a hereditary disease found primarily in the descendants of Eastern European Jews. **Hydrocephalus** is an overproduction of fluid in the brain. It usually occurs at birth (although it can occur in adults with infections or tumors) and is treated with a shunt placed from the ventricle of the brain to the peritoneal space to relieve pressure by draining fluid. Figure 8-7 illustrates an infant with a shunt for relief of the pressure of hydrocephalus.

Degenerative Diseases

Degenerative diseases of the central nervous system can affect almost any part of the body. Deterioration in mental capacity is found in **dementia** and **Alzheimer's disease.** Some Alzheimer's symptoms are **amnesia** (loss of memory), **apraxia** (inability to properly use familiar objects), and **agnosia** (inability to receive and understand outside stimuli).

FIGURE 8-7 A shunt relieves the brain pressure of newborns with hydrocephalus.

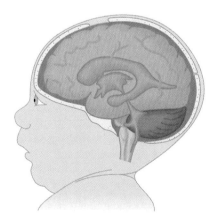
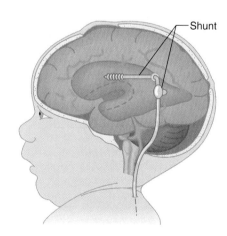

Shunt

Amyotrophic lateral sclerosis (ALS) is a degenerative disease of the motor neurons leading to loss of muscular control and death. It is also known as **Lou Gehrig's disease.** Several other degenerative diseases are not necessarily fatal. **Huntington's chorea** is a hereditary disease with uncontrollable, jerking movements and progressive loss of neural control. **Multiple sclerosis (MS)** is the destruction of the myelin sheath, called **demyelination,** leading to muscle weakness, unsteady **gait** (walking), **paresthesias** (odd sensations, of tingling, stinging, etc.), extreme fatigue, and some paralysis. In certain cases, it can lead to death. **Myasthenia gravis** is disease with muscle weakness. **Parkinson's disease** is a degeneration of nerves in the brain. It is treated with drugs that increase the levels of **dopamine** in the brain.

Most neurological disorders and diseases are helped by national organizations that maintain Web sites. See www.alz.org for information on Alzheimer's disease and www.nmss.org for information on multiple sclerosis. For other diseases, use a search engine and type in the name of the disease to find the Web site for the organization.

Nondegenerative Disorders

Severe neurological disorders cause paralysis, convulsions, and other symptoms, but are not necessarily degenerative or congenital. **Palsy** is partial or complete paralysis. **Cerebral palsy** includes lack of motor coordination from cerebral damage during gestation or birth. **Bell's palsy** is paralysis of one side of the face. It usually disappears after treatment. **Ataxia** is lack of voluntary muscle coordination.

Epilepsy is chronic, recurrent seizure activity. The seizures caused by this activity can be preceded by an **aura,** a collection of symptoms felt just before the actual seizure. **Absence seizures (petit mal seizures)** are mild and usually include only a momentary disorientation with the environment. **Tonic-clonic seizures (grand mal seizures)** are much more severe and include loss of consciousness, convulsions, and twitching of limbs. **Tourette syndrome** is a neurological disorder that causes uncontrollable sounds and twitching (**tics**).

Infectious Diseases

Infectious diseases of the nervous system include **shingles** (Figure 8-8), a viral disease, and **meningitis.** Several types of meningitis, inflammation of

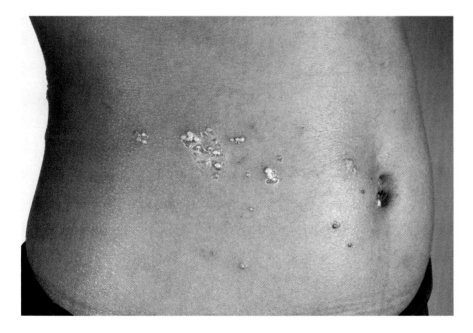

FIGURE 8-8   Shingles can cause severe pain.

the meninges, can be infectious. **Pyrogenic meningitis** (also called **bacterial meningitis**) is caused by bacteria and includes such symptoms as fever, headache, and stiff neck. It is usually treated with antibiotics. In some severe cases, it can be fatal. **Viral meningitis** is caused by any of several viruses. Inflammation can also occur in the nerves (**neuritis**), the spinal cord (**myelitis**), the brain (**encephalitis**), the cerebellum (**cerebellitis**), the dura mater (**duritis**), the ganglion (**gangliitis**), or the spinal nerve roots (**radiculitis**). Some specific nerve inflammations, such as **sciatica,** cause pain in the area served by the nerve.

Abnormal Growths

Abnormal growths in the nervous system usually occur in the brain or the meninges. **Gliomas** (tumors that arise from neuroglia) and **meningiomas** (tumors that arise from the meninges) can be either benign or malignant. Both may be removed surgically. **Astrocytoma, oligodendroglioma,** and **glioblastoma multiforme** are all types of gliomas, with the latter being the most malignant. A **ganglion** is any group of nerve cells bunched together to form a growth or a cyst, usually arising from a wrist tendon.

Vascular Disorders

Vascular problems, such as *arteriosclerosis,* may cause a **cerebrovascular accident (CVA),** a disruption in the normal blood supply to the brain. Various types of **strokes (cerebral infarctions)** result from this disruption. A **thrombus** (stationary blood clot) may cause **occlusion** (blocking of a blood vessel), which in turn may cause a **thrombotic stroke.** Short, strokelike incidents are known as **transient ischemic attacks (TIAs).** TIAs may be symptomless or may cause brief disorientation and speech and motor difficulty. An **embolic stroke** is caused by an **embolus,** a clot that travels from somewhere in the body to the cerebral arteries and blocks a small vessel, causing a sudden stroke. A **hemorrhagic stroke** is caused by blood escaping from a damaged cerebral artery. It may be caused by sudden trauma or an **aneurysm,** bursting of the wall of an artery after abnormal widening. Common symptoms of stroke are thought disorders, **dysphasia** (speech difficulty), **aphasia,** (loss of speech), loss of muscular control, some paralysis, and disorientation.

MORE ABOUT...

Tourette Syndrome

Medications for Tourette syndrome do not always work. People who have Tourette syndrome may not be able to function in social and work environments because of their inability to control sounds, often scatalogical in nature, and twitching, often extreme and repetitive. The National Tourette Syndrome Association publicizes information about the syndrome, holds conventions for people with the syndrome, and provides information and support to its members. This large support group holds social events where members feel comfortable with their fellow sufferers. More information is available from the Association's Web site (www.tsa-usa.org) or from conducting a search for the word *tourette.*

Some states of consciousness are changed by lack of oxygen or brain abnormalities that affect the flow of blood and oxygen to the brain. **Fainting** or **syncope** is caused by lack of oxygen to the brain. **Somnolence** (extreme sleepiness), **somnambulism** (sleepwalking), and **narcolepsy** (uncontrollable, sudden lapses into deep sleep) are all altered states of consciousness.

VOCABULARY REVIEW

In the previous section, you learned terms relating to pathology. Before going on to the exercises, read the definitions below. Pronunciations are provided for certain terms.

Term	Definition
absence seizure [SĔ-zhŭr]	Mild epileptic seizure consisting of brief disorientation with the environment.
agnosia [ăg-NŌ-zhē-ă] Greek, ignorance	Inability to receive and understand outside stimuli.
Alzheimer's [ĂLTS-hī-mĕrz] **disease**	A type of degenerative brain disease causing thought disorders, gradual loss of muscle control, and, eventually, death.
amnesia [ăm-NĒ-zhē-ă]	Loss of memory.
amyotrophic lateral sclerosis [ă-mī-ō-TRŌ-fĭk LĂT-ĕr-ăl sklĕ-RŌ-sĭs] **(ALS)**	Degenerative disease of the motor neurons leading to loss of muscular control and death.
aneurysm [ĂN-yū-rĭzm]	Abnormal widening of an artery wall that bursts and releases blood.
aphasia [ă-FĀ-zhē-ă]	Loss of speech.
apraxia [ă-PRĂK-sē-ă]	Inability to properly use familiar objects.
astrocytoma [ĂS-trō-sī-TŌ-mă]	Type of glioma formed from astrocytes.
ataxia [ă-TĂK-sē-ă]	Condition with uncoordinated voluntary muscular movement, usually resulting from disorders of the cerebellum or spinal cord.
aura [ĂW-ră]	Group of symptoms that precede a seizure.
bacterial meningitis [mĕn-ĭn-JĪ-tĭs]	Meningitis caused by a bacteria; pyrogenic meningitis.
Bell's palsy [PĂWL-zē]	Paralysis of one side of the face; usually temporary.
brain contusion [kŏn-TŪ-zhŭn]	Bruising of the surface of the brain without penetration.
cerebellitis [sĕr-ĕ-bĕl-Ī-tĭs]	Inflammation of the cerebellum.
cerebral infarction [SĔR-ē-brăl ĭn-FĂRK-shŭn]	*See* cerebrovascular accident.
cerebral palsy [PĂWL-zē]	Congenital disease caused by damage to the cerebrum during gestation or birth and resulting in lack of motor coordination.

Term	Definition
cerebrovascular [SĔR-ē-brō-VĂS-kyū-lăr] **accident (CVA)**	Neurological incident caused by disruption in the normal blood supply to the brain; stroke.
coma [KŌ-mă]	Abnormally deep sleep with little or no response to stimuli.
concussion [kŏn-KŬSH-ŭn]	Brain injury due to trauma.
dementia [dē-MĔN-shē-ă]	Deterioration in mental capacity, usually in the elderly.
demyelination [dē-MĪ-ĕ-lĭ-NĀ-shŭn]	Destruction of myelin sheath, particularly in MS.
dopamine [DŌ-pă-mēn]	Substance in the brain or manufactured substance that helps relieve symptoms of Parkinson's disease.
duritis [dū-RĪ-tĭs]	Inflammation of the dura mater.
dysphasia [dĭs-FĀ-zhē-ă]	Speech difficulty.
embolic [ĕm-BŎL-ĭk] **stroke**	Sudden stroke caused by an embolus.
embolus [ĔM-bō-lŭs]	Clot from somewhere in the body that blocks a small blood vessel in the brain.
encephalitis [ĕn-sĕf-ă-LĪ-tĭs]	Inflammation of the brain.
epilepsy [ĔP-ĭ-LĔP-sē]	Chronic recurrent seizure activity.
fainting	*See* syncope.
gait [gāt]	Manner of walking.
gangliitis [găng-glē-Ī-tĭs]	Inflammation of a ganglion.
ganglion (*pl.,* **ganglia, ganglions**) [GĂNG-glē-ŏn (-ă, -ŏns)]	Any group of nerve cell bodies forming a mass or a cyst in the peripheral nervous system; usually forms in the wrist.
glioblastoma multiforme [GLĪ-ō-blăs-TŌ-mă MŬL-tĭ-fŏrm]	Most malignant type of glioma.
glioma [glĭ-Ō-mă]	Tumor that arises from neuroglia.
grand mal [măhl] **seizure**	*See* tonic-clonic seizure.
hemorrhagic [hĕm-ō-RĂJ-ĭk] **stroke**	Stroke caused by blood escaping from a damaged cerebral artery.
Huntington's chorea [kōr-Ē-ă]	Hereditary disorder with uncontrollable, jerking movements.
hydrocephalus [hī-drō-SĔF-ă-lŭs]	Overproduction of fluid in the brain.
Lou Gehrig's [GĔR-ĭgz] **disease**	*See* amyotrophic lateral sclerosis.
meningioma [mĕ-NĬN-jē-Ō-mă]	Tumor that arises from the meninges.
meningitis [mĕ-nĭn-JĪ-tĭs]	Inflammation of the meninges.
meningocele [mĕ-NĬNG-gō-sēl]	In spina bifida cystica, protrusion of the spinal meninges above the surface of the skin.

Term	Definition
meningomyelocele [mĕ-nĭng-gō-MĪ-ĕ-lō-sēl]	In spina bifida cystica, protrusion of the meninges and spinal cord above the surface of the skin.
multiple sclerosis [MŬL-tĭ-pŭl sklĕ-RŌ-sĭs] **(MS)**	Degenerative disease with loss of myelin, resulting in muscle weakness, extreme fatigue, and some paralysis.
myasthenia gravis [mī-ăs-THĒ-nē-ă GRĂV-ĭs]	Disease involving overproduction of antibodies that block certain neurotransmitters; causes muscle weakness.
myelitis [mī-ĕ-LĪ-tĭs]	Inflammation of the spinal cord.
narcolepsy [NĂR-kō-lĕp-sē]	Nervous system disorder that causes uncontrollable, sudden lapses into deep sleep.
neuritis [nū-RĪ-tĭs]	Inflammation of the nerves.
occlusion [ō-KLŪ-zhŭn]	Blocking of a blood vessel.
oligodendroglioma [ŎL-ĭ-gō-DĔN-drŏ-glī-Ō-mă]	Type of glioma formed from oligodendroglia.
palsy [PĂWL-zē]	Partial or complete paralysis.
paresthesia [păr-ĕs-THĒ-zhē-ă]	Abnormal sensation, such as tingling.
Parkinson's disease	Degeneration of nerves in the brain caused by lack of sufficient dopamine.
petit mal [PĔ-tē măhl] **seizure**	*See* absence seizure.
pyrogenic [pī-rō-JĔN-ĭk] **meningitis**	Meningitis caused by bacteria; can be fatal; bacterial meningitis.
radiculitis [ră-dĭk-yū-LĪ-tĭs]	Inflammation of the spinal nerve roots.
sciatica [sī-ĂT-ĭ-kă]	Inflammation of the sciatic nerve.
shingles [SHĬNG-glz]	Viral disease affecting the peripheral nerves.
somnambulism [sŏm-NĂM-byū-lĭzm]	Sleepwalking.
somnolence [SŎM-nō-lĕns]	Extreme sleepiness caused by a neurological disorder.
spina bifida [SPĪ-nă BĬF-ĭ-dă]	Congenital defect of the spinal column.
stroke [strōk]	*See* cerebrovascular accident (CVA).
syncope [SĬN-kŏ-pē]	Loss of consciousness due to a sudden lack of oxygen in the brain.
Tay-Sachs [TĀ-săks] **disease**	Hereditary disease that causes deterioration in the central nervous system and, eventually, death.
thrombotic [thrŏm-BŎT-ĭk] **stroke**	Stroke caused by a thrombus.
thrombus [THRŎM-bŭs]	Stationary blood clot.
tics [tĭks]	Twitching movements that accompany some neurological disorders.

Term	Definition
tonic-clonic [TŎN-ĭk KLŎN-nĭk] seizure	Severe epileptic seizure accompanied by convulsions, twitching, and loss of consciousness.
Tourette [tū-RĔT] syndrome	Neurological disorder that causes uncontrollable speech sounds and tics.
transient ischemic [ĭs-KĒ-mĭk] attack (TIA)	Short neurological incident usually not resulting in permanent injury, but usually signaling that a larger stroke may occur.
viral meningitis	Meningitis caused by a virus and not as severe as pyrogenic meningitis.

CASE STUDY

Adjusting the Dosage

When Mr. Gutierrez returns to Dr. Stanley's office after three weeks, he reports that he can button his shirt again and that his walking has improved. He complains, however, that some of his cognitive symptoms have not improved. Dr. Stanley is encouraged that some of the physical symptoms have begun to improve. He will increase the dosage of the anti-Parkinson's medication he has prescribed. He is confident that Mr. Gutierrez will stabilize and possibly even gain strength.

Critical Thinking

67. Many medications cure the symptoms, but not the disease. How might exercise help Mr. Gutierrez regain mobility?
68. What compound does Mr. Gutierrez's medication contain?

PATHOLOGICAL TERMS EXERCISES

Check Your Knowledge

Fill in the blanks.

69. Palsy is partial or complete _____.

70. Dopamine sometimes helps the symptoms of _____ disease.

71. Inflammation of the spinal nerve roots is called _____.

72. A stationary blood clot is called a(n) _____.

73. A blood clot that moves is called a(n) _____

74. Abnormally deep sleep with lack of responsiveness is a(n) _____.

75. A mild stroke that may be a signal that a larger stroke will occur is called a(n) _____

_____ _____.

76. _____ seizures are milder than _____ seizures.

77. Multiple sclerosis is usually associated with loss of _____, a covering for nerves.

78. ALS is a disease of the _____ neurons.

Make a Match

Match the definition in the right-hand column with the correct word in the left-hand column.

79. ____ coma	**a.** speech difficulty
80. ____ aneurysm	**b.** fainting
81. ____ glioma	**c.** disruption in brain's blood supply
82. ____ duritis	**d.** loss of speech
83. ____ aphasia	**e.** short, mild stroke
84. ____ CVA	**f.** congenital spinal cord disorder
85. ____ spina bifida	**g.** abnormally deep sleep
86. ____ TIA	**h.** bursting of artery wall
87. ____ syncope	**i.** neurological tumor
88. ____ dysphasia	**j.** meningeal inflammation

Surgical Terms

Neurosurgeons are the specialists who perform surgery on the brain and spinal cord. A **lobectomy** is removal of a portion of the brain to treat epilepsy and other disorders, such as brain cancer. A **lobotomy,** severing of nerves in the frontal lobe of the brain, was once considered a primary method for treating mental illness. Now it is rarely used.

When it is necessary to operate directly on the brain (as in the case of a tumor), a **craniectomy,** removal of part of the skull, or a **craniotomy,** incision into the skull, may be performed. **Trephination** (or **trepanation**) is a circular opening into the skull to operate on the brain or to relieve pressure when there is fluid buildup. **Stereotaxy** or **stereotactic surgery** is the destruction of deep-seated brain structures using three-dimensional coordinates to locate the structures.

Neuroplasty is the surgical repair of a nerve. **Neurectomy** is the surgical removal of a nerve. A **neurotomy** is the dissection of a nerve. A **neurorrhaphy** is the suturing of a severed nerve. A **vagotomy** is the severing of the vagus nerve to relieve pain. **Cordotomy** is an operation to resect (remove part of) the spinal cord.

> Brain surgery is often performed using computers and minimal incisions. For up-to-date information, go to www.brain-surgery.com.

VOCABULARY REVIEW

In the previous section, you learned terms relating to surgery. Before going on to the exercises, read the definitions below. Pronunciations are provided for certain terms.

Term	Definition
cordotomy [kŏr-DŎT-ō-mē]	Removing part of the spinal cord.
craniectomy [krā-nē-ĔK-tō-mē] l	Removal of a part of the skull.
craniotomy [krā-nē-ŎT-ō-mē]	Incision into the skull.

Term	Definition
lobectomy [lō-BĔK-tō-mē]	Removal of a portion of the brain to treat certain disorders.
lobotomy [lō-BŎT-ō-mē]	Incision into the frontal lobe of the brain.
neurectomy [nū-RĔK-tō-mē]	Surgical removal of a nerve.
neuroplasty [NŪR-ō-PLĂS-tē]	Surgical repair of a nerve.
neurorrhaphy [nūr-ŎR-ă-fē]	Suturing of a severed nerve.
neurosurgeon [nūr-ō-SĔR-jŭn]	Medical specialist who performs surgery on the brain and spinal cord.
neurotomy [nū-RŎT-ō-mē]	Dissection of a nerve.
stereotaxy, stereotactic [stĕr-ē-ō-TĂK-sē, stĕr-ē-ō-TĂK-tĭk] surgery	Destruction of deep-seated brain structures using three-dimensional coordinates to locate the structures.
trephination, trepanation [trĕf-ĭ-NĀ-shŭn, trĕp-ă-NĀ-shŭn]	Circular incision into the skull.
vagotomy [vā-GŎT-ō-mē]	Surgical severing of the vagus nerve.

CASE STUDY

Repairing a Neurological Injury

Later in the year, Mr. Gutierrez was seriously injured in a car accident. He experienced some nerve damage in his leg. A neurosurgeon was called in to see if she could repair enough of the leg nerves to allow Mr. Gutierrez to walk. She operated, and the results were mixed. The trauma of the accident seemed to worsen some of the symptoms of Parkinson's disease, but Mr. Gutierrez experienced improvement with his walking after undergoing physical therapy. The neurologist decided not to increase Mr. Gutierrez's medication and to give him time to overcome the trauma.

Critical Thinking

89. The damaged leg nerves could actually be a result of an injury elsewhere in the body. What particular nerves or areas might the neurosurgeon examine before determining exactly where to operate?
90. Traumas can temporarily change body chemistry. The body produces dopamine naturally. Why did the doctor not increase the dosage?

SURGICAL TERMS EXERCISES

Check Your Knowledge

Fill in the blanks.

91. An incision into the skull is a(n) _____.
92. Removal of a portion of the skull is a(n) _____.
93. A circular skull incision is _____.
94. The incision into the frontal lobe is called a(n) _____.
95. The removal of a portion of the brain is called a(n) _____.

96. Suturing of a severed nerve is _____.

97. Removal of a nerve is _____.

98. Repair of a nerve is _____.

99. Vagotomy is severing the _____ nerve.

100. Removing a part of the spinal cord is a _____.

TERMINOLOGY IN ACTION

The following chart is for a 30-year-old. Write a brief paragraph discussing his current health and what steps he should be taking in light of his genetic profile.

Patient: Elijah Cannon   December 24, 2XXX

SUBJECTIVE: Patient has had daily headaches for 5 days. He has intermittent nausea and vomiting with the headaches. He also complains of flashing lights in the right eye for a few minutes before the onset of a headache. The headaches are not associated with any time of the day or activity. He is in general good health. Anti-inflammatory medications do not offer improvement. Cafergot has been prescribed in the past. Mother died after complications following a CVA at age 55.

OBJECTIVE:

EARS: TMs are clear.

EYES: Normal discs and venous pulsations.

MOUTH AND THROAT: Clear.

FACE: Sinus percussion reveals no tenderness.

NECK: Supple without tenderness or rigidity.

NEUROLOGIC: Cranial nerves II–XII are intact. Muscle strength and coordination normal.

ASSESSMENT: Vascular, cluster, or migraine variant.

PLAN: Midrin capsules two q.4h. p.r.n. at first sign of headache. Recheck p.r.n. or immmediately if symptoms worsen. Discuss long-term issues relating to mother's early death following a CVA.

USING THE INTERNET

Go to the Alzheimer's Association Web site (http://www.alz.org) and write a paragraph on recent developments in Alzheimer's research. Also, list the stages of Alzheimer's disease.

CHAPTER REVIEW

The material that follows is to help you review all the material in this chapter.

DEFINITIONS

Define the following terms and combining forms. Review the chapter before starting. Make sure you know how to pronounce each term as you define it. The blue words in curly brackets are references to the Spanish glossary on the Web site.

WORD	DEFINITION
absence seizure [SĒ-zhŭr]	
afferent [ĂF-ĕr-ĕnt] (sensory) neuron	
agnosia [ăg-NŌ-zhē-ă] {agnosia}	
Alzheimer's [ĂLTS-hī-mĕrz] disease	
amnesia [ăm-NĒ-zhē-ă] {amnesia}	
amyotrophic lateral sclerosis [ă-mī-ō-TRŌ-fĭk LĂT-ĕr-ăl sklĕ-RŌ-sĭs] (ALS)	
anesthetic [ăn-ĕs-THĚT-ĭk]	
aneurysm [ĂN-yū-rĭzm] {aneurisma}	
aphasia [ă-FĀ-zhē-ă] {afasia}	
apraxia [ă-PRĂK-sē-ă] {apraxia}	
arachnoid [ă-RĂK-nŏyd] {aracnoideo}	
astrocyte [ĂS-trō-sīt], astroglia [ăs-TRŎG-lē-ă] {astrocito, astroglia}	
astrocytoma[ĂS-trō-sī-TŌ-mă] {astrocitoma}	
ataxia [ă-TĂK-sē-ă] {ataxia}	
aura [ĂW-ră] {aura}	
autonomic [ăw-tō-NŎM-ĭk] nervous system	
axon [ĂK-sŏn] {axón}	
bacterial meningitis [měn-ĭn-JĪ-tĭs]	
Babinski's [bă-BĬN-skēz] reflex	
Bell's palsy [PĂWL-zē]	
brain [brān] {cerebro}	
brain contusion [kŏn-TŪ-zhŭn]	
brainstem {tronco encefálico}	

WORD	DEFINITION
cell body	
central nervous system (CNS)	
cerebell(o)	
cerebellitis [sĕr-ĕ-bĕl-Ī-tĭs] {cerebelitis}	
cerebellum [sĕr-ĕ-BĔL-ŭm]	
cerebr(o), cerebri	
cerebral [SĔR-ē-brăl] angiogram	
cerebral cortex [KŌR-tĕks]	
cerebral infarction [ĭn-FĂRK-shŭn]	
cerebral palsy [PĂWL-zē]	
cerebrospinal [SĔR-ĕ-brō-spī-năl] fluid (CSF)	
cerebrovascular [SĔR-ĕ-brō-VĂS-kyū-lăr] accident (CVA)	
cerebrum [SĔR-ĕ-brŭm, sĕ-RĒ-brŭm] {cerebrum}	
coma [KŌ-mă] {coma}	
computerized (axial) tomography [(ĂKS-ē-ăl) tō-MŎG-ră-fē] (CT or CAT) scan	
concussion [kŏn-KŬSH-ŭn] {concusión}	
conductivity [kŏn-dŭk-TĬV-ĭ-tē] {conductividad}	
convolution [kŏn-vō-LŪ-shŭn] {circunvolución}	
cordotomy [kōr-DŎT-ō-mē] {cordotomía}	
corpus callosum [KŌR-pŭs kă-LŌ-sŭm]	
crani(o)	
cranial [KRĀ-nē-ăl] nerves	
craniectomy [krā-nē-ĔK-tō-mē] {craniectomía}	
craniotomy [krā-nē-ŎT-ō-mē] {craneotomía}	
cranium [KRĀ-nē-ŭm] {cráneo}	
dementia [dē-MĔN-shē-ă] {demencia}	
demyelination [dē-MĪ-ĕ-lĭ-NĀ-shŭn] {desmielinación}	
dendrite [DĔN-drīt] {dendrita}	

WORD	DEFINITION

diencephalon [dī-ĕn-SĔF-ă-lŏn]
  {diencéfalo}

dopamine [DŌ-pă-mēn] {dopamina}

dura mater [DŪ-ră MĀ-tĕr]

duritis [dū-RĪ-tĭs]

dysphasia [dĭs-FĀ-zhē-ă] {disfasia}

efferent [ĔF-ĕr-ĕnt] (motor) neuron

electroencephalogram [ē-LĔK-trō-ĕn-
  SĔF-ă-lō-grăm] (EEG)
  {electroencefalógrafo}

embolic [ĕm-BŎL-ĭk] stroke

embolus [ĔM-bō-lŭs] {émbolo}

encephal(o)

encephalitis [ĕn-sĕf-ă-LĪ-tĭs]
  {encefalitis}

encephalogram [ĕn-SĔF-ă-lō-grăm]
  {encefalograma}

epidural [ĕp-ĭ-DŪ-răl space

epilepsy [ĔP-ĭ-LĔP-sē] {epilepsia}

epithalamus [ĔP-ĭ-THĂL-ă-mŭs]
  {epitálamo}

evoked potentials [ē-VŌKT pō-
  TĔN-shălz]

excitability [ĕk-SĪ-tă-BĬL-ĭ-tē]
  {excitabilidad}

fainting

fissure [FĬSH-ŭr] {fisura}

frontal lobe

gait [gāt] {marcha}

gangli(o)

gangliitis [găng-glē-Ī-tĭs] {ganglitis}

ganglion (*pl.* ganglia, ganglions)
  [GĂNG-glē-ŏn (-a, -ons)] {ganglio}

gli(o)

glioblastoma multiforme [GLĪ-ō-blăs-
  TŌ-mă MŬL-tĭ-fŏrm]

glioma [glī-Ō-mă] {glioma}

grand mal [măhl] seizure

WORD	DEFINITION

gyrus (*pl.*, gyri) [JĪ-rŭs (JĪ-rī)]
  {circunvolución}

hemorrhagic [hĕm-ō-RĂJ-ĭk] stroke

Huntington's chorea [kōr-Ē-ă]

hydrocephalus [hī-drō-SĔF-ă-lŭs]
  {hidrocefalia}

hypothalamus [HĪ-pō-THĂL-ă-mŭs]
  {hipotálamo}

interneuron [ĬN-tĕr-NŪ-rŏn]
  {interneurona}

lobectomy [lō-BĔK-tō-mē] {lobotomía}

lobotomy [lō-BŎT-ō-mē]

Lou Gehrig's [GĔR-ĭgz] disease

lumbar [LŬM-băr] (spinal) puncture

medulla oblongata [mĕ-DŪL-ă ŏb-lŏng-
  GĂ-tă]

mening(o), meningi(o)

meninges (*sing.*, meninx) [mĕ-NĬN-jēz
  (MĒ-nĭngks)] {meninges}

meningioma [mĕ-NĬN-jē-Ō-mă]
  {meningioma}

meningitis [mĕn-ĭn-JĪ-tĭs] {meningitis}

meningocele [mĕ-NĬNG-gō-sēl]
  {meningocele}

meningomyelocele [mĕ-nĭng-gō-MĪ-
  ĕ-lō-sēl] {meningomielocele}

microglia [mī-KRŎG-lē-ă] {microglia}

midbrain {cerebro medio}

multiple sclerosis [MŬL-tĭ-pŭl sklĕ-
  RŌ-sĭs] (MS)

myasthenia gravis [mī-ăs-THĒ-nē-ă
  GRĂV-ĭs]

myel(o)

myelin sheath [MĪ-ĕ-lĭn shēth]

myelitis [mī-ĕ-LĪ-tĭs]

myelogram [MĪ-ĕ-lō-grăm]
  {mielograma}

narcolepsy [NĂR-kō-lĕp-sē]
  {narcolepsia}

Word	Definition
nerve [nĕrv] {nervio}	_____
nerve cell	_____
nerve conduction velocity	_____
nerve impulse	_____
neur(o), neuri	_____
neurectomy [nū-RĔK-tō-mē] {neurectomía}	_____
neurilemma [nūr-ĭ-LĔM-ă] {neurilema}	_____
neuritis [nū-RĪ-tĭs] {neuritis}	_____
neuroglia [nū-RŎG-lē-ă], neuroglial [nū-RŎG-lē-ăl] cell	_____
neuron [NŪR-ŏn] {neurona}	_____
neuroplasty [NŪR-ō-PLĂS-tē]	_____
neurorrhaphy [nūr-ŎR-ă-fē]	_____
neurosurgeon [nūr-ō-SĔR-jŭn] {neurocirujano}	_____
neurotomy [nū-RŎT-ō-mē]	_____
neurotransmitter [NŪR-ō-trăns-MĬT-ĕr] {neurotramisor}	_____
occipital lobe [ŏk-SĬP-ĭ-tăl lōb]	_____
occlusion [ō-KLŪ-zhŭn] {oclusión}	_____
oligodendroglia [ŌL-ĭ-gō-dĕn-DRŎG-lē-ă] {oligodendroglia}	_____
oligodendroglioma [ŌL-ĭ-gō-DĔN-drŏ-glī-Ō-mă] {oligodendroglioma}	_____
palsy [PĂWL-zē] {parálisis}	_____
parasympathetic [păr-ă-sĭm-pă-THĔT-ĭk] nervous system	_____
paresthesia [pār-ĕs-THĒ-zhē-ă]	_____
parietal lobe [pă-RĪ-ĕ-tăl lōb]	_____
Parkinson's disease	_____
PET (positron emission tomography) {TEP}	_____
petit mal [PĔ-tē măhl] seizure	_____
pia mater [PĪ-ă, PĒ-ă MĀ-tĕr, MĂ-tĕr)] {piamadre}	_____
polysomnography [PŎL-ē-sŏm-NŎG-ră-fē] (PSG)	_____

WORD	DEFINITION

pons [pŏnz] {pons}

pyrogenic [pī-rō-JĔN-ĭk] meningitis

radiculitis [ră-dĭk-yū-LĪ-tĭs] {radiculitis}

receptor [rē-SĔP-tĕr] {receptor}

reflex [RĒ-flĕks] {reflejo}

sciatica [sī-ĂT-ĭ-kă] {ciática}

shingles [SHĬNG-glz] {culebrilla}

somatic [sō-MĂT-ĭk] nervous system

somnambulism [sŏm-NĂM-byū-lĭzm]
    {sonambulismo}

somnolence [SŎM-nō-lĕns]
    {somnolencia}

SPECT (single photon emission
    computed tomography) brain scan

spin(o)

spina bifida [SPĪ-nă BĬF-ĭ-dă]

spinal cord

spinal nerves

stereotaxy [stĕr-ē-ō-TĂK-sē],
    stereotactic [stĕr-ē-ō-TĂK-tĭk]
    surgery

stimulus (pl., stimuli) [STĬM-yū-lŭs
    (STĬM-yū-lī)] {estimulo}

stroke [strōk] {accidente
    cerebrovascular}

subdural [sŭb-DŪR-ăl] space

sulcus (pl., sulci) [SŬL-kŭs (SŬL-sī)]
    {surco}

sympathetic [sĭm-pă-THĔT-ĭk]
    nervous system

synapse [SĬN-ăps] {sinapsis}

syncope [SĬN-kŏ-pē] {síncope}

Tay-Sachs [TĀ-săks] disease

temporal lobe [TĔM-pō-răl lōb]

terminal end fibers

thalam(o)

thalamus [THĂL-ă-mŭs] {tálamo}

thrombotic [thrŏm-BŎT-ĭk] stroke

WORD	DEFINITION
thrombus [THRŎM-bŭs] {trombo}	_____
tic [tĭk] {tic}	_____
tonic-clonic [TŎN-ĭk KLŎN-nĭk] seizure	_____
transcranial sonogram [trănz-KRĀ-nē-ăl SŎN-ō-grăm]	_____
trephination [trĕf-ĭ-NĀ-shŭn], trepanation [trĕp-ă-NĀ-shŭn]	_____
Tourette [tū-RĔT] syndrome	_____
transient ischemic [ĭs-KĒ-mĭk] attack (TIA)	_____
vag(o)	_____
vagotomy [vā-GŎT-ō-mē]	_____
ventral thalamus	_____
ventricle [VĔN-trĭ-kl] {ventrículo}	_____
ventricul(o)	_____
viral meningitis	_____

Answers to Chapter Exercises

1. brainstem, frontal lobe, temporal lobe
2. symptoms may point to one or two specific disorders
3. a. dura mater
   b. arachnoid
   c. pia mater
4. d
5. h
6. i
7. c
8. g
9. j
10. a
11. e
12. b
13. f
14. receptors
15. myelin sheath
16. dendrites
17. axons
18. medulla oblongata
19. cerebrum
20. pons
21. cranium, or skull
22. cerebrospinal fluid
23. diencephalon
24. meninges
25. thalamus
26. ganglia
27. C
28. C
29. axon
30. C
31. convolutions
32. neuroglia
33. cerebellum
34. Mr. Gutierrez has normal blood pressure and no history of CVA. He does, however, have neurological impairments and may well have a neurological disorder.

35. Yes, a stroke or other blood vessel condition can cause them.
36. encephalo-, brain; myelo-, spinal cord
37. cranio-, skull; meningo-, meninges
38. glio-, neuroglia; neuro-, nerve
39. cerebro-, cerebrum; meningo-, meninges
40. spino-, spine; neur-, nerve
41. neuro-, nerve, encephalo-, brain, myelo-, spinal cord
42. vago-
43. neur-
44. glio-
45. mening-
46. encephal-, brain
47. neur-, nerve
48. cephalo-, head
49. myel-, spinal cord
50. meningo-, meninges
51. neuro-, nerve
52. cranio-, cranium
53. vago-, vagus nerve
54. glio-, neuroglia
55. cerebro-, cerebrum
56. to see how the medicine is helping to reduce symptoms and to adjust the dosage as necessary
57. weakened reflexes, particularly in the legs and hands
58. F
59. F
60. T
61. F
62. T
63. T
64. T
65. F
66. F
67. Once the weakness symptoms are relieved, exercise can

strengthen muscles in the legs and arms.
68. dopamine
69. paralysis
70. Parkinson's
71. radiculitis
72. thrombus
73. embolus
74. coma
75. transient ischemic attack
76. absence, tonic-clonic (or petit mal, grand mal)
77. myelin
78. motor
79. g
80. h
81. i
82. j
83. d
84. c
85. f
86. e
87. b
88. a
89. spinal, brainstem
90. because Mr. Gutierrez may normalize within a short time and an overdose might cause other problems
91. craniotomy
92. craniectomy
93. trephination (or trepanation)
94. lobotomy
95. lobectomy
96. neurorrhaphy
97. neurectomy
98. neuroplasty
99. vagus
100. cordotomy

9

The Urinary System

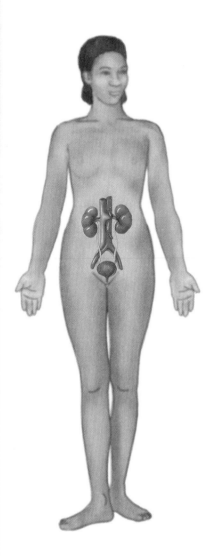

After studying this chapter, you will be able to:

▶ Name the parts of the urinary system and discuss the function of each part
▶ Define combining forms used in building words that relate to the urinary system
▶ Name the common diagnoses, clinical procedures, and laboratory tests used in treating disorders of the urinary system
▶ List and define the major pathological conditions of the urinary system
▶ Explain the meaning of surgical terms related to the urinary system

Structure and Function

The **urinary system** (also called the *renal system* or *excretory system*) maintains the proper amount of water in the body and removes waste products from the blood by excreting them in the urine. The urinary system consists of:

- Two **kidneys**, organs that remove dissolved waste and other substances from the blood and urine
- Two **ureters**, tubes that transport urine from the kidneys to the bladder
- The **bladder**, the organ that stores urine
- The **urethra**, a tubular structure that transports urine through the **meatus**, the external opening of a canal, to the outside of the body

Figure 9-1a shows the urinary system, and Figure 9-1b diagrams the path of urine through the system.

Kidneys

The kidneys are located in the **retroperitoneal** (posterior to the peritoneum) space. Urine is produced by **filtration** of water, salts, sugar, **urea**, and other nitrogenous waste materials such as **creatine** (and its component **creatinine**) and **uric acid**. The kidneys have an outer protective portion, the **cortex**, and an inner soft portion, the **medulla**, which is a term used for the inner, soft portion of any organ. In the middle of the concave side of the kidney is a depression, the **hilum**, through which the blood vessels, the nerves, and the ureters enter and exit the kidney.

The functional unit of the kidney is the **nephron** (Figure 9-2), which produces **urine**. Each nephron contains a *renal corpuscle* made up of a group

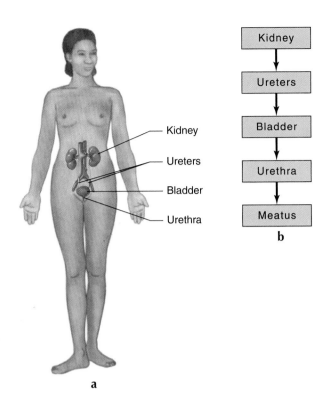

a

Kidney

Ureters

Bladder

Urethra

Meatus

b

of capillaries called a **glomerulus** (*pl.*, **glomeruli**) (Figure 9-3). The kidney produces **renin**, a substance that causes an increase in the blood pressure in order to maintain the filtration rate of blood. Each glomerulus is surrounded by a capsule, **Bowman's capsule**, where this fluid collects.

Urine travels to the **renal pelvis**, a collecting area in the center of the kidney. The renal pelvis contains small cuplike structures called **calices** (also spelled **calyces;** singular **calyx),** that collect urine. Figure 9-4 shows a kidney.

MORE ABOUT...

Blood Pressure and the Kidneys

The kidneys have mechanisms to maintain *homeostasis* (equilibrium) in the filtration rate of the glomeruli. The constant flow of water and its substances back into the bloodstream and the flow of water and waste substances into the renal tubule maintain the body's balance of water, salts (the most common salt in the body is sodium chloride), sugars (the most common sugar in the body is glucose), and other substances. To do this, the kidneys have two lines of action. The first is the automatic dilating and constricting of the arterioles as needed to increase or decrease the flow of blood into the glomeruli. The second is to release renin to increase the blood pressure and thus the filtration rate of blood to maintain a constant supply. Maintaining homeostasis affects blood pressure either by lowering it when blood is flowing too quickly or by increasing it when blood is flowing too slowly. Some forms of high blood pressure are caused by the effort of poorly functioning kidneys to maintain homeostasis.

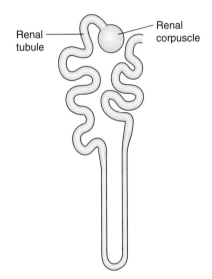

Renal tubule

Renal corpuscle

FIGURE 9-2 A nephron contains both a renal corpuscle and a renal tubule.

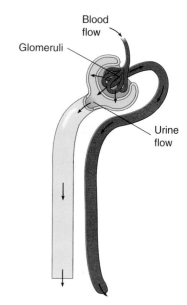

FIGURE 9-3 Blood flows into the glomeruli where urine is excreted and moved to the kidney's cortex.

FIGURE 9-4 The kidneys form urine for excretion and retain essential substances for reabsorption.

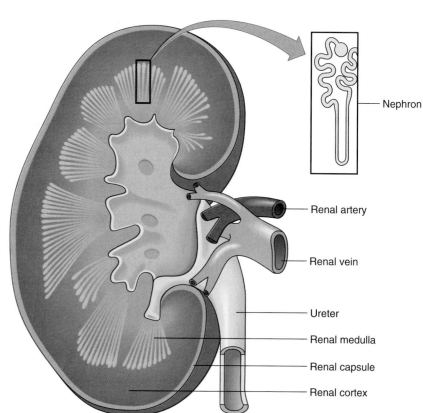

Ureters

Attached to each kidney is a ureter, a tube (usually 16 to 18 centimeters long) that transports urine from the renal pelvis to the urinary bladder.

Bladder

The **urinary bladder** (Figure 9-5) is a hollow, muscular organ that stores urine until it is ready to be excreted from the body.

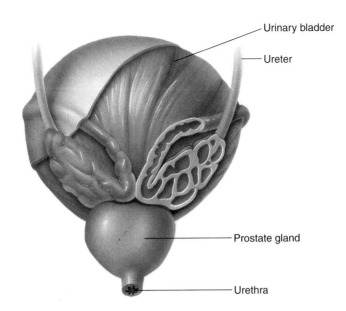

Urinary bladder

Ureter

Prostate gland

Urethra

FIGURE 9-5 Bladders store urine to be released into the urethra to exit the body.

Urethra

Urine is excreted outside the body through the urethra, a tube of smooth muscle with a mucous lining.

VOCABULARY REVIEW

In the previous section, you learned terms relating to the urinary system. Before going on to the exercises, read the definitions below. Pronunciations are provided for certain terms.

Term	Definition
bladder [BLĂD-ĕr]	Organ where urine collects before being excreted from the body.
Bowman's [BŌ-măns] **capsule**	Capsule surrounding a glomerulus and serving as a collection site for urine.
calices, calyces (*sing.*, **calix, calyx**) [KĂL-ĭ-sēz (KĀ-lĭks)]	Cup-shaped structures in the renal pelvis for the collection of urine.
cortex [KŌR-tĕks]	Outer portion of the kidney.
creatine [KRĒ-ă-tēn]	Substance found in urine; elevated levels may indicate muscular dystrophy.
creatinine [krē-ĂT-ĭ-nēn]	A component of creatine.
filtration [fĭl-TRĀ-shŭn]	Process of separating solids from a liquid by passing it through a porous substance.
glomerulus (*pl.*, **glomeruli**) [glō-MĂR-yū-lŏs (glō-MĂR-yū-lī)]	Group of capillaries in a nephron.

Term	Definition
hilum [HĪ-lŭm]	Portion of the kidney where blood vessels and nerves enter and exit.
kidney [KĬD-nē]	Organ that forms urine and reabsorbs essential substances back into the bloodstream.
meatus [mē-Ă-tŭs]	External opening of a canal, such as the urethra.
medulla [mĕ-DŪL-ă]	Soft, central portion of the kidney.
nephron [NĔF-rŏn]	Functional unit of a kidney.
renal pelvis	Collecting area for urine in the center of the kidney.
renin [RĔ-nĭn]	Enzyme produced in the kidneys to regulate the filtration rate of blood by increasing blood pressure as necessary.
retroperitoneal [RĔ-trō-PĔR-ĭ-tō-nē-ăl]	Posterior to the peritoneum.
urea [yū-RĒ-ă]	Waste product of nitrogen metabolism excreted in normal adult urine.
ureter [yū-RĒ-tēr]	One of two tubes that conduct urine from the kidney to the bladder.
urethra [yū-RĒ-thră]	Tube through which urine is transported from the bladder to the exterior of the body.
uric [YŪR-ĭk] **acid**	Nitrogenous waste excreted in the urine.
urinary [YŪR-ĭ-nār-ē] **bladder**	*See* bladder.
urinary system	Body system that forms and excretes urine and helps in the reabsorption of essential substances.
urine [YŪR-ĭn]	Fluid excreted by the urinary system.

STRUCTURE AND FUNCTION EXERCISES

Check Your Knowledge

Fill in the blanks.

1. Urine is transported within the urinary system via the _____.

2. Urine is transported to the outside of the body via the _____.

3. Each kidney has about one million _____.

4. The renal corpuscle contains a mass of capillaries termed a _____.

5. The collecting area in the center of the kidney is called the _____ _____.

6. The external opening of the urethra is the _____.

7. The urethra draws urine from the _____.

8. Removal of waste from the blood takes place in the _____.

9. A fluid collection site in a nephron is called a _____ _____.

10. A waste product excreted in urine is _____.

Check Your Accuracy

Circle T for true or F for false.

11. The urethra transports urine from the kidney to the bladder. T F

12. Renin increases blood flow through the kidneys. T F

13. Two fluid collection sites within the kidney are the calices and the Bowman's capsule. T F

14. The female urethra opens into the vagina. T F

Go with the Flow

Put the following steps, which describe the flow of urine, in order by placing the letters a through g in the space provided.

15. Urine flows from the ureters into the bladder._____

16. Fluid collects in the Bowman's capsule._____

17. Urine flows through the renal tubules to ducts in the kidney. _____

18. Urine exits the body. _____

19. Urine flows from the bladder to the urethra. _____

20. Urine flows from the kidneys into the ureter. _____

21. Fluid flows from the Bowman's capsule to the renal tubule. _____

CASE STUDY

Visiting a Clinic

Central Valley HMO is located in a large medical office building next to a hospital complex. The first floor is a large clinic where patients are evaluated first. Later, they may be referred to specialists located in the same building.

Three of the morning patients complained of problems relating to the urinary system. The first, Mr. Delgado, was having difficulty urinating. The second, Ms. Margolis, showed blood in her urine, and the third, Ms. Jones, complained of frequent, painful, and scanty urination. All three were seen by Dr. Chorzik, a family practitioner employed by the HMO.

Critical Thinking

22. Is blood normally seen in the urine? Why or why not?

23. Does the fact that Mr. Delgado and Ms. Jones are of different sexes make the diagnosis of their urinary problems different?

Combining Forms

The list below includes combining forms that relate specifically to the urinary system. Pronunciations are provided for the examples.

Combining Form	Meaning	Example
cali(o), calic(o)	calix	*calioplasty* [KĂ-lē-ō-plăs-tē], surgical reconstruction of a calix
cyst(o)	bladder, especially the urinary bladder	*cystitis* [sĭs-TĪ-tĭs], bladder inflammation
glomerul(o)	glomerulus	*glomerulitis* [glō-MĀR-yū-LĪ-tĭs], inflammation of the glomeruli
meat(o)	meatus	*meatotomy* [mē-ă-TŎT-ō-mē], surgical enlargement of the meatus
nephr(o)	kidney	*nephritis* [nĕ-FRĪ-tĭs], kidney inflammation
pyel(o)	renal pelvis	*pyeloplasty* [PĪ-ĕ-lō-plăs-tē], surgical repair of the renal pelvis
ren(o)	kidney	*renomegaly* [RĒ-nō-MĔG-ă-lē], enlargement of the kidney
trigon(o)	trigone, structure at the base of the bladder	*trigonitis* [TRĪ-gō-NĪ-tĭs], inflammation of the trigone of the bladder
ur(o), urin(o)	urine	*uremia* [yū-RĒ-mē-ă], excess of urea and other nitrogenous wastes in the blood
ureter(o)	ureter	*ureterostenosis* [yū-RĒ-tĕr-ō-stĕ-NŌ-sĭs], narrowing of a ureter
urethr(o)	urethra	*urethrorrhea* [yū-rē-thrō-RĒ-ă], abnormal discharge from the urethra
-uria	of urine	*anuria* [ăn-yū-RĒ-ă], lack of urine formation
vesic(o)	bladder, generally used when describing something in relation to a bladder	*vesicoabdominal* [VĔS-ĭ-kō-ăb-DŎM-ĭ-năl], relating to the urinary bladder and the abdominal wall

Using Tests for Diagnosis

Dr. Chorzik ordered a urinalysis for each of the three patients. The results give some clues to a possible diagnosis. Note that the column marked Flag indicates when something is out of the range of normal. The reference column gives the normal ranges, and the results column gives the actual readings for the patients' tests. A clean catch urine test is one in which the urine is collected once the area has been cleaned and some urine has been excreted first.

Critical Thinking

24. Whose tests had the most abnormal readings?
25. Name at least three of the items being tested for.

Dr. Joel Chorzik
1420 Glen Road
Meadowvale, OK 44444
111-222-3333

Run Date: 09/22/XX
Run Time: 1507

Page 1
Specimen Report

Patient: James Delgado	Acct #: A994584732	Loc: ED	U #:
Reg Dr: S. Anders, M.D.	Age/Sx: 55/M	Room:	Reg: 09/22/XX
	Status: Reg ER	Bed:	Des:

Spec #: 0922 : U0009A   Coll: 09/22/XX   Status: Comp   Req #: 77744444
                         Recd.: 09/22/XX   Subm Dr:

Entered: 09/22/XX–0841   Other Dr:
Ordered: UA with micro
Comments: Urine Description: Clean catch urine

Test	Result	Flag	Reference
Urinalysis			
UA with micro			
COLOR	YELLOW		
APPEARANCE	HAZY	**	
SP GRAVITY	1.018		1.001-1.030
GLUCOSE	NORMAL		NORMAL mg/dl
BILIRUBIN	NEGATIVE		NEG
KETONE	NEGATIVE		NEG mg/dl
BLOOD	2+	**	NEG
PH	5.0		4.5-8.0
PROTEIN	TRACE	**	NEG mg/dl
UROBILINOGEN	NORMAL		NORMAL-1.0 mg/dl
NITRITES	NEGATIVE		NEG
LEUKOCYTES	2+	**	NEG
WBC	20-50	**	0-5 /HPF
RBC	2-5		0-5 /HPF
EPI CELLS	20-50		/HPF
BACTERIA	2+	**	
MUCUS			

Patient 1

continued on page 250

	Dr. Joel Chorzik		
Run Date: 09/22/XX	1420 Glen Road		Page 1
Run Time: 1507	Meadowvale, OK 44444		Specimen Report
	111-222-3333		

Patient: Sarah Margolis	Acct #: E005792849	Loc:	U #:
Reg Dr: S. Anders, M.D.	Age/Sx: 45/F	Room:	Reg: 09/22/XX
	Status: Reg ER	Bed:	Des:

Spec #: 0922 : U00010R   Coll: 09/22/XX   Status: Comp   Req #: 00704181
Recd.: 09/22/XX   Subm Dr:

Entered: 09/22/XX–0936   Other Dr:
Ordered: UA with micro
Comments: Urine Description: Clean catch urine

Test	Result	Flag	Reference
Urinalysis			
UA with micro			
COLOR	BROWNISH	***	
APPEARANCE	HAZY	***	
SP GRAVITY	1.017		1.001-1.030
GLUCOSE	NORMAL		NORMAL mg/dl
BILIRUBIN	NEGATIVE		NEG
KETONE	NEGATIVE		NEG mg/dl
BLOOD	TRACE	**	NEG
PH	5.0		4.5-8.0
PROTEIN	NEGATIVE		NEG mg/dl
UROBILINOGEN	NORMAL		NORMAL-1.0 mg/dl
NITRITES	NEGATIVE		NEG
LEUKOCYTES	NEGATIVE		NEG
WBC	NO CELLS		0-5 /HPF
RBC	2-5		0-5 /HPF
EPI CELLS	0-2		/HPF
MUCUS	1+		

Patient 2

	Dr. Joel Chorzik		
Run Date: 09/22/XX	1420 Glen Road		Page 1
Run Time: 1507	Meadowvale, OK 44444		Specimen Report
	111-222-3333		

Patient: Lisa Jones	Acct #: F009435543	Loc:	U #:
Reg Dr: S. Anders, M.D.	Age/Sx: 35/F	Room:	Reg: 09/22/XX
	Status: Reg ER	Bed:	Des:

Spec #: 0922 : U0008A   Coll: 09/22/XX   Status: Comp   Req #: 00704876
Recd.: 09/22/XX   Subm Dr:

Entered: 09/22/XX–0925   Other Dr:
Ordered: UA with micro
Comments: Urine Description: Clean catch urine

Test	Result	Flag	Reference
Urinalysis			
UA with micro			
COLOR	BROWNISH	***	
APPEARANCE	HAZY	***	
SP GRAVITY	1.017		1.001-1.030
GLUCOSE	NORMAL		NORMAL mg/dl
BILIRUBIN	NEGATIVE		NEG
KETONE	NEGATIVE		NEG mg/dl
BLOOD	TRACE	***	NEG
PH	5.0		4.5-8.0
PROTEIN	NEGATIVE		NEG mg/dl
UROBILINOGEN	NORMAL		NORMAL-1.0 mg/dl
NITRITES	NEGATIVE		NEG
LEUKOCYTES	POSITIVE	***	NEG
WBC	6-7	***	0-5 /HPF
RBC	7-8	***	0-5 /HPF
EPI CELLS	0-2		/HPF
MUCUS	1+		

Patient 3

COMBINING FORMS EXERCISES

Build Your Medical Vocabulary

Complete the words by adding combining forms, suffixes, or prefixes you have learned in this chapter and in Chapters 1, 2, and 3.

26. Lack of urination: _____urea.

27. Inflammation of the renal pelvis: _____itis

28. Excessive urination: _____uria

29. Kidney disease: _____pathy

30. Scanty urination: olig_____

31. Bladder paralysis: _____plegia

32. Lipids in the urine: lip_____

33. Abnormally large bladder: mega_____

34. Relating to the bladder and the urethra: vesico_____al

35. Kidney enlargement: reno_____

36. Inflammation of the tissues surrounding the bladder: _____cystitis

37. Medical specialty concerned with kidney disease: _____logy

38. Inflammation of the renal pelvis and other kidney parts: pyelo_____itis

39. Suturing of a calix: calio_____

40. Between the two kidneys: inter_____

41. Abnormal urethral discharge: urethro_____

42. Hemorrhage from a ureter: _____rrhagia

43. Softening of the kidneys: nephro_____

44. Within the urinary bladder: _____cystic

45. Removal of a kidney stone: _____litho_____

46. Imaging of the kidney: _____graphy

47. Kidney-shaped: reni _____

Root Out the Meaning

Divide the following words into parts. Write the urinary combining forms in the space at the right and define the word shown.

48. glomerulonephritis

49. nephrocystosis

50. urethrostenosis

41. ureterovesicostomy

52. urocyanosis

53. urolithology

54. pyeloureterectasis

55. calicotomy

56. cystolithotomy

57. nephroma

58. meatorrhaphy

59. nephrosclerosis

60. renopulmonary

61. trigonitis

Diagnostic, Procedural, and Laboratory Terms

Specialists in the urinary system are *urologists*, who treat disorders of the male and female urinary tracts and the male reproductive system, and *nephrologists*, who treat disorders of the kidneys. **Urinalysis** is the most common diagnostic and laboratory test of the urinary system.

Urinalysis

Urinalysis is the examination of urine for its physical and chemical and microscopic properties (Figure 9-6). Some patients do not have bladder control or may have certain conditions that require catheters to aid in urination. A **Foley catheter** (Figure 9-7) is **indwelling** (left in the bladder). Other types of catheters may be disposable units. **Condom catheters** are changed at least once a day (Figure 9-8).

There are three phases of a complete urinalysis:

1. The first phase is the *macroscopic* or *physical phase*. During this phase, the color, turbidity (cloudiness caused by suspended sediment), and **specific gravity** (ratio of density of a substance) of urine give certain diagnostic clues.
2. The second phase is the *chemical phase*, which determines what chemicals are present in the urine. It also determines the **pH** range of urine. The normal pH range is from 5 to 7.
3. The third phase is the *microscopic phase* during which urine sediment is examined for solids (including cellular material) or **casts**, which are formed when protein accumulates in the urine.

Appendix C gives the chemical analyses and ranges commonly used in urinalysis.

In addition, tests of urine are designed to detect various substances indicative of specific conditions. Table 9-1 lists some of the substances found in urine and what they indicate.

TABLE 9-1 Substances found in urinalysis.

Substance	What It May Indicate
acetone	diabetes
ketones	starvation or diabetes
albumin	nephron disease
glucose	diabetes
bacteria	infection
calcium	rickets
bilirubin	liver disease

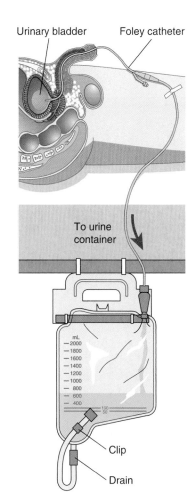

FIGURE 9-7 A Foley catheter remains in place; the collection bag is drained and cleaned.

Meadow Health Systems, Inc.
1420 Glen Road
Meadowvale, OK 44444
111-222-3333

Run Date: 02/22/XX
Run Time: 1632

Page 1
Specimen Report

Patient: Maria Bozutti
Reg Dr: S. Anders, M.D.

Acct #: C038642
Age/Sx: 28/F
Status: Reg ER

Loc:
Room:
Bed:

U #:
Reg: 02/22/XX
Des:

Spec #: 0222 : U00022

Coll: 02/22/XX
Recd.: 02/22/XX

Status: Comp
Subm Dr:

Req #: 77744590

Entered: 02/22/XX–0841
Ordered: UA with micro
Comments: Urine Description: Clean catch urine

Other Dr:

Test	Result	Flag	Reference
Urinalysis			
UA with micro			
COLOR	YELLOW		
APPEARANCE	HAZY		
SP GRAVITY	1.018		1.001-1.030
GLUCOSE	2.604	***	NORMAL mg/dl
BILIRUBIN	NEGATIVE		NEG
KETONE	NEGATIVE		NEG mg/dl
BLOOD	NEGATIVE		NEG
PH	5.0		4.5-8.0
PROTEIN	NEGATIVE		NEG mg/dl
UROBILINOGEN	NORMAL		NORMAL-1.0 mg/dl
NITRITES	NEGATIVE		NEG
LEUKOCYTES	NEGATIVE		NEG
WBC	3		0-5 /HPF
RBC	3.5		0-5 /HPF
EPI CELLS	20-50		/HPF
BACTERIA	NEGATIVE		
MUCUS			

FIGURE 9-6 Urinalysis is a crucial diagnostic test. Dissolved wastes in the urine may reveal any of a number of diseases. For example, in the test results shown here, the patient's glucose is higher than normal, indicating possible diabetes.

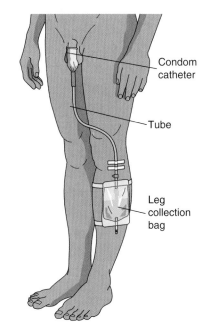

FIGURE 9-8 A condom catheter is changed daily.

Blood Tests

Two important blood tests of kidney function are the *blood urea nitrogen* (*BUN*) and the *creatinine clearance test*. **Phenylketones** in the blood show a lack of an important enzyme that can lead to mental retardation in infants unless a strict diet is followed into adulthood.

Imaging Tests

Various tests are used to visually diagnose stones, growths, obstructions, or abnormalities in the urinary system. Table 9-2 lists imaging tests of the urinary system.

Urinary Tract Procedures

Certain procedures, particularly **dialysis**, can mechanically maintain kidney or renal function when kidney failure occurs. **Hemodialysis** is the process of

TABLE 9-2 Urinary imaging tests.

Imaging Tests	Description
cystoscopy	uses a **cystocope** to examine the bladder (Figure 9-9)
kidney, ureter, bladder (KUB)	x-ray of three parts of the urinary system
retrograde pyelogram (RP)	x-ray taken after contrast medium is introduced
voiding (urinating) cystourethrogram (VCU, VCUG)	x-ray taken during urination
renogram	scan of kidney function

filtering blood outside the body in an artificial kidney machine and returning it to the body after filtering. **Peritoneal dialysis** is the insertion and removal of a dialysis solution into the peritoneal cavity (Figure 9-10).

Extracorporeal shock wave lithotripsy (ESWL) is the breaking up of urinary stones by using shock waves from outside the body.

FIGURE 9-9   Using a cystoscope, a urologist can view the inside of the urinary bladder.

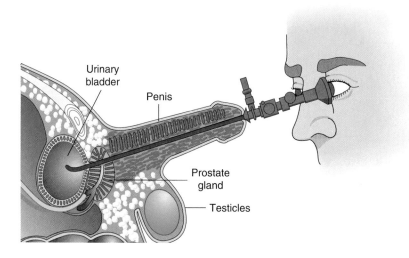

Urinary bladder

Penis

Prostate gland

Testicles

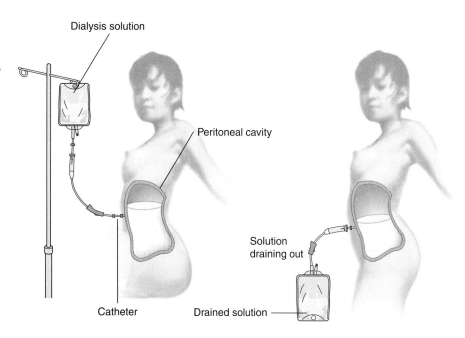

FIGURE 9-10 In peritoneal dialysis, the inserted fluid stays in the peritoneal cavity for about 6 hours until it is drained out through the opening in the peritoneum.

Dialysis solution

Peritoneal cavity

Solution draining out

Catheter

Drained solution

VOCABULARY REVIEW

In the previous section, you learned terms relating to diagnosis, clinical procedures, and laboratory tests. Before going on to the exercises, read the definitions below. Pronunciations are provided for certain terms.

Term	Definition
acetone [ĂS-ĕ-tōn]	Type of ketone normally found in urine in small quantities; found in larger quantities in diabetic urine.
albumin [ăl-BYŪ-mĭn]	Simple protein; when leaked into urine, may indicate a kidney problem.
bilirubin [bĭl-ĭ-RŪ-bĭn]	Substance produced in the liver; elevated levels may indicate liver disease or hepatitis when found in urine.
casts	Materials formed in urine when protein accumulates; may indicate renal disease.
condom catheter [KŎN-dŏm KĂTH-ĕ-tĕr]	Disposable catheter for urinary sample collection or incontinence.
cystoscope [SĬS-tō-skōp]	Tubular instrument for examining the interior of the bladder.
cystoscopy [sĭs-TŎS-kō-pē]	The insertion of a cystoscope to examine the bladder with light.
dialysis [dī-ĂL-ĭ-sĭs]	Method of filtration used when kidneys fail.
extracorporeal shock wave lithotripsy [ĔKS-tră-kōr-PŌR-ē-ăl shŏk wāv LĬTH-ō-trĭp-sē] **(ESWL)**	Breaking of kidney stones by using shock waves from outside the body.

Term	Definition
Foley [FŌ-lē] **catheter**	Indwelling catheter held in place by a balloon that inflates inside the bladder.
glucose [GLŪ-kōs]	Form of sugar found in the blood; may indicate diabetes when found in the urine.
hemodialysis [HĒ-mō-dī-ĂL-ĭ-sĭs]	Dialysis performed by passing blood through a filter outside the body and returning filtered blood to the body.
indwelling [ĬN-dwĕ-lĭng]	Of a type of catheter inserted into the body.
ketone [KĒ-tōn]	Substance that results from the breakdown of fat; indicates diabetes or starvation when present in the urine.
kidney, ureter, bladder (KUB)	X-ray of three parts of the urinary system.
peritoneal [PĔR-ĭ-tō-NĒ-ăl] **dialysis**	Type of dialysis in which liquid that extracts substances from blood is inserted into the peritoneal cavity and later emptied outside the body.
pH	Measurement of the acidity or alkalinity of a solution such as urine.
phenylketones [FĔN-ĭl-KĒ-tōns]	Substances that, if accumulated in the urine of infants, indicate phenylketonuria (PKU), a disease treated by diet.
renogram [RĒ-nō-grăm]	Radioactive imaging of kidney function after introduction of a substance that is filtered through the kidney while it is observed.
retrograde pyelogram [RĔT-rō-grād PĪ-ĕl-ō-grăm] **(RP)**	X-ray of the bladder and ureters after a contrast medium is injected into the bladder.
specific gravity	Measurement of the concentration of wastes, minerals, and solids in urine.
urinalysis [yū-rĭ-NĂL-ĭ-sĭs]	Examination of the properties of urine.
voiding (urinating) cystourethrogram [sĭs-tō-yū-RĒ-thrō-grăm] **(VCU, VCUG)**	X-ray image made after introduction of a contrast medium and while urination is taking place.

Case Study

Examining the Symptoms

Ms. Jones is a 77-year-old female who complained to Dr. Chorzik of painful, scanty, and frequent urination for the past two days. She says that she normally drinks 7 to 8 glasses of water a day, but lately has cut down because of the frequent urination. Her urine was cloudy with a strong odor.

Critical Thinking

62. What did the cloudy urine most likely indicate?
63. What might be present in cloudy urine to indicate infection?

Find the Test

In the space provided, put Y for those properties or substances tested for in urinalysis and N for those substances that are not tested for in urinalysis.

64. glucose _____

65. sodium _____

66. albumin _____

67. cholesterol _____

68. protein _____

69. lipids _____

70. specific gravity _____

70. pH _____

72. bilirubin _____

73. acetone _____

74. phenylketones _____

75. ketones _____

76. homocysteine _____

Finish the Thought

Fill in the blanks.

77. Removing wastes from the blood outside the body is called _____.

78. Removing wastes from the peritoneal cavity using a portable apparatus is called _____ _____.

79. A type of indwelling catheter is (a) _____ catheter.

80. A catheter changed at least once a day is called a(n)_____ catheter.

71. Two substances found in the urine that may indicate diabetes are _____ and _____.

82. Lithotripsy is used to break up _____ that have formed.

83. Solids found in urine are called _____.

84. Dialysis is a method of _____ used in _____ failure.

85. Kidney disorders may be diagnosed by blood tests such as the _____ _____

_____ or _____ _____ _____.

86. An x-ray image taken during urination is a(n) _____ _____.

Pathological Terms

Infections can occur anywhere in the urinary tract. A **urinary tract infection (UTI)** commonly refers to a bladder or urethra infection.

> The National Kidney and Urologic Diseases Information Clearinghouse gives facts about UTI prevention and treatment on their Web site (http://kidney.niddk.nih.gov/kudiseases/pubs/utiadult/index.htm).

MORE ABOUT...

Bed-wetting

Some children, particularly boys, may wet their beds at night (a condition called *nocturnal enuresis*) up to their teenage years. For years, parents have tried everything from humiliation and restricting fluids, to some sort of shock therapy, such as awakening with a loud sound. Most of these methods have not worked. Usually the problem resolves by itself by the teenage years or earlier. In most cases, the children are found to have immature development of the urinary tract, allergies, or such sound sleep habits that they are unable to awaken. Medications are now available to control or treat enuresis.

Some additional photos of interesting kidney stones can be seen at http://www.herringlab.com/photos/.

A number of infections and inflammations affect the urinary system. Table 9-3 lists some of the infections, inflammations, conditions, and disorders that affect the urinary system.

TABLE 9-3 Urinary system disorders.

Urinary System Disorder	Where It Occurs	Description
nephritis	kidney	inflammation
glomulerulonephritis or Bright's disease	glomuleri	inflammation
pyelitis	renal pelvis	inflammation
nephrosis	syndrome that shows protein in the urine	may cause edema (swelling)
hydronephrosis	kidney blockage	urine is not released from kidneys
polycystic kidney disease	kidney cysts	hereditary condition
kidney failure	kidneys	often a result of another disease such as diabetes
uremia, azotemia	excess urea and other waste in the urinary system	may result from kidney failure
end-stage renal disease (ESRD)	kidneys	often fatal
Wilms' tumor or nephroblastoma	kidneys	malignant tumor
nephroma	kidney	tumor
cystitis	bladder	inflammation
bladder cancer	bladder	
cystocele	hernia of the bladder	
cystolith	bladder	stone
anuria	no urine output	
enuresis	lack of bladder control	
dysuria	painful urination	
nocturia	frequent nighttime urination	
oliguria	scanty urination	
polyuria	excessive urination	
incontinence	involuntary discharge of urine or feces	
albuminuria or proteinuria	albumin in urine	
hematuria	blood in urine	
ketonuria	ketones in urine	
pyuria	pus in urine	
calculi or stones	urinary tract	can cause pain and blockages
atresia	narrowing of the ureters or urethra	

VOCABULARY REVIEW

In the previous section, you learned terms relating to pathology. Before going on to the exercises, read the definitions below. Pronunciations are provided for certain terms.

Term	Definition
albuminuria [ăl-byū-mĭ-NŪ-rē-ă]	Presence of albumin in urine, usually indicative of disease.
anuria [ăn-YŪ-rē-ă]	Lack of urine formation.
atresia [ă-TRĒ-zhē-ă]	Abnormal narrowing, as of the ureters or urethra.
azotemia [ăz-ō-TĒ-mē-ă]	*See* uremia.
bladder cancer	Malignancy of the bladder.
Bright's disease	Inflammation of the glomeruli that can result in kidney failure.
cystitis [sĭs-TĪ-tĭs]	Inflammation of the bladder.
cystocele [SĬS-tō-sēl]	Hernia of the bladder.
cystolith [SĬS-tō-lĭth]	Bladder stone.
dysuria [dĭs-YŪ-rē-ă]	Painful urination.
edema [ĕ-DĒ-mă]	Retention of water in cells, tissues, and cavities, sometimes due to kidney disease.
end-stage renal disease (ESRD)	The last stages of kidney failure.
enuresis [ĕn-yū-RĒ-sĭs]	Urinary incontinence.
glomerulonephritis [glō-MĀR-yū-lō-nĕf-RĪ-tĭs]	Inflammation of the glomeruli of the kidneys.
hematuria [hē-mă-TŪ-rē-ă]	Blood in the urine.
hydronephrosis [HĪ-drō-nĕ-FRŌ-sĭs]	Abnormal collection of urine in the kidneys due to a blockage.
incontinence [ĭn-KŎN-tĭ-nĕns]	Inability to prevent excretion of urine or feces.
ketonuria [kē-tō-NŪ-rē-ă]	Increased urinary excretion of ketones, usually indicative of diabetes or starvation.
kidney failure	Loss of kidney function.
nephritis [nĕ-FRĪ-tĭs]	Inflammation of the kidneys.
nephroblastoma [NĔF-rō-blăs-TŌ-mă]	*See* Wilms' tumor.
nephroma [nĕ-FRŌ-mă]	Any renal tumor.
nephrosis [nĕ-FRŌ-sĭs]	Disorder indicated by protein in the urine.
nocturia [nŏk-TŪ-rē-ă]	Frequent nighttime urination.

Term	Definition
oliguria [ŏl-ĭ-GŪ-rē-ă]	Scanty urine production.
polycystic [pŏl-ē-SĬS-tĭk] kidney disease	Condition with many cysts on and within the kidneys.
polyuria [pŏl-ē-ŬR-ē-ă]	Excessive urination.
proteinuria [prō-tē-NŪ-rē-ă]	Abnormal presence of protein in the urine.
pyelitis [pī-ĕ-LĪ-tĭs]	Inflammation of the renal pelvis.
pyuria [pī-YŪ-rē-ă]	Pus in the urine.
uremia [yū-RĒ-mē-ă]	Excess of urea and other nitrogenous wastes in the blood.
urinary tract infection (UTI)	Infection of the urinary tract.
Wilms' [vĭlmz] tumor	Malignant kidney tumor found primarily in young children; nephroblastoma.

CASE STUDY

Seeing a Specialist

Mr. Delgado had a fairly normal urinalysis with slight abnormalities, but restricted urination indicated some other urinary tract problem. Dr. Chorzik referred Mr. Delgado to a urologist. Ms. Margolis had blood in her urine and some signs of infection. Ms. Jones had pus in her urine, and it was cloudy. She had complained about painful, scanty, and excessive urination at various times. Dr. Chorzik concluded that she had a urinary tract infection.

Critical Thinking

87. What are the medical terms for the symptoms Ms. Jones experienced?
88. What course of treatment will likely be prescribed for Ms. Jones?

PATHOLOGICAL TERMS EXERCISES

Build Your Medical Vocabulary

Using the combining forms in this chapter, complete the names of the disorders.

89. Inflammation of the urethra: _____ itis

90. Inflammation of the ureter: _____ itis

91. Inflammation of the bladder and urethra: _____ itis

92. Inflammation of the kidneys: _____ itis

93. Tumor in the kidneys: _____ oma

Spell It Correctly

Check the spelling of the following words. Write C if the spelling is correct. If it is incorrect, write the correct spelling in the space provided.

94. ureteritis_____

95. cystitis_____

96. dysuria_____

97. uretheritis_____

98. cytorrhaphy_____

Check Your Knowledge

Circle T for true or F for false.

99. Wilms' tumor is found only in middle-aged adults. T F

100. Urine collects in the renal pelvis. T F

101. Edema is swelling that may be due to kidney disease. T F

102. Oliguria is abnormally high production of urine. T F

103. Anuresis means the same as enuresis. T F

Surgical Terms

Urology is the practice of medicine specializing in the urinary tract. The practitioner is called a urologist.

Parts of the urinary system may be surgically removed, repaired, biopsied, or otherwise treated. Table 9-4 gives urinary system surgical procedures.

TABLE 9-4 Urinary system surgical procedures.

Surgical Procedure	Where Located	Purpose
nephrectomy	kidney	removal
nephrolysis	kidney	removal of adhesions
nephrostomy	kidney	creation of an opening in the kidney
nephrolithotomy	kidney	removal of a stone
nephropexy	kidney	affixing in place of a floating kidney
nephrorrhaphy	kidney	suturing of damage
pyelotomy	renal pelvis	incision
pyeloplasty	renal pelvis	repair
ureteroplasty	ureter	repair
ureterorrhaphy	ureter	suture
ureterectomy	ureter	removal

TABLE 9-4 Urinary system surgical procedures (*cont.*).

Surgical Procedure	Where Located	Purpose
lithotomy	bladder or other area	removal of a stone or stones
cystectomy	bladder	removal
cystoplasty	bladder	repair
cystopexy	bladder	fixing in place
urethropexy	urethra	fixing in place
urethroplasty	urethra	repair
urethrorrhaphy	urethra	suturing
urethrostomy	urethra	creation of an opening to the outside
urethrotomy	urethra	incision to enlarge
meatotomy	enlargement of the meatus	
urostomy	abdomen	creation of an opening to release urine
intracorporeal electrohydraulic lithotripsy	urinary tract	use of an endoscope to examine and break up stones
resectoscope	urinary system	cut and remove lesions

VOCABULARY REVIEW

In the previous section, you learned terms relating to surgery. Before going on to the exercises, read the definitions below. Pronunciations are provided for certain terms.

Term	Definition
cystectomy [sĭs-TĔK-tō-mē]	Surgical removal of the bladder.
cystopexy [SĬS-tō-pĕk-sē]	Surgical fixing of the bladder to the abdominal wall.
cystoplasty [SĬS-tō-plăs-tē]	Surgical repair of the bladder.
cystorrhaphy [sĭs-TŌR-ă-fē]	Suturing of a damaged bladder.
intracorporeal electrohydraulic lithotripsy [ĬN-tră-kōr-PŌ-rē-ăl ē-LĔK-trō-hī-DRŌ-lĭk LĬTH-ō-trĭp-sē]	Use of an endoscope to break up stones.
lithotomy [lĭ-THŎT-ō-mē]	Surgical removal of bladder stones.
meatotomy [mē-ă-TŎT-ō-mē]	Surgical enlargement of the meatus.
nephrectomy [nĕ-FRĔK-tō-mē]	Removal of a kidney.
nephrolithotomy [NĔF-rō-lĭ-THŎT-ō-mē]	Surgical removal of a kidney stone.
nephrolysis [nĕ-FRŎL-ĭ-sĭs]	Removal of kidney adhesions.

Term	Definition
nephropexy [NĔF-rō-pĕk-sĕ]	Surgical fixing of a kidney to the abdominal wall.
nephrorrhaphy [nĕf-RŌR-ă-fē]	Suturing of a damaged kidney.
nephrostomy [nĕ-FRŎS-tō-mē]	Establishment of an opening from the renal pelvis to the outside of the body.
pyeloplasty [PĪ-ĕ-lō-PLĂS-tē]	Surgical repair of the renal pelvis.
pyelotomy [pī-ĕ-LŎT-ō-mē]	Incision into the renal pelvis.
resectoscope [rē-SĔK-tō-skōp]	Type of endoscope for removal of lesions.
ureterectomy [yū-rē-tĕr-ĔK-tō-mē]	Surgical removal of all or some of a ureter.
ureteroplasty [yū-RĒ-tĕr-ō-PLĂS-tē]	Surgical repair of a ureter.
ureterorrhaphy [yū-rē-tĕr-ŌR-ă-fē]	Suturing of a ureter.
urethropexy [yū-RĒ-thrō-pĕk-sē]	Surgical fixing of the urethra.
urethroplasty [yū-RĒ-thrō-PLĂS-tē]	Surgical repair of the urethra.
urethrorrhaphy [yū-rē-THRŌR-ă-fē]	Suturing of the urethra.
urethrostomy [yū-rē-THRŎS-tō-mē]	Establishment of an opening between the urethra and the exterior of the body.
urethrotomy [yū-rē-THRŎT-ō-mē]	Surgical incision of a narrowing in the urethra.
urology [yū-RŎL-ō-jē]	Medical specialty that diagnoses and treats the urinary system and the male reproductive system.
urostomy [yū-RŎS-tō-mē]	Establishment of an opening in the abdomen to the exterior of the body for the release of urine.

CASE STUDY

Getting the Diagnosis

Patient #1: Mr. Delgado's appointment with the urologist was scheduled for the next day. During a physical examination, the urologist noticed some swelling in the prostate gland, but did not think this was enough to cause Mr. Delgado's difficulties. The urologist ordered a blood test (PSA) to determine if there were another possible cause. The PSA results were normal. The urologist then ordered imaging tests. One test showed a narrowing of the urethra.

Patient #2: Ms. Margolis, a 45-year-old female, had additional tests and was found to have serious kidney disease in one kidney. A nephrectomy was performed, and eventually her symptoms subsided.

Critical Thinking

104. What procedure might relieve Mr. Delgado's symptoms?

105. Ms. Margolis had one kidney removed. The other one is healthy. Does she need dialysis?

Build Your Medical Vocabulary

Complete the name of the operation by adding one or more combining forms.

106. Removal of kidney stones: _____ tomy

107. Removal of kidney adhesions: _____ lysis

108. Removal of a kidney: _____ ectomy

109. Removal of a ureter: _____ ectomy

110. Creation of an artificial opening in the urinary tract: _____ stomy

Check Your Knowledge

Circle T for true or F for false.

111. Surgical repair of the urethra is ureteroplasty. T F

112. Several organs and structures in the urinary system may need surgical attaching to be held in position. T F

113. A resectoscope is an instrument used to remove lesions. T F

114. A urethrostomy and a urostomy serve the same function. T F

TERMINOLOGY IN ACTION

Below is a urinalysis for a 55-year old woman. Write a short paragraph explaining what pathology the abnormal readings might indicate.

```
                        Meadow Health Systems, Inc.
                              1420 Glen Road
    Run Date: 09/22/XX       Meadowvale, OK 44444        Page 1
    Run Time: 1507               111-222-3333            Specimen Report
```

Patient: Mary Langado	Acct #: E115592848	Loc:	U #:
Reg Dr: S. Anders, M.D.	Age/Sx: 55/F	Room:	Reg: 06/10/XX
	Status: Reg ER	Bed:	Des:

Spec #: 0922 : U00010R	Coll: 09/22/XX	Status: Comp	Req #: 00704181
	Recd.: 09/22/XX	Subm Dr:	

Entered: 06/10/XX–0936
Ordered: UA with micro
Comments: Urine Description: Clean catch urine

Test	Result	Flag	Reference
Urinalysis			
UA with micro			
COLOR	BROWNISH	***	
APPEARANCE	HAZY	***	
SP GRAVITY	1.017		1.001-1.030
GLUCOSE	5.2	**	NEG
BILIRUBIN	NEGATIVE		NEG
KETONE	NEGATIVE		NEG mg/dl
BLOOD	TRACE	***	NEG
PH	5.0		4.5-8.0
PROTEIN	NEGATIVE		NEG mg/dl
UROBILINOGEN	NORMAL		NORMAL-1.0 mg/dl
NITRITES	NEGATIVE		NEG
LEUKOCYTES	NEGATIVE		NEG
WBC	8-10	**	0-5 /HPF
RBC	2-5		0-5 /HPF
EPI CELLS	0-2		/HPF
MUCUS	1+		

Patient 5

USING THE INTERNET

Go to the National Kidney Foundation's Web site (http://www.kidney.org) and enter the cyberNephrology site by typing *cybernephrology* in the search window. Write a short paragraph on what's new in transplantation or dialysis.

CHAPTER REVIEW

The material that follows is to help you review all the material in this chapter.

DEFINITIONS

Define the following terms and combining forms. Review the chapter before starting. Make sure you know how to pronounce each term as you define it. The blue words in brackets are references to the Spanish glossary on the Web site.

WORD	DEFINITION
acetone [ĂS-ĕ-tōn] {acetona}	_____
albumin [ăl-BYŪ-mĭn] {albúmina}	_____
albuminuria [ăl-byū-mĭ-NŪ-rē-ă] {albuminuria}	_____
anuria [ăn-YŪ-rē-ă] {anuria}	_____
atresia [ă-TRĒ-zhē-ă] {atresia}	_____
azotemia [ăz-ō-TĒ-mē-ă] {azoemia}	_____
bilirubin [bĭl-ĭ-RŪ-bĭn] {bilirrubina}	_____
bladder [BLĂD-ĕr] {vejiga}	_____
bladder cancer	_____
Bowman's capsule	_____
Bright's disease	_____
cali(o), calic(o)	_____
calices, calyces (_sing._ calix, calyx) [KĂL-ĭ-sēz (KĀ-lĭks)] {calices}	_____
casts	_____
condom catheter [KŎN-dŏm KĂTH-ĕ-tĕr]	_____
cortex [KŌR-tĕks] {corteza}	_____
creatine [KRĒ-ă-tēn] {creatina}	_____
creatinine [krē-ĂT-ĭ-nēn] {creatinina}	_____
cyst(o)	_____
cystectomy [sĭs-TĔK-tō-mē] {cistectomía}	_____
cystitis [sĭs-TĪ-tĭs] {cistitis}	_____
cystocele [SĬS-tō-sēl] {cistocele}	_____
cystolith [SĬS-tō-lĭth] {cistolito}	_____

WORD	DEFINITION
cystopexy [SĬS-tō-pĕk-sē]	
cystoplasty [SĬS-tō-plăs-tē]	
cystorrhaphy [sĭs-TŌR-ă-fē] {cistorrafia}	
cystoscope [SĬS-tō-skōp] {cistoscopio}	
cystoscopy [sĭs-TŎS-kō-pē]	
dialysis [dī-ĂL-ĭ-sĭs] {dialysis}	
dysuria [dĭs-YŪ-rē-ă] {disuria}	
edema [ĕ-DĒ-mă] {edema}	
end-stage renal disease (ESRD)	
enuresis [ĕn-yū-RĒ-sĭs] {enuresis}	
extracorporeal shock wave lithotripsy [ĔKS-tră-kōr-PŌR-ē-ăl shŏk wāv LĬTH-ō-trĭp-sē] (ESWL)	
filtration [fĭl-TRĀ-shŭn] {filtración}	
Foley [FŌ-lē] catheter	
glomerul(o)	
glomerulonephritis [glō-MĀR-yū-lō-nĕf-RĪ-tĭs]	
glomerulus (pl., glomeruli) [glō-MĀR-yū-lŏs (glō-MĀR-yū-lī)] {glomérulo}	
glucose [GLŪ-kōs] {glucose}	
hematuria [hē-mă-TŪ-rē-ă] {hematuria}	
hemodialysis [HĒ-mō-dī-ĂL-ĭ-sĭs] {hemodiálisis}	
hilum [HĪ-lŭm] {hilio}	
hydronephrosis [HĪ-drō-nĕ-FRŌ-sĭs]	
incontinence [ĭn-KŎN-tĭ-nĕns] {incontinecia}	
indwelling [ĬN-dwĕ-lĭng]	
intracorporeal electrohydraulic lithotripsy [ĬN-tră-kōr-PŌ-rē-ăl ē-LĔK-trō-hī-DRŌ-lĭk LĬTH-ō-trĭp-sē]	
ketone [KĒ-tōn] {cetona}	
ketonuria [kē-tō-NŪ-rē-ă] {cetonuria}	
kidney [KĬD-nē] {riñón}	
kidney failure	
kidney, ureter, bladder (KUB)	
lithotomy [lĭ-THŎT-ō-mē]	

meat(o)

meatotomy [mē-ă-TŎT-ō-mē]

meatus [mē-Ă-tŭs] {meato}

medulla [mĕ-DŪL-ă] {médula}

nephrectomy [nĕ-FRĔK-tō-mē]

nephritis [nĕ-FRĪ-tĭs] {nefritis}

nephr(o)

nephroblastoma [NĔF-rō-blăs-TŌ-mă]

nephrolithotomy [NĔF-rō-lĭ-THŎT-ō-mē]

nephrolysis [nĕ-FRŎL-ĭ-sĭs] {nefrólisis}

nephroma [nĕ-FRŌ-mă] {nefroma}

nephron [NĔF-rŏn] {nefrona}

nephropexy [NĔF-rō-pĕk-sē]

nephrorrhaphy [nĕf-RŌR-ă-fē]

nephrosis [nĕ-FRŌ-sĭs] {nefrosis}

nephrostomy [nĕ-FRŎS-tō-mē]

nocturia [nŏk-TŪ-rē-ă] {nocturia}

oliguria [ŏl-ĭ-GŪ-rē-ă] {oliguria}

peritoneal [PĔR-ĭ-tō-NĒ-ăl] dialysis

pH {pH}

phenylketones [FĔN-ĭl-KĒ-tōns]

polycystic [pŏl-ē-SĬS-tĭk] kidney disease

polyuria [pŏl-ē-ŬR-ē-ă] {poliuria}

proteinuria [prō-tē-NŪ-rē-ă]

pyel(o)

pyelitis [pī-ĕ-LĪ-tĭs] {pielitis}

pyeloplasty [PĪ-ĕ-lō-PLĂS-tē]

pyelotomy [pī-ĕ-LŎT-ō-mē]

pyuria [pī-YŪ-rē-ă] {piuria}

ren(o)

renal pelvis

renin [RĔ-nĭn] {renina}

renogram [RĒ-nō-grăm] {renograma}

resectoscope [rē-SĔK-tō-skōp] {resectoscopio}

WORD	DEFINITION
retrograde pyelogram [RĚT-rō-grād PĪ-ĕl-ō-grăm] (RP)	
retroperitoneal [RĚ-trō-PĚR-ĭ-tō-nē-ăl] {retroperitoneal}	
specific gravity	
trigon(o)	
ur(o), urin(o)	
urea [yū-RĒ-ă] {urea}	
uremia [yū-RĒ-mē-ă] {uremia}	
ureter(o)	
ureter [yū-RĒ-tĕr] {uréter}	
ureterectomy [yū-rē-tĕr-ĔK-tō-mē]	
ureteroplasty [yū-RĒ-tĕr-ō-PLĂS-tē]	
ureterorrhaphy [yū-rē-tĕr-ŌR-ă-fē]	
urethr(o)	
urethra [yū-RĒ-thră] {uretra}	
urethropexy [yū-RĒ-thrō-pĕk-sē]	
urethroplasty [yū-RĒ-thrō-PLĂS-tē]	
urethrorrhaphy [yū-rē-THRŌR-ă-fē]	
urethrostomy [yū-rē-THRŎS-tō-mē]	
urethrotomy [yū-rē-THRŎT-ō-mē]	
-uria	
uric [YŪR-ĭk] acid	
urinalysis [yū-rĭ-NĂL-ĭ-sĭs] {análisis de orina}	
urinary [YŪR-ĭ-nār-ē] bladder	
urinary system	
urinary tract infection (UTI)	
urine [YŪR-ĭn] {orina}	
urology [yū-RŎL-ō-jē] {urología}	
urostomy [yū-RŎS-tō-mē]	
vesic(o)	
voiding (urinating) cystourethrogram [sĭs-tō-yū-RĒ-thrō-grăm] (VCU, VCUG)	
Wilms' [vĭlmz] tumor	

Answers to Chapter Exercises

1. ureters
2. urethra
3. nephrons
4. glomerulus
5. renal pelvis
6. meatus
7. bladder
8. kidneys
9. Bowman's capsule
10. urea
11. F
12. T
13. T
14. F
15. e
16. a
17. c
18. g
19. f
20. d
21. b
22. No, blood is normally filtered in the kidneys and returned to the bloodstream.
23. Yes, males have prostates, external urethral exits, and other anatomical features different from females, whose urethras are shorter than those of males.
24. Patient 1
25. sample answer: white blood count, red blood count, ketones
26. anurea
27. pyelitis
28. polyuria
29. nephropathy
30. oliguria
31. cystoplegia
32. lipuria
33. megacystis
34. vesicourethral
35. renomegaly
36. pericystitis
37. nephrology
38. pyelonephritis
39. caliorrhaphy

40. interrenal
41. urethrorrhea
42. ureterorrhagia
43. nephromalacia
44. intracystic
45. nephrolithotomy
46. nephrography
47. reniform
48. glomerulero-, glomerulus; nephro-, kidney; kidney disease located in the glomulerus
49. nephro-, kidney; condition with cysts in the kidneys
50. urethro-, urethra; condition with narrowing of the urethra
51. uretero-, ureter; vesico-, bladder; surgical connection of the ureter to the bladder
52. uro-, urine; condition with bluish color in the urine
53. uro-, urine; study of stones in the urinary system
54. pyelo-, renal pelvis; ureter-, ureter; dilation of the renal pelvis and ureter
55. calico-, calix; removal of a calix
56. cysto-, bladder; removal of stones in the bladder
57. nephr-, kidney; kidney tumor
58. meato-, meatus; suture of the meatus
59. nephr-, kidney; hardening of kidney tissue
60. reno-, kidney; pertaining to the kidneys and lungs
61. trigon-, trigone; inflammation of the trigone
62. infection
63. pus
64. Y
65. Y
66. Y
67. N
68. Y
69. N
70. Y
71. Y

72. Y
73. Y
74. Y
75. Y
76. N
77. hemodialysis
78. peritoneal dialysis
79. Foley
80. condom
81. glucose, ketones
82. stones or calculi
83. casts
84. filtration, kidney
85. blood urea nitrogen, creatinine clearance test
86. voiding cystourethrogram
87. dysuria, oliguria, polyuria
88. antibiotics
89. urethritis
90. ureteritis
91. urethrocystitis
92. nephritis
93. nephroma
94. C
95. C
96. C
97. urethritis
98. cystorrhaphy
99. F
100. T
101. T
102. F
103. F
104. urethrotomy
105. No. One kidney can filter the blood for the whole body.
106. nephrolithotomy
107. nephrolysis
108. nephrectomy
109. ureterectomy
110. urostomy
111. F
112. T
113. T
114. T

10 The Female Reproductive System

After studying this chapter, you will be able to:

▶ Name the parts of the female reproductive system and discuss the function of each part

▶ Define combining forms used in building words that relate to the female reproductive system

▶ Name the common diagnoses, clinical procedures, and laboratory tests used in treating disorders of the female reproductive system

▶ List and define the major pathological conditions of the female reproductive system

▶ Explain the meaning of surgical terms related to the female reproductive system

Structure and Function

The female reproductive system is a group of organs and glands that produce **ova** (singular, **ovum**) or *egg cells* (female sex cells), move them to the site of fertilization, and, if they are fertilized by a sperm (male sex cell), nurture them until birth. The major parts of the female reproductive system (Figure 10-1) are the **ovaries, fallopian tubes, uterus,** and **vagina**.

Reproductive Organs

The **ovaries** (also known as the female **gonads**) are two small, solid, oval structures in the pelvic cavity. The ovaries lie on either side of the uterus. In the monthly cycle of egg production one ovary usually releases only one mature ovum. In most women, the ovaries alternate this release, called **ovulation,** each month. Within the ovaries are sex cells, also known as **gametes.** Before being released from an ovary, the cells develop in a part of the ovary called the **graafian follicle.** These sex cells have the potential to become fertilized and develop. In their immature stage, they are called **oocytes;** once mature (normally 5-7 days), they are known as ova. The ovum is then released from the graafian follicle to the **uterine** or **fallopian tubes,** the two tubes with fingerlike ends called **fimbriae,** that lead from the ovaries to the uterus (Figure 10-2).

The **uterus** is the female reproductive organ in which the fertilized ovum develops or, if not fertilized the cycle of menstruation occurs. The fertilized ovum implants into the lining of the uterus and develops for a period

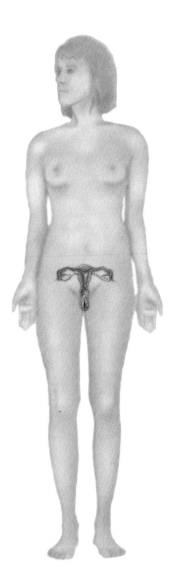

Fertility Friend is a commercial Web site (www.fertilityfriend.com) that has good information about tracking ovulation for people who are trying to get pregnant.

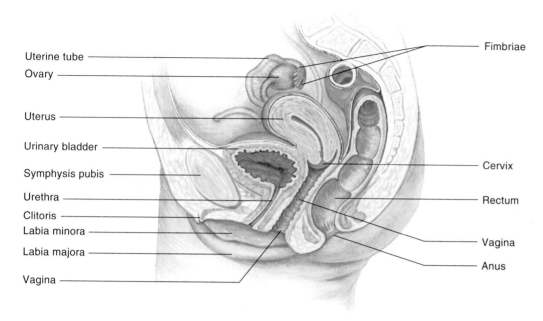

Uterine tube

Ovary

Uterus

Urinary bladder

Symphysis pubis

Urethra

Clitoris

Labia minora

Labia majora

Vagina

Fimbriae

Cervix

Rectum

Vagina

Anus

FIGURE 10-1 The female reproductive system has cycles that determine fertility.

of approximately 40 weeks (**gestation**) until birth (**parturition**). The infant is born through the **vagina** or birth canal in a routine delivery or delivered surgically by *caesarean section*. The female breast or **mammary gland** is also part of the female reproductive system, providing milk (*lactation*) produce in the **lactiferous** ducts and **sinuses** that transport milk to the **nipple** to nurse the infant after birth. The nipple is surrounded by the **areola.**

The uterus is made up of three layers of tissue:

1. the **perimetrium**, the outer layer
2. the **myometrium**, the middle layer
3. the **endometrium**, the inner layer

The upper portion of the uterus, the **fundus**, is where a nutrient-rich organ (the **placenta**) grows in the uterine wall. The middle portion of the uterus is called the **body**. It leads to a narrow region, the **isthmus**. The lower region of the uterus, the **cervix**, leads to the **vagina** or birth canal, which leads to the external genitalia or **vulva**. The vagina has a **hymen** at the external opening (the **introitus**).

The vulva consists of a mound of soft tissue, the **mons pubis**, which is coved by pubic hair after **puberty**. Two folds of skin below the mons pubis are the **labia majora** and the **labia minora**, which form the **foreskin** of the **clitoris**. The **Bartholin's glands** embedded in vaginal tissue produce lubricating fluid. The space between the bottom of the labia majora and the anus is the **perineum**.

Hormones and Cycles

The ovaries secrete **estrogen** and **progesterone,** the primary female **hormones.** Other hormones help in childbirth and milk production. Table 10-1

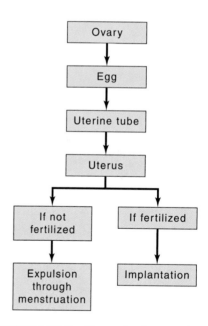

FIGURE 10-2 The path of an egg in the ovarian cycle.

The Museum of Menstruation and Women's Health online (www.mum. org) has many facts about menstruation and how it has been regarded throughout history.

TABLE 10-1 Major reproductive hormones.

Hormone	Purpose	Source
estrogen	stimulates development of female sex characteristics and uterine wall thickening; inhibits FSH and increases LH	ovarian follicle; corpus luteum
progesterone	stimulates uterine wall thickening and formation of mammary ducts	corpus luteum
prolactin	promotes lactation	pituitary gland
oxytocin	stimulates labor and lactation	pituitary gland
FSH (follicle-stimulating hormone)	stimulates oocyte maturation; increasing estrogen	pituitary
HCG (human chorionic gonadotropin)	stimulates estrogen and progesterone from corpus luteum	placenta, embryo
LH (luteinizing hormone)	stimulates oocyte maturation; increases progesterone	pituitary

lists the major reproductive hormones and their functions. In the chapter on the endocrine system (Chapter 15), hormones that stimulate glands in the female reproductive system are discussed.

Ovulation and Menstruation

Ovulation and **menstruation** are contained within the average 28-day female cycle (Figure 10-3). A female's first menstruation (**menarche**) occurs around 10–14 years of age. Although the timing of cycles may vary, the average female cycle is divided into four phases as follows:

1. Days 1-5. Menstruation takes place during the first five days.
2. Days 6-12. The **follicle-stimulating hormone (FSH)** is released from the anterior pituitary.
3. Days 13-14. The next two days, approximately two weeks after the beginning of menstruation, is the time of ovulation or the egg's release from the graafian follicle and the beginning of its trip down the fallopian tube.
4. Days 15-28. In the second 14 days of the cycle, either fertilization occurs or the built-up endometrium starts to break down as estrogen and progesterone levels drop.

It is at the point of ovulation that fertilization can occur or be prevented. Prevention of fertilization is accomplished with **contraception.** Contraceptive devices include the **intrauterine device (IUD)**, *intravaginal ring*, **condom** (both male and female), **spermicide, diaphragm,** or **sponge.** Chemical and surgical conception are also available.

Pregnancy

As a result of contact between the sperm and an ova usually through sexual intercourse (**coitus** or **copulation**), fertilization may occur. A pregnant

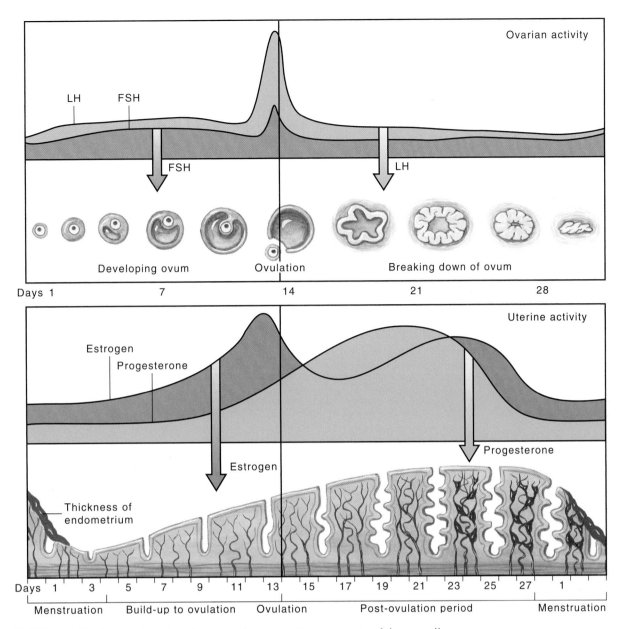

FIGURE 10-3 The cycles of ovulation and menstruation are parts of the overall female cycle.

woman is known as a **gravida,** with gravida I being the first pregnancy, gravida II being the second, and so on. Fertilization may also occur with medical assistance as in *in vitro fertilization*.

An **umbilical cord** connects the placenta to the navel of the fetus so that the mother's blood and the fetal blood do not mix, but nutrients and waste products are exchanged. The fetus develops in a sac containing the **chorion,** the outermost membrane covering the fetus, and the **amnion,** the innermost membrane next to the fluid surrounding the fetus (**amniotic fluid**). The placenta separates from the uterus after delivery and is expelled from the body as the **afterbirth.** The umbilical cord is then severed and tied so that the infant is physically separated from its mother. At the end of this process, the woman is known as a **para** (one who has maintained a pregnancy to the point of viability). Para I refers to the first such pregnancy, para II the second, and so on.

Baby Center (www.babycenter.com) is a commercial site that shows fetal development during pregnancy.

The North American Menopause Society (www.menopause.org) provides information to consumers and health professionals regarding menopause.

Menopause

Menopause, the cessation of menstruation, takes place after levels of estrogen decline. Most women experience menopause between the ages of 45 and 55. However, some women may experience it earlier than that or later. The period of hormonal changes leading up to menopause is called the **climacteric.** The three to five years of decreasing estrogen levels prior to menopause is called **perimenopause.**

VOCABULARY REVIEW

In the previous section, you learned terms relating to the female reproductive system. Before going on to the exercises, read the definitions below. Pronunciations are provided for certain terms.

Term	Definition
afterbirth [ĂF-tĕr-bĕrth]	Placenta and membranes that are expelled from the uterus after birth.
amnion [ĂM-nē-ŏn]	Innermost membrane of the sac surrounding the fetus during gestation.
amniotic [ăm-nē-ŎT-ĭk] **fluid**	Fluid surrounding the fetus and held by the amnion.
areola [ă-RĒ-ō-lă]	Darkish area surrounding the nipple on a breast.
Bartholin's [BĂR-thō-lĕnz] **gland**	One of two glands on either side of the vagina that secrete fluid into the vagina.
body	Middle portion of the uterus.
cervix [SĔR-vĭks]	Protective part of uterus, located at the bottom and protruding through the vaginal wall; contains glands that secrete fluid into the vagina.
chorion [KŌ-rē-ŏn]	Outermost membrane of the sac surrounding the fetus during gestation.
climacteric [klī-MĂK-tĕr-ĭk, klī-măk-TĔR-ĭk]	Period of hormonal changes just prior to menopause.
clitoris [KLĬT-ō-rĭs]	Primary organ of female sexual stimulation, located at the top of the labia minora.
coitus [KŌ-ĭ-tŭs]	Sexual intercourse.
condom [KŎN-dŏm]	Contraceptive device consisting of a rubber or vinyl sheath placed over the penis or as a lining that covers the vaginal canal, blocking contact between the sperm and the female sex organs.
contraception [kŏn-tră-SĔP-shŭn]	Method of controlling conception by blocking access or interrupting reproductive cycles; birth control.
copulation [kŏp-yū-LĀ-shŭn]	Sexual intercourse.

Term	Definition
diaphragm [DĪ-ă-frăm]	Contraceptive device that covers the cervix and blocks sperm from entering; used in conjunction with spermicide.
endometrium [ĔN-dō-MĒ-trē-ŭm]	Inner mucous layer of the uterus.
estrogen [ĔS-trō-jĕn]	One of the primary female hormones produced by the ovaries.
fallopian [fă-LŌ-pē-ăn] **tube**	One of the two tubes that lead from the ovaries to the uterus; uterine tube.
fimbriae [FĬM-brē-ē]	Hairlike ends of the uterine tubes that sweep the ovum into the uterus.
follicle [FŎL-Ĭ-kl] **-stimulating hormone (FSH)**	Hormone necessary for maturation of oocytes and ovulation.
foreskin [FŌR-skĭn]	Fold of skin at the top of the labia minora.
fundus [FŬN-dŭs]	Top portion of the uterus.
gamete [GĂM-ēt]	Sex cell; *see* ovum.
gestation [jĕs-TĀ-shŭn]	Period of fetal development in the uterus; usually about 40 weeks.
gonad [GŌ-năd]	Male or female sex organ; *see* ovary.
graafian follicle [gră-FĒ-ăn FŎL-ĭ-kl]	Follicle in the ovary that holds an oocyte during development and then releases it.
gravida [GRĂV-ĭ-dă]	Pregnant woman.
hormone [HŌR-mōn]	Chemical secretion from glands such as the ovaries.
hymen [HĪ-mĕn]	Fold of mucous membranes covering the vagina of a young female; usually ruptures during first intercourse.
intrauterine [ĬN-tră-YŪ-tĕr-ĭn] **device (IUD)**	Contraceptive device consisting of a coil placed in the uterus to block implantation of a fertilized ovum.
introitus [ĭn-TRŌ-ĭ-tŭs]	External opening or entrance to a hollow organ, such as a vagina.
isthmus [ĬS-mŭs]	Narrow region at the bottom of the uterus opening into the cervix.
labia majora [LĀ-bē-ă mă-JŌR-ă]	Two folds of skin that form the borders of the vulva.
labia minora [mĭ-NŌR-ă]	Two folds of skin between the labia majora.
lactiferous [lăk-TĬF-ĕr-ŭs]	Producing milk.
luteinizing [LŪ-tē-ĭn-Ī-zĭng] **hormone (LH)**	Hormone essential to ovulation.
mammary [MĂM-ă-rē] **glands**	Glandular tissue that forms the breasts and responds to cycles of menstruation and birth.

Term	Definition
menarche [mĕ-NĂR-kē]	First menstruation.
menopause [MĔN-ō-păwz]	Time when menstruation ceases; usually between ages 45 and 55.
menstruation [mĕn-strū-Ā-shŭn]	Cyclical release of uterine lining through the vagina; usually every 28 days.
mons pubis [mŏnz pyū-BĬS]	Mound of soft tissue in the external genitalia covered by pubic hair after puberty.
myometrium [MĪ-ō-MĒ-trē-ŭm]	Middle layer of muscle tissue of the uterus.
nipple [NĬP-l]	Projection at the apex of the breast through which milk flows during lactation.
oocyte [Ō-ō-sīt]	Immature ovum produced in the gonads.
ovary [Ō-vă-rē]	One of two glands that produce ova, usually in alternate months. One ovary can produce every month.
ovulation [ŎV-yū-LĀ-shŭn]	Release of an ovum (or rarely, more than one ovum) as part of a monthly cycle that leads to fertilization or menstruation.
ovum (*pl.*, **ova**) [Ō-vŭm (Ō-vă)]	Mature female sex cell produced by the ovaries, which then travels to the uterus. If fertilized, it implants in the uterus; if not, it is released during menstruation to the outside of the body.
para [PĂ-ră]	Woman who has given birth to one or more viable infants.
parturition [păr-tūr-ĬSH-ŭn]	Birth.
perimenopause [pĕr-ĭ-MĔN-ō-păws]	Three- to five-year period of decreasing estrogen levels prior to menopause.
perimetrium [pĕr-ĭ-MĒ-trē-ŭm]	Outer layer of the uterus.
perineum [PĔR-ĭ-NĒ-ŭm]	Space between the labia majora and the anus.
placenta [plă-SĔN-tă]	Nutrient-rich organ that develops in the uterus during pregnancy; supplies nutrients to the fetus.
progesterone [prō-JĔS-tĕr-ōn]	One of the primary female hormones.
puberty [PYŪ-bĕr-tē]	Preteen or early teen period when secondary sex characteristics develop and menstruation begins.
sinus [SĪ-nŭs]	Space between the lactiferous ducts and the nipple.
spermicide [SPĔR-mĭ-sīd]	Contraceptive chemical that destroys sperm; usually in cream or jelly form.

Term	Definition
sponge [spŭnj]	Polyurethane contraceptive device filled with spermicide and placed in the vagina near the cervix.
umbilical [ŭm-BĬL-ĭ-kăl] **cord**	Cord that connects the placenta in the mother's uterus to the navel of the fetus during gestation for nourishment of the fetus.
uterine [YŪ-tĕr-ĭn] **tube**	One of two tubes through which ova travel from an ovary to the uterus.
uterus [YŪ-tĕr-ŭs]	Female reproductive organ; site of implantation after fertilization or release of the lining during menstruation.
vagina [vă-JĪ-nă]	Genital canal leading from the uterus to the vulva.
vulva [VŬL-vă]	External female genitalia.

CASE STUDY

Examining the Patient

Dr. Liana Malvern is an internist on the staff of Crestwood HMO. She examined Jane Smits and entered the following notes on Jane's record.

Critical Thinking

1. The patient was afebrile. What does afebrile mean?
2. Patient has normal menstruation, but she has only one ovary. How is that possible?

S: Patient is a 29-year-old female who reports generalized lower abdominal pain for the past three days, which seems to have worsened today. She had trouble sleeping last night because of it. States she threw up one time last night but it was after she coughed. She ate today, had no problems digesting her food. She has been afebrile, not taking any medicines. Patient denies burning upon urination; no appreciable vaginal discharge. Her last menstrual period was eleven days ago.

Past history—she has had ovarian cysts on the right ovary. The right ovary and right fallopian tube were removed surgically. She states that her appendix was removed ten years ago. She states she has fairly normal periods.

O: Exam shows her to be afebrile. She has bilateral lower quadrant discomfort but no rebound and no remarkable guarding. Pelvic exam done. Normal appearing introitus; cervix is viewed. No remarkable discharge. She is minimally uncomfortable to manipulation of the cervix but does have more discomfort with palpation toward the uterus. Rectal exam is negative.

Lab: White count: 15,500 with 70 segs. UA: 3-5 red cells, no white cells.

A: Probable pelvic inflammatory infection

P: Prescription for Velosef (antibiotic) for infection and recommended ibuprofen for pain. To return to office if any increased symptoms appear such as fever, nausea, vomiting, or increased pain.

Follow the Path

Using letters a through d, put the following in order according to the path of an ovum from its production to implantation.

3. uterine tube _____   **5.** fimbriae _____

4. ovary _____   **6.** uterus _____

Check Your Knowledge

Fill in the blanks.

7. The oocyte is first released from the _____.

8. Implantation usually takes place in the _____.

9. The monthly cycle of egg production is called _____.

10. The release of the uterine lining on a cyclical basis is called _____.

11. The upper portion of the uterus where the placenta usually develops is the _____.

12. The opening at the bottom of the uterus into the vagina is called the _____.

13. The outermost layer of the uterus is the _____.

14. The mammary glands make up the tissue of the _____.

15. The first menstruation is known as _____.

16. The time when menstruation is beginning to cease is called_____.

17. The primary female hormones are _____ and _____.

18. Birth control pills or implants are chemical forms of _____.

19. The fetus gestates in a sac containing the _____, the outermost membrane, and the _____, the innermost membrane.

20. When the placenta is expelled from the body, it is called the _____.

Combining Forms

The list below includes combining forms that relate specifically to the female reproductive system. Pronunciations are provided for the examples.

COMBINING FORM	MEANING	EXAMPLE
amni(o)	amnion	*amniocentesis* [ĂM-nē-ō-sĕn-TĒ-sĭs], test of amniotic fluid obtained by insertion of a needle into the amnion
cervic(o)	cervix	*cervicitis* [sĕr-vĭ-SĪ-tĭs], inflammation of the cervix

Combining Form	Meaning	Example
colp(o)	vagina	*colporrhagia* [kōl-pō-RĀ-jē-ă], vaginal hemorrhage
episi(o)	vulva	*episiotomy* [ě-pēz-ē-ŌT-tō-mē] surgical incision into the perineum to prevent tearing during childbirth
galact(o)	milk	*galactopoiesis* [gă-LĂK-tō-pǒy-Ē-sĭs], milk production
gynec(o)	female	*gynecology* [gī-ně-KŎL-ō-jē], medical specialty that diagnoses and treats disorders of the female reproductive system
hyster(o)	uterus	*hysterectomy* [hĭs-těr-ĚK-tō-mē], surgical removal of the uterus
lact(o), lacti	milk	*lactogenesis* [lăk-tō-JĚN-ě-sĭs], milk production
mamm(o)	breast	*mammography* [mă-MŎG-ră-fē], imaging of the breast
mast(o)	breast	*mastitis* [măs-TĪ-tĭs], inflammation of the breast
men(o)	menstruation	*menopause* [MĚN-ō-păwz], cessation of menstruation
metr(o)	uterus	*metropathy* [mě-TRŎP-ă-thē], disease of the uterus
oo	egg	*oogenesis* [ō-ō-JĚN-ě-sĭs], production of eggs
oophor(o)	ovary	*oophoritis* [ō-ŏf-ōr-Ī-tĭs], inflammation of an ovary
ov(i), ov(o)	egg	*ovoid* [Ō-vǒyd], egg-shaped
ovari(o)	ovary	*ovariocele* [ō-VĂR-ē-ō-sēl], hernia of an ovary
perine(o)	perineum	*perineocele* [pěr-ĭ-NĒ-ō-sēl], hernia in the perineum
salping(o)	fallopian tube	*salpingoplasty* [săl-PĬNG-ō-plăs-tē], surgical repair of a fallopian tube
uter(o)	uterus	*uteroplasty* [YŪ-těr-ō-plăs-tē], surgical repair of the uterus
vagin(o)	vagina	*vaginitis* [văj-ĭ-NĪ-tĭs], inflammation of the vagina
vulv(o)	vulva	*vulvitis* [vŭl-VĪ-tĭs], inflammation of the vulva

CASE STUDY

Treating an Unusual Occurrence

Dr. Alvino's next patient, Sarah Messer, was having a heavier than usual menstrual flow. After the visit, her record read as follows.

Critical Thinking

21. Did the laboratory tests confirm that the patient was pregnant?
22. What do BP and P mean, and were Sarah Messer's BP and P normal?

S: Patient is a 22-year-old white female who presents with a heavier than usual menstrual flow. Patient states she is using 12–15 pads per day. She states her period started two days ago but is much heavier than usual. Period was about two days late. She is sexually active, no form of birth control, does not think she could be pregnant. She is worried about going to work where she is on her feet all day, and that she seems to flow heavier when she is on her feet. Patient reports cramping. She has had a persistent problem with her right ovary. A previous ultrasound showed problems with the ovary, most likely benign ovarian cysts.

O: Examination shows a young, white female who does not appear in any remarkable distress. She is afebrile. BP 122/70, P 80. Abdomen is soft, no remarkable discomfort, no guarding or rebound present. Pelvic exam was performed. Cervix was closed, significant amount of blood in the cervical vault. There was no remarkable discharge otherwise noted. No discomfort at cervix. No remarkable discomfort or mass in the LLQ on bimanual exam. Lab shows negative serum pregnancy. White count 5500 with 62 segs, HCG 11.5.

A: Menorrhagia. Persistent right ovarian pain.

P: Prescribed Naprosyn 250 mg., one b.i.d. for pain. Provided patient with note to take off work for next two days. Patient to rest and report blood flow tomorrow. Patient to return if problems continue; will monitor HCG.

COMBINING FORMS EXERCISES

Build Your Medical Vocabulary

For the following definitions, provide a medical term. Use the combining forms listed in this chapter and in Chapters 1, 2, and 3.

23. narrowing of the vulva _____
24. x-ray of the breast _____
25. production of milk _____
26. hernia of an ovary _____
27. agent that stimulates milk production _____
28. suture of the perineum _____
29. vaginal infection due to a fungus _____
30. uterine pain _____
31. inflammation of the vulva _____
32. vaginal hemorrhage _____

33. formation and development of the egg _____
34. any disease of the breast _____
35. plastic surgery of the uterus _____
36. inflammation of a fallopian tube _____
37. removal of the cervix _____
38. ovarian tumor _____
39. incision into an ovary _____
40. narrowing of the uterine cavity _____
41. resembling a woman _____
42. rupture of the amniotic membrane _____

Make a Match

Match the definition in the right-hand column with the correct term in the left-hand column.

43. _____ episioperineorrhapy   a. rupture of an ovary

44. _____ galactophoritis   b. vaginal pain

45. _____ ovariorrhexis   c. surgical repair of the perineum

46. _____ oviduct   d. egg movement

47. _____ colpodynia   e. inflammation of the milk ducts

48. _____ metritis   f. escape of amniotic fluid

49. _____ perineoplasty   g. uterine tube

50. _____ ookinesis   h. inflammation of the uterus and fallopian tubes

51. _____ amniorrhea   i. inflammation of the uterus

52. _____ metrosalpingitis   j. surgical repair of a tear in the vulva and perineum

Diagnostic, Procedural, and Laboratory Terms

The major function of the female reproductive system is to bear children. There are several basic tests for pregnancy. Diagnosis of fertility problems involves more sophisticated technology. Aside from pregnancy, the health of the female reproductive system is monitored on a regular basis by a **gynecologist,** a physician who diagnoses and treats disorders of the female reproductive system. An **obstetrician** diagnoses and treats both normal and abnormal pregnancies and childbirths.

A routine gynecological exam usually includes a **Papanicolaou (Pap) smear,** a gathering of cells from the cervix to detect cervical or vaginal cancer or other anomalies. The vagina is held open by a vaginal *speculum*, a device that holds open any cavity or canal for examination. The cervix and vagina may also be examined by **colposcopy,** use of a lighted instrument (a *colposcope*) for viewing into the vagina. **Hysteroscopy** is the use of a *hysteroscope*, a lighted instrument for examination of the interior of the uterus. **Culdoscopy** is the use of an endoscope to examine the contents of the pelvic cavity.

Depending on a woman's age, a routine gynecological exam usually includes a prescription for a *mammogram*, a cancer screening test that can detect tumors before they can be felt. **Mammography** is a procedure that produces radiograms of the breasts.

A pregnancy test is a blood or urine test to detect a hormone that stimulates growth during the first trimester of pregnancy. A pregnancy test may also involve palpation of the uterus during an internal examination by the gynecologist or an obstetrician.

Several tests for fertility problems include **hysterosalpingography,** a procedure to x-ray the uterus and uterine tubes after a contrast medium is injected; *pelvic ultrasonography*, imaging of the pelvic region using sound waves (used both for detection of tumors and for examination of the fetus); and *transvaginal ultrasound*, also a sound wave image of the pelvic area

An e-mail can be sent to you regularly to remind you when you need a Pap smear or mammogram. Go to www.myhealthtestreminder.com and register to get the regular e-mails.

but done with a probe inserted into the vagina. Male fertility tests are discussed in Chapter 11. During pregnancy, the dimensions of the pelvis are measured by **pelvimetry,** an examination to see if the pelvis is large enough to allow delivery.

VOCABULARY REVIEW

In the previous section, you learned terms related to diagnosis, clinical procedures, and laboratory tests. Before going on to the exercises, read the definitions below. Pronunciations are provided for certain terms.

Term	Definition
colposcopy [kŏl-PŎS-kō-pē]	Examination of the vagina with a colposcope.
culdoscopy [kŭl-DŎS-kō-pē] py	Examination of the pelvic cavity using an endoscope.
gynecologist [gī-nĕ-KŎL-ō-jĭst]	Specialist who diagnoses and treats the processes and disorders of the female reproductive system.
hysterosalpingography [HĬS-tĕr-ō-săl-pĭng-GŎG-ră-fē]	X-ray of the uterus and uterine tubes after a contrast medium has been injected.
hysteroscopy [hĭs-tĕr-ŎS-kō-pē]	Examination of the uterus using a hysteroscope.
mammography [mă-MŎG-ră-fē]	X-ray imaging of the breast as a cancer screening method.
obstetrician [ŏb-stĕ-TRĬSH-ŭn]	Physician who specializes in pregnancy and childbirth care.
Papanicolaou [pă-pă-NĒ-kō-lū] **(Pap) smear**	Gathering of cells from the cervix and vagina to observe for abnormalities.
pelvimetry [pĕl-VĬM-ĕ-trē]	Measurement of the pelvis during pregnancy.

CASE STUDY

Seeing a Specialist

The first patient, Jane Smits, called two days after her visit to say that the pain in her lower abdomen seemed to have increased. Also, she said that she had had some unusual bleeding from her vagina yesterday. She was told to come in and see Dr. Maurice Alvino, a gynecologist. He discussed her health history, examined her with a colposcope, and scheduled her for x-rays.

Critical Thinking

53. Why did Dr. Alvino use a colposcope?
54. What are some of the specific areas he might want to view on an x-ray?

Check Your Knowledge

Fill in the blanks.

55. Viewing of the cervix and vagina may be done with a _____.

56. Viewing of the uterus may be done with a _____.

57. Pap smears and mammograms are both _____ screening tests.

58. A pregnancy test can be performed on _____ or _____.

59. A physician who cares for pregnant women is called a(n) _____.

Pathological Terms

Pregnancy is a normal process, with gestation taking about 40 weeks and ending in the birth of an infant. Some pregnancies are not in themselves normal and spontaneously end in **abortion.** Abortion is a controversial term in public discourse, but in medicine, it simply means the premature end of a pregnancy, whether spontaneously during a **miscarriage,** or surgically. There are several types of abortion, such as *habitual abortion*—three or more consecutive abortions; *spontaneous abortions*—those that appear to occur for no specific medical reason; and *missed abortion*, an abortion in which the fetus is dead in the womb for two months or more.

Complications of Pregnancy and Birth

Pregnancies can involve many complications. The initial pregnancy can implant abnormally outside the uterus as in an *ectopic pregnancy*, which requires surgery to remove the fetus because it will die due to lack of nourishment. A *tubal pregnancy* is implantation of the fertilized egg within the fallopian tube or partially within the tube and partially within the abdominal cavity or uterus, and also requires immediate surgical intervention to avoid rupture as the fertilized egg grows.

The placenta may break away from the uterine wall (**abruptio placentae**) and require immediate delivery of the infant. **Placenta previa** is a condition in which the placenta blocks the birth canal, and usually requires a caesarean delivery. Even though a pregnancy appears normal, a *stillbirth*, birth of a dead fetus, may occur. The typical pregnancy lasts from 37 to 40 weeks. An infant may be born *prematurely*, before 37 week's gestation. A toxic condition during pregnancy is called **preeclampsia.**

One of the most dangerous conditions if untreated in pregnancy occurs when a mother has a different Rh factor from the father (blood types are discussed in Chapter 12). The fetus may then carry an Rh factor different from the mother's, in which case *Rh incompatibility* or *erythroblastosis fetalis*, a potentially dangerous fetal condition, may occur in subsequent pregnancies.

> The Preeclampsia Foundation (www.preeclampsia.org) gives helpful information about this disease of pregnancy.

Abnormalities in the Female Cycle

Menstrual abnormalities or other cycle abnormalities sometimes occur. Table 10-2 lists some of those abnormalities. **Amenorrhea,** the absence of menstruation,

TABLE 10-2 Abnormalities in the female cycle.

Abnormality	Description
amenorrhea	lack of menstruation
dysmenorrhea	painful menstruation
menorrhagia	excessive menstrual bleeding
oligomenorrhea	scanty menstrual period
menometrorrhagia	irregular bleeding during or between periods
metrorrhagia	uterine bleeding between menstrual periods
anovulation	absence of ovulation
oligo-ovulation	irregular ovulation
leukorrhea	abnormal vaginal discharge

may result from a normal condition (pregnancy or menopause) or an abnormal condition (excessive dieting or extremely strenuous exercise). It may also occur for no apparent reason. **Dysmenorrhea** is painful cramping associated with menstruation. **Menorrhagia** is excessive menstrual bleeding. **Oligomenorrhea** is a scanty menstrual period. **Menometrorrhagia** is irregular and often excessive bleeding during or between menstrual periods. **Metro-rrhagia** is uterine bleeding between menstrual periods.

Other abnormal conditions in the female cycle also occur. **Anovulation** is the absence of ovulation. **Oligo-ovulation** is irregular ovulation. **Leuko-rrhea** is an abnormal vaginal discharge.

Abnormalities and Infections in the Reproductive System

The Website www.endometriosis.org has information about the prevalence of endometriosis.

Abnormalities and infections occur throughout the reproductive system. Some have an effect on pregnancy. Table 10-3 lists some of those conditions.

Sexually Transmitted Diseases

The American Social Health Association (www.ashastd.org) gives information about the ways to avoid STDs.

Sexually transmitted diseases (STDs) are diseases that are transmitted primarily through sexual contact. **Syphilis,** an infectious disease treatable with antibiotics; **gonorrhea,** a contagious infection of the genital mucous membrane; *herpes II*, a contagious and recurring infection with lesions on the genitalia; *human papilloma virus* (HPV), a contagious infection that causes genital warts; **chlamydia,** a microorganism that causes several sexually transmitted diseases; and *HIV* (which leads to *AIDS*) are some common sexually transmitted diseases.

TABLE 10-3 Abnormalities and infections of the female reproductive system.

Condition	Description
dyspareunia	painful sexual intercourse
anteflexion	abnormal bending forward of the uterus
retroflexion	abnormal bending backward of the uterus
retroversion	backward turning of the uterus
cervicitis	inflammation of the cervix
mastitis	inflammation of the breast
salpingitis	inflammation of the fallopian tubes
vaginitis	inflammation of the vagina
condyloma	growth on the outside of the genitalia
fibroids	benign uterine tumors
endometriosis	abnormal location of uterine lining in the abdominal wall
carcinoma in situ	localized cancer in any area of the reproductive system

MORE ABOUT...

Diagnosing Breast Cancer

Breast cancer is often seen on a mammogram as an unusual growth. The next step is a biopsy to determine whether the growth is malignant or benign. Research is in progress on a number of fronts. Some so-called "breast cancer genes" have been identified. Women who have such a gene are many times more likely to develop breast cancer than those in the general population. However, few of the overall cases of breast cancer are of the inherited type. The best outcome results from the earliest possible diagnosis. Breast self-examination and mammography are used widely for early detection.

The National Breast Cancer Foundation (www.nationalbreastcancer.org) discusses the myths and truths about breast cancer.

VOCABULARY REVIEW

In the previous section, you learned terms related to pathology. Before going on to the exercises, read the definitions below. Pronunciations are provided for certain terms.

Term	Definition
abortion [ă-BŎR-shŭn]	Premature ending of a pregnancy.

Term	Definition
abruptio placentae [ăb-RŬP-shē-ō plă-SĔN-tē]	Breaking away of the placenta from the uterine wall.
amenorrhea [ă-měn-ō-RĒ-ă]	Lack of menstruation.
anovulation [ăn-ŏv-yū-LĀ-shŭn]	Lack of ovulation.
anteflexion [ăn-tē-FLĔK-shŭn]	Bending forward, as of the uterus.
carcinoma in situ [kăr-sĭ-NŌ-mă ĭn SĪ-tū]	Localized malignancy that has not spread.
cervicitis [sĕr-vĭ-SĪ-tĭs]	Inflammation of the cervix.
chlamydia [klă-MĬD-ē-ă]	Sexually transmitted bacterial infection affecting various parts of the male or female reproductive systems; the bacterial agent itself.
condyloma [kŏn-dĭ-LŌ-mă]	Growth on the external genitalia.
dysmenorrhea [dĭs-měn-ōr-Ē-ă]	Painful menstruation.
dyspareunia [dĭs-pă-RŪ-nē-ă]	Painful sexual intercourse due to any of various conditions, such as cysts, infection, or dryness, in the vagina.
endometriosis [ĔN-dō-mē-trē-Ō-sĭs]	Abnormal condition in which uterine wall tissue is found in the pelvis or on the abdominal wall.
fibroid [FĪ-brŏyd]	Benign tumor commonly found in the uterus.
gonorrhea [gŏn-ō-RĒ-ă]	Sexually transmitted inflammation of the genital membranes.
leukorrhea [lū-kō-RĒ-ă]	Abnormal vaginal discharge; usually whitish.
mastitis [măs-TĪ-tĭs]	Inflammation of the breast.
menometrorrhagia [MĔN-ō-mě-trō-RĀ-jē-ă]	Irregular or excessive bleeding between or during menstruation.
menorrhagia [měn-ō-RĀ-jē-ă]	Excessive menstrual bleeding.
metrorrhagia [mě-trŏ-RĀ-jē-ă]	Uterine bleeding between menstrual periods.
miscarriage [mĭs-KĂR-ăj]	Spontaneous, premature ending of a pregnancy.
oligomenorrhea [ŎL-ĭ-gō-měn-ō-RĒ-ă]	Scanty menstrual period.
oligo-ovulation [ŎL-ĭ-gō-ŎV-ū-LĀ-shŭn]	Irregular ovulation.
placenta previa [plă-SĔN-tă PRĒ-vē-ă]	Placement of the placenta so it blocks the birth canal.
preeclampsia [prē-ě-KLĂMP-sē-ă]	Toxic condition during pregnancy.
retroflexion [rě-trō-FLĔK-shŭn]	Bending backward of the uterus.
retroversion [rě-trō-VĔR-zhŭn]	Backward turn of the uterus.
salpingitis [săl-pĭn-JĪ-tĭs]	Inflammation of the fallopian tubes.
syphilis [SĬF-ĭ-lĭs]	Sexually transmitted infection.
vaginitis [văj-ĭ-NĪ-tĭs]	Inflammation of the vagina.

Finding the Cause

Sarah Messer recovered from menorrhagia and persistent ovarian pain, and was able to return to work after two days off. Six months later, however, Sarah experienced heavy bleeding and painful cramps after missing one menstrual period. She did not think she was pregnant, but Dr. Alvino had her HCG level checked and it showed that she was indeed pregnant. Sarah's bleeding turned out to be an early miscarriage. Dr. Alvino prescribed medication for the pain, and again told Sarah to take two days off from work, during which the bleeding should stop. If not, she was to call him.

Dr. Alvino talked to Sarah about the benefits of birth control. He particularly thought that condoms would be appropriate for now, while Sarah remains sexually active with more than one partner.

Critical Thinking

60. What diseases might Sarah contract if she does not use condoms?
61. Does the birth control pill protect you from sexually transmitted diseases?

PATHOLOGICAL TERMS EXERCISES

Check Your Knowledge

Fill in the blanks.

62. A premature end of a pregnancy is a _____.
63. Lack of menstruation is called _____.
64. Painful menstruation is called _____.
65. Scanty menstruation is called _____.
66. Pap smears test for _____ cancer.
67. Benign tumors found in the uterus are _____.
68. Inflammation of the fallopian tubes is called _____.
69. Chlamydia is an agent that can cause _____ _____ diseases.
70. An abortion is the premature ending of a _____, whether spontaneously or by choice.
71. A placenta blocking the birth canal is called _____ _____.
72. A toxic infection during pregnancy is _____.
73. AIDS is caused by _____, a sexually transmitted virus.
74. A localized cancer is called a _____ _____ _____.
75. Uterine bleeding other than that associated with menstruation is called _____.
76. A dangerous pregnancy condition occurs when a father has a different _____ _____ from the mother.
77. Premature birth occurs before _____ weeks of gestation.

Surgical Terms

Surgery of the female reproductive system is performed for a variety of reasons. During pregnancy, it may be necessary to terminate a pregnancy prematurely (*abortion*), to remove a fetus through an abdominal incision (*caesarean birth*), to open and scrape the lining of the uterus (*dilation and curettage* [*D & C*]), or to puncture the amniotic sac to obtain a sample of the fluid for examination (**amniocentesis**). In **culdocentesis,** a sample of fluid extracted from the base of the pelvic cavity may show if an ectopic pregnancy has ruptured. An ectopic pregnancy can be removed through a *salpingotomy,* an incision into one of the fallopian tubes.

Surgery may also be performed as a form of birth control. *Tubal ligation,* a method of female sterilization, blocks the fallopian tubes by cutting or tying and, therefore, blocking the passage of ova. It is usually performed using a *laparoscope,* a thin tube inserted through a woman's navel during **laparoscopy.**

Cryosurgery and **cauterization** are two methods of destroying tissue (such as polyps). Parts of the female reproductive system may have to be removed. A **conization** is the removal of a cone-shaped section of the cervix for examination. Breast cancer may be diagnosed by **aspiration,** a type of biopsy in which fluid is withdrawn through a needle by suction. A **hysterectomy** is removal of the uterus that may be done through the abdomen (*abdominal hysterectomy*) or through the vagina (*vaginal hysterectomy*). Figure 10-4 shows the two types of hysterectomies. New procedures such as *laparascopic hysterectomies* are reducing recovery time.

A **myomectomy** is the removal of fibroid tumors. An **oophorectomy** is the removal of an ovary. A **salpingectomy** is the removal of a fallopian tube. A **salpingotomy** is an incision into the fallopian tubes (usually to remove blockages).

Breast cancer may be treated surgically. A **lumpectomy** is the removal of the tumor itself along with surrounding tissue. During a **mastectomy,** a breast is removed, which may mean the breast and underlying muscle as in a simple mastectomy; the breast, underlying muscles, and the lymph nodes, as in a *radical mastectomy;* or removal of the breast and lymph nodes, as in a *modified radical mastectomy.*

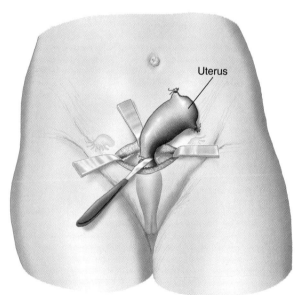

Abdominal hysterectomy

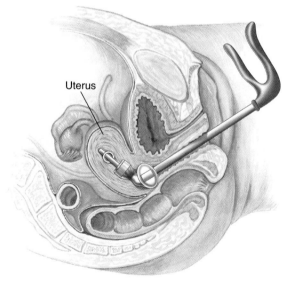

Vaginal hysterectomy

FIGURE 10-4 Hysterectomies can be performed abdominally or vaginally. A surgical instrument is inserted through the cervix in a vaginal hysterectomy.

Breast surgery may include plastic surgery after mastectomy (**mammo-plasty**) or reduction of the size of the breast (*reduction mammoplasty*). Some women have pendulous breast tissue raised (**mastopexy**) or have small breasts augmented by surgical insertion of implants (*augmentation mammoplasty*).

VOCABULARY REVIEW

In the previous section, you learned terms relating to surgery. Before going on to the exercises, read the definitions below. Pronunciations are provided for certain terms.

Term	Meaning
amniocentesis [ĂM-nē-ō-sĕn-TĒ-sĭs]	Removal of a sample of amniotic fluid through a needle inserted in the amniotic sac.
aspiration [ăs-pĭ-RĀ-shŭn]	Biopsy in which fluid is withdrawn through a needle by suction.
cauterization [kăw-tĕr-ĭ-ZĀ-shŭn]	Removal or destruction of tissue using chemicals or devices such as laser-guided equipment.
conization [kō-nĭ-ZĀ-shŭn]	Removal of a cone-shaped section of the cervix for examination.
cryosurgery [krī-ō-SĔR-jĕr-ē]	Removal or destruction of tissue using cold temperatures.
culdocentesis [KŬL-dō-sĕn-TĒ-sĭs]	Taking of a fluid sample from the base of the pelvic cavity to see if an ectopic pregnancy has ruptured.
hysterectomy [hĭs-tĕr-ĔK-tō-mē]	Removal of the uterus.
laparoscopy [lăp-ă-RŎS-kō-pē]	Use of a lighted tubular instrument inserted through a woman's navel to perform a tubal ligation or to examine the fallopian tubes.
lumpectomy [lŭm-PĔK-tō-mē]	Removal of a breast tumor.
mammoplasty [MĂM-ō-plăs-tē]	Plastic surgery to reconstruct the breast, particularly after a mastectomy.
mastectomy [măs-TĔK-tō-mē]	Removal of a breast.
mastopexy [MĂS-tō-pĕk-sē]	Surgical procedure to attach sagging breasts in a more normal position.
myomectomy [mī-ō-MĔK-tō-mē]	Removal of fibroids from the uterus.
oophorectomy [ō-ŏf-ōr-ĔK-tō-mē]	Removal of an ovary.
salpingectomy [săl-pĭn-JĔK-tō-mē]	Removal of a fallopian tube.
salpingotomy [săl-pĭng-GŎT-ō-mē]	Incision into the fallopian tubes.

CASE STUDY

Treating the Problem

Smits learned in her next exam that she now has some cysts on her left ovary. Her right ovary had been removed earlier because of cysts. Jane wants to have a child and expresses her concern to Dr. Alvino.

Critical Thinking

78. Jane had a surgery in which one ovary and one fallopian tube were removed. What is the medical term for this surgery?
79. Jane wants to have children. How might her current condition present a problem?

SURGICAL TERMS EXERCISES

Know the Parts

In the following list, write the name of the part(s) to be removed or altered in the surgery indicated.

80. salpingectomy _____

81. hysterectomy _____

82. tubal ligation _____

TERMINOLOGY IN ACTION

The following are chart notes for a routine gynecological exam:

Patient: Marina Telly   March 30, 2XXX

S: Marina is a 47-year-old, gravida 4, para 4-0-0-4, being seen for an annual gynecological exam. She has had amenorrhea for 3 years and has a lot of trouble with hot flashes. She was placed on estrogen 4 months ago but that made her very sick. She has otherwise been well.

Gyn. History: Menses began at age 14 with PMS as a teenager. She has had 2 C-sections: 1 for eclampsia and 1 for cephalopelvic disproportion.

O: Breasts are pendulous with no discernible masses. Abdomen is soft; no organs or masses noted. Pelvic exam shows external genitalia are normal. Vagina and cervix show mild atropic changes. Uterus is in midposition and feels normal in size. Stool is guaiac negative. Pap smear is done. Mammogram results sent in about two weeks ago are normal.

A: Annual gynecological examination.

P: Patient is undecided about trying another HRT treatment. I gave her all appropriate literature and she will let me know if she wants to try a different hormone. I am scheduling a bone density study.

From the chart, how many children does Marina have? How regular are her periods? What is likely causing her discomfort?

USING THE INTERNET

Go to the Centers for Disease Control site for Women's Health Risks (http://www.cdc.gov/health/womensmenu.htm) and write a paragraph on the latest news in breast and cervical cancer prevention.

CHAPTER REVIEW

The material that follows is to help you review all the material in this chapter.

DEFINITIONS

Define the following terms and combining forms. Review the chapter before starting. Make sure you know how to pronounce each term as you define it. The blue words in brackets are references to the Spanish glossary on the Web site.

WORD	DEFINITION
abortion [ă-BŎR-shŭn] {aborto}	
abruptio placentae [ăb-RŬP-shē-ō plă-SĔN-tē]	
afterbirth [ĂF-tĕr-bĕrth] {secundina}	
amenorrhea [ā-mĕn-ō-RĒ-ă] {amenorrea}	
amni(o)	
amniocentesis [ĂM-nē-ō-sĕn-TĒ-sĭs] {amniocentesis}	
amnion [ĂM-nē-ŏn] {amnios}	
amniotic [ăm-nē-ŎT-ĭk] fluid {amniótico}	
anovulation [ăn-ŏv-yū-LĀ-shŭn]	
anteflexion [ăn-tē-FLĔK-shŭn] {anteflexión}	
areola [ă-RĒ-ō-lă] {areola}	
aspiration [ăs-pĭ-RĀ-shŭn] {aspiración}	
Bartholin's [BĂR-thō-lĕnz] gland	
body {cuerpo}	
carcinoma in situ [kăr-sĭ-NŌ-mă ĭn SĪ-tū]	
cauterization [kăw-tĕr-ĭ-ZĀ-shŭn] {cauterización}	
cervic(o)	
cervicitis [sĕr-vĭ-SĪ-tĭs]	
cervix [SĔR-vĭks] {cervix}	
chlamydia [klă-MĬD-ē-ă] {clamidia}	
chorion [KŌ-rē-ŏn] {corion}	

WORD	DEFINITION
climacteric [klī-MĂK-tēr-ĭk, klī-măk-TĔR-ĭk] {climaterio}	_____
clitoris [KLĬT-ō-rĭs] {clítoris}	_____
coitus [KŌ-ĭ-tŭs] {coito}	_____
colp(o)	_____
colposcopy [kōl-PŎS-kō-pē]	_____
condom [KŎN-dŏm] {condón}	_____
condyloma [kŏn-dĭ-LŌ-mă] {condiloma}	_____
conization [kō-nĭ-ZĀ-shŭn] {conización}	_____
contraception [kŏn-tră-SĔP-shŭn] {anticoncepción}	_____
copulation [kŏp-yū-LĀ-shŭn] {copulación}	_____
cryosurgery [krī-ō-SĔR-jĕr-ē] {criocirugía}	_____
culdocentesis [KŬL-dō-sĕn-tē-sĭs]	_____
culdoscopy [kŭl-DŎS-kō-pē]	_____
diaphragm [DĪ-ă-frăm] {diafragma}	_____
dysmenorrhea [dĭs-mĕn-ōr-Ē-ă] {dismenorrea}	_____
dyspareunia [dĭs-pă-RŪ-nē-ă] {dispareunia}	_____
endometriosis [ĔN-dō-mē-trē-Ō-sĭs] {endometriosis}	_____
endometrium [ĔN-dō-MĒ-trē-ŭm] {endometrio}	_____
episi(o)	_____
estrogen [ĔS-trō-jĕn] {estrógeno}	_____
fallopian [fă-LŌ-pē-ăn] tube	_____
fibroid [FĪ-brŏyd] {fibroide}	_____
fimbriae [FĬM-brē-ē] {fimbrias}	_____
follicle-stimulating hormone (FSH)	_____
foreskin [FŌR-skĭn] {prepucio}	_____
fundus [FŬN-dŭs] {fondo}	_____
galact(o)	_____
gamete [GĂM-ēt] {gameto}	_____
gestation [jĕs-TĀ-shŭn] {gestación}	_____
gonad [GŌ-năd] {gónada}	_____

Word	Definition
gonorrhea [gŏn-ō-RĒ-ă] {gonorrea}	
graafian follicle [gră-FĒ-ăn FŎL-ĭ-kl]	
gravida [GRĂV-ĭ-dă] {grávida}	
gynec(o)	
gynecologist [gī-nĕ-KŎL-ō-jĭst] {ginecólogo}	
hormone [HŌR-mōn] {hormona}	
hymen [HĪ-mĕn] {himen}	
hyster(o)	
hysterectomy [hĭs-tĕr-ĔK-tō-mē] {histerectomía}	
hysterosalpingography [HĬS-tĕr-ō-săl-pĭng-GŎG-ră-fē] {histerosalpingografía}	
hysteroscopy [hĭs-tĕr-ŎS-kō-pē] {histeroscopia}	
intrauterine [ĬN-tră-YŪ-tĕr-ĭn] device (IUD)	
introitus [ĭn-TRŌ-ĭ-tŭs] {introito}	
isthmus [ĬS-mŭs] {istmo}	
labia majora [LĀ-bē-ă mă-JŌR-ă]	
labia minora [mī-NŌR-ă]	
lact(o), lacti	
lactiferous [lăk-TĬF-ĕr-ŭs] {lactífero}	
laparoscopy [lăp-ă-RŎS-kō-pē] {laparoscopia}	
leukorrhea [lū-kō-RĒ-ă] {leucorrea}	
lumpectomy [lŭm-PĔK-tō-mē] {nodulectomía}	
luteinizing [LŪ-tē-ĭn-Ī-zĭng] hormone (LH)	
mamm(o)	
mammary [MĂM-ă-rē] glands	
mammography [mă-MŎG-ră-fē] {mamografía}	
mammoplasty [MĂM-ō-plăs-tē] {mamoplastia}	
mast(o)	

WORD	DEFINITION
mastectomy [măs-TĔK-tō-mē] {mastectomía}	
mastitis [măs-TĪ-tĭs] {mastitis}	
mastopexy [MĂS-tō-pĕk-sē]	
men(o)	
menarche [mĕ-NĂR-kē] {menarca}	
menometrorrhagia [MĔN-ō-mĕ-trō-RĀ-jē-ă]	
menopause [MĔN-ō-păwz] {menopausia}	
menorrhagia [mĕn-ō-RĀ-jē-ă] {menorragia}	
menstruation [mĕn-strū-Ā-shŭn] {menstruación}	
metr(o)	
metrorrhagia [mĕ-trō-RĀ-jē-ă] {metrorragia}	
miscarriage [mĭs-KĂR-ăj] {aborto espontáneo}	
mons pubis [mŏnz PYŪ-bĭs]	
myomectomy [mī-ō-MĔK-tō-mē] {miomectomía}	
myometrium [MĪ-ō-MĒ-trē-ŭm] {miometrio}	
nipple [NĬP-l] {pezón}	
obstetrician [ŏb-stĕ-TRĬSH-ŭn] {obstetra}	
oligomenorrhea [ŎL-ĭ-gō-mĕn-ō-RĒ-ă] {oligomenorrea}	
oligo-ovulation [ŎL-ĭ-gō-ŎV-ū-LĀ-shŭn]	
oo	
oocyte [Ō-ō-sīt] {oocito}	
oophor(o)	
oophorectomy [ō-ŏf-ōr-ĔK-tō-mē] {ooforectomía}	
ov(i), ov(o)	
ovari(o)	
ovary [Ō-vă-rē] {ovario}	

WORD	DEFINITION
ovulation [ŎV-yū-LĀ-shŭn] {ovulación}	
ovum (pl. ova) [Ō-vŭm (Ō-vă)] {óvulo}	
Papanicolaou [pă-pă-NĒ-kō-lū] (Pap) smear	
para [PĂ-ră]	
parturition [păr-tūr-ĬSH-ŭn] {parturición}	
pelvimetry [pĕl-VĬM-ĕ-trē]	
perimenopause [pĕr-ĭ-MĔN-ō-păws]	
perimetrium [pĕr-ĭ-MĒ-trē-ŭm] {perimetrio}	
perine(o)	
perineum [PĔR-ĭ-NĒ-ŭm]	
placenta [plă-SĔN-tă] {placenta}	
placenta previa [plă-SĔN-tă PRĒ-vē-ă]	
preeclampsia [prē-ĕ-KLĂMP-sē-ă]	
progesterone [prō-JĔS-tĕr-ōn] {progesterona}	
puberty [PYŪ-bĕr-tē] {pubertad}	
retroflexion [rĕ-trō-FLĔK-shŭn] {retroflexión}	
retroversion [rĕ-trō-VĔR-zhŭn] {retroversión}	
salping(o)	
salpingectomy [săl-pĭn-JĔK-tō-mē]	
salpingitis [săl-pĭn-JĪ-tĭs] {salpingitis}	
salpingotomy [săl-pĭng-GŎT-ō-mē]	
sinus [SĪ-nŭs] {seno}	
spermicide [SPĔR-mĭ-sīd] {espermicida}	
sponge [spŭnj] {esponja}	
syphilis [SĬF-ĭ-lĭs] {sífilis}	
umbilical [ŭm-BĬL-ĭ-kăl] cord	
uter(o)	
uterine [YŪ-tĕr-ĭn] tube	
uterus [YŪ-tĕr-ŭs] {útero}	
vagin(o)	

vagina [vă-JĪ-nă] {vagina} _____

vaginitis [văj-ĭ-NĪ-tĭs] {vaginitis} _____

vulv(o) _____

vulva [VŬL-vă] {vulva} _____

Answers to Chapter Exercises

1. Without fever.
2. Ovaries do not always alternate ovulation by month. Her single ovary has taken over the function of both.
3. c
4. a
5. b
6. d
7. ovary
8. uterus
9. ovulation
10. menstruation
11. fundus
12. cervix
13. perimetrium
14. breasts
15. menarche
16. menopause
17. estrogen, progesterone
18. contraception
19. chorion, amnion
20. afterbirth
21. no
22. blood pressure, pulse, yes
23. episiostenosis
24. mammogram
25. galactopoiesis
26. ovariocele
27. lactogen
28. perineorrhaphy
29. vaginomycosis
30. metralgia, metrodynia
31. vulvitis
32. colporrhagia
33. oogenesis
34. mastopathy
35. uteroplasty
36. salpingitis
37. cervicectomy
38. oophoroma
39. ovariotomy
40. metrostenosis
41. gynecoid
42. amniorrhexis
43. j
44. e
45. a
46. g
47. b
48. i
49. c
50. d
51. f
52. h
53. Jane's suggested diagnosis was pelvic inflammatory disease (PID). Examination of the vagina is a first step to confirming the diagnosis and seeing if there is an additional problem.
54. uterus, ovaries, fallopian tubes
55. colposcope
56. hysteroscope
57. cancer
58. blood, urine
59. obstetrician
60. a sexually transmitted disease, such as HIV, gonorrhea, herpes II, HPV, or chlamydia
61. No; it does not block fluid-to-fluid contact.
62. miscarriage
63. amenorrhia
64. dysmenorrhea
65. oligomenorrhea
66. cervical
67. fibroids
68. salpingitis
69. sexually transmitted
70. pregnancy
71. Placenta previa
72. preeclampsia
73. HIV
74. carcinoma in situ
75. metrorrhagia
76. Rh factor
77. 37
78. salpingo-oophorectomy
79. If her left ovary needs to be removed, Jane will not be able to get pregnant.
80. uterine/fallopian tube
81. uterus
82. uterine tubes

11

The Male Reproductive System

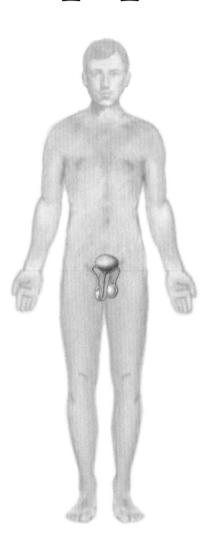

After studying this chapter, you will be able to

▶ Name the parts of the male reproductive system and discuss the function of each part

▶ Define combining forms used in building words that relate to the male reproductive system

▶ Name the common diagnoses, clinical procedures, and laboratory tests used in treating disorders of the male reproductive system

▶ List and define the major pathological conditions of the male reproductive system

▶ Explain the meaning of surgical terms related to the male reproductive system

Structure and Function

The sex cell or **spermatozoon** (plural, **spermatozoa**) or **sperm** is produced in the male gonads or **testes** (singular **testis**). The testes are also called **testicles** and are contained within the **scrotum,** a sac outside the body. The scrotal sack holds and protects the testes as well as regulating the temperature of the testicles. If the testicles are too cold, the scrotum contracts to draw them closer to the body for warmth. If the testicles are too warm, then the scrotum relaxes to draw the testicles away from the body's heat.

The development of sperm (**spermatogenesis**) takes place in the scrotum. **Testosterone,** the most important male hormone, aids in sperm production. Table 11-1 lists the male reproductive hormones and their purpose.

At the top part of each testis is the **epididymis,** a group of ducts for storing sperm. The sperm develop to maturity and become *motile* (able to move) in the epididymis. They leave the epididymis and enter a narrow tube called the **vas deferens.** The sperm then travel to the *seminal vesicles* (which secrete material to help the sperm move) and to the *ejaculatory duct* leading to the **prostate gland** and the urethra. The prostate gland also secretes *prostatic fluid*, which provides a milky color to **semen** (a mixture of sperm and secretions from the seminal vesicles, Cowper's glands, and prostate) and helps the sperm move.

Just below the prostate are the two **bulbourethral glands (Cowper's glands)** that also secrete a fluid that neutralizes the acidity of the male urethra prior to ejaculation. The urethra passes through the **penis** to the outside

TABLE 11-1 Male reproductive hormones.

Hormone	Purpose	Source
testosterone	stimulates development of male sex characteristics; increases sperm; inhibits LH	testes
FSH (follicle-stimulating hormone)	increases testosterone; aids in sperm production	pituitary gland
LH	stimulates testosterone secretion	pituitary gland
inhibin	inhibits FSH	testes

of the body. The tip of the penis is called the **glans penis,** a sensitive area covered by the **foreskin** (*prepuce*). Between the penis and the anus is the area called the **perineum.** Figure 11-1a shows the male reproductive system. Figure 11-1b is a diagram of the path of sperm through the system.

The spermatozoon is a microscopic cell, much smaller than an ovum. It has a head region that carries genetic material (*chromosomes*) and a tail (**flagellum**) that propels the sperm forward. During **ejaculation,** hundreds of millions of sperm are released. Usually only one sperm can fertilize a single ovum. In rare instances, two or more ova are fertilized at a single time, resulting in twins, triplets, quadruplets, and so on. *Identical twins* are the result of one ovum's splitting after it has been fertilized by a single sperm. *Fraternal twins* are the result of two sperm fertilizing two ova.

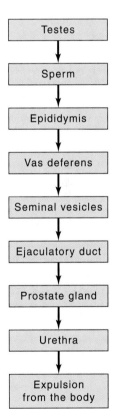

FIGURE 11-1b A diagram of the path that sperm travel.

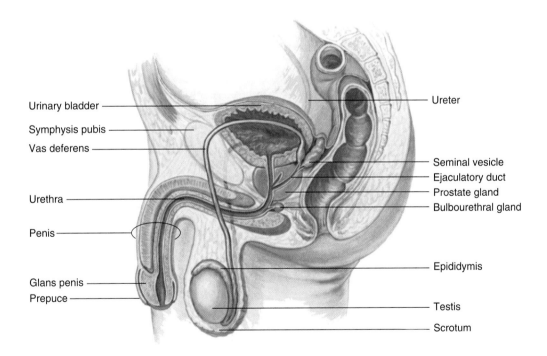

FIGURE 11-1a The male reproductive system usually maintains fertility well into old age.

MORE ABOUT...

Male Hormones

Traditionally, the term *menopause* has referred to women only. In recent years, some researchers have studied the hormonal cycle of males. While males do not experience menstruation and its ultimate cessation, they do seem to experience reduced hormone production, particularly testosterone. This can cause symptoms similar to those of female menopause, including mood swings, decreased libido, and increased fatigue. Some men require treatment with hormones.

VOCABULARY REVIEW

In the previous section, you learned terms relating to the male reproductive system. Before going on to the exercises, read the definitions below. Pronunciations are provided for certain terms.

Term	Definition
bulbourethral [BŬL-bō-yū-RĒ-thrăl] gland	*See* Cowper's gland.
Cowper's [KŎW-pĕrs] gland	One of two glands below the prostate that secrete a fluid to lubricate the inside of the urethra.
ejaculation [ē-jăk-yū-LĀ-shŭn]	Expulsion of semen outside the body.
epididymis [ĕp-ĭ-DĬD-ĭ-mĭs]	Group of ducts at the top of the testis where sperm are stored.
flagellum [flă-JĔL-ŭm]	Tail at the end of a sperm that helps it move.
foreskin [FŌR-skĭn]	Flap of skin covering the glans penis; removed by circumcision in many cultures.
glans penis [glănz PĒ-nĭs]	Sensitive area at the tip of the penis.
penis [PĒ-nĭs]	Male reproductive part that covers the urethra on the outside of the body.
perineum [PĔR-ĭ-NĒ-ŭm]	Area between the penis and the anus.
prostate [PRŎS-tāt] gland	Gland surrounding the urethra that emits a fluid to help the sperm move and contracts its muscular tissue during ejaculation to help the sperm exit the body.
scrotum [SKRŌ-tŭm]	Sac outside the body containing the testicles.
semen [SĒ-mĕn]	Thick, whitish fluid containing spermatozoa and secretions from the seminal vesicles, Cowper's glands, and prostate; ejaculated from the penis.
sperm [spĕrm]	Male sex cell that contains chromosomes.
spermatogenesis [SPĔR-mă-tō-JĔN-ĕ-sĭs]	Production of sperm.

Term	Definition
spermatozoon (*pl.*, **spermatozoa**) [SPĔR-mă-tō-ZŌ-ŏn (SPĔR-mă-tō-ZŌ-ă)]	*See* sperm.
testicle [TĔS-tĭ-kl]	*See* testis.
testis (*pl.*, **testes**) [TĔS-tĭs (TĔS-tēz)]	One of a pair of male organs that produce sperm and are contained in the scrotum.
testosterone [tĕs-TŎS-tĕ-rōn]	Primary male hormone.
vas deferens [văs DĔF-ĕr-ĕns]	Narrow tube through which sperm leave the epididymis and travel to the seminal vesicles and into the urethra.

CASE STUDY

Getting Help

Marta and Luis Consalvo have been trying to have a baby for two years. They are both young and healthy. Recently, Marta's obstetrician-gynecologist referred the couple to an infertility clinic. The doctors at the clinic found nothing in Marta that would cause infertility. They found, however, that Luis had a low sperm count. Marta's ob-gyn referred Luis to a urologist, Dr. Medina, for an examination.

Critical Thinking

1. Why did Marta's physician refer Luis to a urologist?
2. What parts of the male reproductive system might Dr. Medina examine for the cause of Luis's low sperm count?

STRUCTURE AND FUNCTION EXERCISES

Check Your Knowledge

Choose answer a, b, or c to identify each of the following parts of the reproductive system.

a. only in males   b. only in females   c. in both males and females

3. sex cell _____

4. prostate gland _____

5. perineum _____

6. foreskin _____

7. scrotum _____

8. epididymis _____

9. fallopian tube _____

10. gamete _____

11. ova _____

12. spermatozoa _____

Put in order the following sites through which sperm travel, starting with the letter a.

13. epididymis _____

14. seminal vesicles _____

15. testes _____

16. ejaculatory ducts _____

17. vas deferens _____

18. urethra _____

Check Your Understanding

Circle T for true or F for false.

19. Urine is stored in the prostate gland. T F

20. Cowper's gland is another name for the prostate gland. T F

21. Identical twins result from two sperm and one ovum. T F

22. Male genetic material is called testosterone. T F

23. In many cultures, the glans penis is removed during circumcision. T F

Combining Forms

The list below includes combining forms that relate specifically to the male reproductive system. Pronunciations are provided for the examples.

COMBINING FORM	MEANING	EXAMPLE
andr(o)	men	*andropathy* [ăn-DRŎP-ă-thē], any disease peculiar to men
balan(o)	glans penis	*balanitis* [băl-ă-NĪ-tĭs], inflammation of the glans penis
epididym(o)	epididymis	*epididymoplasty* [ĕp-ĭ-DĬD-ĭ-mō-plăs-tē], surgical repair of the epididymis
orch(o), orchi(o), orchid(o)	testes	*orchitis* [ŏr-KĪ-tĭs], inflammation of the testis
prostat(o)	prostate gland	*prostatitis* [prŏs-tă-TĪ-tĭs], inflammation of the prostate
sperm(o), spermat(o)	sperm	*spermatogenesis* [SPĔR-mă-tō-JĔN-ĕ-sĭs], sperm production

COMBINING FORMS EXERCISES

Build Your Medical Vocabulary

Build words for the following definitions using at least one combining form from this chapter. You can refer to Chapters 1, 2, and 3 for general combining forms.

24. Morbid fear of men: _____

25. Surgical reconstruction of the glans penis: _____

26. Killer of sperm: _____

27. Incision into a testis: _____

28. Abnormal discharge of prostate fluid: _____

Put the reproductive system combining form and its meaning in the space following the sentence.

29. A prostatectomy is usually performed only in cases of cancer. _____

30. Androgens cause the development of male secondary sex characteristics. _____

31. An orchiectomy is done in cases of cancer. _____

32. Balanoplasty may be necessary in cases of injury. _____

CASE STUDY

Achieving Results

Dr. Medina was able to help Luis by giving him prescription hormones for his low sperm count and telling him about certain techniques that can increase sperm count. Within six months, Marta was pregnant.

As a urologist, Dr. Medina treats both the reproductive and urinary systems of males. Men who have fertility problems account for a small percentage of Dr. Medina's practice. A slightly larger group sees Dr. Medina about difficulties in sexual functioning. Most of Dr. Medina's patients are much older than Luis. Middle-aged and elderly men tend to have urinary tract problems more frequently than younger men.

Bernard McCoy, who is 35 years old, called for an appointment after his urethrogram. The receptionist scheduled a visit for 10:00 a.m. on November 15. McCoy was escorted to the examining room where the nurse made notes about his complaints (difficulty in urination). A digital rectal exam showed extensive swelling but his previous PSA test was normal. The doctor examined Mr. McCoy. The doctor spoke to Mr. McCoy about the results of his urethrogram.

Critical Thinking

33. What part of the urinary tract is tested for by a PSA test?

34. What condition does Dr. Medina think Mr. McCoy has?

11/15/XX TW: Bernard McCoy, age 35, complains of frequent urination, small stream, and stop and start urine flow; inability to achieve erection. RM: Lab: CBC, chem screen panel, PSA normal. Urethrogram showed swelling. Diagnosis: BPH. A. Medina, M. D.

Diagnostic, Procedural, and Laboratory Terms

A normal male medical checkup may include a *digital rectal exam (DRE)*, the insertion of a finger into the rectum to check the prostate for abnormalities, tenderness, or irregularities. A medical check-up for males usually includes a **prostate-specific antigen (PSA) test,** a blood test to screen for abnormal prostatic growth. If a couple is having fertility problems, a **semen analysis** is done to determine the quantity and quality of the male partner's sperm.

X-ray or imaging procedures are used to further test for abnormalities or blockages. A **urethrogram** is an x-ray of the urethra and prostate. A sonogram may be used when needle biopsies are taken, as of the testicles or prostate. If cancer is present, surgery, chemotherapy, or radiation may

The Prostate Cancer Research Institute (www-prostate-cancer.org) offers free booklets and a wealth of information about this disease.

Visit the American Fertility Association Web site (www.theafa.org) to find out what is normal in a semen analysis.

be used. Hormone replacement therapy is given to males who have a deficiency of male hormones. Men who have erectile dysfunction may be treated chemically or with a *penile prosthesis*, a device implanted in the penis to treat impotence.

VOCABULARY REVIEW

In the previous section, you learned terms relating to diagnosis, clinical procedures, and laboratory tests. Before going on to the exercises, read the definitions below. Pronunciations are provided for certain terms.

Term	Definition
prostate-specific antigen [ĂN-tĭ-jĕn] (PSA) test	Blood test for prostate cancer.
semen analysis	Observation of semen for viability of sperm.
urethrogram [yū-RĒ-thrō-grăm]	X-ray of the urethra and prostate.

CASE STUDY

Testing Further

Alan Salvo is a 58-year-old male with a complaint of difficulty urinating. His blood work is normal including his PSA test. Dr. Medina schedules Mr. Salvo for a urethrogram.

Critical Thinking

35. The normal PSA test virtually eliminated one possible diagnosis. What did it likely eliminate?
36. What might the urethrogram show?

DIAGNOSTIC, PROCEDURAL, AND LABORATORY TERMS EXERCISES

Check Your Knowledge

Fill in the blanks.

37. A semen analysis examines the _____ and _____ of sperm.
38. A digital rectal exam is for finding any abnormalities in the _____ and _____.
39. A PSA tests for _____ cancer.
40. Erectile problems may be treated chemically or with a _____ _____.

The National Kidney and Urologic Diseases Clearinghouse (http://kidney.niddk.nih.gov/kudiseases/pubs/peyronie/index.htm) provides information about Peyronie's disease.

Pathological Terms

Birth defects, infections, and various other medical conditions affect the male reproductive system. Table 11-2 lists some of them.

TABLE 11-2 Conditions of the male reproductive system.

Condition	Description
cryptorchism (Figure 11-2)	undescended testicle
anorchism or **anorchia**	lack of one or both testes
hypospadias (Figure 11-3)	abnormal opening of the urethra on the underside of the penis
epispadias (Figure 11-3)	abnormal opening on the top side of the penis
phimosis	abnormal narrowing of the foreskin over the glans penis
infertility	inability to produce enough viable sperm
aspermia	inability to produce sperm
azoospermia	semen without living sperm
oligospermia	scanty production of sperm
impotence or *penile erectile dysfunction (PED)*	inability to maintain an erection for ejaculation
priapism	persistent, painful erection
hernia	abnormal protrusion of parts of tissue
hydrocele (Figure 11-4)	fluid-containing hernia in a testicle
varicocele	herniated veins near the testicles
prostatitis	inflammation of the prostate
balanitis	inflammation of the glans penis
epididymitis	inflammation of the epididymis
Peyronie's disease	abnormal curvature of the penis
seminoma	malignant tumor in the testicle
chancroids	STD with venereal sores

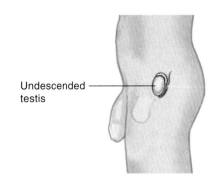

Undescended testis

FIGURE 11-2 Cryptorchism is also known as an undescended testicle.

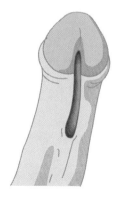

Hypospadias

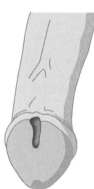

Epispadias

FIGURE 11-3 Hypospadias and epispadias are two congenital urethral abnormalities.

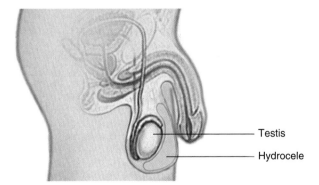

Testis

Hydrocele

FIGURE 11-4 Hydroceles commonly occur in the scrotal sac.

VOCABULARY REVIEW

In the previous section, you learned terms relating to pathology. Before going on to the exercises, read the definitions below. Pronunciations are provided for certain terms.

Term	Definition
anorchism [ăn-ŌR-kĭzm], **anorchia** [-kē-ă]	Congenital absence of one or both testicles.
aspermia [ā-SPĔR-mē-ă]	Inability to produce sperm.
azoospermia [ā-zō-ō-SPĔR-mē-ă]	Semen without living sperm.
balanitis [băl-ă-NĪ-tĭs]	Inflammation of the glans penis.
chancroids [SHĂNG-krŏyds]	Open sores on the penis, urethra, or anus, resulting from a sexually transmitted bacterial infection.
cryptorchism [krĭp-TŌR-kĭzm]	Birth defect with the failure of one or both of the testicles to descend into the scrotal sac.
epididymitis [ĕp-ĭ-dĭd-ĭ-MĪ-tĭs]	Inflammation of the epididymis.
epispadias [ĕp-ĭ-SPĀ-dē-ăs]	Birth defect with abnormal opening of the urethra on the top side of the penis.
hernia [HĔR-nē-ă]	Abnormal protrusion of tissue through muscle that contains it.
hydrocele [HĪ-drō-sēl]	Fluid-containing hernia of the testis.
hypospadias [HĪ-pō-SPĀ-dē-ăs]	Birth defect with abnormal opening of the urethra on the bottom side of the penis.
impotence [ĬM-pō-tĕns]	Inability to maintain an erection for ejaculation.
infertility [ĭn-fĕr-TĬL-ĭ-tē]	Inability to fertilize ova.
oligospermia [ŏl-ĭ-gō-SPĔR-mē-ă]	Scanty production of sperm.
Peyronie's [pā-RŌN-ēz] **disease**	Abnormal curvature of the penis caused by hardening in the interior of the penis.
phimosis [fī-MŌ-sĭs]	Abnormal narrowing of the opening of the foreskin.
priapism [PRĪ-ă-pĭzm]	Persistent, painful erection of the penis.
prostatitis [prŏs-tă-TĪ-tĭs]	Inflammation of the prostate.
seminoma [sĕm-ĭ-NŌ-mă]	Malignant tumor of the testicle.
varicocele [VĂR-ĭ-kō-sēl]	Enlargement of veins of the spermatic cord.

PATHOLOGICAL TERMS EXERCISES

Find a Match

Match the definitions in the right-hand column with the terms in the left-hand column.

41. ____ anorchism   **a.** inflammation of the glans penis

42. ____ aspermia   **b.** hernia in the testis

43. ____ seminoma   **c.** inability to maintain an erection

44. ____ balinitis   **d.** inability to fertilize an ovum

45. ____ hydrocele   **e.** undescended testicle

46. ____ impotence   **f.** lacking sperm

47. ____ infertility   **g.** abnormal urethral opening

48. ____ hypospadias   **h.** lacking testicles

49. ____ cryptorchism   **i.** having no living sperm

50. ____ azoospermia   **j.** testicular tumor

CASE STUDY

Resolving Problems

Marta and Luis Consalvo's baby, an 8-pound boy, was healthy except for hypospadias. Dr. Medina told the Consalvos that an operation to properly place the urethral opening would be needed, but as long as the baby remained in diapers, they could wait until he was a bit older for the surgery. The parents were also told to delay circumcision, so that any excess skin might be used to repair the penis.

Critical Thinking

51. Why might hypospadias cause urination problems once the baby is out of diapers and trained to use a toilet?

52. Hypospadias, if left untreated, may cause fertility problems later in life. How?

Surgical Terms

The most common surgery of the male reproductive system is **circumcision,** the removal of the foreskin or prepuce (Figure 11-5).

Other surgeries are to prevent or enhance the possibility of conception, diagnose or remove cancerous tumors, remove or reduce blockages, and remove or repair parts of the system. Biopsies are commonly taken of the testicles and prostate when cancer is suspected.

Various operations to remove cancerous or infected parts of the reproductive system are an **epididymectomy,** removal of an epididymis; an **orchiectomy** or **orchidectomy,** removal of a testicle; a **prostatectomy,** removal of the prostate gland, which may be done through the perineum or above the pubic bone; and a *transurethral resection of the prostate (TURP)*, removal of a portion of the prostate through the urethra (Figure 11-6). A **vasectomy** is the removal of part of the vas deferens as a method of birth control. A **vasovasostomy** is the reversing of a vasectomy so the male regains fertility. **Castration** is the removal of the testicles. A penile prosthesis can be surgically implanted to increase sexual functioning.

FIGURE 11-5 Circumcision is usually determined by cultural preference.

The practice of circumcising infant males is the subject of controversy. There is a Web site (www.circumcision.org) that gives reasons against the practice, while other Web sites give information about the surgery.

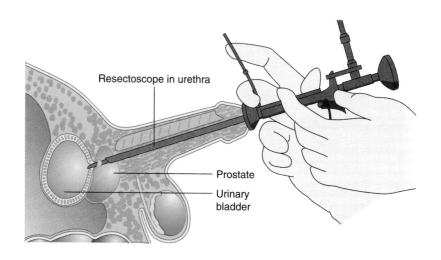

FIGURE 11-6 A TURP (transurethral resection of the prostate) is the removal of some prostate tissue through the urethra.

Resectoscope in urethra

Prostate

Urinary bladder

VOCABULARY REVIEW

In the previous section, you learned terms relating to surgery. Before going on to the exercises, read the definition below and refer to the previous section if you have any questions. Pronunciations are provided for certain terms.

Term	Definition
castration [kăs-TRĀ-shŭn]	Removal of the testicles.
circumcision [sĭr-kŭm-SĬZH-ŭn]	Removal of the foreskin.
epididymectomy [ĔP-ĭ-dĭd-ĭ-MĔK-tō-mē]	Removal of an epididymis.
orchidectomy [ōr-kĭ-DĔK-tō-mē]	Removal of a testicle.
orchiectomy [ōr-kē-ĔK-tō-mē]	Removal of a testicle.
prostatectomy [prŏs-tă-TĔK-tō-mē]	Removal of the prostate.
vasectomy [vă-SĔK-tō-mē]	Removal of part of the vas deferens to prevent conception.
vasovasostomy [VĀ-sō-vă-SŎS-tō-mē]	Reversal of a vasectomy.

MORE ABOUT...

Birth Control

An operation is not the only form of male birth control. Other options available to males are a *condom*, a sheath worn over the penis to collect the semen after ejaculation, *coitus interruptus*, removal of the penis from the vagina before ejaculation (although this is not very safe), and a forthcoming *male birth control pill*, which will block the production of sperm.

CASE STUDY

Surgical Relief

Dr. Medina checked the results of Mr. McCoy's urethrogram. There did not seem to be any abnormalities other than in the prostate. He scheduled Mr. McCoy for a TURP, which is done as cryogenic surgery (surgery using cold to numb an area prior to operating). The procedure is done on an outpatient basis, and one week later, Mr. McCoy is improving rapidly. Dr. Medina wants to wait a while to see if the TURP also helps improve erectile function, before exploring other options. One such option is new medication that can improve erectile function.

Critical Thinking

53. Why did Dr. Medina schedule Mr. McCoy for a TURP?
54. If medication does not work to improve sexual function, what is another option for men with impaired erectile function?

SURGICAL TERMS EXERCISES

Check Your Knowledge

Fill in the blanks.

55. Circumcision is removal of the _____ and is commonly practiced in various cultures.
56. An _____ or _____ is removal of a testicle.
57. A prostatectomy is a general term for removal of the _____.
58. A contraceptive operation is a(n) _____.
59. An operation to reverse a previously done contraceptive one is a(n) _____.

TERMINOLOGY IN ACTION

From the following letter, can you determine why the doctor did *not* suspect prostate cancer?

Dr. Robert Thorkild, MD
Department of General Surgery
555 Tenth Avenue
New York, NY 99999

Dear Dr. Thorkild:

Thank you for agreeing to see John Roberts, a patient of mine, on an urgent basis. He is the 30-year-old male I mentioned in my telephone conversation.

Mr. Roberts complains of right inguinal cramping and sharp, constant pain radiating into the scrotum and right testicle. The pain occurred after lifting several heavy objects at work. He works for a moving company and does constant heavy lifting.

(continued)

On examination, abdomen is soft and non tender. There is fullness in the right groin area. Palpation of the inguinal canal reveals a bulge that is made worse with coughing. It is reducible and there is no question of strangulation. Rectal examination is normal. Prostate is normal in size and texture.

My assessment is right inguinal hernia.

Because of his difficult financial situation, he needs to have this repaired as soon as possible. He agrees to seeing you and having you perform a herniorrhaphy.

Thank you for seeing Mr. Roberts.

Sincerely,

Robert Thorkild, MD

USING THE INTERNET

Google the words "prostate cancer" and write a short paragraph on recent news about prostate cancer.

CHAPTER REVIEW

The material that follows is to help you review all the material in this chapter.

DEFINITIONS

Define the following terms and combining forms. Review the chapter before starting. Make sure you know how to pronounce each term as you define it. The blue words in curly brackets are references to the Spanish glossary on the Web site.

WORD	DEFINITION
andr(o)	
anorchism, anorchia [ăn-ŌR-kĭzm, -kē-ă] {anorquia}	
aspermia [ā-SPĔR-mē-ă] {aspermia}	
azoospermia [ā-zō-ō-SPĔR-mē-ă] {azoospermia}	
balan(o)	
balanitis [băl-ă-NĪ-tĭs] {balanitis}	
bulbourethral [BŬL-bō-yū-RĒ-thrăl] gland	
castration [kăs-TRĀ-shŭn] {castración}	
chancroids [SHĂNG-krŏyds]	
circumcision [sĕr-kŭm-SĬZH-ŭn] {circuncisión}	
Cowper's [KŎW-pĕrs] gland	
cryptorchism [krĭp-TŌR-kĭzm]	
ejaculation [ē-jăk-yū-LĀ-shŭn] {eyaculación}	
epididym(o)	
epididymectomy [ĔP-ĭ-dĭd-ĭ-MĔK-tō-mē]	
epididymis [ĕp-ĭ-DĬD-ĭ-mĭs] {epidídimo}	
epididymitis [ĕp-ĭ-dĭd-ĭ-MĪ-tĭs] {epididimitis}	
epispadias [ĕp-ĭ-SPĀ-dē-ăs] {epispadias}	
flagellum [flă-JĔL-ŭm] {flagelo}	
foreskin [FŌR-skĭn] {prepucio}	
glans penis [glănz PĒ-nĭs]	

hernia [HĔR-nē-ă] {hernia} _____

hydrocele [HĪ-drō-sēl] {hidrocele} _____

hypospadias [HĪ-pō-SPĀ-dē-ăs]
{hipospadias} _____

impotence [ĬM-pō-tĕns] {impotencia} _____

infertility [ĭn-fĕr-TĬL-ĭ-tē] {infertilidad} _____

oligospermia [ŏl-ĭ-gō-SPĔR-mē-ă]
{oligospermia} _____

orch(o), orchi(o), orchid(o) _____

orchidectomy [ōr-kĭ-DĔK-tō-mĕ]
{orquidectomía} _____

orchiectomy [ōr-kē-ĔK-tō-mē]
{orquietomía} _____

penis [PĒ-nĭs] {pene} _____

perineum [PĔR-ĭ-NĒ-ŭm] {perineo} _____

Peyronie's [pā-RŌN-ēz] disease _____

phimosis [fĭ-MŌ-sĭs] {fimosis} _____

priapism [PRĪ-ă-pĭzm] {priapismo} _____

prostat(o) _____

prostate [PRŎS-tāt] gland {próstata} _____

prostatectomy [prŏs-tă-TĔK-tō-mē]
{prostatectomía} _____

prostate-specific antigen [ĂN-tĭ-jĕn]
(PSA) test _____

prostatitis [prŏs-tă-TĪ-tĭs] {prostatitis} _____

scrotum [SKRŌ-tŭm] {escroto} _____

semen [SĒ-mĕn] {semen} _____

semen analysis _____

seminoma [sĕm-ĭ-NŌ-mă] _____

sperm [spĕrm] {esperma} _____

sperm(o), spermat(o) _____

spermatogenesis [SPĔR-mă-tō-JĔN-
ĕ-sĭs] _____

spermatozoon (pl., spermatozoa)
[SPĔR-mă-tō-ZŌ-ōn (SPĔR-mă-
tō-ZŌ-ă)] {espermatozoo} _____

testicle [TĔS-tĭ-kl] {testículo} _____

testis (pl., testes) [TĔS-tĭs (TĔS-tēz)]
{testículo} _____

WORD	DEFINITION
testosterone [tĕs-TŎS-tĕ-rōn] {testosterona}	
urethrogram [yū-RĒ-thrō-grăm]	
varicocele [VĂR-ĭ-kō-sēl] {varicocele}	
vas deferens [văs DĔF-ĕr-ĕns]	
vasectomy [vă-SĔK-tō-mē] {vasectomía}	
vasovasostomy [VĀ-sō-vă-SŎS-tō-mē] {vasovasostomía}	

Answers to Chapter Exercises

1. Ob-gyns do not treat male infertility.
2. testicles, seminal vesicles, epididymis, prostate, and vas deferens
3. c
4. a
5. c
6. c
7. a
8. a
9. b
10. c
11. b
12. a
13. b
14. d
15. a
16. e
17. c
18. f
19. F
20. F
21. F
22. F

23. F
24. androphobia
25. balanoplasty
26. spermicide, spermatocide
27. orchiotomy
28. prostatorrhea
29. prostat-, prostate
30. andro-, male
31. orchi-, testes
32. balano-, glans penis
33. prostate
34. benign prostatic hypertrophy
35. Prostate cancer is probably not present.
36. swelling or other abnormalities in the urethra or prostate
37. quantity, quality
38. rectum, prostate
39. prostate
40. penile prosthesis
41. h
42. f
43. j
44. a
45. b

46. c
47. d
48. g
49. e
50. i
51. If the urethra opens on the bottom, the child will urinate straight down and probably find it difficult to keep his urine from splattering.
52. Delivery of sperm to the cervix during male ejaculation usually requires a centered meatus.
53. The prostate was enlarged and interfering with urination. A TURP removes some prostate tissue.
54. penile prosthesis
55. foreskin
56. orchidectomy, orchiectomy
57. prostate
58. vasectomy
59. vasovasostomy

CHAPTER

12

The Blood System

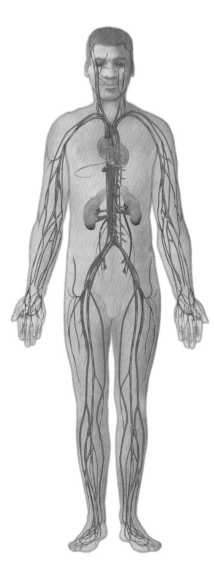

After studying this chapter, you will be able to

▶ Name the parts of the blood system and discuss the function of each part

▶ Define combining forms used in building words that relate to the blood system

▶ Name the common diagnoses, clinical procedures, and laboratory tests used in treating disorders of the blood system

▶ List and define the major pathological conditions of the blood system

▶ Explain the meaning of surgical terms related to the blood system

Structure and Function

Blood is a complex mixture of cells, water, and various biochemical agents, such as proteins and sugars. It transports life-sustaining nutrients, oxygen, and hormones to all parts of the body. As a transport medium for waste products from cells of the body, it prevents toxic buildup. It helps maintain the stability of the fluid volume that exists within body tissues (a form of *homeostasis,* the maintaining of a balance), and it helps regulate body temperature. Without blood, human life is not possible. Figure 12-1a illustrates the blood system, with arteries shown in red and veins shown in blue. Figure 12-1b is a schematic showing the path of blood through the body.

Blood is a thick liquid made up of a fluid part, **plasma,** and a solid part containing **red blood cells (RBCs), white blood cells (WBCs),** and **platelets.** When blood clots (a process called coagulation), the resulting fluid is called **serum.** *Serology* is the science that deals with the properties of serum, such as the presence of immunity-provoking agents.

Plasma

When blood is separated, the plasma (about 55 percent of the blood) is the clear liquid made up of 92 percent water and 8 percent organic and inorganic chemicals. The 8 percent consists of proteins, nutrients, gases, electrolytes, and other substances.

The main groups of plasma proteins are **albumin, globulin, fibrinogen,** and **prothrombin.**

1. **Albumin** helps regulate water movement between blood and tissue.
2. **Globulins** have different functions, depending on their type. The *alpha* and *beta globulins,* which are joined in the liver, transport lipids and fat-soluble

To learn about blood donation, go to the National Heart, Lung, and Blood Institute's Web site (www.nhlbi.nih.gov).

314

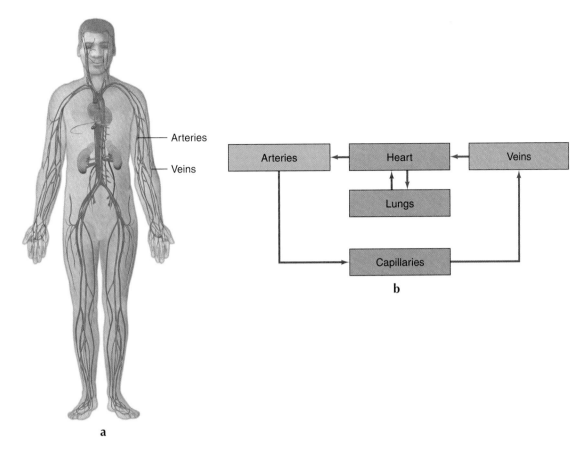

FIGURE 12-1 (a) The blood system transports life-sustaining nutrients to all parts of the body; (b) a schematic showing the path of blood through the body.

vitamins. **Gamma globulins** arise in the lymphatic tissues and function as part of the immune system. Globulins can be separated from each other through a process called **electrophoresis.** Blood may also be *centrifuged,* put in a device that separates blood elements by spinning. **Plasmapheresis** is a process that takes a patient's blood and uses centrifuging to return only red cells to that patient.

3. **Fibrinogen** and **prothrombin** are essential for blood **coagulation,** the process of *clotting.* Platelets clump at the clot site and release a protein, **thromboplastin,** which combines with calcium and various clotting factors (I-V and VII-XIII) to form the **fibrin clot** (Figure 12-2). **Thrombin,** an enzyme, helps in formation of the clot. Without it, one would bleed to death. Blood clotting inside blood vessels, however, can cause major cardiovascular problems. Some elements of the blood, such as **heparin,** prevent clots from forming during normal circulation.

Blood Cells

The solid part of the blood that is suspended in the plasma consists of the **red blood cells (RBCs),** also called **erythrocytes, white blood cells (WBCs),** also called **leukocytes,** and platelets, also referred to as **thrombocytes.** The measurement of the percentage of packed red blood cells is known as the **hematocrit.** Most blood cells are formed as **stem cells (hematocytoblasts)** or immature blood cells in the bone marrow. Stem cells mature in the bone

Stem cells can be gotten from umbilical cord blood. To find out about how to donate cord blood once a baby is born, go to the Stem Cell Research Foundation's Web site (www.stemcellresearchfoundation.org).

FIGURE 12-2 A fibrin clot is formed at the site of an injury.

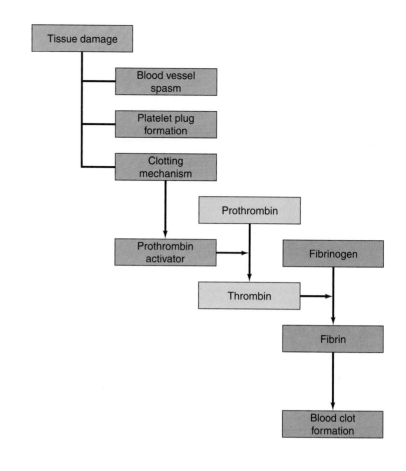

marrow before entering the bloodstream and becoming specialized in their purpose. Figure 12-3 shows the stages of blood cell development.

Erythrocytes or Red Blood Cells

A hormone produced in the kidneys, **erythropoietin,** stimulates the production of red blood cells in the bone marrow. A protein within red blood cells, **hemoglobin,** aids in the transport of oxygen to the cells of the body. Hemoglobin is composed of **heme,** a pigment containing iron, and **globin,** a protein. The average number of red blood cells in a cubic millimeter of blood is 4.6 to 6.4 million for adult males and 4.2 to 5.4 million for adult females. This measurement is known as the **red blood cell count.**

Leukocytes

Leukocytes or white blood cells protect against disease in various ways—for example, by destroying foreign substances. There are two main groups of leukocytes—granulocytes and agranulocytes.

The first group, **granulocytes,** have a granular cytoplasm. There are three types of granulocytes:

1. **Neutrophils** are the most plentiful leukocytes (over half of the white blood cells in the bloodstream).
2. **Eosinophils** are only about 1 to 3 percent of the leukocytes in the bloodstream.
3. **Basophils** are less than 1 percent of the leukocytes in the bloodstream. They release heparin, an anticlotting factor, and **histamine,** a substance involved in allergic reactions.

MORE ABOUT...

Stem Cells

In recent years, researchers have found that stem cells can be used to combat some diseases. It is theorized that stem cells may be the ultimate cure for many chronic and devastating ailments. Because most usable stem cells must come from human embryos obtained from abortions or in vitro fertilization, their use has become controversial.

Erythropoietin is used in the treatment of AIDS patients to encourage red blood cell production.

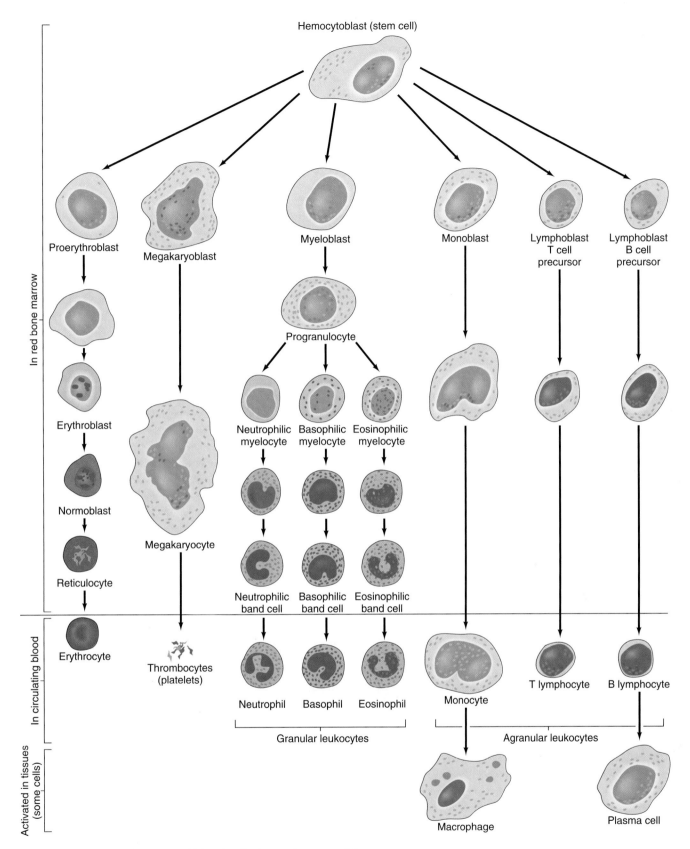

FIGURE 12-3 Development of blood cells from a hemocytoblast.

MORE ABOUT...

Blood

In an emergency situation, in which a person is hemorrhaging, a quick response can save a life. First, make sure the person can breathe. The most effective way to control hemorrhaging is to apply direct pressure on the wound, elevate the area (whenever possible, to a level above the heart), and apply pressure to the nearest pressure point. The points shown here are just some of the most common pressure points.

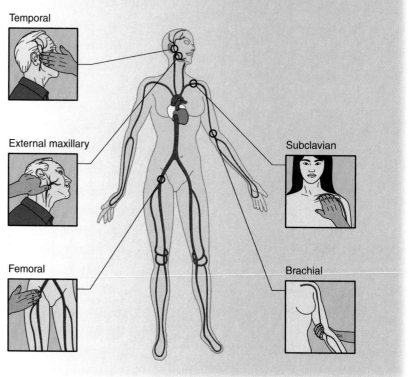

Temporal

External maxillary

Femoral

Subclavian

Brachial

The second group of leukocytes, **agranulocytes,** have cytoplasm with no granules. There are two types of agranulocytes:

1. **Monocytes,** the largest blood cells, make up about 3 to 9 percent of the leukocytes in the bloodstream.
2. **Lymphocytes** make up about 25 to 33 percent of the leukocytes in the bloodstream. They are essential to the immune system, discussed in Chapter 13.

Table 12-1 lists the types of white blood cells.

Platelets

Platelets or thrombocytes are fragments that break off from large cells in red bone marrow called **megakaryocytes.** Platelets adhere to damaged tissue and to each other and group together to control blood loss from a blood vessel. Figure 12-4 shows platelets clumping together.

TABLE 12-1 Types of leukocytes.

Leukocytes	Percentage of Leukocytes in Blood	Function
granulocytes		
basophils	minimal—under 1 percent	release heparin and histamine
eosinophils	minimal—under 3 percent	kill parasites and help control inflammation
neutrophils	most plentiful—over 50 percent	remove unwanted particles
agranulocytes		
lymphocytes	plentiful—25 to 33 percent	important to immune system
monocytes	minimal—3 to 9 percent	destroy large unwanted particles

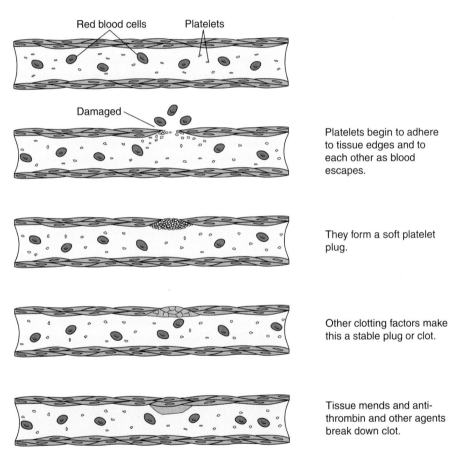

FIGURE 12-4 Platelets clumping together to form a clot.

Platelets begin to adhere to tissue edges and to each other as blood escapes.

They form a soft platelet plug.

Other clotting factors make this a stable plug or clot.

Tissue mends and anti-thrombin and other agents break down clot.

Blood Types

When blood is needed for **transfusion,** the blood being donated is tested for type and put into one of four human **blood types** or **groups.** The donated blood must be tested since an incompatible blood type from a donor can cause adverse reactions. Blood typing is based on the antigens (substances

MORE ABOUT...

Transfusions

Two early scientists attempted various experimental transfusions. Sir Christopher Wren (1632–1723), a famous English architect and scientist, did biological experiments in which he injected fluids into the veins of animals. This process is regarded as an early attempt at blood transfusions. During the same century, a French physician, Jean Baptiste Denis (1643–1704), tried unsuccessfully to transfuse sheep's blood into a human. Later, experiments with transfusing human blood succeeded somewhat, but the majority of people receiving transfusions died, until the advent of blood typing in the twentieth century. Once blood factors and typing became routine, transfusions were widely used in surgery. Later, it was found that some infections (hepatitis, AIDS) were transmitted by blood. Now, donated blood is carefully screened for infections.

The lives of some animals are saved by blood transfusions. Go to www.cvm.uiuc.edu/petcolumns/showarticle.cfm?id=114 to read about the similarities between human and some pet transfusions.

that promote an immune response) and antibodies (special proteins) present in the blood. (Chapter 13 describes the work of antigens and antibodies in the immune system.) The most common type of blood in the population is O, followed by A, B, and AB in descending order. Table 12-2 lists the four blood types and their characteristics.

The danger in transfusing blood of a different type is that **agglutination** or clumping of the antigens stops the flow of blood, which can be fatal. In addition to the four human blood types, there is a positive or negative element in the blood. **Rh factor** is a type of antigen first identified in rhesus monkeys. **Rh-positive** blood contains this factor and **Rh-negative** blood does not. The factor contains any of more than 30 types of **agglutinogens,** substances that cause agglutination, and can be fatal to anyone who receives blood with an Rh factor different from the donor.

Rh factor is particularly important during pregnancy. The fetus of parents with different Rh factors could be harmed by a fatal disease or a type of anemia if preventive measures are not taken prior to birth. Figure 12-5 shows how a combination of Rh factors affects pregnancy.

TABLE 12-2 Blood types.

Blood Type	Antigen	Antibody	Percent of Population with This Type
A	A	Anti-B	41
B	B	Anti-A	10
AB	A and B	Neither anti-A nor anti-B	4
O	Neither A nor B	Both anti-A and anti-B	45

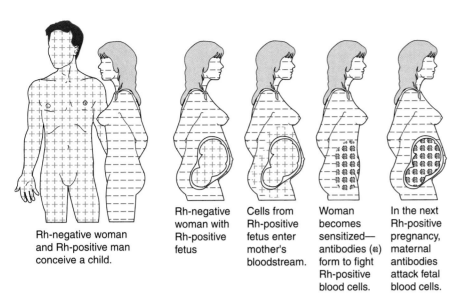

Rh-negative woman
and Rh-positive man
conceive a child.

Rh-negative
woman with
Rh-positive
fetus

Cells from
Rh-positive
fetus enter
mother's
bloodstream.

Woman
becomes
sensitized—
antibodies (◖)
form to fight
Rh-positive
blood cells.

In the next
Rh-positive
pregnancy,
maternal
antibodies
attack fetal
blood cells.

FIGURE 12-5 How the Rh factor affects pregnancy.

VOCABULARY REVIEW

In the previous section, you learned terms relating to the blood system. Before going on to the exercises, read the definitions below. Pronunciations are provided for certain terms.

Term	Definition
agglutination [ă-glū-tĭ-NĀ-shŭn]	Clumping of cells and particles in blood.
agglutinogen [ă-glū-TĬN-ō-jĕn]	Substance that causes agglutination.
agranulocyte [ā-GRĂN-yū-lō-sĭt]	Leukocyte with nongranular cytoplasm.
albumin [ăl-BYŪ-mĭn]	Simple protein found in plasma.
basophil [BĀ-sō-fĭl]	Leukocyte containing heparin and histamine.
blood [blŭd]	Fluid (containing plasma, red blood cells, white blood cells, and platelets) circulated throughout the arteries, veins, capillaries, and heart.
blood types or **groups**	Classification of blood according to its antigen and antibody qualities.
coagulation [kō-ăg-yū-LĀ-shŭn]	Changing of a liquid, especially blood, into a semi-solid.
electrophoresis [ē-lĕk-trō-FŌR-ē-sĭs]	Process of separating particles in a solution by passing electricity through the liquid.
eosinophil [ē-ō-SĬN-ō-fĭl]	Type of granulocyte.
erythrocyte [ĕ-RĬTH-rō-sĭt]	Mature red blood cell.

Term	Definition
erythropoietin [ĕ-rĭth-rō-POY-ĕ-tĭn]	Hormone released by the kidneys to stimulate red blood cell production.
fibrin [FĪ-brĭn] **clot**	Clot-forming threads formed at the site of an injury during coagulation where platelets clump together with various other substances.
fibrinogen [fĭ-BRĬN-ō-jĕn]	Protein in plasma that aids in clotting.
gamma globulin [GĂ-mă GLŎB-yū-lĭn]	Globulin that arises in lymphatic tissue and functions as part of the immune system.
globin [GLŌ-bĭn]	Protein molecule in the blood, a part of hemoglobin.
globulin [GLŎB-yū-lĭn]	Any of a family of proteins in blood plasma.
granulocyte [GRĂN-yū-lō-sīt]	Leukocyte with granular cytoplasm.
hematocrit [HĒ-mă-tō-krĭt, HĔM-ă-tō-krĭt]	Measure of the percentage of red blood cells in a blood sample.
hematocytoblast [HĒ-mă-tō-SĪ-tō-blăst]	Most immature blood cell.
heme [hēm]	Pigment containing iron in hemoglobin.
hemoglobin [hē-mō-GLŌ-bĭn]	Protein in red blood cells essential to the transport of oxygen.
heparin [HĔP-ă-rĭn]	Substance in blood that prevents clotting.
histamine [HĬS-tă-mēn]	Substance released by basophils and eosinophils; involved in allergic reactions.
leukocyte [LŪ-kō-sīt]	Mature white blood cell.
lymphocyte [LĬM-fō-sīt]	Type of agranulocyte.
megakaryocyte [mĕg-ă-KĀR-ē-ō-sīt]	Large cells in red bone marrow that form platelets.
monocyte [MŎN-ō-sīt]	Type of agranulocyte.
neutrophil [NŪ-trō-fĭl]	Type of leukocyte; granulocyte.
plasma [PLĂZ-mă]	Liquid portion of unclotted blood.
plasmapheresis [PLĂZ-mă-fĕ-RĒ-sĭs]	Process of removing blood from a person, centrifuging it, and returning only red blood cells to that person.
platelet [PLĀT-lĕt]	Thrombocyte; part of a megakaryocyte that initiates clotting.
prothrombin [prō-THRŎM-bĭn]	Type of plasma protein that aids in clotting.
red blood cell (RBC)	One of the solid parts of blood formed from stem cells and having hemoglobin within; erythrocyte.
red blood cell count	Measurement of red blood cells in a cubic millimeter of blood.

Term	Definition
Rh factor	Type of antigen in blood that can cause a transfusion reaction.
Rh-negative	Lacking Rh factor on surface of blood cells.
Rh-positive	Having Rh factor on surface of blood cells.
serum [SĒR-ŭm]	The liquid left after blood has clotted.
stem cell	Immature cell formed in bone marrow that becomes differentiated into either a red or a white blood cell.
thrombin [THRŎM-bĭn]	Enzyme that helps in clot formation.
thrombocyte [THRŎM-bō-sīt]	Platelet; cell fragment that produces thrombin.
thromboplastin [thrŏm-bō-PLĂS-tĭn]	Protein that aids in forming a fibrin clot.
transfusion [trăns-FYŪ-zhŭn]	Injection of donor blood into a person needing blood.
white blood cell (WBC)	One of the solid parts of blood from stem cells that plays a role in defense against disease; leukocyte.

CASE STUDY

Getting Treatment

John Maynard was admitted to the hospital on April 2, 2XXX, complaining of respiratory problems and left-sided lower abdominal pain. The doctor on call ordered blood tests, and Mr. Maynard was found to be anemic.

Because of Mr. Maynard's multiple medical problems, a hematologist was called in to consult about the disease and treatment of this patient. The history as written in his medical record is as follows:

> HISTORY OF PRESENT ILLNESS: John Maynard is an 83-year-old man who was admitted on April 2, 2XXX, with acute exacerbation of chronic obstructive pulmonary disease and left-sided lower abdominal pain. He has been admitted in the past with a similar kind of pain but on the right side. He was evaluated by Dr. Evans in the past, but no obvious additional problem was identified. During this present admission, he was also found to be anemic.
>
> On direct interviewing: Mr. Maynard denies any acute blood loss. His stool and urine color are normal. He has a history of a stroke and has not been ambulatory. He lives with his nephew, who takes care of him. He denies any night sweats. He did not notice any new lumps or bruising anywhere. No new bone pain. He feels short of breath with minimal activity. He denies any chest pain or palpitations. He feels dizzy at times.

Critical Thinking

1. Blood tests can reveal problems almost anywhere in the body. Why are the elements in blood a good measure of many bodily functions?

2. Does Mr. Maynard's blood type (O positive) make him more susceptible to illnesses? Why or why not?

STRUCTURE AND FUNCTION EXERCISES

Check Your Knowledge

After each of the following, write the letter of the component of blood that is most closely related to either a, b, or c.

      a. red blood cell   b. white blood cell   c. component of plasma

3. albumin _____

4. hemoglobin _____

5. leukocyte _____

6. eosinophils _____

7. gamma globulin _____

8. fibrinogen _____

9. basophils _____

10. beta globulin _____

11. monocyte _____

12. neutrophils _____

13. histamine _____

14. alpha globulin _____

15. lymphocytes _____

Find the Type

Write the correct blood type, A, B, AB, or O, in the space following each phrase.

16. Has A and B antigens _____

17. Has neither A nor B antigens _____

18. Has only B antigens _____

19. Has only A antigens _____

20. Has both anti-A and anti-B antibodies _____

21. Has neither anti-A nor anti-B antibodies _____

22. Has only anti-A antibodies _____

23. Has only anti-B antibodies _____

Find a Match

Match the term in the left column with its correct definition in the right column.

24. _____ coagulation

25. _____ heparin

26. _____ neutrophil

27. _____ albumin

28. _____ agglutination

29. _____ Rh factor

30. _____ erythrocyte

31. _____ platelet

a. type of leukocyte

b. a blood protein

c. clumping of incompatible blood cells

d. process of clotting

e. antigen

f. cell that activates clotting

g. an anticoagulant

h. red blood cell

Combining Forms

The list below includes combining forms that relate specifically to the blood system. Pronunciations are provided for the examples.

COMBINING FORM	MEANING	EXAMPLE
agglutin(o)	agglutinin	*agglutinogenic* [ă-GLŪ-tĭn-ō-JĔN-ĭk], causing the production of agglutinin
eosino	eosinophil	*eosinopenia* [Ē-ŏ-sĭn-ō-PĒ-nē-ă], abnormally low count of eosinophils
erythr(o)	red	*erythrocyte* [ĕ-RĬTH-rō-sīt], red blood cell
hemo, hemat(o)	blood	*hemodialysis* [HĒ-mō-dī-ĂL-ĭ-sĭs], external dialysis performed by separating solid substances and water from the blood
leuk(o)	white	*leukoblast* [LŪ-kō-blăst], immature white blood cell
phag(o)	eating, devouring	*phagocyte* [FĂG-ō-sīt], cell that consumes other substances, such as bacteria
thromb(o)	blood clot	*thrombocyte* [THRŎM-bō-sīt], cell involved in blood clotting

CASE STUDY

Interpreting Results

The laboratory data on Mr. Maynard's record is as follows.

April 2, 2XXX: PSA 1.8
April 2, 2XXX: BUN 6, creatinine .7, calcium 8.3, uric acid 8.7, SGOT 42, SGPT 38,
alkaline phosphatase 86, total bilirubin 0.7.
April 2, 2XXX: White blood cell count 5.8, hemo-globin 10.4, HCT 31.1, platelet count 275,000.
December 4, 2XXX: vitamin B12 1,230,
folate 16.1.
December 6, 2XXX: HCT 38.9.
December 10, 2XXX: HCT 32.3.

Critical Thinking

32. What procedure is used to obtain the blood samples needed in Mr. Maynard's case? Is it safe to take several blood samples at once? Why or why not?

33. What is the difference between an RBC and a WBC?

Find a Match

Match the terms on the left that contain blood system combining forms with the correct definition on the right. You will be using the combining forms, suffixes, or prefixes you have learned in this chapter and in Chapters 1, 2, and 3.

34. _____ leukocytolysis   a. development of white blood cells

35. _____ hemotoxin   b. instrument for counting red blood cells

36. _____ thrombogenic   c. destruction of a clot

37. _____ hemostasis   d. painful skin redness

38. _____ eosinopenia   e. destruction of white blood cells

39. _____ erythrocytometer   f. substance that causes blood poisoning

40. _____ hemanalysis   g. causing blood coagulation

41. _____ thrombolysis   h. stoppage of bleeding

42. _____ erythralgia   i. blood analysis

43. _____ leukopoiesis   j. low number of eosinophils

Build Your Medical Vocabulary

Define the following words using the list of blood system combining forms above and the prefixes, suffixes, and combining forms in Chapters 1, 2, and 3.

44. agglutinophilic   51. polycythemia

45. thrombectomy   52. cytology

46. erythroblast   53. leukocyte

47. hematopathology   54. leukemia

48. eosinotaxis   55. thrombocytopenia

49. lymphoblast   56. hematoma

50. phagosome   57. erythrocytosis

Diagnostic, Procedural, and Laboratory Terms

Phlebotomy or **venipuncture,** the withdrawal of blood for examination, is probably the most frequently used diagnostic tool in medicine. Various measurements provide a clue as to someone's general health and aid in diagnosing specific conditions. Table 12-3 lists common blood analyses, and Figure 12-6 shows laboratory results for specific blood tests.

Most of the blood tests described in Table 12-3 are performed in a laboratory. Names of tests may vary according to the region of the country or the practice of a particular doctor. For example, a biochemistry panel is sometimes called a **chemistry profile,** and a blood chemistry is sometimes known as an **SMA (sequential multiple analyzer),** the name of the first machine used to analyze blood chemistries.

Elyse Armadian, M.D. 3 South Windsor Street Fairfield, MN 00219 300-546-7890	Laboratory Report Sunview Diagnostics 6712 Adams Drive Fairfield, MN 00220 300-546-7000		

Patient: Janine Josephs	Patient ID: 099-00-1200	Date of Birth: 08/07/43
Date Collected: 09/30/XXXX	Time Collected: 16:05	Total Volume: 2000
Date Received: 09/30/XXXX	Date Reported: 10/06/XXXX	

Test	Result	Flag	Reference
Complete Blood Count			
WBC	4.0		3.9-11.1
RBC	4.11		3.80-5.20
HCT	39.7		34.0-47.0
MCV	96.5		80.0-98.0
MCH	32.9		27.1-34.0
MCHC	34.0		32.0-36.0
MPV	8.6		7.5-11.5
NEUTROPHILS %	45.6		38.0-80.0
NEUTROPHILS ABS.	1.82		1.70-8.50
LYMPHOCYTES %	36.1		15.0-49.0
LYMPHOCYTES ABS.	1.44		1.00-3.50
EOSINOPHILS %	4.5		0.0-8.0
EOSINOPHILS ABS.	0.18		0.03-0.55
BASOPHILS %	0.7		0.0-2.0
BASOPHILS ABS.	0.03		0.000-0.185
PLATELET COUNT	229		150-400
Automated Chemistries			
GLUCOSE	80		65-109
UREA NITROGEN	17		6-30
CREATININE (SERUM)	0.6		0.5-1.3
UREA NITROGEN/CREATININE	28		10-29
SODIUM	140		135-145
POTASSIUM	4.4		3.5-5.3
CHLORIDE	106		96-109
CO_2	28		20-31
ANION GAP	6		3-19
CALCIUM	9.8		8.6-10.4
PHOSPHORUS	3.6		2.2-4.6
AST (SGOT)	28		0-30
ALT (SGPT)	19		0-34
BILIRUBIN, TOTAL	0.5		0.2-1.2
PROTEIN, TOTAL	7.8		6.2-8.2
ALBUMIN	4.3		3.5-5.0
GLOBULIN	3.5		2.1-3.8
URIC ACID	2.4		2.0-7.5
CHOLESTEROL	232		120-199
TRIGLYCERIDES	68		40-199
IRON	85		30-150
HDL CHOLESTEROL	73		35-59
CHOLESTEROL/HDL RATIO	3.2		3.2-5.7
LDL, CALCULATED	148		70-129
T3, UPTAKE	32		24-37
T4, TOTAL	6.9		4.5-12.8

FIGURE 12-6 A laboratory report showing a number of tests and the expected range of results for each type of test.

TABLE 12-3 Common blood analyses (see Appendix D for normal laboratory values).

Test or Procedure	Purpose of Test	Common Diseases/Disorders That May Be Indicated
complete blood count (CBC)	common screen for basic medical checkup (Figure 12-6)	iron-deficiency anemia bacterial or viral infection internal bleeding dehydration aplastic anemia impaired renal function liver disease circulatory disorder
blood chemistry	test of plasma for presence of most substances, such as glucose, cholesterol, uric acid, and electrolytes	diabetes hyperlipidemia gout circulatory disorders impaired renal function liver diseases general metabolic disorder
biochemistry panel	group of automated tests for various common diseases or disorders	same as blood chemistry
blood indices	measurement of size, volume, and content of red blood cells	classification of anemias
blood culture	test of a blood specimen in a culture in which microorganisms are observed; test for infections	septicemia bacterial infections
erythrocyte sedimentation rate (ESR); sedimentation rate (SR)	test for rate at which red blood cells fall through plasma; indicator of inflammation and/or tissue injury	infections joint inflammation sickle cell anemia liver and kidney disorders
white blood cell differential and **red blood cell morphology**	test for number of types of leukocytes and shape of red blood cells	infection anemia leukemia poikilocytosis anisocytosis
platelet count (PLT)	test for number of thrombocytes in a blood sample	hemorrhage infections malignancy hypersplenism aplastic anemia thrombocytopenia
partial thromboplastin time (PTT)	test for coagulation defects	vitamin K deficiency hepatic disease hemophilia hemorrhagic disorders
prothrombin time (PT)	test for coagulation defects	vitamin K deficiency hepatic disease hemorrhagic disorders hemophilia

TABLE 12-3 Common Blood Analyses (see Appendix D for Normal Laboratory Values) (*cont.*).

Test or Procedure	Purpose of Test	Common Diseases/Disorders That May Be Indicated
antiglobulin test; Coombs' test	test for antibodies on red blood cells	Rh factor and anemia
white blood count (WBC)	number of white blood cells in a sample (usually done as part of complete blood count)	bacterial or viral infection aplastic anemia leukemia leukocytosis
red blood count (RBC)	number of red blood cells in a sample (usually done as part of complete blood count)	polycythemia dehydration iron-deficiency anemia blood loss erythropoiesis
hemoglobin (HGB, Hgb)	level of hemoglobin in blood (usually done as part of complete blood count)	polycythemia dehydration anemia sickle cell anemia recent hemorrhage
hematocrit (HCT, Hct)	measure of packed red blood cells in a sample (usually done as part of complete blood count). This shows the percent of red blood cells.	polycythemia dehydration blood loss anemia
mean corpuscular volume (MCV)	volume of individual cells (usually part of blood indices)	microcytic or macrocytic anemia
mean corpuscular hemoglobin (MCH)	weight of hemoglobin in average red blood cell (usually part of blood indices)	classification of anemia
mean corpuscular hemoglobin concentration (MCHC)	concentration of hemoglobin in a red blood cell (usually part of blood indices)	hyperchromic or hypochromic anemia

VOCABULARY REVIEW

In the previous section, you learned diagnostic, procedural, and laboratory terms. Before going on to the exercises, read the definitions below. Pronunciations are provided for certain terms.

Term	Definition
antiglobulin [ĂN-tē-GLŎB-yū-lĭn] **test**	Test for antibodies on red blood cells.
biochemistry panel	Common group of automated tests run on one blood sample.
blood chemistry	Test of plasma for presence of a particular substance such as glucose.
blood culture	Test of a blood specimen in a culture medium to observe for particular microorganisms.

Term	Definition
blood indices [ĬN-dĭ-sēz]	Measurement of the characteristics of red blood cells.
chemistry profile	*See* biochemistry panel.
complete blood count (CBC)	Most common blood test for a number of factors.
erythrocyte sedimentation rate (ESR)	Test for rate at which red blood cells fall through plasma.
partial thromboplastin time (PTT)	Test for ability of blood to coagulate.
phlebotomy [flĕ-BŎT-ō-mē]	*See* venipuncture.
platelet count (PLT)	Measurement of number of platelets in a blood sample.
prothrombin time (PT)	Test for ability of blood to coagulate.
red blood cell morphology	Observation of shape of red blood cells.
sedimentation rate (SR)	*See* erythrocyte sedimentation rate.
SMA (sequential multiple analyzer)	Original blood chemistry machine; now a synonym for blood chemistry.
venipuncture [VĔN-ĭ-pŭnk-chŭr, VĒ-nĭ-pŭnk-chŭr]	Insertion of a needle into a vein, usually for the purpose of extracting a blood sample.

CASE STUDY

Evaluating the Tests

Mr. Maynard's record has the following notes from the hematologist's evaluation.

ASSESSMENT: Mr. Maynard has multiple medical problems. He has recently been admitted with abdominal discomfort, the etiology of which is unclear at this point. He was also found to have anemia. A review of his laboratory data shows that his hematocrit has been fluctuating between 27 and 38. His hematocrit on December 6 was 38.9, but within four days it dropped to 32.3. Since then there have also been several incidences in which his hematocrit dropped further, but then improved. This variation in the hematocrit is suggestive of some ongoing blood loss.

Critical Thinking

58. Other than blood loss, name at least two other conditions the HCT results might indicate.
59. What is the name of a test for leukocytes?

DIAGNOSTIC, PROCEDURAL, AND LABORATORY TERMS EXERCISES

Match the Test

Match the name of the test in the column on the left to its correct description in the column on the right.

60. _____ blood culture   **a.** average red blood cell volume

61. _____ hematocrit   **b.** antibodies on red blood cells

62. ____ sedimentation rate
63. ____ white blood count
64. ____ antiglobulin test
65. ____ mean corpuscular hemoglobin concentration
66. ____ mean corpuscular volume
67. ____ complete blood count
68. ____ prothrombin time
69. ____ biochemistry panel

c. rate at which red blood cells fall
d. group of automated tests
e. most common blood test
f. clotting factors test
g. number of white blood cells
h. measure of packed red blood cells
i. concentration of hemoglobin in red blood cells
j. growing of microorganisms in a culture

Find the Value

Give the expected (normal) range for each of the following laboratory measurements.

70. cholesterol _____
71. sodium _____
72. iron _____
73. thyroid (T4) _____
74. MCV _____

75. PLT _____
76. HCT _____
77. RBC _____
78. WBC _____
79. MCHC _____

Pathological Terms

Many diseases and disorders have some effect on the blood, but they are really diseases of other body systems. For example, diabetes is a disorder of the endocrine system, but its diagnosis includes an analysis of blood glucose levels. Actual diseases of the blood are characterized by changes in the supply or characteristics of blood cells, presence of microorganisms affecting the blood, or presence or lack of certain substances in the blood. Table 12-4 lists some common blood disorders.

The Anemia Institute (www. anemiainstitute.org) provides detailed information about many types of anemia.

TABLE 12-4 Blood disorders.

Disorder	Characteristics
dyscrasia	blood disease with abnormal material present
anemia (Figure 12-7)	deficiency in number or quality of red blood cells
pernicious anemia	lack of sufficient vitamin B_{12}
iron-deficiency anemia	lack of enough iron in blood
aplastic anemaia	failure of bone marrow to produce enough red blood cells
sickle cell anemia	sickle-shaped red blood cells that deliver less oxygen
hemolytic anemia	destruction of red blood cells
thalassemia	inability to produce sufficient hemoglobin

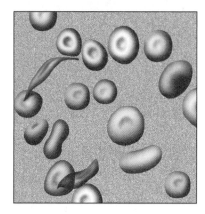

FIGURE 12-7 Characteristics of blood cells in certain anemias.

TABLE 12-4 Blood disorders (*cont.*).

Disorder	Characteristics
hemophilia	excessive bleeding
purpura	multiple tiny hemorrhages under the skin
thrombocytopenia	excessive bleeding
pancytopenia	low number of all blood cell components
erythropenia	low number of red blood cells
hemochromatosis	excessive iron in the blood
polycythemia	abnormal increase in red blood cells and hemoglobin
anisocytosis	variations in red blood cell size and shape
macrocytosis	abnormally large red blood cells
microcytosis	abnormally small red blood cells
poikilocytosis	irregularly-shaped red blood cells
leukemia	excessive number of white blood cells
acute myelogenous leukemia (AML)	immature granulocytes or **myeloblasts** invade the bone marrow
chronic myelogenous leukemia (CML) or *chronic granulocytic leukemia*	mature and immature granulocytes in blood and marrow
acute lymphocytic leukemia (ALL)	abnormal number of immature lymphocytes
chronic lymphocytic leukemia (CLL)	abnormal number of mature lymphocytes
multiple myeloma	tumor of the bone marrow

The Leukemia and Lymphoma Society's Web site (www.leukemia-lymphoma.org) has up-to-date information about various kinds of leukemia.

At www.multiplemyeloma.org, you can learn about the treatment options for multiple myeloma.

VOCABULARY REVIEW

In the previous section, you learned terms relating to pathology. Before going on to the exercises, read the definitions below. Pronunciations are provided for certain terms.

Term	Definition
anemia [ă-NĒ-mē-ă]	Condition in which red blood cells do not transport enough oxygen to the tissues.
anisocytosis [ăn-Ī-sō-sī-TŌ-sĭs]	Condition with abnormal variation in the size of red blood cells.
dyscrasia [dĭs-KRĀ-zhē-ă]	Any disease with abnormal particles in the blood.

Term	Definition
erythropenia [ĕ-rĭth-rō-PĒ-nē-ă]	Disorder with abnormally low number of red blood cells.
hemochromatosis [HĒ-mō-krō-mă-TŌ-sĭs]	Hereditary condition with excessive iron buildup in the blood.
hemophilia [hē-mō-FĬL-ē-ă]	Hereditary disorder with lack of clotting factor in the blood.
leukemia [lū-KĒ-mē-ă]	General term for a number of disorders with excessive white blood cells in the bloodstream and bone marrow.
macrocytosis [MĂK-rō-sī-TŌ-sĭs]	Disorder with abnormally large red blood cells.
microcytosis [MĬK-rō-sī-TŌ-sĭs]	Disorder with abnormally small red blood cells.
multiple myeloma [mī-ĕ-LŌ-mă]	Malignant tumor of the bone marrow.
myeloblast [MĪ-ĕ-lō-blăst]	Immature granulocytes.
pancytopenia [PĂN-sī-tō-PĒ-nē-ă]	Condition with a low number of blood components.
poikilocytosis [PŎY-kĭ-lō-sī-TŌ-sĭs]	Disorder with irregularly shaped red blood cells.
polycythemia [PŎL-ē-sī-THĒ-mē-ă]	Disorder with an abnormal increase in red blood cells and hemoglobin.
purpura [PŬR-pū-ră]	Condition with multiple tiny hemorrhages under the skin.
thalassemia [thăl-ă-SĒ-mē-ă]	Hereditary disorder characterized by inability to produce sufficient hemoglobin.
thrombocytopenia [THRŎM-bō-sī-tō-PĒ-nē-ă]	Bleeding condition with insufficient production of platelets.

PATHOLOGICAL TERMS EXERCISES

Spell It Correctly

The following terms are either spelled correctly or incorrectly. Put C in the space following correctly spelled words. Put the correct spelling in the space following incorrectly spelled words.

80. hemphilia _____

81. pancypenia _____

82. macrocytosis _____

83. anemia _____

84. alplastic anemia _____

85. pupura _____

86. thrombocytenia _____

87. poikilocytosis _____

Check Your Knowledge

Circle T for true or F for false.

88. A sudden loss of blood can cause anemia. T F

89. Multiple myeloma is a form of cancer. T F

90. Rh factor incompatibility can cause hemochromatosis. T F

91. Pernicious anemia may result from a deficiency of vitamin B_{12}. T F

92. Leukemia is a type of cancer. T F

93. Too many red blood cells can be a symptom of a disorder. T F

Find the Meaning

Describe the cause of each of the following forms of anemia.

94. aplastic anemia

95. iron-deficiency anemia

96. pernicious anemia

97. thalassemia

98. sickle cell anemia

CASE STUDY

Reading the X-Rays

Next, the radiology report is added to Mr. Maynard's record, and the hematologist adds notes.

Critical Thinking

99. Does a CBC provide enough information for a diagnosis of anemia or chronic blood loss?

100. Is Rh factor important for an 83-year-old man? Why or why not?

RADIOLOGY: Abdomen: Adynamic ileus.

April 2, 2XXX: Chest; bibasilar changes compatible with a small pleural effusion. Increased density in the right lung and small localized density because of rotation.

December 4, 2XXX: Abdominal ultrasound; normal biliary examination. Bilateral multiple renal cysts. Liver; fatty texture.

In summary, I have initiated more workup for anemia. The possibilities include anemia of chronic disease, myelo-dysplasia, or chronic blood loss. If his workup is inconclusive, then he might require bone marrow aspiration and biopsy to establish the diagnosis.

Surgical Terms

Surgery is not generally performed on the blood system. Sometimes venipuncture is considered a minor surgical procedure. (In this text, we have classified it as a diagnostic procedure.) The exceptions are **bone marrow biopsy** and **bone marrow transplant.** A bone marrow biopsy is used in the diagnosis of various blood disorders, such as anemia and leukemia. A bone marrow transplant is performed for serious ailments, such as leukemia and cancer. In this procedure, a donor's marrow is introduced into the bone marrow of the patient.

The National Marrow Donor Program (www.marrow.org) tells you how to become a bone marrow donor.

VOCABULARY REVIEW

In the previous section, you learned terms relating to surgery. Before going to the exercises, read the definitions below. Pronunciations are provided for certain terms.

Term	Definition
bone marrow biopsy	Extraction of bone marrow, by means of a needle, for observation.
bone marrow transplant	Injection of donor bone marrow into a patient whose diseased cells have been killed through radiation and chemotherapy.

CASE STUDY

Getting Confirmation

In addition to his other problems, Mr. Maynard has prostate cancer. His PSA has remained normal for a few years, so the cancer is thought to be in remission. However, the cause of the anemia was not confirmed. His diagnosis is also not confirmed, so a bone marrow biopsy is ordered. The bone marrow biopsy confirms aplastic anemia.

Critical Thinking

101. Describe the abnormality that the bone marrow biopsy reveals.
102. Does Mr. Maynard's condition require treatment before he has any surgery?

TERMINOLOGY IN ACTION

Alicia Minot is a 21-year-old student who is prone to migraine headaches. Her latest visit to her family doctor included a general physical and a CBC as well as a urinalysis. All test results were normal except for a low hemoglobin count. What are some steps Alicia can take in her daily life to raise her hemoglobin count?

USING THE INTERNET

Go to the Web site of the Aplastic Anemia Association (www.aplastic.org). Choose one of their online articles and write a paragraph summarizing its content.

CHAPTER REVIEW

The material that follows is to help you review all the material in this chapter.

DEFINITIONS

Define the following terms and combining forms. Review the chapter before starting. Make sure you know how to pronounce each term as you define it. The blue words in curly brackets are references to the Spanish Glossary on the Web site.

TERM	DEFINITION
agglutin(o)	
agglutination [ă-glū-tĭ-NĀ-shŭn] {aglutinación}	
agglutinogen [ă-glū-TĬN-ō-jĕn] {aglutinógeno}	
agranulocyte [ă-GRĂN-yū-lō-sĭt] {agranulocito}	
albumin [ăl-BYŪ-mĭn] {albúmina}	
anemia [ă-NĒ-mē-ă] {anemia}	
anisocytosis [ăn-Ī-sō-sĭ-TŌ-sĭs] {anisocitosis}	
antiglobulin [ĂN-tē-GLŎB-yū-lĭn] test	
basophil [BĀ-sō-fĭl] {basófilo}	
biochemistry panel	
blood [blŭd] {sangre}	
blood chemistry	
blood culture	
blood indices [ĬN-dĭ-sēz]	
blood types or groups	
bone marrow biopsy	
bone marrow transplant	
chemistry profile	
coagulation [kō-ăg-yū-LĀ-shŭn] {coagulación}	
complete blood count (CBC)	
dyscrasia [dĭs-KRĀ-zhē-ă] {discrasia}	

TERM	DEFINITION

electrophoresis [ē-lĕk-trō-FŌR-ē-sĭs] {electroforesis}

_____

eosino

_____

eosinophil [ē-ō-SĬN-ō-fĭl] {eosinófilo}

_____

erythr(o)

_____

erythrocyte [ĕ-RĬTH-rō-sīt] {eritrocito}

_____

erythrocyte sedimentation rate (ESR)

_____

erythropenia [ĕ-rĭth-rō-PĒ-nē-ă] {eritropenia}

_____

erythropoietin [ĕ-rĭth-rō-PŎY-ĕ-tĭn] {eritropoyetina}

_____

fibrin [FĪ-brĭn] clot

_____

fibrinogen [fĭ-BRĬN-ō-jĕn] {fibrinógeno}

_____

gamma globulin [GĂ-mă GLŎB-yū-lĭn]

_____

globin [GLŌ-bĭn] {globina}

_____

globulin [GLŎB-yū-lĭn] {globulina}

_____

granulocyte [GRĂN-yū-lō-sīt]

_____

hematocrit [HĒ-mă-tō-krĭt, HĔM-ă-tō-krĭt] {hematócrito}

_____

hematocytoblast [HĒ-mă-tō-SĪ-tō-blăst] {hematocitoblasto}

_____

heme [hēm]

_____

hemo, hemat(o)

_____

hemochromatosis [HĒ-mō-krō-mă-TŌ-sĭs]

_____

hemoglobin [hē-mō-GLŌ-bĭn] {hemoglobina}

_____

hemophilia [hē-mō-FĬL-ē-ă] {hemofilia}

_____

heparin [HĔP-ă-rĭn] {heparina}

_____

histamine [HĬS-tă-mēn] {histamine}

_____

leuk(o)

_____

leukocyte [LŪ-kō-sīt] {leucocito}

_____

leukemia [lū-KĒ-mē-ă] {leucemia}

_____

lymphocyte [LĬM-fō-sīt] {linfocito}

_____

macrocytosis [MĂK-rō-sī-TŌ-sĭs] {macrocitosis}

_____

TERM	DEFINITION
megakaryocyte [mĕg-ă-KĀR-ē-ō-sīt] {megacariocito}	
microcytosis [MĪK-rō-sī-TŌ-sĭs] {microcitosis}	
monocyte [MŎN-ō-sīt] {monocito}	
multiple myeloma [mī-ĕ-LŌ-mă]	
myeloblast [MĪ-ĕ-lŏ-blăst] {mieloblasto}	
neutrophil [NŪ-trō-fĭl] {neutrófilo}	
pancytopenia [PĂN-sī-tō-PĒ-nē-ă] {pancitopenia}	
partial thromboplastin time (PTT)	
phag(o)	
phlebotomy [flĕ-BŎT-ō-mē] {flebotomía}	
plasma [PLĂZ-mă] {plasma}	
plasmapheresis [PLĂZ-mă-fĕ-RĒ-sĭs] {plasmaféresis}	
platelet [PLĀT-lĕt] {plaqueta}	
platelet count (PLT)	
poikilocytosis [PŎY-kĭ-lō-sī-TŌ-sĭs] {poiquilocitosis}	
polycythemia [PŎL-ē-sī-THĒ-mē-ă] {policetemia}	
prothrombin [prō-THRŎM-bĭn] {protrombina}	
prothrombin time (PT)	
purpura [PŬR-pū-ră] {púrpura}	
red blood cell (RBC)	
red blood cell count	
red blood cell morphology	
Rh factor	
Rh-negative	
Rh-positive	
sedimentation rate (SR)	
serum [SĒR-ŭm] {suero}	
SMA (sequential multiple analyzer)	
stem cell	
thalassemia [thăl-ă-SĒ-mē-ă] {talasemia}	

Term	Definition
thromb(o)	_____
thrombin [THRŎM-bĭn] {trombina}	_____
thrombocyte [THRŎM-bō-sīt] {trombocito}	_____
thrombocytopenia [THRŎM-bō-sī-tō-PĒ-nē-ă]	_____
thromboplastin [thrŏm-bō-PLĂS-tĭn]	_____
transfusion [trăns-FYŪ-zhŭn] {transfusión}	_____
venipuncture [VĔN-ĭ-pŭnk-chŭr, VĒ-nĭ-pŭnk-chŭr] {venipuntura}	_____
white blood cell (WBC)	_____

Answers to Chapter Exercises

1. Blood circulates throughout the body and exchanges substances with most of the body's cells.
2. No; blood type does not make one more susceptible.
3. c
4. a
5. b
6. b
7. c
8. c
9. b
10. c
11. b
12. b
13. b
14. c
15. b
16. AB
17. O
18. B
19. A
20. O
21. AB
22. B
23. A
24. d
25. g
26. a
27. b
28. c
29. e
30. h
31. f
32. Venipuncture; Yes; small amounts of blood are replaced within a day or so.
33. RBC measures red blood cells and WBC measures white blood cells.
34. e
35. f
36. g
37. h
38. j

39. b
40. i
41. c
42. d
43. a
44. tending to clump together
45. removal of a thrombus
46. immature red blood cell
47. study of diseases of the blood
48. movement of eosinophils
49. immature white blood cell
50. part of the cell that aids a cell in digesting unwanted particles
51. disease with increased red blood cells
52. study of cells
53. white blood cell
54. disease (type of cancer) with abnormal number of white blood cells
55. abnormally small amount of platelets in the blood
56. blood-filled mass
57. disease with increased red blood cell counts
58. anemia; dehydration; polycythemia
59. white blood count (WBC)
60. j
61. h
62. c
63. g
64. b
65. i
66. a
67. e
68. f
69. d
70. 120–199
71. 135–145
72. 30–150
73. 4.5–12.8
74. 80.0–98.0
75. 150–400
76. 34.0–47.0

77. 3.80–5.20
78. 3.9–11.1
79. 32.0–36.0
80. hemophilia
81. pancytopenia
82. C
83. C
84. aplastic anemia
85. purpura
86. thrombocytopenia
87. C
88. T
89. T
90. F
91. T
92. T
93. T
94. failure in production of red blood cells
95. lack of enough iron either in diet or absorption, which causes insufficient production of hemoglobin
96. insufficient vitamin B_{12}, which causes abnormal red blood cell shape
97. blood disorder with insufficient hemoglobin production
98. red blood cell disorder with problems with carrying oxygen to the tissues
99. Yes. Anemia and chronic blood loss are indicated by the percentage of red blood cells noted in a CBC.
100. Yes; it is important for everybody who might need a transfusion.
101. aplastic anemia, a failure of the bone marrow to produce enough red blood cells
102. Yes; anemia is a complication that should be dealt with first because of the probability of further blood loss during surgery.

The Lymphatic and Immune Systems

13

After studying this chapter, you will be able to:

▶ Name the parts of the lymphatic and immune systems and discuss the function of each part

▶ Define combining forms used in building words that relate to the lymphatic and immune system

▶ Name the common diagnoses, clinical procedures, and laboratory tests used in treating disorders of the lymphatic and immune systems

▶ List and define the major pathological conditions of the lymphatic and immune systems

▶ Explain the meaning of surgical terms related to the lymphatic and immune systems

Structure and Function

The lymphatic and immune systems share some of the same structures and functions. The immune system utilizes other systems to maintain its functions. Both the lymphatic and immune systems contain the lymph nodes, spleen, thymus gland, and some of the disease-fighting immune cells.

The lymphatic system has the following functions:

- It reduces tissue edema by removing fluid from capillary beds.
- It returns the proteins from the fluids to the blood.
- It traps and filters cellular debris including cancer cells, microbes, etc. with the help of cells called macrophages.
- It recycles body fluid to various parts of the body.
- It circulates lymphocytes to assist with the immune response.
- It moves fats from the GI tract to the blood.

The immune system has the following functions:

- The immune system protects the body against foreign body invasion.
- In normal function, the immune system coordinates activities in the blood, body tissues, and the lymphatic system to protect the body from invasion.
- It fights off infections and protects against future infections by producing a variety of immune responses.
- It produces antibodies (immunoglobulins).

Figure 13-1a shows the lymphatic and immune systems. Figure 13-1b shows how lymph circulates throughout the body.

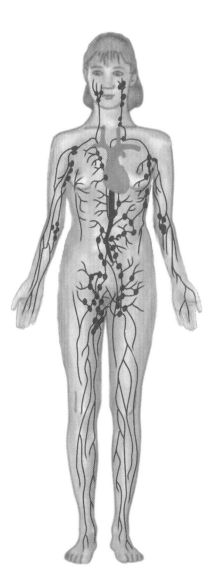

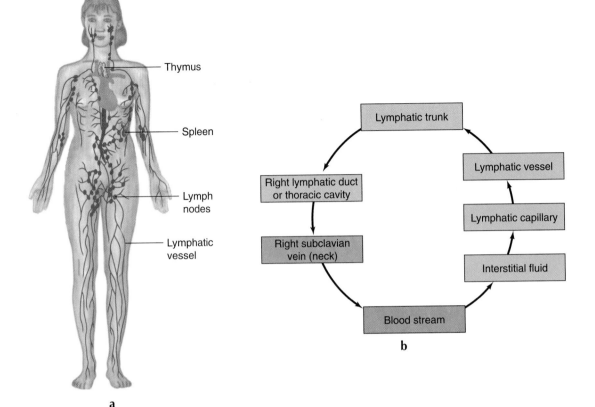

FIGURE 13-1 (a) The lymphatic and immune systems are the body's major defense against foreign substances; (b) flowchart of the path of lymph through the body.

Lymphatic Organs and Structures

The lymphatic system is similar to both the cardiovascular and blood systems in that it involves a network of vessels that transports fluid around the body.

The lymphatic system consists of the following parts:

1. The *lymphatic pathways* are the vessels that transport **lymph** (the fluid of the lymphatic system) around the body. The smallest part of these pathways are the *microscopic capillaries* located in the capillary beds of the body. Figure 13-2 illustrates lymph flow.
2. Located along the lymphatic vessels are the **lymph nodes**, small lumps of lymphatic tissue that serve as a collecting point to filter the lymph.
3. The largest lymphatic organ, the **spleen**, is located in the upper left portion of the abdominal cavity, where unfortunately it can easily be injured and ruptured. In such cases, it must be repaired or removed (its functions are taken over by the lymph nodes, liver, and bone marrow).
4. The **thymus gland** is a two-lobed, soft gland located in the thoracic cavity (Figure 13-3). The thymus gland contains a high number of **T lymphocytes (T cells)** and a decreased number of **B lymphocytes (B cells)**. The movement of T cells is aided by **thymosin**, a hormone secreted by the thymus.

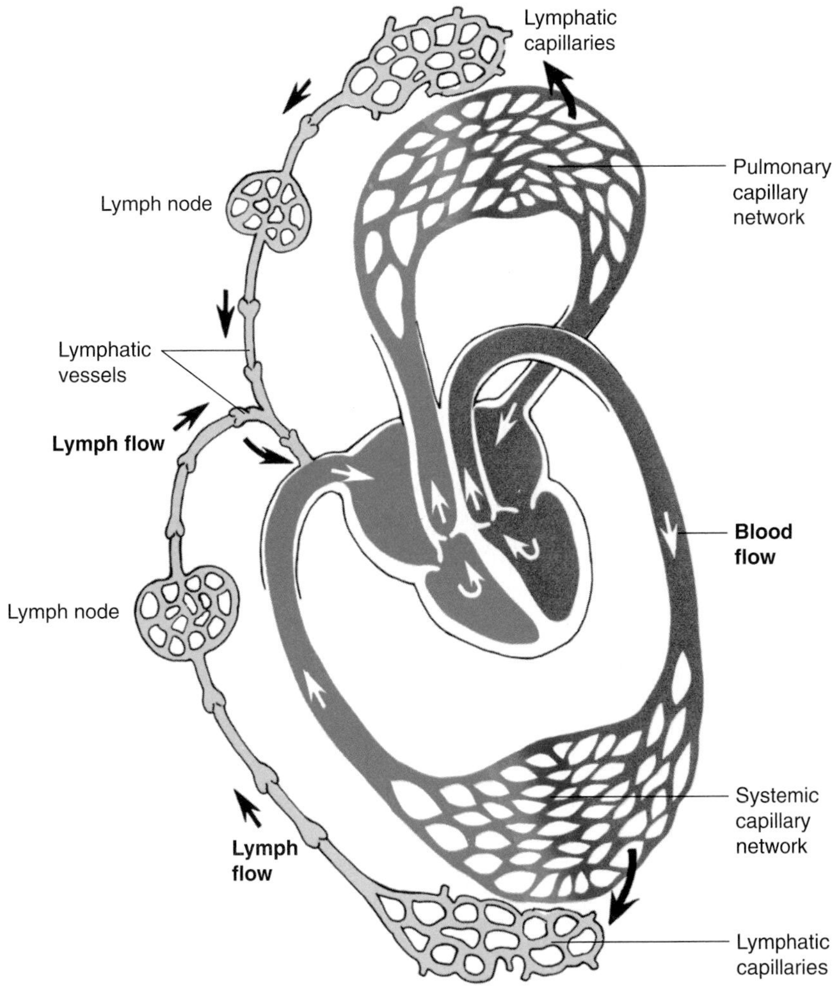

FIGURE 13-2 Lymphatic capillaries gather the lymph from the space between tissues.

Lymphatic capillaries

Lymph node

Lymphatic vessels

Lymph flow

Lymph node

Lymph flow

Pulmonary capillary network

Blood flow

Systemic capillary network

Lymphatic capillaries

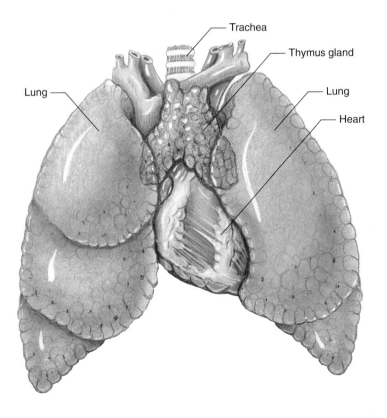

FIGURE 13-3 The thymus gland is located between the lungs.

Trachea

Thymus gland

Lung

Lung

Heart

Lung

The Immune System

The immune system relies on several other systems to accomplish its duties. Leukocytes (white blood cells) from the blood system, include **lymphocytes**, monocytes, and granulocytes (*polymorphonucleated cells* or PMN). Phagocytes of the blood are called **macrophages** and **microphages**. Phagocytes remove foreign particles from the body by the process of **phagocytosis**, the internalization or "eating" of the particles. The immune response is divided into two kinds: the *cellular response* and the *humoral* or *immunoglobulin (antibody) response*.

Lymphocytes are one kind of leukocyte that are intimately involved in the immune system. Included in the classification of lymphocytes are the T lymphocytes (T cells) and the B lymphocytes (B cells). T cells are involved in both types of the immune response. The B cells are responsible for the production of **antibodies** (also called immunoglobulins). The humoral response, or the antibody production, requires the assistance of the T cells through their production of other chemical substances that act as signals to the B cells to begin antibody production.

The immune system shares several parts with the lymphatic system (lymph nodes, spleen, and thymus gland). These parts serve as defense mechanisms protecting the body. Parts of other systems, such as the skin, also play an important role in protecting the body from disease. The immune system of the body consists of all the processes that perform a series of defenses to protect from and respond to disease.

The National Institute of Allergies and Infectious Diseases (http://www.niaid.nih.gov/final/immun/immun.htm) gives detailed information about the immune system on their Web site.

Mechanical and Chemical Defenses

The human body includes a number of mechanical, chemical, and other defenses against disease. When disease-causing agents, **pathogens**, try to enter the body, they are often stopped by the skin, the cilia in the nostrils, and by various mucous membranes—all of which are mechanical barriers to intrusion.

If some pathogens get past the mechanical defenses, they may be stopped by chemical barriers, such as gastric juices in the stomach. Pathogens in the bloodstream may be destroyed by phagocytosis.

Some pathogens prefer the environment of the human body as opposed to that of other animals, so they affect humans but not animals. Some tick-borne diseases such as Lyme disease can have devastating consequences to humans but remain dormant in animals. Some bacteria are beneficial in humans because they help ward off disease. In the bloodstream, certain substances called **antigens** may provoke an immune response to certain diseases.

The Immune Process

Mechanical or chemical defenses work together to avert or attack disease. In addition, the body has specific defenses of the immune system called **immunity** that provide resistance to particular pathogens. There are three major types of immunity—natural immunity, acquired active immunity, and acquired passive immunity.

Natural Immunity

Natural immunity is the human body's natural resistance to certain diseases. This natural resistance varies for individuals, even to the extent that persons of certain racial backgrounds tend to have more or less resistance to certain diseases. Natural resistance depends on the individual's genetic characteristics and on some of the natural chemical defenses.

Acquired Active Immunity

The body develops **acquired active immunity** either by having a disease and producing natural antibodies to it or by being vaccinated against the disease. **Immunization** or **vaccination** is the injection of an **antigen**, a substance that provokes an immune response, from a different organism that causes active immunity via the production of antibodies. The substance is called a **vaccine.**

Acquired active immunity is further divided into two types. The first, **humoral immunity**, is immunity provided by **plasma cells**, which produce antibodies called **immunoglobulins**. There are five major types of immunoglobulins:

- *Immunoglobulin G (IgG)* is effective against bacteria, viruses, and toxins.
- *Immunoglobulin A (IgA)* is common in exocrine gland secretions, such as breast milk, tears, nasal fluid, gastric juice, and so on. IgA transfers immunity from mother to infant through breast milk.
- *Immunoglobulin M (IgM)* develops in the blood plasma in response to certain antigens within the body or from foreign sources. It is the first antibody to be produced after infection.
- *Immunoglobulin D (IgD)* is important in B cell activation, which helps immunity by transforming itself into a plasma cell in the presence of a specific type of antigen.
- *Immunoglobulin E (IgE)* appears in glandular secretions and is associated with allergic reactions.

The second type of acquired active immunity, or **cell-mediated immunity**, is provided by the action of T cells. The T cells respond to antigens by multiplying rapidly and producing proteins called *lymphokines* (for example, **interferons** and **interleukins**) that have antiviral properties or properties that affect the actions of other cells in the body. T cells also produce substances to stimulate B cells to differentiate into plasma cells and to produce antibodies.

Three types of other specialized T cells are:

- **Helper cells** or CD4 cells that stimulate the immune response.
- **Cytotoxic cells** or CD8 cells that help in the destruction of infected cells.
- **Suppressor cells** or T cells (mainly CD8 and some CD4) that suppress B cells and other immune cells.

MORE ABOUT...

Immunization

Most children are immunized against childhood diseases routinely and those vaccines are thought to be safe and effective. There is a very small incidence of bad reactions to vaccines that have harmed some children. Recently, some groups have studied what is thought to be the higher incidence of autism since the introduction of routine vaccinations. So far, the evidence is that there is no connection between autism and childhood immunization through vaccine. Also, the risk of getting some of the diseases which the vaccines prevent is thought to have the potential for much greater harm to children.

Acquired Passive Immunity

Acquired passive immunity is immunity provided in the form of antibodies or antitoxins that have been developed in another person or another species. Acquired passive immunity is necessary in cases of snakebite and tetanus or any problem where immediate immunity is needed. In such cases, a dose of **antitoxin** (antibody directed against specific toxins) is given to provide antibodies. Passive immunity may also be administered to lessen the chance of catching a disease or to lessen the severity of the course of the disease. **Gamma globulin** is a preparation of collected antibodies given to prevent or lessen certain diseases, such as hepatitis A, varicella, and rabies.

VOCABULARY REVIEW

In the previous section, you learned terms relating to the lymphatic and immune systems. Before going on to the exercises, read the definitions below. Pronunciations are provided for certain terms.

Term	Definition
acquired active immunity	Resistance to a disease acquired naturally or developed by previous exposure or vaccination.
acquired passive immunity	Inoculation against disease or poison, using antitoxins or antibodies from or in another person or another species.
antibody [ĂN-tē-bŏd-ē]	Specialized protein that fights disease; also called immunoglobulin.
antigen [ĂN-tĭ-jĕn]	Any substance that can provoke an immune response.
antitoxin [ăn-tē-TŎK-sĭn]	Antibodies directed against a particular disease or poison.
B lymphocytes [LĬM-fō-sīts], B cells	A kind of lymphocyte that manufactures antibodies.
cell-mediated immunity	Resistance to disease mediated by T cells.
cytotoxic [sī-tō-TŎK-sĭk] cell	T cell that helps in destruction of infected cells throughout the body.
gamma globulin [GĂ-mă GLŎB-yū-lĭn]	Antibodies given to prevent or lessen certain diseases.
helper cell	T cell that stimulates the immune response.
humoral [HYŪ-mōr-ăl] immunity	Resistance to disease provided by plasma cells and antibody production.
immunity [ĭ-MYŪ-nĭ-tē]	Resistance to particular pathogens.
immunization [ĬM-yū-nĭ-ZĀ-shŭn]	Vaccination.
immunoglobulin [ĬM-yū-nō-GLŎB-yū-lĭn]	Antibody.

Term	Definition
interferon [ĭn-tĕr-FĒR-ŏn]	Protein produced by T cells and other cells; destroys disease-causing cells with its antiviral properties.
interleukin [ĭn-tĕr-LŪ-kĭn]	Protein produced by T cells; helps regulate immune system.
lymph [lĭmf]	Fluid that contains white blood cells and other substances and flows in the lymphatic vessels.
lymph node	Specialized organ that filters harmful substances from the tissues and assists in the immune response.
lymphocytes [LĬM-fō-sīts]	White blood cells made in the bone marrow that are critical to the body's defense against disease and infection.
macrophage [MĂK-rō-fāj]	Special cell that devours foreign substances.
microphage [MĪK-rō-fāj]	Small phagocytic cell that devours foreign substances.
natural immunity	Inherent resistance to disease found in a species, race, family group, or certain individuals.
pathogen [PĂTH-ō-jĕn]	Disease-causing agent.
phagocytosis [FĂG-ō-sī-TŌ-sĭs]	Ingestion of foreign substances by specialized cells.
plasma [PLĂZ-mă] **cell**	Specialized lymphocyte that produces immunoglobulins.
spleen [splēn]	Organ of lymph system that filters and stores blood, removes old red blood cells, and activates lymphocytes.
suppressor [sŭ-PRĔS-ōr] **cell**	T cell that suppresses B cells and other immune cells.
T cells	Specialized white blood cells that receive markers in the thymus, are responsible for cellular immunity, and assist with humoral immunity.
thymosin [THĪ-mō-sĭn]	Hormone secreted by the thymus gland that aids in distribution of thymocytes and lymphocytes.
thymus [THĪ-mŭs] **gland**	Soft gland with two lobes that is involved in immune responses; located in mediastinum.
T lymphocytes	*See* T cells.
vaccination [VĂK-sĭ-NĀ-shŭn]	Injection of an antigen from a different organism to cause active immunity.
vaccine [văk-SĒN, VĂK-sēn]	Antigen developed from a different organism that causes active immunity in the recipient.

CASE STUDY

Researching a Cure

Some hospitals are part of large university complexes. These hospitals often do many kinds of research and offer tertiary care, medical care at a center that has a unit specializing in certain diseases. They may provide data on drug trials. They may work on improving diagnostic testing. Some research is focused on diseases that are infectious and for which there is not yet a cure. The goal of many studies is to produce a vaccine.

Critical Thinking

1. Why would researchers want to produce a vaccine?
2. What form of immunity would a vaccination provide?

STRUCTURE AND FUNCTION EXERCISES

Find a Match

Match the correct definition in the right-hand column with the terms in the left-hand column.

3. _____ T cell
4. _____ pathogen
5. _____ immunoglobulin E
6. _____ IgD
7. _____ helper cell
8. _____ cytotoxic cell
9. _____ suppressor cell
10. _____ antitoxin
11. _____ antibody
12. _____ gamma globulin

a. T cell that helps destroy foreign cells or substances
b. T cell that regulates the amounts of antibody
c. T cell that stimulates antibody production
d. antibody important in B-cell activation
e. agent given to prevent or lessen disease
f. lymphocyte associated with cellular immunity
g. helps produce resistance to a disease or a poison
h. protein produced by B cells that fight foreign cells
i. disease-causing agent
j. antibody associated with allergic reactions

Check Your Knowledge

Fill in the blanks

13. People are born with some _____ immunity.
14. Vaccinations give _____ _____ immunity.
15. Antitoxins give _____ _____ immunity.
16. The special cells that ingest foreign substances are _____ or _____.
17. Lymph contains _____ blood cells.
18. The thymus gland produces the hormone _____.
19. Agents of T cells that destroy disease-causing cells are _____ and _____.
20. Antibodies are called _____.

Combining Forms

The list below includes combining forms that relate specifically to the lymphatic and immune systems. Pronunciations are provided for the examples.

COMBINING FORM	MEANING	EXAMPLE
aden(o)	gland	*adenocarcinoma* [ĂD-ē-nō-kăr-sĭ-NŌ-mă], glandular cancer
immun(o)	immunity	*immunosuppressor* [ĬM-yū-nō-sŭ-PRĔS-ōr], agent that suppresses the immune response
lymph(o)	lymph	*lymphocyte* [LĬM-fō-sīt], white blood cell associated with the immune response
lymphaden(o)	lymph nodes	*lymphadenopathy* [lĭm-făd-ĕ-NŎP-ă-thē], disease affecting the lymph nodes
lymphangi(o)	lymphatic vessels	*lymphangitis* [lĭm-făn-JĪ-tĭs], inflammation of the lymphatic vessels
splen(o)	spleen	*splenectomy* [splē-NĔK-tō-mē], removal of the spleen
thym(o)	thymus	*thymectomy* [thī-MĔK-tō-mē], removal of the thymus
tox(o), toxi, toxico	poison	*toxicosis* [tŏk-sĭ-KŌ-sĭs], systemic poisoning

CASE STUDY

Checking for Immunity

Jill, a three-year-old girl, was playing barefoot in her backyard when she stepped on a rusty nail. The nail punctured her skin and made her vulnerable to tetanus. Jill is up to date on all her vaccinations. The most common early childhood vacinnation is DPT (diphtheria, pertussis, and tetanus). The vaccinations last for a number of years.

Critical Thinking

21. Is it likely that Jill will contract tetanus? Why or why not?

22. What type of immunity to tetanus does Jill have?

COMBINING FORMS EXERCISES

Build Your Medical Vocabulary

Fill in the missing word part.

23. Removal of lymph nodes: _____ectomy

24. Hemorrhage from a spleen: _____rrhagia

25. Tumor of the thymus: _____oma

26. Lacking in some immune function: _____deficient

27. Cell of a gland: _____cyte

28. Skin disease caused by a poison: _____derma

29. Dilation of the lymphatic vessels: _____ectasis

30. Resembling lymph: _____oid

Find a Match

Match the term on the left with the correct definition on the right.

31. _____ toxicologist

32. _____ splenomegaly

33. _____ lymphangiosarcoma

34. _____ splenomyelomalacia

35. _____ lymphocele

36. _____ lymphadenitis

37. _____ toxanemia

a. anemia resulting from a poison

b. malignancy in the lymphatic vessels

c. cystic mass containing lymph

d. inflammation of a lymph node

e. spleen enlargement

f. expert in the science of poisons

g. softening of the spleen and bone marrow

Diagnostic, Procedural, and Laboratory Terms

Abnormalities of lymph organs can be checked in a CAT scan. Several blood tests that indicate the number and condition of white blood cells are used in diagnosing lymph and immune systems diseases. HIV infection is diagnosed mainly with two blood serum tests, **enzyme-linked immunosorbent assay (EIA, ELISA)** and **Western blot**. ELISA tests blood for the antibody to the HIV virus (as well as antibodies to other specific viruses, such as hepatitis B), and the Western blot is a confirming test for the presence of HIV antibodies. A diagnosis of AIDS is made on the basis of the presence of opportunistic infections and T cell counts in specified ranges.

Allergy tests are performed by an allergist. Tests usually consist of some form of exposure to a small amount of the suspected allergen to see if a reaction occurs. Now there are even home allergy tests available that can detect allergies by testing a small amount of blood.

VOCABULARY REVIEW

In the previous section, you learned terms relating to diagnosis, clinical procedures, and laboratory tests. Before going on to the exercises, read the definitions below. Pronunciations are provided for certain terms.

Term	Definition
enzyme-linked immunosorbent assay (EIA, ELISA [ĕ-LĪ-ză, ĕ-LĪ-să])	Test used to screen blood for the presence of antibodies to different viruses or bacteria.
Western blot	Test primarily used to check for antibodies to HIV in serum.

CASE STUDY

Handling the Emergency

Kyle, a seven-year-old boy, came to the emergency room at the hospital in respiratory distress. His mother says that he often has respiratory allergies. He was taken to the imaging area for chest x-rays. His lungs show some restricted areas. He is also given a thorough medical exam to make sure that nothing other than an allergic reaction is causing the breathing difficulties. If the examination is normal, Kyle will be sent to an allergist to determine the cause of his allergic reaction. The resident performing the exam marks the patient's record as shown below.

Critical Thinking

38. Why did Kyle need a thorough physical exam?
39. Did the physical exam show any abnormalities other than respiratory allergies?

GENERAL: He is a well-developed, well-nourished male in moderate respiratory distress.

HEENT: Tympanic membranes unremarkable. Eyes, nose, mouth, and throat normal.

NECK: No masses. Supple.

LUNGS: Breath sounds clear bilaterally with somewhat decreased air exchange and diffuse expiratory wheeze. Work of breathing is mildly to moderately increased.

CARDIAC: No murmur or gallop. Pulses 2+ and symmetrical.

ABDOMEN: Soft and nontender without organomegaly or mass.

GU: Normal male.

EXTREMITIES: Unremarkable.

NEUROLOGIC: Alert and appropriate. Cranial nerves intact. Reflexes 2+ and symmetrical.

DIAGNOSTIC, PROCEDURAL, AND LABORATORY TERMS EXERCISES

Check Your Knowledge

Circle T for true or F for false.

40. The ELISA tests for HIV. T F
41. A Western blot determines if Hepatitis B is present. T F
42. An analysis of white blood cells can help in diagnosing lymph and immune system diseases. T F

Pathological Terms

Diseases of the lymph and immune systems include diseases that attack lymph tissue itself; diseases that are spread through the lymphatic pathways; and diseases that flourish because of a suppression of the immune response. Disorders of the lymph and immune systems can be caused by an overly vigorous response to an immune system invader. This is the case with some diseases of other body systems, such as multiple sclerosis, in which the immune

FIGURE 13-4 The red dots on the white T cell are HIV virus particles.

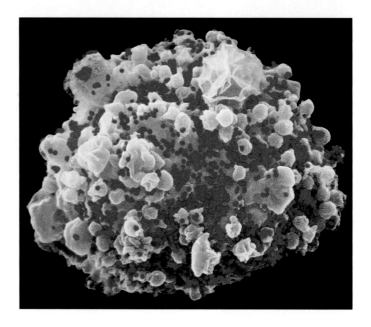

system attacks some of the nervous system's protective covering, myelin. It is also the case with **allergy**, an immune overresponse to a stimulus.

The most widespread virus that attacks the immune system is the **human immunodeficiency virus (HIV)**, a virus spread by sexual contact, exchange of bodily fluids, or intravenous exposure. Figure 13-4 shows a T cell infected with HIV.

AIDS

AIDS or **acquired immunodeficiency syndrome** is the most widespread **immunosuppressive disease**, a disease that suppresses the ability of the immune system to defend against infection. AIDS is a complex of symptoms and is caused by the HIV virus. The HIV virus is a type of **retrovirus**, a ribonucleic acid (RNA) that causes reversal of normal cell copying. The retro- (reverse) is the opposite of the ordinary method of DNA copying itself onto RNA.

AIDS patients are subject to a number of **opportunistic infections**, infections that a healthy immune system can easily fight off but take hold because of the lowered immune response. Many of these infections are present in other body systems. Table 13-1 lists some opportunistic infections commonly present in AIDS patients and the parts of the body affected. AIDS affects the entire body, with diseases such as herpes, candidiasis, and Kaposi's sarcoma appearing on the skin, and Pneumocystis carinii pneumonia (PCP) appearing in the lungs.

Other Immune System Disorders

Opportunistic infections also attack the immune systems of people with immunosuppressive disorders other than AIDS. Any recipient of an organ transplant must take immunosuppressive drugs to avoid organ rejection. These drugs leave the patient open to opportunistic infections. There are a number of other immunosuppressive disorders. Some are congenital and may be inherited. Others are a result of disease; for example, a severe case of diabetes can weaken the immune system.

Lymphoma, cancer of the lymph nodes, is a relatively common cancer with high cure rates. Some AIDS patients are especially susceptible to lym-

The CDC has a group called the Divisions of HIV/AIDS prevention (http://www.cdc.gov/hiv/dhap.htm) that provides up-to-date information on prevention, research, and testing.

The Lymphoma Research Foundation (www.lymphoma.org) is dedicated to assisting people with lymphoma and related diseases and ultimately to eradicating the disease.

TABLE 13-1 Some opportunistic malignancies and infections that often accompany AIDS.

Opportunistic Infection	Type of Malignancy or Infection	Areas Affected
candidiasis	caused by fungus—Candida albicans	digestive tract, respiratory tract, skin, and some reproductive organs (particularly the vagina)
cytomegalovirus	Herpesviridae	can infect various cells or organs (like the eyes); causes swelling
Kaposi's sarcoma	malignancy arising from capillary linings	skin and lymph nodes
Mycobacterium avium-intracellulare (MAI)	caused by bacterium found in soil and water	systemic infection with fever, diarrhea, lung and blood disease, and wasting
Pneumocystis carinii pneumonia (PCP)	caused by parasite—Pneumocystis carinii	lungs—a particularly dangerous type of pneumonia

phomas because of their lowered immune systems. There are many different types of lymphomas. Two of the most common are **Hodgkin's lymphoma (Hodgkin's disease)**, a type of lymph cancer of uncertain origin that generally appears in early adulthood, and **non-Hodgkin's lymphoma**, a cancer of the lymph nodes with some cells resembling healthy cells and spreading in a diffuse pattern. It usually appears in mid-life. Depending on how far the disease has spread (**metastasis**), both types can be arrested with chemo-

More About...

Contracting AIDS

When the AIDS epidemic began in the United States, many people feared that the HIV virus could be spread by casual contact. In fact, time has shown that there are only a few specific ways it can be transmitted. These are the ways that AIDS is transmitted and how it is not transmitted.

How HIV Is Transmitted

Sexual contact, particularly vaginal, anal, and oral intercourse

Contaminated needles (intravenous drug use, accidental needle stick in medical setting)

During birth from an infected mother

Receiving infected blood or other tissue (rare; precautions usually prevent this)

How HIV Is NOT Transmitted

Casual contact (social kissing, hugging, handshakes)

Objects—toilet seats, deodorant sticks, doorknobs

Mosquitoes

Sneezing and coughing

Sharing food

Swimming in the same water as an infected person

therapy and radiation. Surgery (bone marrow transplantation) is also useful in Hodgkin's lymphoma.

Malignant tumors appear in many places in the lymph system. A **thymoma** is a tumor of the thymus gland. Hodgkin's lymphoma is a malignancy of the lymph nodes and spleen. Enlarged lymph nodes, enlarged spleen (**splenomegaly**), and overactive spleen (**hypersplenism**) characterize this disease. Non-Hodgkin's lymphoma is a disease with malignant cells that resemble large lymphocytes (**lymphocytic lymphoma**) or large macrophages called *histiocytes* (hence the name **histiocytic lymphoma**).

Nonmalignant lesions on the lymph nodes, lungs, spleen, skin, and liver can indicate the presences of **sarcoidosis**, an inflammatory condition that can affect lung function. Swollen lymph nodes (**lymphadenopathy**) can also indicate the presence of **infectious mononucleosis**, an acute infectious disease caused by the Epstein-Barr virus.

The Allergic Response

Allergies are a problem of the immune system that affect millions of people. They are due to the production of IgE antibodies against an **allergen**, an allergy-causing substance. Antibodies and some antigens cause a histamine to be released into the tissues. This histamine release is the cause of the symptoms of allergies.

Allergies vary for different people depending on time of year, amount of exposure to different allergens, and other immunological problems. **Hypersensitivity** increases as exposure increases, sometimes resulting in **anaphylaxis** (or *anaphylactic reaction* or *shock*), a reaction so severe that it can be life-threatening by decreasing blood pressure, affecting breathing, and causing loss of consciousness.

The Food Allergy and Anaphylaxis Network (www.foodallergy.org) provides up-to-date information about foods that have been recalled due to undeclared potentially allergic products such as peanuts and milk hidden in them.

Autoimmune Disorders

The immune system can also turn against its own healthy tissue. **Autoimmune diseases**, such as rheumatoid arthritis, lupus, and scleroderma, result from the proliferation of T cells that react as though they were fighting a virus, but are actually destroying healthy cells. **Autoimmune responses** often result from the body's need to fight an actual infection, during which the immune system becomes overactive.

The American Autoimmune and Related Diseases Association (www.aarda.org) keeps track of autoimmune diseases and provides helpful patient information.

VOCABULARY REVIEW

In the previous section, you learned terms relating to pathology. Before going on to the exercises, read the definitions below. Pronunciations are provided for certain terms.

Term	Definitions
acquired immunodeficiency [ĬM-yū-nō-dē-FĬSH-ĕn-sē] **syndrome**	AIDS.
AIDS [ādz]	Most widespread immunosuppressive disease; caused by the HIV virus.

Term	Definitions
allergen [ĂL-ěr-jēn]	Substance to which exposure causes an allergic response.
allergy [ĂL-ěr-jē]	Production of IgE antibodies against an allergen.
anaphylaxis [ĂN-ă-fĭ-LĂK-sĭs]	Life-threatening allergic reaction.
autoimmune [ăw-tō-ĭ-MYŪN] **disease**	Any of a number of diseases, such as rheumatoid arthritis, lupus, and scleroderma, caused by an autoimmune response.
autoimmune response	Overactivity in the immune system against the body, causing destruction of one's own healthy cells.
histiocytic [HĬS-tē-ō-SĬT-ĭk] **lymphoma**	Lymphoma with malignant cells that resemble histiocytes.
Hodgkin's lymphoma, Hodgkin's disease	Type of lymph cancer of uncertain origin that generally appears in early adulthood.
human immunodeficiency [ĬM-yū-nō-dē-FĬSH-ěn-sē] **virus (HIV)**	Virus that causes AIDS; spread by sexual contact, exchange of body fluids, and shared use of needles.
hypersensitivity [HĪ-pěr-sěn-sĭ-TĬV-ĭ-tē]	Abnormal reaction to an allergen.
hypersplenism [hī-pěr-SPLĒN-ĭzm]	Overactive spleen.
immunosuppressive [ĬM-yū-nō-sŭ-PRĔS-ĭv] **disease**	Disease that flourishes because of lowered immune response.
infectious mononucleosis [MŎN-ō-nū-klē-Ō-sĭs]	Acute infectious disease caused by the Epstein-Barr virus.
lymphadenopathy [lĭm-făd-ě-NŎP-ă-thē]	Swollen lymph nodes.
lymphocytic [lĭm-fō-SĬT-ĭk] **lymphoma**	Lymphoma with malignant cells that resemble large lymphocytes.
lymphoma [lĭm-FŌ-mă]	Cancer of the lymph nodes.
metastasis [mě-TĂS-tă-sĭs]	Spread of a cancer from a localized area.
non-Hodgkin's lymphoma	Cancer of the lymph nodes with some cells resembling healthy cells and spreading in a diffuse pattern.
opportunistic [ŏp-ōr-tū-NĬS-tĭk] **infection**	Infection that takes hold because of lowered immune response.
retrovirus [rě-trō-VĪ-rŭs]	Type of virus that spreads by using the body's DNA to help it replicate its RNA.
sarcoidosis [săr-kŏy-DŌ-sĭs]	Inflammatory condition with lesions on the lymph nodes and other organs.
splenomegaly [splēn-ō-MĔG-ă-lē]	Enlarged spleen.
thymoma [thī-MŌ-mă]	Tumor of the thymus gland.

Helping to Manage a Disease

University Hospital has an extensive oncology department involved in research. Jane Bryant is a 32-year-old woman with AIDS. Recently, Kaposi's sarcoma has appeared on her arms and back. She was referred to the oncology department for chemotherapy. In addition, her doctors prescribed a new medication that increases T cell count and the effectiveness of the immune response.

Critical Thinking

43. What might be the advantage for a chronically ill person to be treated in a research hospital?
44. Jane has AIDS, an immunosuppressive disease. Why is she being referred to the oncology department?

Pathological Terms Exercises

Spell It Correctly

Put a C after each word that is spelled correctly; if a word is incorrectly spelled, write it correctly.

45. retorvirus_____
46. immunosuppressive_____
47. imunodeficiency_____
48. sarcodosis_____
49. lumphoma_____

50. mononucleosis_____
51. anphylaxis_____
52. histocytic_____
53. metastasis_____
54. thimoma_____

Check Your Knowledge

For each of the following statements, write either lymph or immune in the blank to complete the sentence.

55. Allergies involve a(n) _____ response.
56. Splenomegaly is a symptom of _____ system disease.
57. Multiple sclerosis is a disease in which the _____ system attacks some of the body's cells.
58. Sarcoidosis is an inflammatory condition of the _____ system.
59. AIDS is a disease of the _____ system.

Surgical Terms

Cancers of the lymph system may require a **lymph node dissection**, removal of cancerous lymph nodes for microscopic examination. A **lymphadenectomy** is the removal of a lymph node, and a **lymphadenotomy** is an incision into a lymph node. A **splenectomy** is removal of the spleen, which is usually required if it is ruptured. Other organs of the body, such as the liver, will take over the functions of the spleen if it is removed. A **thymectomy** is the removal of the thymus gland, which is very important to the maturation process but not as serious once a patient reaches adulthood.

MORE ABOUT...

Lymph Node Surgery

A person with a malignant neoplasm in the breast must have further tests to determine if the cancer has metastasized. In the past, biopsies included removal of many lymph nodes until one without cancer was found. Now, a procedure called sentinel node biopsy is commonly used. The first node it reaches is the sentinel node. It is checked for malignancy. If that node is clean, then no further biopsy is done on the other lymph nodes, and the patient is spared painful surgical side effects.

VOCABULARY REVIEW

In the previous section, you learned terms relating to surgery. Before going on to the exercises, read the definitions below. Pronunciations are provided for certain terms.

Term	Definition
lymphadenectomy [lĭm-făd-ĕ-NĚK-tō-mē]	Removal of a lymph node.
lymphadenotomy [lĭm-făd-ĕ-NŎ-tō-mē]	Incision into a lymph node.
lymph node dissection	Removal of a cancerous node for microscopic examination.
splenectomy [splē-NĚK-tō-mē]	Removal of the spleen.
thymectomy [thī-MĚK-tō-mē]	Removal of the thymus gland.

CASE STUDY

Getting an Examination

John Latella, a patient with AIDS, came to the hospital's clinic for his monthly T cell test and to review the medications he is taking. He seems to be feeling more energetic, so John believes his T cell test will show improvement. During the examination, however, the doctor notices an enlargement in John's lymph nodes. He sends John to the outpatient surgical unit for a biopsy.

Critical Thinking

60. If the node is malignant, what kind of surgery will most likely be performed?
61. A malignancy may have to be treated with radiation, which may destroy some healthy cells at the same time that they destroy malignant cells. Why is treatment be especially risky for an AIDS patient?

SURGICAL TERMS EXERCISES

Build Your Medical Vocabulary

Write and define the lymph and immune system combining forms in the following words.

62. splenectomy

63. lymphadenotomy

64. thymectomy

65. lymphangioma

USING THE INTERNET

Go to the CDC's National Prevention Information Network (http://www.cdcnpin.org) and choose an article from one of their featured publications. Write a paragraph summarizing the content of the article.

CHAPTER REVIEW

The material that follows is to help you review this chapter.

DEFINITIONS

Define the following terms and combining forms. Review the chapter before starting. Make sure you know how to pronounce each term as you define it. The blue words in curly brackets are references to the Spanish Glossary on the Web site. Write the definitions in the space provided.

WORD	DEFINITION
acquired active immunity	
acquired passive immunity	
acquired immunodeficiency [ĬM-yū-nō-dē-FĬSH-ĕn-sē] syndrome	
aden(o)	
AIDS	
allergen [ĂL-ĕr-jĕn] {alergeno}	
allergy [ĂL-ĕr-jē] {alergia}	
anaphylaxis [ĂN-ă-fĭ-LĂK-sĭs] {anafilaxia o anafilaxis}	
antibody [ĂN-tē-bŏd-ē] {anticuerpo}	
antigen [ĂN-tĭ-jĕn] {antígeno}	
antitoxin [ăn-tē-TŎK-sĭn] {antitoxina}	
autoimmune [ăw-tō-ĭ-MYŪN] disease	
autoimmune response	
B lymphocytes [LĬM-fō-sīts], B cells	
cell-mediated immunity	
cytotoxic [sī-tō-TŎK-sĭk] cell	
enzyme-linked immunosorbent assay (EIA, ELISA)	
gamma globulin [GĂ-mă GLŎB-yū-lĭn]	
helper cell	
histiocytic [HĬS-tē-ō-SĪT-ĭk] lymphoma	
Hodgkin's lymphoma, Hodgkin's disease	
human immunodeficiency [ĬM-yū-nō-dē-FĬSH-ĕn-sē] virus (HIV)	
humoral [HYŪ-mōr-ăl] immunity	

WORD	DEFINITION

hypersensitivity [HĪ-pĕr-sĕn-sĭ-TĬV-ĭ-tē] {hipersensibilidad}

_____

hypersplenism [hĭ-pĕr-SPLĒN-izm]

_____

immun(o)

_____

immunity [ĭ-MYŪ-nĭ-tē] {inmunidad}

_____

immunization [ĬM-yū-nĭ-ZĀ-shŭn]

_____

immunoglobulin [ĬM-yū-nō-GLŎB-yū-lĭn] {inmunoglobina}

_____

immunosuppressive [ĬM-yū-nō-sŭ-PRĔS-ĭv] disease

_____

infectious mononucleosis [MŎN-ō-nū-klē-Ō-sĭs]

_____

interferon [ĭn-tĕr-FĒR-ŏn]

_____

interleukin [ĭn-tĕr-LŪ-kĭn] {interleucina}

_____

lymph [lĭmf] {linfa}

_____

lymph(o)

_____

lymphaden(o)

_____

lymphadenectomy [lĭm-făd-ĕ-NĔK-tō-mē] {linfadenectomía}

_____

lymphadenopathy [lĭm-făd-ĕ-NŎP-ă-thē] {linfadenopatía}

_____

lymphadenotomy [lĭm-făd-ĕ-NŎ-tō-mē]

_____

lymphangi(o)

_____

lymph node

_____

lymph node dissection

_____

lymphocytes [LĬM-fō-sīts] {linfocitos}

_____

lymphocytic [lĭm-fō-SĬT-ĭk] lymphoma

_____

lymphoma [lĭm-FŌ-mă] {linfoma}

_____

macrophage [MĂK-rō-fāj] {macrófago}

_____

metastasis [mĕ-TĂS-tă-sĭs] {metastasis}

_____

microphage [MĪK-rō-fāj] {micrófago}

_____

natural immunity

_____

non-Hodgkin's lymphoma

_____

opportunistic [ŏp-ōr-tū-NĬS-tĭk] infection

_____

pathogen [PĂTH-ō-jěn] {patógeno} _____

phagocytosis [FĂG-ō-sī-TŌ-sĭs] {fagocitosis} _____

plasma [PLĂZ-mă] cell _____

retrovirus [rĕ-trō-VĪ-rŭs] {retrovirus} _____

sarcoidosis [săr-kŏy-DŌ-sĭs] {sarcoidosis} _____

spleen [splēn] {bazo} _____

splen(o) _____

splenectomy [splē-NĔK-tō-mē] {esplenectomía} _____

splenomegaly [splēn-ō-MĔG-ă-lē] _____

suppressor [sŭ-PRĔS-ōr] cell _____

T cells _____

thym(o) _____

thymectomy [thī-MĔK-tō-mē] {timectomía} _____

thymoma [thī-MŌ-mă] {timoma} _____

thymosin [THĪ-mō-sĭn] {timosina} _____

thymus [THĪ-mŭs] gland _____

T lymphocytes _____

tox(o), toxi, toxico _____

vaccination [VĂK-sĭ-NĀ-shŭn] {vacunación} _____

vaccine [văk-SĒN, VĂK-sēn] {vacuna} _____

Western blot _____

Answers to Chapter Exercises

1. to lessen the progress of or to prevent disease
2. acquired active immunity
3. f
4. i
5. j
6. d
7. c
8. a
9. b
10. g
11. h
12. e
13. natural
14. acquired active
15. acquired passive
16. macrophages, microphages
17. white
18. thymosin
19. interferon, interleukin
20. immunoglobins
21. No, since she has already been vaccinated, tetanus should not develop.
22. acquired active immunity
23. lymphaden
24. spleno

25. thym
26. immuno
27. adeno
28. toxi
29. lymphangi
30. lymph
31. f
32. e
33. b
34. g
35. c
36. d
37. a
38. to see if his breathing problems are caused by something other than allergies
39. no, just the blocked breathing caused by allergies
40. T
41. F
42. T
43. The patient might be eligible to be part of a new drug testing program.
44. Jane has a type of cancer—Kaposi's sarcoma.
45. retrovirus

46. C
47. immunodeficiency
48. sarcoidosis
49. lymphoma
50. C
51. anaphylaxis
52. histiocytic
53. C
54. thymoma
55. immune
56. lymph
57. immune
58. lymph
59. immune
60. lymphadenectomy
61. AIDS patients already have compromised immune systems. Any destruction of healthy cells can be damaging to their immune system and may allow other infections to take hold.
62. splen-, spleen
63. lymphadeno-, lymph node
64. thym-, thymus gland
65. lymphangi-, lymphatic vessels

14

The Digestive System

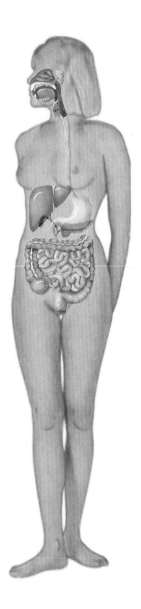

After studying this chapter, you will be able to:

▶ Name the parts of the digestive system and discuss the function of each part

▶ Define combining forms used in building words that relate to the digestive system

▶ Name the common diagnoses, clinical procedures, and laboratory tests used in treating disorders of the digestive system

▶ List and define the major pathological conditions of the digestive system

▶ Explain the meaning of surgical terms related to the digestive system

Structure and Function

The three basic functions of the digestive system are as follows:

1. **Digestion** is the process of breaking down foods into nutrients that can be absorbed by cells. *Mechanical digestion* takes place in the mouth by chewing and in the stomach by churning actions. *Chemical digestion* takes place in the mouth by the addition of the saliva and continues in the stomach with the addition of digestive juices to chemically break down the food into simpler elements.

2. **Absorption** is the passing of digested nutrients into the bloodstream. This primarily occurs in the small intestines.

3. **Elimination** is the conversion of any residual material from a liquid to a solid and removal of that material from the alimentary canal via defecation.

The digestive system consists of the **alimentary canal** (digestive tract or gastrointestinal tract) and several accessory organs. Food enters the alimentary canal through the **mouth,** passes through the **pharynx** and **esophagus** into the **stomach,** then into the **small intestine** and **large intestine** or **bowels,** and then into the **anal canal.** Figure 14-1a shows the digestive system, and Figure 14-1b diagrams the digestive process.

The alimentary canal is a tube that extends from the mouth to the **anus.** The wall of the alimentary canal has four layers that aid in the digestion of the food that passes through it.

• The outer covering is a serous (watery) layer of tissue that protects the canal and lubricates the outer surface so that organs within the abdominal cavity can slide freely near the canal.

Colorado State University has a Web site (http://arbl.cvmbs.colostate.edu/hbooks/pathphys/digestion) that describes a voyage through the digestive tract.

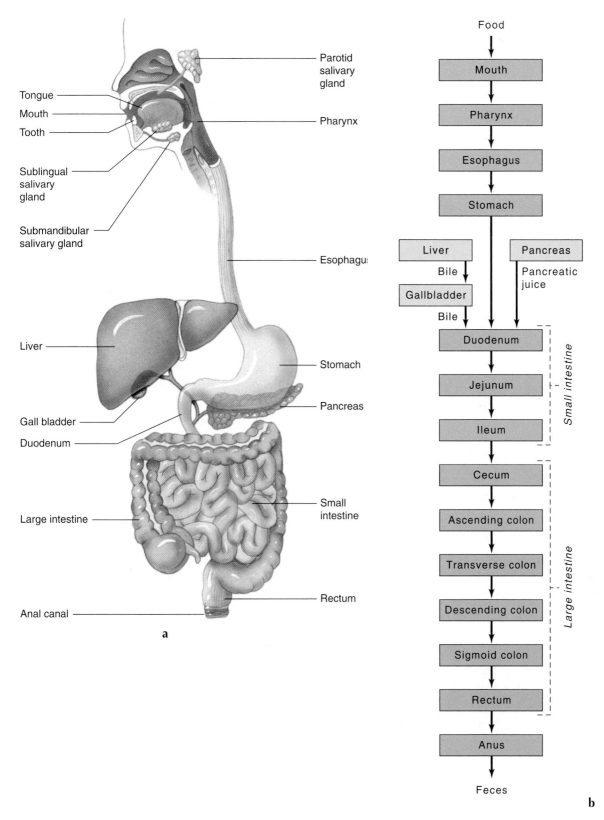

FIGURE 14-1 (a) The process of digestion begins in the mouth. (b) A diagram of the pathway of food through the body.

- The next layer is the muscular layer, which contracts and expands in wavelike motions called **peristalsis,** to move food along the canal.
- The third layer is made of loose connective tissue that holds various vessels, glands, and nerves that both nourish and carry away waste from surrounding tissue.
- The innermost layer is a mucous membrane that secretes mucus and digestive enzymes while protecting the tissues within the canal.

Digestive **enzymes** convert complex proteins into **amino acids,** compounds that can be absorbed by the body. Complex sugars are reduced to **glucose** and other simpler sugars, and fat molecules are reduced to **fatty acids** and other substances through the action of the digestive enzymes.

Mouth

Food enters the mouth at the **lips.** It then passes through the parts of the mouth where digestion starts. Table 14-1 lists the parts of the mouth.

Pharynx

From the mouth, food goes through the pharynx (**throat**). Both food and air share this passageway. The pharynx is a muscular tube (about 5 inches long in adults) that moves food into the esophagus. Air moves through the trachea (windpipe). When we eat and swallow food, a flap of tissue (the **epiglottis**) covers the trachea until the food is moved into the esophagus. The epiglottis prevents food from entering the larynx (the voice box). Food that happens to get into the larynx when we are eating causes choking.

Esophagus

The esophagus is a muscular tube (9 to 10 inches long in the average adult) that contracts rhythmically (peristalsis) to push food toward the stomach. As

TABLE 14-1 Parts of the mouth.

Part	Description
cheeks	walls of the mouth with muscles
tongue	moves the food during **mastication** (chewing) until **deglutition** (swallowing)
papillae	small, raised areas on the tongue that contain the taste buds
frenulum	mucous membrane that connects the tongue to the floor of the mouth
lingual tonsils	mounds of tissue at the back of the tongue
hard palate	roof of the mouth with **rugae**, ridges of membrane
soft palate	soft posterior part of the palate with a downward projection called the **uvula**
palatine tonsils	lymphatic tissue on either side of the back of the mouth
gums	fleshy sockets that hold the teeth
teeth	structures held by the gums; essential to chewing
salivary glands	glands that surround the oral cavity and secrete **saliva**, a fluid containing enzymes, such as **amylase**, that aid in breaking down food.

Choking

People have died of choking, even when efforts were made to save them. If an object such as a chicken bone became lodged in the windpipe, it was difficult to remove it while still allowing the person to breathe. A doctor, Harry J. Heimlich, discovered that a simple series of movements can prevent choking to death in most cases. The movements involve placing arms around the abdomen just below the diaphragm, grasping fists, and thrusting upward to dislodge the item. Testimony from around the world affirms that this maneuver is put to good use every day.

the swallowed food is advanced toward the stomach by the peristaltic wave, the cardiac sphincter (a group of muscles) will open briefly. Once the food is in the stomach, it will close. This prevents **reflux** (backflow) and **emesis** or **regurgitation** (vomiting). Every time more food comes through the esophagus to the stomach, the muscles relax and allow the food to pass.

Stomach

The stomach is a pouchlike organ in the left hypochondriac region of the abdominal cavity. The stomach receives food from the esophagus and mixes it with gastric juice. The enzyme **pepsin** in the gastric juice begins protein digestion. Table 14-2 shows the major components of gastric juice.

The stomach has four regions (Figure 14-2).

- The *cardiac region*, the region closest to the heart, is where the cardiac sphincter allows food to enter the stomach and prevents regurgitation.
- The **fundus** is the upper, rounded portion of the stomach.
- The **body** is the middle portion.
- The **pylorus,** the narrowed bottom part of the stomach, has a powerful, circular muscle at its base, the *pyloric sphincter.* This sphincter controls the emptying of the stomach's contents into the small intestine.

After eating, the muscular movements of the stomach and the mixing of food with gastric juice forms a semifluid mass called **chyme.** The muscles of the stomach release the chyme in small batches at regular intervals into the small intestine, where further digestion takes place.

TABLE 14-2 Major components of gastric juice.

Component	Function
pepsin	digests almost all types of protein
hydrochloric acid	provides acidic environment for action of pepsin
mucus	provides alkaline protective layer on the inside of the stomach wall

FIGURE 14-2 The stomach has four regions and rugae in its lining.

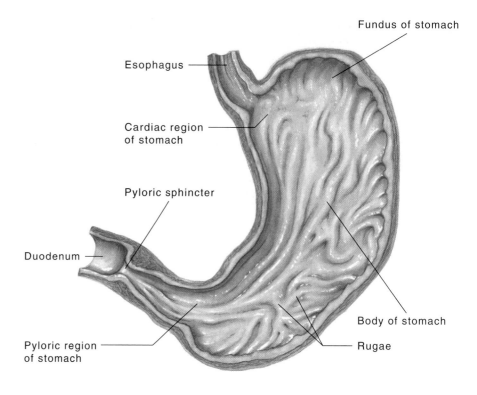

Esophagus

Cardiac region of stomach

Pyloric sphincter

Duodenum

Pyloric region of stomach

Fundus of stomach

Body of stomach

Rugae

Small Intestine

The small intestine receives chyme from the stomach, bile from the liver, and pancreatic juice from the pancreas. The small intestine has the following three parts (Figure 14-3):

1. The **duodenum** is only about 10 inches long. In it, chyme mixes with bile to aid in fat digestion; with pancreatic juice to aid in digestion of starch,

FIGURE 14-3 The small intestine connects the stomach to the large intestine.

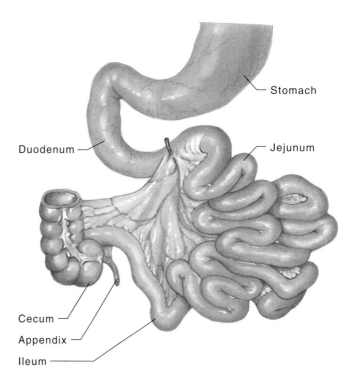

Duodenum

Stomach

Jejunum

Cecum

Appendix

Ileum

proteins, and fat; and with intestinal juice to aid in digesting sugars (glucose). The juices also help change starch (**glycogen**) into glucose. The entire small intestine is lubricated by secretions from mucous glands. The small intestine is lined with **villi** (singular, **villus**), tiny, one-cell-thick fingerlike projections with capillaries through which digested nutrients are absorbed into the bloodstream and lymphatic system.

2. The **jejunum** is an eight-foot long section of the small intestine in which the digestive process continues.

3. The **ileum** connects the small intestine to the large intestine. Located at the bottom of the ileum is the *ileocecal sphincter muscle* that relaxes to allow undigested and unabsorbed food material into the large intestine in fairly regular waves.

Together, the three sections of the small intestine are about 20 feet long from the stomach to the large intestine. The small intestine lies within the abdominopelvic cavity, where it is held in place by the **mesentery.** Chyme takes from one to six hours to travel through the small intestine before it enters the large intestine.

Large Intestine

The large intestine (Figure 14-4), which is about five feet long, has the following four parts:

1. The **cecum** is a pouch attached to the bottom of the ileum of the small intestine. The cecum has three openings: one from the ileum into the cecum; one from the cecum into the colon; and another from the cecum into a wormlike pouch on the side, the **appendix** (also called the *vermiform appendix*). The appendix is filled with lymphatic tissue, but is considered an **appendage,** an accessory part of the body that has no central function.

2. The next section is the **colon.** The colon is further divided into three parts—the *ascending colon*, the *transverse colon*, and the *descending colon*.

3. The colon connects to the **sigmoid colon,** an s-shaped body that goes across the pelvis to the middle of the sacrum, where it connects to the rectum.

4. The **rectum** attaches to the *anal canal*. **Feces (stool)** pass from the anal canal into the anus. The anus and anal canal open during the release of feces from the body (**defecation**).

Liver

The **liver** is an important digestive organ located in the right, upper quadrant of the abdominal cavity. Although it is not within the digestive tract, it performs many digestive functions.

MORE ABOUT...

Intestinal Health

Intestinal health is often directly related to the amount of fiber in a person's diet. In 2005, the federal nutritional guidelines specifically recommended an increase in fibrous foods as a boost to general health and especially to digestive health. The most fibrous foods include vegetables, fruits, and whole grains. Nutritional labels on food give the amount of dietary fiber per serving. It is generally recommended that a person ingest 25 grams of fiber per day.

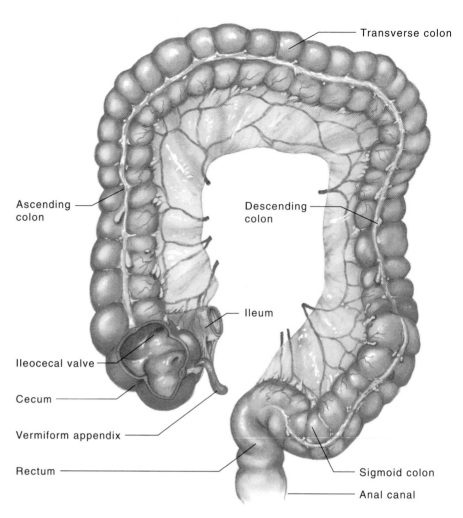

FIGURE 14-4 The large intestine leads from the small intestine to the anal canal.

Transverse colon

Ascending colon

Descending colon

Ileum

Ileocecal valve

Cecum

Vermiform appendix

Rectum

Sigmoid colon

Anal canal

Aside from changing food nutrients into usable substances, the liver also secretes **bile** (a yellowish-brown to greenish fluid), which is stored in the gallbladder for use in breaking down fats and other digestive functions. It stores glucose and certain vitamins for release when the body needs them. The liver also secretes **bilirubin,** a bile pigment that is combined with bile and excreted into the duodenum.

Gallbladder

The bile released from the liver to the *hepatic duct* is then released into the *cystic duct*, which brings the substance into the **gallbladder.** At the entrance to the duodenum, bile mixes with pancreatic juices and enters the duodenum from the *common bile duct.* There the bile aids in **emulsification,** the breaking down of fats.

Pancreas

The chyme that empties into the small intestine mixes with secretions from the pancreas and liver. The **pancreas** is five to six inches long and lies across the posterior side of the stomach. The pancreas is a digestive organ in that it secretes digestive fluids called *pancreatic juice*, which includes various enzymes such as *amylase* and **lipase.** The pancreas is also an endocrine gland that regulates blood sugar through the release of insulin (a hormone) and, as such, is discussed in Chapter 15.

VOCABULARY REVIEW

In the previous section, you learned terms relating to the digestive system. Before going on to the exercises, read the definitions below. Pronunciations are provided for certain terms.

Term	Meaning
absorption [ăb-SŎRP-shŭn]	Passing of nutrients into the bloodstream.
alimentary [ăl-ĭ-MĔN-tĕr-ē] **canal**	Muscular tube from the mouth to the anus; digestive tract; gastrointestinal tract.
amino [ă-MĒ-nō] **acid**	Chemical compound that results from digestion of complex proteins.
amylase [ĂM-ĭl-ās]	Enzyme that is part of pancreatic juice and saliva and that begins the digestion of carbohydrates.
anal [Ā-năl] **canal**	Part of the digestive tract extending from the rectum to the anus.
anus [Ā-nŭs]	Place from which feces exit the body.
appendage [ă-PĔN-dĭj]	Any body part (inside or outside) either subordinate to a larger part or having no specific central function.
appendix [ă-PĔN-dĭks]	Wormlike appendage to the cecum.
bile [bīl]	Yellowish-brown to greenish fluid secreted by the liver and stored in the gallbladder; aids in fat digestion.
bilirubin [bĭl-ĭ-RŪ-bĭn]	Pigment contained in bile.
body	Middle section of the stomach.
bowel [bŏw-l]	Intestine.
cecum [SĒ-kŭm]	Pouch at the top of the large intestine connected to the bottom of the ileum.
cheeks	Walls of the oral cavity.
chyme [kīm]	Semisolid mass of partially digested food and gastric juices that passes from the stomach to the small intestine.
colon [KŌ-lŏn]	Major portion of the large intestine.
defecation [dĕ-fĕ-KĀ-shŭn]	Release of feces from the anus.
deglutition [dē-glū-TĬSH-ŭn]	Swallowing.
digestion [dī-JĔS-chŭn]	Conversion of food into nutrients for the body and into waste products for release from the body.
duodenum [dū-ō-DĒ-nŭm]	Top part of the small intestine where chyme mixes with bile, pancreatic juices, and intestinal juice to continue the digestive process.

Term	Meaning
elimination [ē-lĭm-ĭ-NĀ-shŭn]	The conversion of waste material from a liquid to a semisolid and removal of that material via defecation.
emesis [ĕ-MĒ-sĭs]	*See* regurgitation.
emulsification [ĕ-MŬL-sĭ-fĭ-KĀ-shŭn]	Breaking down of fats.
enzyme [ĔN-zīm]	Protein that causes chemical changes in substances in the digestive tract.
epiglottis [ĕ-pĭ-GLŎ-tĭs]	Movable flap of tissue that covers the trachea.
esophagus [ĕ-SŎF-ă-gŭs]	Part of alimentary canal from the pharynx to the stomach.
fatty acid	Acid derived from fat during the digestive process.
feces [FĒ-sēz]	Semisolid waste that moves through the large intestine to the anus, where it is released from the body.
frenulum [FRĔN-yū-lŭm]	Mucous membrane that attaches the tongue to the floor of the mouth.
fundus [FŬN-dŭs]	Upper portion of the stomach.
gallbladder [GĂWL-blăd-ĕr]	Organ on lower surface of liver; stores bile.
glucose [GLŪ-kōs]	Sugar found in fruits and plants and stored in various parts of the body.
glycogen [GLĪ-kō-jĕn]	Starch that can be converted into glucose.
gums [gŭmz]	Fleshy sockets that hold the teeth.
hard palate [PĂL-ăt]	Hard anterior portion of the palate at the roof of the mouth.
ileum [ĬL-ē-ŭm]	Bottom part of the small intestine that connects to the large intestine.
jejunum [jĕ-JŪ-nŭm]	Middle section of the small intestine.
large intestine	Passageway in intestinal tract for waste received from small intestine to be excreted through the anus; also, place where water reabsorption takes place.
lingual tonsils [LĬNG-gwăl TŎN-sĭls]	Two mounds of lymph tissue at the back of the tongue.
lipase [LĬP-ās]	Enzyme contained in pancreatic juice.
lips	Two muscular folds formed around the outside boundary of the mouth.
liver [LĬV-ĕr]	Organ important in digestive and metabolic functions; secretes bile.
mastication [măs-tĭ-KĀ-shŭn]	Chewing.

Term	Meaning
mesentery [MĔS-ĕn-tĕr-ē, MĔZ-ĕn-tĕr-ē]	Membranous tissue that attaches small and large intestines to the muscular wall at the dorsal part of the abdomen.
mouth	Cavity in the face in which food and water is ingested.
palatine [PĂL-ă-tīn] **tonsils**	Mounds of lymphatic tissue on either side of the pharynx.
pancreas [PĂN-krē-ăs]	Digestive organ that secretes digestive fluids; endocrine gland that regulates blood sugar.
papilla (*pl.*, **papillae**) [pă-PĬL-ă (-ē)]	Tiny projection on the superior surface of the tongue that contains taste buds.
pepsin [PĔP-sĭn]	Digestive enzyme in gastric juice.
peristalsis [pĕr-ĭ-STĂL-sĭs]	Coordinated, rhythmic contractions of smooth muscle that force food through the digestive tract.
pharynx [FĂR-ĭngks]	Tube through which food passes to the esophagus.
pylorus [pī-LŌR-ŭs]	Narrowed bottom part of the stomach.
rectum [RĔK-tŭm]	Bottom portion of large intestine; connected to anal canal.
reflux [RĒ-flŭks]	*See* regurgitation.
regurgitation [rē-GŬR-jĭ-TĀ-shŭn]	Backward flow from the normal direction.
rugae [RŪ-gē]	Folds in stomach lining; also, irregular ridges of mucous membrane on the hard palate.
saliva [să-LĪ-vă]	Fluid secreted by salivary glands; contains amylase.
salivary [SĂL-ĭ-vār-ē] **glands**	Glands in the mouth that secrete fluids that aid in breaking down food.
sigmoid [SĬG-mŏyd] **colon**	S-shaped part of large intestine connecting at the bottom to the rectum.
small intestine	Twenty-foot long tube that continues the process of digestion started in the stomach; place where most absorption takes place.
soft palate [PĂL-ăt]	Soft posterior part of the palate in the mouth.
stomach [STŎM-ăk]	Large sac between the esophagus and small intestine; place where food is broken down.
stool [stūl]	Feces.
teeth [tēth]	Structures held by the gums; aid in chewing.
throat	Pharynx.
tongue [tŭng]	Fleshy part of the mouth that moves food during mastication (and speech).

Term	Meaning
uvula [YŪ-vyū-lă]	Cone-shaped projection hanging down from soft palate.
villus (*pl.*, **villi**) [VĬL-ŭs (-ī)]	Tiny, fingerlike projection on the lining of the small intestine with capillaries through which digested nutrients are absorbed into the bloodstream and lymphatic system.

CASE STUDY

Getting a Referral

Asmin Sahib reported burning chest pains to her general practitioner. Ms. Sahib feared that the pains indicated that she was having a heart attack. After a thorough examination, including an ECG, the physician found Ms. Sahib to have no cardiovascular pathology. The general practitioner referred Asmin to Dr. Mary Walker, a gastroenterologist (specialist in the digestive system).

Critical Thinking

1. Why might Asmin feel she is having a heart attack?
2. What parts of the body will the gastroenterologist treat?

STRUCTURE AND FUNCTION EXERCISES

Complete the Diagram

3. Label the digestive system parts in the illustration on the right.

   a. _____
   b. _____
   c. _____
   d. _____
   e. _____

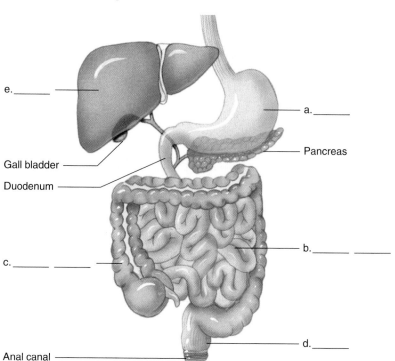

e._____
Gall bladder
Duodenum
c._____ _____
Anal canal
a._____
Pancreas
b._____ _____
d._____

Check Your Knowledge

For each of the following words, write C in the space provided if the word is spelled correctly. If it is not, spell the word correctly.

4. papilae _____

5. frenelum _____

6. deglutition _____

7. chime _____

8. glycogen _____

9. villi _____

10. amylase _____

11. lypase _____

12. bilirubin _____

Fill in the blanks.

13. Food is moved along the alimentary canal by a process called _____.

14. The four areas of the stomach are _____ _____, _____, _____, and _____.

15. The three parts of the small intestine are the _____, _____, and _____.

16. The four parts of the large intestine are the _____, _____, _____ _____, and _____.

17. The longest intestine is the _____ intestine.

18. Chemical compound that results from the digestion of complex proteins: _____ _____.

19. Two enzymes in pancreatic juice are _____ and _____.

20. Bile aids in the breaking down of fats, a process called _____.

Combining Forms

The list belows include combining forms that relate specifically to the digestive system. Pronunciations are provided for the examples.

COMBINING FORM	MEANING	EXAMPLE
an(o)	anus	*anoplasty* [ā-nō-PLĂS-tē], surgical repair of the anus
append(o), appendic(o)	appendix	*appendicitis* [ă-pĕn-dĭ-SĪ-tĭs], inflammation of the appendix
bil(o), bili	bile	*biliverdin* [bĭl-ĭ-VĔR-dĭn], green bile pigment
bucc(o)	cheek	*buccogingival* [bŭk-ō-JĬN-jĭ-văl], pertaining to the cheeks and gums
cec(o)	cecum	*cecopexy* [SĒ-kō-pĕk-sē], surgical repair or fixing of the cecum to correct excessive mobility

Combining Form	Meaning	Example
celi(o)	abdomen	*celioma* [SĒ-lē-ō-mă], tumor in the abdomen
chol(e), cholo	bile	*choleic* [kō-LĒ-ĭk], pertaining to bile
cholangi(o)	bile vessel	*cholangiogram* [kō-LĂN-jē-ō-grăm], x-ray image of the bile vessels
cholecyst(o)	gallbladder	*cholecystectomy* [kō-lē-sĭs-TĔK-tō-mē], removal of the gallbladder
choledoch(o)	common bile duct	*choledochotomy* [kō-lĕd-ō-KŎT-ō-mē], incision into the common bile duct
col(o), colon(o)	colon	*colectomy* [kō-LĔK-tō-mē], removal of all or part of the colon
duoden(o)	duodenum	*duodenitis* [dū-ŏd-ĕ-NĪ-tĭs], inflammation of the duodenum
enter(o)	intestines	*enteropathy* [ĕn-tĕr-ŎP-ă-thē], any intestinal disease
esophag(o)	esophagus	*esophagoscopy* [ĕ-sŏf-ă-GŎS-kō-pē], examination of the interior of the esophagus
gastr(o)	stomach	*gastralgia* [găs-TRĂL-jē-ă], stomachache
gloss(o)	tongue	*glossopharyngeal* [GLŎS-ō-fă-RĬN-jē-ăl], of the tongue and pharynx
gluc(o)	glucose	*glucogenesis* [glū-kō-JĔN-ĕ-sĭs], formation of glucose
glyc(o)	sugar	*glycosuria* [glī-kō-SŪ-rē-ă], abnormal excretion of carbohydrates in urine
glycogen(o)	glycogen	*glycogenolysis* [GLĪ-kō-jĕ-NŎL-ĭ-sĭs], breakdown of glycogen to glucose
hepat(o)	liver	*hepatitis* [hĕp-ă-TĪ-tĭs], liver disease or inflammation
ile(o)	ileum	*ileitis* [ĭl-ē-Ī-tĭs], inflammation of the ileum
jejun(o)	jejunum	*jejunostomy* [jĕ-jū-NŎS-tō-mē], surgical opening to the outside of the body for the jejunum
labi(o)	lip	*labioplasty* [LĀ-bē-ō-plăs-tē], surgical repair of lips
lingu(o)	tongue	*linguodental* [lĭng-gwō-DĔN-tăl], pertaining to tongue and teeth
or(o)	mouth	*orofacial* [ōr-ō-FĀ-shăl], pertaining to mouth and face
pancreat(o)	pancreas	*pancreatitis* [păn-krē-ă-TĪ-tĭs], inflammation of the pancreas

COMBINING FORM	MEANING	EXAMPLE
periton(eo)	peritoneum	*peritonitis* [PĔR-ĭ-tō-NĪ-tĭs], inflammation of the peritoneum
pharyng(o)	pharynx	*pharyngotonsillitis* [fă-RĬN-jō-tŏn-sĭ-LĬ-tĭs], inflammation of tonsils and pharynx
proct(o)	anus, rectum	*proctologist* [prŏk-TŎL-ō-jĭst], specialist in study and treatment of diseases of the anus and rectum
pylor(o)	pylorus	*pylorospasm* [pī-LŌR-ō-spăzm], involuntary contraction of the pylorus
rect(o)	rectum	*rectoabdominal* [RĔK-tō-ăb-DŎM-ĭ-năl], of the rectum and abdomen
sial(o)	saliva, salivary gland	*sialism* [SĪ-ă-lĭzm], excessive secretion of saliva
sialaden(o)	salivary gland	*sialoadenitis* [SĪ-ă-lō-ă-dĕ-NĪ-tĭs], inflammation of the salivary glands
sigmoid(o)	sigmoid colon	*sigmoidoscopy* [SĬG-mŏy-DŎS-kō-pē], visual examination of the sigmoid colon
steat(o)	fats	*steatorrhea* [stē-ă-tō-RĒ-ă], greater than normal amounts of fat in the feces
stomat(o)	mouth	*stomatitis* [STŌ-mă-TĪ-tĭs], inflammation of the lining of the mouth

CASE STUDY

Seeing a Specialist

Dr. Walker reviewed Asmin Sahib's family history. It showed that two members of her immediate family had died from cancer of the digestive tract. Her father had stomach cancer, and her sister had liver cancer. Since Asmin has always known the risks associated with digestive cancers, she has maintained a healthy diet and has had regular checkups to detect any signs of the kinds of cancer that have afflicted her family.

Critical Thinking

21. Why is family history important in evaluating a patient?
22. Before cancer was detected in her family members, they suffered from chronic stomach and liver inflammations. What are the medical names for these two conditions?

COMBINING FORMS EXERCISES

Build Your Medical Vocabulary

Use the following combining forms or roots along with suffixes you learned in Chapter 2 to give the missing term.
gastr(o) esophag(o) proct(o) chol(o) cholecyst(o) choledoch(o) hepat(o) pancreat(o) colon(o) duoden(o) rect(o)

23. Excision (removal) of the stomach: _____

24. Inflammation of the esophagus: _____

25. Hernia of the rectum: _____

26. Pertaining to the duodenum: _____

27. Excision of a part of the common bile duct: _____

28. Inflammation of the pancreas: _____

29. Pain in the rectum: _____

30. Visual examination of the colon: _____

31. Enlargement of the liver: _____

32. Suture of the stomach: _____

33. Specialist in the study of diseases and treatment of the rectum and anus: _____

34. Inflammation of the gallbladder: _____

35. Liver tumor: _____

Find the Combining Forms

For the following terms, write the gastrointestinal combining form(s) in the space provided and define each term.

36. pyloroduodenal

37. perianal

38. enterocolostomy

39. ileocecal

40. sublingual

CASE STUDY

Treating the Symptoms

Dr. Walker finds Asmin to be a healthy 49-year-old except for the burning sensations in her chest. Dr. Walker has decided to have Asmin try a bland diet (avoidance of spicy food, alcohol, and caffeine) and sleeping with the head of the bed raised. She prescribes a mild antacid. Dr. Walker suggests a return visit in three weeks to see if the steps to avoid esophageal reflux are showing improvement.

After three weeks, Asmin has shown marked improvement. Dr. Walker tells her she can add some spicy foods back into her diet slowly, but to continue to avoid alcohol and caffeine. Asmin will need a checkup with Dr. Walker in six months.

Critical Thinking

41. What diagnostic test will Dr. Walker use to check Asmin's reflux condition in six months?

42. What other tests might Dr. Walker prescribe for someone with a family history of intestinal cancer?

Diagnostic, Procedural, and Laboratory Terms

The digestive or gastrointestinal system is examined in many different ways to diagnose a number of problems. Gastroenterologists (specialists in the digestive system) perform procedures to examine the internal health of various organs. They order blood tests to look for signs of infection or disease and also use some of the extensive number of imaging procedures available for this body system.

A stool specimen may be tested to identify disease-causing organisms such as parasites. This test is called a *stool culture*. A *stool culture and sensitivity test (C & S)* is used to try out different medications on *microorganisms* to check for effectiveness. A *chemical test of a stool specimen (hemoccult test* or *stool guaiac*) indicates whether there is bleeding in the digestive tract. Guaiac is a substance added to the stool sample that reacts with any occult (not visible) blood.

Various types of endoscopes are used to examine the digestive system, either through the mouth, the anus, or an opening into the abdominal cavity. The following list includes some of the endoscopic procedures used in the digestive system:

- **esophagoscopy**—use of an *esophagoscope* to examine the esophagus
- **gastroscopy**—use of a *gastroscope* to examine the stomach
- **colonoscopy**—examination of the colon
- **proctoscopy**—examination of the rectum and anus
- **sigmoidoscopy**—examination of the sigmoid colon
- **peritoneoscopy**—examination of the abdominal cavity

X-rays and other imaging techniques are used extensively to search for abnormalities. An MRI shows the major organs of the digestive system. A CAT scan provides a visual image of the abdominal cavity and the digestive tract. To examine more specific areas, patients are usually given a contrast medium or other substance that stands out against the background of the x-ray produced. A *barium swallow* is the ingestion of a barium solution before an x-ray of the esophagus, which is generally used to locate foreign objects that have been swallowed. A *barium enema* is the administration of a barium solution through an enema before taking a series of x-rays of the colon called a *lower GI series*. An *upper GI series* (UGIS) provides x-rays of the esophagus, stomach, and duodenum, usually after the patient swallows a barium solution or other contrast medium. A *cholangiogram* is an image of the bile vessels taken in **cholangiography,** an x-ray of the bile ducts. A *cholecystogram* is an image of the gallbladder taken in **cholecystography,** an x-ray of the gallbladder taken after the patient swallows iodine. A liver scan, done after injection of radioactive material, can reveal abnormalities. Ultrasound is used to provide images of the entire abdominal area, as in *abdominal ultrasonography*.

Several serum tests indicate how the liver is functioning. A *serum glutamic oxaloacetic transaminase* (SGOT) or an *aspartate transaminase* (AST) measures the enzyme levels in serum that has leaked from damaged liver cells. Another serum test for liver function is the *serum glutamic pyruvic transaminase* (SGPT). This test is also known as an *alanine transaminase* (ALT, AT). A *serum bilirubin* measures bilirubin in the blood as an indicator of jaundice. An *alkaline phosphatase* reveals levels of the enzyme alkaline phosphatase in serum as an indicator of liver disease, especially liver cancer.

A *nasogastric (NG) tube* is passed through the nose to the stomach to relieve fluid buildup or to take stomach content samples for analysis (Figure 14-5). This process is called *nasogastric intubation*.

FIGURE 14-5 Liquid nourishment can be provided through a nasogastric (NG) tube. This type of tube may also be used to relieve fluid buildup in the stomach or to take stomach content samples.

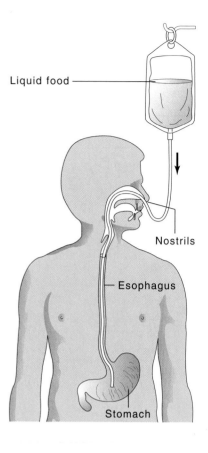

Liquid food

Nostrils

Esophagus

Stomach

VOCABULARY REVIEW

In the previous section, you learned terms relating to diagnosis, clinical procedures, and laboratory tests. Before going on to the exercises, read the definitions below. Pronunciations are provided for certain terms.

Term	Meaning
cholangiography [kō-lăn-jē-ŎG-ră-fē]	X-ray of the bile ducts.
cholecystography [kō-lē-sĭs-TŎG-ră-fē]	X-ray of the gallbladder.
colonoscopy [kō-lŏn-ŎS-kō-pē]	Examination of the colon using an endoscope.
esophagoscopy [ĕ-sŏf-ă-GŎS-kō-pē]	Examination of the esophagus with an esophagoscope.
gastroscopy [găs-TRŎS-kō-pē]	Examination of the stomach using an endoscope.
peritoneoscopy [PĔR-ĭ-tō-nē-ŎS-kō-pē]	Examination of the abdominal cavity using a peritoneoscope.
proctoscopy [prŏk-TŎS-kō-pē]	Examination of the rectum and anus using a proctoscope.
sigmoidoscopy [SĬG-mŏy-DŎS-kō-pē]	Examination of the sigmoid colon using a sigmoidoscope.

CASE STUDY

Testing and Diagnosing

Dr. Walker has morning hours at a local hospital several days a week. Today, Jim Santarelli is scheduled for a colonoscopy. His medical record is shown below:

Critical Thinking

43. What might Dr. Walker be looking for in this procedure?

44. If the examination shows a clear colon, what lifestyle changes might Dr. Walker recommend?

PROCEDURE: colonoscopy

SURGEON: Dr. Walker

INDICATION: This man has a two-year history of increasing, intermittent, sudden bouts of diarrhea without mucus or blood. Antispasmodic treatment with Bentyl has failed. He had a negative barium enema 3 1/2 months ago. Stools have been hemoccult negative. There are no systemic symptoms. The frequency of the diarrhea is once every other day to twice a week.

With the patient turned onto his left side, he was monitored using continuous SAO2 pulse monitoring and intermittent blood pressure monitoring. An IV was started in the left forearm. Mr. Santarelli was given 50 mg of Demerol and 10 mg of Valium by slow intravenous injection. After adequate sedation was achieved, the colonoscopy was performed.

DIAGNOSTIC, PROCEDURAL, AND LABORATORY TERMS EXERCISES

Find a Match

Match the diagnostic test in the left-hand column with the definition or possible diagnosis resulting from the test in the right-hand column.

45. _____ serum bilirubin

46. _____ alkaline phosphatase

47. _____ upper GI series

48. _____ image of bile vessels

49. _____ testing of waste for disease-causing organisms

50. _____ tube to retrieve stomach contents for examination

51. _____ element in a solution used in x-rays

52. _____ test for liver function

53. _____ x-rays of the intestines and anal canal

54. _____ hemoccult test

a. x-ray of esophagus, stomach, and duodenum

b. barium

c. cholangiogram

d. nasogastric tube

e. SGOT

f. stool guaiac

g. jaundice

h. liver cancer

i. stool culture

j. lower GI series

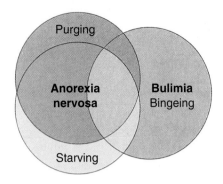

FIGURE 14-6 Starving, bingeing, and purging are symptoms that can overlap in both anorexia nervosa and bulimia.

The National Association of Anorexia Nervosa and Related Disorders (www. anad.org) offers support for eating disorders at their Web site.

Pathological Terms

The digestive system is both the site and the source of many diseases and disorders. What we take into our mouths determines the type of nutrition our body receives. Eating disorders can be the catalyst for disease processes to start.

Eating Disorders

Anorexia is a loss of appetite. In its most severe form, **anorexia nervosa,** it is a morbid refusal to eat because the person wishes to be dangerously thin. **Bulimia** is a disease wherein bingeing on food and then purposely purging or vomiting is also a quest for abnormal weight loss. Figure 14-6 shows problems in both anorexia nervosa and bulimia. **Obesity** is often the result of overeating, although recent gene studies indicate a possible hereditary defect in many obese people.

Disorders of the Mouth, Pharynx, and Esophagus

Areas in the mouth can become inflamed from an infection, allergy, injury, or internal disorder. **Cheilitis** occurs on the lips; **glossitis** occurs on the tongue; **sialoadenitis** occurs in the salivary glands; and **parotitis** or **parotiditis** occurs in the parotid glands. *Gastroesophageal reflux disease (GERD)* disease can irritate the esophagus. Various other dental disorders may similarly cause inflammation. Disorders of the mouth and pharynx include:

- **halitosis**—unusually bad breath
- **ankyloglossia**—tongue completely attached to the floor of the mouth
- **aphagia**—inability to swallow
- **dysphagia**—difficulty in swallowing
- **esophagitis**—inflammation of the esophagus
- **achalasia**—esophageal disorder that interferes with the intake of nutrients

Stomach Disorders

The stomach is also the site of many disorders.

- **achlorhydria**—lack of the proper acid in the stomach for digestion
- **dyspepsia**—difficulty in digesting
- **gastritis**—inflammation of the stomach
- **gastroenteritis**—inflammation of the stomach and small intestine
- **flatulence**—gas in the stomach and/or intestines
- **eructation** (belching)—release of gas through the mouth
- **nausea**—sick feeling in the stomach
- **hematemesis**—vomiting of blood from the stomach
- **peptic ulcer**—ulcer in any part of the gastrointestinal tract, especially the stomach
- **hiatal hernia**—hernia of part of the stomach through the diaphragm.

Disorders of the Liver, Pancreas, and Gallbladder

Secretions of the liver, pancreas, and gallbladder mix with the stomach contents that move into the duodenum. The liver can be the site of **jaundice** or icterus, when excessive bilirubin in the blood (**hyperbilirubinemia**) causes a yellow discoloration of the skin. Newborn jaundice may be a result of liver disease or many other factors. It is sometimes treated with exposure to artificial lights or sunlight. **Hepatomegaly** is an enlarged liver. **Hepatopathy** is a general term for liver disease, and **hepatitis** is a term for several types of contagious diseases, some of which are sexually transmitted (see Chapter 10). **Cirrhosis** is a chronic liver disease usually caused by poor nutrition and excessive alcohol consumption. **Pancreatitis** is an inflammation of the pancreas. (Other pancreatic diseases are discussed in Chapter 15.)

The gallbladder can be the site of calculi (**gallstones** or **cholelithiasis**) that block the bile from leaving the gallbladder. The presence of gallstones in the common bile duct is called *choledocholithiasis*. **Cholangitis** is any inflammation of the bile ducts. **Cholecystitis** is any inflammation of the gallbladder, either acute or chronic. The duodenum can be the site of **duodenal ulcers. Appendicitis,** which usually requires surgery, is an inflammation of the appendix.

The American Liver Foundation (www. liverfoundation.org) supports research into the causes and cure of liver disease.

Intestinal Disorders

The small and large intestines can have ulcers, obstructions, irritations (such as **dysentery**), inflammations, abnormalities, and cancer.

- **ileus**—intestinal blockage
- **enteritis** and **colitis**—inflammation of the small intestine
- **ulcerative colitis**—chronic type of *irritable bowel disease (IBD)* with ulcers and inflammation
- **Crohn's disease**—a type of IBD often with **fistulas**, abnormal openings in tissue walls
- **colic**—gastrointestinal distress, usually in infants
- **diverticulosis**—condition in which **diverticula**, small intestinal pouches, trap food
- **diverticulitis**—inflammation of the diverticula
- **ileitis**—inflammation of the ileum
- **polyposis**—polyps in the intestinal tract
- **volvulus**—intestinal blocking caused by twisting (Figure 14-7)
- **intussusception**—telescoping of the intestine (Figure 14-8)
- **ascites**—fluid in the abdominal and peritoneal regions
- **peritonitis**—inflammation of the peritoneal region

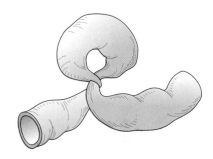

FIGURE 14-7 A volvulus is a twisting of the intestine that causes a blockage and requires surgery.

The Rectum and Anus

The rectum, anus, and stool may play a role in some disorders. **Proctitis** is an inflammation of the rectum and anus. **Constipation** is a condition with infrequent or difficult release of bowel movements, sometimes the result of insufficient moisture to soften and move stools. **Diarrhea** is loose, watery stools that may be the result of insufficient roughage or of an internal disorder. **Flatus** is the release of gas through the anus.

The analysis of stool for blood, bacteria, and other elements can provide a clue to various ailments. **Melena** is a condition in which blood that is not fresh appears in the stool as a black, tarry mass. **Hematochezia** is bright red blood in the stool. **Steatorrhea** is fat in the stool.

A small opening in the anal canal is called an **anal fistula.** Waste material can enter the abdominal cavity through a fistula. The anus may be the site of **hemorrhoids,** swollen, twisted veins that can cause great discomfort.

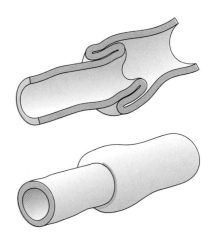

FIGURE 14-8 An intussusception occurs most often in children and requires surgical correction.

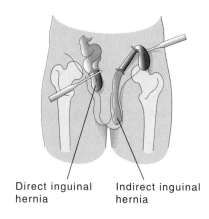

Direct inguinal
hernia · Indirect inguinal
hernia

FIGURE 14-9 An inguinal hernia usually requires surgery.

Hernias

A *hernia* is any loop or twist of an intestine or other organ not positioned correctly in the abdomen. There are many types of hernias. Some common ones are as follows:

- A *hiatal* hernia is the protrusion of the stomach through the esophageal hiatus of the diaphragm.
- An *inguinal hernia* is a protrusion of the intestine through a weakness in the abdominal wall (Figure 14-9).
- A *strangulated hernia* is one in which blood flow is restricted or absent.
- A *femoral hernia* is a protrusion of a loop of intestine into the femoral canal.
- An *umbilical hernia* is a protrusion of part of the intestine into the umbilicus.
- An *incarcerated hernia* is one in which movement of bowel is restricted or obstructed.

VOCABULARY REVIEW

In the previous section, you learned terms relating to pathology. Before going on to the exercises, read the definition below. Pronunciations are provided for certain terms.

Term	Definition
achalasia [ăk-ă-LĀ-zhē-ă]	Inability of a muscle, particularly the cardiac sphincter, to relax.
achlorhydria [ā-klōr-HĪ-drē-ă]	Lack of hydrochloric acid in the stomach.
anal fistula [Ā-năl FĬS-tyū-lă]	Small opening in the anal canal through which waste matter can leak into the abdominal cavity.
ankyloglossia [ĂNG-kĭ-lō-GLŎS-ē-ă]	Condition of the tongue being partially or completely attached to the bottom of the mouth.
anorexia nervosa [ăn-ō-RĔK-sē-ă nĕr-VŌ-să]	Eating disorder with extreme weight loss.
aphagia [ă-FĀ-jē-ă]	Inability to swallow.
appendicitis [ă-pĕn-dĭ-SĪ-tĭs]	Inflammation of the appendix.
ascites [ă-SĪ-tēs]	Fluid buildup in the abdominal and peritoneal cavities.
bulimia [bū-LĒM-ē-ă]	Eating disorder with bingeing and purging.
cheilitis [kī-LĪ-tĭs]	Inflammation of the lips.
cholangitis [kō-lăn-JĪ-tĭs]	Inflammation of the bile ducts.
cholecystitis [KŌ-lē-sĭs-TĪ-tĭs]	Inflammation of the gallbladder.
cholelithiasis [KŌ-lē-lĭ-THĪ-ă-sĭs]	Gallstones in the gallbladder.
cirrhosis [sĭr-RŌ-sĭs]	Liver disease, often caused by alcoholism.
colic [KŎL-ĭk]	Gastrointestinal distress, especially of infants.
colitis [kō-LĪ-tĭs]	Inflammation of the colon.

Term	Definition
constipation [kŏn-stĭ-PĀ-shŭn]	Difficult or infrequent defecation.
Crohn's [krōnz] **disease**	Type of irritable bowel disease with no ulcers.
diarrhea [dī-ă-RĒ-ă]	Loose, watery stool.
diverticula [dī-věr-TĬK-yū-lă]	Small pouches in the intestinal walls.
diverticulitis [DĪ-věr-tĭk-yū-LĪ-tĭs]	Inflammation of the diverticula.
diverticulosis [DĪ-věr-tĭk-yū-LŌ-sĭs]	Condition in which diverticula trap food or bacteria.
duodenal [DŪ-ō-DĒ-năl] **ulcer**	Ulcer in the duodenum.
dysentery [DĬS-ĕn-tĕr-ē]	Irritation of the intestinal tract with loose stools.
dyspepsia [dĭs-PĔP-sē-ă]	Indigestion.
dysphagia [dĭs-FĀ-jē-ă]	Difficulty in swallowing.
enteritis [ĕn-tĕr-Ī-tĭs]	Inflammation of the small intestine.
eructation [ē-rŭk-TĀ-shŭn]	Belching.
esophagitis [ĕ-sŏf-ă-JĪ-tĭs]	Inflammation of the esophagus.
fistula [FĬS-tyū-lă]	Abnormal opening in tissue.
flatulence [FLĂT-yū-lĕns]	Gas in the stomach or intestines.
flatus [FLĂ-tŭs]	Gas in the lower intestinal tract that can be released through the anus.
gallstones	Calculi in the gallbladder.
gastritis [găs-TRĪ-tĭs]	Inflammation of the stomach.
gastroenteritis [GĂS-trō-ĕn-tĕr-Ī-tĭs]	Inflammation of the stomach and small intestine.
glossitis [glŏ-SĪ-tĭs]	Inflammation of the tongue.
halitosis [hăl-ĭ-TŌ-sĭs]	Foul mouth odor.
hematemesis [hē-mă-TĔM-ē-sĭs]	Blood in vomit.
hematochezia [HĒ-mă-tō-KĒ-zhē-ă]	Red blood in stool.
hemorrhoids [HĔM-ō-rŏydz]	Swollen, twisted veins in the anus.
hepatitis [hĕp-ă-TĪ-tĭs]	Inflammation or disease of the liver.
hepatomegaly [HĔP-ă-tō-MĔG-ă-lē]	Enlarged liver.
hepatopathy [hĕp-ă-TŎP-ă-thē]	Liver disease.
hiatal hernia [hī-Ā-tăl HĔR-nē-ă]	Protrusion of the stomach through an opening in the diaphragm.
hyperbilirubinemia [HĪ-pĕr-BĬL-ĭ-rū-bĭ-NĒ-mē-ă]	Excessive bilirubin in the blood.
icterus [ĬK-tĕr-ŭs]	Jaundice.

Term	Definition
ileitis [ĬL-ē-Ī-tĭs]	Inflammation of the ileum.
ileus [ĬL-ē-ŭs]	Intestinal blockage.
intussusception [ĬN-tŭs-sŭ-SĔP-shŭn]	Prolapse or collapse of an intestinal part into a neighboring part. One section collapses into another like a telescope.
jaundice [JĂWN-dĭs]	Excessive bilirubin in the blood causing yellowing of the skin.
melena [mĕ-LĒ-nă]	Old blood in the stool.
nausea [NĂW-zhē-ă]	Sick feeling in the stomach.
obesity [ō-BĒS-ĭ-tē]	Abnormal accumulation of fat in the body.
pancreatitis [PĂN-krē-ă-TĪ-tĭs]	Inflammation of the pancreas.
parotitis, parotiditis [păr-ō-TĪ-tĭs, pă-rŏt-ĭ-DĪ-tĭs]	Inflammation of the parotid gland.
peptic ulcer	Sore on the mucous membrane of the digestive system; stomach ulcer or gastric ulcer.
peritonitis [PĔR-ĭ-tō-NĪ-tĭs]	Inflammation of the peritoneum.
polyposis [PŎL-ĭ-PŌ-sĭs]	Condition with polyps, as in the intestines.
proctitis [prŏk-TĪ-tĭs]	Inflammation of the rectum and anus.
sialoadenitis [SĪ-ă-lō-ăd-ĕ-NĪ-tĭs]	Inflammation of the salivary glands.
steatorrhea [STĒ-ă-tō-RĒ-ă]	Fat in the stool.
ulcerative colitis [kō-LĪ-tĭs]	Inflammation of the colon with ulcers.
volvulus [VŎL-vyū-lŭs]	Intestinal blockage caused by the intestine twisting on itself.

CASE STUDY

Performing Surgery

Dr. Walker has another patient scheduled for a colonoscopy. Laura Martinez had an earlier colonoscopy, which was negative. Since then, she has experienced some rectal bleeding. This time her colonoscopy shows several suspicious-looking polyps near the rectum. Dr. Walker biopsies several of them. The result is positive for cancer, but the area of malignancy that needs to be removed is limited.

Critical Thinking

55. What operation will likely be performed?
56. Why might the operation include a colostomy?

PATHOLOGICAL TERMS EXERCISES

Find a Match

Match the terms in the left-hand column with the correct definition in the right-hand column.

57. ____ bulimia
58. ____ colitis
59. ____ diverticula
60. ____ eructation
61. ____ hematochezia
62. ____ intussusception
63. ____ jaundice
64. ____ peritonitis
65. ____ steatorrhea
66. ____ volvulus

a. intestinal blockage caused by the intestine twisting on itself
b. red blood in the stool
c. prolapse of an intestinal part into a neighboring part
d. eating disorder with bingeing and purging
e. inflammation of the colon
f. inflammation of the peritoneum
g. fat in the stool
h. small pouches in the intestinal wall
i. icterus
j. belching

Check Your Knowledge

Circle the correct term that completes the sentence.

67. Jane's parents have brought her to see an internist. Jane is 5'10" and weighs 105 pounds. Jane thinks she is fat. The doctor suspects Jane's problem is _____. (obesity, anorexia, aphagia)

68. John was seen in the emergency room. He complained of abdominal pain with cramping and diarrhea. He was concerned that he might have _____. (constipation, irritable bowel disease, hemorrhoids)

69. Jean has been complaining of severe pain in the RUQ following the ingestion of food, especially foods like nuts and ice cream. She believes she might have _____. (pancreatitis, appendicitis, cholecystitis)

70. Dora is feeling sluggish and unwell. She complains to her doctor that she has been unable to have a bowel movement for the past 5 days. She is diagnosed with _____. (diarrhea, hematochezia, constipation)

71. Many people cannot lie flat after eating because of a burning sensation in the chest and throat. The pain makes the person feel that he or she is having a heart attack. This condition, seen frequently in the emergency room, is called _____. (inguinal hernia, dysentery, gastroesophageal reflux)

Spell It Correctly

For each of the following words, write C if the spelling is correct. If it is not, write the correct spelling.

72. dypepsia _____
73. hyperbilirubinemia _____
74. diverticuli _____
75. hematochazia _____
76. inginal hernia _____
77. iliitis _____
78. polyposis _____
79. cirrosis _____
80. hietal hernia _____
81. achlorhydria _____
82. flatusence _____

Surgical Terms

Treating the digestive tract often includes biopsies, surgeries, and observation using endoscopes. The following is a list of some of the surgical procedures performed on the digestive system.

- **Abdominocentesis** or **paracentesis** is a surgical puncture to remove fluid or relieve pressure in the abdomal cavity, as in ascites.
- **Cholelithotomy** is an incision into the gallbladder for the removal of stones. **Choledocholithotomy** is an incision for removal of stones in the common bile duct. **Cholelithotripsy** is the crushing of gallstones using sound waves or other techniques.
- Surgical repair of the digestive tract includes **cheiloplasty** (lip repair); **glossorrhaphy** (tongue suturing); **esophagoplasty** (esophagus repair); and **proctoplasty** (repair of the rectum and anus).

Some parts of the digestive system may require partial or complete removal because of malignancies, inflammation, or other conditions. Listed below are some of these types of removal surgeries.

- **glossectomy**—removal of the tongue
- **polypectomy**—removal of polyps
- **appendectomy**—removal of the appendix
- **cholecystectomy**—removal of the gallbladder
- **diverticulectomy**—removal of diverticula
- **gastrectomy**—removal of some or all of the stomach
- **gastric resection** or **gastric bypass**—removes a portion of the stomach to limit overeating
- **colectomy**—removal of some or all of the colon
- **pancreatectomy**—removal of the pancreas
- **hemorrhoidectomy**—removal of hemorrhoids
- **hepatic lobectomy**—removal of one or more lobes of the liver, usually after a **liver biopsy** to determine the extent of disease
- **anastomosis**—surgical union of two hollow tubes, such as parts of the intestines

Openings may have to be made in the gastrointestinal tract. Sometimes they are temporary to allow evacuation of waste material. In some cases, they are permanent, as when intestinal parts cannot be reconnected. An **ileostomy** is the creation of an opening in the abdomen, which is attached to the ileum to allow fecal matter to discharge into a bag outside the body. A **colostomy** is an opening in the colon to the abdominal wall to create a place for waste to exit the body other than through the anus.

VOCABULARY REVIEW

In the previous section, you learned terms relating to surgery. Before going on to the exercises, read the definitions below. Pronunciations are provided for certain terms.

Term	Definition
abdominocentesis [ăb-DŎM-ĭ-nō-sĕn-TĒ-sĭs]	Incision into the abdomen to remove fluid or relieve pressure.

Term	Definition
anastomosis [ă-NĂS-tō-MŌ-sĭs]	Surgical union of two hollow structures.
appendectomy [ăp-pĕn-DĚK-tō-mē]	Removal of the appendix.
cheiloplasty [KĪ-lō-plăs-tē]	Repair of the lips.
cholecystectomy [KŌ-lē-sĭs-TĚK-tō-mē]	Removal of the gallbladder.
choledocholithotomy [kō-LĚD-ō-kō-lĭ-THŎT-ō-mē]	Removal of stones from the common bile duct.
cholelithotomy [KŌ-lē-lĭ-THŎT-ō-mē]	Removal of gallstones.
cholelithotripsy [kō-lē-LĬTH-ō-trĭp-sē]	Breaking up or crushing of stones in the body, especially gallstones.
colectomy [kō-LĚK-tō-mē]	Removal of some or all of the colon.
colostomy [kō-LŎS-tō-mē]	Creation of an opening from the colon into the abdominal wall.
diverticulectomy [dĭ-vĕr-tĭk-ū-LĚK-tō-mē]	Removal of diverticula.
esophagoplasty [ĕ-SŎF-ă-gō-plăs-tē]	Repair of the esophagus.
gastrectomy [găs-TRĚK-tō-mē]	Removal of some or all of part or all of the stomach.
gastric resection or **gastric bypass**	Removal of part of the stomach and repair of the remaining part.
glossectomy [glŏ-SĚK-tō-mē]	Removal of the tongue.
glossorrhaphy [glŏ-SŌR-ă-fē]	Suture of the tongue.
hemorrhoidectomy [HĚM-ō-rŏy-DĚK-tō-mē]	Removal of hemorrhoids.
hepatic lobectomy [hĕ-PĂT-ĭk lō-BĚK-tō-mē]	Removal of one or more lobes of the liver.
ileostomy [ĬL-ē-ŎS-tō-mē]	Creation of an opening into the ileum.
liver biopsy	Removal of a small amount of liver tissue to examine for disease.
pancreatectomy [PĂN-krē-ă-TĚK-tō-mē]	Removal of the pancreas.
paracentesis [PĂR-ă-sĕn-TĒ-sĭs]	Incision into the abdominal cavity to remove fluid or relieve pressure.
polypectomy [pŏl-ĭ-PĚK-tō-mē]	Removal of polyps.
proctoplasty [PRŎK-tō-plăs-tē]	Repair of the rectum and anus.

SURGICAL TERMS EXERCISES

Fill in the blanks.

83. Removal of a liver lobe is a(n) _____ _____.

84. Repair of a part of the stomach is a(n) _____ _____.

85. Two openings that allow waste to exit the body other than through the anus are a(n) _____ and a(n) _____.

86. The crushing of gallstones is called _____.

87. Incision into the intestinal tract to remove fluid is _____ or _____.

CASE STUDY

Resolving a Complaint

Dora, a patient complaining of constipation, was given a laxative to regulate her bowel movements. Doctors found that Dora avoided foods high in roughage because of an acid condition in her stomach.

Critical Thinking

88. Why is it important that Dora eat foods with high roughage content?

89. What condition may occur if acid backs up into Dora's esophagus?

TERMINOLOGY IN ACTION

The patient record for Manny Ramos lists two procedures and four diagnostic terms. Define all six terms and break them down into their word parts.

MEDICAL RECORD	PROGRESS NOTES
DATE 6/28/XX	Patient complains of intermittent stomach pains, some rectal bleeding, heartburn. Schedule tests on two
	successive days in three weeks.
7/22/XX	8:00 Colonoscopy. Four polyps removed and biopsied. Otherwise normal. J Phelps, M.D.
7/23/XX	8:00 Esophagoscopy. Numerous lesions present. J. Phelps, M.D.
7/23/XX	Colonoscopy shows precancerous polyps. Recommend 6-month follow-up. Gastric reflux present—treat with
	Nexium; Stomach ulcers, give 4-week course of treatment and list of dietary restrictions. Recheck stool in
	6 weeks. Recommend dental visit for persistent halitosis.

PATIENT'S IDENTIFICATION *(For typed or written entries give: Name—last, first, middle; grade; rank; hospital or medical facility)*

Manny Ramos
000-33-5555

REGISTER NO. | WARD NO. 4B

PROGRESS NOTES
STANDARD FORM 509

USING THE INTERNET

Go to the American Gastroenterological Association site (http://www.gastro.org), click the public section, then click the digestive health resource center, and then choose a gastroenterological disease site. Write a brief one-paragraph summary of some of the information you gather about the disease.

CHAPTER REVIEW

The material that follows is to help you review this chapter.

DEFINITIONS

Define the following terms and combining forms. Review the chapter before starting. Make sure you know how to pronounce each term as you define it.

WORD	DEFINITION
abdominocentesis [ăb-DŎM-ĭ-nō-sĕn-TĒ-sĭs]	
absorption [ăb-SŎRP-shŭn] {absorción}	
achalasia [ăk-ă-LĀ-zhē-ă] {acalasia}	
achlorhydria [ā-klōr-HĪ-drē-ă]	
alimentary [ăl-ĭ-MĔN-tĕr-ē] canal	
amino [ă-MĒ-nō] acid {aminoácido}	
amylase [ĂM-ĭl-ās] {amilasa}	
anal [Ā-năl] canal	
anal fistula [FĬS-tyū-lă]	
anastomosis [ă-NĂS-tō-MŌ-sĭs] {anastomosis}	
ankyloglossia [ĂNG-kĭ-lō-GLŎS-ē-ă] {anquiloglosia}	
an(o)	
anorexia nervosa [ăn-ō-RĔK-sē-ă nĕr-VŌ-să]	
anus [Ā-nŭs] {ano}	
aphagia [ă-FĀ-jē-ă] {afagia}	
append(o), appendic(o)	
appendage [ă-PĔN-dĭj] {apéndice}	
appendectomy [ăp-pĕn-DĔK-tō-mē] {apendectomía}	
appendicitis [ă-pĕn-dĭ-SĪ-tĭs] {apendicitis}	
appendix [ă-PĔN-dĭks] {apéndice}	
ascites [ă-SĪ-tēs] {ascitis}	
bil(o), bili	
bile [bīl] {bilis}	

WORD	DEFINITION
bilirubin [bĭl-ĭ-RŪ-bĭn] {bilirrubina}	_____
body {cuerpo}	_____
bowel [bŏw-l] {intestine}	_____
bucc(o)	_____
bulimia [bū-LĒM-ē-ă]	_____
cec(o)	_____
cecum [SĒ-kŭm] {ciego}	_____
celi(o)	_____
cheeks {carrillos}	_____
cheilitis [kī-LĪ-tĭs] {queilitis}	_____
cheiloplasty [KĪ-lō-plăs-tē]	_____
chol(e), cholo	_____
cholangi(o)	_____
cholangiography [kō-lăn-jē-ŎG-ră-fē]	_____
cholangitis [kō-lăn-JĪ-tĭs] {colangitis}	_____
cholecyst(o)	_____
cholecystectomy [KŌ-lē-sĭs-TĔK-tō-mē]	_____
cholecystitis [KŌ-lē-sĭs-TĪ-tĭs] {colecistitis}	_____
cholecystography [kō-lē-sĭs-TŎG-ră-fē] {colecistografía}	_____
choledoch(o)	_____
choledocholithotomy [kō-LĔD-ō-kō-lĭ-THŎT-ō-mē]	_____
cholelithiasis [KŌ-lē-lĭ-THĪ-ă-sĭs]	_____
cholelithotomy [KŌ-lē-lĭ-THŎT-ō-mē]	_____
cholelithotripsy [kō-lē-LĬTH-ō-trĭp-sē]	_____
chyme [kīm] {quimo}	_____
cirrhosis [sĭr-RŌ-sĭs] {cirrosis}	_____
col(o), colon(o)	_____
colectomy [kō-LĔK-tō-mē] {colectomía}	_____
colic [KŎL-ĭk] {cólico}	_____
colitis [kō-LĪ-tĭs] {colitis}	_____
colon [KŌ-lŏn] {colon}	_____

WORD	DEFINITION
colonoscopy [kō-lŏn-ŎS-kō-pē] {colonoscopia}	
colostomy [kō-LŎS-tō-mē] {colostomía}	
constipation [kŏn-stĭ-PĀ-shŭn] {constipación}	
Crohn's [krōnz] disease	
defecation [dĕ-fĕ-KĀ-shŭn] {defecación}	
deglutition [dē-glū-TĬSH-ŭn] {deglución}	
diarrhea [dī-ā-RĒ-ă] {diarrea}	
digestion [dī-JĔS-chŭn] {digestión}	
diverticula [dī-vĕr-TĬK-yū-lă]	
diverticulectomy [dī-vĕr-tĭk-ū-LĔK-tō-mē]	
diverticulitis [DĪ-vĕr-tĭk-yū-LĪ-tĭs] {diverticulitis}	
diverticulosis [DĪ-vĕr-tĭk-yū-LŌ-sĭs] {diverticulosis}	
duoden(o)	
duodenal [DŪ-ō-DĒ-năl] ulcer	
duodenum [dū-ō-DĒ-nŭm] {duodeno}	
dysentery [DĬS-ĕn-tĕr-ē] {disentería}	
dyspepsia [dĭs-PĔP-sē-ă] {dyspepsia}	
dysphagia [dĭs-FĀ-jē-ă] {disfagia}	
elimination [ē-lĭm-ĭ-NĀ-shŭn]	
emesis [ĕ-MĒ-sĭs] {emesis}	
emulsification [ĕ-MŬL-sĭ-fĭ-KĀ-shŭn]	
enter(o)	
enteritis [ĕn-tĕr-Ī-tĭs] {enteritis}	
enzyme [ĔN-zīm] {enzima}	
epiglottis [ĕp-ĭ-GLŎ-tĭs] {epiglotis}	
eructation [ē-rŭk-TĀ-shŭn] {eructación}	
esophag(o)	
esophagitis [ĕ-sŏf-ă-JĪ-tĭs] {esofagitis}	

WORD	DEFINITION
esophagoplasty [ĕ-SŎF-ă-gō-plăs-tē] {esofagoplastia}	
esophagoscopy [ĕ-sŏf-ă-GŎS-kō-pē] {esofagoscopia}	
esophagus [ĕ-SŎF-ă-gŭs] {esófago}	
fatty acid	
feces [FĒ-sēz] {heces}	
fistula [FĬS-tyū-lă] {fistula}	
flatulence [FLĂT-yū-lĕns] {flatulencia}	
flatus [FLĂ-tŭs] {flato}	
frenulum [FRĔN-yū-lŭm] {frenillo}	
fundus [FŬN-dŭs] {fondo}	
gallbladder [GĂWL-blăd-ĕr] {vesícula biliar}	
gallstone {cálculo biliar}	
gastrectomy [găs-TRĔK-tŏ-mē] {gastrectomía}	
gastric bypass	
gastric resection	
gastritis [găs-TRĪ-tĭs] {gastritis}	
gastr(o)	
gastroenteritis [GĂS-trō-ĕn-tĕr-Ī-tĭs] {gastroenteritis}	
gastroscopy [găs-TRŎS-kō-pē] {gastroscopia}	
gloss(o)	
glossectomy [glŏ-SĔK-tō-mē]	
glossitis [glŏ-SĪ-tĭs] {glositis}	
glossorrhaphy [glō-SŌR-ă-fē]	
gluc(o)	
glucose [GLŪ-kōs] {glucosa}	
glyc(o)	
glycogen(o)	
glycogen [GLĪ-kō-jĕn] {glucógeno}	
gums [gŭmz] {encía}	
halitosis [hăl-ĭ-TŌ-sĭs] {halitosis}	
hard palate [PĂL-ăt]	

hematemesis [hē-mă-TĔM-ē-sĭs]
{hematemesis}

_____

hematochezia [HĒ-mă-tō-KĒ-zhē-ă]

_____

hemorrhoidectomy [HĔM-ō-rŏy-DĔK-
tō-mē] {hemorroidectomía}

_____

hemorrhoids [HĔM-ō-rŏydz]
{hemorroides}

_____

hepat(o)

_____

hepatic lobectomy [hĕ-PĂT-ĭk lō-
BĔK-tō-mē]

_____

hepatitis [hĕp-ă-TĪ-tĭs] {hepatitis}

_____

hepatomegaly [HĔP-ă-tō-MĔG-ă-lē]
{hepatomegalia}

_____

hepatopathy [hĕp-ă-TŎP-ă-thē]
{hepatopatía}

_____

hiatal hernia [hī-Ā-tăl HĔR-nē-ă]

_____

hyperbilirubinemia [HĪ-pĕr-BĬL-ĭ-rū-
bĭ-NĒ-mē-ă]

_____

icterus [ĬK-tĕr-ŭs] {icterus}

_____

ile(o)

_____

ileitis [ĬL-ē-Ī-tĭs] {ileitis}

_____

ileostomy [ĬL-ē-ŎS-tō-mē] {ileostomía}

_____

ileum [ĬL-ē-ŭm] {íleon}

_____

ileus [ĬL-ē-ŭs] {íleo}

_____

intussusception [ĬN-tŭs-sŭ-SĔP-shŭn]

_____

jaundice [JĂWN-dĭs] {ictericia}

_____

jejun(o)

_____

jejunum [jĕ-JŪ-nŭm] {yeyuno}

_____

labi(o)

_____

large intestine

_____

lingu(o)

_____

lingual tonsils [LĬNG-gwăl TŎN-sĭls]

_____

lipase [LĬP-ās] {lipasa}

_____

lips {labios}

_____

liver [LĬV-ĕr] {hígado}

_____

liver biopsy

_____

mastication [măs-tĭ-KĀ-shŭn]
{masticación}

_____

melena [mĕ-LĒ-nă] {melena}

_____

WORD	DEFINITION
mesentery [MĔS-ĕn-tĕr-ē, MĔZ-ĕn-tĕr-ē] {mesenterio}	
mouth {boca}	
nausea [NĂW-zhē-ă] {náusea}	
obesity [ō-BĒS-ĭ-tē] {obesidad}	
or(o)	
palatine [PĂL-ă-tĭn] tonsils	
pancreas [PĂN-krē-ăs] {páncreas}	
pancreat(o)	
pancreatectomy [PĂN-krē-ă-TĔK-tō-mē] {pancreatectomía}	
pancreatitis [PĂN-krē-ă-TĪ-tĭs] {pancreatitis}	
papilla (pl., papillae) [pă-PĬL-ă (-ē)] {papilas}	
paracentesis [PĂR-ă-sĕn-TĒ-sĭs]	
parotitis, parotiditis [păr-ō-TĪ-tĭs, pă-rŏt-ĭ-DĪ-tĭs]	
pepsin [PĔP-sĭn] {pepsina}	
peptic ulcer	
peristalsis [pĕr-ĭ-STĂL-sĭs] {peristaltismo}	
periton(eo)	
peritoneoscopy [PĔR-ĭ-tō-nē-ŎS-kō-pē] {peritoneoscopia}	
peritonitis [PĔR-ĭ-tō-NĪ-tĭs] {peritonitis}	
pharyng(o)	
pharynx [FĂR-ĭngks] {faringe}	
polypectomy [pŏl-ĭ-PĔK-tō-mē] {polipectomía}	
polyposis [PŎL-ĭ-PŌ-sĭs] {poliposis}	
proct(o)	
proctitis [prŏk-TĪ-tĭs] {proctitis}	
proctoplasty [PRŎK-tō-plăs-tē]	
proctoscopy [prŏk-TŎS-kō-pē]	
pylor(o)	
pylorus [pī-LŌR-ŭs] {píloro}	

WORD	DEFINITION
rect(o)	_____
rectum [RĔK-tŭm] {recto}	_____
reflux [RĒ-flŭks] {reflujo}	_____
regurgitation [rē-GŬR-jǐ-TĀ-shŭn] {regurgitación}	_____
rugae [RŪ-gē] {rugae}	_____
saliva [să-LĪ-vă] {saliva}	_____
salivary [SĂL-ǐ-vār-ē] glands	_____
sial(o)	_____
sialaden(o)	_____
sialoadenitis [SĪ-ă-lō-ăd-ě-NĪ-tǐs]	_____
sigmoid(o)	_____
sigmoid [SĬG-mŏyd] colon	_____
sigmoidoscopy [SĬG-mŏy-DŎS-kō-pē]	_____
small intestine	_____
soft palate [PĂL-ăt]	_____
steat(o)	_____
steatorrhea [STĒ-ă-tō-RĒ-ă] {esteatorrea}	_____
stomach [STŎM-ăk] {estómago}	_____
stomat(o)	_____
stool [stūl] {heces}	_____
teeth [tēth]	_____
throat [thrōwt] {garganta}	_____
tongue [tŭng] {lengua}	_____
ulcerative colitis [ŬL-sěr-ă-tǐv kō-LĪ-tǐs]	_____
uvula [YŪ-vyū-lă] {uvula}	_____
villus (pl., villi) [VĬL-ŭs (-ī)] {vellosidad}	_____
volvulus [VŎL-vyū-lŭs] {vólvulo}	_____

Answers to Chapter Exercises

1. Burning chest pains may also be a sign of a heart attack.
2. esophagus and stomach
3. a. stomach; b. small intestine; c. large intestine; d. rectum; e. liver
4. papillae
5. frenulum
6. C
7. chyme
8. C
9. C
10. C
11. lipase
12. C
13. peristalsis
14. cardiac region, fundus, body, pylorus
15. duodenum, jejunum, ileum
16. cecum, colon, sigmoid colon, rectum
17. small
18. amino acid
19. amylase, lipase
20. emulsification
21. Many diseases are either directly hereditary or may be the result of a hereditary tendency. Early detection may enable better treatment.
22. gastritis and hepatitis
23. gastrectomy
24. esophagitis
25. rectocele
26. duodenal
27. choledochectomy
28. pancreatitis

29. rectodynia, rectalgia
30. colonoscopy
31. hepatomegaly
32. gastrorrhaphy
33. proctologist
34. cholecystitis
35. hepatoma
36. pyloro, duoden, of the pylorus and duodenum
37. an-, around the anus
38. entero, colo-, opening between the small intestine and colon
39. ileo-, cec-, of the ileum and cecum
40. lingu-, under the tongue
41. gastroscopy
42. biopsies for cancer, blood tests for liver function
43. colitis, colon cancer, or other colon disorders
44. bland diet, avoiding alcohol and caffeine
45. g
46. h
47. a
48. c
49. i
50. d
51. b
52. e
53. j
54. f
55. colectomy
56. At least until reconstructive surgery is done, an alternative waste excretion site will be needed.

57. d
58. e
59. h
60. j
61. b
62. c
63. i
64. f
65. g
66. a
67. anorexia
68. irritable bowel disease
69. cholecystitis
70. constipation
71. gastroesophageal reflux
72. dyspepsia
73. C
74. diverticula
75. hematochezia
76. inguinal hernia
77. ileitis
78. C
79. cirrhosis
80. hiatal hernia
81. C
82. flatulence
83. hepatic lobectomy
84. gastric resection
85. ileostomy, colostomy
86. cholelithotripsy
87. abdominocentesis or paracentesis
88. A diet high in roughage may eliminate constipation.
89. gastroesophageal reflux disease (GERD)

The Endocrine System

15

After studying this chapter, you will be able to:

▶ Name the parts of the endocrine system and discuss the function of each part

▶ Define combining forms used in building words that relate to the endocrine system

▶ Name the common diagnoses, clinical procedures, and laboratory tests used in treating disorders of the endocrine system

▶ List and define the major pathological conditions of the endocrine system

▶ Define surgical terms related to the endocrine system

Structure and Function

The endocrine system is a group of glands that act as the body's master regulator (Figure 15-1a). It regulates many bodily functions as diagrammed in Figure 15-1b. The endocrine system is made up of various **glands** and other tissue that secrete **hormones,** specialized chemicals, into the bloodstream. The hormones are effective only in specific **target cells,** cells that have **receptors** that recognize a compatible hormone. A group of such cells forms *target tissue*. Minute amounts of hormones can initiate a strong reaction in some target cells.

Unlike **exocrine glands,** which secrete substances into ducts directed toward a specific location, **endocrine glands** or tissue secrete hormones into the bloodstream. They are also known as **ductless glands.** Some endocrine glands are also exocrine glands.

Hypothalamus

The **hypothalamus** is a part of the nervous system that serves as an endocrine gland because it analyzes the body's condition and directs the release of hormones that regulate pituitary hormones. The hormones released by the hypothalamus have either a **releasing factor** (allowing the secretion of other hormones to take place) or an **inhibiting factor** (preventing the secretion of other hormones). The hypothalamus regulates the body's temperature, blood pressure, heartbeat, metabolism of fats and carbohydrates, and sugar levels in the blood. The hypothalamus is located in the brain superior to the pituitary gland.

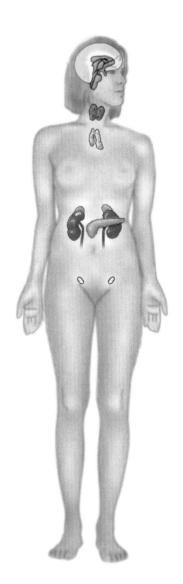

To see pictures of endocrine glands, go to a special Web site run by the University of Delaware (http://www.udel.edu/Biology/Wags/histopage/colorpage/cen/cen.htm). Note: Use uppercase letters where indicated.

FIGURE 15-1 (a) The endocrine system secretes hormones that affect all parts of the body. (b) The bodily functions affected by the endocrine hormones.

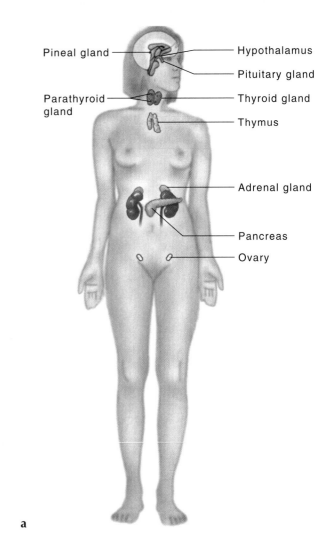

a

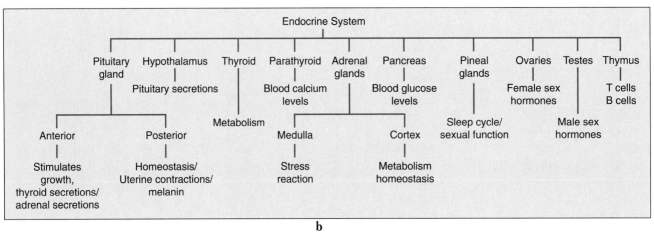

b

Pineal Gland

The **pineal gland** is located superior and posterior to the pituitary gland. It releases **melatonin,** a hormone that is believed to affect sleep and the functioning of the gonads.

Pituitary Gland

The **pituitary gland,** also called the **hypophysis,** is located at the base of the brain in an area called the *sella turcica.* The pituitary is the body's master gland, regulating or aiding in the secretion of essential hormones. Table 15-1 describes the functions of all parts of the endocrine system. The pituitary consists of an *anterior lobe* (**adenohypophysis**) and a *posterior lobe* (**neurohypophysis**).

TABLE 15-1 Endocrine glands, their secretions, and their functions.

Endocrine Gland or Tissue	Hormone	Function
hypothalamus	pituitary-regulating hormones	either stimulate or inhibit pituitary secretions
neurohypophysis (pituitary gland—posterior)	**antidiuretic hormone (ADH), vasopressin**	increase water reabsorption
	oxytocin	stimulates uterine contractions and lactation
	melanocyte-stimulating hormone (MSH)	stimulates the production of melanin
adenohypophysis (pituitary gland—anterior)	**growth hormone (GH), somatotrophic hormone (STH)**	stimulate bone and muscle growth; regulate some metabolic functions, such as the rate that cells utilize carbohydrates and fats
	thyroid-stimulating hormone (TSH)	stimulates thyroid gland to secrete hormones
	adrenocorticotropic hormone (ACTH)	stimulates secretion of adrenal cortex hormones
	follicle-stimulating hormone (FSH), luteinizing hormone (LH)	stimulate development of ova and production of female hormones
	prolactin	stimulates breast development and milk production
thyroid	thyroxine (T4); triiodothyronine (T3) calcitonin	regulates metabolism; stimulates growth lowers blood calcium as necessary to maintain homeostasis
parathyroid	**parathormone, parathyroid hormone (PTH)**	increase blood calcium as necessary to maintain homeostasis
adrenal medulla	**epinephrine (adrenaline), norepinephrine** (*noradrenaline*)	work with the sympathetic nervous system to react to stress
adrenal cortex	**glucocorticoids (cortisol, corticosteroids,** *corticosterone*), **mineralocorticoids (aldosterone),** gonadocorticoids (androgens)	affect metabolism, growth, and aid in electrolyte and fluid balances
pancreas (in islets of Langerhans)	insulin, glucagon	maintain homeostasis in blood glucose concentration
pineal gland	melatonin	affects sexual functions and wake-sleep cycles
ovaries	estrogen (estradiol, the most powerful estrogen), progesterone	promote development of female sex characteristics, menstrual cycle, reproductive functions
testes	androgen, testosterone	promote development of male sex characteristics, sperm production
thymus gland	thymosin, thymic humoral factor (THF), factor thymic serum (FTS)	aid in development of T cells and some B cells; function not well understood

Thyroid Gland

The **thyroid gland** consists of a left lobe and a right lobe. The lobes sit on either side of the trachea. The two lobes are connected by the **isthmus,** a narrow strip of tissue on the ventral surface of the trachea. Above the thyroid gland sits the *thyroid cartilage*, a large piece of cartilage that covers the larynx and produces the protrusion on the neck known as the **Adam's apple.** Thyroid secretions control **metabolism** (the chemical changes in cells that provide energy for vital processes and activities and through which new material is assimilated) and blood calcium concentrations. Two of the hormones secreted, **thyroxine** or *tetraiodothyronine* (T_4) and **triiodothyronine** (T_3), are produced in the thyroid gland. **Calcitonin** is secreted from the outside surface of thyroid cells. It is a hormone that helps lower blood calcium concentration.

Parathyroid Glands

The **parathyroid glands** are four oval-shaped glands located on the dorsal side of the thyroid. The parathyroids helps regulate calcium and phosphate levels, two elements necessary to maintain homeostasis.

Thymus Gland

The **thymus gland** is considered an endocrine gland because it secretes a hormone and is ductless; however, it is also part of the immune system. (Chapter 13 discusses the immune system.)

Adrenal Glands

The **adrenal glands** (or **suprarenal glands**) are a pair of glands. Each of the glands sits atop a kidney. Each gland consists of two parts—the **adrenal cortex** (the outer portion) and the **adrenal medulla** (the inner portion). The adrenal glands regulate **electrolytes** (essential mineral salts that conduct electricity and are decomposed by it) in the body. The mineral salts affect metabolism and blood pressure. The adrenal glands are also **sympathomimetic,** imitative of the sympathetic nervous system, as in response to stress. The adrenal medulla secretes a class of hormones, **catecholamines** (*epinephrine* and *norepinephrine*), in response to stress.

Pancreas

The **pancreas** helps in maintaining a proper level of blood glucose. Within the pancreas, the **islets of Langerhans,** specialized hormone-producing cells, secrete **insulin** to lower blood sugar when blood sugar levels are high and **glucagon** to raise blood sugar levels when they are low. Insulin is produced by **beta cells** in the islets of Langerhans, and glucagon is produced by **alpha cells** in the islets. When insulin is released in response to high blood sugar levels, it stimulates the glucose to be sent to the body's cells for energy as needed and to be converted to a starchy substance, **glycogen,** that is stored for later use in the liver.

Ovaries

The **ovaries** are in the female pelvic region, one at the top of each fallopian tube. (Chapter 10 describes the female reproductive system.)

Testes

The two **testes** (or **testicles**) are located in the scrotum, a sac on the outside of the male body. The testes produce spermatozoa, which fertilize ova. The testes also produce male sex hormones called **androgens.** (Chapter 11 describes the male reproductive system.)

VOCABULARY REVIEW

In the previous section you learned terms related to the endocrine system. Before going on to the exercises, read the definitions below. Pronunciations are provided for certain terms.

Term	Meaning
Adam's apple	Protrusion in the neck caused by a fold of thyroid cartilage.
adenohypophysis [ĂD-ĕ-nō-hī-PŎF-ĭ-sĭs]	Anterior lobe of the pituitary gland.
adrenal cortex [ă-DRĒ-năl KŎR-tĕks]	Outer portion of the adrenal gland; helps control metabolism, inflammations, sodium and potassium retention, and effects of stress.
adrenal gland	One of two glands, each of which is situated on top of each kidney.
adrenaline [ă-DRĔ-nă-lĭn]	Epinephrine; secreted by adrenal medulla.
adrenal medulla [mĕ-DŪL-lă]	Inner portion of adrenal glands; releases large quantities of hormones during stress.
adrenocorticotropic [ă-DRĒ-nō-KŎR-tĭ-kō-TRŌ-pĭk] **hormone (ACTH)**	Hormone secreted by anterior pituitary; involved in the control of the adrenal cortex.
aldosterone [ăl-DŎS-tēr-ōn]	Hormone secreted by adrenal cortex; mineralocorticoid.
alpha [ĂL-fă] **cells**	Specialized cells that produce glucagon in the pancreas.
androgen [ĂN-drō-jĕn]	Any male hormone, such as testosterone.
antidiuretic [ĂN-tē-dī-yū-RĔT-ĭk] **hormone (ADH)**	Posterior pituitary hormone that increases water reabsorption.
beta [BĀ-tă] **cells**	Specialized cells that produce insulin in the pancreas.
calcitonin [kăl-sĕ-TŌ-nĭn]	Hormone secreted by the thyroid gland and other endocrine glands; helps control blood calcium levels.
catecholamines [kăt-ĕ-KŌL-ă-mĕnz]	Hormones, such as epinephrine, released in response to stress.
corticosteroids [KŎR-tĭ-kō-STĒR-ŏydz]	Steroids produced by the adrenal cortex.

Term	Meaning
cortisol [KŎR-tĭ-sōl]	Hydrocortisone.
ductless gland	Endocrine gland.
electrolyte [ē-LĔK-trō-līt]	Any substance that conducts electricity and is decomposed by it.
endocrine [ĔN-dō-krĭn] gland	Gland that secretes substances into the bloodstream instead of into ducts.
epinephrine [ĔP-ĭ-NĔF-rĭn]	Hormone released by the adrenal medulla in response to stress; adrenaline.
exocrine [ĔK-sō-krĭn] gland	Any gland that releases substances through ducts to a specific location.
follicle-stimulating hormone (FSH)	Hormone released by the anterior pituitary to aid in production of ova and sperm.
gland	Any organized mass of tissue secreting or excreting substances.
glucagon [GLŪ-kă-gŏn]	Hormone released by the pancreas to increase blood sugar.
glucocorticoids [glū-kō-KŎR-tĭ-kŏydz]	Hormones released by the adrenal cortex.
glycogen [GLĪ-kō-jĕn]	Converted glucose stored in the liver for future use.
growth hormone (GH)	Hormone released by the anterior pituitary.
hormone [HŌR-mōn]	Substance secreted by glands and carried in the bloodstream to various parts of the body.
hypophysis [hī-PŎF-ĭ-sĭs]	Pituitary gland.
hypothalamus [HĪ-pō-THĂL-ă-mŭs]	Gland in the nervous system that releases hormones to aid in regulating pituitary hormones.
inhibiting factor	Substance in a hormone that prevents the secretion of other hormones.
insulin [ĬN-sū-lĭn]	Substance released by the pancreas to lower blood sugar.
islets of Langerhans [LĂN-gĕr-hănz]	Specialized cells in the pancreas that release insulin and glucagon.
isthmus [ĬS-mŭs]	Narrow band of tissue connecting the two lobes of the thyroid gland.
luteinizing [LŪ-tē-ĭn-ĪZ-ĭng] hormone (LH)	Hormone released to aid in maturation of ova and ovulation.
melanocyte-stimulating [mĕ-LĂN-ō-sīt, MĔL-ă-nō-sīt] hormone (MSH)	Hormone released by the pituitary gland.

Term	Meaning
melatonin [měl-ă-TŌN-ĭn]	Hormone released by the pineal gland; affects sexual function and sleep patterns.
metabolism [mě-TĂB-ō-lĭzm]	The chemical changes in cells that provide energy for vital processes and activities and through which new material is assimilated.
mineralocorticoid [MĬN-ĕr-ăl-ō-KŌR-tĭ-kŏyd]	Steroid secreted by adrenal cortex.
neurohypophysis [NŪR-ō-hī-PŎF-ĭ-sĭs]	Posterior lobe of pituitary gland.
norepinephrine [NŌR-ĕp-ĭ-NĚF-rĭn]	Hormone secreted by adrenal medulla.
ovary [Ō-văr-ē]	One of two female reproductive glands that secrete hormones in the endocrine system.
oxytocin [ŏk-sĭ-TŌ-sĭn]	Hormone released by the posterior pituitary gland to aid in uterine contractions and lactation.
pancreas [PĂN-krē-ăs]	Gland of both the endocrine system (blood sugar control) and the digestive system (as an exocrine gland).
parathormone [păr-ă-THŌR-mōn] **(PTH)**	Parathyroid hormone.
parathyroid [păr-ă-THĪ-rŏyd] **gland**	One of four glands located adjacent to the thyroid gland on its dorsal surface that help maintain levels of blood calcium.
parathyroid hormone (PTH)	Hormone released by parathyroid glands to help raise blood calcium levels.
pineal [PĬN-ē-ăl] **gland**	Gland located above pituitary gland; secretes melatonin.
pituitary [pĭ-TŪ-ĭ-tār-ē] **gland**	Major endocrine gland; secretes hormones essential to metabolic functions.
receptor [rē-SĚP-tōr]	Part of a target cell with properties compatible with a particular substance (hormone).
releasing factor	Substance in a hormone that allows secretion of other hormones.
somatotrophic [SŌ-mă-tō-TRŌF-ĭk] **hormone (STH)**	Hormone secreted by anterior pituitary gland; important in growth and development.
suprarenal [SŪ-pră-RĒ-năl] **gland**	Adrenal gland.
sympathomimetic [SĬM-pă-thō-mĭ-MĚT-ĭk]	Mimicking functions of the sympathetic nervous system.
target cell	Cell with receptors that are compatible with specific hormones.
testis (*pl.*, **testes**) [TĚS-tĭs (TĚS-tēz)], **testicle** [TĚS-tĭ-kl]	One of two male organs that secrete hormones in the endocrine system.

Term	Meaning
thymus [THĪ-mŭs] **gland**	Gland that is part of the immune system as well as part of the endocrine system; aids in the maturation of T and B cells.
thyroid [THĪ-rŏyd] **gland**	Gland with two lobes located on either side of the trachea; helps control blood calcium levels and metabolic functions.
thyroid-stimulating hormone (TSH)	Hormone secreted by anterior pituitary gland; stimulates release of thyroid hormones.
thyroxine [thī-RŎK-sēn, -sĭn] **(T₄)**	Compound found in or manufactured for thyroid gland; helps regulate metabolism.
triiodothyronine [trī-Ī-ō-dō-THĪ-rō-nēn] **(T₃)**	Thyroid hormone that stimulates growth.
vasopressin [vă-sō-PRĔS-ĭn]	Hormone secreted by pituitary gland; raises blood pressure.

CASE STUDY

Checking the Symptoms

Gail Woods is a 45-year-old woman who has noticed some disturbing symptoms, such as unusual fatigue, since her last checkup. She called her physician, Dr. Tyler, for an appointment. Dr. Tyler examined her and sent her to a lab for several tests.

Critical Thinking

1. Dr. Tyler ordered a urinalysis and blood tests. Why?
2. If Dr. Tyler is able to limit the symptoms to one body system, is he likely to send Gail to a specialist?

STRUCTURE AND FUNCTION EXERCISES

Find a Match

Match each hormone with its function by writing the name of the hormone on the appropriate line.

ADH   prolactin   insulin   aldosterone   oxytocin   thyroxine   testosterone   thymosin   melatonin   epinephrine

3. may affect sleep habits: _____

4. reacts to stress: _____

5. decreases urine output: _____

6. stimulates uterine contractions and lactation: _____

7. helps transport glucose to cells and decreases blood sugar: _____

8. stimulates breast development and lactation: _____

9. affects electrolyte and fluid balances: _____

10. regulates rate of cellular metabolism: _____

11. promotes growth and maintenance of male sex characteristics and sperm production: _____

12. aids in development of the immune system: _____

Check Your Knowledge

For each of the following words, write C if the spelling is correct. If it is not, write the correct spelling.

13. adenohypophysis _____

14. adenal _____

15. hypophisis _____

16. suparenal _____

17. sympathomimetic _____

18. pituatary _____

19. lutinizing _____

20. triiodothyronine _____

CASE STUDY

Getting the Results

Gail's tests came back with abnormally high blood sugar. Her lab results are shown at right:

Critical Thinking

21. Were any other tests abnormal?

22. What body system is the likely origin of Gail's abnormal tests?

John Colter, M.D. 3 Windsor Street Nome, AK 66660 777-546-7890	Laboratory Report Grandview Diagnostics 12 Settlers Drive Nome, AK 66661 777-546-7000	
Patient: Gail Woods Date Collected: 04/27/XXXX Date Received: 04/27/XXXX	Patient ID: 099-00-1200 Time Collected: 16:05 Date Reported: 10/06/XXXX	Date of Birth: 06/10/59 Total Volume: 2000

Test	Result	Flag	Reference
Complete Blood Count			
WBC	4.0		3.9-11.1
RBC	4.11		3.80-5.20
HCT	39.7		34.0-47.0
MCV	96.5		80.0-98.0
MCH	32.9		27.1-34.0
MCHC	34.0		32.0-36.0
MPV	8.6		7.5-11.5
NEUTROPHILS %	45.6		38.0-80.0
NEUTROPHILS ABS.	1.82		1.70-8.50
LYMPHOCYTES %	36.1		15.0-49.0
LYMPHOCYTES ABS.	1.44		1.00-3.50
EOSINOPHILS %	4.5		0.0-8.0
EOSINOPHILS ABS.	0.18		0.03-0.55
BASOPHILS %	0.7		0.0-2.0
BASOPHILS ABS.	0.03		0.000-0.185
PLATELET COUNT	229		150-400

continued

Automated Chemistries

GLUCOSE	275	*	65-109
UREA NITROGEN	17		6-30
CREATININE (SERUM)	0.6		0.5-1.3
UREA NITROGEN/CREATININE	28		10-29
SODIUM	152	*	135-145
POTASSIUM	4.4		3.5-5.3
CHLORIDE	106		96-109
CO$_2$	28		20-31
ANION GAP	6		3-19
CALCIUM	9.8		8.6-10.4
PHOSPHORUS	3.6		2.2-4.6
AST (SGOT)	28		0-30
ALT (SGPT)	19		0-34
BILIRUBIN, TOTAL	0.5		0.2-1.2
PROTEIN, TOTAL	7.8		6.2-8.2
ALBUMIN	4.3		3.5-5.0
GLOBULIN	3.5		2.1-3.8
URIC ACID	2.4		2.0-7.5
CHOLESTEROL	195		120-199
TRIGLYCERIDES	68		40-199
IRON	85		30-150
HDL CHOLESTEROL	73		35-59
CHOLESTEROL/HDL RATIO	3.2		3.2-5.7
LDL, CALCULATED	126		70-129
T3, UPTAKE	32		24-37
T4, TOTAL	6.9		4.5-12.8

Combining Forms

The list below includes combining forms that relate specifically to the endocrine system. Pronunciations are provided for the examples.

COMBINING FORM	MEANING	EXAMPLE
aden(o)	gland	*adenopathy* [ă-dĕ-NŎP-ă-thē], glandular or lymph node disease
adren(o), adrenal(o)	adrenal glands	*adrenomegaly* [ă-drē-nō-MĔG-ă-lē], enlargement of the adrenal glands
gluc(o)	glucose	*glucogenesis* [glū-kō-JĔN-ĕ-sĭs], production of glucose
glyc(o)	glycogen	*glycolysis* [glī-KŎL-ĭ-sĭs], conversion of glycogen to glucose
gonad(o)	sex glands	*gonadotropin* [gō-NĂD-ō-trō-pĭn], hormone that aids in growth of gonads
pancreat(o)	pancreas	*pancreatitis* [păn-krē-ă-TĪ-tĭs], inflammation of the pancreas

COMBINING FORM	MEANING	EXAMPLE
parathyroid(o)	parathyroid	*parathyroidectomy* [PĂ-ră-thī-rŏy-DĔK-tō-mē], excision of the parathyroid glands
thyr(o), thyroid(o)	thyroid gland	*thyrotoxic* [thī-rō-TŎK-sĭk], having excessive amounts of thyroid hormones

COMBINING FORMS EXERCISES

Build Your Medical Vocabulary

Using the combining forms learned in this chapter, construct five words about the endocrine system that fit the definitions provided.

23. inflammation of a gland: _____

24. disease of the pancreas: _____

25. production of glycogen: _____

26. enlargement of the thyroid gland: _____

27. beneficial thyroid function: _____

Know the Meaning

Write the definitions for the following terms.

28. adrenalectomy: _____

29. pancreatectomy: _____

30. adenoma: _____

31. gonadotropin: _____

32. thyromegaly: _____

Diagnostic, Procedural, and Laboratory Terms

Endocrine functions affect *homeostasis*, the maintenance of fluid balance in the body. Levels of hormones, minerals, glucose, and other substances affect overall health. Blood and urine test results can often confirm a suspected diagnosis (usually based on symptoms such as sudden weight loss, fatigue, and abnormal thirst as in the case of diabetes). Blood sugar levels vary depending on when the last meal was eaten. A **fasting blood sugar** test and a **glucose tolerance test (GTT)** are both taken after a 12-hour fast. However, in the glucose tolerance, the blood sugar test is repeated every 3-5 hours after the patient ingests a concentrated glucose solution. Patients can check **blood sugar** or **blood glucose** levels themselves to track fluctuations in blood sugar. A **postprandial** (after eating) **blood sugar** is a test for blood sugar usually taken about 2 hours after a meal. A **urine sugar** is a test for ketones and/or sugar in urine, both of which may indicate diabetes. For people already diagnosed with diabetes, a **glycated hemoglobin** test tracks average blood sugar readings over the previous 2–3 months.

Overall endocrine functioning is tested in a serum test. Many hormones and electrolytes are present in serum. Endocrine function can be tested in the plasma by using a **radioactive immunoassay (RIA),** a test using radioactive iodine to locate various substances in the plasma. Thyroid functioning can be tested in a **thyroid function test,** which is a blood test for various hormones secreted by the thyroid. A **radioactive iodine uptake** is a measure of how quickly ingested iodine is taken into the thyroid gland. A **thyroid scan** is a test for cancer or other abnormality using radionuclide imaging.

VOCABULARY REVIEW

In the previous section you learned terms related to diagnosis, clinical procedures, and laboratory tests. Before going on to the exercises, read the definitions below. Pronunciations are provided for certain terms.

Term	Meaning
blood sugar, blood glucose	Test for glucose in blood.
fasting blood sugar	Test for glucose in blood following a fast of 12 hours.
glucose tolerance test (GTT)	Blood test for body's ability to metabolize carbohydrates; taken after a 12-hour fast, then repeated every hour for 4 to 6 hours after ingestion of a sugar solution.
glycated [GLĪ-kā-tĕd] hemoglobin	Blood test for an average of glucose levels over the previous 2–3 months.
postprandial [pōst-PRĂN-dē-ăl] blood sugar	Test for glucose in blood, usually about two hours after a meal.
radioactive immunoassay (RIA)	Test for measuring hormone levels in plasma; taken after radioactive solution is ingested.
radioactive iodine uptake	Test for how quickly the thyroid gland pulls in ingested iodine.
thyroid function test or study	Test for levels of TSH, T_3, and T_4 in blood plasma to determine thyroid function.
thyroid scan	Imaging test for thyroid abnormalities.
urine sugar	Test for diabetes; determined by presence of ketones or sugar in urine.

CASE STUDY

Referring to a Specialist

Dr. Tyler reviewed Gail's symptoms and test results with her. She has lost 12 pounds rapidly over the last couple of months, is feeling abnormally tired, and is unusually thirsty. Dr. Tyler referred her to an endocrinologist.

Critical Thinking

33. What disease does Dr. Tyler think Gail has?

34. What test for blood glucose is taken after a meal?

DIAGNOSTIC, PROCEDURAL, AND LABORATORY TERMS EXERCISES

Match the Test

Match the test with the possible diagnosis. Write D if it is a test for diabetes or T if it is a test for thyroid function.

35. fasting blood sugar _____

36. radioactive iodine uptake _____

37. radioactive immunoassay _____

38. urine sugar _____

39. glucose tolerance test _____

MORE ABOUT...

Diabetes and Diet

For many years, doctors prescribed a high-protein, low-carbohydrate diet for diabetics. In recent years, increased understanding of how food is metabolized by the body has led to changes in diets prescribed for diabetics. Most newly diagnosed diabetics are given a varied diet by a physician or a dietitian that is tailored to their specific needs—current weight, level of diabetes (mild, moderate, severe), and lifestyle. The American Dietetic Association and the American Diabetes Association provide the dietary information on which most diets for diabetics are based. A diabetic's personalized daily diet might include four fruit exchanges, three protein exchanges, three bread exchanges, and seven vegetable exchanges. Many suppliers of processed food, particularly those foods aimed at the health-conscious consumer, now list exchanges as part of their nutrition labels as shown here.

Nutrition Facts

Serving Size 1 cup (246g)
Servings Per Container about 2

Amount Per Serving

Calories 100	Calories from Fat 5

	% Daily Value*
Total Fat 0.5g	1%
Saturated Fat 0g	0%
Cholesterol 0mg	0%
Sodium 430mg	18%
Total Carbohydrate 23g	8%
Dietary Fiber 2g	8%
Sugars 1g	
Protein	4g

Vitamin A 30%	•	Vitamin C 15%
Calcium 4%	•	Iron 6%

* Percent Daily Values are based on a 2,000 calorie diet

DIETARY EXCHANGES PER SERVING:
1 Bread
1 Vegetable

Diet exchanges are based on Exchange Lists for Meal Planning, © 1989, the American Diabetes Assoc., Inc. and the American Dietetic Assoc.

Pathological Terms

Diseases of the endocrine system commonly involve lack of homeostasis. In other words, either too much or too little of a hormone or substance in the body creates an imbalance and, often, a disorder or disease. Most endocrine illnesses are the result of **hypersecretion** (oversecretion) or **hyposecretion** (undersecretion) of one or more hormones.

Pituitary Disorders

Pituitary abnormalities include:

- Hypersecretion of growth hormone before puberty may result in gigantism, abnormal growth, even to over 8 feet tall. After puberty, it causes **acromegaly,** enlarged features.
- Hyposecretion of the same growth hormone may result in dwarfism, which is stunted growth. **Dwarfism** with disproportionate features is usually caused by the congenital absence of the thyroid gland or by another genetic defect. Figure 15-2 shows three people, one of normal height, another with gigantism, and a third with dwarfism.
- Hyposecretion of vasopressin or antidiuretic hormone causes **diabetes insipidus,** a disease with **polyuria** (excessive amount of water excreted in the urine) and **polydipsia** (excessive and constant thirst).
- Hypersecretion of antidiuretic hormone causes **syndrome of inappropriate ADH (SIADH),** which results in excessive water retention.

Thyroid Disorders

The thyroid gland may become overactive, causing **hyperthyroidism,** also known as **Graves' disease** or **thyrotoxicosis.** Symptoms of Graves' disease are consistent with increased T3 and T4, which cause increased metabolic rate, weight loss, insomnia, and sweating. **Exophthalmos,** bulging of the eyes, is a complication that usually occurs in Graves' disease. A **goiter** can also be caused by hypersecretion from the thyroid gland, a tumor, or lack of iodine in the diet.

Hypothyroidism, underactivity of the thyroid gland, causes sluggishness and slow metabolism, often resulting in obesity. **Myxedema** is a specific type of hypothyroidism in adults.

Parathyroid Disorders

The parathyroid glands help control blood calcium levels. **Hyperparathyroidism** (overactivity of the parathyroid glands) is usually caused by a tumor in the parathyroid gland. **Hypoparathyroidism** (underactivity of the parathyroid glands) results in low blood calcium levels, causing many symptoms such as bone loss and some muscle paralysis (**tetany**).

Adrenal Disorders

The adrenal glands may be overactive (**hyperadrenalism**) or underactive (**hypoadrenalism**). Hyperadrenalism is usually caused by an adrenal tumor and can cause the production of excessive androgens both in men and women, which, in turn, can result in **hirsutism,** abnormal hair growth. **Virilism** is also a condition

The Web site www.dwarfism.org is a centralized site for links to many organizations and sites with information about dwarfism.

FIGURE 15-2 The person in the center has gigantism. He is holding a person with dwarfism. The person on the right is of normal height. Human growth hormone is a factor in both conditions.

with excessive androgen secretion. Virilism results in mature masculine features in children. **Cushing's syndrome** results from an oversecretion of ACTH. Hypoadrenalism is also known as **Addison's disease.** It may result in anemia, abnormal skin pigment, and general malaise. It can be controlled with cortisone.

Pancreas Disorders

Sometimes, the pancreas may become inflamed, as in **pancreatitis.** *Hyperinsulinism* is the hypersecretion of insulin and may cause **hypoglycemia,** a lowering of blood sugar levels. Hyposecretion of insulin can cause **diabetes mellitus,** a widespread disease.

Diabetes or Failure of the Beta Cells

Diabetes occurs either as **Type I diabetes (insulin-dependent diabetes mellitus or IDDM)** or as **Type II diabetes (noninsulin-dependent diabetes mellitus or NIDDM).** Type I diabetes usually occurs in childhood and is the result of underproduction of insulin by the beta cells. Glucose accumulates and overflows into the urine (**glucosuria, glycosuria**). Type I diabetes can be treated with controlled doses of insulin. Type II diabetes used to occur only in adulthood (but now also occurs in younger people and even in teens and children), usually in overweight people whose responsiveness to insulin is abnormally low. This lack of response is called *insulin resistance*.

Complications of diabetes cover a wide range of ailments from circulatory problems to infections to organ failure. **Diabetic nephropathy** is a kidney disease resulting from serious diabetes. **Diabetic neuropathy** includes loss of sensation in the extremities. **Diabetic retinopathy** is gradual visual loss leading to blindness. The body uses stored fat to replace glucose, thereby causing **acidosis, ketoacidosis,** and **ketosis,** all of which are marked by the abnormal presence of ketone bodies in the blood and urine.

> The American Diabetes Association (www.diabetes.org) provides information for people with diabetes or those who wish to prevent it.

Cancers of the Endocrine System

Cancers occur commonly in the endocrine system. Many, such as thyroid cancer, can be treated with removal of the affected gland and supplementation with a synthetic version of the necessary hormones that are then missing from the body. Some cancers, such as pancreatic cancer, are almost always fatal since no good treatments are available.

MORE ABOUT...

Misleading Common Terms

In certain parts of the country, both types of diabetes are simply called *sugar,* as in the phrase, "he has sugar." Sometimes common terms for diseases seem to misrepresent what the disease is. Diabetes is in fact an underproduction of or resistance to *insulin,* although in the past, many people thought it was caused by sugar alone.

VOCABULARY REVIEW

In the previous section you learned terms related to pathology. Before going on to the exercises, read the definitions on the following pages. Pronunciations are provided for certain terms.

Term	Meaning
acidosis [ăs-ĭ-DŌ-sĭs]	Abnormal release of ketones in the body.
acromegaly [ăk-rō-MĔG-ă-lē]	Abnormally enlarged features resulting from hypersecretion of growth hormone after puberty.
Addison's [ĂD-ĭ-sŏnz] **disease**	Underactivity of the adrenal glands.
Cushing's [KŪSH-ĭngs] **syndrome**	Group of symptoms caused by overactivity of the adrenal glands.
diabetes [dī-ă-BĒ-tēz]	*See* Type I diabetes, Type II diabetes.
diabetes insipidus [ĭn-SĬP-ĭ-dŭs]	Condition caused by hyposecretion of antidiuretic hormone.
diabetes mellitus [MĔL-ĭ-tŭs, mĕ-LĪ-tŭs]	*See* Type I diabetes, Type II diabetes.
diabetic nephropathy [dī-ă-BĔT-ĭk nĕ-FRŎP-ă-thē]	Kidney disease due to diabetes.
diabetic neuropathy [nū-RŎP-ă-thē]	Loss of sensation in the extremities due to diabetes.
diabetic retinopathy [rĕt-ĭ-NŎP-ă-thē]	Gradual loss of vision due to diabetes.
dwarfism [DWŌRF-ĭzm]	Abnormally stunted growth caused by hyposecretion of growth hormone, congenital lack of a thyroid gland, or a genetic defect.
exophthalmos [ĕk-sŏf-THĂL-mŏs]	Abnormal protrusion of the eyes typical of Graves' disease.
gigantism [JĪ-găn-tĭzm]	Abnormally fast and large growth caused by hypersecretion of growth hormone.
glucosuria [glū-kō-SŪ-rē-ă]	Glucose in the urine.
glycosuria [glī-kō-SŪ-rē-ă]	Glucose in the urine.
goiter [GŎY-tĕr]	Abnormal enlargement of the thyroid gland as a result of its overactivity or lack of iodine in the diet.
Graves' [grāvz] **disease**	Overactivity of the thyroid gland.
hirsutism [HĔR-sū-tĭzm]	Abnormal hair growth due to an excess of androgens.
hyperadrenalism [HĪ-pĕr-ă-DRĔN-ă-lĭzm]	Overactivity of the adrenal glands.
hyperparathyroidism [HĪ-pĕr-pă-ră-THĪ-rŏyd-ĭzm]	Overactivity of the parathyroid glands.
hypersecretion [HĪ-pĕr-sĕ-KRĒ-shŭn]	Abnormally high secretion, as from a gland.
hyperthyroidism [HĪ-pĕr-THĪ-rŏyd-ĭzm]	Overactivity of the thyroid gland.
hypoadrenalism [HĪ-pō-ă-DRĔN-ă-lĭzm]	Underactivity of the adrenal glands.
hypoglycemia [HĪ-pō-glī-SĒ-mē-ă]	Abnormally low level of glucose in the blood.
hypoparathyroidism [HĪ-pō-pă-ră-THĪ-rŏyd-ĭzm]	Underactivity of the parathyroid glands.
hyposecretion [HĪ-pō-sĕ-KRĒ-shŭn]	Abnormally low secretion, as from a gland.
hypothyroidism [HĪ-pō-THĪ-rŏyd-ĭzm]	Underactivity of the thyroid gland.

Term	Meaning
insulin-dependent diabetes mellitus (IDDM)	*See* Type I diabetes.
ketoacidosis [KĒ-tō-ă-sĭ-DŌ-sĭs]	Condition of high acid levels marked by the abnormal release of ketones in the body.
ketosis [kē-TŌ-sĭs]	Condition caused by the abnormal release of ketones in the body.
myxedema [mĭk-sĕ-DĒ-mă]	Advanced adult hypothyroidism.
noninsulin-dependent diabetes mellitus (NIDDM)	*See* Type II diabetes.
pancreatitis [PĂN-krē-ă-TĪ-tĭs]	Inflammation of the pancreas.
polydipsia [pŏl-ē-DĬP-sē-ă]	Excessive thirst.
polyuria [pŏl-ē-YŪ-rē-ă]	Excessive amount of water in the urine.
syndrome of inappropriate ADH (SIADH)	Excessive secretion of antidiuretic hormone.
tetany [TĔT-ă-nē]	Muscle paralysis, usually due to decreased levels of ionized calcium in the blood.
thyrotoxicosis [THĪ-rō-tŏk-sĭ-KŌ-sĭs]	Overactivity of the thyroid gland.
Type I diabetes	Endocrine disorder with abnormally low levels of insulin; also known as insulin-dependent diabetes mellitus (IDDM).
Type II diabetes	Disease caused by failure of the body to recognize insulin that is present or by an abnormally low level of insulin; also known as noninsulin-dependent diabetes mellitus (NIDDM); usually adult onset.
virilism [VĬR-ĭ-lĭzm]	Condition with excessive androgen production, often resulting in the appearance of mature male characteristics in young.

CASE STUDY

Getting a Diagnosis

Gail decides to wait until after the holidays to maker her appointment with the endocrinologist. She thinks that she will watch what she eats and then go to the doctor when she is less busy. For a few days, she moderates her eating and feels a little better. However, on the big holiday weekend, Gail goes to several parties, drinks, and overeats. When she wakes up in the morning, she feels dizzy, is in a cold sweat, and feels very hungry. Right away, she realizes that something is terribly wrong. Since it is a holiday weekend, she has a friend take her to the emergency room. Once there, her symptoms are worse. The emergency room doctor tests her blood sugar and finds it is very low. After she has eaten something, he tests it again. Because Gail is overweight, the doctor suspects that her body is not sensitive to insulin. Gail is sent to Dr. Malpas, an endocrinologist, the very next day.

Critical Thinking

40. What type of diabetes does Gail appear to have?

41. What might some recommendations be for Gail's diet?

PATHOLOGICAL TERMS EXERCISES

Write A for adrenal, PA for pancreas, PI for pituitary, and T for thyroid to indicate the gland from which each of the following diseases arises.

42. acromegaly: _____

43. diabetes mellitus: _____

44. exophthalmos: _____

45. gigantism: _____

46. goiter: _____

47. myxedema: _____

48. Cushing's syndrome: _____

49. Graves' disease: _____

50. Addison's disease: _____

51. dwarfism: _____

52. cretinism: _____

Surgical Terms

Certain endocrine glands that become diseased can be surgically removed. Synthetic versions of the hormones they produce are given to the patients to help their bodies perform the necessary endocrine functions once the glands are removed.

An **adenectomy** is the removal of any gland. An **adrenalectomy** is the removal of an adrenal gland. Removal of the pituitary gland is a **hypophysectomy.** The pancreas is removed in a **pancreatectomy.** Removal of the parathyroid gland is performed in a **parathyroidectomy,** and removal of the thymus gland is performed in a **thymectomy.** A **thyroidectomy** is the removal of the thyroid. Some of these operations may remove only the diseased part of a gland, leaving the remaining part to continue the endocrine function.

VOCABULARY REVIEW

In the previous section you learned terms related to surgery. Before going on to the exercises, read the definitions below. Pronunciations are provided for certain terms.

Term	Meaning
adenectomy [ă-dĕ-NĔK-tō-mē]	Removal of a gland.
adrenalectomy [ă-drē-năl-ĔK-tō-mē]	Removal of an adrenal gland.
hypophysectomy [hī-pŏf-ĭ-SĔK-tō-mē]	Removal of the pituitary gland.
pancreatectomy [PĂN-krē-ă-TĔK-tō-mē]	Removal of the pancreas.
parathyroidectomy [PĂ-ră-thī-rŏy-DĔK-tō-mē]	Removal of one or more of the parathyroid glands.
thymectomy [thī-MĔK-tō-mē]	Removal of the thymus gland.
thyroidectomy [thī-rŏy-DĔK-tō-mē]	Removal of the thyroid.

Controlling the Disease

After the emergency room incident, Gail goes to her appointment with the endocrinologist, where she is given medication to make her body more sensitive to insulin, and told to diet sensibly and exercise. When she returns three months later, Dr. Malpas is pleased to see that Gail is controlling her diabetes, losing weight slowly, and exercising regularly. Her outlook is favorable. Dr. Malpas has another patient, Will Burns, who has had an overactive thyroid since he was a child. Lately, Will's hyperthy-roidism has increased. Dr. Malpas biopsies Will's thyroid and tells Will it would be best to remove the thyroid.

Critical Thinking

53. What did Dr. Malpas probably find that necessitated thyroid removal?
54. What medications should Will be given after the operation?

SURGICAL TERMS EXERCISES

Build Your Medical Vocabulary

Supply the missing part of the term:

55. removal of a gland: _____ectomy

56. removal of the pituitary gland: _____ectomy

57. removal of an adrenal gland: _____ectomy

58. removal of the thymus gland: _____ectomy

59. removal of part of the pancreas: _____ectomy

60. removal of the thyroid gland: _____ectomy

61. removal of one or more of the parathyroid glands: _____ectomy

After completing the terms in items 55 through 61, use them to define the following treatments:

62. Treatment for Graves' disease: _____

63. Treatment for severe virilism: _____

64. Treatment for a cancerous gland: _____

65. Treatment for hyperparathyroidism: _____

66. Treatment for acromegaly: _____

TERMINOLOGY IN ACTION

On the following page is a lab report for a 55-year-old patient. Which items indicate abnormalities in the endocrine system?

_____

_____

Claudia Dinavo, M.D.	Laboratory Report		
20 Ridge Road	Lab Services		
Tuscaloosa, AL 99999	University Square		
555-111-4444	Tuscaloosa, AL 99999		
	555-111-2222		

Patient: Sam Oscar	Patient ID: 099-00-1200	Date of Birth: 4/3/XXXX
Date Collected: 03/28/XXXX	Time Collected: 09:10	Total Volume: 2000
Date Received: 03/28/XXXX	Date Reported: 3/31/XXXX	

Test	Result	Flag	Reference
Complete Blood Count			
WBC	5.2		3.9-11.1
RBC	4.11		3.80-5.20
HCT	39.7		34.0-47.0
MCV	96.5		80.0-98.0
MCH	32.9		27.1-34.0
MCHC	34.0		32.0-36.0
MPV	8.6		7.5-11.5
NEUTROPHILS %	45.6		38.0-80.0
NEUTROPHILS ABS.	3.4		1.70-8.50
LYMPHOCYTES %	36.1		15.0-49.0
LYMPHOCYTES ABS.	1.44		1.00-3.50
EOSINOPHILS %	4.5		0.0-8.0
EOSINOPHILS ABS.	0.18		0.03-0.55
BASOPHILS %	0.7		0.0-2.0
BASOPHILS ABS.	0.03		0.000-0.185
PLATELET COUNT	325		150-400
Automated Chemistries			
GLUCOSE	405	*	65-109
UREA NITROGEN	17		6-30
CREATININE (SERUM)	0.6		0.5-1.3
UREA NITROGEN/CREATININE	28		10-29
SODIUM	152	*	135-145
POTASSIUM	4.4		3.5-5.3
CHLORIDE	106		96-109
CO_2	28		20-31
ANION GAP	6		3-19
CALCIUM	9.8		8.6-10.4
PHOSPHORUS	3.6		2.2-4.6
AST (SGOT)	28		0-30
ALT (SGPT)	19		0-34
BILIRUBIN, TOTAL	0.5		0.2-1.2
PROTEIN, TOTAL	7.8		6.2-8.2
ALBUMIN	4.3		3.5-5.0
GLOBULIN	3.5		2.1-3.8
URIC ACID	2.4		2.0-7.5
CHOLESTEROL	195		120-199
TRIGLYCERIDES	68		40-199
IRON	85		30-150
HDL CHOLESTEROL	73		35-59
CHOLESTEROL/HDL RATIO	3.2		3.2-5.7
LDL, CALCULATED	126		70-129
T3, UPTAKE	42	*	24-37
T4, TOTAL	13.6	*	4.5-12.8

USING THE INTERNET

Go to the site of The Endocrine Society (http://www.endo-society.org), click the news and fact section, then click the fact sheet, and click on an article about an endocrinological disease. Write a brief summary of the information you collect.

CHAPTER REVIEW

The material that follows is to help you review this chapter.

DEFINITIONS

Define the following terms and combining forms. Review the chapter before starting. Make sure you know how to pronounce each term as you define it.

WORD	DEFINITION
acidosis [ăs-ĭ-DŌ-sĭs] {acidosis}	
acromegaly [ăk-rō-MĔG-ă-lē] {acromegalia}	
Adam's apple	
Addison's [ĂD-ĭ-sŏnz] disease	
aden(o)	
adenectomy [ă-dĕ-NĔK-tō-mē]	
adenohypophysis [ĂD-ĕ-nō-hī-PŎF-ĭ-sĭs]	
adren(o), adrenal(o)	
adrenal cortex [ă-DRĒ-năl KŌR-tĕks]	
adrenalectomy [ă-drē-năl-ĔK-tō-mē] {adrenalectomía}	
adrenal gland {adrenal glándula}	
adrenaline [ă-DRĔ-nă-lĭn] {adrenalina}	
adrenal medulla [mĕ-DŪL-lă]	
adrenocorticotropic [ă-DRĒ-nō-KŌR-tĭ-kō-TRŌ-pĭk] hormone (ACTH)	
aldosterone [ăl-DŎS-tēr-ōn] {aldosterina}	
alpha [ĂL-fă] cells	
androgen [ĂN-drō-jĕn] {andrógeno}	
antidiuretic [ĂN-tē-dī-yū-RĔT-ĭk] hormone (ADH)	
beta [BĀ-tă] cells	
blood sugar, blood glucose	
calcitonin [kăl-sĕ-TŌ-nĭn] {calcitonia}	
catecholamines [kăt-ĕ-KŌL-ă-mēnz] {catecolaminas}	

WORD	DEFINITION
corticosteroids [KŎR-tǐ-kō-STĒR-ŏydz] {corticosteroides}	_____
cortisol [KŎR-tǐ-sōl] {cortisol}	_____
Cushing's [KŪSH-ǐngs] syndrome	_____
diabetes [dī-ă-BĒ-tēz] {diabetes}	_____
diabetes insipidus [ǐn-SǏP-ǐ-dŭs]	_____
diabetes mellitus [MĔL-ǐ-tŭs, mĕ-LĪ-tŭs]	_____
diabetic nephropathy [dī-ă-BĔT-ǐk nĕ-FRŎP-ă-thē]	_____
diabetic neuropathy [nū-RŎP-ă-thē]	_____
diabetic retinopathy [rĕt-ǐ-NŎP-ă-thē]	_____
ductless gland	_____
dwarfism [DWŌRF-ǐzm] {enanismo}	_____
electrolyte [ē-LĔK-trō-līt] {electrólito}	_____
endocrine [ĔN-dō-krǐn] gland {glándula endocrina}	_____
epinephrine [ĔP-ǐ-NĔF-rǐn] {epinefrina}	_____
exocrine [ĔK-sō-krǐn] gland {glándula exocrina}	_____
exophthalmos [ĕk-sŏf-THĂL-mŏs] {exoftalmía}	_____
fasting blood sugar	_____
follicle-stimulating hormone (FSH)	_____
gigantism [JĪ-găn-tǐzm] {gigantismo}	_____
gland {glándula}	_____
gluc(o)	_____
glucagon [GLŪ-kă-gŏn] {glucagon}	_____
glucocorticoids [glū-kō-KŌR-tǐ-kŏydz]	_____
glucose tolerance test (GTT)	_____
glucosuria [glū-kō-SŪ-rē-ă]	_____
glycated [GLĪ-kā-tĕd] hemoglobin	_____
glyc(o)	_____
glycogen [GLĪ-kō-jĕn] {glucógeno}	_____
glycosuria [glī-kō-SŪ-rē-ă]	_____

WORD	DEFINITION
goiter [GŎY-tĕr] {bocio}	_____
gonad(o)	_____
Graves' [grāvz] disease	_____
growth hormone (GH)	_____
hirsutism [HĔR-sū-tĭzm] {hirsutismo}	_____
hormone [HŌR-mōn] {hormona}	_____
hormone replacement therapy (HRT)	_____
hyperadrenalism [HĪ-pĕr-ă-DRĒN-ă-lĭzm]	_____
hyperparathyroidism [HĪ-pĕr-pă-ră-THĪ-rŏyd-ĭzm] {hiperparatiroidismo}	_____
hypersecretion [HĪ-pĕr-sĕ-KRĒ-shŭn]	_____
hyperthyroidism [HĪ-pĕr-THĪ-rŏyd-ĭzm] {hipertiroidismo}	_____
hypoadrenalism [HĪ-pō-ă-DRĒN-ă-lĭzm] {hipoadrenalismo}	_____
hypoglycemia [HĪ-pō-glī-SĒ-mē-ă] {hipoglucemia}	_____
hypoparathyroidism [HĪ-pō-pă-ră-THĪ-rŏyd-ĭzm] {hipoparatiroidismo}	_____
hypophysectomy [hī-pŏf-ĭ-SĔK-tō-mē]	_____
hypophysis [hī-PŎF-ĭ-sĭs] {hipófisis}	_____
hyposecretion [HĪ-pō-sĕ-KRĒ-shŭn]	_____
hypothalamus [HĪ-pō-THĂL-ă-mŭs] {hipotálamo}	_____
hypothyroidism [HĪ-pō-THĪ-rŏyd-ĭzm] {hipotiroidismo}	_____
inhibiting factor	_____
insulin [ĬN-sū-lĭn] {insulina}	_____
insulin-dependent diabetes mellitus (IDDM)	_____
islets of Langerhans [LĂN-gĕr-hănz]	_____
isthmus [ĬS-mŭs] {istmo}	_____
ketoacidosis [KĒ-tō-ă-sĭ-DŌ-sĭs] {cetoacidosis}	_____
ketosis [kē-TŌ-sĭs] {cetosis}	_____
luteinizing [LŪ-tē-ĭn-ĪZ-ĭng] hormone (LH)	_____

WORD	DEFINITION

melanocyte-stimulating [mě-LĂN-ō-sīt, MĚL-ă-nō-sīt] hormone (MSH) _____

melatonin [měl-ă-TŌN-ĭn] _____

metabolism [mě-TĂB-ō-lĭzm] _____

mineralocorticoid [MĬN-ěr-ăl-ō-KŌR-tĭ-kŏyd] _____

myxedema [mĭk-sě-DĒ-mă] {mixedema} _____

neurohypophysis [NŪR-ō-hī-PŎF-ĭ-sĭs] _____

noninsulin-dependent diabetes mellitus (NIDDM) _____

norepinephrine [NŌR-ěp-ĭ-NĚF-rĭn] {norepinefrina} _____

ovary [Ō-văr-ē] {ovario} _____

oxytocin [ŏk-sĭ-TŌ-sĭn] {oxitocina} _____

pancreas [PĂN-krē-ăs] {páncreas} _____

pancreat(o) _____

pancreatectomy [PĂN-krē-ă-TĚK-tō-mē] _____

pancreatitis [PĂN-krē-ă-TĪ-tĭs] {pancreatitis} _____

parathormone [păr-ă-THŌR-mōn] (PTH) {parathormona} _____

parathyroid(o) _____

parathyroidectomy [PĂ-ră-thī-rŏy-DĚK-tō-mē] _____

parathyroid [păr-ă-THĪ-rŏyd] gland {paratiroide} _____

parathyroid hormone (PTH) _____

pineal [PĬN-ē-ăl] gland _____

pituitary [pĭ-TŪ-ĭ-tār-ē] gland _____

polydipsia [pŏl-ē-DĬP-sē-ă] {polidipsa} _____

polyuria [pŏl-ē-YŪ-rē-ă] {poliuria} _____

postprandial [pōst-PRĂN-dē-ăl] blood sugar _____

radioactive immunoassay (RIA) _____

radioactive iodine uptake _____

receptor [rē-SĚP-tōr] {receptor} _____

releasing factor _____

somatotrophic [SŌ-mă-tō-TRŌF-ĭk] hormone (STH)

suprarenal [SŪ-pră-RĒ-năl] gland

sympathomimetic [SĬM-pă-thō-mĭ-MĚT-ĭk] {simpatomimético}

syndrome of inappropriate ADH (SIADH)

target cell

testis (pl., testes) [TĔS-tĭs (TĔS-tēz)], testicle [TĔS-tĭ-kl] {testículo}

tetany [TĔT-ă-nē] {tetania}

thymectomy [thī-MĔK-tō-mē] {timectomía}

thymus [THĪ-mŭs] gland

thyr(o), thyroid(o)

thyroidectomy [thī-rŏy-DĔK-tō-mē] {tiroidectomía}

thyroid function test or study

thyroid [THĪ-rŏyd] gland

thyroid scan

thyroid-stimulating hormone (TSH)

thyrotoxicosis [THĪ-rō-tŏk-sĭ-KŌ-sĭs]

thyroxine [thī-RŎK-sēn, -sĭn] (T_4)

triiodothyronine [trī-Ī-ō-dō-THĪ-rō-nēn] (T_3)

Type I diabetes

Type II diabetes

urine sugar

vasopressin [vā-sō-PRĔS-ĭn]

virilism [VĬR-ĭ-lĭzm] {virilismo}

Answers to Chapter Exercises

1. to eliminate various diseases and to test for others
2. possibly yes, if her symptoms are serious enough
3. melatonin
4. epinephrine
5. ADH
6. oxytocin
7. insulin
8. prolactin
9. aldosterone
10. thyroxine
11. testosterone
12. thymosin
13. C
14. adrenal
15. hypophysis
16. suprarenal
17. C
18. pituitary
19. luteinizing
20. C
21. yes, sodium
22. endocrine

23. adenitis
24. pancreatopathy
25. glycogenesis
26. thyromegaly
27. euthyroid
28. removal of an adrenal gland
29. removal of part of the pancreas
30. glandular tumor
31. aid in sex cell development
32. abnormally large thyroid
33. diabetes
34. postprandial blood sugar
35. D
36. T
37. T
38. D
39. D
40. Type II diabetes
41. Gail has to pay attention to food quantities, as well as to the kinds of foods she should avoid.
42. PI
43. PA
44. T

45. PI
46. T
47. T
48. A
49. T
50. A
51. PI
52. T
53. cancer
54. thyroid hormones
55. adenectomy
56. hypophysectomy
57. adrenalectomy
58. thymectomy
59. pancreatectomy
60. thyroidectomy
61. parathyroidectomy
62. thyroidectomy
63. adrenalectomy
64. adenectomy
65. parathyroidectomy
66. hypophysectomy

The Sensory System

After studying this chapter, you will be able to:

▶ Name the parts of the sensory system and discuss the function of each part

▶ Define combining forms used in building words that relate to the sensory system

▶ Name the common diagnoses, clinical procedures, and laboratory tests used in treating disorders of the sensory system

▶ List and define the major pathological conditions of the sensory system

▶ Explain the meaning of surgical terms related to the sensory system

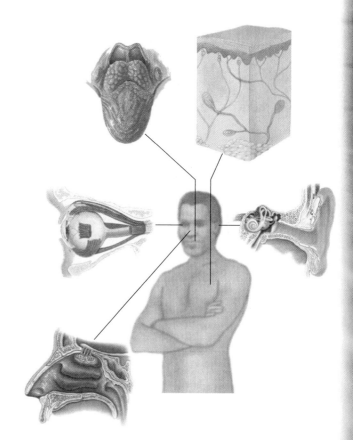

Structure and Function

The **sensory system** includes any organ or part involved in the perceiving and receiving of stimuli from the outside world and from within our bodies. Aristotle, a Greek philosopher who lived more than 2000 years ago, identified the five senses—**sight, touch, hearing, smell,** and **taste.** These senses are popularly thought of as the sensory system even though most of the senses are based on stimulation of nerves in the nervous system.

Figure 16-1a shows the major organs of the sensory system. Figure 16-1b charts the location in the body where stimuli are sensed.

Sensory organs are also known as **sensory receptors.** All sensory receptors contain specialized receptor cells that are able to receive stimuli. They are designed to receive only certain stimuli (such as sound in the ear and light waves in the eye).

Sight—the Eye

The **eyes,** organs of sight, contain about 70 percent of all the receptors in the human body. Each eye is made up of three layers—the sclera, the choroid, and the retinal layer. The parts of the eye are listed in Table 16-1.

> The Howard Hughes Medical Institute (http://www.hhmi.org/senses) has an informational Web site called "Seeing, Hearing, and Smelling the World."

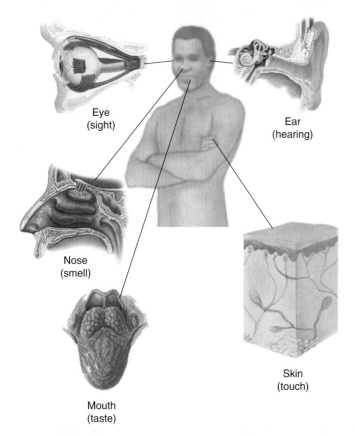

Eye
(sight)

Ear
(hearing)

Nose
(smell)

Skin
(touch)

Mouth
(taste)

Sense		Sensory Organ
Sight	⟶	Eyes
Touch	⟶	Skin
Hearing	⟶	Ears
Smell	⟶	Nose
Taste	⟶	Mouth

FIGURE 16-1a The sensory system includes organs of the five senses.

FIGURE 16-1b The locations where stimuli are sensed.

TABLE 16-1 Parts of the eye.

Eye Part	Description
sclera	thick, tough outer layer
cornea	transparent anterior section where light is first bent in a process called **refraction**
eyelid	outer layer that covers the eye
conjunctiva	mucous membrane that lines the eyelid and the surface of the eye
choroid	membrane in the middle layer of the eye containing blood vessels
ciliary body	membranous section next to the choroid used for focusing
pupil	black circular center of the eye through which light passes
iris	colored part of the eye which contracts and expands in response to light
lens	transparent section behind the iris through which light passes
uvea	section of the eye including the choroid, iris, and ciliary body
retina	part in the interior of the eye that decodes the light waves
neuroretina	layer of the retina containing nervous tissue
rods	sensors of black and white in the neuroretina

TABLE 16-1 Parts of the eye (*cont.*).

Eye Part	Description
cones	sensors of color and bright light in the neuroretina
optic nerve	nerve through which information is transmitted from the neuroretina to the brain
macula lutea	small, yellowish spot at the center of the retina
fovea centralis	depression in the macula lutea; area of sharpest focus
chambers	three cavities of the eye, two of which hold the third holds the *aqueous humor* and the *vitreous humor*, liquids that nourish and support the eye

MORE ABOUT...

Eye Color

Newborns with light skin are almost always born with blue eyes, even though their eyes may later turn brown or green. Eye color is determined by heredity. It takes several months for the melanocytes to be distributed to the anterior portion of the eye. Babies with darker skin normally have a higher concentration of melanocytes to begin with, and their eyes at birth are almost always dark. Albinos are born with no melanocytes in their body and they are, therefore, much more sensitive to light and have no pigment in the iris of their eyes.

Several other structures are important to the eye. The eyelids close to protect the eyes or to allow rest and sleep. The **eyebrows** and **eyelashes** help keep foreign particles from entering the eye. The **lacrimal glands** secrete moisture into the *lacrimal ducts* or *tear ducts*. The resulting **tears** moisten the eyes, wash foreign particles off the eye, and distribute water and nutrients to parts of the eye. Figure 16-2 shows the eye.

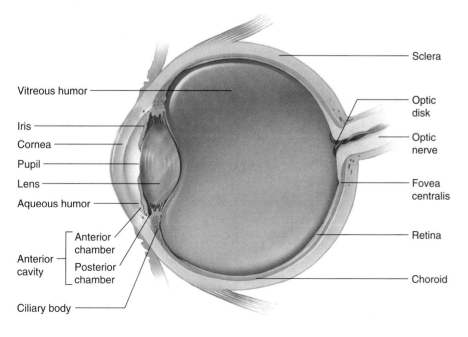

FIGURE 16-2 The eye is the organ of sight.

Ears

Driving down a mountain sometimes causes you to feel and hear a popping sound. The eustachian tubes react quickly to equalize the pressure caused by exposure to a high altitude when the eardrum membrane is stretched. The eardrum "pops" back into place when pressure is equalized.

Dangerous Decibels (http://www.dangerousdecibels.org) is an organization dedicated to the prevention of noise-induced hearing loss.

Hearing and Equilibrium—the Ear

The **ear** (Figure 16-3) is an organ of hearing and **equilibrium** (balance). The three major divisions of the ear are discussed below:

1. The *external ear* begins on the outside of the head with a funnel-like structure called the **auricle** or **pinna.** This structure leads through part of the skull known as the *temporal bone* (which itself has a bony projection called the *mastoid process*) to an S-shaped tube called the *external auditory meatus*. The external auditory meatus contains glands that secrete *cerumen* or earwax, a brownish yellow, waxy substance.

2. The *middle ear* includes the *tympanic cavity*, in which sit the **eardrum (tympanic membrane)** and the **auditory ossicles,** three small, specially shaped bones. The eardrum is an oval, semitransparent membrane with skin on its outer surface and a mucous membrane on the inside. Sound waves change the pressure on the eardrum, which moves back and forth, thereby producing vibrations. The three ossicles are the **malleus** (hammer), **incus** (anvil), and **stapes** (stirrup). The middle ear is connected to the pharynx through the **eustachian tube** (*auditory tube*).

3. The *inner ear* is a system of two tubes—the **osseus labyrinth** and the **membranous labyrinth.** The osseus labyrinth is a bony canal in the temporal bone. The membranous labyrinth is a tube within the osseus labyrinth and separated from it by **perilymph,** a liquid secreted by the walls of the osseus labyrinth. Inside the membranous labyrinth is another fluid, **endolymph.** The labyrinths include three **semicircular canals,** structures important to equilibrium, and a **cochlea,** a snail-shaped structure important to hearing. The cochlea is further divided into the *scala vestibuli*, which leads from the oval window to the apex of the cochlea, and the *scala tympani*. The cochlea has a membrane called the *basilar membrane* that has hairlike receptor cells located in the **organ of Corti** on the membrane's surface. The hairs move back and forth in response to sound waves and eventually send messages via neurotransmitters through the eighth cranial nerve and to the brain for interpretation. Table 16-2 shows various **decibel** (intensity of sound) levels that can be heard by a normal human ear.

TABLE 16-2 Decibel levels.

Decibel Level	Intensity of Sound	Effect on Hearing
40dB	10,000 times as great as 10dB	A whisper—perceptible to most people with normal hearing
60dB	1 million (1,000,000) times as great as 10dB	Regular conversational speech
80dB	100 million (100,000,000) times as great as 10dB	High noise such as in a crowded room or heavy traffic
130dB	10 trillion times as great as 10dB	Extremely loud rock concert; can cause ear damage.
140dB	100 trillion times as great as 10dB	Sound of a jet engine on takeoff. Hearing can be damaged.

MORE ABOUT...

Skin

One of the remarkable advances in genetic engineering is the ability to grow replacement skin. The new skin is grown from cells of skin from various parts of the body and can be used to replace burned or injured areas. If the skin is working once it is put in place, it will continue to grow and function like normal skin—helping to regulate body temperature, preventing foreign material from entering the body, and protecting inner organs from bruises.

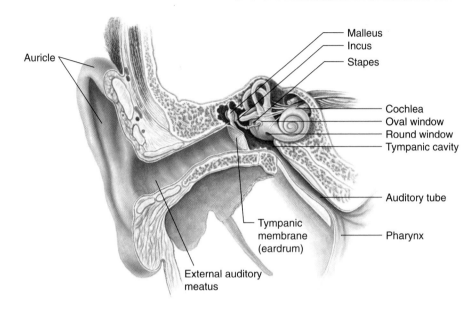

FIGURE 16-3 The ear is the organ of hearing.

The sense of **equilibrium** is the ability to maintain steady balance either when still, *static equilibrium*, or when moving, *dynamic equilibrium*. The bony chamber between the semicircular canals and the cochlea is called the **vestibule.** The vestibule contains a membranous labyrinth divided into two chambers, the *utricle* and *saccule*. Both of these chambers contain a **macula,** a structure with many hairlike sensory receptors that move forward, backward, or upward to move the gelatinous mass inside the inner ear. This mass contains **otoliths,** small calcifications that move to maintain gravitational balance. The semicircular canals also respond to movement and aid in maintaining balance.

Touch, Pain, and Temperature—the Skin

The skin's layers sense different intensities of touch. Light touch is felt in the top layer of skin, whereas touch with harder pressure is felt in the middle or bottom layer. The skin's receptors can sense touch, pressure, pain, and hot and cold temperatures. Chapter 4 discusses the integumentary system, which is incorporated within the skin.

Smell—the Nose

The sense of smell or *olfactory stimulation* is activated by *olfactory receptors* located at the top of the nasal cavity. The receptors are located within the **olfactory organs,** yellowish-brown masses along the top of the nasal cavity.

Taste—the Tongue and Oral Cavity

Taste buds are organs that sense the taste of food. Most taste buds are on the surface of the tongue in small raised structures called **papillae,** but some also line the roof of the mouth and the walls of the pharynx. Each taste bud contains receptor cells, called **taste cells.** Nerve fibers wrapped around the taste cells transmit impulses to the brain.

VOCABULARY REVIEW

In the previous section, you learned terms relating to the sensory system. Before going on to the exercises, read the definitions below. Pronunciations are provided for certain terms.

Term	Meaning
auditory ossicles [ĂW-dĭ-tōr-ē ŎS-ĭ-klz]	Three specially shaped bones in the middle ear that anchor the eardrum to the tympanic cavity and that transmit vibrations to the inner ear.
auricle [ĂW-rĭ-kl]	Funnel-like structure leading from the external ear to the external auditory meatus; also called pinna.
choroid [KŌ-rŏyd]	Thin posterior membrane in the middle layer of the eye.
ciliary [SĬL-ē-ăr-ē] **body**	Thick anterior membrane in the middle layer of the eye.
cochlea [KŌK-lē-ă]	Snail-shaped structure in the inner ear that contains the organ of Corti.
cones [kōnz]	Specialized receptor cells in the retina that perceive color and bright light.
conjunctiva (*pl.,* **conjunctivae**) [kŏn-JŬNK-tĭ-vă (kŏn-JŬNK-tĭ-vē)]	Mucous membrane lining the eyelid.
cornea [KŌR-nē-ă]	Transparent anterior section of the eyeball that bends light in a process called refraction.
decibel [DĔS-ĭ-bĕl]	Measure of the intensity of sound.
ear [ēr]	Organ of hearing.
eardrum [ĒR-drŭm]	Oval, semitransparent membrane that moves in response to sound waves and produces vibrations.
endolymph [ĔN-dō-lĭmf]	Fluid inside the membranous labyrinth.
equilibrium [ē-kwĭ-LĬB-rē-ŭm]	Sense of balance.
eustachian [yū-STĀ-shŭn, yū-STĀ-kē-ăn] **tube**	Tube that connects the middle ear to the pharynx.
eye [ī]	Organ of sight.
eyebrow [Ī-brŏw]	Clump of hair, usually about a half an inch above the eye, that helps to keep foreign particles from entering the eye.

Term	Meaning
eyelashes [Ī-lăsh-ĕz]	Group of hairs protruding from the end of the eyelid; helps to keep foreign particles from entering the eye.
eyelid [Ī-lĭd]	Moveable covering over the eye.
fovea centralis [FŌ-vē-ă sĕn-TRĂL-ĭs]	Depression in the center of the macula lutea; perceives sharpest images.
hearing	Ability to perceive sound.
incus [ĬN-kŭs]	One of the three auditory ossicles; the anvil.
iris [Ī-rĭs]	Colored part of the eye; contains muscles that expand and contract in response to light.
lacrimal [LĂK-rĭ-măl] glands	Glands that secrete liquid to moisten the eyes and produce tears.
lens [lĕnz]	Colorless, flexible transparent body behind the iris.
macula [MĂK-yū-lă]	Inner ear structure containing hairlike sensors that move to maintain equilibrium.
macula lutea [lū-TĒ-ă]	Small, yellowish area located in the center of the retina, which has a depression called the fovea centralis.
malleus [MĂL-ē-ŭs]	One of the three auditory ossicles; the hammer.
membranous labyrinth [LĂB-ĭ-rĭnth]	One of the two tubes that make up the semicircular canals.
neuroretina [nūr-ō-RĔT-ĭ-nă]	Thick layer of nervous tissue in the retina.
olfactory [ōl-FĂK-tō-rē] organs	Organs at the top of the nasal cavity containing olfactory receptors.
optic nerve	Nerve that transmits nerve impulses from the eye to the brain.
organ of Corti [KŌR-tī]	Structure on the basilar membrane with hairlike receptors that receive and transmit sound waves.
osseus [ŎS-sē-ŭs] labyrinth	One of the two tubes that make up the semicircular canals.
otoliths [Ō-tō-lĭths]	Small calcifications in the inner ear that help to maintain balance.
papillae [pă-PĬL-ē]	Small, raised structures that contain the taste buds.
perilymph [PĔR-ĭ-lĭmf]	Liquid secreted by the walls of the osseus labyrinth.
pinna [PĬN-ă]	Auricle.
pupil [PYŪ-pĭl]	Black circular center of the eye; opens and closes when muscles in the iris expand and contract in response to light.
refraction [rē-FRĂK-shŭn]	Process of bending light rays.

Term	Meaning
retina [RĔT-ĭ-nă]	Oval, light-sensitive membrane in the interior layer of the eye; decodes light waves and transmits information to the brain.
rods [rŏdz]	Specialized receptor cells in the retina that perceive black to white shades.
sclera (*pl.*, **sclerae**) [SKLĒR-ă (SKLĒR-ē)]	Thick, tough membrane in the outer eye layer; supports eyeball structure.
semicircular canals	Structures in the inner ear important to equilibrium.
sensory receptors	Specialized tissue containing cells that can receive stimuli.
sensory system	Organs or tissue that perceive and receive stimuli from outside or within the body.
sight	Ability to see.
smell	Ability to perceive odors.
stapes (*pl.*, **stapes, stapedes**) [STĀ-pēz (STĀ-pĕ-dēz)]	One of the three auditory ossicles; the stirrup.
taste	Ability to perceive the qualities of ingested matter.
taste buds	Organs that sense the taste of food.
taste cells	Specialized receptor cells within the taste buds.
tears [tērz]	Moisture secreted from the lacrimal glands.
touch	Ability to perceive sensation on the skin.
tympanic [tĭm-PĂN-ĭk] **membrane**	Eardrum.
uvea [YŪ-vē-ă]	Region of the eye containing the iris, choroid membrane, and ciliary bodies.
vestibule [VĔS-tĭ-būl]	Bony chamber between the semicircular canals and the cochlea.

CASE STUDY

Checking Symptoms

John James, a 67-year-old male, presented at his family doctor's office very nervous and upset. His general health is excellent and, although he was widowed one year ago, he is proud of the way he has maintained his independence. His only complaint is diminished vision. He says his night vision is so bad that he has given up night driving. His family doctor gives him a general physical including laboratory tests. All of the test results prove normal. Mr. James is then referred to an ophthalmologist (eye specialist).

Critical Thinking

1. In addition to the general physical, why did the family doctor refer Mr. James to an ophthalmologist?
2. Why is a general physical necessary?

Find a Match

Match the terms in the left-hand column with the definitions in the right-hand column.

3. ____ iris
4. ____ sclera
5. ____ pupil
6. ____ optic disc
7. ____ eustachian
8. ____ incus
9. ____ malleus
10. ____ stapes
11. ____ tympanic membrane
12. ____ auricle
13. ____ cerumen

a. tough, white, outer coating of eyeball
b. dark opening of the eye, surrounded by the iris
c. earwax
d. hammer
e. eardrum
f. anvil
g. stirrup
h. auditory tube
i. pinna
j. blind spot of the eye
k. colored portion of the eye

Check Your Knowledge

Circle T for true or F for false.

14. The aqueous humor is a thick, gelatinous substance. T F
15. The sharpest images are perceived in the optic disk. T F
16. Cones are receptor cells that sense color. T F
17. Olfactory receptors perceive light rays. T F
18. Semicircular canals in the ears are important to equilibrium. T F
19. Refraction is the focusing on distant objects. T F
20. The papillae house the taste buds. T F

Combining Forms

The list below includes combining forms that relate specifically to the sensory system. Pronunciations are provided for the examples.

COMBINING FORM	MEANING	EXAMPLE
audi(o), audit(o)	hearing	*audiometer* [ăw-dē-ŎM-ĕ-tĕr], instrument for measuring hearing
aur(o), auricul(o)	hearing	*auriculocranial* [ăw-RĬK-yū-lō-KRĀ-nē-ăl], pertaining to the auricle of the ear and the cranium
blephar(o)	eyelid	*blepharitis* [blĕf-ă-RĪ-tĭs], inflammation of the eyelid

Combining Form	Meaning	Example
cerumin(o)	wax	*ceruminolytic* [sĕ-rū-mĭ-nō-LĬT-ĭk], agent for softening earwax
cochle(o)	cochlea	*cochleovestibular* [kōk-lē-ō-vĕs-TĬB-yū-lăr], pertaining to the cochlea and the vestibule of the ear
conjunctiv(o)	conjunctiva	*conjunctivoplasty* [kŏn-JŬNK-tĭ-vō-plăs-tē], plastic surgery on the conjunctiva
cor(o), core(o)	pupil	*coreoplasty* [KŌR-ē-ō-plăs-tē], surgical correction of the size and shape of a pupil
corne(o)	cornea	*corneoscleral* [kōr-nē-ō-SKLĔR-ăl], pertaining to the cornea and sclera
cycl(o)	ciliary body	*cyclodialysis* [sī-klō-dī-ĂL-ĭ-sĭs], method of relieving intraocular pressure in glaucoma
dacry(o)	tears	*dacryolith* [DĂK-rē-ō-lĭth], calculus in the tear duct
ir(o), irid(o)	iris	*iridoptosis* [ĭr-ĭ-dŏp-TŌ-sĭs], prolapse of the iris
kerat(o)	cornea	*keratoconus* [kĕr-ă-tō-KŌ-nŭs], abnormal protrusion of the cornea
lacrim(o)	tears	*lacrimotomy* [LĂK-rĭ-mŏ-tō-mē], incision into the lacrimal duct
mastoid(o)	mastoid process	*mastoiditis* [măs-tŏy-DĪ-tĭs], inflammation of the mastoid process
myring(o)	eardrum, middle ear	*myringitis* [mĭr-ĭn-JĪ-tĭs], inflammation of the tympanic membrane
nas(o)	nose	*nasosinusitis* [nās-zō-sī-nŭ-SĪ-tĭs], inflammation of the nasal and sinus cavities
ocul(o)	eye	*oculodynia* [ŏk-yū-lō-DĬN-ē-ă], pain in the eyeball
ophthalm(o)	eye	*ophthalmoscope* [ŏf-THĂL-mō-skōp], instrument for studying the interior of the eyeball
opt(o), optic(o)	eye	*optometer* [ŏp-TŎM-ĕ-tĕr], instrument for determining eye refraction
ossicul(o)	ossicle	*ossiculectomy* [ōt-ĭ-kyū-LĔK-tō-mē], removal of one of the ossicles of the middle ear
ot(o)	ear	*otitis* [ō-TĪ-tĭs] inflammation of the ear
phac(o), phak(o)	lens	*phacoma* [fā-KŌ-mă], tumor of the lens

COMBINING FORM	MEANING	EXAMPLE
pupill(o)	pupil	*pupillometer* [pyū-pǐ-LŎM-ě-těr], instrument for measuring the diameter of the pupil
retin(o)	retina	*retinitis* [rět-ǐ-NĪ-tǐs], inflammation of the retina
scler(o)	white of the eye	*sclerectasia* [sklěr-ěk-TĀ-zhē-ǎ], bulging of the sclera
scot(o)	darkness	*scotometer* [skō-TŎM-ě-těr], instrument for evaluating a scotoma or blind spot
tympan(o)	eardrum, middle ear	*tympanoplasty* [tǐm-pǎ-nō-PLĂS-tē], repair of a damaged middle ear
uve(o)	uvea	*uveitis* [yū-vē-Ī-tǐs], inflammation of the uvea

CASE STUDY

Seeing a Specialist

Mr. James was next referred to an ophthalmologist who discovered that Mr. James had a cataract in his right eye that should be removed. He also had one in the left eye that did not need treatment at this time. During surgery, an intraocular lens implant was placed in the right eye. After surgery, the ophthalmologist prescribed eyeglasses. The prescription form is used to instruct the optometrist or optician as to what corrective powers are necessary.

Critical Thinking

21. Through which eye can Mr. James see distant objects more clearly?
22. Did Mr. James need a corrective lens for his left eye?

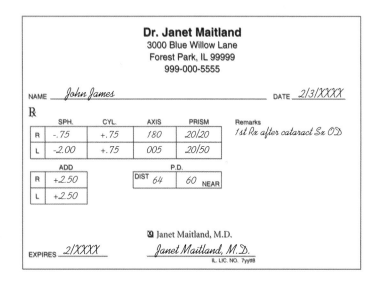

COMBINING FORMS EXERCISES

Find the Roots

From the following list of combining forms and from the list of suffixes in Chapter 2, write the word that matches the definition.

audi(o)   blephar(o)   core(o)   dacryocyst(o)   irid(o)   kerat(o)   opt(o)   ot(o)   retin(o)   scler(o)

23. _____ inflammation of the ear

24. _____ instrument for determining eye refraction

25. _____ study of the ear

26. _____ inflammation of the cornea

27. _____ instrument to examine
the cornea

28. _____ disease of the iris

29. _____ pain in the tear sac

30. _____ repair of the pupil

31. _____ softening of the sclera

32. _____ inflammation of the sclera
and cornea

33. _____ swelling in the eyelid

34. _____ pertaining to the retina

35. _____ paralysis of the iris

36. _____ earache

37. _____ study of hearing (disorders)

38. _____ inflammation of the eyelid

39. _____ hemorrhage from the ear

40. _____ instrument to measure hearing

Diagnostic, Procedural, and Laboratory Terms

Diagnosis of the sensory system usually includes testing of the sense in question and examination of the sensory structures. Loss of a sense can cause serious problems for an individual. In some cases, senses can be partially or totally restored through the use of prosthetic devices, transplants, or medication. In other cases, patients must adapt to the loss of a sense.

Diagnosing the Eye

An **ophthalmologist** (medical doctor who specializes in treatment and surgeries of the eye) and an **optometrist** (a trained nonmedical specialist who can examine patients for vision problems and prescribe lenses) both perform routine eye examinations. The most common diagnostic test of the eye is the visual acuity test, which measures the ability to see objects clearly at measured distances. The most common chart is the *Snellen Chart*. Perfect vision measures 20/20 on such a test. The first number, 20, is the distance (typically 20 feet) from which the person being tested reads a chart with black letters of different size. The second number is the distance from which the person being tested can read the size of the letters in relation to someone with normal vision.

The next step in a routine eye examination is to examine peripheral vision, the area one is able to see to the side with the eyes looking straight ahead. Depending on the patient's age, most routine eye examinations also include **tonometry,** a measurement of pressure within the eye (a test for glaucoma) and **ophthalmoscopy** (visual examination of the interior of the eye). If the patient needs corrective lenses, an **optician** (trained technician who makes and fits corrective lenses) can fill the prescription written by an ophthalmologist or an optometrist. A prescription includes the **diopter,** the unit of refracting power needed in a lens.

Diagnosing the Ear

Hearing tests are routinely given to young children to see if they have any hearing deficit. Later, hearing is checked when a person notices hearing loss or when that person's friends and family suspect it. An **otologist** is an ear specialist, and

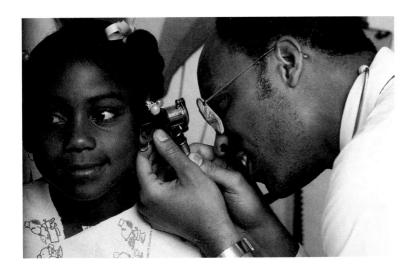

an **audiologist** is a nonmedical hearing specialist. **Otorhinolaryngologists** are specialists who practice *otorhinolaryngology*, the medical specialty covering the ear, nose, and throat. They all perform thorough examinations that include **otoscopy**, visual examination of the ear using an *otoscope*, a lighted viewing device (Figure 16-4). Such an examination might also include **audiometry**, the measurement of various acoustic frequencies to determine what frequencies the patient can or cannot hear. The device used is an *audiometer*, and the results of the test are plotted on a graph, an **audiogram.**

Diagnosing Other Senses

The nose is usually observed as part of a general examination or, more specifically, a respiratory examination. Loss of the sense of smell is often the result of a disease process or of aging. The tongue and other parts of the mouth and the skin are also observed during a general examination. Loss of taste or touch may also be part of a disease process or of aging.

VOCABULARY REVIEW

In the previous section, you learned diagnostic, procedural, and laboratory terms. Before going on to the exercises, read the definitions below. Pronunciations are provided for certain terms.

Term	Meaning
audiogram [ĂW-dē-ō-grăm]	Graph that plots the acoustic frequencies being tested.
audiologist [ăw-dē-ŎL-ō-jĭst]	Specialist in evaluating hearing function.
audiometry [ăw-dē-ŎM-ĕ-trē]	Measurement of acoustic frequencies using an audiometer.
diopter [dī-ŎP-tĕr]	Unit of refracting power of a lens.
ophthalmologist [ŏf-thăl-MŎL-ō-jĭst]	Medical specialist who diagnoses and treats eye disorders.
ophthalmoscopy [ŏf-thăl-MŎS-kō-pē]	Visual examination of the interior of the eye.

Term	Meaning
optician [ŏp-TĬSH-ŭn]	Technician who makes and fits corrective lenses.
optometrist [ŏp-TŎM-ĕ-trĭst]	Nonmedical specialist who examines the eyes and prescribes lenses.
otologist [ō-TŎL-ō-jĭst]	Medical specialist in ear disorders.
otorhinolaryngologist [ō-tō-rī-nō-lăr-ĭng-GŎL-ō-jĭst]	Medical specialist who treats ear, nose, and throat disorders.
otoscopy [ō-TŎS-kō-pē]	Inspection of the ear using an otoscope.
tonometry [tō-NŎM-ĕ-trē]	Measurement of tension or pressure within the eye.

CASE STUDY

Another Problem Arises

Mr. James returned to the ophthalmologist in four months complaining of cloudy vision in his left eye. The ophthalmologist determined that it was time to remove the cataract in the left eye and replace it with an artificial lens or IOL. After a few weeks, Mr. James had regained night vision, even proclaiming that he could see better now than he had years before. His eyeglass prescription was changed. He only really needed his glasses for reading. The ophthalmologist also recommended sunglasses for most outdoor daytime activities, because ultraviolet rays can harm the eyes.

Critical Thinking

41. An artificial lens replaces what part of the eye?

42. Does a lens implant change eye color?

DIAGNOSTIC, PROCEDURAL, AND LABORATORY TERMS EXERCISES

Know Your Senses

For each of the following diagnostic tests or devices, write A for eye, B for ear, or C for both eye and ear.

43. audiogram _____

44. otoscope _____

45. diopter _____

46. visual acuity _____

47. audiometer _____

48. Snellen chart _____

49. tonometer _____

50. ophthalmoscope _____

Pathological Terms

Lost or damaged senses are illnesses in themselves. The disruption of losing or damaging a sense organ can lead to related illnesses. Much of the pathology of the sensory system results from age-related disorders or just age-related wear and tear on the sensory organs.

Eye Disorders

The most common eye disorders involve defects in the curvature of the cornea and/or lens or defects in the refractive ability of the eye due to an abnormally short or long eyeball. Such disorders are usually managed with corrective lenses. Corrective lenses may be placed in frames to be worn on the face or may be in the form of **contact lenses,** which are placed directly over the cornea of the eye centered on the pupil. An eye examination may reveal a number of conditions. Table 16-3 describes eye conditions.

There are a number of organizations dedicated to fighting blindness or providing services for the blind. Prevent Blindness (www.preventblindness.org) is one example.

TABLE 16-3 Eye conditions.

Condition	Description
astigmatism (Figure 16-5)	distortion of sight
hyperopia (farsightedness) (Figure 16-6)	focusing of light rays behind the retina
myopia (nearsigtedness) (Figure 16-6)	focusing of light in front of the retina
presbyopia	loss of close reading vision
strabismus	eye misalignment (sometimes called "cross-eyed")
esotropia	deviation of one eye inward
exotropia	deviation of one eye outward
asthenopia or **eyestrain**	eyes tire easily
diplopia	double vision
photophobia	extreme sensitivity to light
cataracts (Figure 16-7)	cloudiness of the lens of the eye
aphakia	absence of a lens as when removed in a cataract operation
pseudophakia	implanted lens
scotoma	blind spot in vision
glaucoma (Figure 16-8)	increased intraocular pressure; can lead to **blindness,** loss of vision
macular degeneration (Figure 16-9)	breakdown of macular tissue leading to loss of central vision
retinitis pigmentosa	scarring on the retina caused by a hereditary disorder
nyctalopia	night blindness
exophthalmus, exophthalmos	protruding eyeballs usually caused by hyperthyroidism.
lacrimation or **epiphora**	excessive tearing
nystagmus	excessive eyeball movement
blepharitis	inflammation of the eyelid
blepharospasm	involuntary eyelid movement
blepharoptosis	drooping of the eyelid.
conjunctivitis or **pinkeye**	inflammation of the conjunctiva
hordeolum or **sty**	infection of a sebaceous gland in the eyelid

TABLE 16-3 Eye conditions (*cont.*).

Condition	Description
iritis	inflammation of the iris
keratitis	inflammation of the cornea
retinitis	inflammation of the retina
scleritis	inflammation of the sclera
dacryoadenitis	inflammation of a lacrimal gland
dacryocystitis	inflammation of a tear duct

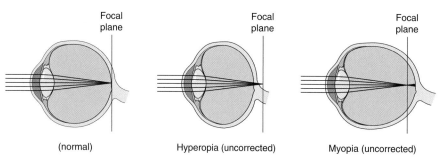

Astigmatism   Correction

FIGURE 16-5   An astigmatism distorts light rays.

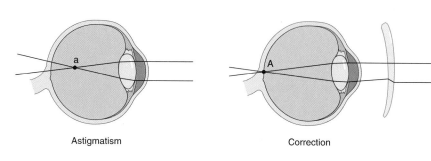

(normal)   Hyperopia (uncorrected)   Myopia (uncorrected)

FIGURE 16-6   Hyperopia and myopia are errors of refraction.

FIGURE 16-7   The blurry image of two children holding balls is seen through the eye of a patient with cataracts.

FIGURE 16-8   The same image as in Figure 16-8 seen through the eyes of someone with glaucoma.

FIGURE 16-9   The same image as in Figure 16-8 seen through the eyes of a patient with macular degeneration.

The Deafness Research Foundation (www.drf.org) provides research grants and disseminates information about deafness.

Ear Disorders

The sense of hearing can be diminished or lost in a number of situations. Hearing problems may result from aging, disease, injury, or birth defect. Table 16-4 describes conditions related to the ear.

TABLE 16-4 Ear conditions.

Condition	Description
anacusis	absence of hearing
paracusis	impaired hearing
deafness	partial or total hearing loss
presbyacusis	age-related hearing loss
otosclerosis	hardening of bone within the ear
tinnitus	constant ringing or buzzing in the ear
otalgia	ear pain; earache
otorrhagia	bleeding in the ear
otorrhea	pus draining from the ear
otitis media	inflammation of the middle ear
otitis externa	fungal infection of the external ear canal
labyrinthitis	inflammation of the labyrinth
myringitis or tympanitis	inflammation of the eardrum
mastoiditis	inflammation of the mastoid process
aerotitis media	inflammation of the middle ear resulting from changes in atmospheric pressure
cholesteatoma	fatty cyst in the middle ear
Meniere's disease	elevated fluid pressure causing **vertigo** (dizziness)

VOCABULARY REVIEW

In the previous section, you learned terms relating to pathology. Before going on to the exercises, read the definitions below. Pronunciations are provided for certain terms.

TERM	MEANING
aerotitis media [ār-ō-TĪ-tĭs MĒ-dē-ă]	Inflammation of the middle ear caused by air pressure changes, as in air travel.
anacusis [ăn-ă-KŪ-sĭs]	Lack of hearing.
aphakia [ă-FĀ-kē-ă]	Absence of a lens.
asthenopia [ăs-thĕ-NŌ-pē-ă]	Weakness of the ocular or ciliary muscles that causes the eyes to tire easily.
astigmatism [ă-STĬG-mă-tĭzm]	Distortion of sight because of lack of focus of light rays at one point on the retina.

Term	Meaning
blepharitis [blĕf-ă-RĪ-tĭs]	Inflammation of the eyelid.
blepharoptosis [blĕf-ă-RŎP-tō-sĭs]	Drooping of the eyelid.
blepharospasm [BLĔF-ă-rō-spăzm]	Involuntary eyelid movement; excessive blinking.
blindness	Loss or absence of vision.
cataract [CĂT-ă-răkt]	Cloudiness of the lens of the eye.
cholesteatoma [kō-lĕs-tē-ă-TŌ-mă]	Fatty cyst within the middle ear.
conjunctivitis [kŏn-jŭnk-tĭ-VĪ-tĭs]	Inflammation of the conjunctiva of the eyelid.
contact lenses	Corrective lenses worn on the surface of the eye.
dacryoadenitis [DĂK-rē-ō-ăd-ĕ-NĪ-tĭs]	Inflammation of the lacrimal glands.
dacryocystitis [DĂK-rē-ō-sĭs-TĪ-tĭs]	Inflammation of a tear duct.
deafness	Loss or absence of hearing.
diplopia [dĭ-PLŌ-pē-ă]	Double vision.
epiphora [ĕ-PĬF-ō-ră]	Excessive tearing.
esotropia [ĕs-ō-TRŌ-pē-ă]	Deviation of one eye inward.
exophthalmos, exophthalmus [ĕk-sŏf-THĂL-mōs]	Abnormal protrusion of the eyeballs.
exotropia [ĕk-sō-TRŌ-pē-ă]	Deviation of one eye outward.
eyestrain	Asthenopia.
farsightedness	Hyperopia.
glaucoma [glăw-KŌ-mă]	Any of various diseases caused by abnormally high eye pressure.
hordeolum [hōr-DĒ-ō-lŭm]	Infection of a sebaceous gland of the eyelid; sty.
hyperopia [hī-pĕr-Ō-pē-ă]	Focusing behind the retina causing vision distortion; farsightedness.
iritis [ī-RĪ-tĭs]	Inflammation of the iris.
keratitis [kĕr-ă-TĪ-tĭs]	Inflammation of the cornea.
labyrinthitis [LĂB-ĭ-rĭn-THĪ-tĭs]	Inflammation of the labyrinth.
lacrimation [lăk-rĭ-MĀ-shŭn]	Secretion of tears, usually excessively.
macular [MĂK-yū-lăr] **degeneration**	Gradual loss of vision caused by degeneration of tissue in the macula.
mastoiditis [măs-tŏy-DĪ-tĭs]	Inflammation of the mastoid process.
Meniere's disease [mĕn-YĒRZ]	Elevated pressure within the cochlea.

TERM	MEANING
myopia [mī-Ō-pē-ă]	Focusing in front of the retina causing vision distortion; nearsightedness.
myringitis [mĭr-ĭn-JĪ-tĭs]	Inflammation of the eardrum.
nearsightedness	Myopia.
nyctalopia [nĭk-tă-LŌ-pē-ă]	Night blindness.
nystagmus [nĭs-STĂG-mŭs]	Excessive involuntary eyeball movement.
otalgia [ō-TĂL-jē-ă]	Pain in the ear.
otitis externa [ō-TĪ-tĭs ĕks-TĔR-nă]	Fungal infection of the external ear canal.
otitis media [MĒ-dē-ă]	Inflammation of the middle ear.
otorrhagia [ō-tō-RĀ-jē-ă]	Bleeding from the ear.
otorrhea [ō-tō-RĒ-ă]	Purulent discharge from the ear.
otosclerosis [ō-tō-sklĕ-RŌ-sĭs]	Hardening of bones of the ear.
paracusis [PĂR-ă-KŪ-sĭs]	Impaired hearing.
photophobia [fō-tō-FŌ-bē-ă]	Extreme sensitivity to light.
pinkeye	Conjunctivitis.
presbyacusis [prĕz-bē-ă-KŪ-sĭs]	Age-related hearing loss.
presbyopia [prĕz-bē-Ō-pē-ă]	Age-related diminished ability to focus or accommodate.
pseudophakia [sū-dō-FĀ-kē-ă]	Eye with an implanted lens after cataract surgery.
retinitis [rĕt-ĭ-NĪ-tĭs]	Inflammation of the retina.
retinitis pigmentosa [pĭg-mĕn-TŌ-să]	Progressive, inherited disease with a pigmented spot on the retina and poor night vision.
scleritis [sklĕ-RĪ-tĭs]	Inflammation of the sclera.
scotoma [skō-TŌ-mă]	Blind spot in vision.
strabismus [stră-BĬZ-mŭs]	Eye misalignment.
sty, stye [stī]	Hordeolum.
tinnitus [tĭ-NĪ-tŭs, TĬ-nĭ-tŭs]	Constant ringing or buzzing in the ear.
tympanitis [tĭm-pă-NĪ-tĭs]	Inflammation of the eardrum.
vertigo [VĔR-tĭ-gō, vĕr-TĪ-gō]	Dizziness.

Getting Treatment

After his 69th birthday, Mr. James noticed that his hearing had seriously diminished in the last year. His physician referred him to a specialist. It was found that Mr. James had a buildup of wax in his ear. After treatment, his hearing improved slightly, but not enough for Mr. James to feel comfortable.

Critical Thinking

51. What other condition might explain this patient's hearing loss?
52. What type of specialist should Mr. James be referred to?

PATHOLOGICAL TERMS EXERCISES

Sense the Diseases

For each of the diseases listed below, write A for eye, B for ear, or C for nose to indicate the organ associated with that disease.

53. conjunctivitis _____

54. cataract _____

55. nyctalopia _____

56. aerotitis media _____

57. presbyopia _____

58. allergic rhinitis _____

59. scotoma _____

60. nasosinusitis _____

61. Meniere's disease _____

Check Your Knowledge

Circle T for true or F for false.

62. A hordeolum is a sty. T F

63. The focusing of light rays behind the retina is myopia. T F

64. Myringitis is an inflammation of the tympanic membrane. T F

65. Labyrinthitis occurs in the labyrinth of the eye. T F

Surgical Terms

Some of the sense organs require surgery at various times. Some surgeries performed on parts of the sensory system are to enhance beauty, as in a "nose job" to change the shape of one's nose. Others may involve removal of a part that has become cancerous. Table 16-5 lists some of the common surgeries of the sensory system.

TABLE 16-5 Surgeries of the sensory system.

Surgery	Purpose
keratoplasty	corneal transplant to restore or give sight
blepharoplasty	eyelid repair
otoplasty	repair of the outer ear
tympanoplasty	eardrum repair
cataract extraction	to remove a cloudy lens, usually followed by an *intraocular lens (IOL) implant*
phacoemulsification	breaking up and removal of cataracts using ultrasound
dacryocystectomy	removal of a lacrimal sac
enucleation	removal of an eyeball
iridectomy	removal of part of the iris
stapedectomy	removal of the stapes to correct otosclerosis
myringotomy	insertion of a small tube to help drain fluid, used for children or infants with recurring ear infections

VOCABULARY REVIEW

In the previous section, you learned terms relating to surgery. Before going on to the exercises, read the definitions below. Pronunciations are provided for certain terms.

Term	Meaning
blepharoplasty [BLĔF-ă-rō-plăst-ē]	Surgical repair of the eyelid.
dacryocystectomy [dăk-rē-ō-sĭs-TĔK-tō-mē] removal	Removal of a lacrimal sac.
enucleation [ē-nū-klē-Ā-shŭn]	Removal of an eyeball.
iridectomy [ĭr-ĭ-DĔK-tō-mē]	Removal of part of the iris.
keratoplasty [KĔR-ă-tō-plăs-tē]	Corneal transplant.
myringotomy [mĭr-ĭng-GŎT-ō-mē]	Insertion of a small tube to help drain fluid from the ears (particularly of children).
otoplasty [Ō-tō-plăs-tē]	Surgical repair of the outer ear.
phacoemulsification [FĀ-kō-ē-mŭls-ĭ-fĭ-KĀ-shŭn]	Use of ultrasound to break up and remove cataracts.
stapedectomy [stā-pĕ-DĔK-tō-mē]	Removal of the stapes to correct otosclerosis.

Term	Meaning
tympanoplasty [TĬM-pă-nō-plăs-tē]	Repair of an eardrum.

CASE STUDY

Getting Help

Mr. James's great grandson came for a few days' visit with his mother. The two-year-old had had fairly frequent ear infections, but they seemed to have subsided for a month or two, so his mother decided to risk the overnight stay. The boy woke up screaming and clutching his ear. A local 24-hour clinic diagnosed severe otitis media and prescribed medication. When the boy returned home, his pediatrician wrote the note below in his medical record.

Critical Thinking

66. Is the child's otitis media infectious for Mr. James?

67. Why did the doctor suggest a myringotomy?

Patient name _Everett James_	Age _2_	Current Diagnosis _____

DATE/TIME	
3/3/XXXX	Notes: Frequent otitis media (7 times in the last 11 months). Suggest
	myringotomy. (Note: schedule during mother's work vacation 5/4–5/11.)
	J. Redpine, M.D.

SURGICAL TERMS EXERCISES

Check Your Knowledge

68. A patient sustaining a third-degree burn to the pinna would likely require _____.

69. A stapedectomy would be performed to correct _____.

70. Otoplasty can correct a deformed _____.

71. A corneal _____ may restore sight.

72. A child with chronic otitis media may need a _____.

Terminology in Action

This prescription is for eyeglasses for a 55-year-old woman. What condition or conditions are being corrected?

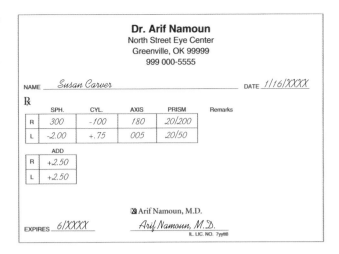

Using the Internet

Go to the site of the American Society of Cataract and Refractive Surgery (http://www.ascrs.org). Write a brief description of any discussion of cataracts, including what type of surgery is available.

CHAPTER REVIEW

The material that follows is to help you review all the material in this chapter.

DEFINITIONS

Define the following terms and combining forms. Review the chapter before starting. Make sure you know how to pronounce each term as you define it. The blue words in curly brackets are references to the Spanish glossary on the Web site.

WORD	DEFINITION
aerotitis media [ār-ō-TĪ-tĭs MĒ-dē-ă]	
anacusis [ăn-ă-KŪ-sĭs] {anacusia}	
aphakia [ă-FĀ-kē-ă] {afaquia}	
asthenopia [ăs-thĕ-NŌ-pē-ă] {astenopía}	
astigmatism [ă-STĬG-mă-tĭzm] {astimagtismo}	
audi(o), audit(o)	
audiogram [ĂW-dē-ō-grăm] {audiograma}	
audiologist [ăw-dē-ŎL-ō-jĭst] {audiólogo}	
audiometry [ăw-dē-ŎM-ĕ-trē] {audiometría}	
auditory ossicles [ĂW-dĭ-tōr-ē ŎS-ĭ-klz]	
aur(o), auricul(o)	
auricle [ĂW-rĭ-kl] {auricula}	
blephar(o)	
blepharitis [blĕf-ă-RĪ-tĭs] {blefaritis}	
blepharoplasty [BLĔF-ă-rō-plăst-ē]	
blepharoptosis [blĕf-ă-RŎP-tō-sĭs]	
blepharospasm [BLĔF-ă-rō-spăzm]	
blindness {ceguera}	
cataract [CĂT-ă-răkt] {catarata}	
cerumin(o)	
cholesteatoma [kō-lĕs-tē-ă-TŌ-mă]	
choroid [KŌ-rŏyd] {coroides}	

Word	Definition
ciliary [SĬL-ē-ăr-ē] body	
cochle(o)	
cochlea [KŌK-lē-ă] {caracol}	
cones [kōnz] {conos}	
conjunctiv(o)	
conjunctiva (*pl.*, conjunctivae) [kŏn-JŬNK-tĭ-vă (-vē)] {conjuntiva}	
conjunctivitis [kŏn-jŭnk-tĭ-VĪ-tĭs] {conjuntivitis}	
contact lenses	
cor(o), core(o)	
corne(o)	
cornea [KŌR-nē-ă] {cornea}	
cycl(o)	
dacry(o)	
dacryoadenitis [DĂK-rē-ō-ăd-ĕ-NĪ-tĭs]	
dacryocystectomy [dăk-rē-ō-sĭs-TĔK-tō-mē]	
dacryocystitis [DĂK-rē-ō-sĭs-TĪ-tĭs]	
deafness {sordera}	
decibel [DĔS-ĭ-bĕl] {decibel}	
diopter [dī-ŎP-tĕr]	
diplopia [dĭ-PLŌ-pē-ă] {diplopía}	
ear [ēr] {oreja, oído}	
eardrum [ĒR-drŭm] {tambor de oído}	
endolymph [ĔN-dō-lĭmf] {endolinfa}	
enucleation [ē-nū-klē-Ā-shŭn] {enucleación}	
epiphora [ĕ-PĬF-ō-ră] {epífora}	
equilibrium [ē-kwĭ-LĬB-rē-ŭm] {equilibrio}	
esotropia [ĕs-ō-TRŌ-pē-ă] {esotropía}	
eustachian [yū-STĀ-shŭn, yū-STĀ-kē-ăn] tube	
exophthalmos, exophthalmus [ĕk-sŏf-THĂL-mōs]	
exotropia [ĕk-sō-TRŌ-pē-ă]	

WORD	DEFINITION

eye [ī] {ojo} _____

eyebrow [Ī-brŏw] {ceja} _____

eyelashes [Ī-lăsh-ĕz] {pestañas} _____

eyelid [Ī-lĭd] {párpado} _____

eyestrain {vista fatigada} _____

farsightedness {hiperopía} _____

fovea centralis [FŌ-vē-ă sĕn-TRĂL-ĭs] _____

glaucoma [glăw-KŌ-mă] {glaucoma} _____

hearing {audición} _____

hordeolum [hōr-DĒ-ō-lŭm] {orzuelo} _____

hyperopia [hī-pĕr-Ō-pē-ă] _____

incus [ĬN-kŭs] {incus} _____

ir(o), irid(o) _____

iridectomy [ĭr-ĭ-DĔK-tō-mē] {iridectomía} _____

iris [Ī-rĭs] {iris} _____

iritis [ī-RĪ-tĭs] {iritis} _____

kerat(o) _____

keratitis [kĕr-ă-TĪ-tĭs] {queratitis} _____

keratoplasty [KĔR-ă-tō-plăs-tē] {queratoplastia} _____

labyrinthitis [LĂB-ĭ-rĭn-THĪ-tĭs] {laberintitis} _____

lacrim(o) _____

lacrimal [LĂK-rĭ-măl] glands _____

lacrimation [lăk-rĭ-MĀ-shŭn] {lagrimeo} _____

lens [lĕnz] {lens, lente} _____

macula [MĂK-yū-lă] {macula} _____

macula lutea [lū-TĒ-ă] _____

macular [MĂK-yū-lăr] degeneration _____

malleus [MĂL-ē-ŭs] {malleus} _____

mastoid(o) _____

mastoiditis [măs-tŏy-DĪ-tĭs] _____

membranous labyrinth [LĂB-ĭ-rĭnth] _____

Meniere's [mĕn-YĒRZ] disease _____

WORD	DEFINITION
myopia [mī-Ō-pē-ă] {miopía}	_____
myring(o)	_____
myringitis [mĭr-ĭn-JĪ-tĭs] {miringitis}	_____
myringotomy [mĭr-ĭng-GŎT-ŏ-mē]	_____
nas(o)	_____
nearsightedness {miopía}	_____
neuroretina [nūr-ō-RĔT-ĭ-nă]	_____
nyctalopia [nĭk-tă-LŌ-pē-ă] {nictalopía}	_____
nystagmus [nĭs-STĂG-mŭs] {nistagmo}	_____
ocul(o)	_____
olfactory [ōl-FĂK-tō-rē] organs	_____
ophthalm(o)	_____
ophthalmologist [ŏf-thăl-MŎL-ō-jĭst] {oftalmólogo}	_____
ophthalmoscopy [ŏf-thăl-MŎS-kō-pē] {oftalmoscopia}	_____
opt(o), optic(o)	_____
optician [ŏp-TĬSH-ŭn]	_____
optic nerve	_____
optometrist [ŏp-TŎM-ĕ-trĭst] {optometrista}	_____
organ of Corti [KŌR-tĭ]	_____
osseus [ŎS-sē-ŭs] labyrinth	_____
ossicul(o)	_____
ot(o)	_____
otalgia [ō-TĂL-jē-ă] {otalgia}	_____
otitis externa [ō-TĪ-tĭs ĕks-TĔR-nă] {otitis externa}	_____
otitis media [MĒ-dē-ă] {otitis media}	_____
otoliths [Ō-tō-lĭths] {otolitos}	_____
otologist [ō-TŎL-ō-jĭst] {otólogo}	_____
otoplasty [Ō-tō-plăs-tē] {otoplastia}	_____
otorhinolaryngologist [ō-tō-rī-nō-lăr-ĭng-GŎL-ō-jĭst]	_____
otorrhagia [ō-tō-RĀ-jē-ă] {otorragia}	_____
otorrhea [ō-tō-RĒ-ă] {otorrea}	_____

WORD	DEFINITION
otosclerosis [ō-tō-sklĕ-RŌ-sĭs] {otosclerosis}	
otoscopy [ō-TŎS-kō-pē] {otoscopia}	
papillae [pă-PĬL-ē] {papilas}	
paracusis [PĂR-ă-KŪ-sĭs] {paracusia}	
perilymph [PĔR-ĭ-lĭmf]	
phac(o), phak(o)	
phacoemulsification [FĀ-kō-ē-mŭls-ĭ-fĭ-KĀ-shŭn]	
photophobia [fō-tō-FŌ-bē-ă] {fotofobia}	
pinkeye [PĬNK-Ī]	
pinna [PĬN-ă]	
presbyacusis [prĕz-bē-ă-KŪ-sĭs] {presbiacusia}	
presbyopia [prĕz-bē-Ō-pē-ă] {presbiopía}	
pseudophakia [sū-dō-FĀ-kē-ă] {seudofaquia}	
pupil [PYŪ-pĭl] {pupila}	
pupill(o)	
refraction [rē-FRĂK-shŭn] {refracción}	
retin(o)	
retina [RĔT-ĭ-nă] {retina}	
retinitis [rĕt-ĭ-NĪ-tĭs] {retinitis}	
retinitis pigmentosa [pĭg-mĕn-TŌ-să]	
rods [rŏdz] {bastoncillos}	
scler(o)	
sclera (pl., sclerae) [SKLĒR-ă (SKLĒR-ē)] {sclera}	
scleritis [sklĕ-RĪ-tĭs] {escleritis}	
scot(o)	
scotoma [skō-TŌ-mă] {escotoma}	
semicircular canals	
sensory receptors	
sensory system	
sight {vista}	

smell {olfacción, oler} _____

stapedectomy [stā-pē-DĚK-tō-mē] _____

stapes (*pl.*, stapes, stapedes) [STĀ-pēz (STĀ-pē-dēz)] {estribo} _____

strabismus [stră-BĬZ-mŭs] {estrabismo} _____

sty, stye [stī] {orzuelo} _____

taste _____

taste buds _____

taste cells _____

tears [tērz] {lágrimas} _____

tinnitus [tĭ-NĪ-tŭs, TĬN-ĭ-tŭs] {tinnitus} _____

tonometry [tō-NŎM-ĕ-trē] {tonometría} _____

touch {tacto} _____

tympan(o) _____

tympanic [tĭm-PĂN-ĭk] membrane _____

tympanitis [tĭm-pă-NĪ-tĭs] _____

tympanoplasty [TĬM-pă-nō-plăs-tē] _____

uve(o) _____

uvea [YŪ-vē-ă] {úvea} _____

vertigo [VĚR-tĭ-gō, vĕr-TĪ-gō] {vértigo} _____

vestibule [VĚS-tĭ-būl] {vestíbulo} _____

Answers to Chapter Exercises

1. None of the general tests showed abnormal results so Mr. James's problem needs further investigation.
2. Eye disease can be part of a systemic problem.
3. k
4. a
5. b
6. j
7. h
8. f
9. d
10. g
11. e
12. i
13. c
14. F
15. F
16. T
17. F
18. T
19. F
20. T
21. right eye
22. yes
23. otitis

24. optometer
25. otology
26. keratitis
27. keratometer
28. iridopathy
29. dacryocystalgia
30. coreoplasty
31. scleromalacia
32. sclerokeratitis
33. blepharedema
34. retinal
35. iridoplegia
36. otalgia
37. otology/audiology
38. blepharitis
39. otorrhagia
40. otometer/ audiometer
41. lens
42. No, the lens is inside the eye; the iris determines eye color.
43. B
44. B
45. A
46. A
47. B
48. A
49. A

50. A
51. nerve deafness of old age or other systemic condition such as an infection
52. otologist
53. A
54. A
55. A
56. B
57. A
58. C
59. A
60. C
61. B
62. T
63. F
64. T
65. F
66. No—it is an inflammation of the middle ear.
67. to relieve the recurring ear infections
68. otoplasty
69. otosclerosis
70. ear
71. transplant
72. myringotomy

Terms in Pharmacology

After studying this chapter, you will be able to:

► Describe the source and types of drugs
► List various generic and trade names for common drugs
► Identify the various ways drugs are administered
► Describe some of the ways in which drugs affect the body
► Identify the meaning of related abbreviations

Drug Sources, Types, Function, and Administration

Drugs are biological or chemical agents. They are *therapeutic* when they are used to cure, alleviate, diagnose, treat, or prevent illness. They are *addictive* or habit-forming when they are used in unregulated and excessive quantities to stimulate or depress someone's moods. Therapeutic drugs are also called **medicines** or **medications.**

Drugs come from plants, animals, or through chemical synthesis in a laboratory. **Vitamins,** organic substances found in food, are also a form of drugs. The federal *Food and Drug Administration (FDA)* regulates the testing, manufacture, content, and distribution of all drugs that are not part of or derived from food. The standards for approval are set by an independent committee in publications collected and published as the *United States Pharmacopeia (U.S.P.)*. When the letters U.S.P. follow a drug name on the package, it means that the drug has met the stringent standards set by the committee.

Aside from the *Pharmacopeia*, doctors generally use one of two references in gathering drug information. The first, the *Hospital Formulary*, lists drugs that are approved for patient care in that particular facility. The second, the *Physician's Desk Reference (PDR)*, is a widely used reference for physicians. The PDR lists drugs by their drug class, and includes information such as indication for use, known side effects, appropriate dosages, and routes of administration. Figure 17-1 shows the PDR entry for aspirin.

Pharmacology is the science that studies, develops, and tests drugs. Some of the scientists who work in pharmacology specialize in the various subdivisions of the field. For example, *medicinal chemistry* is the study of new drugs, their structure, and how they work. **Pharmacodynamics** is the study of how

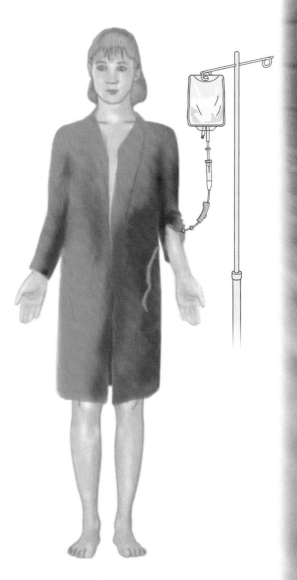

Ecotrin® OTC
Enteric-Coated Aspirin
Antiarthritic, Antiplatelet

DESCRIPTION
"Ecotrin" is enteric-coated aspirin (acetylsalicylic acid, ASA) available in tablet form in 81 mg., 325 mg., and 500 mg. dosage units.
The enteric coating covers a core of aspirin and is designed to resist disintegration in the stomach, dissolving in the more neutral-to-alkaline environment of the duodenum. Such action helps to protect the stomach from injury that may result from ingestion of plain, buffered or highly buffered aspirin (see SAFETY).

INDICATIONS
'Ecotrin' is indicated for:
• Conditions requiring chronic or long-term aspirin therapy for pain and/or inflammation, e.g., rheumatoid arthritis, juvenile rheumatoid arthritis, systemic lupus

The publishers of the PDR run a Web site (/www.gettingwell.com/drug_info/index.html) where it is possible to search for information about specific drugs.

drugs affect the body. **Toxicology** is the study of harmful effects of drugs on the body and of **antidotes,** substances able to cancel out unwanted effects. **Pharmacokinetics** is the study of how drugs are **absorbed, metabolized** (chemically changed so it can be used in the body), and **excreted** over time.

Some drugs are available **over-the-counter (OTC),** sold without a doctor's **prescription,** which is an order for medication with the dosages, directions, route, and timing of administration included. Prescription drugs are dispensed by a **pharmacist** or **druggist** in a pharmacy or drug store. Drugs are also available from mail-order companies and from companies on the Internet. Drugs usually come with instructions about how and how often to take the medication and a listing of the potential side effects. Sometimes other drugs or even foods are **contraindicated** (advised against) to be taken along with the medication being given.

Drugs can have several different names. First is a chemical name that describes the chemical formula of the drug. Second is a **generic** name that is the official name of the drug and is often a shortened or simpler version of the chemical name for legal purposes. Third is a **trade, brand,** or **proprietary name** that is given and copyrighted by the manufacturer for a specific drug. Each drug has only one chemical name and only one generic name, but it may have many trade names. For example, acetylsalicylic acid is the chemical name for *aspirin*, the generic name packaged under various trade names, such as Bayer aspirin. Table 17-1 lists some generic and trade names of drugs according to their function (what class of drug it is).

Dosages of drugs vary depending on the age, size, severity of symptoms, and other medications in use. Some drugs are *tapered*; that is, they are given at a higher dose initially and then the dose is gradually reduced as the symptoms subside. Many drugs are synthesized to perform like substances in the body. For example, manufactured **hormones** (chemical substances in the body that form in one organ and have an effect on another organ or part) are widely used in hormone replacement therapy.

Drugs are classified by their use in the body. For example, **antibiotics** or **anti-infectives** stop or slow the growth of harmful microorganisms, such as bacteria, fungi, or parasites. Subclassifications of antibiotics include the more

TABLE 17-1 Pharmacological agents, their functions, and examples.

Drug Class	Purpose	Generic	Trade Name
analgesic	relieves pain without causing loss of consciousness	acetaminophen	Tylenol
anesthetic	produces a lack of feeling either locally or generally throughout the body	lidocaine procaine	Novacaine Xylocaine
antacid	neutralizes stomach acid	calcium carbonate and magnesia alumina, magnesia, simethicone	Rolaids Mylanta
antianemic	replaces iron	ferrous sulfate erythropoietin	Feosol, Slow Fe Procrit
antianginal	dilates coronary arteries to increase blood flow and reduce angina	nitroglycerine	Nitrocot
antianxiety	relieves anxiety	alprazolam lorazepam	Xanax Ativan
antiarrhythmic	controls cardiac arrhythmias	quinidine amiodarone	Cardioquin, Quinaglute Cordarone
antibiotic, anti-infective, antibacterial	destroys or inhibits the growth of harmful microorganisms	ciprofloxacin levofloxacin amoxicillin penicillin	Cipro Levaquin Amoxil, Wymox various
anticholinergic	blocks certain nerve impulses and muscular reactions, as in the movements of Parkinson's disease, or in cases of nausea	atropine homatropine propantheline	Atropair Homapin Pro-Banthine
anticoagulant	prevents blood clotting	warfarin sodium heparin dipyrimadole	Coumadin various Persantine
anticonvulsant	inhibits convulsions	phenytoin clonazepam carbamazepine	Dilantin Klonipin Tegetrol
antidepressant	prevents or relieves symptoms of depression	fluoxentine sertraline paroxetine	Prozac Zoloft Paxil
antidiabetic	lowers blood sugar or increases insulin sensitivity	insulin glyburide rosiglitazone	Humulin, Novolin Diabeta, Micronase Avandia
antidiarrheal	prevents or slows diarrhea	bismuth subsalicylate loperamide	Pepto-Bismol Imodium

TABLE 17-1 Pharmacological agents, their functions, and examples (*cont.*).

Drug Class	Purpose	Generic	Trade Name
antiemetic	prevents or relieves nausea and vomiting	dimenhydrenate meclizine	Dramamine Bonine, Antivert
antifungal	destroys or inhibits fungal growth	tolnaftate ketoconazole	Tinactin, Desenex Nizoral
antihistamine	slows allergic reactions by counteracting histamines	loratidine diphenhydramine fexofenadine	Claritin Benadryl Allegra
antihypertensive	controls high blood pressure	clonidine prazosin guanethidine metoprolol	Catapres Minipress Ismelin Lopressor
anti-inflammatory, **nonsteroidal anti-inflammatory drug (NSAID)**	counteracts inflammations	ibuprofen naprosyn celecoxib valdecoxib	Advil, Motrin Aleve Celebrex Bextra
antineoplastic	destroys malignant cells	cyclophosphamide vincristine doxorubicin	Cytoxan Oncovin Adriamycin
antiparkinson	controls symptoms of Parkinson's disease	levodopa benztropine biperiden	Sinemet Cogentin Akineton
antipsychotic	controls symptoms of schizophrenia and some psychoses	aripiprazole risperidone olanzapine	Abilify Risperdal Zyprexa
antipyretic	reduces fever	acetylsalicylic acid (aspirin)	Bayer, Excedrin, various
antitubercular	decreases growth of microorganisms that cause tuberculosis	isoniazid ethambutol rifampin	Laniazid Myambutol Rifadin
antitussive, expectorant	prevents or relieves coughing	guaifenesin dextromethorphan	Humibid, Robitussin Vicks Formula 44
antiulcer	relieves and heals ulcers	cimetidine omeprazole ranitidine	Tagamet Prilosec Zantac
antiviral	controls the growth of viral microorganisms	didanosine zidovudine amantadine	Videx AZT, Retrovir Symmetrel
barbiturate	controls epileptic seizures	pentobarbital secobarbital	Nembutal Seconal
bronchodilator	dilates bronchial passages	albuterol ephredrine	Ventolin Bronkaid, Primatene
decongestant	reduces nasal congestion and/or swelling	pseudoephedrine	Drixoral, Sudafed

TABLE 17-1 Pharmacological agents, their functions, and examples (*cont.*).

Drug Class	Purpose	Generic	Trade Name
diuretic	increases excretion of urine	furosemide bumetanide	Lasix Bumex
hemostatic	controls or stops bleeding	aminocaproic acid recombinant factor VIIa	Amicar NovoSeven
hypnotic, sedative	produces sleep or a hypnotic state	diazepam zolpidem methaqualone	Valium Ambien Quaalude
hypoglycemic	lowers blood glucose levels	glucagon	Glucagon Diagnostic Kit
laxative	loosens stool and promotes normal bowel elimination	psyllium bisacodyl docusate	Metamucil Dulcolax, Theralax Therevac
vasodilator	decreases blood pressure by relaxing blood vessels	hydralazine enalapril benazepril	Apresoline Vasotec Lotensin

specific purposes of the drug; for example, an **antifungal** is an antibiotic that kills fungi. Table 17-1 lists the major drug classes, their functions, and generic and trade name examples for each class.

Drugs come in many forms—pills, liquids, semiliquids, suppositories, foams, lotions, creams, powders, transdermal patches, sprays, or gases—depending on how the drug is to be administered to the patient. Pills or tablets (usually stored in a small bottle called a **vial**) may be available as the standard solid small tablet or they may be in the form of capsules, a tablet with a gelatin covering encasing a powder or a liquid. They may also be coated (**enteric-coated** capsules dissolve slowly in the intestine so as not to irritate the stomach) or delayed- or timed-release (as with a transdermal patch), which spreads the dosage of the medicine gradually over a period of hours. Pills may also be in the form of lozenges, tablets meant to be dissolved slowly in the mouth, not swallowed. Tablets and some liquids can also be placed **sublingually,** under the tongue, or **buccally,** inside the cheek, where they are left to dissolve. **Oral administration** is the most common method for giving pills and some liquids.

Liquid and semiliquid drugs may come in various forms, such as syrups, heavy solutions of sugar, flavoring, and water added to the medication, and emulsions, suspensions of oil or fat in water along with the medication. Liquids can be swallowed, sprayed (as on a wound or in an inhalant form), or injected. They may also be released directly into the body from an implantable drug pump controlled by the patient. Patients with diabetes can use a pump to release amounts of insulin as needed rather than in a specific dose. Specific types of liquid and semiliquid medications are:

- *elixir*, oral liquid dissolved in alcohol
- *tincture*, topical liquid dissolved in alcohol
- *solution*, drug dissolved in liquid
- *suspension*, drug particles suspended in liquid, must shake before administration

- *emulsion*, drug particles suspended with oil or fat in water
- *lozenge*, drug in a candy-like base, dissolves slowly and coats the oral pharynx
- *syrup*, oral liquid drug in a thick solution, coats the oral pharynx

Drugs that are meant to go throughout the body are *systemic* (able to travel throughout the bloodstream to affect any part of the body); for example, aspirin tablets are taken internally for various pains. **Suppositories,** drugs mixed with a semisolid melting substance, are inserted into the vagina, rectum, or urethra are either *topical* or systemic drugs. Foams are generally inserted into the vagina. Lotions and creams are applied **topically** to the surface of the skin. Topical drugs are meant to work where they are placed. Powders may be inserted into a gelatin capsule or mixed with a liquid. Liquids or gases can be administered in **inhalation** form, in which tiny droplets are inhaled through an inhaler, nebulizer, or spray. Inhalants are usually given in metered doses (for example, 2 puffs q4h). Sprays can be applied topically to the skin, into the nose (*intranasal*), or into the mouth.

Injection of a drug is called **parenteral administration.** Parenteral administration may be done by health care professionals. Most drugs given by parenteral administration are meant for systemic use. The closer to the bloodstream, the faster the drug will work. Some parenteral administration is topical; for example, **intradermal** or **intracutaneous** administration is the injection of a needle or **syringe** just beneath the outer layer of skin to check for local reactions. **Subcutaneous** administration is injection of the substance into the fatty layer of tissue below the outer portion of the skin. **Intramuscular** administration is the injection of drugs deep into the muscles. Intravenous administration is the injection of drugs through an **intravenous (IV)** tube. Generally the liquid drugs are titrated, put into solution in a specific volume. An IV **infusion** is the slow intravenous administration of a drug so that fluid is added to the bloodstream at a slow and steady rate. IV tubes can also be put into a pump system controlled by the patient. Figure 17-2 shows the methods of parenteral administration. There are other types of parenteral injection that can only be performed by a physician. These types of injection are: **intracardiac** (directly into heart muscle), **intra-arterial** (directly into an artery), **intraspinal** or **intrathecal** (directly into spinal spaces as in a case of severe pain or cancer), and **intraosseus** (directly into bone). For *steroids* and **anesthetics,** injections are done *intra-articularly*, or directly into a joint.

MORE ABOUT...

Drugs

When doctors prescribe drugs, the pharmacist usually provides instructions regarding side effects and what to avoid (incompatible or contraindicated with certain other drugs, alcohol, and so on). Those instructions do not usually discuss what types of food can interact with drugs. The National Consumers League and the Food and Drug Administration have published a brochure listing potentially harmful drug-food combinations. For example, grapefruit juice taken along with certain heart drugs can be fatal. Cheeses and sausages contain the substance tyramine, which can cause extremely high blood pressure when taken along with certain antidepressants.

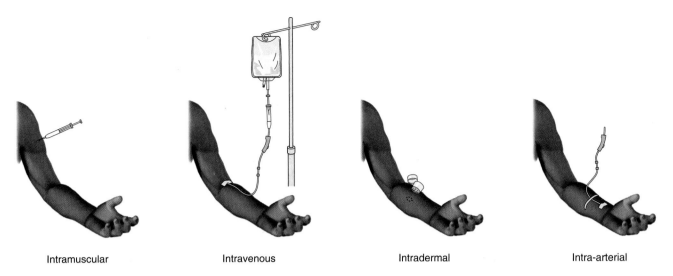

| Intramuscular | Intravenous | Intradermal | Intra-arterial |

FIGURE 17-2 Parenteral administration is the general term for administration by injection. These are only some types of parenteral administration.

VOCABULARY REVIEW

In the previous section, you learned terms relating to pharmacology. Before going on to the exercises, read the definitions below. Pronunciations are provided for certain terms.

Term	Definition
absorb [ăb-SŎRB]	To take into.
analgesic [ăn-ăl-JĒ-zĭk]	Drug that lessens or blocks pain.
anesthetic [ăn-ĕs-THĔT-ĭk]	Drug that causes temporary loss of ability to perceive sensations at a conscious level.
antacid [ănt-ĂS-ĭd]	Drug that lessens or neutralizes acidity.
antibacterial [ĂN-tē-băk-TĒR-ē-ăl]	Drug that stops or slows bacterial growth.
antibiotic [ĂN-tē-bī-ŎT-ĭk]	Drug that stops or slows the growth of harmful microorganisms.
antidiabetic [ĂN-tē-dī-ă-BĔT-ĭk]	Drug that lowers blood sugar or increases insulin sensitivity.
antidote [ĂN-tē-dōt]	Substance able to cancel out unwanted effects of another substance.
antifungal [ĂN-tē-FŬNG-găl]	Drug that stops or slows the growth of fungus.
antihistamine [ĂN-tē-HĬS-tă-mēn]	Drug that reduces the action of histamines; used in allergy treatments.
anti-infective [ĂN-tē-ĭn-FĔK-tĭv]	Antibiotic.
antitubercular [ĂN-tē-tū-BĔR-kyū-lăr]	Drug that stops the spread of tuberculosis.

Term	Definition
antiviral [ĂN-tē-VĪ-răl]	Drug that stops or slows the spread of a virus.
brand name	See Trade name.
buccally [BŪK-ăl-lē]	Inside the cheek.
contraindicated [kŏn-tră-ĬN-dĭ-kă-tĕd]	Inadvisable to use; said especially of a drug that might cause complications when used in combination with other drugs or when used on a patient with a particular set of symptoms.
drug [drŭg]	Biological or chemical agents that can aid or alter body functions.
druggist [DRŬG-ĭst]	Pharmacist.
enteric-coated [ĕn-TĒR-ĭk]	Having a coating (as on a capsule) that prevents stomach irritation.
excrete [ĕks-KRĒT]	To separate out and expel.
generic [jĕ-NĂR-ĭk]	Shortened version of a chemical name; official drug name.
hormone [HŌR-mōn]	Chemical substance in the body that forms in one organ and moves to another organ or part on which the substance has an effect; manufactured version of that chemical substance.
infusion [ĭn-FYŪ-zhŭn]	Administration of a fluid through an intravenous tube at a slow and steady rate.
inhalation [ĭn-hă-LĀ-shŭn]	Taking in of drugs in a fine spray of droplets.
intra-arterial [ĬN-tră-ăr-TĒ-rē-ăl]	Injected directly into an artery.
intracardiac [ĬN-tră-KĂR-dē-ăk]	Injected directly into heart muscle.
intracutaneous [ĬN-tră-kyū-TĀ-nē-ŭs]	Injected just beneath the outer layer of skin.
intradermal [ĬN-tră-DĔR-măl]	Intracutaneous.
intramuscular [ĬN-tră-MŬS-kyū-lăr]	Injected deep into muscle tissue.
intraosseus [ĬN-tră-ŎS-ē-ŭs]	Injected directly into bone.
intraspinal [ĬN-tră-SPĪ-năl]	Injected directly into spinal spaces.
intrathecal [ĬN-tră-THĒ-kăl]	Intraspinal.
intravenous [ĬN-tră-VĒ-nŭs] **(IV)**	Administered through a tube into a vein.
medication, medicine [mĕd-ĭ-KĀ-shŭn, MĔD-ĭ-sĭn]	Drug that serves a therapeutic purpose.
metabolize [mĕ-TĂB-ō-līz]	To change chemically or physically so as to make useful.
nonsteroidal anti-inflammatory drug (NSAID)	Anti-inflammatory drug that does not include steroids.

Term	Definition
oral administration	Swallowing of pills or liquids via the mouth.
over-the-counter (OTC)	Available for sale without a doctor's prescription.
parenteral [pă-RĚN-tēr-ăl] **administration**	Administration of a drug by injection.
pharmacist [FĂR-mă-sĭst]	Person licensed to dispense medications.
pharmacodynamics [FĂR-mă-kō-dĭ-NĂM-ĭks]	Study of how drugs affect the body.
pharmacokinetics [FĂR-mă-kō-kĭ-NĔT-ĭks]	Study of how the body absorbs, metabolizes, and excretes drugs.
pharmacology [făr-mă-KŎL-ō-jē]	Science that studies, develops, and tests new drugs.
prescription [prē-SKRĬP-shŭn]	Order given by a doctor for medication dosage, route, and timing of administration.
proprietary [prō-PRĪ-ĕ-tār-ē] **name**	Trade name.
subcutaneous [sŭb-kyū-TĀ-nē-ŭs]	Injected into the fatty layer of tissue beneath the outer layer of skin.
sublingually [sŭb-LĬNG-gwă-lē]	Under the tongue.
suppository [sŭ-PŎZ-ĭ-tōr-ē]	Drug mixed with a semisolid melting substance meant for administration by insertion into the vagina, rectum, or urethra.
syringe [sĭ-RĬNJ]	Instrument used for injection or withdrawal of fluids.
topically [TŎP-ĭ-căl-lē]	On the surface of the skin.
toxicology [tŏk-sĭ-KŎL-ō-jē]	Study of harmful effects of drugs.
trade name	Name copyrighted by the manufacturer for a particular version of a drug.
vial [VĪ-ăl]	A small receptacle for holding liquid or pill medications.
vitamin [VĪT-ă-mĭn]	Organic substance found in food.

Drug Sources, Types, Function, and Administration Exercises

Follow the Route

Name the route of drug administration or type of drug from its description.

1. Drug is administered via a semisolid into the rectum: _____

2. Drug is administered via vapor or gas into the nose or mouth: _____

3. Drug is administered under the tongue: _____

4. Drug is applied locally on skin or mucous membrane: _____

5. Drug is injected through a syringe under the skin, into a vein, into a muscle, or into a body cavity: _____

6. Drug is given by mouth and absorbed through the stomach or intestinal wall: _____

Find the Class

Give the class (not the name) of a drug that does the following. For example: stops diarrhea = antidiarrheal.

7. prevents/stops angina: _____

8. increases excretion of urine: _____

9. reduces blood pressure: _____

10. corrects abnormal heart rhythms: _____

11. relieves symptoms of depression: _____

12. prevents blood clotting: _____

13. inhibits vomiting: _____

14. relieves pain: _____

15. neutralizes stomach acid: _____

CASE STUDY

Getting an Evaluation

Many elderly people go to different doctors for different ailments without being monitored by one regular physician. Some people take so many medications that it affects their health adversely. Helen Metrone is an 86-year-old woman with high blood pressure, a tendency to retain water, skin allergies, and minor heart disease. Her preferred provider organization (PPO) allows her to see different doctors. Helen likes to go to various doctors. She almost always gets new prescriptions because of her symptoms. Often, she neglects to tell each doctor what medications she is already taking. When asked to list her medications, Helen will put one or two that she can remember. Also, Helen sometimes forgets which pills she has already taken in one day. This has led to several instances of fainting, disorientation, and dizziness. Helen's family is very concerned. They are looking into an assisted living arrangement where a nurse would give Helen her medication. They have also made an appointment with a gerontologist to review Helen's medications, outlook, and general health.

Critical Thinking

16. Why is it important for patients to inform their physician of all medications they are taking?

17. Why is it important for Helen to understand the instructions that come with her medication?

Combining Forms and Abbreviations

The lists below include combining forms that relate specifically to pharmacology. Pronunciations are provided for the examples.

COMBINING FORM	MEANING	EXAMPLE
chem(o)	chemical	*chemotherapy* [KĒ-mō-thār-ă-pē], treatment of a disease with chemical substances
pyret(o)	fever	*pyretogenous* [pī-rĕ-TŎJ-ĕ-nŭs], causing fever
tox(o), toxi, toxico	poison	*toxicogenic* [TŎK-sĭ-kō-JĔN-ĭk], caused by a poison

ABBREVIATION	MEANING	ABBREVIATION	MEANING
aa, āā	of each	ex aq.	in water
a.c.	before meals (Latin *ante cibum*), usually one-half hour preceding a meal	ext.	extract
ad	up to	FDA	Food and Drug Administration
a.d., AD	right ear (Latin *auris dexter*)	fld. ext.	fluid extract
ad lib	freely (Latin *ad libitum*), as often as desired	FUO	fever of unknown origin
AM, a.m., A	morning (Latin *ante meridiem*)	g, gm	gram
a.s., AS	left ear (Latin *auris sinister*)	gr	grain, gram
a.u., AU	each ear (Latin *auris uterque*)	gtt	drop
BID, b.i.d.	twice a day (Latin *bis in die*)	H	hypodermic
c, c̄	with	h.	every hour (Latin *hora*)
cap., caps.	capsule	h.s.	at bedtime (Latin *hora somni* [hour of sleep])
cc., cc	cubic centimeter	IM	intramuscular
comp.	compound	inj	injection
cx	contraindicated	IV	intravenous
DAW	dispense as written	mcg	microgram
dil.	dilute	mEq	milliequivalent
disc, DC, dc	discontinue	mg	milligram
disp.	dispense	ml	milliliter
div.	divide	n., noct.	night (Latin *nocte*)
DW	distilled water	non rep.	do not repeat
D₅W	dextrose 5% in water	NPO	nothing by mouth
dx, Dx	diagnosis	NPO p MN	nothing by mouth after midnight
elix.	elixir	N.S., NS	normal saline
e.m.p.	as directed (Latin *ex modo praescripto*)	NSAID	nonsteroidal anti-inflammatory drug

Abbreviation	Meaning	Abbreviation	Meaning
N&V	nausea and vomiting	s, s̄	without
o.d., OD	right eye (Latin *oculus dexter*)	Sig.	patient directions such as route and timing of medication (Latin *signa*, inscription)
oint., ung.	ointment, unguent	SL	sublingual
o.l.	left eye	sol., soln.	solution
o.s.	left eye (Latin *oculus sinister*)	s.o.s.	if there is need
OTC	over the counter	sp.	spirit
o.u.	each eye	ss, s̄s̄	one-half
oz.	ounce	stat	immediately
p	post, after	subc, subq, s.c.	subcutaneously
p.c.	after meals (Latin *post cibum*), one-half hour after a meal	supp., suppos	suppository
PDR	*Physician's Desk Reference*	susp.	suspension
PM, p.m., P	afternoon (Latin *post meridiem*)	sym, Sym, Sx	symptom
p.o.	by mouth (Latin *per os*)	syr.	syrup
PRN, p.r.n.	repeat as needed (Latin *pro re nata*)	tab.	tablet
pulv., pwdr	powder	tbsp.	tablespoonful
qam	every morning	t.i.d.	three times a day
q.d.	every day (Latin *quaque dies*)	tinct., tr.	tincture
q.h.	every hour	TPN	total parenteral nutrition
q.i.d.	four times a day	TPR	temperature, pulse, respirations
QNS	quantity not sufficient	tsp.	teaspoonful
q.o.d.	every other day	U, u	unit
q.s.	sufficient quantity	u.d.	as directed
R	rectal	ung.	ointment
Rx	prescription	U.S.P.	*United States Pharmacopeia*

CASE STUDY

Visiting a Specialist

Helen finally did go to a gerontologist—this time with her niece. Her niece brought along a list of all her medications. The doctor advised coming off several of the medications over the next few weeks. The gerontologist also asked Helen to see her in three weeks for a medication evaluation. She asked Helen to bring in the prescription vials, but her niece also had her regular nurse provide the following list of her medications.

Lopressor 10 mg. b.i.d.
Synthroid 50 mcg q.d.
Motrin as needed
Lasix 10 mg. b.i.d.

NDC 0075-1505-43

Nasacort®
(triamcinolone acetonide) U.S. Pat. No. 49999999999

Black's Pharmacy   #3333 ph. 879-000-0000
36 Main St.
Norfolk, VA 34444

Rx: **666777**   Dr. Esteves, Marion D.
                   St: B3456789

Use 2 sprays in each nostril once daily.

Nasacort Nasal inhaler RHO

You may refill this script 10 times before 4/26/XXXX.

Critical Thinking

18. How many times a day does Helen take Synthroid?

19. How many milligrams of Lopressor does Helen take daily?

COMBINING FORMS AND ABBREVIATIONS EXERCISES

Check Your Knowledge

Give abbreviations for the following.

20. three times a day _____

21. before meals _____

22. intramuscular _____

23. two times a day _____

24. intravenous _____

25. nothing by mouth _____

26. after meals _____

27. every hour _____

28. every morning _____

29. at bedtime _____

30. four times a day _____

31. when requested _____

32. every day _____

33. drops _____

Find the Root

Add the combining form to complete the word.

34. Resistance to the effects of chemicals: _____ resistance

35. Treatment of fever: _____ therapy

36. Study of poisons: _____ logy

USING THE INTERNET

Go to the FDA's Web site (www.fda.gov/opacom/hpnews.html) and find information about the approval of at least one drug. Explain what the medication is for. In addition, describe at least one new procedure aimed at monitoring drug safety once the drug is on the market.

CHAPTER REVIEW

The material that follows is to help you review this chapter.

DEFINITIONS

Define the following terms and combining forms. Review the chapter before starting. Make sure you know how to pronounce each term as you define it. The blue words in curly brackets are references to the Spanish glossary on the Web site.

TERM	DEFINITION
absorb [ăb-SŎRB]	
analgesic [ăn-ăl-JĒ-zĭk] {analgésico}	
anesthetic [ăn-ĕs-THĔT-ĭk] {anestésico}	
antacid [ănt-ĂS-ĭd] {antiácido}	
antibacterial [ĂN-tē-băk-TĒR-ē-ăl] {antibacteriano}	
antibiotic [ĂN-tē-bī-ŎT-ĭk] {antibiótico}	
antidiabetic [ĂN-tē-dī-ă-BĔT-ĭk] {antidiabético}	
antidote [ĂN-tē-dōt] {antidote}	
antifungal [ĂN-tē-FŬNG-găl] {antifúngico}	
antihistamine [ĂN-tē-HĬS-tă-mēn] {antihistamina}	
anti-infective [ĂN-tē-ĭn-FĔK-tĭv]	
antitubercular [ĂN-tē-tū-BĔR-kyū-lăr]	
antiviral [ĂN-tē-VĪ-răl]	
brand name	
buccally [BŬK-ăl-lē]	
chem(o)	
contraindicated [kŏn-tră-ĬN-dĭ-kā-tĕd]	
drug [drŭg] {droga}	
druggist [DRŬG-ĭst] {boticario}	
enteric-coated [ĕn-TĒR-ĭk]	
excrete [ĕks-KRĒT]	

Term	Definition
generic [jĕ-NĀR-ĭk] {genérico}	_____
hormone [HŌR-mōn] {hormona}	_____
infusion [ĭn-FYŪ-zhŭn]	_____
inhalation [ĭn-hă-LĀ-shŭn]	_____
intra-arterial [ĬN-tră-ăr-TĒ-rē-ăl]	_____
intracardiac [ĬN-tră-KĂR-dē-ăk]	_____
intracutaneous [ĬN-tră-kyū-TĀ-nē-ŭs]	_____
intradermal [ĬN-tră-DĔR-măl]	_____
intramuscular [ĬN-tră-MŬS-kyū-lăr]	_____
intraosseus [ĬN-tră-ŎS-ē-ŭs]	_____
intraspinal [ĬN-tră-SPĪ-năl]	_____
intrathecal [ĬN-tră-THĒ-kăl]	_____
intravenous [ĬN-tră-VĒ-nŭs] (IV) {intravenoso (IV)}	_____
medication, medicine [mĕd-ĭ-KĀ-shŭn, MĔD-ĭ-sĭn] {medicación, medicina}	_____
metabolize [mĕ-TĂB-ō-līz]	_____
nonsteroidal anti-inflammatory drug (NSAID) {agentes de antiiflamatorios no esteroideos, AINE}	_____
oral administration	_____
over-the-counter (OTC)	_____
parenteral [pă-RĔN-tēr-ăl] administration	_____
pharmacist [FĂR-mă-sĭst]	_____
pharmacodynamics [FĂR-mă-kō-dī-NĂM-ĭks]	_____
pharmacokinetics [FĂR-mă-kō-kĭ-NĔT-ĭks]	_____
pharmacology [făr-mă-KŎL-ō-jē] {farmacología}	_____
prescription [prē-SKRĬP-shŭn] {prescripción}	_____
proprietary [prō-PRĪ-ĕ-tār-ē] name	_____
pyret(o)	_____
subcutaneous [sŭb-kyū-TĀ-nē-ŭs]	_____
sublingually [sŭb-LĬNG-gwă-lē]	_____

suppository [sŭ-PŎZ-ĭ-tōr-ē]
{supositorio}

syringe [sĭ-RĬNJ] {jeringa}

topically [TŎP-ĭ-căl-lē]

tox(o), toxi, toxico

toxicology [tŏk-sĭ-KŎL-ō-jē]
{toxicología}

trade name

vial [VĪ-ăl] {vial}

vitamin [VĪT-ă-mĭn] {vitamina}

Answers to Chapter Exercises

1. suppository
2. inhalation
3. sublingually
4. topically
5. parenteral administration
6. oral administration
7. antianginal
8. diuretic
9. antihypertensive, vasodilator
10. antiarrhythmic
11. antidepressant
12. anticoagulant
13. antiemetic
14. analgesic
15. antacid
16. Medications can cause interactions or side effects.
17. Instructions, such as "take with food," can help avoid side effects.
18. once
19. 20 mg.
20. t.i.d.
21. a. c.
22. IM
23. b.i.d.
24. IV
25. NPO
26. p.c.
27. q.h. or h.
28. qam
29. h.s.
30. q.i.d.
31. ad lib
32. q.d.
33. gtt
34. chemoresistance
35. pyretotherapy
36. toxicology

Combining Forms, Prefixes, and Suffixes

Listed below are the word parts that appear throughout this textbook. The page numbers given indicate those pages on which the parts are defined and used in an example of a medical term. When a combining form ends in a vowel, the vowel is surrounded with parentheses only in those cases where the term may also appear used in words without the vowel. For example: *abdomin(o)* represents the combining form used both in *abdominoskeletal* and in *abdominal*.

a-, 24
aa, a̅a̅, 463
ab-, 24
abdomin(o), 48
abs-, 24
acetabul(o), 106
acromi(o), 106
actin(o), 7
-ad, 27
ad-, 24
aden(o), 349, 406
adenoid(o), 184
adip(o), 48, 66
adren(o), 49, 406
adrenal(o), 406
aer(o), 7
agglutin(o), 325
alge, 7
algesi, 7
-algia, 27
algio, 7
algo, 7
alveoli(o), 184
ambi-, 24
amni(o), 278
an-, 24
an(o), 373
ana-, 24
andr(o), 7, 302
angi(o), 49, 144
ankyl(o), 106
ante-, 24
anti-, 24
apo-, 24
aort(o), 49, 144
append(o), 373
appendic(o), 49, 373
arter(o), 144
arteri(o), 49, 144

arthr(o), 49, 106
-asthenia, 27
ather(o), 7, 145
atri(o), 145
audi(o), 431
audit(o), 431
aur(o), 431
auricul(o), 431
aut(o)-, 24

bacteri(o), 8
balan(o), 302
bar(o), 8
bas(o), 8
basi(o), 8
bi-, 24
bil(o), 373
bili, 373
bio-, 8
-blast, 27
blasto, 8
blephar(o), 431
brachi(o), 106
brachy-, 24
brady-, 24
bronch(o), 184
bronchi(o), 184
bronchiol(o), 184
bucc(o), 373
burs(o), 107

calc(o), 8
calcane(o), 107
calci(o), 8, 107
cali(o), 248
calic(o), 248
capn(o), 184
carcin(o), 8
cardi(o), 49,145

carp(o), 107
cata-, 24
cec(o), 373
-cele, 27
celi(o), 374
cephal(o), 49, 107
cerebell(o), 49, 219
cerebr(o), 49, 219
cerumin(o), 432
cervic(o), 49, 107, 278
chem(o), 8, 462
chir(o), 49
chlor(o), 8
chol(e), 49, 373
cholangi(o), 374
cholecyst(o), 374
choledoch(o), 374
cholo, 49, 373
chondr(o), 8, 107
chondri(o), 8
chrom, 8
chromat, 8
chromo, 8
chrono, 8
-cidal, 27
-cide, 27
circum-, 24
-clasis, 28
-clast, 28
co-, 24
cochle(o), 432
col-, 24
col(o), 49, 374
colon(o), 374
colp(o), 279
com-, 24
con-, 24
condyl(o), 107
conjunctiv(o), 432

contra-, 24
cor-, 24
cor(o), 432
core(o), 432
corne(o), 432
cost(o), 107
crani(o), 107, 219
-crine, 28
-crit, 28
cry(o), 8
crypt(o), 8
cyan(o), 8
cycl(o), 8, 432
cyst(i), 49
cyst(o), 8, 49, 248
cysti, 8
cyt(o), 8, 49
-cyte, 28
-cytosis, 28

dacry(o), 432
dactyl(o), 107
de-, 24
dent(i), 49
dento, 49
derm(o), 66
-derma, 28
dermat(o), 66
-desis, 28
dextr(o), 8
di-, 24
dia-, 24
dif-, 24
dips(o), 8
dir-, 24
dis-, 24
disc, 463
dors(o), 9
dorsi, 9

duoden(o), 50, 374
-dynia, 28
dys-, 25

echo, 9
ect(o)-, 25
-ectasia, 28
-ectasis, 28
-ectomy, 28
-edema, 28
electr(o), 9
-emesis, 28
-emia, 28
-emic, 28
encephal(o), 50, 219
end(o)-, 25
enter(o), 374
epi-, 25
epididym(o), 302
epiglott(o), 184
episi(o), 279
erythr(o), 9, 325
esophag(o), 374
-esthesia, 28
esthesio, 9
etio, 9
eu-, 25
ex-, 25
exo-, 25
extra-, 25

fasci(o), 107
femor(o), 107
fibr(o), 9, 107
fluor(o), 9
-form, 28

galact(o), 279
gangli(o), 220
gastr(o), 50, 374
-gen, 28
gen(o), 9
-genesis, 29
-genic, 29
gero, 9
geront(o), 9
gingiv(o), 50
gli(o), 220
-globin, 29
-globulin, 29
glomerul(o), 248
gloss(o), 50, 374
gluc(o), 9, 374, 406
glyc(o), 9, 374, 406
glycogen(o), 374
gonad(o), 406
gonio, 9
-gram, 29
granulo, 9
-graph, 29
-graphy, 29

gyn(o), 9
gyne, 9
gynec(o), 9, 279

hem(a), 50
hemangi(o), 145
hemat(o), 325
heme, 316, 322
hemi-, 25
hemo, 50, 325
hepat(o), 374
hidr(o), 50, 66
histi(o), 50
histo, 50
home(o), 9
homo, 9
humer(o), 107
hydr(o), 10
hyper-, 25
hypn(o), 10
hypo-, 25
hyster(o), 279

-iasis, 29
iatr(o), 10
-ic, 29
ichthy(o), 66
-ics, 29
ile(o), 374
ili(o), 107
immun(o), 10, 349
infra-, 25
inter-, 25
intra-, 25
ir(o), 432
irid(o), 432
ischi(o), 50, 107
iso-, 25
-ism, 29
-itides, 29
-itis, 29

jejun(o), 374

kerat(o), 50, 66, 432
kines(o), 10
-kinesia, 29
kinesi(o), 10
kyph(o), 107

labi(o), 50, 374
lacrim(o), 432
lact(o), 279
lacti, 10, 279
lamin(o), 107
lapar(o), 50
laryng(o), 184
latero, 10
leiomy(o), 107
-lepsy, 29
-leptic, 29

leuk(o), 325
linguo, 50
lip(o), 10, 66
lith(o), 10
lob(o), 184
log(o), 10
-logist, 29
-logy, 29
lumb(o), 108
lymph(o), 50
lymphaden(o), 349
lymphangi(o), 349
-lysis, 29
-lytic, 29

macr(o), 10
mal-, 25
-malacia, 29
mamm(o), 279
-mania, 29
mast(o), 279
mastoid(o), 432
maxill(o), 108
meat(o), 248
medi(o), 10
medistin(o), 184
megal(o)-, 10, 25
-megaly, 30
melan(o), 10, 66
men(o), 279
mening(o), 220
mes(o)-, 25
mes(o), 10
meta-, 25
metacarp(o), 108
-meter, 30
metr(o), 279
-metry, 30
micr(o)-, 10, 26
mio, 10
mon(o)-, 26
morph(o), 10
multi-, 26
my(o), 50, 108
myc(o), 66
myel(o), 50, 108, 220
myring(o), 432

narco, 11
nas(o), 184, 432
necr(o), 11
nephr(o), 50, 248
neur(o), 50, 220
neuri, 220
noct(i), 11
nucle(o), 11
nyct(o), 11

ocul(o), 432
odont(o), 50
-oid, 30

olig(o)-, 26
-oma, 30
-omata, 30
oncho, 11
onco, 11
onych(o), 66
oo, 279
oophor(o), 279
ophthalm(o), 50, 432
-opia, 30
opsia, 30
-opsy, 30
opt(o), 51, 432
optic(o), 51, 432
or(o), 51, 184, 374
orch(o), 302
orchi(o), 51, 302
orchid(o), 51, 302
orth(o), 11
-oses, 30
-osis, 30
ossicul(o), 432
oste(o), 51, 108
-ostomy, 30
ot(o), 51
ov(i), 279
ov(o), 279
ovari(o), 279
ox(o), 184
oxi-, 184
-oxia, 30
oxy, 11, 184

pan-, 26
pancreat(o), 374, 406
pant(o)-, 26
par(a)-, 26
-para, 30
para, 273, 276
parathyroid(o), 407
-paresis, 30
-parous, 30
patell(o), 108
path(o), 11
-pathy, 30
ped(i), 51, 108
ped(o), 51, 108
pelv(i), 108
-penia, 30
-pepsia, 30
per-, 26
peri-, 26
pericardi(o), 145
perine(o), 279
periton(eo), 375
-pexy, 30
phac(o), 432
phag(o), 11, 325
-phage, 30
-phagia, 30
-phagy, 30

B Abbreviations—Ones to Use and Ones to Avoid

Recently, medical abbreviations have been linked to some of the worst medical errors, particularly those involving wrong doses of medication. As a result, the Joint Commission on Accreditation of Hospital Organizations (JCAHO) has come up with a list of nine prohibited abbreviations plus several recommended for elimination in medical communication. For the prohibited abbreviations, it is suggested that the full words be substituted. Table A-1 shows the prohibited abbreviations, what they can be confused with, and what should be substituted. Table A-2 shows suggested replacements for abbreviations that have the potential to cause medical errors. JCAHO has also suggested that each healthcare organization come up with their own list of frequently used and potentially misunderstood abbreviations.

TABLE A-1. Prohibited Abbreviations.

Abbreviation	Potential Problem	Solution
1. U (for unit)	Mistaken as zero, four or cc.	Write or speak "unit"
2. IU (for international unit)	Mistaken as IV (intravenous) or 10 (ten).	Write or speak "international unit"
3. Q.D. (once daily) 4. Q.O.D. (every other day)	Mistaken for each other. The period after the Q can be mistaken for an "I" and the "O" can be mistaken for "I".	Write or speak "daily" and "every other day"
5. Trailing zero (X.0 mg) [*Note: Prohibited only for medication-related notations*] 6. Lack of leading zero (.X mg)	Decimal point is missed and dosage is either too large or too small.	Never write a zero by itself after a decimal point (X mg), and always use a zero before a decimal point (0.X mg)
7. MS 8. MSO$_4$ 9. MgSO$_4$	Can mean morphine sulfate or magnesium sulfate. Potentially confused for one another.	Write or speak "morphine sulfate" or "magnesium sulfate"

TABLE A-2. Suggested Additional Abbreviations to Avoid.

Abbreviation	Potential Problem	Solution
μg (for microgram)	Mistaken for mg (milligrams) resulting in one thousand-fold dosing overdose.	Write "mcg" or speak microgram
H.S. (for half-strength or Latin abbreviation for bedtime)	Mistaken for either half-strength or hour of sleep (at bedtime). q.H.S. mistaken for every hour. All can result in a dosing error.	Write out or speak "half-strength" or "at bedtime"
T.I.W. (for three times a week)	Mistaken for three times a day or twice weekly resulting in an overdose.	Write or speak "3 times weekly" or "three times weekly"
S.C. or S.Q. (for subcutaneous)	Mistaken as SL for sublingual, or "5 every".	Write or speak "Sub-Q","subQ", or "subcutaneously"
D/C (for discharge)	Interpreted as discontinue whatever medications follow (typically discharge meds).	Write "discharge"
c.c. (for cubic centimeter)	Mistaken for U (units) when poorly written.	Write or speak "ml" for milliliters
A.S., A.D., A.U. (Latin abbreviation for left, right, or both ears)	Mistaken for OS, OD, and OU, etc.).	Write or speak "left ear," "right ear" or "both ears"

Listed below are the medical abbreviations that you should learn while studying medical terminology.

Abbreviation	Meaning
–	minus/concave
+	plus/convex
aa, $\overline{aa}$	of each
ABG	arterial blood gases
a.c.	before meals (Latin *ante cibum*), usually one-half hour preceding
acc.	accommodation
Ach	acetylcholine
ACTH	adrenocorticotropic hormone
ad	up to
a. d., AD	right ear (Latin *auris dexter*)
ad lib	freely (Latin *ad libitum*), as often as desired
ADH	antidiuretic hormone
AF	atrial fibrillation
AFB	acid-fast bacillus (causes tuberculosis)
AIDS	acquired immunodeficiency syndrome
AIH	artificial insemination homologous
A-K	above the knee
ALL	acute lymphocytic leukemia
ALS	amyotrophic lateral sclerosis
AM, a.m., A	morning (Latin *ante meridiem*)
AML	acute myelogenous leukemia
AP	anteroposterior
A&P	auscultation and percussion
APTT	activated partial thromboplastin time
ARD	acute respiratory disease
ARDS	adult respiratory distress syndrome
ARF	acute respiratory failure, acute renal failure
a. s., AS	left ear (Latin *auris sinister*)
AS	aortic stenosis
ASD	atrial septal defect
a. u., AU	each ear (Latin *auris uterque*)
AV	atrioventricular
AZT	Azidothymidine
B-K	below the knee
Ba	barium
BaE	barium enema
baso	basophil
BBB	blood-brain barrier
BCP	biochemistry panel
BID, b.i.d.	twice a day (Latin *bis in die*)
BMT	bone marrow transplant
BP	blood pressure
BPH	benign prostatic hypertrophy
BS	breath sounds
BUN	blood urea nitrogen
bx	biopsy
c, $\overline{c}$	with
C-section	caesarean section
C-spine	cervical spine (film)
C_1	first cervical vertebra
ca	calcium
CA	carcinoma
CABG	coronary artery bypass graft
CAD	coronary artery disease
cap., caps.	capsule
CAT	computerized axial tomography
cath	catheter
CBC	complete blood count
cc., $\overline{cc}$	cubic centimeter
CCU	coronary care unit
CHD	coronary heart disease

Abbreviation	Meaning
CHF	congestive heart failure
CIS	carcinoma in situ
Cl	chlorine
CLL	chronic lymphocytic leukemia
CML	chronic myelogenous leukemia
CMV	cytomegalovirus
CNS	central nervous system
CO	cardiac output
COLD	chronic obstructive lung disease
comp.	compound
COPD	chronic obstructive pulmonary disease
CP	cerebral palsy
CPK	creatine phosphokinase
CPR	cardiopulmonary resuscitation
CRF	chronic renal failure
CS	caesarean section
CSF	cerebrospinal fluid
CT	computed tomography
CT or CAT scan	computerized (axial) tomography
CTA	clear to auscultation
CTS	carpal tunnel syndrome
CVA	cerebrovascular accident
CVD	cerebrovascular disease
cx	contraindicated
Cx	cervix
CXR	chest x-ray
cysto	cystoscopy
D	diopter
D & C	dilation and curettage
d.t.d.	give of such doses
DAW	dispense as written
dB	decibel
DDS	doctor of dental surgery
def	decayed, extracted, or filled (primary teeth)
DEF	decayed, extracted, or filled (permanent teeth)
diff	differential blood count
dil.	dilute
disc, D. C.	discontinue
disp.	dispense
div.	divide
DLE	discoid lupus erythematosus
DM	diabetes mellitus
dmf	decayed, missing, or filled (primary teeth)
DMF	decayed, missing, or filled (permanent teeth)
DNA	deoxyribonucleic acid
DOE	dyspnea on exertion
DPT	diphtheria, pertussis, tetanus (combined vaccination)
DRE	digital rectal exam
DSA	digital subtraction angiography
DT	delirium tremens
DVT	deep venous thrombosis
dx, Dx	diagnosis
e.m.p.	as directed
EBV	Epstein-Barr virus
ECCE	extracapsular cataract extraction
ECG, EKG	electrocardiogram
ECHO	echocardiogram
ECT	electroconvulsive therapy
EEG	electroencephalogram
EENT	eye, ear, nose, and throat
EIA, ELISA	Enzyme-linked immunosorbent assay

ABBREVIATION	MEANING	ABBREVIATION	MEANING
elix.	elixir	MCP	metacarpophalangeal
ENT	ear, nose, and throat	MCV	mean corpuscular volume
ERT	estrogen replacement therapy	MDI	metered dose inhaler
ESR	erythrocyte sedimentation rate	mg	milligram
ESRD	end-stage renal disease	MI	mitral insufficiency; myocardial infarction
ET tube	endotracheal intubation tube	ml	milliliter
ETT	exercise tolerance test	mono	monocyte
ex aq.	in water	MR	mitral regurgitation
ext.	extract	MRA	magnetic resonance angiography
fld. ext.	fluid extract	MRI	magnetic resonance imaging
FUO	fever of unknown origin	MS	multiple sclerosis
fx	fracture	MS	mitral stenosis
Fx	fracture	MUGA	multiple-gated acquisition scan
g, gm	gram	multip	multiparous
G	gravida (pregnancy)	MVP	mitral valve prolapse
G-CSF	granulocyte colony-stimulating factor	n., noct.	night (Latin, *nocte*)
GERD	gastroesophageal reflux disease	N.S., NS	normal saline
GH	growth hormone	N&V	nausea and vomiting
GI	gastrointestinal	Na	sodium
GOT	glutamic oxaloacetic transaminase	NHL	non-Hodgkin's lymphoma
gr	grain, gram	NIDDM	noninsulin-dependent diabetes mellitus
gtt	drop	NMR	nuclear magnetic resonance (imaging)
GTT	glucose tolerance test	non rep.	do not repeat
Gy	unit of radiation equal to 100 rads	NPO	nothing by mouth
gyn	gynecology	NPO p MN	nothing by mouth after midnight
H	hypodermic	NSAID	nonsteroidal anti-inflammatory drug
h.	every hour (Latin *hora*)	NVA	near visual acuity
h.s.	hour of sleep (Latin *hora somni*)	OB	obstetrics
HCG	human chorionic gonadotropin	OCD	obsessive-compulsive disorder
HCT, Hct	hematocrit	OCP	oral contraceptive pill
HD	hemodialysis	o.d., OD	right eye
HDL	high-density lipoprotein	oint., ung.	ointment, unguent
HGB, Hgb, HB	hemoglobin	o.l., OL	left eye
HIV	human immunodeficiency virus	OM	otitis media
HRT	hormone replacement therapy	o.s., OS	left eye
HSV	herpes simplex virus	OTC	over the counter
ICCE	intracapsular cataract cryoextraction	o.u., OU	each eye
ICD	International Classification of Diseases	oz.	ounce
ICP	intracranial pressure	p	post, after
IDDM	insulin-dependent diabetes mellitus	P	para (live births)
IM	intramuscular	P	phosphorus
inj	injection	p.c.	after meals (Latin *post cibum*), one-half hour after a meal
IOL	intraocular lens		
IOP	intraocular pressure	p.o.	by mouth (Latin *per os*)
IPPB	intermittent positive pressure breathing	PA	posteroanterior
IQ	intelligence quotient	Pap smear	Papanicolaou smear
IRDS	infant respiratory distress syndrome	PCP	Pneumocystis carinii pneumonia
IRV	inspiratory reserve volume	PCV	packed cell volume
IUD	intrauterine device	PDR	*Physician's Desk Reference*
IV	intravenous	PE tube	polyethylene ventilating tube (placed in the eardrum)
K	potassium		
KUB	kidney, ureter, bladder		
L1	first lumbar vertebra	PED	penile erectile dysfunction
LDL	low-density lipoprotein	PEEP	positive end expiratory pressure
LLL	left lower lobe [of the lungs]	PERRLA	pupils equal, round, reactive to light and accommodation
LMP	last menstrual period		
LP	lumbar puncture	PET	positron emission tomography
LUL	left upper lobe [of the lungs]	PFT	pulmonary function tests
LV	left ventricle	pH	power of hydrogen concentration
LVH	left ventricular hypertrophy	PID	pelvic inflammatory disease
M.	mix	PKU	phenylketonuria
MBC	maximal breathing capacity	PLT	platelet count
mcg	microgram	PM, p.m., P	afternoon (Latin *post meridiem*)
MCH	mean corpuscular hemoglobin	PMP	previous menstrual period
MCHC	mean corpuscular hemoglobin concentration	PMS	premenstrual syndrome
		PND	paroxysmal nocturnal dyspnea; postnasal drip

ABBREVIATION	MEANING	ABBREVIATION	MEANING
PPD	purified protein derivative	SR; sed. rate	sedimentation rate
primip	primiparous	ss, s̄s̄	one-half
PRN, p.r.n.	repeat as needed (Latin *pro re nata*)	stat	immediately
PSA	prostate-specific antigen	subc, subq, s.c.	subcutaneously
PT	prothrombin time	sup., supp.	suppository
PTCA	percutaneous transluminal coronary angioplasty	susp.	suspension
		SV	stroke volume
PTSD	post-traumatic stress disorder	Sx	symptoms
PTT	partial thromboplastin time	syr.	syrup
pulv.	powder	t.i.d.	three times a day
PUVA	psoralen—ultraviolet A light therapy	T&A	tonsillectomy and adenoidectomy
PVC	premature ventricular contraction	T_1	first thoracic verterbra
q. s.	sufficient quantity	tab.	tablet
q.d.	every day (Latin *quaque dies*)	tal.	such
q.h.	every hour	tal. dos.	such doses
q.i.d.	four times a day	TB	tuberculosis
q.o.d.	every other day	tbsp.	tablespoonful
qam	every morning	TDM	therapeutic drug monitoring
QNS	quantity not sufficient	TIA	transient ischemic attack
r	roentgen	tinct., tr.	tincture
R	rectal	TLC	total lung capacity
Ra	radium	TMJ	temporomandibular joint
rad	radiation absorbed dose	TNM	tumor, nodes, metastasis
RAI	radioactive iodine	tPA, TPA	tissue plasminogen activator
RBC	red blood cell count	TPN	total parenteral nutrition
RD	respiratory disease	TPR	temperature, pulse, and respiration
RDH	registered dental hygienist	TSH	thyroid-stimulating hormone
RDS	respiratory distress syndrome	tsp.	teaspoonful
RIA	radioimmunoassay	TSS	toxic shock syndrome
RNA	ribonucleic acid	TURP	transurethral resection of the prostate
ROM	range of motion	Tx	treatment
RT	radiation therapy	U, u	unit
Rx	prescription	U/S	ultrasound
s,s̄	without	u.d.	as directed
s.o.s.	if there is need	U.S.P.	*United States Pharmacopeia*
seg	segmented mature white blood cells	UA	urinalysis
SG	specific gravity	ung.	ointment
SIDS	sudden infant death syndrome	URI	upper respiratory infection
Sig.	patient directions such as route and timing of medication (Latin signa, inscription)	UTI	urinary tract infection
		V/Q, V/Q scan	ventilation/perfusion scan
SL	sublingual	VA	visual acuity
SLE	systemic lupus erythematosus	VC	vital capacity
SNOMED	Systematized Nomenclature of Medicine	VCU, VCUG	voiding cystourethrogram
SOB	shortness of breath	VSD	ventricular septal defect
sol., soln.	solution	VT	ventricular tachycardia
SOM	serious otitis media	WBC	white blood cell count
sp.	spirit	XRT	x-ray or radiation therapy
SPECT	single photon emission computed tomography	ZDV	Zidovudine

C Normal Laboratory Values

The table below lists a number of common laboratory tests taken either in normal CBCs (complete blood counts) or a urinalysis or as separate diagnostic tools.

Abbreviations used in table:

W	women	mol	mole
M	men	l	liter
d	deci	m	milli
g	gram	μ	micro
k	kilo	n	nano
kat	katal (unit of catalytic activity)	p	pico

Note that "normal" values can vary depending on a variety of factors, including the patient's age or gender, time of day test was taken, and so on. In addition, as new medical advances are made, the understanding of what is the best range for some readings has changed. For example, optimal blood pressure readings are now lower than they were ten years ago.

Laboratory Test	Normal Range in US Units	Normal Range in SI Units	To Convert US to SI Units
ALT (Alanine *aminotransferase)	W 7-30 units/liter M 10-55 units/liter	W 0.12-0.50 μkat/liter M 0.17-0.92 μkat/liter	x 0.01667
Albumin	3.1–4.3 g/dl	31–43 g/liter	x 10
Alkaline Phosphatase	W 30-100 units/liter M 45-115 units/liter	W 0.5-1.67 μkat/liter M 0.75-1.92 μkat/liter	x 0.01667
Aspartate aminotransferase	W 9-25 units/liter M 10-40 units/liter	W 0.15-0.42 μkat/liter M 0.17-0.67 μkat/liter	x 0.01667
Basophils	0-3% of lymphocytes	0.0-0.3 fraction of white blood cells	x 0.01
Bilirubin – Direct	0.0-0.4 mg/dl	0-7 μmol/liter	x 17.1
Bilirubin – Total	0.0-1.0 mg/dl	0-17 μmol/liter	x 17.1

*variant of transaminase.

Laboratory Test	Normal Range in US Units	Normal Range in SI Units	To Convert US to SI Units
Blood pressure	120/80 millimeters of mercury (mmHg). Top number is systolic pressure, when heart is pumping. Bottom number is diastolic pressure when heart is at rest. Blood pressure can be too low (hypotension) or too high (hypertension).		No conversion
Cholesterol, total Desirable Marginal High	<200 mg/dL 200–239 mg/dL >239 mg/dL	<5.17 mmol/liter 5.17–6.18 mmol/liter >6.18 mmol/liter	x 0.02586
Cholesterol, LDL Desirable Marginal High Very high	<100 mg/dL 100–159 mg/dL 160–189 mg/dL >190 mg/dL	<2.59 mmol/liter 2.59–4.14 mmol/liter 4.14–4.89 mmol/liter >4.91 mmol/liter	x 0.02586
Cholesterol, HDL Desirable Moderate Low (heart risk)	>60 mg/dL 40-60 mg/dL <40 mg/dL	>1.55 mmol/liter 1.03–1.55 mmol/liter <1.03 mmol/liter	x 0.02586
Eosinophils	0-8% of white blood cells	0.0–0.8 fraction of white blood cells	x 0.01
Erythrocytes RBC	4.0–6.0 ml (females slightly lower than males)	4.0–6.0 10^{12} /liter	
Glucose, urine	<0.05 g/dl	<0.003 mmol/liter	x 0.05551
Glucose, plasma fasting reading—often in self-test	70–110 mg/dl (nonfasting not to exceed 140 mg/dl)	3.9–6.1 mmol/liter	x 0.05551
Hematocrit	W 36.0%–46.0% of red blood cells M 37.0%–49.0% of red blood cells	W 0.36–0.46 fraction of red blood cells M 0.37–0.49 fraction of red blood cells	x 0.01
Hemoglobin	W 12.0–16.0 g/dl M 13.0–18.0 g/dl	W 7.4–9.9 mmol/liter M 8.1–11.2 mmol/liter	x 0.6206
Leukocytes (WBC)	4.5–11.0x10^3/mm^3	4.5–11.0x10^9/liter	x 10^6
Lymphocytes	16%–46% of white blood cells	0.16–0.46 fraction of white blood cells	x 0.01
Mean corpuscular hemoglobin (MCH)	25.0–35.0 pg/cell	25.0–35.0 pg/cell	No conversion
Mean corpuscular hemoglobin concentration (MCHC)	31.0–37.0 g/dl	310–370 g/liter	x 10

Laboratory Test	Normal Range in US Units	Normal Range in SI Units	To Convert US to SI Units
Mean corpuscular volume (MCV)	W 78–102 μm^3 M 78–100 μm^3 M 78–100 fl	W 78–102 fl	No conversion
Monocytes	4–11% of white blood cells	0.04–0.11 fraction of white blood cells	x 0.01
Neutrophils	45%–75% of white blood cells	0.45–0.75 fraction of white blood cells	x 0.01
Potassium	3.4–5.0 mmol/liter	3.4–5.0 mmol/liter	No conversion
Prostate specific antigen (PSA)	0–2.5 ng/ml		
Serum calcium	8.5–10.5 mg/dl	2.1–2.6 mmol/liter	x 0.25
Sodium	135–145 mmol/liter	135–145 mmol/liter	No conversion
Testosterone, total (morning sample)	W 6–86 ng/dl M 270-1070 ng/dl	W 0.21–2.98 nmol/liter M 9.36-37.10 nmol/liter	x 0.03467
Testosterone, unbound Age 20–40 Age 41–60 Age 61–80	W 0.6–3.1, M 15.0–40.0 pg/ml W 0.4–2.5, M 13.0–35.0 pg/ml W 0.2–2.0, M 12.0–28.0 pg/ml	W 20.8–107.5, M 520–1387 pmol/liter W 13.9–86.7, M 451–1213 pmol/liter W 6.9–69.3, M 416–971 pmol/liter	x 34.67
Triglycerides, fasting Normal Borderline High Very high	40–150 mg/dl 150–200 mg/dl 200–500 mg/dl >500 mg/dl	0.45–1.69 mmol/liter 1.69–2.26 mmol/liter 2.26–-5.65 mmol/liter >5.65 mmol/liter	x 0.01129
Urea, plasma (BUN)	8–25 mg/dl	2.9–8.9 mmol/liter	x 0.357
Urinalysis: pH Specific gravity	5.0–9.0 1.001–1.035	5.0–9.0 1.001–1.035	No conversion
WBC (White blood cells, leukocytes)	4.5–11.0x10^3/mm^3	4.5–11.0x10^9 liter	x 10^6

Table adapted from www.aidsinfonet.org

Medical Terminology Style

Government agencies, national organizations, and educational institutions vary the rules set up for style of medical terminology. One area with great variation is the spelling of *eponyms*, terms derived from proper names. For example, Alzheimer's disease was named after Alois Alzheimer, a German neurologist. Several major organizations (especially the AMA—American Medical Association and AAMT—American Association for Medical Transcription) have decided to simplify eponyms by dropping the apostrophe S, so that Alzheimer's disease is known by some as Alzheimer disease. The national charitable organizations and the governmental health organizations currently retain the use of the possessive.

The list below shows examples of medical eponyms in the two different styles.

U. S. Government	AMA and AAMT
Alzheimer's disease	Alzheimer disease
Babinski's reflex	Babinski reflex
Bartholin's glands	Bartholin glands
Bell's palsy	Bell palsy
Cooley's anemia	Cooley anemia
Cushing's syndrome	Cushing syndrome
Fontan's operation	Fontan operation
Meniere's disease	Meniere disease
non-Hodgkin's lymphoma	non-Hodgkin lymphoma
Parkinson's disease	Parkinson disease
Raynaud's phenomemon	Raynaud phenomenon
Tinel's sign	Tinel sign
Wilms' tumor	Wilm tumor

For the name of the disease, structure, condition, and so on, the initial capital remains style. However, for words derived from eponyms, some organizations recommend the use of lowercase; for example, *parkinsonian symptom*.

Index

coccyx, 95, 100
cochlea, 426, 428
coitus, 272, 274
cold sore, 73, 76
colectomy, 386, 387
colic, 381, 382
colitis, 381, 382
collagen, 62, 63
Colles' fracture, 115, 118
colon, 367, 369
colonoscopy, 377, 378
colostomy, 386, 387
colposcopy, 281, 282
coma, 224, 228
comedones, 73, 76
comminuted fracture, 115, 118
comp., 463
compact bone, 91, 92, 100
complete blood count (CBC), 328, 330
complex fracture, 115, 118
complicated fracture, 115, 118
compound fracture, 114, 115, 118
compression fracture, 115, 118
computerized (axial) tomography (CT or CAT scan), 221, 222
concussion, 224, 228
condom, 272, 274
condom catheter, 252, 255
conduction system, 139, 141
conductivity, 210, 215
condyle, 93, 100
condyloma, 285, 286
cones, 425, 428
congenital heart disease, 155, 157
congestive heart failure, 155, 157
conjunctiva, 424, 428
conjunctivitis, 437, 440
conization, 288, 289
connective tissue, 36, 39
constipation, 381, 383
constriction, 154, 157
contact lenses, 437, 440
contraception, 272, 274
contracture, 116, 118
contraindicate, 454, 460
convolutions, 212, 215
Coombs' test, 329
copulation, 272, 274
cordotomy, 231
corium, 62, 63
corn, 73, 76
cornea, 424, 428
coronal plane, 42, 45
coronary, 154, 155
coronary angioplasty, 161, 164
coronary artery, 136, 141
coronary artery bypass graft (CABG), 162
coronary artery disease (CAD), 153, 157
coronary bypass surgery, 162, 164
coronary circulation, 136, 139
corpus callosum, 212, 215
cortex, 244, 245
corticosteroids, 399, 401
cortisol, 399, 402
Cowper's gland, 298, 300
CPK, 112, 149
crackles, 190, 193
cranial cavity, 38, 39
cranial nerves, 213, 215
craniectomy, 231
craniotomy, 231
cranium, 212, 216
creatine, 242, 245
creatine phosphokinase (CPK), 112, 149
creatinine clearance test, 253
crest, 93, 100
Crohn's disease, 381, 383
cross-sectional plane, 42, 46
croup, 191, 193

crust, 70, 71, 76
cryosurgery, 81, 288, 289
cryptorchism, 305, 306
CT scan, 221, 222
culdocentesis, 288, 289
culdoscopy, 281, 282
curettage, 81, 82
Cushing's syndrome, 411, 412
cuticle, 63
cyanosis, 154, 157
cyst, 76
cystectomy, 262
cystic fibrosis, 190, 193
cystitis, 258, 259
cystocele, 259
cystolith, 258, 259
cystopexy, 262
cystoplasty, 262
cystorrhaphy, 262
cytoscope, 254, 255
cytoscopy, 254, 255
cytotoxic cell, 345, 346
cx, 463

D

dacryoadentitis, 438, 440
dacryocystectomy, 443
dacryocystitis, 438, 440
dandruff, 73
DAW, 463
DC, dc, 463
deafness, 439, 440
debridement, 81, 82
decibel, 426, 428
decubitus ulcer, 71, 76
deep, 41, 46
deep vein thrombosis, 154, 157
defecation, 367, 369
degenerative arthritis, 118
deglutition, 364, 369
dementia, 224, 228
demyelination, 225, 228
dendrite, 210, 216
densitometer, 112, 113
deoxygenated blood, 136
depigmentation, 73, 76
depolarization, 139, 141
dermabrasion, 81, 82
dermatitis, 72, 76
dermatology, 67–68
dermis, 62, 63
derma, 49
diabetes, 411, 412
diabetes insipidus, 410, 412
diabetes mellitus, 411, 412
diabetes nephropathy, 411, 412
diabetes neuropathy, 411, 412
diabetes retinopathy, 411, 412
diabetes, Type I, 411, 413
diabetes, Type II, 411, 413
dialysis, 253, 255
diaphoresis, 63
diaphragm, 38, 39, 179, 180, 272, 275
diaphysis, 91, 100
diaphysis, 91, 100
diarrhea, 381, 383
diarthroses, 97, 98, 101
diastole, 138, 141
diencephalon, 212, 216
digestion, 362, 363, 369
digestive system, 38, 39, 362–396
digital subtraction angiography (DSA), 148, 150
dil., 463
diopter, 434, 435
diphtheria, 191, 193

diplopia, 437, 440
disc, 463
discography, 112, 113
disk, 93, 101
dislocation, 116, 118
disp., 463
distal, 41, 46
div., 463
diverticula, 381, 383
diverticulectomy, 386, 387
diverticulitis, 381, 383
diverticulosis, 381, 383
dopamine, 225, 228
Doppler ultrasound, 148, 150
dorsal, 41, 46
dorsal cavity, 38, 39
dorsal vertebrae, 95, 101
dorsiflexion, 98
drug, 453, 460
drug-eluting stent, 162, 164
druggist, 454, 460
ductless gland, 397, 402
ductus arteriosus, 140, 142
ductus venosus, 140, 142
duodenal ulcer, 381, 383
duodenum, 366, 369
dura mater, 213, 216
duritis, 226, 228
DW, 463
D₅W, 463
dwarfism, 410, 412
dx, Dx, 463
dyscrasia, 331, 332
dysentery, 383
dysmenorrhea, 284, 286
dyspareunia, 285, 286
dyspepsia, 380, 383
dysphagia, 380, 383
dysphasia, 226, 228
dysphonia, 190, 193
dyspnea, 189, 193
dysrhythmia, 153, 157
dystonia, 116, 118
dysuria, 258, 259

E

ear, 426, 428, 434–435, 438–439
eardrum, 426, 428
ecchymosis, 72, 76
eccrine glands, 63
ECG, 147, 148
echo, 9
echocardiography, 148, 150
eczema, 72, 76
edema, 258, 259
EET, 147
efferent neuron, 210, 216
ejaculation, 299, 300
ejection fraction, 148, 150
EKG, 147
elbow, 96, 97, 101
electrocardiogram, 147, 149
electrocardiography, 147, 150
electrodessiccation, 81, 82
electroencephalogram (EEG), 221, 222
electrolyte, 400, 402
electromyogram, 112, 113
electrophoresis, 315, 321
elimination, 362, 370
elix., 463
embolectomy, 162, 164
embolic stroke, 226, 228
embolus, 154, 157, 226, 228
emesis, 365, 370
e.m.p., 463
emphysema, 191, 193
empyema, 192, 193
emulsification, 368, 370
encephalitis, 226, 228

nonsteroidal anti-inflammatory drug (NSAID), 456, 460
norepinephrine, 399, 403
nose, 176, 181, 427
nosebleed, 191, 194
nostrils, 177, 181
NPO, 463
NPO p MN, 463
N.S., NS, 463
NSAID, 463
N&V, 464
nucleus pulposus, 95, 102
nyctalopia, 437, 441
nystagmus, 437, 441

O

obesity, 380, 384
obstetrician, 281, 282
occipital bone, 94, 102
occipital lobe, 212, 217
occlusion, 158, 226, 229
o.d., OD, 464
oint., 464
o.l., 464
olecranon, 96, 97, 103
olfactory organs, 427, 429
oligodendroglia, 211, 217
oligodendroglioma, 226, 229
oligomenorrhea, 284, 286
oligo-ovulation, 284, 286
oligospermia, 305, 306
oliguria, 258, 260
onychitis, 73, 78
onychopathy, 73, 78
oocyte, 270, 276
oophorectomy, 288, 289
open fracture, 114, 115, 119
ophthalmologist, 434, 435
ophthalmoscopy, 434, 435
opportunistic infection, 352, 355
optician, 434, 436
optic nerve, 425, 429
optometrist, 434, 436
oral administration, 457, 461
orchidectomy, 307, 308
orchiectomy, 307, 308
organ, 37, 40
organ of Corti, 426, 429
origin, 98, 99, 103
oropharynx, 177, 181
orthopedic surgeon, 111, 113
orthopedist, 111, 113
orthopnea, 190, 194
orthosis, 122
orthotic, 122
o.s., 464
osseous tissue, 91, 103
osseus labyrinth, 426, 429
ossification, 91, 103
ostealgia, 116, 119
osteoarthritis, 117, 119
osteoblast, 91, 103
osteoclasis, 122
osteoclast, 91, 103
osteocyte, 91, 103
osteodynia, 116, 119
osteoma, 117, 119
osteomyelitis, 117, 119
osteopath, 111, 113
osteoplasty, 122, 123
osteoporosis, 91, 116, 119
osteosarcoma, 117, 119
osteotomy, 122, 123
otolgia, 439, 441
OTC, 464
otitis externa, 439, 441
otitis media, 439, 441
otoliths, 427, 429
otologist, 434, 436

otoplasty, 443
otorhinolaryngologist, 196, 197, 434, 436
otorrhagia, 439, 441
otorrhea, 439, 441
otosclerosis, 439, 441
otoscopy, 434, 436
o.u., 464
ovary, 270, 276, 400, 403
over-the-counter (OTC), 454, 461
ovulation, 270, 272, 276
ovum, 270, 276
oxytocin, 399, 403
oz., 464

P

P, 464
pacemaker, 139, 142
palatine bone, 95, 103
palatine tonsils, 177, 181, 364, 371
palpitations, 153, 158
palsy, 225, 229
pancreas, 368, 371, 400, 403
pancreatectomy, 386, 387, 414
pancreatitis, 381, 384, 411, 413
pancytopenia, 332, 333
Papanicolaou (Pap) smear, 281, 282
papillae, 364, 371, 428, 429
papillary layer, 62, 64
papule, 70, 71, 78
para, 273, 276
paracentesis, 386, 387
paracusis, 439, 441
paranasal sinuses, 177, 181
parasympathetic nervous system, 214, 217
parathormone (PTH), 399, 403
parathyroid gland, 400, 403
parathyroid hormone (PTH), 399, 403
parathyroidectomy, 414
parenteral administration, 458, 461
paresthesia, 225, 229
Parkinson's disease, 225, 229
parietal bone, 94, 103
parietal lobe, 212, 217
parietal pleura, 179, 181
paronychia, 73, 78
parotiditis, 380, 384
parotitis, 380, 384
paroxysmal, 190, 194
partial thromboplastin time (PTT), 328, 330
parturition, 271, 276
patch, 70, 71, 78
patch test, 68
patent ductus arteriosus, 155, 158
pathogen, 344, 347
pathological fracture, 115, 119
patella, 97, 103
p.c., 464
PDR, 464
peak flow meter, 187, 188
pediculosis, 73, 78
pediculosis capitis, 73
pediculosis pubis, 73
pelvic cavity, 38, 40, 96, 103
pelvic girdle, 96, 103
pelvimetry, 282
pelvis, 103
penis, 299, 300
pepsin, 365, 371
peptic ulcer, 380, 384
percussion, 187, 188
percutaneous transluminal coronary angioplasty (PTCA), 161, 164
perfusion deficit, 154, 158
pericardial fluid, 137
pericarditis, 155, 158
pericardium, 137, 142
perilymph, 426, 429

perimenopause, 275, 276
perimetrium, 271, 276
perineum, 271, 276, 299, 300
periosteum, 91, 103
peripheral nervous system, 213–214
peripheral vascular disease, 154, 158
peristalsis, 364, 371
peritoneal dialysis, 254, 256
peritoneoscopy, 377, 378
peritonitis, 381, 384
pertussis, 194
PET, 221, 223
petechia, 72, 78, 154, 159
petit mal seizure, 225, 229
Peyronie's disease, 305, 306
pH, 252, 256
phacoemulsification, 443
phagocytosis, 344, 347
phalanges, 96, 97, 103
phalanx, 97, 103
phantom limb, 117, 119
phantom pain, 117, 119
pharmacist, 454, 46
pharmacodynamics, 453, 461
pharmacokinetics, 454, 461
pharmacology, terms in, 453–469
  abbreviations, 463–464
  drug sources, types, function, and administration, 453–461
pharyngeal tonsils, 177, 181
pharyngitis, 191, 194
pharynx, 177, 181, 362, 364, 371
phenylketones, 254, 256
phimosis, 305, 306
phlebitis, 154, 159
phlebography, 148, 151
phlebotomy, 162, 164, 326, 330
phosphorus, 91
photophobia, 437, 441
physical therapy, 116, 119
pia mater, 213, 217
pilonidal cyst, 71, 78
pimple, 71
pineal gland, 398, 403
pinkeye, 437, 441
pinna, 426, 429
pituitary gland, 399, 403
placenta, 271, 276
placenta previa, 283, 286
plantar flexion, 98
plaque, 70, 71, 78, 153, 159
plasma, 11, 51, 314–315, 322
plasma cell, 345, 347
plasmapheresis, 315, 322
plastic surgery, 82
platelet, 314, 318, 319, 322
platelet count (PLT), 328, 330
pleura, 51, 179, 182
pleural cavity, 178, 182
pleural effusion, 192, 194
pleurisy, 191, 194
pleuritis, 191, 194
pleurocentesis, 197, 198
pleuropexy, 197, 198
PM, p.m., 464
pneumobronchotomy, 196-197, 198
pneumoconiosis, 191, 194
pneumonectomy, 196, 198
pneumonia, 191, 194
pneumonitis, 191, 194
pneumothorax, 192, 194
p.o., 464
podagra, 117, 120
podiatrist, 111, 113
poikilocytosis, 332, 333
polarization, 139, 142
polycystic kidney disease, 258, 260
polycythemia, 332, 333
polydipsia, 410, 413

skin graft, 82
skin lesions, 70–71
SL, 464
sleep apnea, 221
SMA (sequential multiple analyzer), 326, 330
small intestine, 362, 366–367, 371
smell, 423, 430
smooth muscle, 98, 99, 104
SNOMED CT, 17
SOAP, 16
soft palate, 177, 182, 364, 371
sol., 464
soln., 464
somatic nervous system, 213–214, 217
somatotrophic hormone (STH), 399, 403
somnambulism, 227, 229
somnolence, 227, 229
sonography, 148, 151
s.o.s., 464
sp., 464
spasm, 116, 120
spastic, 120
specific gravity, 252, 256
SPECT brain scan (single photon emission
       computed tomography), 221, 223
sperm, 298, 300
spermatogenesis, 298, 300
spermatozoon, 298, 301
spermicide, 272, 276
sphenoid bone, 94, 104
sphenoid sinus, 94, 104
sphygmomanometer, 147, 151
spina bifida, 116, 120, 224, 229
spinal cavity, 38, 40
spinal column, 93, 104
spinal cord, 213, 217
spinal curvature, 117, 120
spinal nerves, 213, 217
spinous process, 95, 104
spirometer, 187, 188
spleen, 342, 347
splenectomy, 356, 357
splenomegaly, 354, 355
splinting, 122, 123
spondylosyndesis, 122, 123
sponge, 272, 277
spongy bone, 91, 104
sprain, 116, 120
spur, 116, 120
sputum sample/culture, 187, 188
squamous cell carcinoma, 74, 79
squamous epithelium, 61, 64
ss, s̄s̄, 464
stapedectomy, 443
stapes, 426, 430
stat, 464
steatorrhea, 381, 384
stem cell, 315, 323
stenosis, 159
stent, 162, 164
stereotactic surgery, 231, 232
stereotaxy, 231, 232
sternum, 104
stimulus, 210, 217
stomach, 362, 365–366, 371
stool, 367, 371
strabismus, 437, 441
strain, 116, 120
strata, 61
stratum corneum, 61, 64
stratum germinativum, 62, 64
stress test, 147, 151
striated muscle, 97, 99, 104
stridor, 190, 195
stroke, 226, 229
sty, 437, 441
stye, 437, 441
styloid process, 94, 104
subc, subq, 464

subcutaneous, 458, 461
subcutaneous layer, 62, 64
subdural hematoma, 224
subdural space, 213, 217
sublingually, 457, 461
subluxation, 116, 120
sudoriferous glands, 61, 63
sulcus, 93, 104, 212, 217
superior, 41, 47
superior lobe, 179, 182
superior vena cava, 138, 143
supination, 98
supine, 42, 47
supp., suppos, 464
suppository, 458, 461
suppressor cell, 345, 347
suprarenal gland, 400, 403
susp., 464
suture, 93, 104
sweat glands, 61, 63, 64
sweat test, 187, 188
Sx, 464
sym, Sym, 464
sympathetic nervous system, 214, 217
sympathomimetic, 400, 403
symphysis, 97, 104
synapse, 210, 217
synarthrosis, 97, 98, 104
syncope, 227, 229
syndrome of inappropriate ADH (SIADH),
       410, 413
synovectomy, 122, 123
synovial fluid, 97, 104
synovial joint, 97, 104
synovial membrane, 97, 104
syphilis, 284, 286
syr., 464
syringe, 458, 461
system, 37, 40
systemic circulation, 136
systole, 138, 143

T

tab., 464
tachycardia, 153, 159
tachypnea, 189, 195
target cell, 397, 403
tarsal bones, 96, 97, 104
tarsus, 97, 104
taste, 423, 430
taste buds, 428, 430
taste cells, 428, 430
Tay-Sachs disease, 224, 229
tbsp., 464
TB tine, 68, 69
T cells, 342
tears, 425, 430
teeth, 364, 371
telangiectasia, 70, 71, 79
temporal bone, 94, 104
temporal lobe, 212, 217
temporomandibular joint, 94, 104
tendinitis, 120
tendon, 97, 105
tendonitis, 116, 120
tenotomy, 122, 123
terminal end fibers, 210, 217
testicle, 298, 301, 401, 403
testis, 298, 301, 401, 403
testosterone, 298, 301
tetany, 410, 413
tetralogy of Fallot, 159
thalamus, 212, 218
thalassemia, 332, 333
third-degree burn, 73, 79
thoracic cavity, 38, 40
thoracic surgeon, 196, 198
thoracic vertebrae, 95, 105
thoracocentesis, 197, 198

thoracostomy, 197, 198
thoracotomy, 197, 198
thorax, 105, 178, 182
throat, 182, 364, 371
throat culture, 187, 188
thrombectomy, 162, 165
thrombin, 315, 323
thrombocyte, 315, 323
thrombocytopenia, 332, 333
thrombophlebitis, 154, 160
thromboplastin, 315, 323
thrombosis, 154, 160
thrombotic occlusion, 154, 160
thrombotic stroke, 226, 229
thrombus, 154, 160, 226, 229
thymectomy, 356, 357, 414
thymoma, 354, 355
thymosin, 342, 347
thymus gland, 342, 347, 400, 404
thyroid cartilage, 178, 182
thyroidectomy, 414
thyroid function test/study, 408
thyroid gland, 400, 404
thyroid scan, 408
thyroid-stimulating hormone (TSH), 399, 404
thyrotoxicosis, 410, 413
thyroxine (T4), 400, 404
tibia, 96, 97, 105
tics, 225, 229
t.i.d., 464
tinct., 464
tinea, 72, 79
Tinel('s) sign, 112, 113
tine test, 68, 69
tinnitus, 439, 441
tissue, 36, 40
T lymphocytes, 342, 347
TMJ, 94, 104
tongue, 364, 371, 428
tonic-clonic seizure, 225, 230
tonometry, 434, 436
tonsillectomy, 196, 198
tonsillitis, 191, 195
topically, 458, 461
touch, 423, 430
Tourette syndrome, 225, 226, 230
toxicology, 454, 461
TPN, 464
TPR, 464
tr., 464
trachea, 178, 182
tracheitis, 191, 195
tracheoplasty, 196, 198
tracheostomy, 197, 198
tracheotomy, 197, 198
traction, 122, 123
trade name, 454, 461
transcranial sonogram, 222, 223
transfusion, 319, 320, 323
transient ischemic attack (TIA), 226, 230
transverse plane, 42, 47
transverse process, 95, 105
trepanation, 231, 232
trephination, 231, 232
trichiasis, 441
tricuspid stenosis, 155, 160
tricuspid valve, 137, 143
triglycerides, 149, 151
triiodothyronine (T3), 400, 404
trochanter, 93, 105
true ribs, 96, 105
tsp., 464
tubercle, 93, 105
tuberculosis, 191, 195
tuberosity, 93, 105
tumor, 70, 71, 79
tympanic membrane, 426, 430
tympanitis, 439, 441
tympanoplasty, 443, 444